CFO Fundamentals

Founded in 1807, John Wiley & Sons is the oldest independent publishing company in the United States. With offices in North America, Europe, Asia, and Australia, Wiley is globally committed to developing and marketing print and electronic products and services for our customers' professional and personal knowledge and understanding.

The Wiley Corporate F&A series provides information, tools, and insights to corporate professionals responsible for issues affecting the profitability of their companies, from accounting and finance to internal controls and performance management.

CFO Fundamentals

Your Quick Guide to Internal Controls, Financial Reporting, IFRS, Web 2.0, Cloud Computing, and More

JAE K. SHIM

JOEL G. SIEGEL

ALLISON I. SHIM

WILEY

John Wiley & Sons, Inc.

Library of Congress Cataloging-in-Publication Data:

Shim, Jae K.
    CFO fundamentals : your quick guide to internal controls, financial reporting, IFRS, Web 2.0, cloud computing, and more / Jae K. Shim, Joel G. Siegel, and Allison I. Shim. — 4th ed.

        p. cm. — (Wiley corporate F&A)
Rev. ed. of: The vest pocket CFO. 3rd ed. c2008.
    Includes index.
    ISBN 978-1-118-13249-4 (pbk.); ISBN 978-1-118-21955-3 (ebk);
    ISBN 978-1-118-21958-4 (ebk); ISBN 978-1-118-21960-7 (ebk)
        1. Corporations—United States—Finance—Handbooks, manuals, etc.   I. Siegel, Joel G.   II. Shim, Allison I., 1984–   III. Shim, Jae K. Vest pocket CFO.   IV. Title.

    HG4061.S48 2012
    658.15—dc23
    2011037184

Printed in the United States of America

10 9 8 7 6 5 4 3 2 1

To Chung Shim, dedicated wife and mother;
Roberta M. Siegel, loving wife and colleague;
and Sylvia and Arnold Siegel, loving mother and brother.

Contents

PART SIX: FINANCIAL ANALYSIS, INSURANCE AND LEGAL CONSIDERATIONS, AND ECONOMICS

PART SEVEN: LIQUIDITY AND TREASURY

What This Book Will Do for You

HERE IS A handy pocket problem-solver for today's busy chief financial officer (CFO). It's a working guide to help you quickly pinpoint what to look for, what to be aware of, what to do, and how to do it in the complex world of business. You will find checklists, ratios, formulas, measures, guidelines, procedures, rules of thumb, illustrations, step-by-step instructions, real-life examples, tables, charts, and exhibits to help you analyze and evaluate any business-related problem. Throughout, you will find this book practical, quick, comprehensive, and useful.

Uses for this book are as varied as the topics presented. It can be used by CFOs employed by large, medium, or small companies.

You will be able to move quickly to take advantage of favorable situations and avoid unfavorable ones. Here is the guide that will help you make smart decisions. The book provides analysis of recurring problems as well as unusual ones that may occur and posts red flags of potential difficulties. It gives vital suggestions throughout on correcting financial sickness and inefficiency. The latest developments, such as new tax laws, are included.

The book covers the major areas and problems of corporate financial management and accounting. It is directed to the modern CFO who must follow some traditional elements common to controllership and financial management but must be cognizant of the ever-changing financial markets and technology of today. These factors make some of the traditional techniques of financial management obsolete; new strategies and techniques are necessary in order to do an effective job that ensures financial survival.

We present guidelines for evaluating proposals and for analyzing and measuring operations and activities and provide tips for preparing necessary reports.

The book is a practical reference that contains approaches and techniques for understanding and solving problems of:

- Financial reporting: International Financial Reporting Standards (IFRS)
- Cost management and information technology (IT) systems
- Financial planning and budgeting
- Management of assets and liabilities
- Risk management and continuity planning
- Liquidity and treasury
- Financing the business
- Real options and discovery-driven planning
- Taxation

- Mergers and acquisitions
- Divestitures
- Multinational finance
- Forecasting corporate bankruptcy
- Reading economic indicators

Part I (Chapters 1–2) covers the financial reporting responsibilities of the CFO, including the types of reports that must be prepared. Securities and Exchange Commission filings are required by public companies, and compliance with the Sarbanes-Oxley Act is required.

Part II (Chapters 3–8) discusses the financial accounting requirements applicable to the income statement, balance sheet, and statement of cash flows. Generally accepted accounting principles are delved into, including such important topics as leases, pensions, and accounting for income taxes.

Part III (Chapters 9–19) focuses on cost management and IT systems. It covers what the CFO should know about cost management and analysis, break-even analysis, contribution margin analysis, budgeting and financial modeling, variance analysis, risk management, portfolio diversification sustainable growth, capital budgeting, managerial reports, segmental performance, and quantitative techniques. Chapter 19 takes up the issue as to how IT assists CFOs in business decisions. It covers the use of information systems in all phases of business and in all functional areas to analyze and solve business problems in the real world. It covers topics such as cloud computing, Web 2.0, value chain software, and contingency planning.

Part IV (Chapters 20–23) addresses the management of working capital and assets including cash, accounts receivable, and inventory. The management of payables is also highlighted.

Part V (Chapters 24–29) deals with how to adequately obtain financing for the business to meet its goals and financial needs. Short-term, intermediate-term, and long-term financing requirements are discussed, and the circumstances under which each would be appropriate are indicated. Cost of capital determination and capital structure decisions are presented. The factors in establishing a dividend policy are noted. The financial management of overseas operations for multinational companies is explained.

Part VI (Chapters 30–33) is directed toward financial analysis areas, including risk/reward relationships and financial statement analysis for internal evaluation. Ways to analyze and control revenue and expenses are addressed. Proper insurance is needed to ensure the sustenance of the business. Knowledge of law is required to guard against legal exposure such as from product defects. The economic environment by way of economic indicators and statistics has to be studied to determine its impact on the business and what can be done in recessionary times.

Part VII (Chapter 34) covers investment portfolio selection so as to earn a satisfactory return while controlling risk. Current trend in corporate investment and liquidity management is also outlined.

Part VIII (Chapter 35) discusses the tax consequences of making financial decisions. Tax planning is essential to minimizing the tax obligation of the business.

Part IX (Chapters 36–41) presents the planning and financial aspects for mergers and acquisitions. The reasons and ways of divesting of business segments are discussed. The signs of potential business failure must be noted so that timely corrective action may be taken. The steps in a reorganization are discussed. Chapter 40 provides an in-depth treatment as to how to value a security. Chapter 41 addresses a special topic—financial analysis for nonprofit organizations.

The content of the book is clear, concise, and to the point. It is a valuable reference tool with practical applications and how-tos for you, the up-to-date knowledgeable CFO. Keep this book handy for easy reference and daily use.

PART ONE

Reports and Filings

CHAPTER ONE

Chief Financial Officer's Role and Reports

 ## ROLE OF THE CHIEF FINANCIAL OFFICER

The chief financial officer (CFO) plays a strategic role in the company's goal-setting, policy determination, and financial success. The CFO's typical title is vice president of finance (VP Finance). Unless the business is small, no one individual handles all the financial decisions; responsibility is dispersed throughout the organization. The CFO's responsibilities include:

- *Financial analysis and planning:* Determining the amount of funds the company needs; a large company seeking a rapid growth rate will require more funds.
- *Making investment decisions:* Allocating funds to specific assets (things owned by the company). The financial manager makes decisions regarding the mix and type of assets acquired and the possible modification or replacement of assets, particularly when assets are inefficient or obsolete.
- *Making financing and capital structure decisions:* Raising funds on favorable terms (i.e., at a lower interest rate or with few restrictions). Deciding how to raise funds depends on many factors, including interest rate, cash position, and existing debt level; for example, a company with a cash-flow problem may be better off using long-term financing.
- *Managing financial resources:* Managing cash, receivables, and inventory to accomplish higher returns without undue risk.

The CFO affects stockholder wealth maximization by influencing:

- Current and future earnings per share (EPS), equal to net income divided by common shares outstanding

- Timing, duration, and risk of earnings
- Dividend policy
- Manner of financing

Exhibit 1.1 presents the functions of the CFO.

EXHIBIT 1.1 Functions of the CFO

A. Accounting and Control

Establishment of accounting policies and internal control

Development and reporting of accounting data

Cost accounting

Internal auditing

System and procedures

Government reporting and filings

Report and interpretation of results of operations to management

Comparison of performance with operating plans and standards

B. Planning

Long- and short-range financial and corporate planning

Budgeting for operations and capital expenditures

Evaluating performance

Pricing policies and sales forecasting

Analyzing economic factors

Appraising acquisitions and divestment

C. Provision of capital

Short-term sources; cost and arrangements

Long-term sources; cost and arrangements

Internal generation

D. Administration of Funds

Cash management

Banking arrangements

Receipt, custody, and disbursement of company's securities and moneys

Credit and collection management

Pension money management

Investment portfolio management

E. Protection of Assets

Provision for insurance

Establishment of sound internal controls

F. Tax Administration

Establishment of tax policies

Preparation of tax reports

Tax planning

(continued)

EXHIBIT 1.1 *(continued)*

G. Investor Relations

Maintaining liaison with the investment community

Counseling with analyst regarding public financial information

H. Evaluation and Consulting

Consultation with and advice to other corporate executives on company policies, operations, objectives, and their degree of effectiveness

I. Information Technology and Management Information Systems

Development and use of information technology (IT) facilities

Development and use of management information systems

Development and use of IT systems and procedures

How do you differentiate among the controller, treasurer, and CFO?

If you are employed by a large company, the financial responsibilities are probably held by the controller, treasurer, and CFO. The activities of the controller and treasurer fall under the umbrella of finance.

There is no precise distinction between the jobs of controller and treasurer, and the functions may differ slightly between organizations because of size, company policy, and the personality of the office holder. In most businesses, the role of the controller is constantly changing and adapting to the situation at hand. The controller's functions are primarily of an *internal* nature and include record keeping, tracking, and controlling the financial effects of prior and current operations. The *internal* matters of importance to the controller include financial reporting, internal control and compliance, cost and managerial accounting, taxes, control, and audit functions. The controller is the chief accountant and is involved in the preparation of financial statements, tax returns, the annual report, and filings with the Securities and Exchange Commission (SEC). The controller's function is primarily to ensure that funds are used efficiently. He or she is primarily concerned with collecting and presenting financial information. The controller usually looks at what has occurred rather than what should or will happen.

Many controllers are involved with management information and IT systems, and review previous, current, and emerging IT patterns. They report their analysis of the financial implications of decisions to top management. Controllers are called on to establish, monitor, and analyze the internal control structure of the company to the extent that those controls impact the company's financial statements. At times, controllers may be called on to consider operational controls broader in scope. In particular, for SEC registrants that fall under Sarbanes-Oxley 404 requirements, controllers are required to obtain an independent auditor's opinion as to whether the control design and operating effectiveness are able to prevent a material misstatement in the financial statements. For entities that are not SEC registrants, much of the Sarbanes-Oxley 404 requirement could be considered best practice. In this regard, a risk-based control self-assessment program is a useful starting point. Tools such as internal control questionnaires or process maps may be useful. It is important to keep in mind that every company is different, and, therefore, the internal control self-assessment process should be tailored to the particular needs and peculiarities of each company. When designing a control self-assessment process or modifying controls, it would be prudent to obtain the external auditor's view at the onset to facilitate that auditor's function and lessen audit costs.

The treasurer's function, in contrast, is primary external. The treasurer obtains and managers the corporation's capital and is involved with creditors (e.g., bank loan officers), stockholders, investors, underwriters of equity (stock) and bond issuances, and governmental regulatory bodies (e.g., the SEC, Public Company Accounting Oversight Board [PCAOB]). The treasurer is responsible for managing corporate assets (e.g., accounts receivable, inventory) and debt, planning the finances and capital expenditures, obtaining funds, formulating credit policy, and managing the investment portfolio.

The treasurer concentrates on keeping the company afloat by obtaining cash to meet obligations and buying assets to achieve corporate objectives. While the controller concentrates on profitability, the treasurer emphasizes cash flow. Even though a company has been profitable, it may have a significant negative cash flow; for example, there may exist substantial long-term receivables (receivables having a maturity of greater than one year). Without adequate cash flow, even a profitable company may fail. By emphasizing cash flow, the treasurer strives to prevent bankruptcy and achieve corporate goals. The treasurer analyzes the financial statements, formulates additional data, and makes decisions based on the analysis.

The major responsibilities of controllers and treasures are summarized in Exhibit 1.2. Typically, both report to the *chief financial officer.* The CFO is involved with financial policy making and planning. He or she has financial and managerial responsibilities, supervises all phases of financial activity, and serves as the financial advisor to the board of directors. In the post-Enron era, the CFO's role has taken on a whole new level

EXHIBIT 1.2   Functions of Controller and Treasurer

Controller	Treasurer
Internal controls	Obtaining financing
Financial reporting—SOX, SEC, generally accepted accounting principles, International Financial Reporting Standards	Banking relationship
Risk management	Credit appraisal
Custody of records	Investment of funds
Interpretation of financial data	Investor relations
Budgeting and planning	Cash management
Controlling operations	Insuring assets
Appraisal of results and making recommendations	Fostering relationship with creditors and investors
Preparation of taxes	Collecting funds
Managing assets and IT systems	Managing assets

of importance—nearly as important as the job of the chief executive officer (CEO). The new reporting rules instituted by the mandate of the Sarbanes-Oxley Act of 2002 (SOX; the Act) require that CFOs and CEOs sign off on their companies' financials not once but twice. The certification puts CFOs at risk of criminal penalties for materially misrepresenting the numbers. That alone makes the CFO position more daunting.

Exhibit 1.3 shows an organization chart of the finances structure within a company. Note that the controller and treasurer report to the VP Finance. For smaller companies, the controller is usually the CFO.

The CFO must communicate important and accurate financial information to senior-level executives, the board of directors and its audit committee, divisional managers, employees, and various third parties. The reports must be prepared in a timely fashion and be comprehensible and relevant to readers.

The needs of management differ among organizations. Management reports should be sufficiently simple to enable readers to concentrate on problems and difficulties that may arise. The reports should not be cumbersome to read through; they should be consistent and uniform in format. The facts presented should be based on supportable financial and accounting data. The CFO should use less accounting jargon and more operating terminology when reporting to management. Also, the reports should generate questions for top management discussions.

What are prospective financial statements?

Prospective financial statements include financial forecasts and projections. This category excludes pro forma financial statements and partial presentations.

Financial forecasts are prospective financial statements that present the company's expected financial position as well as results of operations and cash flows, based on assumptions about conditions actually anticipated to occur and on the management action expected to be taken.

A financial forecast may be presented in a single dollar amount based on the best estimate or as a reasonable range. However, this range cannot be selected in a misleading way.

In contrast, financial projections are prospective statements that present the company's financial position, results of operations and cash flows, based on assumptions

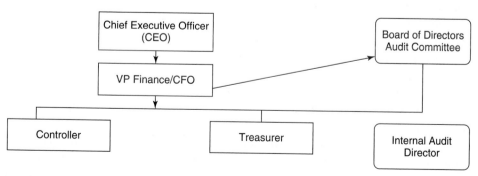

EXHIBIT 1.3 A Typical Financial Structure

about conditions anticipated to exist and the action management is expected to take, given the hypothetical (what-if) assumptions.

Financial projections may be most useful to users who seek answers to hypothetical questions. These users may want to change the scenarios based on expected changing situations. A financial projection may contain a range.

A financial projection may be prepared for general users *only* if it supplements a financial forecast. However, financial projections may not be contained in general-use documents and tax-shelter prospectuses.

What should be contained in financial forecasts and financial projections?

Financial forecasts and financial projections may be in the form of complete basic financial statements or financial statements containing the following minimum items:

- Sales or gross revenues
- Net income
- Gross profit
- Basic and basic diluted EPS
- Income from continuing operations
- Income from discontinued operations
- Unusual income statement items
- Tax provision
- Material changes in financial positions
- Summaries of significant accounting policies and assumptions

Management's intent of preparing the prospective financial statements should be stated. However, there should be a mention that prospective results may not materialize. Also, it should be clearly stated that the assumptions used by management are based on information and circumstances that existed at the time the financial statements were prepared.

What are the various kinds of planning reports that can be prepared?

The CFO can prepare short-term companywide or division-wide planning reports. These include the forecasted balance sheet, forecasted income statement, forecasted statement of cash flows, and projections of capital expenditures.

Special short-term planning studies of specific business segments may also be prepared. These reports may relate to product distribution by territory and market, product line mix analysis, warehouse handling, salesperson performance, and logistics. Long-range planning reports may include 5- to 10-year projections for the company and its major business segments.

Specialized planning and control reports may include the effects of cost-reduction programs, production issues in cost/quality terms, cash flow plans for line-of-credit agreements, evaluation of pension/termination costs in plant closings, contingency and downsizing plans, and appraisal of risk factors in long-term contracts.

Why are information reports useful?

The CFO may prepare information reports for other members of top management. The reports can show and discuss long-term financial and operating trends. For example, the reasons and analytical implications of trends in revenue, production, and costs can be presented over the last three years. Although the format of such reports may vary depending on the environmental considerations and user needs, graphic depiction is often enlightening.

How can reports be used to analyze and control operations?

Reports can be prepared dealing with controlling financial activities and related analytical implications. Analytical procedures include comparing financial and nonfinancial information over time. The reports can highlight the reasons for significant change between prior- and current-year performance. For example, a sharp increase in promotion and entertainment expense or telephone expense may require investigation. Analytical reports are also used to summarize and evaluate variances from forecasts and budgets. Appraisal of variances may be by revenue, expense, profit, assets, product, division, and territory.

Why are exceptions to the norm significant to note?

Exception reports present detailed enumeration of the problems and difficulties faced by the business over a given time period. Such reports might zero in on internal control structure inadequacies or improper employment of accounting or auditing procedures in violation of generally accepted accounting principles (GAAP) and generally accepted auditing standards (GAAS). The computer should automatically output exception reports when a red flag is posted, such as when a customer's balance exceeds the credit limit.

What should the board of directors know?

The board of directors usually is concerned with overall policy matters, general trends in revenue and earnings, and what the competition is doing. It is also interested in short-term and long-term issues. Relevant information in reports directed to the board of directors include company and divisional performance reports, historical and forecasted financial statements, status reports applicable to capital expenditures, and special studies. SOX requires an independent audit committee within the board. The board's audit committee is responsible for the selection and oversight of the auditing certified public accounting (CPA) firm.

What special occurrences should be reported?

Special situations and circumstances may occur that require separate evaluation and study. For example, it may be necessary to identify the cause for a repeated decline in profitability of a given product, service, or territory. There may be a need for a feasibility analysis of whether to open a new store location or plant. Other reports may be in connection with union negotiations, commercial contract reviews, pension plan administration, bonus plans, and product warranty issues. It is essential that the reports contain narrative and statistical analyses of the decision with graphic presentations as needed.

What reports may segment managers find useful in decision making?

Reports prepared to assist divisional managers in evaluating performance and improving operating results include:

- Dollar sales and volume
- Profitability by product line, service, project, program, and territory
- Return on investment and residual income
- Divisional contribution margin, segment margin, and short-term performance margin
- Actual and budgeted costs by cost center
- Cash flow
- Labor and plant utilization
- Backlog
- Comparisons of each division's performance to other divisions within the company and to competing divisions in other companies

The CFO should determine whether current reporting may be improved. In one case, one of the authors, Professor Siegel, consulted with a company in which a maintenance and repair department manager prepared reports focusing solely on machine downtime. The reports concentrated on expenditures for repairs due to equipment breakdowns. Instead, the author recommended that the focus of attention should be on improving the productivity of manufacturing facilities. Hence, it is more constructive to look at uptime (machine usage) rather than downtime and to allocate resources accordingly. A machine uptime index may be computed. One can also analyze the production cycle period. This is the time between the receipt of an order and delivery to the customer, and it should be monitored on a regular basis.

How can reports be directed to improving quality?

Reports can be prepared with the view of improving the quality of goods and/or services while controlling costs. What is the cost effectiveness of contemplated quality improvements? Of course, there is a trade-off between better quality and increased costs. Attention should be directed to curing defects that cause project delays. Cost considerations include overtime, rework, scrap, and capital outlays. The reports should concentrate on the accumulated costs of actions that promote quality. The costs include material inspection, quality control, preventive maintenance, and sampling. The CFO should also consider the increased costs associated with poor-quality products and/or services, such as warranties, promotional expenditures to improve the company's image, and legal liability settlements.

EXHIBIT 1.4 ABC Company Statement of Revenue and Expense for Employees for the Year Ended December 31, 2X12

	Total Amount	Amount per Employee	Costs per Dollar of Receipts
Business Received			
From customers for merchandise or services performed			
Interest			
Dividends			
Total amount received			
Business Expenses Incurred			
For raw materials, supplies, and other expenses			
Depreciation			
Taxes			
Total expenses			
Residual for salaries, dividends, and reinvestment in the company			
This was divided as follows:			
Paid to employees (excluding officers' salaries)			
Paid for employee fringe benefits			
Total			
Executive salaries			
Executive fringe benefits			
Dividends to stockholders			
Reinvested in the company for expansion			
Total division			

What types of information might interest employees?

Reports (see Exhibit 1.4) can be directed toward the interests and concerns of employees and contain this information:

- Revenue and/or profitability per employee
- Revenue relative to employee salaries
- Assets per employee
- Profit margin
- Sales volume or service hours
- Investments made to directly or indirectly benefit employees
- Explanation of changes in benefit programs (e.g., health insurance, pension plan)

- Percentage increase in salaries, fringe benefits, and overtime
- Dividends relative to wages and number of employees
- Corporate annual growth rate; comparison of employee salaries to that of competing companies and industry averages
- Real earnings after adjusting for inflation
- Analytical profit and cost information by responsibility center
- Assets by business segment
- Future prospects and problems in the company, industry, and economy
- Break-even point
- Actual and expected production
- Employee safety
- Compliance with federal, state, and local laws pertaining to employee working conditions
- Sources of financing
- Nature and type of assets held
- Overall financial health of the company

 ## GOVERNMENTAL REPORTING

The CFO may have to prepare reports to federal, state, and city governmental agencies. Antitrust laws, environmental protection laws, pension laws, product liability laws, pollution laws, laws governing international trade and commerce, and tax laws are but a few of the myriad reports with which the company must contend. Penalties may be assessed for failing to file reports on time.

What does the New York Stock Exchange want to know?

The listing application to the New York Stock Exchange (NYSE) contains an agreement to provide annual and interim reports including financial statements and disclosures. The reports must be filed on a timely basis because the information they contain may have a material influence on the market price of stock, bond ratings, and cost of financing.

 ## REPORTING UNDER THE SARBANES-OXLEY ACT

SOX has had a significant impact on CFOs and their reporting responsibilities. It has changed how public companies are audited and has made adjustments to the financial reporting system. The Act has also created the PCAOB to enforce professional standards. In addition, it has increased corporate responsibility and the usefulness of corporate financial disclosures. CFOs must personally attest to the truth and fairness of their company's disclosures. The next provisions and requirements are promulgated under the Act as it applies to CFOs:

- CFOs cannot engage in any action to fraudulently influence, coerce, manipulate, or mislead the independent auditor.
- CFOs must certify in the annual report that they have reviewed the report and that it does not include untrue statements or omissions of material information.
- CFOs must establish and maintain internal controls to ensure proper reporting.
- CFOs are prohibited from falsifying records.
- Pro forma financial data in any report filed with the SEC or in any public release cannot include false or misleading statements or omit significant information needed to preserve the integrity of the financial data.
- The company's audit committee is responsible for the selection and oversight of the auditing CPA firm.
- An independent audit committee is required.
- No insider trading is allowed during pension fund blackout periods.
- Significant off-balance sheet transactions, arrangements, obligations, and other relationships must be disclosed. Disclosure must be made on material aspects related to financial condition, liquidity, resources, capital expenditures, and components of revenue and expense.

 XBRL REPORTING

Extensible Business Reporting Language (XBRL) is an *intelligent* Internet language that can be used in business by preparers and users of financial statements including corporate accountants, CPAs, financial analysts, business managers (in reviewing reports), loan officers at banks, investors, suppliers, securities exchanges (e.g., NYSE), over-the-counter market members of Nasdaq, and federal and local governmental agencies (e.g., the SEC and Internal Revenue Service). By comparison, the Hypertext Markup Language (HTML) format is not intelligent enough as a language to understand and reveal relationships in accounting and financial data. HTML is not designed to be aware of the information it presents. XBRL closes the "communication gap" between the preparers and users of financial data on the Internet.

XBRL represents a major step forward in the preparation, publication, exchange, and analysis of financial data. It results in a simpler process for issuing financial reports and making investment and credit decisions. XBRL standardizes financial reports by clearly specifying and defining each item of data, using clearly defined tags. This allows XBRL-enabled software to accurately read and understand the figures, store them, and compare them.

The precise definitions, or tags, are necessary because terms such as "revenue," "income," "fees," "stock," and "inventory" can have a variety of meanings, depending on the organization. Humans use judgment to interpret financial data, but for computers to make sense of it, they need precise definitions. The SEC requires public companies to prepare interactive financial statement data in XBRL format by 2013. For more on XBRL, see Chapter 19.

OTHER REPORTING

Many groups, such as trade associations, state commerce departments, federal bureaus and agencies, and credit agencies, compile statistics on business performance. These groups receive and complete questionnaires and reports on a wide range of topics.

The CFO's role in reporting information cannot be understated. Besides being able to formulate relevant financial and nonfinancial data, the CFO must be able to effectively and efficiently communicate that information to management, employees, government, investors, creditors, and other interested parties. The CFO should submit these reports in a timely way so that up-to-date information is available for decision-making purposes.

CHAPTER TWO

Securities and Exchange Commission Filings

THE SECURITIES AND EXCHANGE COMMISSION (SEC) requires full and fair disclosure in connection with the offering and issuance of securities to the public. The CFO should be familiar with the major provisions of the Securities Act of 1933 and the Securities Act of 1934.

The SEC's disclosure rules were enhanced by the Sarbanes-Oxley Act of 2002 (SOX), as detailed in Chapter 1. The accounting requirements of the SEC are specified mostly in Articles 3A through 12 of Regulation S-X, Financial Reporting Releases (FRRs), Accounting and Audit Enforcement Releases (AAERs), and industry guides.

 ## SEC RULES

What SEC rules apply to the issuance of securities for the first time?

The Securities Act of 1933 (as amended) pertains to the initial offering and sale of securities. It does not apply to the subsequent trading of securities. The Act requires the filing of a registration statement with the SEC so as to prevent misrepresentation.

What SEC rules apply to the subsequent trading of securities?

The Securities Act of 1934 regulates the subsequent trading of securities on the various national stock exchanges. A scaled-down version of the 1933 Act registration statement must be filed by the company if its securities are to be traded on a national exchange. The annual Form 10-K and the quarterly Form 10-Q are required to be filed.

What should the Basic Information Package contain?

The complexity of the reporting requirements under the 1933 and 1934 Acts was somewhat relieved when the SEC adopted the Integrated Disclosure System, which requires the Basic Information Package (BIP). The BIP includes:

▪ Audited balance sheets for the last two years and audited statements of income, retained earnings, and cash flows for the most recent three years
▪ Management's discussion and analysis of the company's financial position and operating results
▪ A five-year summary consisting of selected financial information

 ## S FORMS

What information is required in the S forms?

Form S-1

Form S-1 is typically used by a company that wants to sell securities and has been subject to the SEC reporting requirements for less than three years. The form typically includes:

▪ A description of the securities being registered
▪ A summary of the business including pertinent industry and segment information
▪ A listing of properties
▪ Background and financial information concerning the company's directors and officers
▪ Selected financial information over the last five years, including sales, profit, divisions, and total assets

Form S-2

Form S-2 is a short form that is used by issuers who have been reporting to the SEC for at least three years and have voting stock held by nonaffiliates of less than $150 million.

Form S-3

Form S-3 generally may be used by a company that has at least $150 million of voting stock owned by nonaffiliates. It may also be used if the company issues $100 million of securities and the annual trading volume is at least 3 million shares.

Form S-4

Form S-4 is filed for securities issuances arising from business combinations.

Form S-8

Form S-8 is filed when registering securities to be offered to employees under an employee benefit plan. Information presented is usually restricted to a description of the securities and the benefit plan.

Form S-18

Form S-18 is filed when the company's objective is to obtain capital of $7.5 million or less. Although disclosures shown in Form S-18 are very similar to those in Form S-1, some differences exist. Form S-18 does not mandate management's discussion and analysis. It also requires only one year's audited balance sheet and two years' audited statements of income and cash flows.

What should the CFO discuss when reporting to stockholders?

Management's discussion and analysis are important elements of the registration filing and provide an explanation of significant changes in financial position and results of operations, including:

- Results of operations
- Unusual or infrequent items
- Liquidity
- Capital resources
- Significant uncertainties

Forecasted data may be presented.

 SEC REGULATIONS

What disclosures are required under Regulation S-X?

In general, the accounting rules under Regulation S-X parallel generally accepted accounting principles (GAAP). However, some disclosure rules under Regulation S-X are more expansive. For example, financial statements filed with the SEC require these disclosures, which usually are not included in financial statements under GAAP:

- Lines of credit
- Compensating balance arrangements
- Current liabilities if they represent in excess of 5 percent of the entity's total liabilities

What disclosures are mandated under Regulation S-K?

Regulation S-K provides disclosures for information that is not part of the financial statements and includes:

- General data, such as the SEC's policies on projections and security ratings
- Selected financial information and changes in and disagreements with the independent auditor applicable to accounting matters and financial disclosures

- Description of the company's securities, market price of such securities, dividends paid, and associated stockholder matters
- Description of the business, its property, and litigation
- Disclosures related to directors and executive officers, executive pay, and security ownership of management
- Recent sales of unregistered securities and indemnification of directors and officers

What does Regulation S-B apply to?

Regulation S-B relates to financial and nonfinancial information in registration statements of small businesses.

What information must be filed annually with the SEC?

To comply with the Securities Act of 1934, most registrants must file a Form 10-K each year. It is due within 60 days after the reporting year-end. Some required disclosures are financial statements, management's discussion of operations, litigation, executive compensation, and related party transactions. The rules apply to public companies having a market value capitalization of $75 million or more.

What if something important suddenly happens?

Form 8-K usually must be filed immediately (within four business days) after a significant event occurs that materially affects the company's financial status and/or operating performance. Such events may include bankruptcy, acquisition or disposition of assets, change in control, change in outside auditor, and other important issues (e.g., litigation).

What information should be filed on an interim basis?

Form 10-Q is a quarterly filing updating for changes in financial position and operations since the filing of the last Form 10-K. Form 10-Q is due within 35 days after the end of each of the first three fiscal quarters.

What about electronic information?

The SEC's Electronic Data-Gathering, Analysis, and Retrieval (EDGAR) system for public companies has registration, documents, and other data available via online databases. The CFO can use EDGAR to obtain information, for research purposes, on how other entities have filed information with the SEC.

What about takeover regulation?

If an investor acquires more than a 5 percent ownership interest of a company, it must file with the SEC, the target business, and its stockholders the investor's identity, the source of financing, and the purpose of the acquisition.

What about unresolved matters?

In 2006, the SEC required most business entities to include a footnote on "unresolved staff comments." The company must disclose any significant comments from an SEC review of its filings issued more than 180 days before year-end or still unresolved by the date of Form 10-K. Examples of such matters include accounting violations, disclosures or procedural questions, and financial statement item restatements.

What about significant financial statement misstatement?

SEC Staff Accounting Bulletin (SAB) No. 108, *Considering the Effects of Prior Year Misstatements when Quantifying Misstatements in Current Year Financial Statements*, gives guidance on quantifying material financial statement misstatements, including the effect of carryover and reversal of prior-year restatements. The SEC will not object to a company making a one-time cumulative-effect adjustment to correct mistakes from prior years that are qualitatively and quantitatively immaterial, based on appropriate use of the registrant's previously used approach.

 ## SOX REPORTING REQUIREMENTS

What are the features of the Sarbanes-Oxley Act reporting?

Section 404(b) of the SOX Act, "Enhanced Financial Disclosures, Management Assessment of Internal Control," mandates sweeping changes. Section 404(b), in conjunction with the related SEC rules and Auditing Standard (AS) No. 5, *An Audit of Internal Control over Financial Reporting That Is Integrated with an Audit of Financial Statements*, established by the Public Company Accounting Oversight Board (PCAOB), requires the audit of internal control to be integrated with the audit of the financial statements. This integrated audit must be included in the company's annual report filed with the SEC.

- Management must report annually on the effectiveness of the company's internal control over financial reporting (ICFR).
- In conjunction with the audit of the company's financial statements, the company's independent auditor must issue a report on ICFR, which includes both an opinion on management's assessment and an opinion on the effectiveness of the company's ICFR.

In the past, a company's internal controls were considered in the context of planning the audit but were not required to be reported publicly, except in response to the SEC's Form 8-K requirements when related to a change in auditor. The new audit and reporting requirements have drastically changed the situation and have brought the concept of ICFR to the forefront for audit committees, management, auditors, and users of financial statements.

AS No. 5 highlights the concept of a significant deficiency in ICFR and mandates that both management and the independent auditor must publicly report any material weaknesses in ICFR that exist as of the fiscal year-end assessment date. Under both PCAOB AS No. 2 (*An Audit of Financial Statements*) and the SEC rules implementing Section 404, the existence of a single material weakness requires management and the independent auditor to conclude that ICFR is not effective. The main features of AS No. 5 are summarized later in the chapter.

How will the new reporting model differ from historical reporting?

In the past, the independent auditor provided an opinion on whether the company's financial statements were presented fairly in all material respects, in accordance with GAAP. The new reporting model maintains this historical requirement for the auditor to express an opinion on the financial statements. Section 404 also institutes additional requirements for management and the independent auditor to report on the effectiveness of ICFR.

Historical Reporting

> Independent auditor's opinion on whether the financial statements are presented fairly in all material respects, in accordance with GAAP

New Reporting

> *Management's report* on its assessment of the effectiveness of the company's ICFR
> *Independent auditor's report* on ICFR, including the auditor's opinions on: (1) whether management's assessment is fairly stated in all material respects (i.e., whether the auditor concurs with management's conclusions about the effectiveness of ICFR), and (2) the effectiveness of the company's ICFR

The auditor may choose to issue separate reports, such as a separate report on ICFR, or a combined report. The combined report on financial statements and ICFR addresses both the financial statements and management's report on ICFR. While the combined report is permitted, the separate report is more common. Exhibit 2.1 identifies the various reports and reflects the fact that management's assessment of ICFR constitutes the starting point for the auditor's reporting. Exhibit 2.2 is an example of the type of disclosure that public companies are now making

What will management's report include?

Neither the SEC nor the PCAOB has issued a standard or illustrative management report on ICFR; thus, there may be differences in the nature and extent of the information companies provide. We advise companies to consult with legal counsel on these matters. At a minimum, management's report on ICFR should include the following information:

- Statement of management's responsibility for establishing and maintaining adequate ICFR

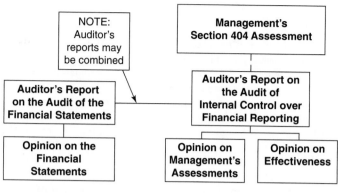

EXHIBIT 2.1   Section 404 Reporting

- Statement identifying the framework used by management to evaluate the effectiveness of ICFR
- Management's assessment of the effectiveness of the company's ICFR as of the end of the company's most recent fiscal year, including an explicit statement as to whether that internal control is effective and a disclosure of any material weaknesses identified by management in that control
- Statement that the registered public accounting firm that audited the financial statements included in the annual report has issued an attestation report on management's internal control assessment

EXHIBIT 2.2   Report on Management's Responsibilities

Home Depot

Management's Responsibility for Financial Statements

The financial statements presented in this Annual Report have been prepared with integrity and objectivity and are the responsibility of the management of The Home Depot, Inc. These financial statements have been prepared in conformity with U.S. generally accepted accounting principles and properly reflect certain estimates and judgments based upon the best available information.

The financial statements of the Company have been audited by KPMG LLP, an independent registered public accounting firm. Their accompanying report is based upon an audit conducted in accordance with the standards of the Public Company Accounting Oversight Board (United States).

The Audit Committee of the Board of Directors, consisting solely of outside directors, meets five times a year with the independent registered public accounting firm, the internal auditors and representatives of management to discuss auditing and financial reporting matters. In addition, a telephonic meeting is held prior to each quarterly earnings release. The Audit Committee retains the independent registered public accounting firm and regularly reviews the internal accounting controls, the activities of the independent registered public accounting firm and internal auditors and the financial condition of the Company. Both the Company's independent registered public accounting firm and the internal auditors have free access to the Audit Committee.

(continued)

EXHIBIT 2.2 *(continued)*

Management's Report an Internal Control over Financial Reporting
Our management is responsible for establishing and maintaining adequate internal control over financial reporting, as such term is defined in Rules 13a-15(f) promulgated under the Securities Exchange Act of 1934, as amended. Under the supervision and with the participation of our management, including our chief executive officer and chief financial officer, we conducted an evaluation of the effectiveness of our internal control over financial reporting as of February 3, 2011 based on the framework in Internal Control—Integrated Framework issued by the Committee of Sponsoring Organizations of the Treadway Commission (COSO). Based on our evaluation, our management concluded that our internal control over financial reporting was effective as of February 3, 2011 in providing reasonable assurance regarding the reliability of financial reporting and the preparation of financial statements for external purposes in accordance with generally accepted accounting principles. The effectiveness of our internal control over financial reporting as of February 3, 2011 has been audited by KPMG LLP, an independent registered public accounting firm, as stated in their report which is included on page 32 in this Form 10-K.

Francis S. Blake, Chairman & Chief Executive Officer
Carol B. Tome, Chief Financial Officer & Executive Vice President—Corporate Services

---

Management's report must indicate that ICFR is either:

- *Effective.* ICFR is effective (i.e., no material weaknesses in ICFR existed as of the assessment date).
- *Ineffective.* Internal control is not effective because one or more material weaknesses existed as of management's assessment date.

Management is required to state *whether or not* the company's ICFR is effective. A negative assurance statement, such as "Nothing has come to management's attention to suggest internal control is ineffective," is not acceptable.

If a material weakness exists as of the assessment date, management is required to conclude that ICFR is not effective and to disclose all material weaknesses that may have been identified. The SEC chief accountant has stated publicly that he expects management's report to disclose the nature of any material weakness in sufficient detail to enable investors and other financial statement users to understand the weakness and evaluate the circumstances underlying it.

Management may not express a qualified conclusion, such as stating that internal control is effective except to the extent that certain problems have been identified. If management is unable to assess certain aspects of internal control that are material to overall control effectiveness, management must conclude that ICFR is ineffective. Although management cannot issue a report with a scope limitation, under specific conditions, newly acquired businesses or certain other consolidated entities may be excluded from the assessment.

What are key points of Auditing Standard No. 5?

AS No. 5 has six key points.

1. *Focus the audit of ICFR on the most important matters.*

   AS No. 5 articulates a key principle that a direct relationship exists between the risk of material weakness and the amount of auditor attention given to that area. It requires auditors to use a top-down, risk-based approach, beginning with the financial statements and company-level controls, and requires the auditor to perform a walk-through for each significant process before selecting the controls to test. Using this assessment, the auditor selects the controls to test based on the risk of a material weakness. AS No. 5 emphasizes the integration of the financial statement audit with the audit of ICFR.

2. *Provide explicit and practical guidance on scaling the audit to fit the size and complexity of the company.*

   These provisions do not create a separate standard for smaller companies. Instead, AS No. 5 explicitly requires the auditor to tailor the nature, extent, and timing of testing to meet the unique characteristics of smaller companies.

3. *Eliminate procedures that are unnecessary to achieve the intended benefits.*

   AS No. 5 links the testing of specific controls to a risk assessment of that control. This means that the risk of a specific control not being effective should drive the nature, extent, and timing of testing performed and evidence of effectiveness obtained for that control.

SOX in Action

In response to the requirements of SOX, companies are placing a renewed focus on their accounting systems to ensure that relevant and reliable information is reported in financial statements. One study of first compliance with the internal-control testing provisions of SOX documented material weaknesses for about 13 percent of companies reporting in 2004 and 2005. Since then, material weaknesses declined, with just 8.33 percent of companies reporting internal control problems in 2006, for example. At the same time, companies reported a 5.4 percent decline in audit costs to comply with SOX internal control audit requirements.

Sources: L. Townsend, "Internal Control Deficiency Disclosures—Interim Alert," Yellow Card—Interim Trend Alert, April 12, 2005, Glass, Lewis & Co., LLC. K. Pany and J. Zhang, "Current Research Questions on Internal Control over Financial Reporting Under Sarbanes-Oxley," *CPA Journal* (February 2008): 42. FEI Audit Fee Survey, "Including Sarbanes-Oxley Section 404 Costs" (April 2008). ▪

4. *Require auditors to consider whether and how to use the work of others.*
   AS No. 5 allows auditors to place greater reliance on testing completed by management and the internal audit function. The scope of the new Auditing Standard applies to both the audit of ICFR and to the audit of financial statements, thus eliminating a barrier to the integrated audit.

5. *Incorporate guidance on efficiency.*
   Many of the audit efficiency practices outlined in AS No. 5's May 16, 2005 guidance are contained in the new standard. AS No. 5 specifically includes the language from the May 16 guidance regarding the baselining of information technology controls. As a result, companies can leverage this guidance to reduce compliance costs on a year-over-year basis.

6. *Establish a simplified standard.*
   AS No. 5 changes the definitions of material weakness from "more than remote" to "reasonably possible" and significant deficiency from "more than inconsequential" to "significant." AS No. 5 defines "significant" as "less than material but merits the attention of those with the responsibility for the oversight of financial reporting." In other words, significant deficiencies are not material weaknesses but items about which those responsible for oversight need to know.

PART TWO

Financial Reporting

CHAPTER THREE

Financial Statement Reporting: The Income Statement

I N PREPARING THE INCOME STATEMENT, revenue and expenses must be properly recognized. Many revenue recognition methods exist. Extraordinary and nonrecurring items must be shown separately. The income statement must be presented in the proper format with earnings per share (EPS) disclosed.

 HOW IS THE INCOME STATEMENT PRESENTED?

The format of the income statement follows.

Income from continuing operations before tax
Less: Taxes
Income from continuing operations after tax
Discontinued operations:
   Income from discontinued operations (net of tax)
   Loss or gain on disposal of a division (net of tax)
Income before extraordinary items
Extraordinary items (net of tax)
Net Income

The EPS effect for each of these items is presented.

What is comprehensive income?

Accounting Standards Codification (ASC) No. 220-10-45-3, *Comprehensive Income: Overall* (Financial Accounting Standards [FAS] No. 130, *Reporting Comprehensive Income*), mandates that companies report comprehensive income and its components.

Comprehensive income consists of two components: net income and "other comprehensive income," which includes:

- Unrealized (holding) loss or gain on available-for-sale securities
- Foreign currency translation gains or losses
- Change in market value of a futures contract that is a hedge of an asset reported at fair value

Although three options exist for how to report comprehensive income, most often it is presented below the net income figure in the income statement, as shown:

Statement of Income and Comprehensive Income		
Net Income		$500,000
Other Comprehensive Income:		
Unrealized loss on available-for-sale securities	($60,000)	
Foreign currency translation gain	80,000	
Total Other Comprehensive Income		20,000
Total Comprehensive Income		$520,000

Note

In the income statement, the "other comprehensive income" reported is for the *current year* only. In the balance sheet, under the stockholders' equity section, the "accumulated (cumulative) other comprehensive income" is reported for all the years. ■

What are extraordinary items?

Extraordinary items are unusual and infrequent. Unusual means the occurrence is abnormal and unrelated to the usual activities of the business. Infrequent means the transaction is not expected to occur in the foreseeable future considering the company's environment. Materiality looks at items individually and not in the aggregate. However, if arising from a single event, extraordinary items are aggregated. Extraordinary items are presented net of tax between income from discontinued operations and cumulative effect of a change in accounting principle. Examples of extraordinary items are:

- Casualty losses
- Gain on troubled debt restructuring
- Losses on expropriation of property by a foreign government
- Gain on life insurance proceeds
- Gain or loss on disposal of a major part of the assets of a previously separate company in a business combination when sale is made within two years after the combination date
- Loss from prohibition under a newly enacted law or regulation

Losses on receivables and inventory take place in the ordinary course of business and therefore are not extraordinary. However, losses on receivables and inventory are extraordinary if they relate to a casualty loss (e.g., earthquake) or governmental expropriation (e.g., withdrawal of a product deemed hazardous to health).

IFRS Treatment

International Financial Reporting Standards (IFRS) do not permit special reporting for extraordinary items. ■

What is a nonrecurring item, and how is it presented?

Nonrecurring items are unusual or infrequent. They are shown separately before tax in arriving at income from continuing operations. An example is the gain or loss on the sale of a fixed asset.

How are discontinued operations presented?

A business segment is a major line of business or customer class. A discontinued operation is one that is discontinued during the year or that will be discontinued shortly after year-end. It may be a segment that has been sold, abandoned, or spun off. The footnote disclosure for a discontinued operation includes an identification of the segment, the manner of disposal, disposal date, and description of the remaining net assets of the segment.

The two components of discontinued operations are: (1) income or loss from operations and (2) loss or gain on disposal of division.

ASC No. 360-10-05 (FAS No. 144), *Accounting for the Impairment or Disposal of Long-Lived Assets*, requires the following accounting and presentation to report discontinued operations:

- In a year in which a component of a company either has been disposed of or is held for sale, the income statement for the current and prior years must separately report the income (loss) on the component, including any gain or loss recognized in discontinued operations.
- The income (loss) of a component held for sale is reported in discontinued operations in the year(s) in which they occur. Therefore, phase-out operating losses are not accrued.
- The net of tax effect of the results of discontinued operations is presented as a separate component of income before extraordinary items and the cumulative effect of a change in accounting principle.
- The income (loss) of a component of a company that either has been disposed of or is held for sale is presented in discontinued operations only if both of the following conditions exist:

1. The company will not have any significant continual involvement in the operations of the component after the disposal transaction.
2. The cash flows and operations of the component have been (or will be) eliminated from the continual operations of the company due to the disposal transaction.

In general, gain or loss from operations of the discontinued component should include operating gain or loss and the gain or loss on disposal of a component incurred in the current year. Gains should not be recognized until the year actually realized.

IFRS Treatment

IFRS defines revenue to include both revenues and gains. U.S. generally accepted accounting principles provide separate definitions for the terms "revenues" and "gains." ■

 ## REVENUE RECOGNITION

Revenue can be recognized under different methods, depending on the circumstances. (Special revenue recognition guidelines exist for franchisors and in right-of-return situations. A product financing arrangement may also exist.) The basic methods of recognition are:

- Realization
- Completion of production
- During production
- Cash basis

When does realization occur?

Revenue is recognized when goods are sold or services are performed. This method is used most of the time. At realization, the earnings process is complete. Furthermore, realization is in conformity with accrual, meaning that revenue is recognized when earned rather than when received. Realization should be used when the selling price is determinable, future costs can be estimated, and an exchange has occurred that can be objectively measured. There are other cases in which another method of revenue recognition should be used, as discussed next.

When can revenue be recorded if production is completed?

Revenue can be recognized before sale or exchange. There must be a stable selling price, absence of significant marketing costs, and interchangeability in units. This approach is used with agricultural products, by-products, and precious metals when the aforementioned criteria are satisfied. It is also used in accounting for construction contracts under the completed-contract method.

When can revenue be recognized in stages?

Revenue can be recognized gradually as work is performed on a long-term contract. There must be an assured selling price and reliable estimation of costs. An example is the percentage of completion method for long-term construction contracts.

CONSTRUCTION CONTRACTS

Under the completed-contract method, revenue is recognized only in the final year the project is completed. The method should be used only when the percentage-of-completion method is inappropriate.

Under the percentage-of-completion method, revenue is recognized with production activity. The gradual recognition of revenue levels out earnings over the years and is more realistic since revenue is recognized as performance occurs. This method is preferred to the completed-contract method and should be used when reliable estimates of the degree of completion are possible. Percentage of completion results in a matching of revenue against expenses in the benefit period.

Using the cost-to-cost method, we see that revenue recognized for the period equals:

$$\frac{\text{Actual costs to date}}{\text{Total estimated costs}} \times \text{Contract price} = \text{Cumulative revenues}$$

Revenue recognized in previous years is deducted from the cumulative revenue to determine the revenue in the current period, for example:

Cumulative revenue (1–4 years)
Revenue recognized (1–3 years)
Revenue (Year 4–Current year)
Revenue less expenses equals profit

Example 3.1

In year 4 of a contract, the actual costs to date were $50,000. Total estimated costs were $200,000, and the contract price was $1 million. Revenue recognized in the prior years (years 1–3) was $185,000.

$$\frac{\$50,000}{\$200,000} \times \$1,00,000 = \$250,000$$

Cumulative revenue	$250,000
Prior year revenue	185,000
Current year revenue	$65,000

(continued)

Regardless of which method is used, conservatism requires that a loss on a contract be recognized immediately.

Journal entries under the construction method using assumed figures include:

	Percentage of Completion		Completed Contract	
Construction in progress (CIP)	$100,000		$100,000	
Cash		$100,000		$100,000
Construction costs				
Progress billings				
Receivable	$80,000		$80,000	
Progress billings on CIP		$80,000		$80,000
Periodic billings				
CIP	$25,000		No entry	
Profit		$25,000		

In the last year when the construction project is completed, the following additional entry is made to record the profit in the final year:

	Percentage of Completion	Completed Contract
Progress billings on CIP	Total billings	Total billings
CIP	Cost + Profit	Cost
Profit	Incremental profit for last year	Profit for all the years

CIP less progress billings is shown net. Typically, a debit figure results that is shown as a current asset. CIP is an inventory account for a construction company. If a credit balance occurs, the net amount is shown as a current liability.

IFRS Treatment

IFRS prohibits the use of the completed-contract method of accounting for long-term construction contracts. Companies must use the percentage-of-completion method. If revenues and costs are difficult to estimate, then companies recognize revenue only to the extent of the cost incurred—a zero-profit approach. ■

When must revenue recognition await cash receipt?

If a company sells inventory, the accrual basis is used. However, when certain circumstances exist, the cash basis of revenue recognition is used. Namely, revenue is recognized when cash is received. The cash basis rather than the accrual basis must be used when one or more of these circumstances exist:

- Selling price is not objectively determinable at the time of sale
- Inability to estimate expenses at the time of sale
- Collection risk
- Uncertain collection period

Revenue recognition under the installment method equals the cash collected times the gross profit percent. Any gross profit not collected is deferred on the balance sheet until collection occurs. When collections are received, realized gross profit is recognized by debiting the deferred gross profit account. The balance sheet presentation is:

Accounts receivable (Cost + Profit)
Less: Deferred gross profit (Profit)
Net accounts receivable (Cost)

Under the cost recovery method, profit is recognized only after all costs have been recovered.

Note

Since a service business does not have inventory, it has the option of using either the accrual basis or cash basis. ■

What if the buyer has the privilege to return the merchandise?

If a buyer has the right to return merchandise, the seller can recognize revenue only at the time of sale, according to ASC No. 605-15-25-1, *Revenue Recognition: Products* (FAS No. 48, *Revenue Recognition when Right of Return Exists*) if all of these criteria are met:

- The selling price is known.
- Buyer has to pay for the product even if the buyer is unable to resell it.
- If the buyer loses or damages the item, the buyer still has to pay for it.
- Purchase by the buyer makes economic sense.
- Seller does not have to perform future services so that the buyer will be able to resell the item.
- Returns may be reasonably estimated.

If any one of these criteria is not satisfied, revenue must be deferred along with deferral of related expenses until the criteria have been met or the right-of-return provision has expired. An alternative to deferring the revenue would be to record a memo entry.

The ability of a company to predict future returns involves consideration of:

- Predictability
  - Technological obsolescence risk of the product, uncertain product demand changes, or other significant external factors detract from predictability.
  - A long time period for returns lessens predictability.
  - The presence of many similar transactions enhances predictability.
- Whether the seller has prior experience in estimating returns for similar products
- Whether the nature of customer relationship and types of products sold is known

What is a product financing arrangement?

According to ASC No. 470-40-25, *Debt: Product Financing Arrangements* (FAS No. 49, *Accounting for Product Financing Arrangements*), the sale and repurchase of inventory is in substance a financing arrangement. The product financing arrangement must be accounted for as a borrowing and not as a sale. In many instances, the product is stored on the company's (sponsor's) premises. Furthermore, the sponsor often guarantees the debt of the other entity.

Product financing arrangements are of two types:

1. Sponsor sells a product to another business and contracts to reacquire it or an identical one. The price paid by the sponsor usually includes financing and storage costs.
2. Sponsor controls the distribution of the product that has been bought by another company based on the aforementioned terms.

In each case, the company (sponsor) either agrees to repurchase the product at specified prices over given time periods or guarantees resale prices to third parties.

When the sponsor sells the product to the other business and in a related transaction agrees to repurchase it, the sponsor records a liability when the proceeds are received. A sale should not be recorded, and the product should be retained as inventory on the sponsor's balance sheet.

If another entity buys the product for the sponsor, inventory is debited, and liability is credited at the time of purchase.

Costs of the product, excluding processing costs, that exceed the sponsor's original cost represent finance and holding costs. The sponsor accounts for these costs based on its customary accounting policies. Interest expense will also be recognized.

Example 3.2

On 1/1/2X12, a sponsor borrows $100,000 from another company and gives the inventory as collateral. The entry is:

Cash	$100,000	
Liability		$100,000

A sale is not recorded, and the inventory continues on the books of the sponsor.

On 12/31/2X12, the sponsor remits payment to the other company. The collateralized inventory item is returned. If the interest rate on the loan is 8 percent and storage costs are $2,000, the journal entry is:

Liability	$100,000	
Interest expense (or		
Deferred interest)	8,000	
Storage expense	2,000	
Cash		$110,000

In most cases, the product in the financing agreement is ultimately used or sold by the sponsor. However, in some instances, small amounts of the product may be sold by the financing entity to other parties.

The entity providing financing to the sponsor is typically an existing creditor, nonbusiness entity, or trust. It is also possible that the financer may have been established for the sole purpose of providing financing to the sponsor.

Footnote disclosure should be made of the product financing terms.

How should franchisors recognize revenue?

According to ASC No. 952-10-25-4, *Franchisors; Revenue Recognition* (FAS No. 45, *Accounting for Franchise Fee Revenue*), the franchisor can record revenue from the initial sale of the franchise only when all significant services and obligations applicable to the sale have been substantially performed. Substantial performance is indicated by these points:

- There is an absence of intent to give cash refunds or relieve the accounts receivable due from the franchisee.
- Nothing material remains to be done by the franchisor.
- Initial services have been rendered.

The earliest date that substantial performance can take place is the franchisee's commencement of operations unless there are special circumstances. When it is probable that the franchisor will eventually repurchase the franchise, the initial fee may be deferred and treated as a reduction of the repurchase price.

If revenue is deferred, the related expenses must be deferred for later matching in the year in which the revenue is recognized, as in the next illustration.

Year of initial fee:
Cash
    Deferred revenue
Deferred expenses
    Cash
Year when substantial performance occurs:
Deferred revenue
    Revenue
Expenses
    Deferred expenses

If the initial fee includes both services and property (real or personal), there should be an allocation based on fair market values.

When part of the initial fee applies to tangible property (e.g., equipment, signs, inventory), revenue recognition is based on the fair value of the assets. Revenue recognition may occur before or after recognizing the portion of the fee related to initial services. For example, part of the fee for equipment may be recognized at the time title passes, with the balance of the fee being recorded as revenue when future services are performed.

Recurring franchise fees are recognized as earned with related costs being expensed. There is one exception. If the price charged for the continuing services or goods to the franchisee is less than the price charged to third parties, it implies that the initial franchise fee was in essence a partial prepayment for the recurring franchise fee. In this case, part of the initial fee has to be deferred and recognized as an adjustment of the revenue from the sale of goods and services at bargain prices.

When there is a probability that continuing franchise fees will not cover the cost of the continuing services and provide for a reasonable profit to the franchisor, part of the initial franchise fee should be deferred to satisfy the deficiency and amortized over the life of the franchise. The deferred amount should be adequate to meet future costs and generate a profit on the recurring services. This situation may arise if the continuing fees are minimal considering the services rendered or if the franchisee has the option to make bargain purchases over a stated time period.

Unearned franchise fees are recorded at present value. Where a part of the initial fee represents a nonrefundable amount for services already performed, revenue should be recognized accordingly.

The initial franchise fee is not usually allocated to specific franchisor services before all services are performed. Such allocations can be made only if actual transaction prices are available for individual services.

If the franchisor sells equipment and inventory to the franchisee at no profit, a receivable and a payable are recorded. There is no revenue or expense recognition.

When there is a repossessed franchise, amounts refunded to the franchisee reduce current revenue. In the absence of a refund, the franchisor records additional revenue for the consideration retained that was not previously recorded. In either case, prospective accounting treatment is given for the repossession. *Warning:* Do not adjust previously recorded revenue for the repossession.

Indirect costs of an operating and recurring nature are expensed immediately. Future costs are accrued no later than the period in which related revenue is recognized. A bad debt provision for uncollectible franchise fees should be recorded in the year of revenue recognition.

Installment or cost recovery accounting may be used to account for franchise fee revenue only if there is a long collection period and future uncollectibility of receivables cannot be estimated reliably.

Footnote disclosure should be made of outstanding obligations, and franchise fee revenue should be segregated between initial and continuing.

We now consider other revenue aspects.

What happens if the vendor gives consideration to a customer?

In general, if the vendor provides the customer something to purchase the vendor's product, such consideration should reduce the vendor's revenue applicable to that sale.

What if the vendor is reimbursed for its "out-of-pocket" expenses?

The vendor records the recovery of reimbursable expenses (e.g., shipping costs billed to customer, travel costs on service contracts) as revenue.

Note

These costs are not netted as a reduction of cost. ■

How are contributions received recorded?

As per ASC No. 958-605-05 *Not-for-Profit Entities: Revenue Recognition* (FAS No. 116, *Accounting for Contributions Received and Contributions Made*), contributions received by a donee are recorded at fair market value by debiting the asset and crediting revenue. The donor debits contribution expense at fair market value. A gain or loss is recorded if fair value differs from the carrying value of the donated asset.

EXPENSE RECOGNITION

How are advertising costs accounted for?

Advertising must be expensed as incurred or when the advertising program first occurs. The cost of a billboard should be deferred and amortized.

How are restructuring charges treated?

Restructuring charges are expensed. In general, an expense and liability is accrued for employee termination costs. Disclosure should be made of the group and number of employees laid off.

Start-up costs including organization costs and moving costs are expensed as incurred.

How are environmental costs accounted for?

Environmental contamination costs typically are expensed as incurred. However, the company may elect to expense or capitalize the costs if (1) the expenditures extend the life of the asset or improve the property's safety or (2) the expenditures reduce environmental contamination that may result from the future activities of property owned.

What are research and development costs, and how are they accounted for?

Research is the testing in search for a new product, process, service, or technique. Research can be directed at substantially improving an existing product or process. *Development* is translating the research into a design for the new product or process. Development may also result in a significant improvement to an existing product or process. According to ASC No. 730-10-05-1, *Research and Development: Overall* (FAS No. 2, *Accounting for Research and Development Costs*), research and development (R&D) costs are expensed as incurred. However, R&D costs incurred under contract for others that are reimbursable are charged to a receivable account. Furthermore, materials, equipment, and intangibles bought from others that have alternative future benefit in R&D activities are capitalized. The depreciation or amortization on such assets is classified as R&D expense. If there is no alternative future use, the costs should be expensed.

R&D cost includes the salaries of personnel involved in R&D efforts. R&D cost also includes a rational allocation of indirect (general and administrative) costs. If a group of assets are acquired, allocation should be made to those that relate to R&D activities. When a business combination is accounted for as a purchase, R&D costs are assigned their fair market value.

Expenditures paid to others to conduct R&D activities are expensed.

Examples of R&D activities include:

- Formulation and design of product alternatives and testing thereof
- Preproduction models and prototypes
- Design of models, tools, and dies involving latest technology
- Laboratory research
- Pilot plant costs
- Engineering functions until the product meets operational guidelines for manu-facture

Examples of activities that are not for R&D include:

- Legal costs to obtain a patent
- Quality control
- Seasonal design modifications
- Market research
- Commercial use of the product
- Rearrangement and start-up operations, including design and construction engineering
- Recurring efforts to improve the product
- Identifying breakdowns during commercial production

FASB No. 2 does not apply to either regulated or extractive (e.g., mining) industries.

According to ASC No. 985-20-25, *Software: Costs of Software to Be Sold, Leased, or Marketed* (FAS No. 86, *Accounting for the Costs of Computer Software to Be Sold, Leased, or Otherwise Marketed*), costs incurred for computer software to be sold, leased, or otherwise marketed are expensed as R&D costs until technological feasibility has been established as evidenced by the development of a detailed program or working model. After technological feasibility, software production costs should be deferred and recorded at the lower of unamortized cost or net realizable value. Examples of such costs include debugging of the software, improvements to subroutines, and adaptations for other uses. Amortization starts when the product is available for customer release. The amortization expense should be based on the higher of the straight-line amortization amount or the percentage of current revenue to total revenue from the product.

As per ASC No. 730-20-25, *Research and Development: Research and Development Arrangements* (FAS No. 68, *Research and Development Arrangements*), if a company enters into an agreement with other parties to fund the R&D efforts, the nature of the obligation must be determined. If the company has an obligation to repay the funds regardless of the R&D results, a liability must be recognized with the related R&D expense. The journal entries are:

Cash	
Liability	
Research and development expense	
Cash	

A liability does not arise when the transfer of financial risk to the other party is substantive. If the financial risk is transferred because repayment depends only on the R&D possessing future benefit, the company accounts for its obligation as a contract to conduct R&D for others. In this case, R&D costs are capitalized, and revenue is recognized as earned and becomes billable under the contract. Footnote disclosure is made of the terms of the R&D agreement, the amount of compensation earned, and the costs incurred under the contract.

When repayment of loans or advances to the company depends only on R&D results, such amounts are considered R&D costs incurred by the company and charged to expense.

If warrants or other financial instruments are issued in an R&D arrangement, the company records part of the proceeds to be provided by the other parties as paid-in capital based on their fair market value on the arrangement date.

How are earnings per share computed?

ASC No. 260-10-50-1, *Earnings per Share: Overall* (FAS No. 128, *Earnings per Share*) requires the computation of basic EPS and diluted EPS. Basic EPS includes only the actual number of outstanding shares during the period. Diluted EPS includes the effect of common shares actually outstanding and the effect of convertible securities, stock options, stock warrants, and their equivalents. Diluted EPS does not include antidilutive securities (contingent issuance of securities increasing EPS or decreasing loss per share).

Basic EPS equals net income available to common stockholders divided by the weighted-average number of common shares outstanding.

Weighted-average common stock shares outstanding considers the number of months in which those shares were outstanding.

Example 3.3

On 1/1/2X12 10,000 shares were issued. On 4/1/2X12, 2,000 of those shares were reacquired. The weighted-average common stock outstanding is:

$$(10,000 \times 3/12) + (8,000 \times 9/12) = 8,500 \text{ shares}$$

Example 3.4

The following information is presented for a business:

Preferred stock, $10 par, 6% cumulative, 30,000 shares issued, and outstanding	$300,000
Common stock, $5 par, 100,000 shares issued and outstanding	$500,000
Net income	$400,000
Cash dividend on preferred stock = $300,000 × 6% =	$18,000

Basic EPS = Net income − preferred dividends/Common shares outstanding

$$\$400,000 - \$18,000 = \$320,000/100,000 \text{ shares} = \$3.82$$

Example 3.5

On 1/1/2X12, a company had the following outstanding shares:

Cumulative preferred stock, 6%, $100 par	150,000 shares
Common stock, $5 par	500,000 shares

During the year, the following occurred:

- On 4/1/2X12, the company issued 100,000 shares of common stock.
- On 9/1/2X12, the company declared and issued a 10 percent stock dividend.
- For the year ended 12/31/2X12, the net income was $2,200,000.

Basic EPS for 2X12 equals $2.06 ($1,300,000/632,500 shares) computed next.

Earnings available to common stockholders:	
Net income	$2,200,000
Less: Preferred dividend (150,000 shares × $6)	900,000
Earnings available to common stockholders	$1,300,000

Weighted-average number of common shares outstanding is computed as:

1/1/2X12–3/31/2X12 (500,000 × 3/12 × 110%)	137,500
4/1/2X12–8/31/2X12 (600,000 × 5/12 × 110%)	275,000
9/1/2X12–12/31/2X12 (660,000 × 4/12)	220,000
Weighted-average common shares outstanding	632,500

Diluted EPS = Net income available to common stockholders + Net of tax interest and/or dividend savings on convertible securities/Weighted average number of common shares outstanding + Effect of convertible securities + Net effect of stock options

Example 3.6

Assume the same information as in Example 3.5. Further assume that potentially diluted securities outstanding include 5 percent convertible bonds (each $1,000 bond is convertible into 25 shares of common stock) having a face value of $5 million. There are options to buy 50,000 shares of common stock at $10 per share. The

(continued)

average market price for common shares is $25 per share for 2X12. The tax rate is 30 percent. Diluted EPS for 2X12 is $1.87 ($1,475,000/787,500 shares) as computed next.

Income for diluted EPS:		
Earnings available to common stockholders		$1,300,000
Interest expense on convertible bonds ($5,000,000 × 0.05)	$250,000	
Less: Tax savings ($250,000 × 0.30)	$ 75,000	
Interest expense (net of tax)		$ 175,000
Income for diluted EPS		$1,475,000
Shares outstanding for diluted EPS:		
Weighted-average outstanding common shares		632,500
Assumed issued common shares for convertible bonds (5,000 bonds × 25 shares)		125,000
Assumed issued common shares from exercise of option	50,000	
Less: Assumed repurchase of treasury shares	20,000	
Net amount of shares		30,000
Shares outstanding for diluted EPS		787,500

    Basic EPS and diluted EPS (if required) must be disclosed on the face of the income statement. A reconciliation is required of the numerators and denominators for both basic and diluted EPS calculations.

    When shares are issued because of a stock dividend or stock split, the computation of weighted-average common stock shares outstanding requires retroactive adjustment as if the shares were outstanding at the beginning of the year.

    The common stock equivalency of options and warrants is determined using the treasury stock method. Options and warrants are assumed exercised at the beginning of the year (or at time of issuance, if later).

Example 3.7

One hundred shares are under option at an option price of $10. The average market price of stock is $25. The common stock equivalent is 60 shares as calculated next:

Issued shares from option	100 shares × $10 = $1,000
Less: Treasury shares	40 shares × $25 = $1,000
Common stock equivalent	60 shares

Convertible securities are accounted for using the "if converted method." The convertible securities are assumed converted at the beginning of the earliest year presented or date of security issuance. Interest or dividends on them are added back to net income since the securities are considered part of equity in the denominator of the EPS calculation.

Net income less preferred dividends is in the numerator of the EPS fraction representing earnings available to common stockholders. On cumulative preferred stock, preferred dividends for the current year are subtracted whether paid or not. Furthermore, preferred dividends are subtracted only for the current year. Thus, if preferred dividends in arrears were for five years, all of which were paid plus the sixth-year dividend, only the sixth-year dividend (current year) would be deducted. Note that preferred dividends for each of the prior years would have been deducted in those years.

In computing EPS, preferred dividends are subtracted only on preferred stock that was not included as a common stock equivalent. If the preferred stock is a common stock equivalent, the preferred dividend will not be deducted because the equivalency of preferred shares into common shares is included in the denominator.

If convertible bonds are included in the denominator of EPS, they are considered as equivalent to common shares. Thus, interest expense (net of tax) has to be added back in the numerator.

Disclosure of EPS should include information on the capital structure, explanation of the computation of EPS, identification of common stock equivalents, number of shares converted, and assumptions made. Rights and privileges of the securities should also be disclosed. Such disclosure includes dividend and participation rights, conversion ratios, call prices, and sinking fund requirements.

A stock conversion occurring during the year, or between year-end and the audit report date, may significantly impact EPS if it occurs at the beginning of the year. Thus, supplementary footnote disclosure should be made reflecting on an as-if basis what the effects of these conversions would have had on EPS if they were made at the start of the accounting period.

If a subsidiary has been acquired under the purchase accounting method during the year, the weighted-average shares outstanding for the year is used from the purchase date.

When comparative financial statements are presented, there is a retroactive adjustment for stock splits and stock dividends. Assume that in 2X12 a 10 percent stock dividend occurs. The weighted-average shares used for previous years' computations has to be increased by 10 percent to make EPS data comparable.

When a prior-period adjustment occurs that results in a restatement of previous years' earnings, EPS should be restated.

CHAPTER FOUR

4

Financial Statement Reporting: The Balance Sheet

O N THE BALANCE sheet, the CFO is concerned with the accounting for and reporting of assets, liabilities, and stockholders' equity.

 ## ASSETS

How are assets recorded?

An asset is recorded at the price paid plus the cost of putting the asset in service (e.g., freight, insurance, installation). If an asset is acquired in exchange for a liability, the asset is recorded at the discounted values of the future payments.

Example 4.1

A machine was bought by taking out a loan requiring ten $10,000 payments. Each payment includes principal and interest. The interest rate is 10 percent. Although the total payments (principal and interest) are $100,000, the present value will be less since the machine is recorded at the present value of the payments. The asset would be recorded at $61,450 ($10,000 × 6.145). The factor is obtained from the present value of an annuity of $1.00 table (Table A.4 in the Appendix) for $n = 10$, $i = 10\%$.

Note

The asset is recorded at the principal amount excluding the interest payments. If an asset is acquired for stock, the asset is recorded at the fair value of the stock issued. If it is impossible to ascertain the fair market value of the stock (e.g., closely held company), the asset will be recorded at its appraised value. ∎

45

Unearned discounts (except for quantity or cost), finance charges, and interest included in the face of receivables should be deducted to arrive at the net receivable.

Some of the major current and noncurrent assets are accounts receivable, inventory, fixed assets, and intangibles.

 ## ACCOUNTS RECEIVABLE

What is an assignment of accounts receivable?

When accounts receivable are assigned, the owner of the receivables borrows cash from a lender in the form of a note payable. The accounts receivable serves as security. New receivables substitute for receivables collected. The assignment of accounts receivable usually involves a financing charge and interest on the note.

The transferor's equity in the assigned receivables equals the difference between the accounts receivable assigned and the balance of the line (e.g., $50,000). When payments on the receivables are received, they are remitted by the company to the lending institution to reduce the liability. Customers are not notified of the assignment. Assignment is with recourse, meaning the company has to make good for uncollectible accounts.

Example 4.2

On 4/1/2X12, X Company assigns accounts receivable totaling $600,000 to A Bank as collateral for a $400,000 note. X Company will continue to receive customer remissions since the customers are not notified of the assignment. There is a 2 percent finance charge of the accounts receivable assigned. Interest on the note is 13 percent. Monthly settlement of the cash received from assigned receivables is made. During April, there were collections of $360,000 of assigned receivables less cash discounts of $5,000. Sales returns were $10,000. On 5/1/2X12, April remissions were made plus accrued interest. In May, the balance of the assigned accounts receivable was collected less $4,000 that were uncollectible. On 6/1/2X12, the balance due was remitted to the bank plus interest for May. The journal entries follow.

4/1/2X12		
Cash	$388,000	
Finance charge (2% × $600,000)	12,000	
Accounts receivable assigned	600,000	
Notes payable		$400,000
Accounts receivable		600,000
During April:		
Cash	355,000	
Sales discount	5,000	
Sales returns	10,000	
Accounts receivable assigned		370,000

5/1/2X12		
Interest expense	4,333[a]	
Notes payable	355,000	
Cash		359,333
During May:		
Cash	226,000	
Allowance for bad debts	4,000	
Accounts receivable assigned ($600,000 – $370,000)		230,000
6/1/2X12		
Interest expense	488[b]	
Notes payable ($400,000 – $355,000)	45,000	
Cash		45,488

[a] $400,000 × 0.13 × 1/12 = $4,333
[b] $45,000 × 0.13 × 1/12 = $488

How does factoring of accounts receivable work?

When factoring accounts receivable, the receivables are sold to a finance company. The factor buys the accounts receivable at a discount from face value (typically a discount of 6 percent). Customers are usually notified. The factoring arrangement is usually without recourse, where the risk of uncollectability of the customer's account rests with the financing institution. Billing and collection is typically done by the factor. The factor charges a commission ranging from 0.75 percent to 1.5 percent of the net receivables acquired. The entry is:

Cash (proceeds)
Loss on sale of receivables
Due from factor (proceeds kept by factor to cover possible adjustments such as sales discounts, sales returns, and allowances)
Accounts receivable (face amount of receivables)

Factoring is usually a continual process. The seller of merchandise receives orders and transmits them to the factor for acceptance; if approved, the goods are shipped; the factor advances the money to the seller; the buyers pay the factor when payment is due; and the factor periodically remits any excess reserve to the seller of the goods. There is a continual circular flow of goods and money among the seller, the buyers, and the factor. Once the agreement is in effect, funds from this source are spontaneous.

Example 4.3

T Company factors $200,000 of accounts receivable. There is a 4 percent finance charge. The factor retains 6 percent of the accounts receivable. Appropriate journal entries are:

Cash	180,000	
Loss on sale of receivables (4% × $200,000)	8,000	
Due from factor (6% × $200,000)	12,000	
Accounts receivable		200,000

Factors provide a dependable source of income for small manufacturers and service businesses.

Example 4.4

You need $100,000 and are considering a factoring arrangement. The factor is willing to buy the accounts receivable and advance the invoice amount less a 4 percent factoring commission on the receivables purchased. Sales are on 30-day terms. A 14 percent interest rate will be charged on the total invoice price and deducted in advance. With the factoring arrangement, the credit department will be eliminated, reducing monthly credit expenses by $1,500. Also, bad debt losses of 8 percent on the factored amount will be avoided.

To net $100,000, the amount of accounts receivable to be factored is:

$$\frac{\$100,000}{1-(0.04+0.14)} = \frac{\$100,000}{0.82} = \$12$$

The effective interest rate on the factoring arrangement is:

$$0.14/0.82 = 17.07\%$$

The annual total dollar cost is:

Interest (0.14 × $121,951)	$17,073
Factoring (0.04 × $121,951)	4,878
Total cost	$21,951

What if receivables are transferred with recourse?

A sale is recorded for the transfer of receivables with recourse if all three of these conditions are met:

1. The transferor gives up control of the future economic benefits applicable to the receivables (e.g., repurchase right).

2. The liability of the transferor under the recourse provisions can be estimated.
3. The transferee cannot require the transferor to repurchase the receivables unless there is a recourse stipulation in the contract.

When the transfer is treated as a sale, gain or loss is recognized for the difference between the selling price and the net receivables. The selling price includes normal servicing fees of the transferor and probable adjustments (e.g., debtor's failure to pay on time, effects of prepayment, and defects in the transferred receivable). Net receivables equals gross receivables plus finance and service charges minus unearned finance and service charges.

If the selling price varies during the term of the receivables because of a variable interest rate provision, the selling price is estimated with the use of an appropriate going market interest rate at the transfer date. Subsequent changes in the rate result in a change in estimated selling price, not in interest income or interest expense.

If one of the aforementioned criteria is not met, a liability is recognized for the amount received.

Footnote disclosure includes amount received by transferor and balance of the receivables at the balance sheet date.

INVENTORY

Inventory may be valued at the lower of cost or market value. Specialized inventory methods may be used such as retail, retail lower of cost or market; retail last-in, first-out (LIFO); and dollar value LIFO. Losses on purchase commitments should be recognized in the accounts.

If ending inventory is understated, cost of sales is overstated, and net income is understated. If beginning inventory is understated, cost of sales is understated, and net income is overstated.

How does the lower-of-cost-or-market value method work?

Inventories are recorded at the lower of cost or market value for conservative purposes applied on a total basis, category basis, or individual basis. The basis selected must be used consistently.

If cost is less than market value (replacement cost), cost is selected. If market value is below cost, we start with market value. However, market value cannot exceed the ceiling, which is net realizable value (selling price less costs to complete and dispose). If it does, the cost is used. Furthermore, market value cannot be less than the floor that is net realizable value less a normal profit margin. If market value is less than the floor, floor value is chosen. Of course, market value is used when it lies between the ceiling and floor. (See Exhibit 4.1.)

EXHIBIT 4.1 Lower of Cost or Market Value

Example 4.5

The lower of cost or market value method is applied on an item-by-item basis. The bold figure is the appropriate valuation.

Product	Cost	Market	Ceiling	Floor
A	**$ 5**	$ 7	$ 9	$ 6
B	14	12	**11**	7
C	18	**15**	16	12
D	20	12	18	**16**
E	**6**	5	12	7

Note that in case E, market value of $5 was originally selected. The market value of $5 exceeded the floor of $7, so the floor value would be used. However, if after applying the lower of cost or market value rule, the valuation derived ($7) exceeds the cost ($6), the cost figure is more conservative and thus is used.

If market (replacement cost) is below the original cost but the selling price has not also declined, no loss should be recognized. To do so would result in an abnormal profit margin in the future period.

The lower of cost or market value method is not used with LIFO since under LIFO, current revenue is matched against current costs.

How does the retail method work?

Some large retail concerns use the retail method. These businesses may carry inventory items at retail selling price. The retail method is used to estimate the ending inventory at cost by employing a cost-to-retail (selling price) ratio. The ending inventory is first determined at selling price and then converted to cost. Markups and markdowns are both considered in arriving at the cost-to-retail ratio, resulting in a higher ending inventory than the retail lower of cost or market value method.

Retail Lower-of-Cost-or-Market Value Method (Conventional Retail)

This is a modification of the retail method and is preferable to it. In computing the cost-to-retail ratio, markups but not markdowns are considered, resulting in a lower inventory figure.

Example 4.6 illustrates the accounting difference between the retail method and the retail lower of cost or market value method.

Example 4.6 Retail Method versus Retail Lower-of-Cost-or-Market Value Method

	Cost	Retail
Inventory—beginning	16,000	30,000
Purchases	30,000	60,000

	Cost	Retail
Purchase returns	(5,000)	(10,000)
Purchase discount	(2,000)	
Freight in	1,000	
Markups	25,000	
Markup cancellations	5,000	20,000
Total (40%)	40,000	100,000
Markdowns	22,000	
Markdown cancellations	2,000	20,000
Cost of goods available (50%)	40,000	80,000
Deduct:		
Sales	55,000	
Less: sales returns	5,000	50,000
Inventory—Retail		30,000
Retail method: At cost 50% × 30,000		15,000
Retail lower of cost or market method:		
40% × 30,000		12,000

Retail LIFO

In computing ending inventory, the mechanics of the retail method are basically used. Beginning inventory is excluded, and both markups and markdowns are included in computing the cost-to-retail ratio. A decrease in inventory during the period is deducted from the most recent layer and then subtracted from layers in the inverse order of addition. A retail price index is used in restating inventory.

Example 4.7

Retail price indices follow.

2X10	100
2X11	104
2X12	110

	Cost	Retail
2X11		
Inventory—Jan. 1 (base inv.)	80,000	130,000
Purchases	240,000	410,000
Markups		10,000
Markdowns		(20,000)

(continued)

	Cost	Retail
Total (exclude beg. inv.) 60%	240,000	400,000
Total (include beg. inv.)	320,000	530,000
Sales		389,600
2X11 inv.—retail		140,400[a]
Cost basis		
2X11 inventory in terms of		
2X10 prices 140,400 ÷ 1.04		135,000
2X10 base	80,000	130,000
2X11 layer in 2X10 prices		5,000
2X11 layer in 2X11 prices		5,200
2X11 LIFO cost 60% × 5,200	3,120	
	83,120	140,000[a]
2X12		
Inventory—Jan. 1	83,120	140,400
Purchases	260,400	430,000
Markups		20,000
Markdowns		(30,000)
Total (exclude beg. inv.) 62%	260,400	420,000
Total (include beg. inv.)	343,520	560,400
Sales		408,600
2X12 inventory—end at retail		151,800
Cost Basis		
2X12 Inventory in 2X10 prices 151,800 ÷ 1.10		138,000
2X10 base	80,000	130,000
Excess over base year		8,000
2X11 layer in 2X11 prices	3,120	5,000
2X12 layer in 2X10 prices		3,000
2X12 layer in 2X12 prices		3,300
2X12 increase in 2X12 prices LIFO cost 62% × 3,300	2,046	
	85,166	151,800[b]

[a] 130,000 × 1.04 = 135,200
    5,000 × 1.04 =   5,200
                   140,400

[b] 130,000 × 1.10 = 143,000
     5,000 × 1.10 =   5,500
     3,000 × 1.10 =   3,300
                    151,800

What are the mechanics of the dollar-value LIFO method?

Dollar-value LIFO is an extension of the historical cost principle. The method aggregates dollars rather than units into homogeneous groupings. The method assumes that an inventory decrease came from the last year.

The procedures under dollar-value LIFO are:

▪ Restate ending inventory in the current year into base dollars by applying a price index.
▪ Subtract the year 0 inventory in base dollars from the current year's inventory in base dollars.
▪ Multiply the incremental inventory in the current year in base dollars by the price index to obtain the incremental inventory in current dollars.
▪ Obtain the reportable inventory for the current year by adding to the year 0 inventory in base dollars the incremental inventory for the current year in current dollars.

Example 4.8

At 12/31/2X12, the ending inventory is $130,000 and the price index is 1.30. The base inventory on 1/1/2X12 was $80,000. The 12/31/2X12 inventory is computed next.

12/31/2X12 inventory in base dollars $130,000/1.30	$100,000
1/1/2X12 beginning base inventory	80,000
2X12 increment in base dollars	$ 20,000
2X12 increment in current-year dollars	× 1.3
	$ 26,000
Inventory in base dollars	$ 80,000
Increment in current-year dollars	26,000
Reportable inventory	$106,000

IFRS Treatment

International Financial Reporting Standards (IFRS) prohibit the use of the LIFO cost flow assumption and define "market" in the lower of cost or market *differently*. First-in, first-out (FIFO) and average cost are the only two acceptable cost flow assumptions permitted under IFRS. Both U.S. generally accepted accounting principles (GAAP) and IFRS permit specific identification where appropriate. In the lower-of-cost-or-market test for inventory valuation, IFRS defines "market" as *net realizable value*. U.S. GAAP, however, defines "market" as replacement cost subject to the constraints of net realizable value (the ceiling) and net realizable value less a normal markup (the floor). In other words, IFRS does not use a ceiling or a floor to determine market. ▪

Losses on Purchase Commitment

Significant net losses on purchase commitments should be recognized at the end of the reporting period.

Example 4.9

In 2X12, ABC Company committed itself to buy raw materials at $1.20 per pound. At the end of the year, before fulfilling the purchase commitment, the price of the materials dropped to $1.00 per pound. Conservatism requires that a loss on purchase commitment of $0.20 per pound be recognized in 2X12. Loss on purchase commitment is debited, and allowance for purchase commitment loss is credited.

Inventory Valuation Problems

Although the basics of inventory cost measurement are easily stated, difficulties exist in cost allocation. For example, idle capacity costs and abnormal spoilage costs may have to be written off immediately in the current year rather than being allocated as a component of inventory valuation. Furthermore, general and administrative expenses are inventoryable when they are directly related to production.

As per Financial Accounting Standards Board (FASB) Statement No. 151, *Inventory Costs*, freight and handling charges are expensed as incurred.

Inventory Stated at Market Value in Excess of Cost

In unusual cases, inventories may be stated in excess of cost. This may arise when there is no basis for cost apportionment (e.g., in the meat-packing industry). Market value may also be used when there is immediate marketability at quoted prices (e.g., certain precious metals or agricultural products). Disclosure is necessary when inventory is stated above cost.

 ## FIXED ASSETS

How do we account for fixed assets?

A fixed asset is recorded at its fair market value or the fair market value of the consideration given, whichever is more clearly evident.

The cost of *buying an asset* includes all costs required to place that asset into existing use and location, including freight, installation, insurance, taxes, and break-in costs (e.g., instruction).

The additions to an existing building (such as constructing a new garage) are capitalized and depreciated over the shorter of the life of the addition or the life of the building. Rearrangement and reinstallation costs are deferred when future benefit exists. If not, they should be expensed. Obsolete fixed assets should be reclassified from property, plant, and equipment to other assets and shown at salvage value, recognizing a loss.

When *two or more assets are purchased for one price*, cost is allocated to the assets based on their relative fair market values. If an old building is demolished to make way for the construction of a new building, the costs of demolishing the old building are capitalized to land.

Self-constructed assets are recorded at the incremental costs to build assuming idle capacity. However, they should not be recorded at more than the outside price.

Example 4.10

Incremental costs to self-construct equipment is $12,000. The equipment could have been bought outside for $9,000. The journal entry is:

Equipment	$9,000	
Loss	$3,000	
Cash		$12,000

A donated fixed asset should be recorded at fair market value. The entry is to debit fixed assets and credit contribution revenue.

Note

Fixed assets cannot be written up except in the case of a discovery of a natural resource or in a purchase combination. In a discovery of a natural resource (e.g., oil), the land account is debited at the appraised value and then depleted by the units of production method. ▪

Land improvements (e.g., driveways, sidewalks, fencing) are capitalized and depreciated over useful life. Land held for investment purposes or for a future plant site should be classified under investments and not fixed assets.

Ordinary repairs (e.g., tune-up for a car) are expensed because they have a benefit period of less than one year.

Extraordinary repairs are deferred since they benefit a period of more than one year. An example is a new motor for a car. Extraordinary repairs increase the life of an asset or make the asset more useful. Capital expenditures improve the quality or quantity of services to be derived from the asset.

What is depreciation, and how is it accounted for?

Depreciation is the allocation of the historical cost of a fixed asset into expense over the period benefited to result in matching expense against revenue.

Fractional-year depreciation is computing depreciation when the asset is bought during the year. A proration is needed.

Example 4.11

On 10/1/2X11, a fixed asset costing $10,000 with a salvage value of $1,000 and a life of five years is acquired.

Depreciation expense for 2X12 using the sum-of-the-years digits method is:

1/1/2X12 – 9/30/2X12 5/15 × $9,000 × 9/12	$2,250
10/1/2X12 – 12/31/2X12 4/15 × $9,000 × 3/12	600
	$2,850

Depreciation expense for 2X12 using double-declining balance is:

Year	Computation	Depreciation	Book Value
0			$10,000
10/1/2X11–12/31/2X11	3/12 × $10,000 × 40%	$1,000	9,000
1/1/2X12–12/31/2X12	$9,000 × 40%	3,600	5,400

What are the group and composite depreciation methods?

Group and composite depreciation methods involve similar accounting. The group method is used for similar assets, whereas the composite method is used for dissimilar assets. Both methods are generally accepted. There is one accumulated depreciation account for the entire group. The depreciation rate equals:

$$\frac{\text{Depreciation}}{\text{Gross cost}}$$

Depreciation expense for a period equals:

$$\text{Depreciation rate} \times \text{Gross cost}$$

The depreciation life equals:

$$\frac{\text{Depreciation cost}}{\text{Depreciation}}$$

When an asset is sold in the group, the entry is:

Cash (proceeds received)
Accumulated depreciation (plug figure)
Fixed asset (cost)

Upon sale of a fixed asset in the group, the difference between the cash received and the cost of the fixed asset is plugged to accumulated depreciation. No gain or loss is recognized upon the sale. The only time a gain or loss is recognized is if all the assets were sold.

Example 4.12

Calculations for composite depreciation follow.

Asset	Cost	Salvage	Depreciable Cost	Life	Depreciation
A	$25,000	$5,000	$20,000	10	$2,000
B	40,000	2,000	38,000	5	7,600
C	52,000	4,000	48,000	6	8,000
	$117,000	$11,000	$106,000		$17,600

$$\text{Composite rate: } \frac{\$17,600}{117,000} = 15.04\%$$

$$\text{Composite life: } \frac{\$106,000}{\$17,600} = 6.02 \text{ years}$$

The entry to record depreciation is:

Depreciation	17,600	
Accumulated depreciation		17,600

The entry to sell asset B for $36,000 is:

Cash	36,000	
Accumulated depreciation	4,000	
Fixed asset		40,000

When is interest deferred?

Disclosure should be made of the interest capitalized and expensed. Interest incurred on borrowed funds is expensed. However, interest on borrowed funds is deferred to the asset and then amortized in the following instances:

- Self-constructed assets for the company's own use: To justify interest capitalization, a time period must exist for assets to be prepared for use.
- Assets for sale or lease constructed as discrete, individual projects (e.g., real estate development).
- Assets purchased for the entity's own use by arrangements requiring a down payment and/or progress payments.

Interest is not capitalized for:

▪ Assets in use or ready for use
▪ Assets not in use and not being prepared for use
▪ Assets produced in large volume or on a recurring basis

Interest capitalized is based on the average accumulated expenditures for that asset. The interest rate used is either:

▪ Interest rate on the specific borrowing
▪ Weighted-average interest rate on corporate debt

Example 4.13

In the purchase of a qualifying asset, a company expends $100,000 on January 1, 2X12, and $150,000 on March 1, 2X12. The average accumulated expenditures for 2X12 are computed as:

Expenditure	Number of Months	Average Expenditure
$100,000	12	$100,000
$150,000	10	$125,000
$250,000		$225,000

The interest capitalization period begins when the following exist:

▪ Interest is being incurred.
▪ Expenditures have been incurred.
▪ Work is taking place to make the asset ready for intended use. These activities are not limited to actual construction but may also include administrative and technical activities before construction. They also include unforeseen events occurring during construction, such as labor instability and litigation.

The capitalization period ends when the asset is substantially complete and usable. When an asset consists of individual elements (e.g., condominium units), the capitalization period of interest costs applicable to one of the separate units ends when the particular unit is substantially finished. Capitalization of interest is not continued when construction ends, except for brief or unanticipated delays.

When the total asset must be completed to be useful, interest capitalization continues until the total asset is materially finished (e.g., a manufacturing plant where sequential production activities must occur).

How are exchanges of assets accounted for?

Nonmonetary transactions covered under Accounting Standards Codification (ASC) No. 845-10-05, *Nonmonetary Transactions: Overall* (Financial Accounting Standard [FAS] No.

153, *Exchanges of Nonmonetary Assets*) deal primarily with exchanges or distributions of fixed assets.

Fair market value in a nonmonetary exchange may be based on:

▪ Quoted market price
▪ Appraisal
▪ Cash transaction for similar items

As per ASC No. 845-10-05, the asset received in a nonmonetary exchange is recorded at fair market value when the transaction has *commercial substance*. Commercial substance exists when future cash flows change because of the transaction arising from a change in economic positions of the two parties. A gain or loss is recorded for the difference between the book value of the asset given up and the fair market value of the asset received. However, if commercial substance does *not* exist, the exchange is recorded based on book values with no gain or loss recognized.

Example 4.14

Erlach Corporation exchanged autos plus cash for land. The autos have a fair market value of $25,000. They cost $32,500 with accumulated depreciation of $12,500, so the book value is $20,000. Cash paid is $8,750. The exchange has commercial substance.

The cost of the land to Erlach Corporation equals:

Fair market value of autos exchanged	$25,000
Cash paid	8,750
Cost of land	$33,750

The journal entry for the exchange transaction is:

Land	33,750	
Accumulated depreciation	12,500	
Autos		32,500
Cash		8,750
Gain		5,000

The gain equals the fair market value of the autos less their book value as calculated next:

Fair market value of autos	$25,000
Book value of autos ($32,500 – $12,500)	20,000
Gain	$ 5,000

What footnote disclosure is required?

Footnote disclosure should be made of the nature of the exchange transaction, method to account for transferred assets, and gain or loss on the exchange.

What happens if a fixed asset is damaged?

There may be an involuntary conversion of nonmonetary assets into monetary assets, followed by replacement of the involuntarily converted assets (e.g., a building is destroyed by a fire, and the insurance recovery is used to buy a similar building). Gain or loss is recognized for the difference between the insurance recovery and the book value of the destroyed asset.

Caution

A contingency arises if the old fixed asset is damaged in one period but the insurance recovery is received in a later period. A contingent gain or loss is reported in the period the old fixed asset was damaged. The gain or loss may be recognized for book and tax purposes in different years, resulting in a temporary difference for income tax allocation purposes. ▪

How do we reflect the impairment or disposal of long-lived assets?

ASC No. 205-20-45-3, *Presentation of Financial Statements: Discontinued Operations* (FAS No. 144, *Accounting for the Impairment or Disposal of Long-Lived Assets*) applies to a company's long-term assets to be retained or to be disposed of.

With regard to long-term assets to be retained and used, an impairment occurs when the fair market value of the long-term asset group is less than its book (carrying) value. The impairment loss is recognized only when the carrying value of the asset group is not recoverable and exceeds its fair value. There is a lack of recoverability when the carrying value of the asset group exceeds the total undiscounted cash flows anticipated from the use and ultimate disposition of the asset group. The impairment loss equals the carrying value of the asset group less its fair value.

Example 4.15

The following information applies to an asset group:

Carrying value	$100,000
Fair value	80,000
Sum of the undiscounted cash flows	95,000

Because the sum of the undiscounted cash flows is less than the carrying value, there is a nonrecoverability situation. The impairment loss to be recognized equals $20,000 ($100,000 – $80,000).

Example 4.16

The following data are given for an asset group:

Carrying value	$100,000
Fair value	106,000
Sum of the undiscounted cash flows	94,000

Because the sum of the undiscounted cash flows is less than the carrying value, a nonrecoverability situation is indicated. However, an impairment loss is not recorded owing to the fact that fair value is more than carrying value.

Example 4.17

Carrying value	$100,000
Fair value	92,000
Sum of the undiscounted cash flows	104,000

Because the sum of the undiscounted cash flows is more than the carrying value, a recoverability situation exists. Thus, no impairment loss exists.

What should be footnoted for an impairment loss?

Footnote disclosure for an impairment loss is:

▪ The business segment associated with the impaired asset
▪ Description of the impaired asset along with impairment circumstances
▪ Method used to derive fair value
▪ Amount of impairment loss and where such loss is included in the income statement

IFRS Treatment

IFRS also uses a fair value test to measure the impairment loss. However, IFRS does not use the first-stage recoverability test used under U.S. GAAP—that is, comparing the *undiscounted* expected future cash flows to the carrying (book) amount. Thus, the IFRS test is more stringent than U.S. GAAP. ▪

How are asset retirement obligations accounted for?

ASC No. 410-20-05, *Asset Retirement and Environmental Obligations: Asset Retirement Obligations* (FAS No. 143, *Accounting for Asset Retirement Obligations*) requires companies to record at fair value a liability when a retirement obligation is incurred, provided that fair value can be reasonably estimated, even though it is years prior to the asset's planned retirement. The asset retirement obligation has to be measured and recorded along with its associated asset retirement cost. Asset retirements may be from sale, recycling, abandonment, or disposal.

When the initial obligation occurs, the company records a liability and defers the cost to the long-term asset for the same amount. After the initial recognition, the liability will change over time, so that the obligation must be accreted to its present value each year. The long-term asset's capitalized cost is depreciated over its useful life. When the liability is settled, the company either settles the liability for the amount recorded or will have a settlement gain or loss.

Any incremental liability incurred in a later year is an additional layer of the initial obligation. Each layer is measured at fair value.

DISCLOSURE

What footnote disclosures are provided for fixed assets?

Footnote disclosures for fixed assets include:

- Idle fixed assets
- Fixed assets subject to pledges, liens, or other commitments
- Fully depreciated assets still in use
- Fixed assets held to be disposed of and anticipated losses
- Contractual agreements to purchase new fixed assets
- Description of depreciation method and estimates
- Fixed assets by major category

How do we account for intangible assets?

Intangible assets have a life of one year or more and lack physical substance (e.g., goodwill), or represent a right granted by the government (e.g., patent) or another company (e.g., franchise fee). ASC No. 350-20-55, *Intangibles—Goodwill and Other: Goodwill* (FAS 142, *Goodwill and Other Intangible Assets*) covers accounting for intangible assets, whether purchased or internally developed. The costs of intangibles acquired from others should be reported as assets. The cost equals the cash or fair market value of the consideration given. The individual intangibles that can be separately identified must be costed separately. If not separately identified, the intangibles are assigned a cost equal to the difference between the total purchase price and the cost of identifiable tangible and intangible assets. Note that "goodwill" does not include identifiable assets.

The cost of developing and maintaining intangibles should be charged against earnings if the assets are not specifically identifiable, have indeterminate lives, or are inherent in the continuing business (e.g., goodwill). An example of internally developed goodwill that is expensed are the costs incurred in developing a name (e.g., Cuisinart).

As per ASC No. 350-20-55, intangibles have either a *limited useful life* or an *indefinite useful life*. An intangible with a limited life is amortized into expense over its useful life.

Examples are trade names, trademarks, patents, licenses, franchises, and copyrights. A loss on impairment is recognized on a *limited-life* intangible asset when its carrying value exceeds its fair market value. After the impairment is recognized, the reduced carrying amount is its new cost basis. An intangible asset with an *indefinite life* is not amortized but rather is subject to a yearly impairment test. An example is goodwill.

The factors in estimating useful lives for limited-life intangibles include:

▪ Legal, contractual, and regulatory provisions
▪ Renewal or extension provisions (if a renewal occurs, the life of the intangible may be increased)
▪ Obsolescence and competitive factors
▪ Product demand
▪ Service lives of key employees within the company

For example, an intangible may be enhanced owing to a strong public relations staff. Footnote disclosure should be made of the amortization period and method.

When the purchase of assets results in goodwill, the subsequent sale of a separable part of the entity acquired requires a proportionate reduction of the goodwill account.

In a business combination accounted for under the purchase method, goodwill is recorded only when the cost to the acquirer exceeds the fair market value of the net assets acquired. Goodwill may be determined by an individual appraiser, a purchase audit done by the acquiring company's public accounting firm, and so on. Goodwill is then subject to an annual impairment test. If the cost to the acquirer is less than the fair market value of the net assets acquired, a credit arises. This credit represents negative goodwill, which is proportionately allocated as a reduction of the acquired assets except for certain deferred assets (e.g., deferred pension and tax assets). If these assets are reduced to zero, the credit balance remaining is recorded as an extraordinary gain.

Goodwill is theoretically equal to the discounted value of future excess earnings of a company over other companies in the industry. However, it is difficult to forecast the years in which superior earnings will occur.

In acquiring a new business, goodwill must be estimated. Two possible methods to value goodwill are (1) capitalization of earnings and (2) capitalization of excess earnings.

Example 4.18

The following information applies to a business we are considering buying:

Expected average annual earnings	$10,000
Expected future value of net assets exclusive of goodwill	$45,000
Normal rate of return	20%

(continued)

Using the capitalization of earnings approach, we estimate goodwill at:

Total asset value implied ($10,000/20%)	$50,000
Estimated fair value of assets	45,000
Estimated goodwill	$ 5,000

Assuming the same facts as above except a capitalization rate of excess earnings of 22 percent and using the capitalization of excess earnings method, we can estimate goodwill at:

Expected average annual earnings	$10,000
Return on expected average assets ($45,000 × 20%)	9,000
Excess earnings	$ 1,000
Goodwill ($1,000/0.22) = $4,545	

Example 4.19

The net worth of ABC Company excluding goodwill is $800,000, and earnings for the last four years were $750,000. The latter figure includes extraordinary gains of $50,000 and nonrecurring losses of $30,000. It is desired to determine a selling price of the business. A 12 percent return on net worth is typical for the industry. The capitalization of excess earnings is 45 percent in determining goodwill.

Net income for 4 years	$750,000
Less: Extraordinary gains	50,000
Add: Nonrecurring losses	30,000
Adjusted 4-year earnings	$730,000
Average earnings ($730,000/4)	$182,500
Normal earnings ($800,000 × 0.12)	96,000
Excess annual earnings	$ 86,500
Excess earnings capitalized at 45%:	

$$\frac{\$86,500}{0.45} = \$192,222$$

Internally generated costs to derive a patented product, such as research and development incurred in developing a new product, are expensed. The patent is recorded at the registration fees to secure and register it, legal fees in successfully defending it, and the cost of acquiring competing patents. The patent is amortized over its useful life not exceeding its nonrenewable legal life of 20 years. If an intangible asset is worthless, it should be written off immediately as a loss.

Trademarks and trade names have legal protection for 10 years and may be renewed an indefinite number of times. Franchises and licenses with limited lives should be

amortized over their useful lives. Copyrights are granted for the life of the creator plus 70 years. Registration fees and successful legal fees are deferred to the intangible asset.
Leaseholds are rent paid in advance and are amortized over the life of the lease.

What disclosures are made for goodwill and other intangible assets?

The footnote disclosures for goodwill and other intangible assets are:

- Description of impaired intangible assets and the reasons for such impairment
- Amortization period for limited-life intangibles and expected amortization expense for the next five years
- Method to compute fair value
- Amount of any significant residual value
- Amount of goodwill included in the gain or loss on disposal of all or a part of a reporting unit

What should be disclosed about recognized intangible assets?

Companies must disclose information about how recognized intangible assets would aid financial statement users to determine how a company's ability to renew or extend an arrangement impacts the company's anticipated cash flows associated with the asset.
Disclosure should be made of:

- Weighted-average period at acquisition or renewal before the next renewal or extension
- Accounting policy for costs incurred to renew or extend an intangible asset's term
- In the event renewal or extension costs are capitalized, the total cost incurred to renew or extend the term of a recognized intangible asset

 **LIABILITIES**

How do we account for and report liabilities?

In accounting for liabilities, the CFO must consider many reporting and disclosure responsibilities:

- Bonds payable may be issued between interest dates at a premium or discount.
- Bonds may be amortized using the straight-line method or effective interest method.
- Debt may be extinguished prior to the maturity date when the company can issue new debt at a lower interest rate.
- Estimated liabilities must be recognized when it is probable that an asset has been impaired or liability has been incurred by year-end, and the amount of loss can be reasonably estimated.
- An accrued liability may be recognized for future absences (e.g., sick leave or vacation time).

- Special termination benefits such as early retirement may also be offered to and accepted by employees.
- Short-term debt may be rolled over to long-term debt, requiring special reporting.
- A callable obligation by the creditor may exist.
- Long-term purchase obligations have to be disclosed.

How are bonds payable handled?

The cost of a corporate bond is expressed in terms of yield. Two types of yield are:

1. Simple yield

$$\text{Nominal interest/Present value of bond}$$

This is not as accurate as yield to maturity.

2. Yield to maturity (effective interest rate)

$$\frac{\text{Nominal interest} + \text{Discount/Years} - \text{Premium/Years}}{(\text{Present value of bond} + \text{Maturity rate})/2}$$

Example 4.20

A $100,000, 10 percent five-year bond is issued at 96. The simple yield is:

$$\frac{\text{Nominal interest}}{\text{Present value of bond}} = \frac{\$10,000}{\$96,000} = 10.42\%$$

The yield to maturity is:

$$\frac{\text{Nominal interest} + \text{Discount/Years}}{(\text{Present value} + \text{Maturity})/2}$$

When a bond is issued at a discount, the yield (effective interest rate) exceeds the nominal (face, coupon) interest rate.

When a bond is issued at a premium, the yield is below the nominal interest rate. The two methods of amortizing bond discount or bond premium are:

1. *Straight-line method.* It results in a constant dollar amount of amortization but a different effective rate each period.
2. *Effective interest method.* It results in a constant rate of interest but different dollar amounts each period. This method is preferred over the straight-line method. The amortization entry is:

Interest expense (Yield × Carrying value of bond at the beginning of the year)
    Discount
    Cash (Nominal interest × Face value of bond)

In the early years, the amortization amount under the effective interest method is lower relative to the straight-line method (either for discount or premium).

Example 4.21

On 1/1/2X12, a $100,000 bond is issued at $95,624. The yield rate is 7 percent, and the nominal interest rate is 6 percent. The following schedule is the basis for the journal entries.

Date	Debit Interest Expense	Credit Cash	Credit Discount	Carrying Value
1/1/2X12				$95,624
12/31/2X12	$6,694	$6,000	$694	96,318
12/31/2X13	6,742	6,000	742	97,060

The entry on 12/31/2X12 is:

Interest expense	6,694	
Cash		6,000
Discount		694

At maturity, the bond will be worth its face value of $100,000. When bonds are issued between interest dates, the entry is:

Cash
    Bonds payable
    Premium (or debit discount)
    Interest expense

Example 4.22

A $100,000, 5 percent bond having a life of five years is issued at 110 on 4/1/2X11. The bonds are dated 1/1/2X11. Interest is payable on 1/1 and 7/1. Straight-line amortization is used. The journal entries are:

4/1/2X11 Cash (110,000 + 1,250)	111,250	
Bonds payable		100,000
Premium on bonds payable		10,000
Bond interest expense		1,250
$(100,000 \times 5\% \times 3/12)$		

(continued)

7/1/2X11 Bond interest expense	2,500	
Cash		2,500
100,000 × 5% × 6/12		
Premium on bonds payable	526.50	
Bond interest expense		526.50
4/1/20X1–1/1/20X5 = 4 years, 9 months = 57 months		
$10,000/57 = $175.50 per month		
$175.50 × 3 months = $526.50		
12/31/2X11 Bond interest expense	2,500	
Interest payable		2,500
Premium on bonds payable	1,053	
Bond interest expense		1,053
1/1/2X12 Interest payable	2,500	
Cash		2,500

Bonds payable is presented on the balance sheet at its present value in this manner:

Bonds payable
Add: Premium
Less: Discount
Carrying value

Bond issue costs are the expenditures in issuing the bonds such as legal, registration, and printing fees. Bond issue costs are preferably deferred and amortized over the life of the bond. They are shown under deferred charges.

In computing the price of a bond, the face amount is discounted using the present value of $1 table. The interest payments are discounted using the present value of an ordinary annuity of $1 table. The yield serves as the discount rate.

Example 4.23

A $50,000, 10-year bond is issued with interest payable semiannually at an 8 percent nominal interest rate. The yield rate is 10 percent. The present value of $1 table factor for $n = 20$, $i = 5\%$ is 0.37689. The present value of annuity of $1 table factor for $n = 20$, $i = 5\%$ is 12.46221. The price of the bond equals:

Present value of principal	
$50,000 × 0.37689	$18,844.50
Present value of interest payments	
$20,000 × 12.46221	24,924.42
	$43,768.92

What if bonds are converted to stock?

In converting a bond into stock, three alternative methods may be used: book value of bond, market value of bond, and market value of stock. Under the book value of bond method, no gain or loss on bond conversion arises because the book value of the bond is the basis to credit equity. This method is preferred. Under the market value methods, gain or loss will result because the book value of the bond will be different from the market value of bond or market value of stock, which is the basis to credit the equity accounts.

Example 4.24

A $100,000 bond with unamortized premium of $8,420.50 is converted to common stock. There are 100 bonds ($100,000/$1,000). Each bond is converted into 50 shares of stock. Thus, there are 5,000 shares of common stock. Par value is $15 per share. The market value of the stock is $25 per share. The market value of the bond is 120. Using the book value method, the entry for the conversion is:

Bonds payable	100,000	
Premium on bonds payable	8,420.50	
Common stock (5,000 × 15)		75,000
Premium on common stock		33,420.50

Using the market value of stock method, the entry is:

Bonds payable	100,000	
Premium on bonds payable	8,420.50	
Loss on conversion	16,579.50	
Common stock		75,000
Premium on common stock		50,000
5,000 × $25 = $125,000		

(continued)

Using the market value of the bond method, the entry is:

Bonds payable	100,000	
Premium on bonds payable	8,420.50	
Loss on conversion	111,579.50	
Common stock		75,000
Premium on common stock		45,000
$100,000 \times 120\% = \$120,000$		

How do we handle an inducement offer to convert debt to equity?

ASC No. 470-20-05, *Debt: Debt with Conversion and Other Options* (FAS No. 84, *Induced Conversions of Convertible Debt*) requires that if convertible debt is converted to stock due to an inducement offer where the debtor changes the conversion privileges (e.g., conversion price), the debtor records an expense. The amount of expense equals the fair market value of the securities transferred in excess of the fair market value of the securities issuable based on the original conversion terms. The fair market value is measured at the earlier of the conversion date or agreement date. If the additional inducement consists of stock, the market value of the stock is credited to common stock at par value, with the excess over par credited to paid-in capital and with the offsetting debit to debt conversion expense. If the additional inducement is assets, the market value of the assets is credited with an offsetting charge to debt conversion expense. For example, the inducement may be in the form of cash or property.

How do we account for the extinguishment of debt?

Long-term debt may be retired when new debt can be issued at a lower interest rate. It can also occur when the company has excess cash and wants to avoid paying interest and having the debt on its balance sheet. The gain or loss on the extinguishment of debt is an ordinary item. Extraordinary classification occurs whether the extinguishment is early, at scheduled maturity, or later.

Debt may be considered extinguished if the debtor is relieved of the principal liability and it is probable the debtor will not have to make future payments.

Example 4.25

A $100,000 bond payable with an unamortized premium of $10,000 is called at 85. The entry is:

Bonds payable	100,000	
Premium on bonds payable	10,000	
Cash (85% × $100,000)		85,000
Ordinary gain		25,000

Footnote disclosures regarding extinguishment of debt include description of extinguishment transaction including the source of funds.

As per ASC No. 860-10-05, *Transfers and Servicing: Overall* (FAS No. 76, *Extinguishment of Debt*), if the debtor puts cash or other assets in a trust to be used only for paying interest and principal on debt on an irrevocable basis, there should be disclosure of the particulars, including a description of the transaction and the amount of debt extinguished.

IFRS Treatment

Under IFRS, the measurement of a provision related to a contingency is based on the best estimate of the expenditure required to settle the obligation. If a range of estimates is predicted and no amount in the range is more likely than any other amount in the range, the *midpoint* of the range is used to measure the liability. In U.S. GAAP, the *minimum* amount in a range is used. ▪

How is recognition given to estimated liabilities?

A loss contingency should be accrued if both of these criteria exist:

▪ At year-end, it is probable (likely to occur) that an asset was impaired or a liability was incurred.
▪ The amount of loss can be reasonably estimated.

The loss contingency is booked based on conservatism. The entry for a probable loss is:

Expense (Loss)
Estimated liability

A probable loss that cannot be estimated should be footnoted.

Example 4.26

On 12/31/2X11 warranty expenses are estimated at $20,000. On 3/15/2X12 actual warranty costs paid were $16,000. The journal entries are:

12/31/2X11 Warranty expense	20,000	
Estimated liability		20,000
3/15/2X12 Estimated liability	16,000	
Cash		16,000

If a loss contingency exists at year-end but no asset impairment or liability incurrence exists (e.g., uninsured equipment), footnote disclosure can be made.

A probable loss occurring after year-end but before the audit report date only requires subsequent event disclosure.

Examples of probable loss contingencies are warranties, lawsuits, claims, and assessments, casualties, catastrophes (e.g., fire), and expropriation of property by a foreign government.

If the amount of loss is within a range, the accrual is based on the best estimate within that range. However, if no amount within the range is better than any other amount, the minimum amount (not maximum amount) of the range is booked. The exposure to additional losses should be disclosed.

There is no accrual for a reasonably possible loss (more than remote but less than likely). However, footnote disclosure is required of the nature of the contingency and the estimate of probable loss or range of loss. If an estimate of loss is not possible, that fact should be noted.

A remote contingency (slight chance of occurring) is usually ignored, and no disclosure is made. There are exceptions when a remote contingency would be disclosed in the case of guarantees of indebtedness, standby letters of credit, and agreements to repurchase receivables or properties.

General (unspecified) contingencies are not accrued. Examples are self-insurance and catastrophic losses. Disclosure and/or an appropriation of retained earnings can be made for general contingencies. To be booked as an estimated liability, the future loss must be specific and measurable, such as parcel post and freight losses.

Gain contingencies cannot be recognized because such recognition violates conservatism. However, footnote disclosure can be made.

 ## ACCOUNTING FOR COMPENSATED ABSENCES

Compensated absences include sick leave, holiday, and vacation time. ASC 710-10-15, *Compensation*—General: Overall (FAS No. 43, *Accounting for Compensated Absences*) is not applicable to severance or termination pay, postretirement benefits, deferred compensation, stock option plans, and other long-term fringe benefits (e.g., disability, insurance).

The employer accrues a liability for employees' compensation for future absences if all of these conditions are satisfied:

■ Employee services have already been performed.
■ Employee rights have vested.
■ Probable payment exists.
■ Amount of estimated liability can reasonably be determined.

Note

If the criteria are met except that the amount is not determinable, only a footnote can be made because an accrual is not possible. ■

The accrual for sick leave is required when the employer allows employees to take accumulated sick leave days off regardless of actual illness. The accrual is not required if employees may take accumulated days off only for actual illness, since losses for these are usually insignificant.

Example 4.27

Estimated compensation for future absences is $30,000. The entry is:

Expense	$30,000	
Estimated liability		$30,000

If at a later date a payment of $28,000 is made, the entry is:

Estimated liability	$28,000	
Cash		$28,000

What if there is a special termination benefit?

An expense is accrued when an employer offers special termination benefits to an employee, the employee accepts the offer, and the amount can be estimated reasonably. The amount equals the current payment plus the discounted value of future payments.

When it can be measured objectively, the effect of changes on the employer's previously accrued expenses applicable to other employee benefits directly associated with employee termination should be included in measuring termination expense.

Example 4.28

On 1/1/2X12, as an incentive for early retirement, the employee receives a lump-sum payment today of $50,000 plus payments of $10,000 for each of the next 10 years. The discount rate is 10 percent. The journal entry is:

Expense	$111,450	
Estimated liability		$111,450
Present value $10,000 × 6.145[a] =	$61,450	
Current payment	50,000	
Total	$111,450	

[a] Present value factor for $n = 10$, $i = 10\%$ is 6.145.

ENVIRONMENTAL OBLIGATIONS

How do we account for environmental liabilities?

In determining a loss contingency to accrue for environmental liabilities, these points should be considered:

- Name and extent of hazardous waste at a site
- Remedial steps
- Level of acceptable remediation
- Other responsible individuals or entities and their degree of liability

The present value of payments associated with a liability may be recognized only when the future cash flows are reliably determinable in amount and timing.

Disclosure is required of environmental difficulties, how environmental liabilities are determined, important factors applicable to the environment as it impacts the business, future contingencies, compliance issues, and contamination.

What if short-term debt is rolled over into long-term debt?

A short-term obligation shall be reclassified as a long-term liability in either of two cases:

1. After the year-end of the financial statements but before the audit report is issued, the short-term debt is rolled over into a long-term obligation or an equity security is issued in substitution, OR
2. Before the audit report date, the company contracts for refinancing the current obligation on a long-term basis and all of the following conditions are satisfied:

   - The agreement does not expire within one year.
   - No violation of the agreement exists.
   - The parties are financially able to meet the requirements of the arrangement.

The proper classification of the refinanced item is under long-term debt and not stockholders' equity, even if equity securities were issued in substitution of the debt. When short-term debt is excluded from current liabilities, a footnote should describe the financing agreement and the terms of any new obligation.

If the amounts under the agreement for refinancing vary, the amount of short-term debt excluded from current liabilities will be the minimum amount expected to be refinanced based on conservatism. The exclusion from current liabilities cannot be greater than the net proceeds of debt or security issuances, or amounts available under the refinancing agreement.

Once cash is paid for the short-term debt, even though the next day long-term debt of a similar amount is issued, the short-term debt is presented under current liabilities since cash was paid.

What if the creditor has the right to call the bond?

A long-term debt callable by the creditor is presented as a current liability because of the debtor's violation of the agreement except if one of these conditions exist:

- The creditor waives or has lost the right to demand repayment for a period in excess of one year from the balance sheet date.
- There is a grace period in which the debtor may correct the violation that makes it callable, and it is probable that the violation will be so rectified.

What footnote information should be presented for long-term purchase commitments?

An unconditional purchase obligation provides funds for goods or services at a determinable future date. An example is a take-or-pay contract in which the buyer must pay specified periodic amounts for products or services. Even if the buyer does not take delivery of the goods, periodic payments still must be made.

When unconditional purchase obligations are recorded in the balance sheet, disclosure is made of payments for recorded unconditional purchase obligations and maturities and sinking fund requirements for long-term borrowings.

Unconditional purchase obligations not reflected in the balance sheet should be disclosed if they meet these conditions:

- Noncancelable; however, it may be cancellable upon a remote contingency
- Negotiated to arrange financing to provide contracted goods or services
- A term exceeding one year

The disclosures for unconditional purchase obligations when not recorded in the accounts are:

- Nature and term
- Fixed and variable amounts
- Total amount for the current year and for the next five years
- Purchases made under the obligation for each year presented

Optional disclosure exists of the amount of imputed interest required to reduce the unconditional purchase obligation to present value.

 ## EXIT OR DISPOSAL ACTIVITIES

How do we account for the costs and obligations associated with exit or disposal activities?

ASC No. 420-10-05-3, *Exit or Disposal Cost Obligations: Overall* (FAS No. 146, *Accounting for Costs Associated with Exit or Disposal Activities*) applies to costs (e.g., costs to consolidate facilities or relocate workers, one-time termination benefits to current workers, operating lease termination costs) applicable to a restructuring, plant closing, discontinued operation, or other exit or disposal activity. These costs are recognized as incurred (not at the commitment date to an exit plan) based on fair value along with the related liability. The best indication of fair value is quoted market prices in active markets. If fair value cannot reasonably be estimated, we must postpone recognizing the liability until it can.

The initiation date of an exit or disposal activity is that date when management obligates itself to a plan to do so or otherwise dispose of a long-lived asset and if the activity includes worker termination.

What footnote disclosures are made for exit or disposal activities?

These points should be footnoted:

- Description of exit or disposal activity and the anticipated completion date
- For each major type of cost applicable to the exit activity, the total anticipated cost, the amount incurred in the current year, and the cumulative amount to date
- If a liability for a cost is not recorded because fair value is not reasonably estimated, along with the reasons
- Where exit or disposal costs are presented in the income statement

 ## FAIR VALUE MEASUREMENTS

What are fair value measurements about?

ASC No. 820-10-05, *Fair Value Measurements and Disclosures: Overall* (FAS No. 157, *Fair Value Measurements*) states that a fair value measurement reflects current market participant assumptions about future inflows of the asset and future outflows of the liability. A fair value measurement incorporates the attributes of the particular asset or liability (e.g., location, condition). In formulating fair value, consideration is given to the *exchange price*, which is the market price at the measurement date in an *orderly transaction* between the parties to sell the asset or transfer the liability. The focus is on the price that would be received to sell the asset or would be paid to transfer the liability (exit price), *not* the price that would be paid to buy the asset or would be received to assume the liability (entry price).

The asset or liability may be by itself (e.g., financial security, operating asset) or a group of assets or liabilities (e.g., asset group, reporting unit).

What about the fair value hierarchy?

A hierarchy list of fair value distinguishes between (1) assumptions based on market data from independent outside sources (observable inputs) and (2) assumptions by the company itself (unobservable inputs). The use of unobservable inputs allows for situations in which there is minimal or no market activity for the asset or liability at the measurement date. Valuation methods used to measure fair value shall maximize the use of observable inputs and minimize the use of unobservable ones.

What about risk and restrictions?

An adjustment for *risk* should be made in a fair value measurement when market participants would include risk in the pricing of the asset or liability. Nonperformance risk of the obligation and the entity's credit risk should be noted. Further, consideration should be given to the effect of a restriction on the sale or use of an asset that impacts its price.

What is the difference between the principal market and the most advantageous market?

In a fair value measurement, we assume that the transaction occurs in the principal (main) market for the asset or liability. This is the market in which the company would sell the asset or transfer the liability with the greatest volume. If a principal market is nonexistent, then the most advantageous market should be used. This is the market in which the business would sell the asset or transfer the liability with the price that maximizes the amount that would be received for the asset or minimizes the amount that would be paid to transfer the liability after taking into account any transaction costs. The fair value measurement should incorporate transportation costs for the asset or liability.

What valuation approaches may be used?

In fair value measurement, valuation techniques based on the market, income, and cost approaches may be used. The *market approach* uses prices for market transactions for identical or comparable assets or liabilities. The *income approach* uses valuation techniques to discount future cash flows to a present value amount. The *cost approach* is based on the current replacement cost, such as the cost to buy or build a substitute comparable asset after adjusting for obsolescence. Input availability and reliability related to the asset or liability may impact the choice of the most suitable valuation method.

A single- or multiple-valuation technique may be needed based on the situation. For example, a single-valuation method would be used for an asset having quoted market prices in an active market for identical assets. A multiple-valuation method would be used to value a reporting unit.

What are the three levels of fair value hierarchy?

The fair value hierarchy prioritizes the *inputs* to valuation techniques used to measure fair value into three broad levels. Level 1, the highest priority, assigns quoted prices (unadjusted) in active markets for identical assets or liabilities. Level 3, the lowest priority, is assigned for unobservable inputs for the assets or liabilities.

Level 2 inputs are those except quoted prices included within Level 1 that are observable for the asset or liability, either directly or indirectly. Level 2 inputs include:

- Quoted price for similar assets or liabilities in active markets
- Quoted prices for similar or identical assets or liabilities in markets that are *not* active, such as markets with few transactions, noncurrent prices, limited public information, and where price quotations show substantial fluctuation
- Inputs excluding quoted prices that are observable for the asset or liability, such as interest rates observable at often quoted intervals and credit risks
- Inputs obtained primarily from observable market information by correlation or other means

In the case of Level 3, unobservable inputs are used to measure fair value to the degree that observable inputs are not available. Unobservable inputs reflect the reporting company's own assumptions about what market participants consider (e.g., risk) in pricing the asset or liability.

What should be disclosed?

Quantitative disclosures in a tabular format should be used for fair value measurements in addition to qualitative (narrative) disclosures about the valuation methods. Emphasis should be placed on the inputs used to measure fair value and the effect of fair value measurements on profit or change in net assets. Any change in valuation techniques should be noted.

FAIR VALUE OPTION FOR FINANCIAL ASSETS AND FINANCIAL LIABILITIES

ASC No. 825-10, *Financial Instruments: Overall* (FAS No. 159, *The Fair Value Option for Financial Assets and Financial Liabilities*) permits business entities to choose to measure most financial instruments and some other items at fair value. Many provisions of the pronouncement apply only to businesses that select the fair value option. The eligible items for the fair value measurement option are:

   a. Recognized financial assets and financial liabilities excluding:

      (1) Investment in a subsidiary or variable interest entity that must be consolidated

      (2) Employers' plan obligations or assets for pension and postretirement benefits

      (3) Financial assets and financial liabilities recognized under leases

      (4) Financial instruments classified by the issuer as a component of stockholders' equity (e.g., convertible bond with a noncontingent beneficial conversion feature)

      (5) Deposit liabilities that can be withdrawn on demand of banks

   b. Written loan commitment

   c. Nonfinancial insurance contracts and warranties that can be settled by the insurer by paying a third party for goods or services

   d. Firm commitments applying to financial instruments, such as a forward purchase contract for a loan not readily convertible to cash

   e. Host financial instruments arising from separating an embedded nonfinancial derivative instrument from a nonfinancial hybrid instrument

ASC No. 825-10 allows a business to select to measure eligible items at fair value at specified election dates. Included in earnings at each reporting date are the unrealized (holding) gains and losses on items for which the fair value option has been elected.

The fair value option is irrevocable (except if a new election date occurs) and is applied solely to *entire* instruments (*not* parts of those instruments or specified risks or specific cash flows). The fair value option may be applied in most cases instrument by instrument including investments otherwise accounted for under the equity method.

FASB No. 159's amendment to ASC No. 805-10 (FAS No. 115, *Accounting for Certain Investments in Debt and Equity Securities*) relates to all companies with trading and available-for-sale securities.

Up-front costs and fees associated to items for which the fair value option is chosen are expensed as incurred.

Electing the Fair Value Option

A business entity may select the fair value option for all eligible items only on the date that *one* of the following occurs:

1. The company first recognizes the eligible item.
2. The company engages in an eligible firm commitment.
3. There is a change in the accounting treatment for an investment in another company because the investment becomes subject to the equity method or the investor no longer consolidates a subsidiary because a majority voting interest no longer exists but still retains some ownership interest.
4. Specialized accounting treatment no longer applies for the financial assets that have been reported at fair value, such as under an American Institute of Certified Public Accountants Audit and Accounting Guide.
5. An event that mandates an eligible item to be measured at fair value on the event date but does not require fair value measurement at each later reporting date.

Events

Some events that require remeasurement of eligible items at fair value, initial recognition of eligible items, or both, and thus create an election date for the fair value option, are:

- Business combination
- Consolidation or deconsolidation of a subsidiary or variable-interest entity
- Major debt modification

Instrument Application

The fair value option may be chosen for a single eligible item without electing it for other identical items except in these four cases:

1. If the fair value option is selected for an investment under the equity method, it must be applied to all of the investor's financial interests in the same entity that are eligible items.

2. If the fair value option is selected to an eligible insurance contract, it must be applied to all claims and obligations under the contract.
3. If the fair value option is chosen for an insurance contract for which integrated or nonintegrated contract features or riders are issued at the same time or subsequently, the fair value option must be applied as well to those features or coverage.
4. If multiple advances are made to one borrower under a single contract, such as a construction loan, and the individual advances lose their identity and become part of the larger loan, the fair value option must be applied to the larger loan balance but *not* to the individual advances.

The fair value option typically does not have to be applied to all financial instruments issued or bought in a single transaction. An investor in stocks or bonds, for example, may apply the fair value option to only some of the stock shares or bonds issued or acquired in a single transaction. In this situation, an individual bond is considered the minimum denomination of that debt security. A financial instrument that is a single contract cannot be broken down into parts when using the fair value option. However, a loan syndication may be in multiple loans to the same debtor by different creditors. Each of the loans is a separate instrument, and the fair value option may be selected for some of the loans but not others.

An investor in an equity security may select the fair value option for its entire investment in that security including any fractional shares.

Balance Sheet

Companies must present assets and liabilities measured at the fair value option in a manner that separates those reported fair values from the book (carrying) values of similar assets and liabilities measured with a different measurement attribute. To accomplish this, a company must either:

- Report the aggregate fair value and nonfinancial fair value amounts in the same line items in the balance sheet and in parentheses disclose the amount measured at fair value included in the aggregate amount
- Report two separate line items to display the fair value and non–fair value carrying amounts

 STATEMENT OF CASH FLOWS

Companies must classify cash receipts and cash payments for items measured at fair value based on their nature and purpose.

Disclosures

Disclosures of fair value are mandated in annual and interim financial statements.

When a balance sheet is presented, these six points must be disclosed:

1. The reasons why the company selected the fair value option for each allowable item or group of similar items.
2. For every line item on the balance sheet that includes an item or items for which the fair value option has been chosen, management must provide information on how each line item relates to major asset and liability categories. Further, management must provide the aggregate carrying amount of items included in each line item that are *not* eligible for the fair value option.
3. When the fair value option is selected for some but not all eligible items within a group of similar items, management must describe those similar items and the reasons for partial election. Further, information must be provided so that financial statement users can understand how the group of similar items applies to individual line items on the balance sheet.
4. Disclosure should be made of investments that would have been reported under the equity method if the company did not elect the fair value option.
5. To be disclosed is the difference between the aggregate fair value and the aggregate unpaid principal balance of loans, long-term receivables, and long-term debt instruments with contractual principal amounts for which the fair value option has been chosen.
6. In the case of loans held as assets for which the fair value option has been selected, management should disclose the aggregate fair value of loans past due by 90 days or more. If the company recognizes interest revenue separately from other changes in fair value, disclosure should be made of the aggregate fair value of loans in the nonaccrual status. Disclosure should also be made of the difference between the aggregate fair value and aggregate unpaid principal balance for loans that are 90 days or more past due and/or in nonaccrual status.

When an income statement is presented, these four points must be disclosed:

1. How dividends and interest are measured and where they are reported in the income statement
2. Gains and losses from changes in fair value included in profit and where they are shown
3. For loans and other receivables, the estimated amount of gains and losses (including how they were calculated) included in earnings applicable to changes in instrument-specific credit risk
4. For liabilities with fair values that have been significantly impacted by changes in the instrument-specific credit risk, the estimated amount of gains and losses from fair value changes (including how they were calculated) related to changes in such credit risk, and the reasons for those changes

Other disclosures include the methods and assumptions used in fair value estimation. Qualitative information concerning the nature of the event as well as quantitative information including the impact on earnings of initially electing the fair value option for an item should also be disclosed.

Eligible Items at Effective Date

A company may elect the fair value option for eligible items at the effective date. The difference between the book (carrying) value and the fair value of eligible items related for the fair value option at the effective date must be removed from the balance sheet and included in the cumulative-effect adjustment. These differences include (1) valuation allowances (e.g., loan loss reserves); (2) unamortized deferred costs, fees, discounts, and premiums; and (3) accrued interest associated with the fair value of the eligible item.

A company that selects the fair value option for items at the effective date must provide in financial statements that include the effective date these five issues:

1. Reasons for choosing the fair value option for each existing *eligible* item or group of similar items.
2. Amount of valuation allowances removed from the balance sheet because they applied to items for which the fair value option was selected.
3. Impact on deferred tax assets and liabilities of selecting the fair value option.
4. If the fair value option is chosen for some but not all eligible items within a group of similar eligible items, there should be a description of similar items and the reasons for the partial election. Further, information should be provided so financial statement users can understand how the group of similar items applies to individual items on the balance sheet.
5. Schedule presenting by line items in the balance sheet: (a) before-tax portion of the cumulative-effect adjustment to retained earnings for the items on that line and (b) fair value at the effective date of eligible items for which the fair value option is selected and the book (carrying) amounts of those same items immediately before opting for the fair value option.

AVAILABLE-FOR-SALE AND HELD-TO-MATURITY SECURITIES

Available-for-sale and held-to-maturity securities held at the effective date are eligible for the fair value option at that date. In the event that the fair value option is selected for any of those securities at the effective date, cumulative holding (unrealized) gains and losses must be included in the cumulative-effect adjustment. Separate disclosure must be made of the holding gains and losses reclassified from accumulated other comprehensive income (for available-for-sale securities) and holding gains and losses previously unrecognized (for held-to-maturity securities).

How is stockholders' equity accounted for?

In accounting for stockholders' equity, consideration is given to preferred stock characteristics, conversion of preferred stock to common stock, stock retirement, appropriation of retained earnings, treasury stock, quasi-reorganization, dividends, fractional share warrants, stock options, stock warrants, and stock splits.

The stockholders' equity section of the balance sheet includes major categories for:

■ Capital stock (stock issued and stock to be issued)
■ Paid-in capital
■ Retained earnings
■ Accumulated other comprehensive income
■ Treasury stock

> **Note**
>
> Disclosure should be made for provisions of capital stock redeemable at given prices on specific dates. ■

What are the types and provisions of preferred stock?

Participating preferred stock is rare. If it does exist, it may be partially or fully participating. In partially participating stock, preferred stockholders participate in excess dividends over the preferred dividend rate proportionately with common stockholders up to a maximum additional rate. For example, a 6 percent preferred stock may allow participation up to 11 percent, so that an extra 5 percent dividend may be added. In fully participating stock, a distribution for the current year is at the preference rate plus any cumulative preference. Furthermore, the preferred stockholders' share in dividend distributions in excess of the preferred stock rate on a proportionate basis using the total par value of the preferred stock and common stock. For example, a 12 percent fully participating preferred stock will get the 12 percent preference rate plus a proportionate share based on the total par value of the common and preferred stock of excess dividends once common stockholders have obtained their matching 12 percent of par of the common stock.

Example 4.29

Assume 5 percent preferred stock, $20 par, 5,000 shares. The preferred stock is partially participating up to an additional 2 percent. Common stock is $10 par, 30,000 shares. A $40,000 dividend is declared. Dividends are distributed as:

	Preferred	Common
Preferred stock, current year ($100,000 × 5%)	$5,000	
Common stock, current year ($300,000 × 5%)		$15,000
Preferred stock, partial ($100,000 × 2%)	2,000	
Common stock, matching ($300,000 × 2%)		6,000
Balance to common stock		12,000
Total	$7,000	$33,000

Example 4.30

Preferred stock having a par value of $300,000 and paid-in capital (preferred stock) of $20,000 are converted into common stock. There are 30,000 preferred shares having a $10 par value per share. Common stock issued is 10,000 shares having a par value of $25.

The journal entry is:

Preferred stock	300,000	
Paid-in capital (preferred stock)	20,000	
Common stock (10,000 × $25)		250,000
Paid-in capital (common stock)		70,000

Cumulative preferred stock means that if dividends are not paid, the dividends accumulate and must be paid before any dividends can be paid to noncumulative stock.

The *liquidation value* of preferred stock means that in corporate liquidation, preferred stockholders will receive the liquidation value (sometimes stated as par value) before any funds may be distributed to common stockholders.

Disclosure for preferred stock includes liquidation preferences, call prices, and cumulative dividends in arrears.

When preferred stock is converted to common stock, the preferred stock and paid-in capital accounts are eliminated, and the common stock and paid-in capital accounts are credited. If a deficit results, retained earnings would be charged.

What is done for retired shares?

A company may retire its stock. If common stock is retired *at par value*, the entry is:

Common stock
Cash   } Par value

If common stock is retired for *less than par value*, the entry is:

Common stock
Cash
Paid-in capital

If common stock is retired for *more than par value*, the entry is:

Common stock
Paid-in capital (original premium per share)
Retained earnings (excess over original premium per share)
Cash

> ## Note
> In retirement of stock, retained earnings can only be debited, not credited. ■

What is done if retained earnings must be restricted?

Appropriation of retained earnings means setting aside retained earnings and making them unavailable for dividends. Examples include appropriations for plant expansion, debt retirement, sinking fund, and general contingencies (e.g., self-insurance).

How is treasury stock accounted for and reported?

Treasury stock is issued shares bought back by the company. The two ways to account for treasury stock are:

1. *Cost method.* Treasury stock is recorded at the cost to purchase it. If treasury stock is later sold above cost, the entry is:

Cash	
	Treasury stock
	Paid-in capital

    If treasury stock is sold instead at below cost, the entry is:

Cash	
Paid-in capital—Treasury stock (up to amount available)	
Retained earnings (if paid-in capital is unavailable)	
	Treasury stock

    If treasury stock is donated, only a memo entry is made. When the treasury shares are later sold, the entry based on the market price at that time is:

Cash	
	Paid-in capital—Donation

    An appropriation of retained earnings equal to the cost of treasury stock on hand is required.
    Treasury stock is shown as a reduction from total stockholders' equity.

2. *Par value method.* Treasury stock is recorded at its par value when bought. If treasury stock is purchased at more than par value, the entry is:

Treasury stock—Par value
Paid-in capital—Original premium per share
Retained earnings—If necessary
    Cash

If treasury stock is purchased at less than par value, the entry is:

Treasury stock—Par value
    Cash
    Paid-in capital

Upon sale of the treasury stock above par value, the entry is:

Cash
    Treasury stock
    Paid-in capital

Upon sale of the treasury stock at less than par value, the entry is:

Cash
Paid-in capital (amount available)
Retained earnings (if paid-in capital is insufficient)
    Treasury stock

An appropriation of retained earnings equal to the cost of the treasury stock on hand is required. Treasury stock is presented as a contra account to the common stock it applies to under the capital stock section of stockholders' equity.

What is a quasi-reorganization?

A *quasi-reorganization* provides a fresh start for a financially troubled firm with a deficit in retained earnings. A quasi-reorganization occurs to avoid bankruptcy. A revaluation of assets is made.

- Stockholders and creditors must consent to the quasi-reorganization. Net assets are reduced to fair market value. If fair value is not readily determinable, then conservative estimates of such value may be made.
- Paid-in capital is reduced to eliminate the deficit in retained earnings. If paid-in capital is insufficient, then capital stock is charged.
- Retained earnings becomes a zero balance. Retained earnings will bear the quasi-reorganization date for 10 years after the reorganization.

The retained earnings account consists of these components:

Retained earnings—Unappropriated	
Dividends	Net income
Appropriations	
Prior-period adjustments	
Quasi-reorganization	

The entry for the quasi-reorganization is:

Paid-in capital
Capital stock (if necessary)
    Assets
    Retained earnings

Caution

If potential losses exist at the readjustment date but the amounts of losses cannot be determined, there should be a provision for the maximum probable loss. If estimates are later shown to be incorrect, the difference adjusts paid-in capital. ■

Note

New or additional common stock or preferred stock may be issued in exchange for existing *indebtedness*. Thus, the current liability account would be charged for the indebtedness and the capital account credited. ■

Example 4.31

A company having a $3.5 million deficit undertakes a quasi-reorganization. There is an overstatement in assets of $800,000 relative to fair market value. The balances in capital stock and paid-in capital are $5 million and $1.5 million, respectively. This entry is made to effect the quasi-reorganization:

Paid-in capital	1,500,000	
Capital stock	2,800,000	
Assets		800,000
Retained earnings		3,500,000

Since the paid-in capital account has been fully wiped out, the residual debit goes to capital stock.

How are dividends accounted for?

Dividends are distributions by the company to stockholders. After the declaration date is the record date. A person is qualified to receive a dividend only if he or she is the registered owner of the stock on the date of record. Several days before the date of record, the stock will be selling "ex-dividend." This is done to alert investors that those owning the stock before the record date are entitled to receive the dividend and that those selling the stock prior to the record date will lose their rights to the dividend.

A dividend is typically in cash or stock. A dividend is based on the outstanding shares (issued shares less treasury shares).

Example 4.32

Issued shares are 5,000, treasury shares are 1,000, and outstanding shares are therefore 4,000. The par value of the stock is $10 per share. If a $0.30 dividend per share is declared, the dividend is:

$$4,000 \times \$0.30 = \$1,200$$

If the dividend rate is 6 percent, the dividend is:

4,000 shares × $10 par value =	$40,000
	× 0.06
	$ 2,400

Assuming a cash dividend of $2,400 is declared, the entry is:

Retained earnings	2,400	
Cash dividend payable		2,400

No entry is made at the record date. The entry at the payment date is:

Cash dividend payable	2,400	
Cash		2,400

A property dividend is payable in assets other than cash. When the property dividend is declared, the company restates the distributed asset to fair market value, recognizing any gain or loss as the difference between the fair market value and carrying value of the property at the declaration date.

Example 4.33

A company transfers investments in marketable securities costing $10,000 to stockholders by declaring a property dividend on December 16, 2X11, to be distributed on January 15, 2X12. At the declaration date, the securities have a market value of $14,000. The entries are:

Declaration:		
12/16/2X11		
Investment in securities	4,000	
Gain on appreciation of securities		4,000
Retained earnings	14,000	
Property dividend payable		14,000

The net reduction is still the $10,000, cost of the asset.

Distribution:		
1/15/2X12		
Property dividend payable	14,000	
Investment in securities		14,000

A stock dividend is issued in the form of stock. Stock dividend distributable is shown in the capital stock section of stockholders' equity. It is not a liability. If the stock dividend is less than 20 to 25 percent of outstanding shares at the declaration date, retained earnings is reduced at the market price of the shares. If the stock dividend is in excess

Example 4.34

A stock dividend of 10 percent is declared on 5,000 shares of $10 par value common stock having a market price of $12. The entry at the declaration and issuance dates follow.

Retained earnings (500 shares × $12)	6,000	
Stock dividend distributable (500 shares × $10)		5,000
Paid-in capital		1,000
Stock dividend distributable	5,000	
Common stock		5,000

(continued)

Assume instead that the stock dividend was 30 percent. The entries would be:

Retained earnings (1,500 × $10)	15,000	
Stock dividend distributable		15,000
Stock dividend distributable	15,000	
Common stock		15,000

of 20 to 25 percent of outstanding shares, retained earnings is charged at par value. Between 20 and 25 percent is a gray area.

A liability dividend (scrip dividend) is payable in the form of a liability (e.g., notes payable). This type of dividend sometimes occurs when a company has financial difficulties.

Example 4.35

On 1/1/2X12, a liability dividend of $20,000 is declared in the form of a one-year, 8 percent note. The entry at the declaration date is:

Retained earnings	20,000	
Scrip dividend payable		20,000

When the scrip dividend is paid, the entry is:

Scrip dividend payable	20,000	
Interest expense	1,600	
Cash		21,600

A liquidating dividend can be deceptive, for it is not actually a dividend. It is a return of capital and not a distribution of earnings. The entry is to debit paid-in capital and credit dividends payable. The recipient of a liquidating dividend pays no tax on it.

How is a stock split handled?

In a *stock split*, the shares are *increased*, and the par value per share is *decreased*. However, total par value is the same.

Only a memo entry is made.

Example 4.36

Before: 1,000 shares, $10 par value = $10,000 total par value 2-for-1 stock
split declared

After: 2,000 shares, $5 par value = $10,000 total par value

How are stock options accounted for and reported?

A stock option gives a company's officers and other employees the right to buy shares of the company's stock, at a stated price, within a specified time period. A stock option is typically in the form of compensation or an incentive for employee services.

Noncompensatory plans are not primarily designed to give employees compensation for services. Compensation expense is not recognized. A noncompensatory plan has all four of these characteristics:

1. All employees are offered stock on some basis (e.g., equally, as percent of salary).
2. Most full-time employees can participate.
3. A reasonable time period exists to exercise the options.
4. The price discount for employees on the stock is not better than that afforded to corporate stockholders if there was an additional issuance.

The objective of a noncompensatory plan is to obtain funds and to reduce widespread ownership in the company among employees.

Accounting for a noncompensatory stock plan is one of simple sale. The option price is the same as the issue price.

A compensatory plan exists if any one of the above four criteria is not met. Consideration received by the firm for the stock equals the cash, assets, or employee services.

ASC No. 718-10-05, *Compensation—Stock Compensation: Overall* (FAS No. 123(R), *Share-Based Payment*) eliminates the intrinsic method to account for stock option plans.

ASC No. 718-10-05 mandates that the total compensation cost that should be recognized for stock-based compensation plans be equal to the grant-date fair value of all share options that vest with employees. This amount is then allocated over the service years based on the amount of service performance that has been, or will be, performed by workers. At the date of grant, the fair value of the share options *locks* and cannot be changed to later changes in stock prices. Typically the service period is the vesting period, which is the time from the grant date to the vesting date. The company must estimate the number of share options that will be given to workers based on services rendered. Compensation cost should be recognized only if performance by the employee is likely to take place. Thus, compensation cost *cannot* be accrued if it is *unlikely* that employee performance will occur. An example is an expected resignation. If at a later date it is ascertained that the initial estimate of the number of share options that are likely to be earned by workers was incorrect, a revision must be made. It is required under ASC No. 718-10-05 that the cumulative effect on current and previous years of a change in the estimated number of share options for which service is expected to be, or has been, performed should be recognized as compensation in the year of the change.

The mathematical models used to measure the fair value of share options do so at a single period in time, usually the grant date. The assumptions underlying the fair value measurement are a function of available information at the time the measurement is made. Models used to value share options include the Black-Scholes-Merton option pricing model and the Lattice-based models.

Footnote disclosure for a stock option plan includes the number of shares under option, status of the plan, option price, number of shares exercisable, and the number of shares issued under the option plan during the year.

What if a bond is issued along with warrants?

If bonds are issued along with *detachable* stock warrants, the portion of the proceeds applicable to the warrants is credited to paid-in capital. The basis for allocation is the relative values of the securities at the time of issuance. If the warrants are *not detachable*, the bonds are accounted for only as convertible debt with no allocation of the proceeds to the conversion right.

Example 4.37

A $20,000 convertible bond is issued at $21,000 with $1,000 applicable to stock warrants. If the warrants are not detachable, the entry is:

Cash	21,000	
Bonds payable		20,000
Premium on bonds payable		1,000

If the warrants are detachable, the entry is:

Cash	21,000	
Bonds payable		20,000
Paid-in capital—Stock warrants		1,000

If the proceeds of the bond issue were only $20,000 rather than $21,000 and $1,000 is attributable to the warrants, the entry is:

Cash	20,000	
Discount	1,000	
Bonds payable		20,000
Paid-in capital—Stock warrants		1,000

How are fractional shares accounted for?

Fractional share warrants can be issued.

Example 4.38

There are 1,000 shares of $10 par value common stock. The common stock has a market price of $15. A 20 percent dividend is declared, resulting in 200 shares (20% × 1,000). The 200 shares include fractional share warrants. Each warrant equals 1/5 of a share of stock. There are 100 warrants resulting in 20 shares of stock (100/5). Therefore, we have 180 regular shares and 20 fractional shares. The journal entries follow.

At the declaration date:		
Retained earnings (200 shares × 15)	3,000	
Stock dividends distributable (180 shares × 10)		1,800
Fractional share warrants (20 shares × 10)		200
Paid-in capital		1,000
At time of issuance:		
Stock dividend distributable	1,800	
Common stock		1,800
Fractional share warrants	200	
Common stock		200

If only 80 percent of the fractional share warrants were turned in, the entry would be:

Fractional share warrants	200	
Common stock		160
Paid-in capital		40

With respect to stockholders' equity, disclosure should be made of the following:

- Unusual voting rights
- Call features
- Participation rights
- Dividend and liquidation preferences
- Dividends in arrears
- Sinking fund provisions
- Conversion terms
- Agreements to issue additional shares

IFRS Treatment

IFRS requires that the issuer of convertible debt record the liability and equity components separately, while GAAP does not. ◼

IFRS Treatment

Both IFRS and U.S. GAAP consider the statement of stockholders' equity a primary financial statement. However, under IFRS, a company has the option of preparing a statement of stockholders' equity similar to U.S. GAAP or preparing a statement of recognized income and expense (SoRIE). The SoRIE reports the items that were charged directly to equity, such as revaluation surplus, and then adds the net income for the period to arrive at total recognized income and expense. In this situation, additional note disclosure is required to provide reconciliations of other equity items. ◼

CHAPTER FIVE

Statement of Cash Flows

I N ACCORDANCE WITH Accounting Standards Codification (ASC) No. 230, *Statement of Cash Flows* (Financial Accounting Standards [FAS] No. 95, *Statement of Cash Flows*) a statement of cash flows is included in the annual report. This chapter discusses how the statement may be prepared as well as the analytical implications for the CFO. The purpose of the statement is to provide useful information about the company's cash receipts and cash payments. A reconciliation between net income and net cash flow from operations is included. There is also disclosure of noncash investments and financing transactions.

CLASSIFICATIONS OF CASH FLOW

What is the definition of "cash flow"?

The statement of cash flows explains the change in cash and cash equivalents for the period. A cash equivalent is a short-term liquid investment having an original maturity of three months or less. Examples are Treasury bills and commercial paper.

The statement of cash flows classifies cash receipts and cash payments as arising from operating, investing, and financing activities.

IFRS Treatment

International Financial Reporting Standards (IFRS) require a statement of cash flows. Both IFRS and U.S. generally accepted accounting principles (GAAP) specify that the cash flows must be classified as operating, investing, or financing. ■

What is included in the operating section?

Operating activities relate to manufacturing and selling goods or the performance of services. They do not apply to investing or financing activities. The term "cash flow from operating activities" usually applies to the cash effects of transactions entering into profit computations. Cash inflows from operating activities include:

- Cash sales or collections on receivables arising from the initial sale of merchandise or rendering of service
- Cash receipts from returns on loans, debt securities (e.g., interest income), or equity securities (e.g., dividend income) of other entities
- Cash received from licensees and lessees
- Receipt of a litigation settlement
- Reimbursement under an insurance policy

Cash outflows for operating activities include:

- Cash paid for raw material or merchandise for resale
- Principal payments on accounts payable
- Payments to suppliers for operating expenses (e.g., office supplies, advertising, insurance)
- Salaries
- Payments to governmental agencies (e.g., taxes, penalties)
- Interest expenses
- Lawsuit payments
- Charitable contributions
- Cash refunds to customers for defective goods

What is included in the investing section?

Investing activities include buying debt and equity securities in other entities, purchasing and selling fixed assets, and making and collecting loans. Cash inflows from investing are receipts from sales of equity or debt securities of other companies, amounts received from selling fixed assets, and collections or sales of loans made by the company. Cash outflows for investing activities include disbursements to buy equity or debt securities of other companies, payments to buy fixed assets, and disbursements for loans made by the company.

What is included in the financing section?

Financing activities include cash flows resulting from changes in long-term liabilities and stockholders' equity items. Financing activities relate to receiving equity funds and providing owners with a return on their investment. They also include debt financing and repayment or settlement of debt. Another element is obtaining and paying for other resources derived from noncurrent creditors. Cash inflows from financing activities are comprised of funds received from the issuance of stock and funds obtained from the incurrence of debt. Cash outflows for financing activities include paying off debt, repurchasing stock, paying dividends, and making other principal payments to long-term creditors.

IFRS Treatment

In certain situations, bank overdrafts are considered part of cash and cash equivalents under IFRS (which is not the case in U.S. GAAP). Under U.S. GAAP, bank overdrafts are classified as financing activities. ■

Are cash inflows and cash outflows shown gross for each major item?

There should be separate presentations of cash inflows and cash outflows from investing and financing activities. For example, the purchase of fixed assets is a use of cash, but the sale of a fixed asset is a source of cash. These are shown separately. The issuance of debt would be a source of cash, and debt payment would be an application. Thus, cash received of $800,000 from debt incurrence would be shown as a source, but the payment of debt of $250,000 would be presented as an application. The net effect is $550,000.

What disclosure is made for noncash activities?

There is separate disclosure for investing and financing activities impacting assets or liabilities that do not affect cash flow. Examples of the noncash activities of an investing and financing nature are bond conversion, purchase of a fixed asset by the incurrence of a mortgage payable, capital lease, and nonmonetary exchange of assets. This disclosure may be footnoted or shown in a schedule.

Example 5.1

Net increase in cash	$980,000
Noncash investing and financing activities:	
Purchase of land by the issuance of common stock	$400,000
Conversion of bonds payable to common stock	200,000
	$600,000

IFRS Treatment

IFRS requires that noncash investing and financing activities be excluded from the statement of cash flows. Instead, these noncash activities should be disclosed in the notes to the financial statements instead of in the financial statements. Under

(continued)

U.S. GAAP, companies may present this information at the bottom of the cash flow statement or in a separate note. ■

What if an item applies to more than one section within the statement?

If a cash receipt or cash payment applies to more than one classification (operating, investing, financing), classification is made as to the activity that is the primary source of that cash flow. For example, the purchase and sale of equipment to be used by the company is usually considered an investing activity.

What about foreign currency exposure?

In the case of foreign currency cash flows, use the exchange rate at the time of the cash flow in reporting the currency equivalent of foreign currency cash flows. The effect of changes in the exchange rate on cash balances held in foreign currencies should be reported as a separate element of the reconciliation of the change in cash and cash equivalents for the period.

How is the direct method different from the indirect method?

The *direct method* is *preferred* in that companies should report cash flows from operating activities by major classes of gross cash receipts and gross cash payments and the resulting net amount in the operating section. A reconciliation of net income to cash flow from operating activities should be shown in a separate schedule after the body of the statement.

Note

This schedule has the same net result as gross cash receipts and cash payments from operating activities. ■

Although the direct method is preferred, a company has the option of using the indirect (reconciliation) method. In practice, most companies use the indirect method because of its easier preparation. Under the indirect method, the company reports net cash flow from operating activities indirectly by adjusting profit to reconcile it to net cash flow from operating activities. This is shown in the operating section within the body of the statement of cash flows or in a separate schedule. If presented in a separate schedule, the net cash flow from operating activities is presented as a single line item. The adjustment to reported earnings for noncash revenues and expenses involves:

- Effects of deferrals of past operating cash receipts and cash payments (e.g., changes in inventory and deferred revenue) and accumulations of expected future operating cash receipts and cash payments (e.g., changes in receivables and payables)

▪ Effects of items whose cash effect applies to investing or financing cash flows (e.g., depreciation, amortization expense, and gain or loss on the sale of fixed assets)

From this discussion, we can see that there is basically one difference in presentation between the direct and indirect method. It relates only to the operating section. Under the direct method, the operating section presents gross cash receipts and gross cash payments from operating activities with a reconciliation of net income to cash flow from operations in a separate schedule. Under the indirect method, gross cash receipts and gross cash payments from operating activities are not shown. Instead, only the reconciliation of net income to cash flow from operations is presented in the operating section or in a separate schedule with the final figure of cash flow from operations reported as a single-line item in the operating section.

Since the indirect method is the one commonly used, we concentrate on it.

Exhibit 5.1 shows the reconciliation process of net income to cash flow from operating activities, and Exhibit 5.2 outlines the indirect method.

EXHIBIT 5.1   Indirect Method of Computing Cash Provided by Operations

Add (+) or Deduct (–) to	Adjust Net Income
Net income	$XXX
Adjustments required to convert net income to cash basis:	
Depreciation, depletion, amortization expense, and loss on sale of noncurrent assets	+
Amortization of deferred revenue, amortization of bond premium, and gain on sale of noncurrent assets	–
Add (deduct) changes in current asset accounts affecting revenue or expenses[a]	
Increase in the account	–
Decrease in the account	+
Add (deduct) changes in current liability accounts affecting revenue or expense[b]	
Increase in the account	+
Decrease in the account	–
Add (deduct) changes in the Deferred Income Taxes account	
Increase in the account	+
Decrease in the account	–
Cash provided by operations	$XXX

[a] Examples include accounts receivable, accrued receivables, inventory, and prepaid expenses.
[b] Examples include accounts payable, accrued liabilities, and deferred revenue.

EXHIBIT 5.2   Format of the Statement of Cash Flows (Indirect Method)

Net cash flow from operating activities:			
Net income	×		
Adjustments for noncash expenses, revenues, losses, and gains included in income	×		
	(×)		
Net cash flow from operating activities		×	
Cash flows from investing activities	×		
	(×)		
Net cash flows provided (used) by investing activities		×	
Cash flows from financing activities	×		
	(×)		
Net cash provided (used) by financing activities		×	
Net increase (decrease) in cash		× ×	

 ## ANALYSIS OF THE STATEMENT OF CASH FLOWS

The statement of cash flows provides CFOs with information about the company's cash receipts and cash payments for operating, investing, and financing activities.

What useful information is obtained from doing a comparative analysis?

Comparative statements of cash flows hold clues to a company's earning potential, risk, and liquidity.

These statements show the repeatability of the company's sources of funds, their costs, and whether such sources may be relied on in the future. The uses of funds for growth and for maintaining competitive position are revealed. An analysis of comparative statements of cash flows helps in understanding the entity's current and prospective financial health.

It facilitates planning future ventures and financing needs. Comparative data help the CFO identify abnormal or cyclical factors and changes in the relationship among each flow element.

The statement is a basis for forecasting earnings based on plant, property, and equipment posture. It assists in appraising growth potential and incorporates cash flow requirements, highlighting specific fund sources and future means of payment. Will the company be able to pay its obligations and dividends?

The statement reveals the type and degree of financing required to expand long-term assets and to bolster operations.

The CFO should compute for analytical purposes cash flow per share equal to net cash flow divided by the number of shares. A high ratio indicates that the company is liquid.

We now discuss the analysis of the operating, investing, and financing sections of the statement of cash flows.

What should you look at in evaluating the operating section?

An analysis of the operating section enables the CFO to determine the adequacy of cash flow from operating activities to satisfy company requirements. Can the firm obtain positive future net cash flows? The reconciliation tracing net income to net cash flow from operating activities should be examined to see the effect of noncash revenue and noncash expense items.

A high ratio of cash from sales to total sales points to quality sales dollars.

The cash debt coverage ratio equals cash flow from operations less dividends divided by total debt. Cash flow from operations less dividends is referred to as retained operating cash flow. The ratio indicates the number of years current cash flows will be needed to pay debt. A high ratio reflects the company's ability to repay debt. Another related ratio is cash flow from operations less dividends divided by the current maturities of long-term debt. These ratios could include adding to the denominator current liabilities or other fixed commitments, such as lease obligations.

The cash dividend coverage ratio equals cash flow from operations divided by total dividends. It reflects the company's ability to pay current dividends from operating cash flow.

The capital acquisitions ratio equals cash flow from operations less dividends divided by cash paid for acquisitions. The ratio reveals the entity's ability to finance capital expenditures from internal sources.

The cash return on assets equals cash flow from operations before interest and taxes divided by total assets. A higher ratio means a greater cash return earned on assets employed. However, this ratio contains no provision for the replacement of assets or for future commitments.

The ratio of cash flow from operations divided by total debt plus stockholders' equity indicates the internal generation of cash available to creditors and investors.

The ratio of cash flow from operations to stockholders' equity indicates the return to stockholders.

An award under a lawsuit is a cash inflow from operating activities that results in a nonrecurring source of revenue.

An operating cash outlay for refunds given to customers for deficient goods indicates a quality problem with merchandise.

Payments of penalties, fines, and lawsuit damages are operating cash outflows that show poor management in that a problem arose that required a nonbeneficial expenditure.

What investing activities should be examined?

An analysis of the investing section identifies an investment in another company that may point to an attempt for ultimate control for diversification purposes. It may also indicate a change in future direction or change in business philosophy.

An increase in fixed assets indicates capital expansion and growth. The CFO should determine which assets have been purchased. Are they assets for risky (specialized) ventures, or are they stable (multipurpose) ones? This is a clue as to risk potential and expected return. The nature of the assets shows future direction and earning potential of product lines, business segments, and territories. Are these directions viable?

The CFO should ascertain whether there is a contraction in the business arising from the sale of fixed assets without adequate replacement. Is the problem corporate (e.g., product line is weakening) or industry-wide (e.g., industry is on the downturn)?

What is the importance of financing activities?

An appraisal of the financing section will help the CFO form an opinion of the company's ability to obtain financing in the money and capital markets as well as its ability to satisfy its obligations. The financial mixture of equity, bonds, and long-term bank loans impacts the cost of financing. A major advantage of debt is the tax deductibility of interest. However, dividends on stock are not tax deductible. In inflation, paying debt back in cheaper dollars will result in purchasing power gains. The risk of debt financing is the required repayment of principal and interest. Will the company have the funds at maturity? The CFO must analyze the stability of the fund source to ascertain whether it may be relied on in the future even in a tight money market. Otherwise, there may be problems in maintaining corporate operations in a recession. The question is: Where can the company go for funds during times of tight money?

By appraising the financing sources, the financing preferences of management are revealed. Is there an inclination toward risk or safety?

The ability of a company to finance with the issuance of common stock on attractive terms (high stock price) indicates that investors are positive about the financial health of the business.

The issuance of preferred stock may be a negative indicator because it may mean the company has a problem issuing common stock.

An appraisal should be made of the company's ability to meet debt. Excessive debt means greater corporate risk especially in an economic downturn. The problem is acute if earnings are unstable or declining. The reduction in long-term debt is favorable, however, because it lessens corporate risk.

The CFO should appraise the company's dividend-paying ability. Stockholders favor a company with a high dividend payout.

Why are noncash activities worth considering?

A bond conversion is positive because it indicates that bondholders are optimistic about the company's financial well-being and/or the market price of stock has increased. A conversion of preferred stock to common stock is favorable because it shows that preferred stockholders are impressed with the company's future and are willing to have a lower priority in liquidation.

How is managerial planning facilitated by analyzing the statement of cash flows?

Profitability is only one important ingredient for success. Current and future cash flows are also important.

Management is responsible for planning how and when cash will be used and obtained. When planned expenditures require more cash than planned activities are likely to produce, managers must decide what to do. They may decide to obtain debt or equity financing or to dispose of some fixed assets or a business segment. Alternatively, they may decide to reduce planned activities by modifying operational plans, such as ending a special advertising campaign or delaying new acquisitions. Or they may decide to revise planned payments to financing sources, such as delaying bond repayment or reducing dividends. Whatever is decided, the managers' goal is to balance, over both the short and the long term, the cash available and the needs for cash.

Management gains insight into cash planning and control when evaluating the statement of cash flows in terms of coordinating dividend policy with other corporate activities, financial planning for new products and types of assets needed, strengthening a weak cash posture and credit availability, and ascertaining the feasibility and implementation of existing top management plans.

The ratio of net cash flows for investing activities divided by net cash flows from financing activities compares the total funds needed for investment to funds generated from financing. Are fund sources adequate to meet investment needs?

Similarly, the ratio of net cash flows for investing divided by net cash flows from operating and financing activities compares the funds needed for investment to the funds obtained from financing and operations.

The analysis and evaluation of cash flows is essential if the CFO is to appraise an entity's cash flows from operating, investing, and financing activities. The company's liquidity and solvency positions as well as future directions are revealed. Inadequacy in cash flow has possible serious implications because it may lead to declining profitability, greater financial risk, and even bankruptcy.

Example 5.2

X Company provides these financial statements:

X Company

Comparative Balance Sheets

December 31

(in millions)

Assets	2X12	2X11
Cash	$ 40	$ 47
Accounts receivable	30	35
Prepaid expenses	4	2
Land	50	35
Building	100	80
Accumulated depreciation	(9)	(6)
Equipment	50	42
Accumulated depreciation	(11)	(7)
Total assets	$254	$228

(continued)

Liabilities and Stockholders' Equity

Accounts payable	$ 20	$ 16
Long-term notes payable	30	20
Common stock	100	100
Retained earnings	104	92
Total liabilities and stockholders' equity	$254	$228

X Company

Income Statement for the Year-End December 31, 2X12

(in millions)

Revenue		$300
Operating expenses (excluding depreciation)	$200	
Depreciation	7	207
Income from operations		$ 93
Income tax expense		32
Net income		$ 61

Additional information:

- Cash dividends paid $49.
- The company issued long-term notes payable for cash.
- Land, building, and equipment were acquired for cash.

We can now prepare the statement of cash flows under the indirect method, as follows.

X Company

Statement of Cash Flows for the Year-End December 31, 2X12

(in millions)

Cash flow from operating activities		
Net income		$61
Add (deduct) items not affecting cash		
Depreciation expense	$ 7	
Decrease in accounts receivable	5	
Increase in prepaid expenses	(2)	
Increase in accounts payable	4	14
Net cash flow from operating activities		$75
Cash flow from investing activities		
Purchase of land	($15)	
Purchase of building	(20)	
Purchase of equipment	(8)	(43)

Cash flow from financing activities		
Issuance of long-term notes payable	$10	
Payment of cash dividends	(49)	(39)
Net decrease in cash		$ 7

A financial analysis of the statement of cash flows reveals that the profitability and operating cash flow of X Company improved. This indicates good earnings performance as well as earnings being backed up by cash. The decrease in accounts receivable reveals better collection efforts. The increase in accounts payable is a sign that suppliers are confident in the company and willing to give interest-free financing. The acquisition of land, building, and equipment points to a growing business undertaking capital expansion. The issuance of long-term notes payable indicates that part of the financing of assets is through debt. Stockholders will be happy with the significant dividend payout of 80.3 percent (dividends divided by net income, or $49/$61). Overall, there was a decrease in cash of $7, but this should not cause alarm because of the company's profitability and the fact that cash was used for capital expansion and dividend payments. We recommend that the dividend payout be reduced from its high level and the funds be reinvested in the profitable business. Also, the curtailment of dividends by more than $7 would result in a positive net cash flow for the year. Cash flow is needed for immediate liquidity needs.

Example 5.3

Y Company presents this statement of cash flows:

Y Company

Statement of Cash Flows for the Year-End December 31, 2X12

Cash flows from operating activities		
Net income	$134,000	
Add (deduct) items not affecting cash		
Depreciation expense	$ 21,000	
Decrease in accounts receivable	10,000	
Increase in prepaid expenses	(6,000)	
Increase in accounts payable	35,000	60,000
Net cash flow from operating activities		$194,000
Cash flows from investing activities		
Purchase of land	$(70,000)	

(continued)

Purchase of building	(200,000)	
Purchase of equipment	(68,000)	
Cash used by investing activities		(338,000)
Cash flows from financing activities		
Issuance of bonds	150,000	
Payment of cash dividends	(18,000)	
Cash provided by financing activities		132,000
Net decrease in cash		$(12,000)

An analysis of the statement of cash flows reveals that the company is profitable. Also, cash flow from operating activities exceeds net income, which indicates good internal cash generation. The ratio of cash flow from operating activities to net income is a solid 1.45 ($194,000/$134,000). A high ratio is desirable because it shows that earnings are backed up by cash. The decline in accounts receivable indicates better collection efforts. The increase in accounts payable shows the company can obtain interest-free financing. The company is in the process of expanding for future growth as evidenced by the purchase of land, building, and equipment. The debt position of the company has increased, indicating greater risk. The dividend payout was 13.4 percent ($18,000/$134,000). Stockholders look positively on a firm that pays dividends. The decrease in cash flow for the year of $12,000 is a negative sign.

CHAPTER SIX

Accounting and Disclosures

THIS CHAPTER DISCUSSES the accounting involved in changes in principle, estimate, and reporting entity. Corrections of errors are also presented. In a troubled debt situation, the debtor wants relief from the creditor. Non–interest-bearing notes and futures contracts are presented. Disclosure about financial instruments with off-balance-sheet risk is discussed.

This chapter also presents disclosures for accounting policies; development-stage company reporting and disclosures; disclosures for capital structure, related parties, inflation, and business interruption insurance; and environmental reporting and disclosures.

 ## ACCOUNTING CHANGES

The types of accounting changes as per Accounting Standards Codification (ASC) No. 250-10-05, *Accounting Changes and Error Corrections: Overall* (Financial Accounting Standard [FAS] No. 154, *Accounting Changes and Error Corrections—A Replacement of APB Opinion No. 20 and FASB Statement No. 3*) are principle, estimate, and reporting entity.

What do we do if an accounting principle is changed?

ASC No. 250-10-05 mandates retroactive application to previous years' financial statements of changes in accounting principle. This approach is the application of a different accounting method to previous years as if that new method had always been used. If it is impractical to ascertain either the year-specific impact or the cumulative effect of the change, the newly adopted accounting method must be applied to the beginning balances of assets or liabilities of the earliest year for practical retrospective application. Further, a corresponding adjustment must be made to the beginning balance of retained earnings for that year. If the cumulative dollar effect of applying an accounting principle change to previous years is impractical, the new accounting principle must be applied as if it were adopted prospectively from the earliest practical date.

A change in depreciation, depletion, or amortization must be accounted for as a change in estimate effected by a change in principle.

What is presented in the retained earnings statement?

The retained earnings statement after a retroactive change for a change in accounting principle follows:

> Retained earnings—beginning of period, as previously reported
> Add: Adjustment for the cumulative effect on prior years of applying retrospectively the new accounting method
> Retained earnings—beginning of period, as adjusted

Example 6.1

Akel Construction Company has in prior years used the completed contract method for construction costs. In 2X12 the company changed to the percentage-of-completion method. The tax rate is 30 percent. This data is presented:

| | Before-Tax Income from | |
| | Percentage-of- | Completed |
Year	Completion	Contract
Before 2X12	$60,000	$40,000
In 2X12	18,000	16,000
Total at beginning of 2X12	78,000	56,000
Total in 2X12	20,000	19,000

The basis for the journal entry to record the change in 2X12 is:

	Difference	Tax (30%)	Net of Tax
Before 2X12	$20,000	$6,000	$14,000
In 2X12	2,000	600	1,400
Total at beginning of 2X12	22,000	6,600	15,400
Total in 2X12	1,000	300	700

The journal entry to record the change in 2X12 is:

Construction in Progress	22,000	
Deferred Tax Liability		6,600
Retained Earnings		15,400

A footnote discloses the nature and justification of a change in principle, including an explanation of why the new principle is preferred. Justification may be a new Financial Accounting Standards Board pronouncement, new tax law, new American Institute of Certified Public Accountants statement of position or industry audit guide, or a change in circumstances, or to more readily conform to industry practice.

If an accounting change in principle is immaterial in the current year, but it is expected to be material in the future, disclosure is needed.

These are *not* considered a change in accounting principle:

- A principle adopted for the first time on new or previously immaterial events or transactions
- A principle adopted or changed because of events or transactions clearly different in substance

A *change in composition* of the cost elements (e.g., material, labor, and overhead) of inventory qualifies as an accounting change.

What if an estimate is revised?

A change in accounting estimate results from new circumstances, such as a change in salvage value or bad debt experience. A change in accounting estimate is recognized prospectively over current and future years. There is no restatement of past years. A footnote describes the nature of a material change.

If a change in estimate is coupled with a change in principle and the effects cannot be distinguished, it is accounted for as a change in estimate. For example, there may be a change from deferring and amortizing a cost to expensing it because future benefits are uncertain. This should be accounted for as a change in estimate.

Example 6.2

Equipment was bought on 1/1/2X08 for $40,000 having an original estimated life of 10 years with a salvage value of $4,000. On 1/1/2X12, the estimated life was revised to eight more years remaining with a new salvage value of $3,200. The journal entry on 12/31/2X12 for depreciation expense is:

Depreciation	2,800	
Accumulated depreciation		2,800

Computations follow.

(continued)

Book value on 1/1/2X12:

Original cost	$40,000
Less: Accumulated depreciation	

$$\frac{\$40,000 - 4,000}{10} = \$3,6000 \times 4 \qquad 14,400$$

Book value	$25,600

Depreciation for 2X12:

Book value	$25,600
Less: New salvage value	3,200
Depreciable cost	$22,400

Depreciable cost/New life = $22,400/8 = $2,800

How do we account for and report when the makeup of the entity is changed?

A change in reporting entity (e.g., two previously separate companies merge) is accounted for by restating previous years' financial statements as if both companies were always combined. The restatement helps to show trends in comparative financial statements and historical summaries. The effect of the change on income before extraordinary items, net income, and per share amounts is reported for all periods presented. The restatement does not have to go back more than five years. Footnote disclosure should be made of the nature of and reason for the change in reporting entity only in the year of change. Examples of changes in reporting entity are:

■ Presenting consolidated statements rather than statements of individual companies
■ Including change in subsidiaries in consolidated statements or combined statements

How is a prior-period adjustment handled?

The two types of prior-period adjustments are:

1. Correction of an error that was made in a previous year
2. Recognition of a tax loss carryforward benefit arising from a purchased subsidiary (curtailed by the 1986 Tax Reform Act)

When a single year is presented, prior-period adjustments adjust the beginning balance of retained earnings. The presentation follows (1/1 represents the beginning of the period; 12/31 represents the end):

Retained earnings—1/1 Unadjusted
    Prior-period adjustments (net of tax)

Retained earnings—1/1 Adjusted
    Add: Net income
    Less: Dividends
Retained earnings—12/31

Errors may arise from mathematical mistakes, misapplication of accounting principles, or misuse of facts existing when the financial statements were prepared. Furthermore, a change in principle from one that is not generally accepted accounting principle (GAAP) to one that is GAAP is an error correction. Disclosure should be made of the nature of the error and the effect of correction on profit.

When comparative statements are prepared, a retroactive adjustment for the error is made to prior years. The retroactive adjustment is disclosed by showing the effects of the adjustment on previous years' earnings and component items of net income.

Example 6.3

In 2X11, a company incorrectly charged furniture for promotion expense amounting to $30,000. The error was discovered in 2X12. The correcting journal entry is:

Retained earnings	30,000	
Furniture		30,000

Example 6.4

At the end of 2X11, a company failed to accrue telephone expense that was paid at the beginning of 2X12. The correcting entry on 12/31/2X12 is:

Retained earnings	16,000	
Telephone expense		16,000

Example 6.5

On 1/1/2X10, an advance retainer fee of $50,000 was received covering a five-year period. In error, revenue was credited for the full amount. The error was discovered on 12/31/2X12 before closing the books. The correcting entry is:

12/31/2X12		
Retained earnings	30,000	
Revenue		10,000
Deferred revenue		20,000

Example 6.6

A company bought a machine on January 1, 2X09, for $32,000 with a $2,000 salvage value and a five-year life. By mistake, repairs expense was charged. The error was uncovered on December 31, 2X12, before closing the books. The correcting entry is:

Depreciation expense	6,000	
Machine	32,000	
Accumulated depreciation		24,000
Retained earnings		14,000

Accumulated depreciation of $24,000 is calculated below:

($32,000 – $2,000)/5 = $6,000 per year × 4 years = $24,000

The credit to retained earnings reflects the difference between the erroneous repairs expense of $32,000 in 2X09 versus showing depreciation expense of $18,000 for three years (2X09–2X11).

Example 6.7

At the beginning of 2X10, a company bought equipment for $300,000 with a salvage value of $20,000 and an expected life of 10 years. Straight-line depreciation is used. In error, salvage value was not deducted in computing depreciation. The correcting journal entries on 12/31/2X12 follow.

	2X10	and	2X11
Depreciation taken $300,000/10 × 2 years			$ 60,000
Depreciation correctly stated $280,000/10 × 2 years			56,000
			$ 4,000
Depreciation	28,000		
Accumulated depreciation			28,000
Depreciation for current year			
Accumulated depreciation	4,000		
Retained earnings			4,000
Correct prior-year depreciation misstatement			

What policies should be disclosed?

Accounting policies are the specific accounting principles and methods of applying them that are selected by management. Accounting policies should be those that are most appropriate in the circumstances to fairly present financial position and operating results. Accounting policies can relate to reporting and measurement methods as well as disclosures. They include:

- A selection from GAAP or unusual applications thereof
- Practices peculiar to the industry

The first footnote or a section preceding the notes to the financial statements should describe the accounting policies used.

The application of GAAP requires the use of judgment when alternative acceptable principles exist and when there are varying methods of applying a principle to a given set of facts. Disclosure of these principles and methods is essential to the full presentation of financial position and operations.

Examples of accounting policy disclosures are inventory pricing method, depreciation method, consolidation bases, and amortization period for intangibles.

Some types of financial statements do not have to describe the accounting policies that are followed. Examples are quarterly unaudited statements when there has not been a policy change since the last year-end and statements only for internal use.

What if the debtor has trouble paying?

In a troubled debt restructuring, the debtor has financial problems and is relieved of part or all of the obligation. The concession arises from the debtor–creditor agreement or law. It also applies to foreclosure and repossession. The types of troubled debt restructurings are:

- Debtor transfers to creditor receivables from third parties or other assets.
- Debtor gives creditor equity securities to satisfy the debt.
- The debt terms are modified, including reducing the interest rate, extending the maturity date, or reducing the principal of the obligation.

The debtor records an extraordinary gain (net of tax) on the restructuring while the creditor recognizes a loss. The loss may be ordinary or extraordinary, depending on whether the arrangement is unusual and infrequent. Typically, the loss is ordinary.

Debtor

The gain to the debtor equals the difference between the fair value of assets exchanged and the book value of the debt, including accrued interest. Furthermore, there may arise a gain on disposal of assets exchanged equal to the difference between the fair market value and the book value of the transferred assets. The latter gain or loss is *not* a gain or loss on restructuring but rather an ordinary gain or loss in connection with asset disposal.

Example 6.8

A debtor transfers assets having a fair market value of $80 and a book value of $65 to settle a payable having a carrying value of $90. The gain on restructuring is $10 ($90 – $80). The ordinary gain is $15 ($80 – $65).

A debtor may give the creditor an equity interest. The debtor records the equity securities issued based on fair market value, not the recorded value of the debt extinguished. The excess of the recorded payable satisfied over the fair value of the issued securities constitutes an extraordinary item.

A modification in terms of an initial debt contract is accounted for prospectively. A new interest rate may be determined based on the new terms. This interest rate is then used to allocate future payments to lower principal and interest. When the new terms of the agreement result in the sum of all the future payments to be *less* than the carrying value of the payable, the payable is reduced, and a restructuring gain is recorded for the difference. The future payments only reduce principal. Interest expense is not recorded.

A troubled debt restructuring may result in a *combination* of concessions to the debtor. This may occur when assets or an equity interest are given in *partial* satisfaction of the obligation and the balance is subject to a modification of terms. There are two steps.

1. The payable is reduced by the fair value of the assets or equity transferred.
2. The balance of the debt is accounted for as a modification-of-terms–type restructuring.

Direct costs, such as legal fees, incurred by the debtor in an equity transfer reduce the fair value of the equity interest. All other costs reduce the gain on restructuring. If there is no gain, they are expensed.

Example 6.9

The debtor owes the creditor $200,000 and because of financial problems may have difficulty making future payments. Both the debtor and creditor should make footnote disclosure of the problem.

Example 6.10

The debtor owes the creditor $80,000. The creditor relieves the debtor of $10,000. The balance of the debt will be paid at a later time.
The journal entry for the debtor is:

Accounts payable	10,000	
Extraordinary gain		10,000

The journal entry for the creditor is:

Ordinary loss	10,000	
Accounts receivable		10,000

Example 6.11

The debtor owes the creditor $90,000. The creditor agrees to accept $70,000 in full satisfaction of the obligation.
    The journal entry for the debtor is:

Accounts payable	90,000	
Extraordinary gain		20,000
Cash		70,000

The journal entry for the creditor is:

Cash	70,000	
Ordinary loss	20,000	
Accounts receivable		90,000

The debtor should disclose in the footnotes:

■ Terms of the restructuring agreement
■ The aggregate and per share amounts of the gain on restructuring
■ Amounts that are contingently payable, including the contingency terms

Creditor

The creditor's loss is the difference between the fair value of assets received and the book value of the investment. When terms are modified, the creditor recognizes interest income to the degree that total future payments are greater than the carrying value of the investment. Interest income is recognized using the effective interest method. Assets received are reflected at fair market value. When the book value of the receivable is in excess of the aggregate payments, an ordinary loss is recognized for the difference. All cash received in the future is accounted for as a recovery of the investment. Direct costs of the creditor are expensed.

The creditor does not recognize contingent interest until the contingency is removed and interest has been earned. Furthermore, future changes in the interest rate are accounted for as a change in estimate.

The creditor discloses in the footnotes:

■ Loan commitments of additional funds to financially troubled companies
■ Loans and/or receivables by major type
■ Debt agreements in which the interest rate has been downwardly adjusted, including an explanation of the circumstances
■ Description of the restructuring provisions

What if a note does not provide for interest?

If the face amount of a note does not represent the present value of the consideration given or received in the exchange, imputation of interest is needed to avoid the misstatement of profit. Interest is imputed on noninterest-bearing notes, notes that provide for an unrealistically low interest rate, and when the face value of the note is substantially different from the "going" selling price of the property or market value of the note.

If a note is issued only for cash, the note should be recorded at the cash exchanged regardless of whether the interest rate is reasonable. The note has a present value at issuance equal to the cash transacted. When a note is exchanged for property, goods, or services, there is a presumption that the interest rate is reasonable. Where the stipulated interest rate is unreasonable, the note is recorded at the fair value of the merchandise or services or at an amount that approximates fair value. If fair value is not ascertainable for the goods or services, the discounted present value of the note is used.

The imputed interest rate is the one that would have resulted if an independent borrower or lender had negotiated an arm's-length transaction. For example, it could be the prevailing interest rate the borrower would have paid for financing. The interest rate is based on economic circumstances and events.

The factors to be taken into account in deriving an appropriate discount rate include:

- Prime interest rate
- Going market rate for similar-quality instruments
- Collateral
- Issuer's credit standing
- Restrictive covenants and other terms in the note agreement
- Tax effects of the arrangement

ASC No. 835-30-05, *Interest: Imputation of Interest* (Accounting Principles Board No. 21, *Interest on Receivables and Payables*) applies to *long-term* payables and receivables. Short-term payables and receivables are typically recorded at face value. The pronouncement is *not* applicable to:

- Receivables or payables occurring within the ordinary course of business
- Security deposits
- Amounts that do not require repayment
- Transactions between parent and subsidiary

The difference between the face value of the note and its present value represents discount or premium that has to be accounted for as an element of interest over the life of the note. Present value of the payments of the note is based on an imputed interest rate.

The interest method is used to amortize the discount or premium on the note. The interest method results in a constant rate of interest. Under the method, amortization equals:

$$\text{Interest rate} \times \frac{\text{Present value of the liability}}{\text{Receivable at the beginning of the year}}$$

Interest expense is recorded for the borrower, whereas interest revenue is recorded for the lender. Issuance costs are treated as a deferred charge.

The note payable and note receivable are presented in the balance sheet in this way:

Notes payable (principal plus interest)
    Less: Discount (interest)
Present value (principal)

Notes receivable (principal plus interest)
    Less: Premium (interest)
Present value (principal)

Example 6.12

On 1/1/2X12, equipment is acquired in exchange for a one-year note payable of $1,000 maturing on 12/31/2X12. The imputed interest rate is 10 percent, resulting in the present value factor for $n = 1$, $i = 10\%$ of 0.91. Relevant journal entries follow.

1/1/2X12		
Equipment	910	
Discount	90	
Notes payable		1,000
12/31/2X12		
Interest expense	90	
Discount		90
Notes payable	1,000	
Cash		1,000

Example 6.13

On 1/1/2X11, a machine is bought for cash of $10,000 and the incurrence of a $30,000, five-year, non-interest-bearing note payable. The imputed interest rate is 10 percent. The present value factor for $n = 5$, $i = 10\%$ is 0.62. Appropriate journal entries follow:

(continued)

1/1/2X11		
Machine (10,000 + 18,600)	28,600	
Discount	11,400	
Notes payable		30,000
Cash		10,000
Present value of note = $30,000 × 0.62 = $18,600		

On 1/1/2X11, the balance sheet shows:

Notes payable	$30,000	
Less: Discount	11,400	
Present value	$18,600	
12/31/2X11		
Interest expense	1,860	
Discount		1,860
10% × $18,600 = $1,860		
1/1/2X12		
Notes payable	$30,000	
Less: Discount (11,400 − 1,860)	9,540	
Present value	$20,460	
12/31/2X12		
Interest expense	2,046	
Discount		2,046
10% × $20,460 = $2,046		

 FUTURES CONTRACTS

Should you engage in futures contracts?

A futures contract is a legal arrangement between the purchaser or seller and a regulated futures exchange in the United States or overseas. Futures contracts involve:

- A buyer or seller receiving or making a delivery of a commodity or financial instrument (e.g., stocks, bonds, commercial paper, mortgages) at a specified date. Cash settlement rather than delivery typically exists (e.g., stock index future).
- The elimination of a futures contract before the delivery date by engaging in an offsetting contract for the particular commodity or financial instrument. For example, a futures contract to buy 200,000 pounds of a commodity by December 31, 2X11, may be canceled by entering into another contract to sell 200,000 pounds of that same commodity on December 31, 2X11.
- Regular (e.g., daily) settlement changes in value of open contracts. The usual contract provides that when a decrease in the contract value occurs, the contract holder has to make a cash deposit for such a decline with the clearinghouse. If the contract increases in value, the holder may withdraw the increased value.

The change in the market value of a futures contract involves a gain or loss that should be recognized in earnings. An exception exists that for certain contracts the timing of income statement recognition relates to the accounting for the applicable asset, liability, commitment, or transaction. This accounting exception applies when the contract is designed as a hedge against price and interest rate fluctuation. When the criteria discussed in the next section are satisfied, the accounting for the contract relates to the accounting for the hedged item. Thus, a change in market value is recognized in the same accounting period that the effects of the related changes in price or interest rate of the hedged item are reflected in income.

What is a hedge?

A *hedge* exists when both of these criteria are met:

1. *The hedged item places price and interest rate risk on the firm.* "Risk" means the sensitivity of corporate earnings to market price changes or rates of return of existing assets, liabilities, commitments, and expected transactions. This criterion is not met in the case that other assets, liabilities, commitments, and anticipated transactions *already* offset the risk.
2. *The contract lowers risk exposure and is entered into as a hedge.* High correlation exists between the change in market value of the contract and the fair value of the hedged item. In effect, the market price change of the contract offsets the price and interest rate changes on the exposed item. An example is a futures contract to sell silver that offsets the changes in the price of silver.

A change in market value of a futures contract that meets the hedging criteria of the related asset or liability adjusts the carrying value of the hedged item. For example, a company has an investment in a government bond that it expects to sell in the future. The company can reduce its susceptibility to changes in fair value of the bonds by entering into a futures contract. The changes in the market value of the futures contract adjusts the book value of the bonds.

A change in market value of a futures contract that is for the purpose of hedging a firm commitment is included in measuring the transaction satisfying the commitment. An example is when the company hedges a firm purchase commitment by using a futures contract. When the acquisition takes place satisfying the purchase commitment, the gain or loss on the futures contract is an element of the cost of the acquired item. Assume ABC Company has a purchase commitment for 30,000 pounds of a commodity at $2 per pound, totaling $60,000. At the time of the consummation of the transaction, the $60,000 cost is *decreased* by any gain (e.g., $5,000) arising from the "hedged" futures contract. The net cost is shown as the carrying value (e.g., $55,000).

A futures contract may apply to transactions the company *expects* to carry out in the ordinary course of business. It is not obligated to do so. These expected transactions do not involve existing assets or liabilities, or transactions applicable to *existing* firm commitments. For example, perhaps your company *anticipates* buying a commodity in the future but has not made a formal purchase commitment. The company may minimize risk exposure to price changes by making a futures contract. The change in market value of this anticipatory hedge contract is included in measuring the subsequent transaction. The change in market value of the futures contract adjusts the cost of the acquired item. The next four criteria must be satisfied for anticipatory hedge accounting. (Note that items 1 and 2 are the same as the criteria for regular hedge contracts related to *existing* assets, liabilities, or firm commitments.)

1. *The hedged item places price and interest rate risk on the firm.*
2. *The contract lowers risk exposure and is entered into as a hedge.*
3. *The major terms of the contemplated transaction have been identified.* This includes the type of commodity or financial instrument, quantity, and expected transaction date. If the financial instrument carries interest, the maturity date should be given.
4. *It is probable that the expected transaction will occur.*

   Probability of occurrence depends on:

- Monetary commitment
- Time period
- Financial soundness to conduct the transaction
- Frequency of previous transactions of a similar nature
- Adverse operational effects of not engaging in the transaction
- Possibility that other types of transactions may be undertaken to accomplish the desired objective

How do we account for and disclose hedge-type contracts?

The accounting for a hedge-type futures contract related to an expected asset acquisition or liability incurrence should be consistent with the company's accounting method used for those assets and liabilities. For example, the company should recognize a loss for a futures contract that is a hedge of an expected inventory acquisition if the amount will not be removed from the sale of inventory.

If a hedged futures contract is closed before the expected transaction, the accumulated value change in the contract should be carried forward in measuring the related transaction. If it is probable that the quantity of an expected transaction will be less than the amount initially hedged, the company should recognize a gain or loss for a pro rata portion of futures results that would have been included in the measurement of the subsequent transaction.

A hedged futures contract requires disclosure of:

- Nature of assets and liabilities
- Accounting method used for the contract, including a description of events resulting in recognizing changes in contract values
- Expected transactions that are hedged with futures contracts
- Firm commitments

What footnote information should be presented for financial instruments?

Disclosure is required of information about financial instruments with off-balance-sheet risk and financial instruments with concentrations of credit risk. A financial instrument is defined as cash, evidence of an ownership interest in another entity, or a contract that *both* (1) imposes on one entity a contractual obligation to deliver cash or another financial instrument to a second entity, or to exchange financial instruments on unfavorable terms, and (2) conveys to the second entity a contractual right to receive cash, another financial instrument, or exchange financial instruments on favorable terms with the first entity. Examples of financial instruments include letters of credit or loan commitments written, foreign currency or interest rate swaps, financial guarantees written, forward or futures contracts, call and put options written, and interest rate caps or floors written.

The company must disclose information about financial instruments that may result in future loss but have not been recognized in the accounts as liabilities and are thus not reported in the income statement or balance sheet. A financial instrument has an off-balance-sheet risk of accounting loss if the risk of loss exceeds the amount recognized as an asset (if any), or if the ultimate obligation may exceed the amount recognized as a liability.

These points must be footnoted:

- The face amounts of the financial instruments
- The extent, nature, and terms of the financial instruments, including any cash requirements
- The entity's policy for requiring security on financial instruments it accepts
- Identification and description of collateral
- A discussion of credit risks associated with financial instruments because of the failure of another party to perform
- A discussion of market risk that will make a financial instrument less valuable, including future changes in market prices caused by foreign exchange and interest rate fluctuations
- Information about a region, activity, or economic factor that may result in a concentration of credit risk
- The *potential* loss from the financial instrument if a party fails to perform under the contract
- The entity's accounting policies for financial instruments

 VARIOUS DISCLOSURES

What environmental reporting and disclosures are required?

CFOs must be cognizant of compliance regulations with respect to environmental matters. Failure to adhere to environmental laws could result in penalties and fines. The

CFO must be assured that the company is following relevant accounting, reporting, and disclosures for environmental issues.

Depending on the circumstances, a liability and/or footnote disclosure may be required for pollution, waste disposal, radiation, ocean dumping, corrosion and leakage, oil spills, and hazardous materials and chemicals. Examples of footnote disclosures are:

- Water or air pollution
- Contamination resulting in health or safety hazards
- Information on site remediation projects
- Legal and regulatory compliance issues (e.g., cleanup responsibility)

Actual environmental costs should be compared to what was budgeted with variances determined. Environmental cost trends should be noted.

What capital structure information should be disclosed?

As per ASC No. 505-10-50, *Equity: Overall* (FAS No. 129, *Disclosure of Information about Capital Structure*), companies must disclose the rights and privileges of common and preferred stockholders, such as conversion terms, sinking fund provisions, redemption requirements, participation rights, liquidation preferences, voting rights, and terms for additional issuances.

What related party disclosures are required?

According to ASC No. 850-10-05, *Related Party Disclosures: Overall* (FAS No. 57, *Related Party Disclosures*), related party relationships and transactions must be disclosed. Related party transactions include parent–subsidiary relationships, activities between affiliates, joint ventures, and transactions between the company and its principal owners. Related party transactions take place when a transacting party can materially influence or exercise control of another transacting party owing to a financial, common ownership, or familial relationship. They may also occur when a nontransacting party can significantly affect the policies of two other transacting parties.

Related party transactions may include sales, purchases, services, loans, rentals, and property transfers.

It is presumed that related party transactions are *not* at arm's length. Examples are services billed at higher-than-usual rates, a loan at a very low interest rate, unusual pledges or guarantees, a very low rental, and merchandise purchased at unusually low prices.

Related party disclosures include:

- Transaction terms and amounts
- Nature and substance of the relationship
- Year-end balances due or owed
- Control relationships

What should be disclosed for business interruption insurance?

Disclosure should be made of the event resulting in losses from business interruption, including the total amount received from insurance and where such amounts are presented in the income statement.

What inflation information should be disclosed?

As per ASC No. 255-10-50, *Accounting Changes and Error Corrections: Overall* (FAS No. 89, *Financial Reporting and Changing Prices*), a company can *voluntarily* disclose inflation data so that management and financial statement users can better appraise inflationary impact on the company. Selected summarized financial data may be presented in both current costs and constant purchasing power (Consumer Price Index adjusted). Inflation disclosures may be for revenue, expenses, income from continuing operations, cash dividends per share, market price of stock, inventory, fixed assets, and liabilities.

What are the reporting, presentation, and disclosure requirements for development-stage companies?

A development-stage company must follow the same GAAP as an established company. A balance sheet, income statement, and statement of cash flows are presented. The balance sheet shows the cumulative net losses as a deficit. The income statement presents both cumulative and current-year figures for revenue and expenses. The statement of cash flows discloses cumulative cash receipts and cash payments. The stockholders' equity statement presents for each equity security from inception the date and number of shares issued and dollar figures per share for cash and noncash consideration. The financial statements must be headed "Development-Stage Company." A footnote should disclose the development-stage activities. In the first year the business is out of the development stage, it should disclose that in prior years it was in the development stage.

7

Key Financial Accounting Areas

THIS CHAPTER DISCUSSES the accounting requirements for major financial areas including consolidation, investing in stocks and bonds, leases, pensions, postretirement benefits excluding pensions, tax allocation, and foreign currency translation and transactions.

CONSOLIDATION

Consolidation occurs when the parent owns more than 50 percent of the voting common stock of the subsidiary. Its primary purpose is to present as one economic unit the financial position and operating results of a parent and subsidiaries. Consolidation shows the group as a single company (with one or more branches or divisions) rather than separate companies. It is an example of theoretical substance over legal form. The companies constituting the consolidated group keep their individual legal identity. Adjustments and eliminations are only for financial statement reporting. Disclosure should be made of the company's consolidation policy in footnotes or by explanatory headings.

A consolidation is negated, even if the parent owns more than 50 percent of voting common stock, in the following situations:

- Parent is not in actual control of subsidiary (e.g., subsidiary is in receivership, subsidiary is in a politically unstable foreign country).
- Parent has sold or contracted to sell subsidiary shortly after year-end. The subsidiary is a temporary investment.
- Minority interest is substantive relative to the parent's interest; thus, individual financial statements are more useful.

Intercompany eliminations include those for intercompany receivables and payables, advances, and profits. However, in the case of certain regulated companies, intercompany profit does not have to be eliminated to the extent that the profit represents a reasonable return on investment. Subsidiary investment in the parent's shares is not consolidated outstanding stock in the consolidated balance sheet. Consolidated statements do not reflect capitalized earnings in the form of stock dividends by subsidiaries subsequent to acquisition.

Minority interest in a subsidiary is the stockholders' equity of those outside to the parent's controlling interest in the partially owned subsidiaries. Minority interest should be shown as a separate component of stockholders' equity. When losses applicable to the minority interest in a subsidiary exceed the minority interest's equity capital, the excess and any subsequent losses related to the minority interest are charged to the parent. If profit subsequently occurs, the parent's interest is credited to the degree prior losses are absorbed.

If a parent acquires a subsidiary in more than one block of stock, each purchase is on a step-by-step basis, and consolidation does not occur until control exists.

If the subsidiary is acquired within the year, it should be included in consolidation as if the subsidiary had been bought at the start of the year with a deduction for the preacquisition part of earnings applicable to each block of stock. An alternative, but less preferable, approach is to include in consolidation the subsidiary's profit after the acquisition date.

The retained earnings of a subsidiary at the acquisition date are not included in the consolidated financial statements.

When the subsidiary is disposed of during the year, the parent should present its equity in the subsidiary's earnings before the sale date as a separate line item in conformity with the equity method.

A subsidiary whose *major business activity* is leasing to a parent should always be consolidated.

Consolidation is allowed without adjustments when the fiscal year-ends of the parent and subsidiary are three months or less apart. However, disclosure is required of significant events in the intervening period.

The equity method of accounting is used for unconsolidated subsidiaries unless there is a foreign investment or a temporary investment. In a case where the equity method is not used, the cost method is followed. The cost method recognizes the difference between the cost of the subsidiary and the equity in net assets at the acquisition date. Depreciation is adjusted for the difference as if consolidation of the subsidiary was made. There is an elimination of intercompany gain or loss for unconsolidated subsidiaries to the extent the gain or loss exceeds the unrecorded equity in undistributed earnings. Unconsolidated subsidiaries accounted for with the cost method should have adequate disclosure of assets, liabilities, and earnings. Such disclosure may be in footnote or supplementary schedule form.

In some cases, combined rather than consolidated financial statements are more meaningful, such as when a person owns a controlling interest in several related operating companies (brother–sister corporation).

There are instances where, besides consolidated statements, parent company statements are required to properly provide information to creditors and preferred stockholders. In this case, *dual columns* are needed—one column for the parent and other columns for subsidiaries.

INVESTMENTS IN STOCKS AND BONDS

Investments in stock may be accounted for under the market value or equity method, depending on the percentage of ownership in the voting common stock.

> **Note**
>
> Nonvoting stock (e.g., preferred stock) is always accounted for under the market value method. ■

When is the market value method used?

The market value method of accounting for investments is used when the holder owns less than 20 percent of the voting common stock of the company. However, the market value method can be used instead of the equity method when the holder owns between 20 and 50 percent of the voting common stock but lacks significant influence (effective control).

Significant influence may be indicated by one or more of these circumstances:

- Investor owns a high percentage of investee's shares compared to other stockholders.
- There is input into the decision making of the owned company.
- Managerial personnel are interchanged between the investor and investee.
- Significant intercompany transactions take place.
- Investor provides investee with technological knowledge.
- Investor has representation on the board of directors of the investee company.

These circumstances signify an absence of significant influence:

- Majority ownership of investee is concentrated among a few stockholders, particularly when the group operates the investee disregarding the investor's viewpoints.
- Investee opposes the investment (e.g., a lawsuit or complaint is filed).
- Investor cannot obtain the financial information required from the investee to use the equity method.
- Investor and investee sign a contract (called a standstill) in which the investor surrenders significant shareholder rights. The standstill agreement is generally used to settle disputes between the parties.

How do we account for the investment portfolio?

The investment portfolio is accounted for in accordance with Accounting Standards Codification (ASC) Nos. 320-10-05-1 and 05-2, *Investments—Debt and Equity Securities: Overall* (Financial Accounting Standards [FAS] No. 115, *Accounting for Certain*

Investments in Debt and Equity Securities). The three types of securities portfolios as per the pronouncement are trading, available for sale, and held to maturity.

Trading securities can be either debt or equity. The intent is to hold them for a short-term period (typically three months or less). They are usually bought and sold to earn a short-term gain. Trading securities are recorded at market value with the unrealized (holding) loss or gain presented as a separate item in the income statement. Trading securities are reported as current assets on the balance sheet.

Example 7.1

On 12/31/2X12, the trading securities portfolio had a cost and market value of $250,000 and $260,000, respectively. The journal entry to account for this portfolio at market value is:

Allowance	10,000	
Unrealized gain		10,000

The allowance account has a debit balance and is added to the cost of the portfolio in the current asset section of the balance sheet as follows.

Trading securities (cost)	$250,000
Add: Allowance	10,000
Trading securities (market value)	$260,000

The unrealized (holding) gain is presented in the income statement under "other revenue."

Example 7.2

On 12/31/2X12, the available-for-sale securities portfolio had a cost and market value of $600,000 and $570,000, respectively. The journal entry to recognize the portfolio at market value is:

Unrealized loss	30,000	
Allowance		30,000

The allowance account has a credit balance and is deducted from the cost of the portfolio in the noncurrent asset section of the balance sheet as follows.

Available-for-sale securities (cost)	$600,000
Less: Allowance	30,000
Available-for-sale securities (market value)	$570,000

Available-for-sale securities may be either debt or equity. These securities are not held for trading purposes, nor is the intent to hold them to maturity. They are reported at market value. The unrealized (holding) loss or gain for the current year is presented under "other comprehensive income" in the income statement, whereas the accumulated (cumulative) unrealized loss or gain for *all the years* is presented in the stockholders' equity section of the balance sheet as "accumulated other comprehensive income." Available-for-sale securities are usually presented as a noncurrent asset.

Held-to-maturity securities (typically long-term bond investments) are only debt securities because debt securities (not equity securities) are the only ones with a maturity date. They are reported as noncurrent assets. Held-to-maturity securities are presented at unamortized cost (initial cost adjusted for discount or premium amortization).

Note

Under ASC Nos. 825-10-15-4 and 15-5 and 825-10-35-4, *Financial Instruments: Overall* (FAS No. 159, *The Fair Value Option for Financial Assets and Financial Liabilities*), a company has the option, if it wishes, to measure held-to-maturity securities at fair market value. If this fair value option is selected, unrealized (holding) gains and losses will be presented separately in the income statement. ■

If securities are sold, a realized loss or realized gain is recognized. The realized loss or gain is presented in the income statement regardless of whether the portfolio is current or noncurrent. The same realized loss or gain on sale appears on the tax return.

The entry to record the sale of securities is:

Cash (proceeds received)
Loss
Securities (at cost)
Gain

If a balance sheet is unclassified, the investment security portfolio is considered noncurrent.

A permanent decline in value of a particular security is recognized immediately with a realized loss being booked shown in the income statement even if it is a noncurrent portfolio. The investment account is credited directly. The new market value becomes the new cost basis, which means it cannot later be written up.

A permanent decline in market price of stock may be indicated when the company has several years of losses, is in a very weak financial condition, and has issued a liquidating dividend. For example, if the company sells some of its major divisions and distributes the proceeds to stockholders, a write-down of the investment may be appropriate.

Example 7.3

In a long-term investment portfolio, one stock in ABC Company has suffered a permanent decline in value from cost of $6,000 to market value of $5,000. The entry is:

Realized loss	1,000	
Long-term investment		1,000

The new cost now becomes $5,000 (the market value). If in a later period, the market value increased above $5,000, the stock would not be written up above $5,000.

If market value of a portfolio significantly declines between year-end and the audit report date, subsequent event disclosure is needed.

There is interperiod income tax allocation with investments because of temporary differences. A deferred tax arises because unrealized losses and gains on securities are not recognized on the tax return.

Example 7.4

On 1/1/2X11, Company X buys long-term securities of $480,000 plus brokerage commissions of $20,000. On 5/12/2X11, a cash dividend of $15,000 is received. On 12/31/2X11, the market value of the portfolio is $490,000. On 2/6/2X12, securities costing $50,000 are sold for $54,000. On 12/31/2X12, the market value of the portfolio is $447,000. The journal entries follow.

1/1/2X11		
Long-term investment	500,000	
Cash		500,000
5/12/2X11		
Cash	15,000	
Dividend revenue		
12/31/2X11		
Unrealized loss	10,000	
Allowance		10,000

The balance sheet presentation of the long-term investments is:

Long-term investments	$500,000
Less: Allowance	10,000
Net balance	$490,000

2/6/2X12		
Cash	54,000	
Long-term investments		50,000
Gain		4,000
12/31/2X12		
Allowance	7,000	
Unrealized loss		7,000

The balance sheet presentation of the long-term securities is:

Long-term investments	$450,000
Less: Allowance	3,000
Net balance	$447,000

If instead market value was $435,000, the entry would have been:

Unrealized loss	5,000	
Allowance		5,000

If instead market value was $452,000, the entry would have been:

Allowance	10,000	
Unrealized gain		10,000

If two or more securities are purchased at one price, the cost is allocated among the securities based on their relative fair market value. In the exchange of one security for another, the new security received in the exchange is valued at its fair market value.

Example 7.5

Preferred stock costing $10,000 is exchanged for 1,000 shares of common stock having a market value of $15,000. The entry is:

Investment in common stock	15,000	
Investment in preferred stock		10,000
Gain		5,000

There is a memo entry for a stock dividend indicating that there are more shares at no additional cost. In consequence, the cost per share decreases.

Example 7.6

The company owns 50 shares at $12 per share of stock for a total cost of $600. A 20 percent stock dividend is declared. A memo entry reflects the additional shares as:

Investment		
50	$12	$800
10		0
50	$12	$800

A stock split increases the shares and reduces the cost basis proportionately. There is a memo entry. Assume 100 shares costing $20 per share were owned. A 2-for-1 split results in 200 shares at a cost per share of $10. Total par value is still $2,000.

When is the equity method used?

If an investor owns between 20 and 50 percent of the voting common stock of an investee, the equity method is used. The equity method also applies if the holder owned less than 20 percent of the voting common stock but had significant influence (effective control). The equity method is also employed if more than 50 percent of the voting common stock was owned but a negating factor for consolidation existed. Furthermore investments in joint ventures have to be accounted for under the equity method.

How does the equity method work?

The accounting under the equity method can be illustrated by examining these T-accounts:

Investment in Investee	
Cost	Dividends
Ordinary profit	Depreciation on excess of fair market value less book value of specific assets
Extraordinary gain	Permanent decline

Equity in Earnings of Investee	
Depreciation	Ordinary profit

Loss	
Permanent decline	

Extraordinary Gain	
	Extraordinary gain

The cost of the investment includes brokerage fees. The investor recognizes his percentage ownership interest in the ordinary profit of the investee by debiting investment in investee and crediting equity in earnings of investee. The investor's share in the investee's earnings is computed after deducting cumulative preferred dividends, whether declared or not. The investor's share of investee net income should be based on the investee's most current income statement applied on a consistent basis. Extraordinary gains or losses and prior period adjustments are also recognized on the investor's books. Dividends reduce the carrying value of the investment account.

The excess paid by the investor for the investee's net assets is first assigned to the specific assets and liabilities and depreciated. The unidentifiable portion of the excess is considered goodwill, which is subject to an annual impairment test. Depreciation on excess value of assets reduces the investment account and is charged to equity in earnings. Temporary decline in price of the investment in the investee is ignored. Permanent decline in value of the investment is reflected by debiting loss and crediting investment in investee.

When the investor's share of the investee's losses is greater than the balance in the investment account, the equity method should be discontinued at the zero amount unless the investor has guaranteed the investee's obligations or where immediate profitability is assured. A return to the equity method is made only after offsetting subsequent profits against the losses not recorded.

When the investee's stock is sold, a realized gain or loss arises for the difference between selling price and the cost of the investment.

The mechanics of consolidation basically apply with the equity method. For example, there is an elimination of intercompany profits and losses. Investee capital transactions affecting the investor's share of equity should be accounted for as in a consolidation. For example, when the investee issues common stock to third parties at a price exceeding book value, there will be an increase in the value of the investment and a related increase in the investor's paid-in capital.

Interperiod income tax allocation occurs because the investor recognizes the investee's earnings for book reporting but dividends for tax purposes result in a deferred income tax liability.

If the ownership goes below 20 percent or the investor for some reason is unable to control the investee, the investor should cease recognizing the investee's earnings. The equity method is discontinued, but the balance in the investment account is maintained. The market value method should then be applied.

If the investor increases ownership in the investee to 20 percent or more, the equity method should be used for current and future years. Furthermore, the effect of using the equity method rather than the market value method on prior years at the old percentage (e.g., 15 percent) should be recognized as an adjustment to retained earnings and other accounts so affected, such as investment in investee. The retroactive adjustment on the investment, earnings, and retained earnings should be applied in the same manner as a step-by-step acquisition of a subsidiary.

Disclosures should be made by the investor (in footnotes, separate schedules, or parenthetically) of:

- Name of investee
- Percent owned

- Investor's accounting policies
- Significant effects of possible conversions and exercises of investee common stock
- Quoted market price (for investees not qualifying as subsidiaries)

Furthermore, summarized financial data as to assets, liabilities, and earnings should be given in footnotes or separate schedules for material investments in unconsolidated subsidiaries. Material realized and unrealized gains and losses relating to the subsidiary's portfolio occurring between the dates of the financial statements of the subsidiary and parent must also be disclosed.

Example 7.7

On 1/1/2X11, X Company bought 30,000 shares for a 40 percent interest in the common stock of AB Company at $25 per share. Brokerage commissions were $10,000. During 2X11 AB's net income was $140,000, and dividends received were $30,000. On 1/1/2X12, X Company received 15,000 shares of common stock as a result of a stock split by AB Company. On 1/4/2X12, X Company sold 2,000 shares at $16 per share of AB stock. The journal entries follow.

1/1/2X11		
Investment in investee	760,000	
Cash		760,000
12/31/2X11		
Investment in investee	56,000	
Equity in earnings of investee		56,000
40% × $140,000 = $56,000		
Cash	30,000	
Investment in investee	30,000	
1/1/2X12 Memo entry for stock split		
1/4/2X12		
Cash (2,000 × $16)	32,000	
Loss on sale of investment	2,940	
Investment in investee (2,000 × $17.47)		34,940
$786,000/45,000= $17.47 per share		

Investment in Investee

1/1/2X11	760,000	12/31/2X11	30,000
12/31/2X11	$56,000		
	816,000		
	786,000		

Example 7.8

On 1/1/2X12, an investor purchased 100,000 shares of investee's 400,000 shares outstanding for $3 million. The book value of net assets acquired was $2.5 million. All of the $500,000 excess paid over book value is attributable to undervalued tangible assets. The depreciation period is 20 years. In 2X12, investee's net income was $800,000, including an extraordinary loss of $200,000. Dividends of $75,000 were paid on June 1, 2X12. The following journal entries are necessary for the acquisition of investee by investor accounted for under the equity method.

1/1/2X12		
Investment in investee	3,000,000	
Cash		3,000,000
6/1/2X12		
Cash	18,750	
Investment in investee		18,750
25% × $75,000		
12/31/2X12		
Investment in investee	250,000	
Equity in earnings of investee		250,000
$1,000,000 × 25 = 250,000		
Extraordinary loss from		
investment	50,000	
Investment in investee		50,000
$200,000 × 25 = 50,000		
Equity in earnings of investee	25,000	
Investment in investee		25,000

Computation:

Undervalued depreciable assets $500,000/20 years = $25,000

Note

Under ASC Nos. 825-10-15-4 and 15-5 and 825-10-35-4 (FAS No. 159), a company using the equity method can *elect* to use the fair value option. If that option is selected, the investment-in-investee account will reflect temporary changes in market value of the investee. The resulting unrealized (holding) loss or gain will be presented as a separate item in the income statement. For example, if the fair market value of the investee decreases, the investor will debit unrealized loss and credit the investment-in-investee account (or a valuation allowance account) for the decrease in value. However, if there is an increase in fair market value, the investment-in-investee account (or valuation allowance account) would be debited and unrealized gain credited for the increase in fair market value. ■

How are held-to-maturity securities (bond investments) handled?

The difference between the cost of a bond and its face value is discount or premium. Discount or premium is amortized over the life of the bond from the *acquisition date.*

The bond investment account is usually recorded net of the discount or premium. If bonds are acquired between interest dates, accrued interest should be recorded separately.

The market price of the bond takes into account the financial health of the company, "prevailing" interest rates in the market, and the maturity date.

The market price is computed by discounting the principal and interest using the yield rate.

Example 7.9

On 3/1/2X11, an investor purchases $100,000, 6 percent, 20-year bonds. Interest is payable on 1/1 and 6/30. The bonds are bought at face value.

3/1/2X11		
Investment in bonds	100,000	
Accrued bond interest receivable	1,000	
Cash		101,000
$100,000 × 6% = $6,000 per year		
$6,000 × 2/12 = $1,000		
6/30/2X11		
Cash	3,000	
Accrued bond interest receivable (2 months)		1,000
Interest income (4 months)		2,000
$6,000 × 6/12 = $3,000		
12/31/2X11		
Accrued bond interest receivable	3,000	
Interest income		3,000
1/1/2X12		
Cash	3,000	
Accrued bond interest receivable		3,000
6/30/2X12		
Cash	3,000	
Interest income		3,000

Example 7.10

On 1/1/2X11, $10,000 of ABC Company's 6 percent, 10-year bonds are bought for $12,000. Interest is payable 1/1 and 6/30. On 4/1/2X12, the bonds are sold for $11,000. There is a commission charge on the bonds of $100. Applicable journal entries follow.

1/1/2X11		
Investment in bonds	12,000	
Cash		12,000
6/30/2X11		
Interest income	100	
Investment in bonds		100

Amortization of premium is computed as:

$2,000/10 years = $200 per year × 6/12 = $100		
Cash	300	
Interest income		300
6 % × $10,000 × 6/12 = $300		
12/31/2X11		
Accrued bond interest receivable	300	
Interest income		300
Interest income	100	
Investment in bonds		100
4/1/2X12		
Accrued bond interest receivable	150	
Interest income		150
6% × $10,000 × 3/12 = $150		
Interest income	50	
Investment in bonds		50

Amortization of premium is computed as:

$200 per year × 3/12 = $50		
Cash (11,000 + 150 − 100)	11,050	
Loss on sale of investments	850	
Investment in bonds (12,000 − 100 − 100 − 50)		11,750
Accrued bond interest receivable		150

What should be disclosed in the footnotes about investments in debt and equity securities?

These points should be disclosed about investments in debt and equity securities:

- Name of companies owned
- Valuation basis used
- Market value and amortized cost by major debt security type
- Method to determine cost

 # LEASES

Leases are usually long-term noncancelable commitments. The lessee acquires the right to use property owned by the lessor. Although there is no legal transfer of title, many leases transfer substantially all the risks and ownership rights. A capital lease is recorded as an asset and liability by the lessee because theoretical substance governs over legal form.

A lease may be between related parties such as when a company has significant control over the operating and financial policies of another business.

The *date of inception* of a lease is the date of the lease *agreement or commitment*, if earlier. A commitment has to be in writing, signed, and provide the major terms. If substantive provisions are to be negotiated in the future, a commitment does not exist.

Lessee

The lessee can account for a lease in two ways: the operating method and the capital method.

What does the operating method entail?

An operating lease is a regular rental of property. As rental payments become payable, rent expense is charged, and cash and/or payables are credited. The lessee does not report anything on the balance sheet. Rent expense is accrued on the straight-line basis unless another method is more suitable.

What criteria must be met for there to be a capital lease?

The lessee uses the capital lease method if any *one* of these four conditions is satisfied:

1. The lessee obtains ownership to the property at the end of the lease term.
2. A bargain purchase option exists where either the lessee can buy the property at a nominal amount or renew the lease at minimal rental payments.

3. The life of the lease is 75 percent or more of the life of the property.
4. The discounted value of minimum lease payments at the inception of the lease equals or exceeds 90 percent of the fair market value of the property. Minimum lease payments exclude executory costs to be paid by the lessee to reimburse the lessor for its costs of maintenance, insurance, and property taxes.

If criterion 1 or 2 is met, the depreciation period is the life of the property. Otherwise, the depreciation period is the life of the lease.

The third and fourth criteria do not apply when the beginning of the lease term falls within the last 25 percent of the total economic life of the property.

The asset and liability are recorded at the present value of the minimum lease payments plus the present value of the bargain purchase option. The lessee is expected to pay the nominal purchase price. If the present value of the minimum lease payments plus the bargain purchase option exceeds the fair value of the leased property at the time of lease inception, the asset should be capitalized at the fair market value of the property. The lessee's discount rate is the *lower* of the lessee's incremental borrowing rate (the rate the lessee would have to borrow at to be able to buy the asset) or the lessor's implicit interest rate. The lessor's implicit interest rate is the one implicit in the recovery of the fair value of the property at lease inception through the present value of minimum lease payments including the lessee's guarantee of salvage value. The liability is divided between current and noncurrent.

The lessee's minimum lease payments (MLPs) usually include MLPs over the lease term plus any guaranteed salvage value. The guarantee is the determinable amount for which the lessor has the right to require the lessee to buy the property at the lease termination. It is the stated amount when the lessee agrees to satisfy any dollar deficiency below a stated amount in the lessor's realization of the residual value. MLPs also include any payment lessee must pay due to failure to extend or renew the lease at expiration. If there exists a bargain purchase option, MLPs include *only* MLPs over the lease term and exercise option payment. MLPs do not include contingent rentals, lessee's guarantee of lessor's debt, and lessee's obligation for executory costs.

Each minimum lease payment is allocated as a reduction of principal (debiting the liability) and as interest (debiting interest expense). The interest method is used to result in a constant periodic rate of interest. Interest expense equals the interest rate times the carrying value of the liability at the beginning of the year.

The balance sheet shows the "Asset under Lease" less "Accumulated Depreciation." The income statement shows interest expense and depreciation expense. In the first year, the expenses under a capital lease (interest expense and depreciation) are greater than the expenses under an operating lease (rent expense).

When a lessee buys during the lease term a leased asset that had originally been capitalized, the transaction is considered an *extension* of a capital lease, not a termination. Thus, the difference between the purchase price and the carrying value of the lease obligation is an *adjustment* of the book value of the asset. There is *no loss recognition* when a capital lease is extended.

Example 7.11

On 1/1/2X11, the lessee enters into a capital lease for property. The minimum rental payment is $20,000 a year for six years to be made at the end of the year. The interest rate is 5 percent. The present value of an ordinary annuity factor for $n = 6$, $i = 5\%$ is 5.0757. The journal entries for the first two years follow.

1/1/2X11		
Asset	101,514	
Liability		101,514
12/31/2X11		
Interest expense	5,076	
Liability	14,924	
Cash		20,000
5% × $101,514 = $5,076		
Depreciation	16,919	
Accumulated depreciation		16,919
$101,514/6 = $16,919		

The liability as of 12/31/2X11 is presented next.

	Liability		
12/31/2X11	14,924	1/1/2X11	101,514
		12/31/2X11	86,590

12/31/2X12		
Interest expense	4,330	
Liability	15,670	
Cash		20,000
5% × $86,590 = $4,330		
Depreciation	16,919	
Accumulated depreciation		16,919

The footnote disclosures under a capital lease are:

- Description of leasing arrangement, including purchase options, escalation clause, renewal terms, and restrictions
- Assets under lease by category
- Future minimum lease payments in total and for each of the next five years
- Total future sublease rentals
- Contingent rentals (rentals based on other than time such as based on profit)

Lessor

The lessor may account for leases under the operating, direct-financing, and sales-type methods.

How does the lessor account under the operating method?

The operating method is a regular rental by the lessor. An example is Hertz rental cars. The income statement shows rental revenue less related expenses. The balance sheet presents the asset under lease less accumulated depreciation to obtain book value.

Rental income is recognized as earned using the *straight-line* basis over the lease term except if there is another preferable method. *Initial direct costs* are deferred and amortized over the lease term on a pro rata basis based on rental income recognized. However, if immaterial relative to the allocation amount, the initial direct costs may be expensed.

Example 7.12

Hall Corporation produced machinery costing $5 million, which it held for resale from January 1, 2X12, to June 30, 2X12, at a price to Travis Company under an operating lease. The lease is for four years with equal monthly payments of $85,000 due on the first of the month. The initial payment was made on July 1, 2X12. The depreciation period is 10 years with no salvage value.

Lessee's rental expense for 2X12:	
$85,000 × 6	$510,000
Lessor's income before taxes for 2X12:	
Rental income	$510,000
Less: Depreciation $\dfrac{\$5,000,000}{10} \times \dfrac{6}{12}$	250,000
Income before taxes	$260,000

What is the accounting and financial statement reporting under the direct financing method?

The direct financing method satisfies one of the four conditions for a capital lease by the lessee plus both of the following two requirements for the lessor:

- Collectability of lease payments is assured.
- No important uncertainties surround future costs to be incurred.

The lessor is not a manufacturer or dealer. The lessor acquires the property for the sole purpose of leasing it out. An example is a bank leasing computers. The carrying value and fair value of the leased property are the same at the inception of the lease.

The lessor uses as the discount rate the interest rate implicit in the lease.

Interest income is only recognized in the financial statements over the life of the lease using the interest method. Unearned interest income is amortized as income over the lease term to result in a constant rate of interest. Interest revenue equals the interest rate times the carrying value of the receivable at the beginning of the year.

Contingent rentals are recognized in earnings as earned.

The lessor's MLPs include the (1) MLPs made by the lessee (net of any executory costs together with any profit thereon) and (2) any guarantee of the salvage value of the leased property, or of rental payments after the lease term, made by a third party unrelated to either party in the lease provided the third party is financially able to satisfy the commitment. A guarantee by a third party related to the lessor makes the residual value unguaranteed. A guarantee by a third party related to the lessee infers a guaranteed residual value by the lessee.

A modification of lease provisions, which would have resulted in a different classification had they occurred at the beginning of the lease, requires that the lease be treated as a new agreement and classified under the new terms. However, exercise of existing renewal options is not considered a lease change. A change in estimate does not result in a new lease.

A provision for escalating the MLPs during a construction or preacquisition period may exist. The resulting increase in MLPs is considered in determining the fair value of the leased property at the lease inception. There may also exist a salvage value increase that takes place from an escalation clause.

Initial direct costs are incurred by the lessor to negotiate and consummate a *completed* lease transaction, including commissions, legal fees, credit investigation, document preparation and processing, and the relevant percentage of salespersons' and other employees' compensation. It does not include costs for leases *not consummated*, nor does it include administrative, supervisory, or other indirect expenses. Initial direct costs of the lease are expensed as incurred. A portion of the unearned income equal to the initial direct costs should be recognized as income in the same accounting period.

If the contract includes a penalty for nonrenewal or becomes inoperative because of a time extension, the unearned interest income account must be adjusted for the difference between the present values of the old and revised agreements. The present value of the future minimum lease payments under the new arrangement should be computed using the original rate for the initial lease.

Lease termination is accounted for by the lessor through eliminating the net investment and recording the leased property at the lower of cost or fair value; the net adjustment is charged against earnings.

The lessor reports on his balance sheet as the gross investment in the lease the total minimum lease payments plus salvage value of the property accruing to the lessor. This represents lease payments receivable. Unearned interest revenue is deducted from lease payments receivable. The balance sheet presentation follows.

Lease payments receivable (Principal + Interest)
Less: Unearned interest revenue (Interest)
Net receivable balance (Principal)

The income statement shows:

Interest revenue
Less: Initial direct costs
Less: Initial direct costs
Net income

Footnote disclosure includes assets leased by type, future lease payments in total and for each of the next five years, contingent rentals, and lease provisions.

How do we account for and present the sales-type method?

The sales-type method must satisfy the same criteria as the direct-financing method. The only difference is that the sales-type method involves a lessor who is a manufacturer or dealer in the leased item. Thus, a manufacturer or dealer profit results. Although legally there is no sale of the item, theoretical substance governs over legal form, and a sale is assumed to have taken place.

> ## Note
>
> The distinction between a sales-type lease and a direct-financing lease affects only the lessor; for the lessee, either type would be a capital lease. ■

If there is a renewal or extension of an existing sales-type or financing lease, it shall not be classified as a sales-type lease. An *exception* may exist when the renewal occurs toward the end of the lease term.

In a sales-type lease, profit on the assumed sale of the item is recognized in the year of lease as well as interest income over the life of the lease. The cost and fair value of the leased property are different at the inception of the lease.

An annual appraisal should be made of the salvage value. Where necessary, the net investment should be reduced and a loss recognized, but the salvage value should not be adjusted.

The cost of the leased property is matched against the selling price in determining the assumed profit in the year of lease. Initial direct costs of the lease are expensed.

Except for the initial entry to record the lease, the entries are the same for the direct-financing and sales-type methods.

Example 7.13

Assume the same facts as in the capital lease example (Example 7.11). The accounting by the lessor assuming a direct-financing lease and a sales-type lease follow.

Direct Financing		
1/1/2X12		
Receivable	120,000	
Asset		101,514
Unearned interest revenue		8,486
Sales Type		
Receivable	120,000	
Cost of sales	85,000	
Inventory		85,000

(continued)

Sales		101,514
Unearned interest revenue		18,486
Direct Financing		
12/31/2X11		
Cash	20,000	
Receivable		20,000
Unearned interest revenue	5,076	
Interest revenue		5,076
12/31/2X12		
Cash	20,000	
Receivable		20,000
Unearned interest revenue	4,330	
Investment revenue		4,330
Sales Type		
Same entries as Direct Financing.		

The income statement for 2X12 presents:

Direct Financing	
Interest revenue	$ 5,076
Sales Type	
Sales	$101,514
Less: Cost of sales	85,000
Gross profit	$ 16,514
Interest revenue	5,076

Example 7.14

On October 1, 2X12, Jones leased equipment to Tape Company. It is a capital lease to the lessee and a sales-type lease to the lessor. The lease is for eight years with equal annual payments of $500,000 due on October 1 each period. The first payment was made on October 1, 2X12. The cost of the equipment to Tape Company is $2.5 million. The equipment has a life of 10 years with no salvage value. The interest rate is 10 percent.

Tape reports the following in its income statement for 2X12:

Asset cost ($500,000 × 5.868 = $2,934,000)

$$\text{Depreciation} \frac{\$2,934,000}{10} \times \frac{3}{12} \qquad \$73,350$$

Interest expense:	
Present value of lease payments	$2,934,00
Less: Initial payment	500,000

Balance	$2,434,000	
Interest expense		
$2,434,000 \times 100\% \times \dfrac{3}{13}$		60,850
Total expenses		134,200
Jones' income before tax is:		
Interest revenue		$ 60,850
Gross profit on assumed sale of property:		
Selling price	$2,934,000	
Less: Cost	2,500,000	
Gross Profit		434,000
Income before tax		$494,850

How do we treat a sales-leaseback?

A sales-leaseback occurs when the lessor sells the property and then leases it back. The lessor may do this when she needs money.

The profit or loss on the sale is deferred and amortized as an adjustment on a proportionate basis to depreciation expense in the case of a capital lease or in proportion to rental expense in the case of an operating lease. However, if the fair value of the property at the time of the sales-leaseback is below its book value, a loss is recognized immediately for the difference between book value and fair value.

Example 7.15

The deferred profit on a sales-leaseback is $50,000. An operating lease is involved where rental expense in the current year is $10,000, and total rental expense is $150,000. Rental expense is adjusted as:

Rental expense	$10,000
Less: Amortization of deferred gross profit	
$50,000 \times \dfrac{\$10,000}{\$150,000}$	3,333
	$ 6,667

What if there is a sublease?

There are three types of transactions. In the first type, the *sublease*, the original lessee leases the property to a third party. The lease agreement of the original parties remains intact. A second possibility involves substituting a new lessee under the original agreement. The original lessee may still be secondarily liable. Finally, the new lessee is substituted in a new agreement. There is a cancellation of the original lease.

The original lessor continues his present accounting method if the original lessee subleases or sells to a third party. If the original lease is replaced by a new agreement with a new lessee, the lessor terminates the initial lease and accounts for the new one in a separate transaction.

In accounting by the original lessee, if the lessee is relieved of primary obligation by a transaction other than a sublease, the original lease should be terminated in these situations:

■ If the original lease was a capital lease, remove the asset and liability, recognize a gain or loss for the difference including any additional consideration paid or received, and accrue a loss contingency where secondary liability exists.
■ If the original lease was an operating one and the initial lessee is secondarily liable, recognize a loss contingency accrual.

If the original lessee is not relieved of *primary* obligation under a sublease, the original lessee (now sublessor) accounts in this manner:

■ If the original lease met lessee criterion 1 or 2, classify the new lease per normal classification criteria by lessor. If the sublease is a sales-type or direct-financing lease, the unamortized asset balance becomes the cost of the leased property. Otherwise, it is an operating lease. Continue to account for the original lease obligation as before.
■ If the original lease met only lessee criterion 3 or 4, classify the new lease using lessee criterion 3 and lessor criterion 1 and 2. Classify as a direct financing lease. The unamortized balance of the asset becomes the cost of the leased property; otherwise, it is an operating lease. Continue to account for original lease obligation as before.

If the original lease was an *operating lease*, account for old and new leases as operating leases.

What is the accounting under a leveraged lease?

A leveraged lease occurs when the lessor (equity participant) finances a small part of the acquisition (retaining total equity ownership) while a third party (debt participant) finances the balance. The lessor maximizes her leveraged return by recognizing lease revenue and income tax shelter (e.g., interest deduction, rapid depreciation).

A leveraged lease meets *all* of these criteria:

■ It satisfies the tests for a direct-financing lease. Sales-type leases are not leveraged leases.
■ It involves at least three parties: lessee, long-term creditor (debt participant), and lessor (equity participant).
■ The long-term creditor provides nonrecourse financing as to the general credit of the lessor. The financing is adequate to give the lessor significant leverage.
■ The lessor's net investment decreases during the initial lease years, then increases in the subsequent years just before its liquidation by sale. These increases and decreases in the net investment balance may take place more than once during the lease life.

The lessee classifies and accounts for leveraged leases in the same way as nonleveraged leases.

The lessor records *investment in the leveraged lease net* of the nonrecourse debt. The net of the following balances represents the initial and continuing investment: rentals receivable (net of the amount applicable to principal and interest on the nonrecourse debt), estimated residual value, and unearned and deferred income. The initial entry to record the leveraged lease is:

Lease receivable
Residual value of asset
Cash investment in asset
Unearned income

The lessor's *net investment in the leveraged lease* for computing net income is the investment in the *leveraged lease less* deferred income taxes. Periodic net income is determined in the following manner using the *net investment in the leveraged lease*:

- Determine annual cash flow equal to the following:
  Gross lease rental (plus residual value of asset in last year of lease term)
  Less: Loan interest payments
  Less: Income tax charges (or add income tax credits)
  Less: Loan principal payments
  Annual cash flow
- Determine the return rate on the net investment *in the leveraged lease*. The rate of return is the one when applied to the net investment in the years when it is positive. The lease agreement will distribute the net income (cash flow) to those positive years. The *net investment* will be positive (but declining rapidly due to accelerated depreciation and interest expense) in the early years; it will be negative during the middle years; and it will again be positive in the later years (because of the declining tax shelter).

 ## PENSION PLANS

The company must conform to the Financial Accounting Standards Board (FASB) and governmental rules on the accounting and reporting for its pension plan.

ASC No. 715-70-50-2, *Compensation—Retirement Benefits: Defined Contribution Plans* (FAS No. 87, *Employers' Accounting for Pensions*) and ASC No. 715-30-25-1, *Compensation—Retirement Benefits: Defined Benefit Plans—Pension* (FAS No. 158, *Employers' Accounting for Defined Benefit Pension and Other Postretirement Plans*) require the accrual of pension expense based on services rendered. The pension plan relationship between the employer, trustee, and employee is shown in Exhibit 7.1.

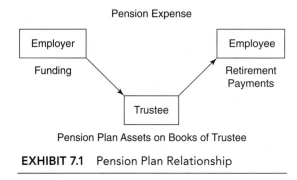

EXHIBIT 7.1   Pension Plan Relationship

What are the two kinds of pension arrangements?

The two types of pension plans are:

1. *Defined contribution.* The employer's annual contribution is specified rather than the benefits to be paid.
2. *Defined benefit.* The determinable pension benefit to be received by participants upon retirement is specified. In determining amounts, consider such factors as salary, service years, and age. The employer makes contributions so that adequate funds are accumulated to pay benefits when due. Typically, there is an annuity of payments. Pension cost for administrative staff is expensed, while pension cost for factory personnel is inventoryable.

What are some important pension plan terms?

The following pension plan terminology should be understood.

Accumulated benefit obligation: The year-end obligation based on current salaries. It is the actuarial present value of benefits (vested and nonvested) applicable to the pension plan based on services rendered prior to a given date based on *current* salaries.

The accumulated and projected benefit obligation figures will be the same in the case of plans having flat-benefit or nonpay-related pension benefit formulas.

Actuarial assumptions: Actuaries make assumptions as to variables in determining pension expense and related funding. Examples of estimates are employee turnover, mortality rate, return rates, and compensation.

Actuarial cost (funding) method: The method actuaries use to compute the employer contribution to assure adequate funds will be available when employees retire. The method used determines the pension expense and related liability.

Actuarial present value of accumulated plan benefits: The discounted amount of money required to meet retirement obligations for active and retired employees.

Benefit information date: The date the actuarial present value of accumulated benefits is presented.

Net assets available for pension benefits: Net assets represents plan assets less plan liabilities. The plan's liabilities exclude participants' accumulated benefits.

Projected benefit obligation: The year-end pension obligation based on future salaries. It is the actuarial present value of vested and nonvested benefits for services performed before a particular actuarial valuation date based on expected future salaries.

Vested benefits: The employee vests when she has accumulated pension rights to receive benefits upon retirement. The employee no longer has to be with the company to receive pension payments.

What are the accounting and disclosures for a defined contribution pension plan?

Pension expense equals the employer's cash contribution for the period. There is no deferred charge or deferred credit. If the defined contribution plan specifies contributions are to be made for years after an employee's performance of services (e.g., after retirement), there should be an accrual of costs during the employee's service period.

Footnote disclosure includes cost recognized for the period, basis of determining contributions, and description of plan including employee groups covered.

Accounting Standards Update

Under Accounting Standards Update (ASU) No. 2010-25 (September 2010), *Plan Accounting—Defined Contribution Pension Plans* (Topic No. 962—*Reporting Loans to Participants*), participant loans should be presented as notes receivable and are to be segregated from plan investments and valued at their unpaid principal amount plus any accrued but unpaid interest. ▪

What is the impact of FASB No. 158?

ASC No. 715-20, *Compensation—Retirement Benefits: Defined Benefit Plans—General* amends ASC No. 962-10-05, *Plan Accounting—Defined Contribution Pension Plans: Overall* (FAS No. 87), FAS No. 88, and FAS No. 106. Pension accounting is segregated between the employer's accounting and the accounting for the pension fund. The employer incurs the cost and makes contributions to the pension fund. The fund (plan) is the entity that receives the contributions, administers plan assets, and makes benefit payments to retirees. The assets and liabilities of a pension plan are *not* included in the employer's financial statements. The pension fund is a distinct legal and accounting entity.

ASC No. 715-30-25-1 applies only to single-employer plans, *not* multiple-employer ones. Upon adoption of this statement, most companies will show a very substantial increase in liabilities as well as a reduction in stockholders' equity because most companies are underfunded.

What are the elements of pension expense?

The components of pension expense in a defined benefit pension plan are:

- Service cost
- Amortization expense of prior service cost
- Return on plan assets
- Interest on projected benefit obligation
- Amortization of actuarial gain or loss (gain reduces pension expense but loss increases pension expense)

Service cost is based on the present value of future payments under the benefit formula for employee services of the current period. It is recognized in full in the current year. The calculation involves actuarial assumptions.

The company must incorporate future salary levels in measuring pension expense and the present obligation if the plan benefit includes them. ASC No. 715-30-25 adopts the *benefits/years-of-service* actuarial method, which computes pension expense based on future compensation levels. The employer must fund at a minimum the annual service cost.

Prior service cost is the pension expense for services performed before the adoption or amendment of a pension plan. The cost of the retroactive benefits is the increase in the projected benefit obligation at the date of amendment. It involves the allocation of amounts of cost to future service years. Prior service cost determination involves actuarial considerations. Amortization is achieved by assigning an equal amount to each service year of active employees at the amendment date who are anticipated to receive plan benefits. The amortization of prior service cost takes into consideration future service years, period employees will receive benefits, change in the projected benefit obligation, and decrement in employees receiving benefits each year.

"Other comprehensive income" is adjusted when amortizing prior service cost. Amortization of prior service cost typically increases pension expense.

The employer recognizes prior service cost as a component of pension expense over the remaining service lives of employees. ASC No. 715-30-25-1 prefers a years-of-service amortization method consisting of three steps:

1. The total number of service years to be worked by eligible participants is calculated.
2. Prior service cost is divided by the total number of service years to compute a cost per service year (unit cost).
3. The number of service years each year is multiplied by the cost per service year to compute the annual amortization charge.

Companies may also use the straight-line method of amortization in which prior service cost is amortized over the average remaining service life of employees.

Prior service cost is reported as a component of "accumulated other comprehensive income" in the stockholders' equity section of the balance sheet.

Example 7.16

X Company changes its pension formula from 2 to 5 percent of the last three years of pay multiplied by the service years on January 1, 2X12. This results in the projected benefit obligation being increased by $500,000. Employees are anticipated to receive benefits over the next 10 years.

$$\text{Total future service years} = \frac{n(n + 1)}{2} \times p$$

where
n = the number of years services are to be made
p = the population decrement each year

$$\frac{10(10 + 1)}{2} \times 9 = 495$$

$$\text{Amortization of prior service cost in 2X11} = \$500,000 \times \frac{10 \times 9}{495} = \$90,909$$

Example 7.17

On 1/1/2X12, a company modifies its pension plan and grants $200,000 of prior service cost to employees. The workers are expected to provide 5,000 service years in the future with 250 service years in 2X12. The amortization of prior service cost for the year 2X12 is:

$$\text{Cost per service year} = \$200,000/5,000 = \underline{\$40}$$
$$\text{2X12 amortization} = 250 \times \$40 = \underline{\$10,000}$$

The return on plan assets (e.g., stocks, bonds) reduces pension expense. Plan assets are valued at the moving average of asset values for the accounting period.

The annual pension expense is adjusted for dividends and interest earned by the pension fund in addition to the appreciation or decline in the market value of plan assets.

Pension assets are increased from employer contributions and actual returns but pension assets are decreased from benefit payments to retirees. Actual return on plan assets increases the fund balance and reduces the net cost to provide workers' pension benefits. Actual return on plan assets is calculated as follows using assumed numbers:

Fair market value of plan assets—beginning of year	$600,000
Add: Contributions	80,000
Less: Benefit payments	(30,000)
Add: Actual return	?
Fair market value of plan assets—end of year	$725,000
Actual return must be $75,000 (the missing number).	$725,000

Interest is on the projected benefit obligation at the beginning of the year. The settlement rate is employed representing the rate that pension benefits could be settled for.

$$\text{Interest} = \text{Interest rate} \times \text{Projected benefit obligation at the beginning of the year}$$

In determining the settlement rate, consideration is given to the return rate on high-quality fixed-income investments, whose cash flows match the amount and timing of the expected benefit obligations.

Actuarial gains and losses are the difference between estimates and actual experience. For example, if the assumed interest rate is 11 percent and the actual interest rate is 14 percent, an actuarial gain results. There may also be a change in actuarial assumptions regarding the future. Actuarial gains and losses are deferred and amortized as an adjustment to pension expense over future years. Actuarial gains and losses related to a single event not related to the pension plan and not in the ordinary course of business are immediately recognized in the current year's income statement. Examples are plant closing and segment disposal.

Gains and losses are changes in the amount of either the projected benefit obligation (PBO) or pension plan assets because of experience different from that assumed from changes in assumptions. Gains and losses that are *not* recognized immediately as a component of pension expense shall be recognized as increases or decreases in "other comprehensive income" as they arise.

When is there an asset or liability gain or loss?

An asset gain or loss occurs on plan assets when the expected return is different from the actual return.

$$\text{Asset gain} = \text{Actual return} > \text{Expected return}$$

$$\text{Asset loss} = \text{Actual return} < \text{Expected return}$$

A liability gain or loss occurs when actuarial assumptions differ from actual experiences related to the computation of the projected benefit obligation.

$$\text{Liability gain} = \text{Unexpected decrease in the PBO}$$

$$\text{Liability loss} = \text{Unexpected increase in the PBO}$$

Asset gains and losses are combined with liability gains and losses to derive a *net gain or loss*. Net gain or loss is the change in the fair market value of plan assets and the amount of change in the projected benefit obligation.

What is the corridor method?

Asset gains and losses and liability gains and losses offset each other. The *corridor method* is used to amortize the "accumulated other comprehensive income" account balance when it becomes excessive. The FASB set a limit of 10 percent of the *greater* of the beginning balances of the market-related value of plan assets or the projected benefit obligation. Above the 10 percent limit, the "accumulated other comprehensive income" account related to gain and loss is too large and must be amortized. For example, if the projected benefit obligation and market-related asset value are $800,000 and $650,000, respectively, the corridor equals $80,000 (10% × $800,000). Any amount exceeding $80,000 would be amortized so if the "accumulated other comprehensive income" account balance was $120,000, the amount to be amortized would be $40,000 ($120,000 − $80,000). However, if the "accumulated other comprehensive income" account had a balance of $80,000 or less, *no* amortization is required.

If amortization is required, the *minimum* amortization is the excess ($40,000) divided by the average remaining service years of active employees to receive benefits. Assuming a 40-year service life, the amortization for the year would be $1,000 ($40,000/40 years). The amortization of a loss increases pension expense while the amortization of a gain reduces it.

Note

A company can use any amortization method for gain and loss provided it is more than the minimum amount. ■

How does a pension asset or pension liability arise?

Pension expense will not typically equal the employer's cash funding; rather, it is usually based on the benefits/years-of-service actuarial method. Under this approach, pension expense and related liability depends on estimating future salaries for total benefits to be paid.

If Pension expense > Cash paid = Pension liability (Credit)

If Pension expense < Cash paid = Pension asset (Charge)

What is the financial statement presentation?

The change in the fair market value of pension plan assets equals:

Fair market value of plan assets—beginning of year
Plus: Actual return on plan assets
Plus: Contributions
Minus: Benefit payments
Fair market value of plan assets—end of year

The change in the projected benefit obligation equals:

Projected benefit obligation—beginning of year
Plus: Service cost
Plus: Interest cost
Plus: Amendments (prior service cost)
Plus: Actuarial loss
Minus: Benefit payments
Projected benefit obligation—end of year

As per ASC No. 715-30-25-1, the employer must measure the funded status (assets and liabilities) of a plan at its fiscal year-end date used for financial reporting.

The net funded status must be recognized on the balance sheet. If the projected benefit obligation exceeds the fair market value of plan assets, the plan is underfunded, and there will be a pension liability. If the fair market value of plan assets exceeds the projected benefit obligation, the plan is overfunded, and there will be a pension asset.

IFRS Treatment

Unlike U.S. generally accepted accounting principles (GAAP), International Financial Reporting Standards (IFRS) allow companies to have the option to report the funded status of their pension plans on the balance sheet. ■

There should be an aggregation of the statuses of all overfunded plans, and the amount should be presented as a noncurrent asset.

Note

No part of a pension asset is reported as a current asset because the pension plan assets are *restricted*. There should be an aggregation of the statuses of all underfunded plans, and the amount should be presented as a liability. The liability for an underfunded plan may be classified as a current liability, noncurrent liability, or a combination of both. The current portion is the amount by which the actuarial present value of benefits included in the benefit obligation payable within the year exceeds the fair market value of plan assets. ■

All underfunded plans should be combined and presented as a pension asset. Similarly, all underfunded plans should be combined and presented as a pension liability. It is *not* allowed to combine all plans and show a net amount as a single net asset or net liability.

Exhibit 7.2 presents a summary of the accounting for pension plans as required by FASB Statement No. 158.

EXHIBIT 7.2   Pension Plan Accounting

Items	Journal Entry Account	Memo Account
Prior service cost (PSC) arising from amendment of plan	Other comprehensive income (OCI) (prior service cost) Dr.	Projected benefit obligation (PBO) Cr.
Service cost	Pension expense (PE) Dr.	PBO Cr.
Interest cost on PBO	PE Dr.	PBO Cr.
Actual return	PE Cr.	Plan assets (PA) Dr.
Amortization of PSC	PE Dr. and OCI (PSC) Cr.	
Contributions	Cash Cr.	PA Dr.
Benefit payments		PBO Dr. and PA Cr.

(continued)

EXHIBIT 7.2 *(continued)*

Items	Journal Entry Account	Memo Account
Unexpected loss (expected return on PA exceeds actual return)	OCI (G/L) Dr. and PE Cr.	
Unexpected gain (actual return on PA exceeds expected return)	PE Dr. and OCI (G/L) Cr.	
Liability (PBO) increase	OCI (G/L) Dr.	PBO Cr.
Liability (PBO) decrease	OCI (G/L) Cr.	PBO Dr.
Amortization of excess loss over the corridor	PE Dr. and OCI(G/L) Cr.	
Amortization of excess gain over the corridor	OCI(G/L) Dr. and PE Cr.	

Example 7.18

Mr. A has six years before retirement. The estimated salary at retirement is $50,000. The pension benefit is 3 percent of final salary for each service year payable at retirement. The retirement benefit is computed below:

Final annual salary	$50,000
Formula rate	× 3%
	$ 1,500
Years of service	× 6
Retirement benefit	$ 9,000

Example 7.19

On 1/1/2X11, a company adopts a defined benefit pension plan. The return and interest rate are both 10 percent. Service cost for 2X11 and 2X12 are $100,000 and $120,000, respectively. The funding amounts for 2X11 and 2X12 are $80,000 and $110,000, respectively.

The entry for 2X11 is:

Pension expense	100,000	
Cash		80,000
Pension liability		20,000

The entry for 2X12 is:

Pension expense	122,000	
Cash		110,000
Pension liability		12,000

(continued)

Computation:

Service cost	$120,000
Interest on projected benefit obligation 10% × $100,000	10,000
Return on plan assets 10% × $80,000	(8,000)
	$122,000

At 12/31/2X12:

Projected benefit obligation = $230,000 ($100,000 + $120,000 + $10,000)

Pension plan assets = $198,000 ($80,000 + $110,000 + $8,000)

Example 7.20

Company X has a defined benefit pension plan for its 100 employees. On 1/1/2X12, pension plan assets have a fair value of $230,000, and the projected benefit obligation is $420,000. Ten employees are expected to resign each year for the next 10 years. They will be eligible to receive benefits. Service cost for 2X12 is $40,000. On 12/31/2X12, the projected benefit obligation is $490,000, and fair value of plan assets is $265,000. The expected return on plan assets and the interest rate are both 8 percent. No actuarial gains or losses occurred during the year. Cash funded for the year is $75,000.

Pension expense equals:

Service cost		$40,000
Interest on projected benefit obligation 8% × $420,000		33,600
Expected return on plan assets 8% × $230,000		(18,400)
Amortization of actuarial gains and losses		—
Amortization of unrecognized transition amount		34,545[a]
Pension expense		$89,745
Projected benefit obligation	$420,000	
Fair value of pension plan assets	230,000	
Initial net obligation	$190,000	

[a] Amortization $190,000/5.5 years = $34,545

$$\frac{n(n+1)}{2} \times p = \frac{10(10+1)}{2} \times = 550$$

550/100 = 5.5 years (average remaining service period)

The journal entry at 12/31/2X12 follows.

Pension expense	89,745	
Cash		75,000
Pension liability		14,745

What disclosures should be made?

Footnote disclosures for a pension plan include:

- Description of the plan, including employee groups covered, benefit formula, funding policy, and retirement age
- Pension assumptions (e.g., employee turnover, interest rate, mortality rate)
- Components of pension expense
- Weighted-average discount rate used to measure the projected benefit obligation
- Weighted-average return rate on pension plan assets
- Present value of vested and nonvested benefits
- Amounts and types of securities held in pension assets
- Approximate annuity benefits to employees
- Nature and amount of changes in pension plan assets and benefit obligations recognized in net income and in "other comprehensive income"
- Amortization method used for the excess of the "accumulated other comprehensive income" balance over the corridor amount
- Reconciliation of how the fair market value of plan assets and the projected benefit obligation changed from the beginning to end of year

What are the major differences between pensions and postretirement?

The major differences between pension benefits versus postretirement benefits are:

- Pension benefits typically are funded, while postretirement benefits are not.
- Pension benefits are well defined within a level dollar amount, while postretirement benefits are usually uncapped and show significant fluctuation.

What if part of the employer's pension obligation is relieved?

According to ASC No. 715-60-0, *Compensation—Retirement Benefits: Defined Benefit Plans—Other Postretirement* (FAS No. 88, *Employer's Accounting for Settlements and Curtailments of Defined Benefit Pension Plans and for Termination Benefits*), and ASC No. 715-30-25-1, a settlement is discharging some or all of the employer's pension benefit obligation. Excess plan assets revert back to the employer. A settlement must meet all of the following conditions:

- Relieves pension benefit responsibility
- Substantially reduces risk of the pension obligation
- Is irrevocable

The amount of gain or loss when a pension obligation is settled is limited to the unrecognized net gain or loss from realized or unrealized changes in either the pension benefit obligation or plan assets arising from the difference between actual experience and assumptions. All or a proportion of the unrecognized gain or loss is recognized when a plan is settled.

If there is a full settlement, all unrecognized gains or losses are recognized. If only a part of the plan is settled, a pro rata share of the unrecognized net gain or loss is recognized.

An example of a settlement involves the employer's paying employees a lump sum to waive their pension rights. The gain or loss is included in the current year's income statement.

What if employee services in the future are to be reduced?

According to ASC Nos. 715-60-05 and 715-30-25-1, a curtailment of the pension plan occurs when an event materially reduces the future service years of current employees or eliminates for most employees the accumulation of defined benefits for future services. An example is a plant closing, terminating employee services before pension plan expectations. The gain or loss is recognized in the current year's income statement and includes the following elements:

- Prior service cost for employee services no longer required
- Change in pension benefit obligation because of the curtailment

The projected benefit obligation may be decreased (a gain) or increased (a loss) by a curtailment. To the extent that such a gain (loss) exceeds any net loss (gain) included in "accumulated other comprehensive income," it is a curtailment gain.

The amount of net periodic benefit cost should include the gain or loss recognized because of settlements or curtailments.

What if there is early retirement?

When termination benefits are offered by the employer, accepted by employees, and the amount can reasonably be determined, an expense and liability are recorded. The amount of the accrual equals the down payment plus the discontinued value of future employer payments. The entry is to debit loss and credit cash (down payment) and liability (future payments). The terms of the arrangement should be disclosed.

 ## POSTRETIREMENT BENEFITS EXCLUDING PENSIONS

What are the major differences between pensions and postretirement?

The major differences between pension benefits versus postretirement benefits are:

- Pension benefits are typically funded, while postretirement benefits are not.
- Pension benefits are well defined within a level dollar amount, while postretirement benefits are usually uncapped and show significant fluctuation.

ASC No. 715-60-05 (FAS No. 106, *Employers' Accounting for Postretirement Benefits Other than Pensions*) and ASC No. 715-30-25-1 deal with all types of postretirement benefits, but they concentrate on postretirement health care benefits. However, brief references are made to long-term care, tuition assistance, legal advisory services, and housing subsidies.

How are postretirement benefits accounted for?

ASC No. 715-60-05 drastically changed the practice of accounting for postretirement benefits on the pay-as-you-go (cash) basis by requiring accrual of the expected cost of postretirement benefits during the years in which active employee services are rendered. These expected postretirement benefits may be paid to employees, employees' beneficiaries, and covered dependents.

Postretirement benefits for current and future retirees constitute deferred compensation. The time period the postretirement benefits accrue is called the *attribution period.*

The *accumulated postretirement benefit obligation* (APBO) is the actuarial present value of future benefits assigned to employees' services performed to a particular date. The *expected postretirement benefit obligation* (EPBO) is the actuarial present value as of a specified date of all benefits the employer expects to pay after retirement to workers, their beneficiaries, or covered dependents. The APBO equals the EPBO for retirees and active employees fully eligible for benefits at the end of the attribution period. Before full eligibility is reached, the APBO is a part of the EPBO. Therefore, the difference between the APBO and the EPBO is the future service costs of active employees who are not yet fully eligible. The employer's obligation for postretirement benefits expected to be provided must be fully accrued by the date that the employee attains full eligibility for all of the benefits expected to be received (the full eligibility date), even if the employee is expected to perform additional services beyond that date.

The beginning of the accrual (attribution) period is the date of employment unless the plan only grants credit for service from a later date, in which instance benefits are generally attributed from the beginning of that credited service period. An equal amount of the anticipated postretirement benefit is attributed to each year of service unless the plan provides a disproportionate share of the expected benefits to early years of service.

The pronouncement requires a single measurement approach to spread costs from the date of hire to the date the employee is fully eligible to receive benefits. If information on gross charges is not available, there is a measurement approach based on net claims cost (e.g., gross changes less deductibles, copayments, Medicare). There is a projection of future retiree healthcare costs based on a healthcare cost trend assumption to current costs.

What are the elements of postretirement benefit expense?

Net periodic postretirement benefit cost is comprised of these components:

- *Service cost:* Actuarial present value of benefits applicable to services performed during the *current year.*
- *Interest cost:* Interest on the accumulated postretirement benefit obligation at the beginning of the period, adjusted for benefit payments during the year.

- *Actual return on plan assets:* Return based on the fair value of plan assets at the beginning and end of the period, adjusted for contributions and benefit payments.
- *Amortization expense on prior service cost:* Expense provision for the current year due to amortization of the prior service cost arising from adoption of or amendment to the plan. Prior service cost applies to credited services *before* adoption or amendment, and is accounted for over current and future years. The typical amortization period, beginning with the amendment date, is the remaining service years to the full eligibility date. There should be amortization of any prior service cost or credit included in "accumulated other comprehensive income."
- *Gain or loss component:* Gains and losses apply to changes in the amount of either the accumulated postretirement benefit obligation or plan assets resulting from actual experience being different from the actuarial assumptions. The gains and losses may also apply to changes in assumptions. Gains and losses may be realized (i.e., sale of securities) or unrealized. Gains and losses that are *not* recognized immediately as a component of net periodic postretirement benefit cost are recognized as increases or decreases in "other comprehensive income" as they occur.

What disclosures are necessary?

Footnote disclosures include:

- A description of the postretirement plan, including employee groups covered, type of benefits provided, funding policy, types of assets held, and liabilities assumed
- The components of net periodic postretirement cost
- The fair value of plan assets
- Accumulated postretirement benefit obligation showing separately the amount applicable to retirees, other fully eligible participants, and other active plan participants
- Funded status of the plan
- Unrecognized net gain or loss
- Unrecognized transition obligation or transition asset
- The amount of net postretirement benefit asset or liability recognized in the balance sheet
- The assumed healthcare cost trends used to measure the expected postretirement benefit cost for the next year
- The discount rate used to determine the accumulated postretirement benefit obligation
- The return rate used on the fair value of plan assets
- The cost of providing termination benefits recognized during the period

What about interim periods?

- With regard to interim reporting, unless a company remeasures both its plan assets and benefit obligations during the fiscal year, the funded status it reports in its interim balance sheet shall be the same asset or liability recognized in the previous year-end balance sheet adjusted for (1) subsequent accruals of net periodic post-retirement cost excluding the amortization of amounts previously recognized in "other comprehensive income" and (2) contributions to the funded plan, or benefit payments. Upon remeasurement, a company shall adjust its balance sheet in a later interim period to take into account the underfunded or overfunded status of the plan consistent with that measurement date.

INCOME TAX ALLOCATION

How do you account for the differences between book income and taxable income?

ASC Nos. 740-10-05-1 through 05-10, *Income Taxes: Overall* (FAS No. 109, *Accounting for Income Taxes*) requires that income taxes be accounted for using the liability method. Tax allocation applies to temporary differences, not permanent ones.

The deferred tax liability or asset is measured at the tax rate under *current* law, which will apply when the temporary difference reverses. Furthermore, the deferred tax liability or asset must be adjusted for tax law changes.

Comprehensive deferred tax accounting is followed where tax expense equals taxes payable plus the tax effects of all temporary differences.

Income taxes are accounted for on the accrual basis providing for *matching* of tax expense to income before tax.

Interperiod tax allocation recognizes current (or deferred) tax liability or asset for the current (or deferred) tax effect of transactions that have occurred at year-end. Tax effects of future events should be recognized in the year they occur. It is incorrect to anticipate them for recognizing a deferred tax liability or asset in the current year.

What are the examples of temporary differences?

Temporary differences are the differences between the years in which transactions affect taxable income and book income. They originate in one year and reverse in another. Temporary differences arise from four types of transactions:

1. Income included in taxable income after being recognized in accounting income (e.g., installment sales)
2. Expenses deducted for taxable income after being recognized for accounting income (e.g., bad debts, warranties)
3. Income included in taxable income before being recognized in accounting income (e.g., revenue received in advance such as a retainer)
4. Expenses deducted for taxable income before being recognized for accounting income (e.g., accelerated depreciation)

If tax rates are graduated based on taxable income, aggregate calculations may be made using an estimated average rate.

What effect do permanent differences have?

Permanent differences do not reverse (turn around) and therefore do not require tax allocation. Examples of expenses that are not tax deductible are premiums on officers' life insurance, fines, and penalties. An example of income that is not taxable is interest on municipal bonds.

How are deferred taxes reported?

In the balance sheet, deferred tax charges and credits are offset and shown (a) net current and (b) net noncurrent. However, offset is not allowed for deferred tax liabilities or assets of different tax jurisdictions.

Deferred tax assets or liabilities are classified according to the related asset or liability to which they apply. For example, a deferred tax liability arising from depreciation on a fixed asset would be noncurrent.

Deferred taxes not applicable to specific assets or liabilities are classified as current or noncurrent based on the expected reversal dates of the temporary differences. Temporary differences reversing within one year are current, whereas those reversing in more than one year are noncurrent.

In the income statement, disclosure is made of the income tax expense currently payable (the liability) and the *deferred portion* of the expense (the portion of the expense based on temporary differences). (The total expense provision is based on financial reporting income excluding permanent differences.)

The presentation of these two expense portions (with numbers and a 40 percent tax rate assumed) are:

Income before income taxes		$200
Income tax expense:		
Amount currently payable	$400	
Deferred portion	(320)	80
Net income		$120

IFRS Treatment

The classification of deferred taxes under IFRS is always noncurrent. U.S. GAAP classifies deferred taxes based on the classification of the asset or liability to which it relates. ■

What is Intraperiod tax allocation?

Intraperiod tax allocation is when tax expense is shown in different parts of the financial statements for the current year. The income statement shows the tax allocated to income from continuing operations, income from discontinued operations, extraordinary items, and cumulative effect of a change in accounting principle. In the retained earnings statement, prior-period adjustments are shown net of tax.

What can be done for current-year losses for tax purposes?

The tax effects of net operating *loss carrybacks* should be allocated to the loss year. The company may carry back a net operating loss two years and receive a refund for taxes paid in those years. The loss is first applied to the earliest year. Any remaining loss is carried forward up to 20 years.

The presentation of a *loss carryback* with recognition of refund during the loss year follows.

Loss before refundable income taxes	$1,000
Refund of prior years' income taxes arising from carryback of operating loss	485
Net loss	$ 515

Note

The refund should be computed at the amount actually refundable regardless of current tax rates. ■

A loss carryforward may be recognized to the extent that there are net taxable amounts in the carryforward period (deferred tax liability) to absorb them. A loss carryforward may also be recognized if there exists more than a 50 percent probability of future realization. In this case, a net deferred tax asset may be recorded for the tax benefit. In other words, the tax benefit of a loss carryforward is recognized as a deferred tax asset if the loss is to be carried forward to offset future amounts of taxable income. The tax benefit is based on the tax rates expected to be in effect for the carryforward period. When the net deferred tax asset is recorded, income tax expense is reduced. In later years, as income is realized, the deferred tax asset is reduced. If there is a 50 percent or less probability of future realization, a net deferred tax asset is not recorded. In this case, the tax effect of the operating loss carryforward cannot be recognized until the year realized (the year in which the tax liability is reduced).

The tax benefit of a loss carryforward recognized when realized in a later year is classified in the same way as the income enabling recognition (typically reducing tax expense).

Presentation of the loss carryforward with recognition of benefit in year realized (numbers and 50 percent rate assumed):

Income before income taxes		$1,000
Income tax expense:		
Without carryforward	$500	
Reduction of income taxes arising from carryforward of prior years' operating losses	(300)	200
Net income		$ 800

The amounts and expiration dates of operating loss carryforwards should be footnoted.

DEFERRED TAX LIABILITY VERSUS DEFERRED TAX ASSET

If book income exceeds taxable income, tax expense exceeds tax payable so that a deferred tax liability results. If book income is less than taxable income, tax expense is less than tax payable so a deferred tax asset results.

How do we account for a deferred tax liability?

Example 7.21

Assume that book income and taxable income are $1,000. Depreciation for book purposes is $50 based on the straight-line method and $100 for tax purposes based on the accelerated cost recovery system. Assuming a tax rate of 34 percent, the entry is:

Income tax expense (950 × 34%)	323	
Income tax payable (900 × 34%)		306
Deferred tax liability		17

At the end of the life of the asset, the deferred tax liability of $17 will be completely reversed.

Example 7.22

At the end of year 1, future recovery of the reported amount of an enterprise's installment receivables will result in taxable amounts totaling $240,000 in years 2 to 4. Also, a $20,000 liability for estimated expenses has been recognized in the financial statements in year 1, and those expenses will be deductible for tax purposes in year 4 when the liability is expected to be paid. Those temporary differences are estimated to result in net taxable amounts in future years as presented next.

	Year 2	Year 3	Year 4
Taxable amounts	$70,000	$110,000	$60,000
Deductible amount	—	—	(20,000)
Net taxable amounts	$70,000	$110,000	$40,000

This example assumes that the enacted tax rates for years 2 to 4 are 20 percent for the first $50,000 of taxable income, 30 percent for the next $50,000, and 40 percent for taxable income over $100,000. The liability for deferred tax consequences is measured as follows.

	Year 2	Year 3	Year 4
20% tax on first $50,000	$10,000	$10,000	$8,000
30% tax on next $50,000	6,000	15,000	—
40% tax on over $100,000	—	4,000	—
	$16,000	$29,000	$8,000

A deferred tax liability is recognized for $53,000 (the total of the taxes payable for years 2 to 4) at the end of year 1.

Source: Financial Accounting Standards Board, FASB No. 96, *Accounting for Income Taxes* (Stamford, CT: Author, December 1987), p. 32.

How do we account for a deferred tax asset?

A net deferred tax asset may be recorded if it is more likely than not (more than a 50 percent probability) that the tax benefit will be realized in the future. The gross deferred tax asset is reduced by a valuation allowance (contra account) if it is more likely than not that some or all of the gross deferred tax asset will not be realized. The net deferred tax asset represents the amount likely to be realized. The deferred tax asset is presented in the following balance sheet, assuming a temporary difference of $1 million, a tax rate of 30 percent, and $700,000 of the tax benefit having more than a 50 percent probability of being realized.

Gross deferred tax asset ($1,000,000 × 0.30)	$300,000
Less: Valuation allowance ($300,000 × 0.30)	90,000
Net deferred tax asset ($700,000 × 0.30)	$210,000

Example 7.23

There is a temporary difference of $600,000, a 40 percent tax rate, and the entire temporary difference has more than a 50 percent probability of being realized. The balance sheet will show:

Gross deferred tax asset ($600,000 × 0.40)	$240,000
Less: Valuation allowance	0
Net deferred tax asset ($600,000 × 0.40)	$240,000

The valuation allowance reduces the deferred tax asset to its realizable value. The determination of whether a valuation allowance is required involves considering the positive and negative factors applied to whether the deferred tax asset is more likely than not to be realized. The valuation allowance account should be reviewed periodically to ascertain whether adjustments are needed. For instance, the valuation allowance account will be completely eliminated if positive evidence now exists that the deferred

Example 7.24

Assume in that the entire deferred tax asset of $600,000 had less than a 50 percent probability of being realized. The balance sheet would present:

Gross deferred tax asset ($600,000 × 0.40)	$240,000
Less: Valuation allowance ($600,000 × 0.40)	240,000
Net deferred tax asset	0

tax asset is no longer impaired. Any entry required to the valuation allowance account is coupled with a related adjustment to income tax expense. The entry is to debit income tax expense and credit valuation allowance.

These factors indicate that there is more than a 50 percent probability of future realization of a temporary difference presented as a deferred tax asset:

- Lucrative contracts and backlog of orders exist.
- Earnings have been strong historically, and future earnings are anticipated.

These factors indicate that there is a 50 percent or less probability of future realization of a deferred tax asset:

- A history of past losses exists.
- Tax benefits have expired.
- Many lawsuits have been filed against the company.

Example 7.25

In 2X11, a company sold a fixed asset reporting a gain of $70,000 for book purposes, which was deferred for tax purposes (installment method) until 2X12. In addition, in 2X11, $40,000 of subscription income was received in advance. The income was recognized for tax purposes in 2X11 but was deferred for book purposes until 2X12.

The deferred tax asset may be recorded because the deductible amount in the future ($40,000) offsets the taxable amount ($70,000). Assuming a 34 percent tax rate and income taxes payable of $100,000, the entry in 2X11 is:

Income tax expense	110,200	
Deferred tax asset ($40,000 × 34%)	13,600	
Deferred tax liability ($70,000 × 34%)		23,800
Income taxes payable		100,000

A deferred tax asset can also be recognized for the tax benefit of deductible amounts realizable by carrying back a loss from future years to reduce taxes paid in the current or a previous year.

TAX RATES

The tax rates over the years may be different. Furthermore, there may be a change in tax law.

What happens when tax rates are different?

Deferred taxes are reflected at the amounts of settlement when the temporary differences reverse.

Example 7.26

Assume in 2X09, a cumulative temporary difference of $200,000 that will reverse in the future, generating the following taxable amounts and tax rate:

	2X10	2X11	2X12	Total
Reversals	$60,000	$90,000	$50,000	$200,000
Tax rate	× 0.34	× 0.30	× 0.25	
Deferred tax liability	$20,400	$27,000	$12,500	$59,900

On December 31, 2X09, the deferred tax liability is recorded at $59,900.

A future tax rate can be used *only* if it has been enacted by law.

Although there may be graduated tax rates, the highest tax rate may be used when the difference is insignificant.

What happens if tax rates change?

A change in tax rate must be immediately recognized by adjusting tax expense and deferred taxes in the year of change.

Example 7.27

Assume at the end of 2X08 that a new tax law reduces the tax rate from 34 to 30 percent beginning in 2X10. In 2X08, there was deferred profit of $100,000 showing a deferred tax liability of $34,000 as of 2X08. The gross profit is to be reflected equally in 2X09, 2X10, 2X11, and 2X12. Thus, the deferred tax liability at the end of 20X2 is $31,000, as shown:

	2X09	2X10	2X11	2X12
Reversals	$25,000	$25,000	$25,000	$25,000
Tax rate	× 0.34	× 0.30	× 0.30	× 0.30
Deferred tax liability	$ 8,500	$ 7,500	$ 7,500	$ 7,500
Total = $31,000				

(continued)

The appropriate entry in 2X08 is:

Deferred tax liability	3,000	
Income tax expense		3,000

How is tax allocation treated in a business combination accounted for under the purchase method?

In a business combination accounted for as a purchase, the net assets acquired are recorded at their gross fair values with a separate deferred tax balance for the tax effects. Furthermore, a temporary difference in amount arises between the financial reporting and tax basis of assets and liabilities acquired. If the acquired company has an operating loss, it reduces the deferred tax liability of the acquired business.

What footnote disclosures should be made?

There should be disclosure of the types of temporary differences and cumulative amounts. An example is the disclosure that warranties are deducted for taxes when paid but are deducted for financial reporting in the year of sale.

If a deferred tax liability is not recognized, disclosure should be made of these items:

■ Description of the types of temporary differences for which no recognition is made to a deferred tax liability and the kinds of occurrences that would result in tax recognition of the temporary differences
■ Cumulative amount of each type of temporary difference

A reconciliation should exist between the reported amount of tax expense and the tax expense that would have occurred using federal statutory tax rates. The reconciliation should be in terms of percentages or dollar amounts. If statutory tax rates do not exist, use the regular tax rates for alternative tax systems. Disclosure should be made of the estimated amount and the nature of each material reconciling item.

There should be disclosure of the terms of intercorporate tax-sharing arrangements and tax-related balances due to or from affiliates.

Other disclosures include:

■ Factors taken into account in determining the realizability of deferred tax assets
■ Government grants that lower tax expense
■ Adjustments to tax expense arising from a change in tax law, tax rates, or tax status
■ Major aspects of the method used by which consolidated tax expense is allocated to subsidiaries

Extensions of tax allocation

ASC No. 740-30-05 (Accounting Principles Board [APB] Opinions Nos. 23, *Accounting for Income Taxes—Special Areas* and 24, *Accounting for Income Taxes*) provide that undistributed earnings (parent/investor share of subsidiary/investee income less dividends received) are temporary differences.

The reasoning for this treatment is the assumption that such earnings ultimately will be transferred.

Temporary Difference

In the case of investee income arising from applying APB No. 18, if evidence indicates ultimate realization by disposition of investment, income taxes should be determined at capital gains or other appropriate rates.

What happens in the case of indefinite reversal?

There is no interperiod tax allocation in the case of indefinite reversal. Indefinite reversal occurs when undistributed earnings in a foreign subsidiary are indefinitely postponed or when earnings are remitted in a tax-free liquidation.

If circumstances change and the presumption of indefinite reversal no longer is valid, an adjustment to tax expense is required.

Disclosure should be made of the declaration to reinvest indefinitely or to remit tax free, and the cumulative amount of undistributed earnings.

Amount of Temporary Difference

Eighty percent of the dividends received from affiliated corporations are generally exempt from tax. Consequently, the temporary difference is equal to 20 percent of the undistributed earnings (parent/investor interest less dividends received).

 FOREIGN CURRENCY ACCOUNTING

How do you account for and report foreign currency translation and transaction gains and losses?

ASC No. 830-10-15, *Foreign Currency Matters: Overall* (FAS No. 52, *Foreign Currency Translation*) applies to foreign currency transactions, such as exports and imports denominated in other than a company's functional currency. It also relates to foreign currency financial statements of branches, divisions, and other investees incorporated in the financial statements of a U.S. company by combination, consolidation, or the equity method.

An objective of translation is to provide information on the expected effects of rate changes on cash flow and equity. Translation also provides data in consolidated financial statements relative to the financial results of each individual foreign consolidated entity.

ASC No. 830-10-15 covers the translation of foreign currency statements and gains and losses on foreign currency transactions. The translation of foreign currency statements is usually required when the statements of a foreign subsidiary having a functional currency other than the U.S. dollar are to be included in the consolidated financial statements of a domestic enterprise. In general, the foreign currency balance sheet should be translated using the exchange rate at the end of the reporting year. The income statement should be translated using the average exchange rate for the year. The resulting translation gains and losses are shown as a separate component in the stockholders' equity section.

Any gains or losses arising from transactions denominated in a foreign currency are presented in the current year's income statement.

What are some important terms in foreign currency?

Some key terms that the CFO should be familiar with are:

Conversion: An exchange of one currency for another.

Currency swap: An exchange between two companies of the currencies of two different countries according to an agreement to re-exchange the two currencies at the same rate of exchange at a specified future date.

Denominate: Pay or receive in that same foreign currency. It can only be denominated in one currency (e.g., yen). It is a real account (asset or liability) fixed in terms of a foreign currency regardless of exchange rate.

Exchange rate: The ratio between a unit of one currency and that of another at a specified date. If there is a *temporary lack of exchangeability* between two currencies at the transaction date or balance sheet date, the first rate available thereafter is used.

Foreign currency: A currency other than the functional currency of the business (e.g., the dollar could be a foreign currency for a foreign entity).

Foreign currency statements: The financial statements using a functional currency as the unit of measure.

Foreign currency transactions: Transactions whose terms are denominated in a currency other than the entity's functional currency. Foreign currency transactions occur when a business:

1. Buys or sells on credit goods or services whose prices are denominated in foreign currency,
2. Borrows or lends funds and the amounts payable or receivable are denominated in foreign currency,
3. Is a party to an unperformed forward exchange contract, or
4. Acquires or disposes of assets, or incurs or settles liabilities denominated in foreign currency.

Foreign currency translation: The expression in the reporting currency of the company those amounts that are denominated or measured in a different currency.

Foreign entity: An operation (e.g., subsidiary, division, branch, joint venture) whose financial statements are prepared in a currency other than the reporting currency of the reporting entity.

Functional currency: An entity's functional currency is the currency of the *primary economic environment* in which the business operates. It is usually the currency of the foreign country that the company primarily obtains and uses cash.

Before translation, the foreign country figures are remeasured in the functional currency. For example, if a company in France is an independent entity and received cash and incurred expenses in France, the euro is the functional currency. However, if the French company was an extension of a British parent, the functional currency is the pound. The functional currency should be consistently used except if unusual material economic changes occur. However, previously issued financial statements are not restated for a change in the functional currency.

If a company's books are *not* kept in its functional currency, remeasurement into the functional currency is required. The remeasurement process occurs before translation into the reporting currency. When a foreign entity's functional currency is the reporting currency, remeasurement into the reporting currency obviates translation. The remeasurement process generates the same result as if the company's books had been kept in the functional currency.

How do you determine the functional currency?

There are guidelines to determine the functional currency of a foreign operation. The "benchmarks" apply to selling price, market, cash flow, financing, expense, and intercompany transactions. A detailed discussion follows.

- *Selling price.* The functional currency is the foreign currency when the foreign operation's selling price of products or services arises primarily from local factors such as government law. It is not caused by changes in exchange rate. The functional currency is the parent's currency when foreign operation's sales prices apply in the short run to fluctuation in the exchange rate emanating from international factors (e.g., worldwide competition).
- *Market.* The functional currency is the foreign currency when the foreign activity has a strong local sales market for products or services even though a significant amount of exports may exist. The functional currency is the parent's currency when the foreign operation's sales market is mostly in the parent's country.
- *Cash flow.* The functional currency is the foreign currency when the foreign operation's cash flows are predominately in foreign currency not directly impacting the parent's cash flow. The functional currency is the parent's currency when the foreign operation's cash flows affect the parent's cash flows. They are typically available for remittance via intercompany accounting settlement.
- *Financing.* The functional currency is the foreign currency if financing the foreign activity is in foreign currency and funds obtained by the foreign activity are adequate to satisfy debt payments. The functional currency is the parent's currency when financing foreign activity is provided by the parent or occurs in U.S. dollars. The funds obtained by the foreign activity are inadequate to meet debt requirements.
- *Expenses.* The functional currency is the foreign currency when a foreign operation's production costs or services are usually incurred locally. However, there may be some foreign imports. The functional currency is the parent's currency when a foreign operation's production and service costs are mostly component costs obtained from the parent's country.

- *Intercompany transactions.* The functional currency is the foreign currency when minor interrelationships exist between the activities of the foreign entity and parent except for competitive advantages (e.g., patents). There are a few intercompany transactions. The functional currency is the parent's currency when significant interrelationships exist between the foreign entity and parent. There are many intercompany transactions.

Consistent use should be made of the functional currency of the foreign entity over the years unless a significant change in circumstances takes place. If a change in the functional currency occurs, it is treated as a change in estimate.

- *Local currency:* The currency of the foreign country.
- *Measure:* A translation into a currency other than the original reporting currency. The foreign financial statements are measured in U.S. dollars by using the appropriate exchange rate.
- *Reporting currency:* The currency in which the business prepares its financial statements is typically U.S. dollars.
- *Spot rate:* The exchange rate for immediate delivery of currencies exchanged.
- *Transaction gain or loss:* Transaction gains or losses arise from a change in exchange rates between the functional currency and the currency in which a foreign currency transaction is denominated. They represent an increase or decrease in (a) the actual functional currency cash flows realized upon settlement of foreign currency transactions and (b) the expected functional currency cash flows on unsettled foreign currency transactions.
- *Translation adjustments:* These arise from translating financial statements from the entity's functional currency into the reporting one.

How is translation accomplished and reported?

The foreign entity's financial statements in a highly *inflationary* economy is not sufficiently stable and should be remeasured as if the functional currency were the reporting currency. Thus, the financial statements of those entities should be remeasured into the reporting currency. (The U.S. dollar becomes the functional currency.) In effect, the reporting currency is used directly.

A *highly inflationary environment* is one that has cumulative inflation of about *100 percent or more over a three-year period.* In other words, the inflation rate must be increasing at a rate of about 35 percent a year for three consecutive years. *Tip:* The International Monetary Fund of Washington, D.C., publishes monthly figures on international inflation rates.

TRANSLATION OF FOREIGN CURRENCY STATEMENTS WHEN THE FOREIGN CURRENCY IS THE FUNCTIONAL CURRENCY

The balance sheet accounts are translated using the current exchange rate. Assets and liabilities are converted at the exchange rate at the balance sheet date. If a current exchange rate is not available at the balance sheet date, use the first exchange rate available after that date. The current exchange rate is also used to translate the statement of cash flows except for those items found in the income statement, which are translated using the weighted-average rate. The income statement items are translated using the weighted-average exchange rate.

A significant change in the exchange rate between year-end and the audit report date should be disclosed as a subsequent event. Disclosure should also be made of the effects on unsettled balances applicable to foreign currency transactions.

What are the steps in the translation process?

The four steps in translating the foreign country's financial statements into U.S. reporting requirements are:

1. Conform the foreign country's financial statements to U.S. GAAP.
2. Determine the functional currency of the foreign entity.
3. Remeasure the financial statements in the functional currency, if necessary. Gains or losses from remeasurement are includable in remeasured current net income.
4. Convert from the foreign currency into U.S. dollars (reporting currency).

If a company's functional currency is a foreign currency, *translation adjustments* arise from translating that company's financial statements into the reporting currency. Translation adjustments are unrealized and should not be included in the income statement but should be reported separately and accumulated in a *separate component of equity*. However, if remeasurement from the recording currency to the functional currency is required before translation, the gain or loss is reflected in the income statement.

Upon sale or liquidation of an investment in a foreign entity, the amount attributable to that entity and accumulated in the translation adjustment component of equity is removed from the stockholders' equity section and considered a part of the gain or loss on sale or liquidation of the investment in the income statement for the period during which the sale or liquidation occurs.

As per ASC No. 830-30-40, *Foreign Currency Matters* (Interpretation 37), a sale of an investment in a foreign entity may include a partial sale of an ownership interest. In that case, a pro rata amount of the cumulative translation adjustment reflected as a stockholders' equity component is includable in arriving at the gain or loss on sale. For example, if a business sells a 40 percent ownership interest in a foreign investment, 40 percent of the translation adjustment applicable to it is included in calculating gain or loss on sale of that ownership interest.

How are foreign currency transactions handled?

Foreign currency transactions are denominated in a currency other than the company's functional currency. Foreign currency transactions may result in receivables or payables fixed in the amount of foreign currency to be received or paid.

A foreign currency transaction requires settlement in a currency other than the functional currency. A change in exchange rates between the functional currency and the currency in which a transaction is denominated increases or decreases the expected amount of functional currency cash flows upon settlement of the transaction. This change in expected functional currency cash flows is a *foreign currency transaction gain or loss* that typically is included in arriving at earnings in the *income statement* for the period in which the exchange rate is changed. An example of a transaction gain or loss would be an Italian subsidiary having a receivable denominated in euros from a British customer.

Similarly, a transaction gain or loss (measured from the *transaction date* or the most recent intervening balance sheet date, whichever is later) realized upon settlement of a foreign currency transaction usually should be included in determining net income for the period in which the transaction is settled.

Example 7.28

An exchange gain or loss occurs when the exchange rate changes between the purchase date and sale date.

Merchandise is bought for £100,000. The exchange rate is £4 to $1. The journal entry is:

Purchases	25,000	
Accounts payable		25,000
100,000/4 = $25,000		

When the merchandise is paid for, the exchange rate is 5 to 1. The journal entry is:

Accounts payable	25,000	
Cash		20,000
Foreign exchange gain		5,000
100,000/5 = $20,000		

The $20,000 using an exchange rate of 5 to 1 can buy £100,000. The transaction gain is the difference between the cash required of $20,000 and the initial liability of $25,000.

Note that a foreign transaction gain or loss has to be determined at each balance sheet date on all recorded foreign transactions that have not been settled.

Example 7.29

A U.S. company sells goods to a customer in England on 11/15/2X11 for £10,000. The exchange rate is £1 equals $0.75. Thus, the transaction is worth $7,500 (£10,000 × 0.75). Payment is due two months later. The entry on 11/15/2X11 is:

Accounts receivable—England	7,500	
Sales		7,500

Accounts receivable and sales are measured in U.S. dollars at the transaction date employing the spot rate. Even though the accounts receivable is measured and reported in U.S. dollars, the receivable is fixed in pounds. Thus, a transaction gain or loss can occur if the exchange rate changes between the transaction date (11/15/2X11) and the settlement date (1/15/2X12).

Since the financial statements are prepared between the transaction date and settlement date, receivables that are denominated in a currency other than the functional currency (U.S. dollar) have to be restated to reflect the spot rate on the balance sheet date. On 12/31/ 2X11, the exchange rate is £1 pound equals $0.80. Hence, the £10,000 are now valued at $8,000 (10,000 × $.80). Therefore, the accounts receivable denominated in pounds should be upwardly adjusted by $500. The required journal entry on 12/31/2X11 is:

Accounts receivable—England	500	
Foreign exchange gain		500

The income statement for the year-ended 12/31/2X11 shows an exchange gain of $500. Note that sales is not affected by the exchange gain since sales relates to operational activity.

On 1/15/2X12, the spot rate is £1 = $0.78. The journal entry is:

Cash	7,800	
Foreign exchange loss	200	
Accounts receivable—England		8,000

The 2X12 income statement shows an exchange loss of $200.

Which transaction gain or loss should not be reported in the income statement?

Gains and losses on the following foreign currency transactions are not included in earnings but rather are reported as translation adjustments:

- Foreign currency transactions designated as *economic hedges* of a net investment in a foreign entity, beginning as of the designation date
- Intercompany foreign currency transactions of a *long-term investment nature* (settlement is not planned or expected in the foreseeable future), when the entities to the transaction are consolidated, combined, or accounted for by the equity method in the reporting company's financial statements

A gain or loss on a forward contract or other foreign currency transaction that is intended to *hedge* an identifiable foreign currency commitment (e.g., an agreement to buy or sell machinery) should be deferred and included in the measurement of the related foreign currency transaction. Losses should *not* be deferred if deferral is expected to result in recognizing losses in later periods. A foreign currency transaction is deemed a hedge of an identifiable foreign currency commitment if both of these conditions are met:

- The foreign currency transaction is designated as a hedge of a foreign currency commitment.
- The foreign currency commitment is firm.

What is a forward exchange contract, and how is it accounted for?

A forward exchange contract is an agreement to exchange different currencies at a specified future date and at a given rate (forward rate). A forward contract is a foreign currency transaction. A gain or loss on a forward contract that does not satisfy the conditions described below is included in earnings.

Note

Currency swaps are accounted for in a similar way. ■

A gain or loss (whether deferred or not) on a forward contract, except a speculative forward contract, should be computed by multiplying the foreign currency amount of the forward contract by the difference between the spot rate at the balance sheet date and the spot rate at the date of inception of the forward contract.

The *discount or premium on a forward contract* (i.e., the foreign currency amount of the contract multiplied by the difference between the contracted forward rate and the spot rate at the date of inception of the contract) should be accounted for separately from the gain or loss on the contract and typically should be included in computing net income over the life of the forward contract.

A gain or loss on *a speculative forward contract* (a contract that does not hedge an exposure) should be computed by multiplying the foreign currency amount of the forward contract by the difference between the forward rate available from the remaining maturity of the contract and the contracted forward rate (or the forward rate last used to measure a gain or loss on that contract for an earlier period). *No separate accounting recognition* is given to the *discount or premium* on a *speculative forward contract*.

How can you hedge foreign currency exposure to reduce risk?

Foreign currency transactions gains and losses on assets and liabilities, denominated in a currency other than the functional currency, can be hedged if the U.S. company engages into a forward exchange contract.

There can be a hedge even if there is not a forward exchange contract. For example, a foreign currency transaction can serve as an economic hedge offsetting a parent's net investment in a foreign entity.

Example 7.30

A U.S. parent owns 100 percent of a French subsidiary having net assets of $3 million in euros. The U.S. parent can borrow $3 million in euros to hedge its net investment in the French subsidiary. Assume the French currency is the functional currency and the $3 million obligation is denominated in euros. The variability in the exchange rate for euros does not have a net effect on the parent's consolidated balance sheet because increases in the translation adjustments balance arising from translation of the net investment will be netted against decreases in this balance arising from the adjustment of the liability denominated in euros.

Accounting Standards Update

Accounting Standards Update (ASU) No. 2010-19 (May 2010), *Foreign Currency* (Topic No. 830), *Foreign Currency Issues*

In the case of a foreign company's financial statements in a highly inflationary environment, there should be a remeasurement assuming the functional currency is the reporting currency. If there is a difference existing before using the mandates of a highly inflationary accounting between the financial reporting balances and the U.S. dollar–denominated balances, it should be reflected in the profit and loss statement. Disclosure should be made of translation and remeasurement rates, why U.S. dollar–denominated balances are different from financial reporting balances, and the reasons why different rates were employed for translation and remeasurement. ■

INTERNATIONAL FINANCIAL REPORTING STANDARDS

International Financial Reporting Standards is the framework used by many publicly traded companies around the world today to report their financial results. With support from the important constituencies, the U.S. Securities and Exchange Commission (SEC) and the FASB have taken several steps toward what will be a major transition from the accounting and reporting framework currently in place in the United States to IFRS. The demand for IFRS is driven by several factors, including the magnitude of multinational corporations, global capital markets, economic interdependence, foreign direct investment, and multinational political organizations such as the European Union.

It appears that the SEC will move to a mandatory adoption of IFRS by all U.S. public companies. As of this writing, however, the SEC has temporarily halted early adoption of IFRS. In the United States, registered companies were scheduled to issue financial statements using IFRS in 2014 as part of a proposed "road map." In an effort to better understand how convergence will affect financial reporting in the United States, this section examines some of the material differences that currently exist between U.S. GAAP and IFRS.

What is the major difference between the proposed presentation of IFRS financial statements and the current presentation under U.S. GAAP?

The major difference between the proposed presentation of IFRS financial statements under IFRS (as opposed to U.S. GAAP) is that all statements would follow the structure of business (operating and investing), financing, income taxes, discontinued operations, and equity. This would cause the most change in the statement of comprehensive income and the statement of financial position.

How do the approaches to income measurement and fair value use under IFRS and U.S. GAAP compare?

Both U.S. GAAP and IFRS recognize accrual accounting as the key concept underlying income measurement. However, IFRS and U.S. GAAP differ in their income measurement in that IFRS emphasizes measurement of assets and liabilities on the balance sheet at fair value and U.S. GAAP emphasizes the matching rule and measurement of items on the income statement. Whereas U.S. GAAP has various notions of value, including fair value, IFRS permits the use of a single concept of fair value as an exit value, that is, the amount an asset may be exchanged for, or a liability settled, between knowledgeable parties in an arm's-length transaction.

What are IFRS differences affecting the statement of financial position?

Cash and Cash Equivalents

Cash and cash equivalents are defined similarly under IFRS and U.S. GAAP. However, U.S. GAAP does not allow bank overdraft offsets to the cash account and reports them as a liability. The only exception that allows offsetting is in the case that two accounts are held by the same bank; an overdrawn account may be offset against another account in the same institution. IFRS allows offsetting of overdrafts to cash as long as it is integral to the entity's cash management.

Receivables

Under U.S. GAAP, receivables are not reported at fair value. However, under IFRS, they are initially reported at fair value, with subsequent adjustments accounted for using amortized cost (effective interest method). In addition, under U.S. GAAP, an estimate of bad debts impacts earnings on the income statement. When a receivable is deemed uncollectible using the allowance method for accounting for bad debts, the write-off of the specific account does not impact earnings; any recovery of a previously written-off account also does not impact earnings. Under IFRS, impairment losses previously recognized on the income statement may be reversed in subsequent years, adjusting earnings. U.S. GAAP prohibits reversals of impairment losses on bad debts.

Inventories

U.S. GAAP generally measures inventory at lower of cost or market; under IFRS, inventory is measured at lower of cost or net realizable value (estimated selling price less estimated costs of completion and sale). IFRS includes distribution and marketing costs in its cost of sales, whereas U.S. GAAP excludes marketing costs in determining cost of sale.

Inventory write-downs under U.S. GAAP are normally determined either on an item-by-item, group, or categorical basis. IFRS writes inventory down to net realizable value (floor) on an item-by-item basis but allows write-downs to occur by groups of similar products in special circumstances. In addition, any inventory write-downs under U.S. GAAP cannot subsequently be reversed, whereas IFRS allows previous inventory write-down reversals to be recognized in the same period as the write-down.

U.S. GAAP allows for the cost of inventory to be calculated using first-in, first-out (FIFO), last-in, first-out (LIFO), or a weighted-average calculation. IFRS allows FIFO and weighted average but prohibits use of LIFO.

Investments

Accounting for trading, available-for-sale, and held-to-maturity instruments is similar between U.S. GAAP and IFRS. The major differences exist with unrealized gains and losses of available-for-sale securities, which are reported in comprehensive income under U.S. GAAP, whereas under IFRS such gains and losses are reported in the equity section of the balance sheet. In addition, IFRS allows for impairment reversals for only available-for-sale debt (not equity) securities and held-to-maturity securities, while U.S. GAAP does not permit impairment reversals of any investments.

Equity Method Investments

Both U.S. GAAP and IFRS account for investments where the investor possesses significant influence over the investee, holding at least 20 percent and up to 50 percent of an investee's outstanding stock, lacking control over the entity. IFRS refers to an equity investment as an investment in associates. Additionally, IFRS requires that the investee and investor firms follow the same accounting policies, while U.S. GAAP does not require such a practice.

Property, Plant, and Equipment

In general, U.S. GAAP and IFRS treat accounting for the property, plant, and equipment (PP&E) category similarly, including the initial accounting for all costs necessary to bring the asset to its intended use. Additionally, there are no differences in depreciation methods used. Differences exist primarily in the treatment of capitalized interest and the subsequent revaluation of the asset's fair value.

Interest incurred is capitalized under U.S. GAAP only during construction of a qualifying asset. Under IFRS, interest costs of borrowing may either be capitalized for the acquisition, construction, or production of a qualifying asset or expensed in the period incurred. Whichever method is selected must be consistently applied.

Another difference between U.S. GAAP and IFRS is in the revaluation of property, plant, and equipment. U.S. GAAP requires that PP&E be accounted for using the cost method. Under IFRS, property, plant, and equipment is reported on a company's books at fair value less accumulated depreciation and impairment losses (if any). The accumulated depreciation account is used to revalue plant and equipment with the permission of two treatments, which use a revaluation surplus account.

Intangible Assets and Goodwill

U.S. GAAP and IFRS are not similar in the definition of an intangible asset, as it lacks physical substance and it is not a financial asset. In addition, U.S. GAAP and IFRS view intangibles as assets that are identifiable if they are separable or as a result of contractual or legal rights. Goodwill, in particular, is viewed similarly by both as a residual that arises from a business combination and is not amortized but is tested annually for impairment. Some significant differences exist. While U.S. GAAP bases amortization of intangibles on historical cost less any impairment, IFRS allows revaluation of the value of the intangible by crediting any upward revision to the asset to a revaluation surplus account and adjusted against equity; downward revisions to fair value reduce the revaluation surplus account (until the account declines to zero). In addition, impairment for intangibles is treated differently under U.S. GAAP and IFRS (see "Impairment" at the end of this chapter).

With regard to research and development (R&D) costs, such costs are segregated into two types: research phase costs and developmental phase costs. Under both U.S. GAAP and IFRS, research phase costs are expensed in the period incurred. Developmental phase costs are expensed in the period incurred under U.S. GAAP. Under IFRS, such costs are similarly expensed unless technological feasibility is achieved. If technical feasibility results, such development costs are capitalized only if there is an intention to complete the developed asset, if there exists an ability to either use or sell the asset, if future economic benefits are reasonably expected to result, and if the entity provides adequate resources to finish development of the asset. With regard to in-process R&D costs that are acquired as part of a business combination, U.S. GAAP and IFRS standards have converged where acquired in-process R&D costs are capitalized and treated as an indefinite-life asset, with annual testing for impairment.

Contingent Liabilities

U.S. GAAP and IFRS measure contingent liabilities similarly in that such a liability can be recognized only if the outcome is probable and can be reasonably estimated. However, IFRS contains a slight difference in estimating the contingent liability: While U.S. GAAP uses a more conservative (low-end) estimate in recording the liability, IFRS recognizes a contingent liability at the midpoint of the estimate range.

Income Tax Deferrals

In accounting for deferred income tax differences, U.S. GAAP and IFRS both use the asset and liability approach in recognizing future tax differences arising from present transactions. There are four differences in approaches.

1. U.S. GAAP's recognition of a deferred tax asset (or liability) is based on the assumption that the underlying asset or liability will eventually be reversed (recovered or settled) in a manner consistent with its use in the business. IFRS recognizes deferred taxes based on the expected manner of settlement or recovery.

2. U.S. GAAP employs an asset valuation account to the extent that it is more likely than not that the deferred tax asset will eventually be realized (reversed) at a future date. Under IFRS, a deferred tax asset is recognized if it is probable that it will eventually be realized (reversed) in the future. Therefore, IFRS has a higher recognition threshold.

3. U.S. GAAP allows for a deferred tax asset or liability classification to be either current or noncurrent, based on the classification of the related asset or liability. IFRS instead classifies all deferred tax differences as noncurrent.

4. IFRS measures the deferred tax based on tax rates that are enacted or substantively enacted at the reporting date, whereas U.S. GAAP uses only the enacted tax rates at the reporting date (and ignores estimated future tax rate adjustments).

Lease Accounting

U.S. GAAP and IFRS recognize the economic substance of recording leases of both the lessor and lessee. There are four relatively significant differences in the accounting treatments. (While U.S. GAAP refers to capital lease treatment, IFRS terminology refers to such leases as finance leases.)

1. Under U.S. GAAP, leased assets consist of only PP&E, whereas under IFRS the leased asset can consist of other types of assets, including leases to explore mineral or natural resources and other licensing agreements (e.g., motion pictures, plays, and manuscripts).

2. U.S. GAAP is more rules based. For example, four criteria are used by the lessee and lessor (plus two required additional criteria for lessor) in determining if a lease should be capitalized. Many of these criteria are quantitative thresholds. IFRS similarly focuses on recording a lease where it transfers substantially all of the risks and rewards of ownership from the lessor to the lessee. Unlike the specific quantitative criteria under U.S. GAAP, IFRS provides a series of indicators that are used to determine if a lease is classified as a finance lease. This criteria determination is much more general than U.S. GAAP and is not rules based.

3. U.S. GAAP expenses and excludes specific costs from the calculation of minimum lease payments, including insurance, maintenance, and taxes, whereas IFRS excludes costs for services and taxes from minimum lease payments.

4. The present value of the minimum lease payment by the lessee is computed under U.S. GAAP as the lower of the lessor's implicit rate (if known by the lessee) or the lessee's incremental borrowing rate. IFRS uses the interest rate implicit in the lease if known by the lessee. If the lessee lacks knowledge of such rate, then the lessee uses its incremental borrowing rate.

Equity

There are several differences in the classification of items in the equity section of the statement of financial position under U.S. GAAP and IFRS. First, "common stock" is referred to as "share capital" under IFRS, "additional paid-in capital" is reported as "share premium" under IFRS, and "retained earnings" are often referred to as "accumulated profit and loss" or "retained profits." Treasury stock under IFRS is reported similar to U.S. GAAP as a reduction to shareholders' equity; however, IFRS allows treasury stock amounts to be offset against specific equity accounts. Further, IFRS does not recognize gains or losses on the disposition of treasury shares and instead makes an adjustment to equity. Under U.S. GAAP, using the cost method, proceeds in excess of the purchase price are generally credited to a specific paid-in capital account from treasury stock, while subsequent losses are reduced from the paid-in capital account (to the extent of its balance) and then any residual is deducted from retained earnings.

In addition to the standard items classified in the equity section of the statement of financial position, two other common classification issues exist: the treatment of convertible bonds and the reporting of noncontrolling (minority) interest in a subsidiary. With regard to corporate bonds that are convertible into common shares, U.S. GAAP reports such financial instruments as debt. However, under IFRS, proceeds of a debt instrument that are convertible into common shares are allocated between debt (reported at fair value) and equity (reported at residual value). U.S. GAAP formerly reported noncontrolling interest in a subsidiary (minority interest) in the "mezzanine" section of the balance sheet. However, U.S. GAAP and IFRS methods converged, and now both report noncontrolling interest in a subsidiary in the equity section.

What are IFRS differences affecting the income statement?

Revenue Recognition

Under U.S. GAAP, revenue is generally recognized when a product has been delivered or a service performed, the sales price is fixed and determinable, and collectability is reasonably assured. Revenue recognition principles are spread over several areas of authority within the literature, particularly with the application of the concepts of realized, recognized, and earned revenues. In addition, the SEC offers specific guidance on revenue recognition for listed companies. The International Accounting Standards Board (IASB) does not receive guidance from a regulatory body like the SEC. Further, U.S. GAAP has several areas of specific industry guidance with regard to revenue recognition; IFRS has no industry guidance.

Under IFRS, revenue is generally recognized when probable economic benefits exist, the item(s) of revenue can be reliably measured, the risks and rewards of ownership are conveyed from the seller to the buyer, and the cost of sale can be measured reliably. In addition, IFRS includes gains in the definition of revenues, which are not reported separately on the income statement, whereas U.S. GAAP records gains separate from revenues and defines it as a specific element on the income statement. One additional difference in revenue recognition is in the area of long-term construction contract accounting. Under U.S. GAAP, the percentage-of-completion method is the most common method, but the completed-contract method is allowed in specific circumstances. IFRS only allows the percentage-of-completion method.

Share-Based Payment

U.S. GAAP and IFRS standards have closely converged in the accounting of share-based payment where the fair value of shares and options that are awarded to employees are recognized over their period of service (period of benefit). One significant difference that remains regarding share-based payment is that U.S. GAAP rules apply only to employee share-based payments, whereas IFRS applies to employee and non-employee share-based payments.

Intangible Impairment

U.S. GAAP measures impairment as the excess of the intangible's carrying value over its fair value (expected future cash flows, undiscounted); IFRS recognizes impairment if the intangible's carrying value exceeds its recoverable amount (which is the higher of the intangible's fair value less costs to dispose of the asset and its value in use). Under U.S. GAAP, recorded impairment losses are not reversed in subsequent periods, as the intangible's revised basis for amortization reflects the written-down asset after impairment loss recognition. IFRS allows for recovery of impairment losses in subsequent periods if there has been a change in economic conditions or a change in the expected use of the asset. Such allowable impairment recoveries (or asset write-ups) are limited to the intangible's pre-impairment carrying value.

Earnings per Share

The calculations of basic and diluted earnings per share (EPS) are similar under U.S. GAAP and IFRS, with some minor differences. Both require EPS to be reported on the face of the income statement if the shares are traded publicly. U.S. GAAP and IFRS each report EPS for income from continuing operations and for net income or loss; however, U.S. GAAP requires EPS for discontinued operations and extraordinary items. In addition, under U.S. GAAP, if the treasury stock method of calculating incremental shares is used, a quarterly calculation of the average stock price is used. IFRS calculates the incremental shares based on a weighted average at the end of the accounting period, not at the end of each quarter. This topic is one that the two boards are jointly working on in order to converge accounting treatments. As of this writing, the treatment has not been resolved.

CHAPTER EIGHT

Interim and Segmental Reporting

T HIS CHAPTER DISCUSSES the requirements for preparing interim financial
statements and segmental disclosures included in the annual report.

 INTERIM REPORTING

What should be reported and disclosed in interim periods?

Interim reports may be issued periodically, such as quarterly or monthly. Complete
financial statements or summarized data may be provided, but interim financial statements do not have to be certified by the outside auditors.

Interim balance sheets and cash flow information should be given. If these statements are not presented, material changes in liquid assets, cash, long-term debt, and
stockholders' equity should be disclosed.

Interim reports typically include results of the current interim-period and the
cumulative year-to-date figures. Usually comparisons are made to the results of comparable interim periods for the previous year.

Interim results should be based on the accounting principles used in the preceding
year's annual report unless a change has been made in the current year.

A gain or loss cannot be deferred to a later interim period except if such deferral
would have been allowable for annual reporting.

Revenue from merchandise sold and services performed should be accounted for as
earned in the interim period in the same manner as in annual reporting. If an advance
is received in the first quarter and benefits the whole year, it should be allocated ratably
to the interim periods affected.

Expenses should be matched to revenue in the interim period. If a cost cannot be traced to revenue in a future interim period, it should be expensed in the current one. Yearly expenses, such as administrative salaries, insurance, pension plan expense, and year-end bonuses, should be allocated to the quarters. The allocation basis can be based on such factors as time spent, benefit obtained, and activity.

The gross profit method can be used to estimate interim inventory and cost of sales. Disclosure should be made of the method, assumptions, and material adjustments by reconciliations with the annual physical inventory.

A permanent inventory loss should be recognized in the interim period when it occurs. A subsequent recovery is considered a gain in the later interim period. However, if the change in inventory value is temporary, no recognition is given in the accounts.

If a temporary liquidation of the last-in, first-out (LIFO) base occurs with replacement expected by year-end, cost of sales should be based on replacement cost.

Example 8.1

The historical cost of an inventory item is $10,000, with replacement cost expected to be $15,000. The entry is:

Cost of sales	15,000	
Inventory		10,000
Reserve for liquidation of LIFO base		5,000

The reserve for liquidation of LIFO base is reported as a current liability. When there is replenishment at year-end, the entry is:

Reserve for liquidation of LIFO base	5,000	
Inventory	10,000	
Cash		15,000

Volume discounts to customers tied into annual purchases should be apportioned to the interim period based on the ratio of:

Purchases for the interim period/Total estimated purchases for the year

When a standard cost system is used, variances expected to be reversed by year-end may be deferred to an asset or liability account.

How are taxes provided for in interim periods?

The income tax provision includes current and deferred taxes. Taxes include federal and local. The tax provision for an interim period should be cumulative (e.g., total tax expense for a nine-month period is shown in the third quarter based on nine months' income). The tax expense for the three-month period based on three months' revenue may also be presented (e.g., third-quarter tax expense based on only the third quarter). In computing tax expense, use the estimated annual effective tax rate based on income from continuing operations. If a reliable estimate is not feasible, the actual year-to-date effective tax rate may be used.

At the end of each interim period, a revision of the effective tax rate may be needed using the best estimates of the annual effective tax rate. The projected tax rate includes adjustment for net deferred credits. Adjustments should be considered in deriving the maximum tax benefit for year-to-date figures.

The estimated effective tax rate should incorporate all available tax credits (e.g., foreign tax credit). A change in taxes arising from a new tax law is reflected immediately in the interim period in which it occurs.

Income statement items shown below income from continuing operations (e.g., income from discontinued operations, extraordinary items, and cumulative effect of a change in accounting principle) should be presented net of taxes. The tax effect on these unusual line items should be reflected only in the interim period when they actually occur. Prior-period adjustments in the retained earnings statement are also shown net of tax.

The tax implication of an interim loss is recognized only when realization of the tax benefit is assured beyond reasonable doubt. If a loss is expected for the remainder of the year and carryback is not possible, the tax benefits typically should not be recognized.

The tax benefit of a previous-year operating loss carryforward is recognized as an extraordinary item in each interim period to the extent that income is available to offset the loss carryforward.

What if a change in principle occurs?

When a change in principle is made in the first interim period, the cumulative effect of a change in principle account should be shown net of tax in the first interim period. If a change in principle is made in a quarter other than the first (e.g., third quarter), we assume the change was made at the beginning of the first quarter showing the cumulative effect in the first quarter. The interim periods will have to be restated using the new principle (e.g., first, second, and third quarters).

When interim data for previous years are presented for comparative purposes, there should be a restatement to conform with newly adopted policies. Alternatively, disclosure can be made of the effect on prior data that the new practice would have had, had it been applied to that period.

If there is a change in principle, disclosure should be made of the nature of and justification for the change. The effect of the change on per share amounts should be given.

There should be disclosure of seasonality affecting interim results. Contingencies should be disclosed. When a change in the estimated effective tax rate occurs, it should be disclosed. Furthermore, if a fourth quarter is not presented, any material adjustments to that quarter must be commented on in the footnotes to the annual report. If an event is immaterial on an annual basis but material in the interim period, it should be disclosed. Purchase transactions should be noted.

What about financial statement presentation?

The financial statement presentation for prior-period adjustments is:

- Include in net income for the current period the portion of the effect related to current operations.

- Restate earnings of impacted prior interim periods of the current year to include the portion related thereto.
- If the prior-period adjustment affects prior years, include it in the earnings of the first interim period of the current year.

The criteria for prior-period adjustments in interim periods are materiality, subject to estimation, and identifiable to a prior interim period. Examples of prior-period adjustments for interim reporting are error corrections, settlement of litigation or claims, renegotiation proceedings, and adjustment of income taxes.

Segmental disposal is shown separately in the interim period in which it occurs.

 SEGMENTAL REPORTING

What is presented in segmental reports?

The financial reporting for business segments is useful in appraising segmental performance, earning prospects, and risk. Segmental reporting may be by industry, foreign geographic area, major customers, and government contracts. The financial statement presentation for segments may appear in the body, footnotes, or separate schedule to the financial statements. Some segmental information is required in interim reports. An industry *segment* sells products or renders services to outside customers.

Segmental data occur when a company prepares a full set of financial statements (balance sheet, income statement, statement of cash flows, and related footnotes). Segmental information is shown for each year presented.

Accounting principles employed in preparing financial statements should be used for segment information, except that intercompany transactions eliminated in consolidation are included in segmental reporting.

What are the requirements of ASC No. 280-10-05 (FAS No. 131)?

Accounting Standards Codification (ASC) No. 280-10-05 (Financial Accounting Standard [FAS] No. 131, *Disclosures about Segments of an Enterprise and Related Information*) mandates that the amount reported for each segment item be based on what is used by the "chief operating decision maker" to determine how many resources to assign to a segment and how to evaluate the performance of that segment. The term "chief operating decision maker" may apply to the chief executive officer or chief operating officer or to a group of executives. It may also relate to a function and not necessarily to a particular person.

Revenue, gains, expenses, losses, and assets should be allocated to a segment only if the chief operating decision maker takes it into account in measuring a segment's profitability to formulate a financial or operating decision. The same applies to allocating to segments eliminations and adjustments applying to the entity's general-purpose financial statements. Any allocation of financial items to a segment should be rationally based.

In measuring a segment's profitability or assets, the following points should be disclosed for explanatory reasons:

- Measurement or valuation basis used
- A change in measurement method
- Differences in measurements used for the general-purpose financial statements compared to the financial data of the segment
- A symmetrical allocation, referring to an allocation of depreciation or amortization to a segment without a related allocation to the associated asset

An operating segment is a distinct revenue-producing component of the business for which internal financial information is generated. Expenses are reported as incurred in that segment. It should be noted that a start-up operation would be considered an operating segment even though revenue is not being earned. The chief operating decision maker periodically reviews an operating segment to analyze performance and to ascertain what and how many resources to allocate to the segment.

What reconciliation is required?

A business need not use the same accounting principles for segmental reporting as are used to prepare the consolidated financial statements. A reconciliation must be made between segmental financial information and general-purpose financial statements. The reconciliation is for revenue, operating profit, and assets. Any differences in measurement approaches between the company as a whole and its segments should be explained. The CFO must describe the reasoning and methods in deriving the composition of its operating segments.

What segments should be reported on?

A segment must be reported if one or more of these conditions are satisfied:

- Revenue is 10 percent or more of total revenue.
- Operating income is 10 percent or more of the combined operating profit.
- Identifiable assets are 10 percent or more of the total identifiable assets.
  The factors to be taken into account when determining industry segments are:
- *Nature of the market.* Similarity exists in geographic markets serviced or types of customers.
- *Nature of the product.* Related products or services have similar purposes or end uses (e.g., similarity in profit margins, risk, and growth).
- *Nature of the production process.* Homogeneity exists when there is interchangeable production of sales facilities, labor force, equipment, or service groups.
  Reportable segments are determined by:
- Identifying specific products and services
- Grouping those products and services by industry line into segments
- Selecting material segments to the company as a whole

There should be a grouping of products and services by industry lines. A number of approaches exist. However, no one method is appropriate in determining industry segments in every case. In many instances, management judgment determines the industry segment. A starting point in deciding on an industry segment is by *profit center.* A profit center is a component that sells mostly to outsiders for a profit.

When the profit center goes across industry lines, it should be broken down into smaller groups. A company in many industries not accumulating financial information on a segregated basis must disaggregate its operations by industry line.

Although worldwide industry segmentation is recommended, it may not be practical to gather. If foreign operations cannot be disaggregated, the firm should disaggregate domestic activities. Foreign operations should be disaggregated where possible, and the remaining foreign operations should be treated as a single segment.

What should you know about the 10 percent and 75 percent rules?

A segment that was significant in previous years, even though not meeting the 10 percent test in the current year, should still be reported on if the segment is expected to be significant in future years.

Segments should represent a substantial portion, meaning 75 percent or more, of the company's total revenue to outside customers. The 75 percent test is applied separately each year. However, in order to derive 75 percent, as a matter of practicality, not more than 10 segments should be shown. If more than 10 are identified, it is possible to combine similar segments.

Even though intersegment transfers are eliminated in the preparation of consolidated financial statements, they are included for segmental disclosure in determining the 10 percent and 75 percent rules.

In applying the 10 percent criterion, the CFO should note these issues:

- *Revenue.* A separation should exist between revenue to unaffiliated customers and revenue to other business segments. Transfer prices are used for intersegmental transfers. Accounting bases followed should be disclosed.
- *Operating profit or loss.* Operating earnings of a segment exclude general corporate revenue and expenses that are not allocable, interest expense (unless the segment is a financial type, such as one involved in banking), domestic and foreign income taxes, income from unconsolidated subsidiaries or investees, income from discontinued operations, extraordinary items, cumulative effect of a change in accounting principles, and minority interest. Traceable and allocable costs should be charged to segments.
- *Identifiable assets.* Assets of a segment include those directly in it and general corporate assets that can rationally be allocated to it. Allocation methods should be applied consistently. Identifiable assets include those consisting of a part of the company's investment in the segment (e.g., goodwill). Identifiable assets do not include advances or loans to other segments except for income therefrom that is used to compute the results of operations (e.g., a segment of a financial nature).

Example 8.2

A company provides the following data regarding its business segments and overall operations:

	Segment A	Segment B	Company[a]
Revenue	$2,000	$1,000	$12,000
Direct costs	500	300	5,000
Company-wide costs (allocable)			800
General company costs (not allocable)			1,700

[a] Excludes segment amounts.

Company-wide costs are allocable based on the ratios of direct costs. The tax rate is 34 percent.

The profits to be reported by segment and for the company as a whole are:

	Segment A	Segment B	Company
Revenues	$2,000	$1,000	$15,000
Less:			
Direct costs	(500)	(300)	(5,800)
Indirect costs (allocated)			
$800 × $500/$5,800	(69)		
$800 × $300/$5,800		(41)	
			(800)
Segment margin	$1,431	$ 659	
General company costs			(1,700)
Income before tax			$ 6,700
Income tax (34%)			2,278
Net income			$ 4,422

What should be disclosed?

Disclosures are not required for 90 percent enterprises (companies that derive 90 percent or more of their revenue, operating profit, and total assets from one segment). In effect, that segment is the business. The dominant industry segment should be identified.

Segmental disclosure includes:

- Allocation method for costs
- Capital expenditures
- Aggregate depreciation, depletion, and amortization expense
- Transfer price used
- Unusual items affecting segmental profit

- Company's equity in vertically integrated unconsolidated subsidiaries and equity method investees. (Note the geographic location of equity method investees.)
- Effect of an accounting principle change on the operating profit of the reportable segment. (Also include its effect on the company.)
- Material segmental accounting policies not already disclosed in the regular financial statements
- Type of products

What if consolidation is involved?

If a segment includes a purchase method consolidated subsidiary, segmental information is based on the consolidated value of the subsidiary (e.g., fair market value and goodwill recognized) and not on the book values recorded in the subsidiary's own financial statements.

Segmental information is not required for unconsolidated subsidiaries or other unconsolidated investees. Each subsidiary or investee is subject to the rules of ASC No. 280-10-05 that segment information be reported.

Some types of typical consolidation eliminations are not eliminated when reporting for segments. For example, revenue of a segment includes intersegmental sales and sales to unrelated customers.

A complete set of financial statements for a foreign investee that is not a subsidiary does not have to disclose segmental information when presented in the same financial report of a primary reporting entity except if the foreign investee's separately issued statements already disclose the required segmental data.

What other reporting requirements are there?

Segmental disclosure is also required when:

- 10 percent or more of revenue or assets is applicable to a foreign area. Presentation must be made of revenue, operating profit or loss, and assets for foreign operations in the aggregate or by geographic locality.
- 10 percent or more of sales is to one customer. A group of customers under common control is considered one customer.
- 10 percent or more of revenue is obtained from domestic government contracts or a foreign government.

In these cases, the source of the segmental revenue should be disclosed along with the percent derived.

The *restatement* of prior-period information may be required for comparative purposes. The nature and effect of restatement should be disclosed. Restatement is needed when financial statements of the company as a whole have been restated. Restatement is also needed when a change has occurred in grouping products or services for segment determination or in grouping foreign activities into geographic segments.

Segmental data are not required in financial statements that are presented in another company's financial report if those statements are:

- Combined in a complete set of statements and both sets are presented in the same report; or
- Presented for a foreign investee (not a subsidiary of the primary enterprise) unless the financial statements disclose segment information (e.g., those foreign investees for which such information is already required by the Securities and Exchange Commission).

If an investee uses the cost or equity method and is not exempted by one of the preceding provisions, its full set of financial statements presented in another enterprise's report must present segment information if such data are significant to statements of the primary enterprise. Significance is determined by applying the percentage tests (i.e., 10 percent tests) in relation to financial statements of the primary enterprise without adjustment for the investee's revenue, operating results, or identifiable assets.

PART THREE

Cost Management and IT Systems

CHAPTER NINE

Cost Management and Analysis

H OW DO FIRMS fare in the world market? Do global companies firms really measure the costs of products and services they offer accurately? Today American managers are finding themselves operating in a highly competitive global economy. Manufacturing and service industries are seeing their profits squeezed by the pinch of foreign price and quality competition. Costs are now of strategic significance in a more intensive way than ever before.

Firms that do know how to measure product costs accurately will find the going tough, whereas firms that fail to recognize and solve cost measurement problems and to analyze cost data are probably destined for extinction.

Today's CFOs bear the tremendous responsibility for analyzing cost data. They are the ones who ensure that their cost accounting systems produce accurate (not distorted) cost data for managerial uses for performance measurement and for strategic decisions on pricing, product mix, process technology, and product design. They must know how to analyze cost information for operational planning and control, how to be competitive in a global economy, and how to make informed decisions, both tactical and strategic.

 ## WHAT IS COST MANAGEMENT AND ANALYSIS?

Cost management and analysis involves obtaining accurate product-costing data and managing it to assist managers in making critical decisions regarding pricing, product mix, and process technology. It also involves measuring and analyzing cost data and translating them into information useful for managerial planning and control and for making short-term and long-term decisions. Activity-based costing (ABC), activity-based management (ABM), just-in-time costing, target costing, and balanced scorecard are a series of developments that enhance product-costing accuracy and cost management as well.

Cost management and analysis facilitates better decision making. Decision making, which can be described as problem solving, is largely a matter of choosing among alternative courses of action. The questions that arise from time to time are many and varied.

- Should the new product be introduced?
- Should one of the products or services in a line be dropped?
- Should a special order be accepted at below the normal selling price?
- Should parts now being manufactured be purchased?
- Should the present equipment be replaced?
- Should equipment be purchased or leased?
- Should production capacity be expanded?

A cost management system is used to support management's needs for better decisions about product design, pricing, marketing, and mix and to encourage continual operating improvements.

Quantitative methods can be used in various phases of cost analysis to determine costs and their financial effects, correlations, and the financial feasibility of adopting alternatives. These methods include learning curves, linear programming, inventory planning techniques, and program evaluation and review technique.

 ## STRATEGIC COST MANAGEMENT

Strategic cost management is concerned with managerial use of cost information for the purpose(s) of establishing organizational strategy (e.g., being globally competitive), employing the success methods to achieve the strategies, and evaluating the level of success in meeting the proclaimed strategies. Four specific principles of strategic cost management are listed next.

1. Managers must try to mold their costs to fit medium- and longer-term corporate objectives. Rather than taking existing costs as a baseline, companies need to shape the costs that they incur. The primary purpose of cost management is not merely to count costs, as has historically been the case, but to manage them in a proactive way.

2. Strategic cost management is an interdisciplinary and multifunctional activity, not something that can be safely left to corporate cost accountants alone. It should draw on the insights of engineers, production managers, design experts, distributors, financial specialists, and many others. It draws on wide expertise to identify and then act on those factors that can radically shift where and how costs are incurred.

3. It accords a new role and status to the business of cost calculation. Instead of the static, periodic, and company-wide accounting of the past, the need now is for specific and localized activity that is repeated time and time again as different options

are considered and evaluated. The role of cost calculation now is creative rather than reactive. Traditional cost accounting systems have proved to be distorted and too inflexible to provide the necessary responses to the rapid pace of changes in global competition.

4. While insights can generate significant changes in costs, in many cases, costs can best be managed by providing comparative and benchmarking information in both a routine and ad hoc way. What are competitors' prices and costs? What can be gauged of competitors' cost structures? Are they differentially sensitive to changes in volume or relative input prices? Where possible, every effort should be made to incorporate such information into regular patterns of reporting. Industry surveys, consultancy reports, and trade press analyses can assist in this regard. Otherwise companies should undertake detailed analyses of the likely cost breakdown of competitors' products or services, the anticipated cost consequences of new technologies and new methods of organization, and the cost implications of variations in product attributes and differential levels of service.

What is wrong with traditional cost systems?

Many companies use a traditional cost system such as job-order costing or process costing, or some hybrid of the two. This traditional system may provide distorted product cost information. In fact, companies selling multiple products are making critical decisions about product pricing, making bids, or product mix, based on inaccurate cost data. In all likelihood, the problem is not with assigning the costs of direct labor or direct materials. These prime costs are traceable to individual products, and most conventional cost systems are designed to ensure that this tracing takes place.

The assignment of overhead costs to individual products is another matter. Using the traditional methods of assigning overhead costs to products, using a single predetermined overhead rate based on any single activity measure, can produce distorted product costs.

 OVERHEAD COSTING

Single-Product Situation

The accuracy of overhead cost assignment becomes an issue only when multiple products are manufactured in a single facility. If only a single product is produced, all overhead costs are caused by it and traceable to it. The overhead cost per unit is simply the total overhead for the year divided by the number of hours or units produced.

The cost calculation for a single-product setting is illustrated in Exhibit 9.1. There is no question that the cost of manufacturing the product illustrated in Exhibit 9.1 is $28.00 per unit. All manufacturing costs were incurred specifically to make this product. Thus, one way to ensure product-costing accuracy is to focus on producing one

EXHIBIT 9.1 Unit Cost Computation: Single Product

	Manufacturing Costs	Units Produced	Unit Cost
Direct materials	$ 800,000	50,000	$16.00
Direct labor	200,000	50,000	4.00
Factory overhead	400,000	50,000	8.00
Total	$1,400,000	50,000	$28.00

product. For this reason, some multiple-product firms choose to dedicate entire plants to the manufacture of a single product.

By focusing on only one or two products, small manufacturers are able to calculate the cost of manufacturing the high-volume products more accurately and price them more effectively.

Multiple-Product Situation

In a multiple-product situation, manufacturing overhead costs are caused jointly by all products.

The problem becomes one of trying to identify the amount of overhead caused or consumed by each. This is accomplished by searching for *cost drivers*, or activity measures that cause costs to be incurred.

In a traditional setting, it is normally assumed that overhead consumption is highly correlated with the volume of production activity, measured in terms of direct labor hours, machine hours, or direct labor dollars. These volume-related cost drivers are

Example 9.1

To illustrate the limitation of this traditional approach, assume that Delta Manufacturing Company has a plant that produces two high-quality fertilizer products: Nitro-X and Nitro-Y. Product costing data are given in Exhibit 9.2. Because the quantity of Nitro-Y produced is five times greater than that of Nitro-X, Nitro-X can be labeled a low-volume product and Nitro-Y a high-volume product.

EXHIBIT 9.2 Product-Costing Data

	Nitro-X	Nitro-Y	Total
Units produced per year	10,000	50,000	60,000
Production runs	20	30	50
Inspection hours	800	1,200	2,000
Kilowatt-hours	5,000	25,000	30,000
Prime costs (direct materials and direct labor)	$50,000	$250,000	$300,000

(continued)

EXHIBIT 9.2 *(continued)*

Departmental Data	Department 1	Department 2	Total
Direct labor hours:			
Nitro-X	4,000	16,000	20,000
Nitro-Y	76,000	24,000	100,000
Total	80,000	40,000	120,000
Machine hours:			
Nitro-X	4,000	6,000	10,000
Nitro-Y	16,000	34,000	50,000
Total	20,000	40,000	60,000
Overhead costs:			
Setup costs	$ 48,000	$ 48,000	$ 96,000
Quality control	37,000	37,000	74,000
Power	14,000	70,000	84,000
Maintenance	13,000	65,000	78,000
Total	$112,000	$220,000	$332,000

For simplicity, only four types of factory overhead costs are assumed: setup, quality control, power, and maintenance. These overhead costs are allocated to the two production departments using the direct method.

Assume that the four service centers do not interact. Setup costs are allocated based on the number of production runs handled by each department. Quality control costs are allocated by the number of inspection hours used by each department. Power costs are allocated in proportion to the kilowatt-hours used. Maintenance costs are allocated in proportion to the machine hours used.

used to assign overhead to products. Volume-related cost drivers use either *plantwide* or *departmental* rates.

Plantwide Overhead Rate

A common method of assigning overhead to products is to compute a plantwide rate, using a volume-related cost driver. This approach assumes that all overhead cost variation can be explained by one cost driver. Assume that machine hours is the chosen driver.

Dividing the total overhead by the total machine hours yields the following overhead rate:

Plantwide rate = $332,000/60,000 = $5.53/machine hour

Using this rate and other information from Exhibit 9.2, we can calculate the unit cost for each product, as given in Exhibit 9.3.

EXHIBIT 9.3   Unit Cost Computation: Plantwide Rate

Nitro-X	
Prime costs	$ 50,000
Overhead costs: $5.53 × 10,000	55,300
	$105,300
Unit cost: $105,300/10,000 units	$10.53

Nitro-Y	
Prime costs	$250,000
Overhead costs: $5.53 × 50,000	276,500
	$526,500
Unit cost: $526,500/50,000 units	$ 10.53

Departmental Rates

Based on the distribution of labor hours and machine hours in Exhibit 9.2, Department 1 is labor intensive and Department 2 is machine oriented. Furthermore, the overhead costs of Department 1 are about one-half those of Department 2. Based on these observations, it is obvious that departmental overhead rates would reflect the consumption of overhead better than a plantwide rate. Product costs would be more accurate, using departmental rates rather than a plantwide rate.

This approach would yield these departmental rates, using direct labor hours for Department 1 and machine hours for Department 2:

$$\text{Department 1 rate} = \$112,000/80,000$$

$$= 1.40/\text{labor hour}$$

$$\text{Department 2 rate} = \$220,000/40,000$$

$$= \$5.50/\text{machine hour}$$

Using these rates and the data from Exhibit 9.2, the computation of the unit costs for each product is shown in Exhibit 9.4.

Plantwide Rate versus Departmental Rates

Using a single, plantwide overhead rate based on machine hours gave the same overhead application and cost per unit for Nitro-X and Nitro-Y, or $10.53. But this would not be an accurate measurement of the underlying relationship because Nitro-X made light use of overhead-incurring factors whereas Nitro-Y made heavy use of such services.

To summarize, when products are heterogeneous, receiving uneven attention and effort as they move through various departments, departmental rates are necessary to achieve more accurate product costs.

EXHIBIT 9.4   Unit Cost Computation: Department Rates

Nitro-X	
Prime costs	$50,000
Overhead costs	
Department 1: $1.40 × 4,000 = $5,600	
Department 2: $5.50 × 6,000 = 33,000	38,600
	$88,600
Unit cost: $88,600/10,000 units	$ 8.86

Nitro-Y	
Prime costs	$250,000
Overhead costs	
Department 1: $1.40 × 76,000 = $106,400	
Department 2: $5.50 × 34,000 = 187,000	293,400
	$543,400
Unit cost: $543,400/50,000 units	$ 10.87

Problems with Costing Accuracy

The accuracy of the overhead cost assignment can be challenged regardless of whether the plantwide or departmental rates are used. The main problem with either procedure is the assumption that machine hours or direct labor hours drive or cause all overhead costs.

From Exhibit 9.2, we know that Nitro-Y—with five times the volume of Nitro-X—uses five times the machine hours and direct labor hours. Thus, if a plantwide rate is used, Nitro-Y will receive five times more overhead costs. But does it make sense? Is all overhead driven by volume? Use of a single driver—especially a volume-related one—is not proper.

Examination of the data in Exhibit 9.2 suggests that a significant portion of overhead costs is not driven or caused by volume. For example, setup costs are probably related to the number of setups and quality control costs to the number of hours of inspection.

Notice that Nitro-Y only has 1.5 times as many setups as the Nitro-X (30/20) and only 1.5 times as many inspection hours (1,200/800). Use of a volume-related cost driver (machine hours or labor hours) and a plantwide rate assigns five times more overhead to the Nitro-Y than to Nitro-X. For quality control and setup costs, then, Nitro-Y is overcosted and Nitro-X is undercosted.

The problems worsened when departmental rates were used. Nitro-Y consumes 19 times as many direct labor hours (76,000/4,000) as Nitro-X and 5.7 times as many machine hours (34,000/6,000). Thus, Nitro-Y receives 19 times more overhead from Department 1 and 5.7 times more overhead from Department 2.

As Exhibit 9.4 shows, with departmental rates, the unit cost of Nitro-X decreases to $8.86 and the unit cost of Nitro-Y increases to $10.87. This change emphasizes the failure of volume-based cost drivers to reflect accurately each product's consumption of setup and quality control costs.

Why do volume-related cost drivers fail?

At least two major factors impair the ability of a volume-related cost driver to assign overhead costs accurately: (1) the proportion of non–volume-related overhead costs to total overhead costs and (2) the degree of product diversity.

Non–Volume-Related Overhead Costs

In our example, there are four overhead activities: quality control, setup, maintenance, and power. Two of them, maintenance and power, are volume related. Quality control and setup are less dependent on volume. As a result, volume-based cost drivers cannot assign these costs accurately to products.

Using volume-based cost drivers to assign non–volume-related overhead costs creates distorted product costs. The severity of this distortion depends on what proportion of total overhead costs these non–volume-related costs represent. For our example, setup costs and quality control costs represent a substantial share—51 percent—of total overhead ($170,000/$332,000). This suggests that some care should be exercised in assigning these costs. If non–volume-related overhead costs are only a small percentage of total overhead costs, the distortion of product costs will be quite small. In such a case, the use of volume-based cost drivers may be acceptable.

Product Diversity

When products consume overhead activities in different proportions, a firm has product diversity.

To illustrate, the proportion of all overhead activities consumed by both Nitro-X and Nitro-Y is computed and displayed in Exhibit 9.5. The proportion of each activity consumed by a product is defined as the consumption ratio. As you can see from the

EXHIBIT 9.5 Product Diversity: Proportion of Consumption

Overhead Activity	Mix[a]	Nitro-X	Nitro-Y	Consumption Measure
Setup	(1)	0.40	0.60	Production runs
Quality control	(2)	0.40	0.60	Inspection hours
Power	(3)	0.17	0.83	Kilowatt-hours
Maintenance	(4)	0.17	0.83	Machine hours

[a] (1) 20/50 (Nitro-X) and 30/50 (Nitro-Y).
(2) 800/2,000 (Nitro-X) and 1,200/2,000 (Nitro-Y).
(3) 5,000/30,000 (Nitro-X) and 25,000/30,000 (Nitro-Y).
(4) 10,000/60,000 (Nitro-X) and 50,000/60,000 (Nitro-Y).

exhibit, the consumption ratios for these two products differ from the non–volume-related categories to the volume-related costs.

Since the non–volume-related overhead costs are a significant proportion of total overhead and their consumption ratio differs from that of the volume-based cost driver, product costs can be distorted if a volume-based cost driver is used. The solution to this costing problem is to use an ABC approach.

 ACTIVITY-BASED COSTING

How does activity-based product costing correct the situation?

An ABC system is one that traces costs first to activities and then to products. Traditional product costing also involves two stages, but in the first stage costs are traced to departments, not to activities. In both traditional and activity-based costing, the second stage consists of tracing costs to the product. The principal difference between the two methods is the number of cost drivers used. ABC uses a much larger number of cost drivers than the one or two volume-based cost drivers typical in a conventional system. In fact, the approach separates overhead costs into overhead cost pools, where each cost pool is associated with a different cost driver. Then a predetermined overhead rate is computed for each cost pool and each cost driver. Consequently, this method has enhanced accuracy.

First-Stage Procedure

In the first stage of ABC, overhead costs are divided into homogeneous cost pools. A *homogeneous cost pool* is a collection of overhead costs for which cost variations can be explained by a single cost driver. Overhead activities are homogeneous whenever they have the same consumption ratios for all products.

Once a cost pool is defined, the cost per unit of the cost driver is computed for that pool. This is referred to as the *pool rate*. Computation of the pool rate completes the first stage. Thus, the first stage produces two outcomes: (1) a set of homogeneous cost pools and (2) a pool rate.

For example, in Exhibit 9.5, quality control costs and setup costs can be combined into one homogeneous cost pool, and maintenance and power costs can be combined into a second. For the first cost pool, the number of production runs or inspection hours could be the cost driver. Since the two cost drivers are perfectly correlated, they will assign the same amount of overhead to both products. For the second pool, machine hours or kilowatt-hours could be selected as the cost driver.

Assume for the purpose of illustration that the number of production runs and machine hours are the cost drivers chosen. Using data from Exhibit 9.2, the first-stage outcomes are illustrated in Exhibit 9.6.

Second-Stage Procedure

In the second stage, the costs of each overhead pool are traced to products. This is done using the pool rate computed in the first stage and the measure of the amount of

EXHIBIT 9.6   Activity-Based Costing: First-Stage Procedure

Pool 1	
Setup costs	$ 96,000
Quality control costs	74,000
Total costs	$170,000
Production runs	50
Pool rate (cost per run): $170,000/50	$ 3,400
Pool 2	
Power cost	$ 84,000
Maintenance	78,000
Total costs	$162,000
Machine hours	60,000
Pool rate (cost per machine hour): $162,000/60,000	$ 2.70

resources consumed by each product. This measure is simply the quantity of the cost driver used by each product. In our example, that would be the number of production runs and machine hours used by each product. Thus, the overhead assigned from each cost pool to each product is computed as:

$$\text{Applied overhead} = \text{Pool rate} \times \text{Cost driver units used}$$

To illustrate, consider the assignment of costs from the first overhead pool to Nitro-X. From Exhibit 9.6, the rate for this pool is $3,400 per production run. From Exhibit 9.2, Nitro-X uses 20 production runs. Thus, the overhead assigned from the first cost pool is $68,000 ($3,400 × 20 runs). Similar assignments would be made for the other cost pool and for the other product (for both cost pools).

The total overhead cost per unit of product is obtained by first tracing the overhead costs from the pools to the individual products. This total is then divided by the number of units produced. The result is the unit overhead cost. Adding the per-unit overhead cost to the per-unit prime cost yields the manufacturing cost per unit. In Exhibit 9.7, the manufacturing cost per unit is computed using ABC.

Comparison of Product Costs

In Exhibit 9.8, the unit cost from ABC is compared with the unit costs produced by conventional costing using either a plantwide or departmental rate. This comparison clearly illustrates the effects of using only volume-based cost drivers to assign overhead costs. The activity-based cost reflects the correct pattern of overhead consumption and is, therefore, the most accurate of the three costs shown in the exhibit.

ABC reveals that the conventional method undercosts the Nitro-X significantly—by at least 37.7% = ($14.50 − 10.53)/$10.53)—and overcosts the Nitro-Y by at least 8.1% = ($10.53 − $9.74)/$9.74.

EXHIBIT 9.7 Activity-Based Costing: Second-Stage Procedure

Nitro-X		
Overhead		
Pool 1: $3,400 × 20	$68,000	
Pool 2: $2.70 × 10,000	27,000	
Total overhead costs		$ 95,000
Prime costs		50,000
Total manufacturing costs		$145,000
Units produced		10,000
Unit cost		$ 14.50

Nitro-Y		
Overhead		
Pool 1: $3,400 × 30	$102,000	
Pool 2: $2.70 × 50,000	135,000	
Total overhead costs		$237,000
Prime costs		$250,000
Total manufacturing costs		$487,000
Units produced		50,000
Unit cost		$ 9.74

Which cost drivers should be used?

At least two major factors should be considered in selecting cost drivers: the cost of measurement and the degree of correlation between the cost driver and the actual consumption of overhead.

Cost of Measurement

In an ABC system, a large number of cost drivers can be selected and used. However, it is preferable to select cost drivers that use information that is readily available. Information that is not available in the existing system must be produced, which will increase the cost of the firm's information system. A homogeneous cost pool could offer a number

EXHIBIT 9.8 Comparison of Unit Costs

	Nitro-X	Nitro-Y	Source
Conventional			
Plantwide rate	10.53	10.53	Exhibit 9.3
Department rates	8.86	10.87	Exhibit 9.4
Activity-based cost	$14.50	$9.74	Exhibit 9.5

> **Note**
>
> Using only volume-based cost drivers can lead to one product subsidizing another. This subsidy could create the appearance that one group of products is highly profitable and could adversely impact the pricing and competitiveness of another group of products. In a highly competitive environment, accurate cost information is critical to sound planning and decision making. ■

of possible cost drivers. For this situation, any cost driver that can be used with existing information should be chosen. This choice minimizes the costs of measurement.

In our example, for instance, quality control costs and setup costs were placed in the same cost pool, giving the choice of using either inspection hours or number of production runs as the cost driver. If the quantities of both cost drivers used by the two products are already being produced by the company's information system, then which is chosen is unimportant. Assume, however, that inspection hours by product are not tracked but data for production runs are available. In this case, production runs should be chosen as the cost driver, avoiding the need to produce any additional information.

Indirect Measures and the Degree of Correlation

The existing information structure can be exploited in another way to minimize the costs of obtaining cost driver quantities. It is sometimes possible to replace a cost driver that directly measures the consumption of an activity with a cost driver that indirectly measures that consumption. For example, inspection hours could be replaced by the actual number of inspections associated with each product; this number is more likely to be known. This replacement works, of course, only if hours used per inspection are reasonably stable for each product. Linear regressions can be utilized to determine the degree of correlation. A list of potential cost drivers is given in Exhibit 9.9.

EXHIBIT 9.9 Potential Cost Drivers

Manufacturing	
Number of setups	Direct labor hours
Weight of material	Number of vendors
Number of units reworked	Machine hours
Number of orders placed	Number of labor transactions
Number of orders received	Number of units scrapped
Number of inspections	Number of parts
Number of material handling operations	Square footage
Nonmanufacturing	
Number of hospital beds occupied	Number of rooms occupied in a hotel
Number of takeoffs and landings for an airline	

Cost drivers that indirectly measure the consumption of an activity usually measure the number of transactions associated with that activity. It is possible to replace a cost driver that directly measures consumption with one that only indirectly measures it without loss of accuracy, provided that the quantities of activity consumed per transaction are stable for each product. In such a case, the indirect cost driver has a high correlation and can be used.

Example 9.2

To further illustrate the limitation of this traditional approach, assume that OC Metals, Inc. has established the overhead cost pools and cost drivers for their product as shown in Exhibit 9.10.

EXHIBIT 9.10 Overhead Cost Pools and Cost Drivers for OC Metals

Overhead Cost Pool	Budgeted Overhead Cost	Cost Driver	Predicted Level for Cost Driver	Predetermined Overhead Rate
Machine setups	$100,000	Number of setups	100	$1,000 per setup
Material handling	100,000	Weight of raw material	50,000 pounds	$2 per pound
Waste control	50,000	Weight of hazardous chemicals used	10,000 pounds	$5 per pound
Inspection	75,000	Number of inspections	1,000	$75 per inspection
Other overhead costs	$200,000	Machine hours	20,000	$10 per machine hour
	$525,000			

Job No. 3941 consists of 2,000 special-purpose machine tools with the following requirements:

Machine setups:	2 setups
Raw material required:	10,000 pounds
Waste materials required:	2,000 pounds
Inspections:	10 inspections
Machine hours:	500 machine hours

The overhead assigned to Job No. 3941 is computed in Exhibit 9.11.

(continued)

EXHIBIT 9.11 Overhead Computation

Overhead Cost Pool	Predetermined Overhead Rate	Level of Cost Driver	Assigned Overhead Cost
Machine setups	$1,000 per setup	2 setups	$ 2,000
Material handling	$2 per pound	10,000 pounds	20,000
Waste control	$5 per pound	2,000 pounds	10,000
Inspection	$75 per inspection	10 inspections	750
Other overhead costs	$10 per machine hour	500 machine hours	5,000
Total			$37,750

The total overhead cost assigned to Job No. 3941 is $37,750, or $18.88 ($37,750/2,000) per tool. Compare this with the overhead cost that is assigned to the job if the firm uses a single predetermined overhead rate based on machine hours:

Total budgeted overhead cost/Total predicted machine hours

$$= \$525,000/20,000$$
$$= \$26.25 \text{ per machine hour}$$

Under this approach, the total overhead cost assigned to Job No. 3941 is $13,125 ($26.25 per machine hour × 500 machine hours). This is only $6.56 ($13,125/2,000) per tool, which is about one-third of the overhead cost per tool computed when multiple cost drivers are used.

The reason for this wide discrepancy is that these special-purpose tools require a relatively large number of machine setups, a sizable amount of waste materials, and several inspections. Thus, they are relatively costly in terms of driving overhead costs. Use of a single predetermined overhead rate obscures that fact.

Inaccurately calculating the overhead cost per unit to the extent illustrated can have serious adverse consequences for the firm. For example, it can lead to poor decisions about pricing, product mix, or contract bidding.

Note

CFOs need to weigh such considerations carefully in designing a product-costing system. A costing system using multiple cost drivers is more expensive to implement and use, but it may save millions through improved decisions. ■

 ### ACTIVITY-BASED MANAGEMENT

ABM is one of the most important ways to be competitive. It is a systemwide, integrated approach that focuses management's attention on activities with the goal of improving customer value, reducing costs, and increasing the resulting profit. The basic premise of ABM is: *Products consume activities; activities consume resources.* To be competitive, you must know both (1) the activities that go into manufacturing the products or providing the services and (2) the cost of those activities. To cut down a product's costs, you will likely have to change the activities the product consumes. An attitude such as "I want across-the-board cuts—everyone reduce cost by 10 percent" rarely obtains the desired results.

In order to achieve desired cost reductions, you must first identify the activities that a product or service consumes. Then you must figure out how to rework those activities to improve productivity and efficiency. *Process value analysis* is used to try to determine why activities are performed and how well they are performed. ABC, discussed in this chapter, is a tool used in activity-based management.

What is process value analysis?

Process value analysis is the process of identifying, describing, and evaluating the activities a company performs. It produces these four outcomes:

1. What activities are done
2. How many people perform the activities
3. The time and resources required to perform the activities
4. An assessment of the value of the activities to the company, including a recommendation to select and keep only those that add value

What causes costs?

Effective cost control requires managers to understand how producing a product requires activities and how activities, in turn, generate costs. Consider the activities of a manufacturer facing a financial crisis. In a system of managing by the members, each department is told to reduce costs in an amount equal to its share of the budget cut. The usual response by department heads is to reduce the number of people and supplies, as these are the only cost items that they can control in the short run. Asking everyone to work harder produces only temporary gains, however, as the pace cannot be sustained in the long run.

Under ABM, the manufacturer reduces costs by studying what activities it conducts and develops plans to eliminate non–value-added activities and to improve the efficiency of value-added activities. Eliminating activities that do not create customer value is a very effective way to cut costs. For example, spending $100 to train all employees to avoid common mistakes will repay itself many times over by reducing customer ill will caused by those mistakes.

How do you differentiate between value-added and non–value-added activities?

A *value-added activity* is an activity that increases the product's service to the customer. For instance, purchasing the raw materials to make a product is a value-added activity. Without the purchase of raw materials, the organization would be unable to make the product. Sanding and varnishing a wooden chair are value-added activities because customers do not want splinters. Value-added activities are evaluated by how they contribute to the final product's service, quality, and cost.

Good management involves finding and, if possible, eliminating non–value-added activities. *Non–value-added activities* are activities that, when eliminated, reduce costs without reducing the product's potential to the customer. In many organizations, poor facility layout may require the work in process to be moved around or temporarily stored during production. For example, a Midwest steel company that we studied had more than 100 miles of railroad track to move things back and forth in a poorly designed facility. Moving work around a factory, an office, or a store is unlikely to add value for the customer. Waiting, inspecting, and storing are other examples of non–value-added activities.

Organizations must change the process that makes non–value-added activities necessary. Elimination of non–value-added activities requires organizations to improve the process so that the activities are no longer required. Organizations strive to reduce or eliminate non–value-added activities because, by doing so, they permanently reduce the costs they must incur to produce goods or services without affecting the value to the customer.

Although managers should pay particular attention to non–value-added activities, they should also carefully evaluate the need for value-added activities. For example, in wine production, classifying storage as a value-added activity assumes the only way to make good-tasting wine is to allow it to age in storage. Think of the advantage that someone could have if she discovered a way to produce wine that tasted as good as conventionally aged wine but did not require long storage periods.

Activity Drivers and Categories

Activity output is measured by activity drivers. An activity driver is a factor (activity) that causes (drives) costs. We can simply identify activity output measures by classifying activities into four general categories: (1) unit level, (2) batch level, (3) product level, and (4) facility level. Classifying activities into these general categories is useful because the costs of activities associated with the different levels respond to different types of activity drivers. Exhibit 9.12 describes what they perform, examples, output measures, and examples of possible cost drivers.

What is the value chain of the business functions?

The value chain concept of the business functions is used to demonstrate how to use cost management to add value to organizations (see Exhibit 9.13). The value chain describes the linked set of activities that increase the usefulness (or value) of the products or services of an organization (value-added activities). Activities are evaluated by how they contribute to the final product's service, quality, and cost. In general, the business functions include the following:

- *Research and development*: The generation and development of ideas related to new products, services, or processes
- *Design*: The detailed planning and engineering of products, services, or processes
- *Production*: The aggregation and assembly of resources to produce a product or deliver a service

EXHIBIT 9.12 Activity Categories and Drivers

	Unit-Level Activities	Batch-Level Activities	Product-Level (Product- and Customer-Sustaining) Activities	Facility-Level (Capacity-Sustaining) Activities
Activities:	Performed each time a unit is produced	Performed each time a batch is produced	Performed as needed to support a product	Sustain a factory's general manufacturing process
Examples:	Direct materials, direct labor, assembly, energy to run machines	Quality inspections, machine setups, production scheduling, material handling	Engineering changes, maintenance of equipment, customer records and files, marketing the product	Plant management, plant security, landscaping, maintaining grounds, heating and lighting, property taxes, rent, plant depreciation
Output measures:	Unit-level drivers	Batch-level drivers	Product-level drivers	Difficult to define
Examples:	Units of product, direct labor hours, machine hours	Number of batches, number of production orders, inspection hours	Number of products, number of changing orders	Plant size (square feet), number of security personnel

- *Marketing*: The process that (a) informs potential customers about the attributes of products or services and (b) leads to the purchase of those products or services
- *Distribution*: The mechanism established to deliver products or services to customers
- *Customer service*: The product or service support activities provided to customers

A strategy and administration function spans all the business activities described. Human resource management, tax planning, legal matters, and the like, for example, potentially affect every step of the value chain. Cost management is a major means of helping managers to run each of the business functions and coordinate their activities within the framework of the entire organization.

Strategic Cost Analysis

Companies can identify strategic advantages in the marketplace by analyzing the value chain and the information about the costs of activities. A company that eliminates non–value-added activities reduces costs without reducing the value of the product to customers. With reduced costs, the company can reduce the price it charges customers, thus giving the company a cost advantage over its competitors. Or the company can use the resources saved from eliminating non–value-added activities to provide greater service to customers. *Strategic cost analysis* is the use of cost data to develop and identify

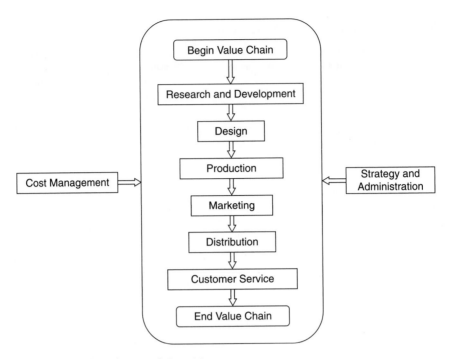

EXHIBIT 9.13 Value Chain and Cost Management

superior strategies that will produce a sustainable competitive advantage. The idea here is simple. Look for activities that are not on the value chain. If the company can safely eliminate non–value-added activities, then it should do so. By identifying and cutting them, you will save the company money and make it more competitive.

Global Strategies

Another approach to gaining a cost advantage is to identify where on the value chain your company has a strategic advantage. Many IT companies, for example, are looking at foreign markets as a way to capitalize on their investment in research and development. The reservoir of intellectual capital gives these firms an advantage over local competitors that have not yet developed this expertise. These competitors would face research and development costs already incurred by established companies, making it difficult for the newcomers to charge competitive prices and still make a profit.

TARGET COSTING AND PRICING

What is the role of target costing? How does it differ from cost-plus pricing?

A firm may determine that market conditions require that a product sell at a given target price. Hence, target cost can be determined by subtracting the desired unit profit margin from the target price. Thus, target costing becomes a particularly useful tool

EXHIBIT 9.14   Cost-Plus Pricing versus Target Costing

	Formula	Implications
Cost-plus pricing	Cost base + markup = selling price	Cost is the base (given). Markup is added (given). The firm puts the product on the market and hopes the selling price is accepted.
Pricing based on target costing	Target selling price − Desired profit = Target cost	Markets determine prices (given). Desired profit must be sustained for survival (given). Target cost is the residual, the variable to be managed.

for establishing cost-reduction goals. Toyota, for example, calculates the lifetime target profit for a new car model by multiplying a target profit ratio times the target sales. It then calculates the estimated profit by subtracting the estimated costs from target sales. Usually, at this point, target profit is greater than estimated profit. The cost-reduction goal is defined by the difference between the target profit and the estimated profit. Toyota then searches for cost-reduction opportunities through better design of the new model. Toyota's management recognizes that more opportunities exist for cost reduction during product planning than in actual development and production.

The Japanese developed target costing to enhance their ability to compete in the global marketplace. This approach to product pricing differs significantly from the cost-based methods just described. Instead of first determining the cost of a product or service and then adding a profit factor to arrive at its price, target costing reverses the procedure. Target costing is a pricing method that involves identifying the price at which a product will be competitive in the marketplace, defining the desired profit to be made on the product, and computing the target cost for the product by subtracting the desired profit from the competitive market price. The formula is

$$\text{Target price} - \text{Desired profit} = \text{Target cost}$$

Target cost is then given to the engineers and product designers, who use it as the maximum cost to be incurred for the materials and other resources needed to design and manufacture the product. It is their responsibility to create the product at or below its target cost.

Exhibit 9.14 compares the cost-plus philosophy with the target costing philosophy.

Example 9.3

A salesperson at Daeji Products Company has reported that a customer is seeking price quotations for two electronic components: a special-purpose battery charger (Product X101) and a small transistorized machine computer (Product Y101). Competing for the customer's order are one French company and two Japanese companies. The current market price ranges for the two products are:

(continued)

Product X101: $310 to $370 per unit

Product Y101: $720 to $820 per unit

    The salesperson feels that if Daeji could quote prices of $325 for Product X101 and $700 for Product Y101, the company would get the order and gain a significant share of the global market for those goods. Daeji's usual profit markup is 25 percent of total unit cost. The company's design engineers and cost accountants put together the following specifications and costs for the new products:

Activity-Based Cost Rates:		
Materials-handling activity	$1.30 per dollar of raw materials and purchased parts cost	
Production activity	$3.50 per machine hour	
Product delivery activity	$24.00 per unit of X101	
	$30.00 per unit of Y101	

	Product X101	Product Y101
Projected unit demand	26,000	18,000
Per unit data:		
Raw materials cost	$30.00	$65.00
Purchased parts cost	$15.00	$45.00
Manufacturing labor		
Hours	2.6	4.8
Hourly labor rate	$12.00	$15.00
Assembly labor		
Hours	3.4	8.2
Hourly labor rate	$14.00	$16.00
Machine hours	12.8	12.4

    The company wants to address three questions:

1. What is the target cost for each product?
2. What is the projected total unit cost of production and delivery?
3. Using the target costing approach, should the company produce the products?
    1. Target cost for each product:

$$\text{Product X101} = \$325.00/1.25 = \$260.00*$$
$$\text{Product Y101} = \$700.00/1.25 = \$560.00$$

*Target price – Desired profit = Target cost (x).
    $\$325.00 - 0.25x = x$
        $\$325.00 = 1.25x$
            $x = \$325.00/1.25 = \$260$

    2. Projected total unit cost of production and delivery:

	Product X101	Product Y101
Raw materials cost	$30.00	$65.00
Purchased parts cost	15.00	45.00

	Product X101	Product Y101
Total cost of raw materials and parts	$45.00	$110.00
Manufacturing labor		
X101 (2.6 hours × 12.00)	31.20	
Y101 (4.8 hours × 15.00)		72.00
Assembly labor		
X101 (3.4 hours × 14.00)	47.60	
Y101 (8.2 hours × 16.00)		131.20
Activity-based costs		
Materials-handling activity		
X101 ($45.00 × $1.30)	58.500	
Y101 ($110.00 × $1.30)		143.00
Production activity		
X101 (12.8 machine hours × $3.50)	44.80	
Y101 (28.4 machine hours × $3.50)		99.40
Product delivery activity		
X101	24.00	
Y101		30.00
Projected total unit cost	$251.10	$585.60
3. Production decision		

	Product X101	Product Y101
Target unit cost	$260.00	$560.00
Less: projected unit cost	251.10	585.60
Difference	$ 8.90	($25.60)

Since product X101 can be produced below its target cost, it should be produced. As currently designed, Product Y101 cannot be produced at or below its target cost; either it needs to be redesigned, or the company should drop plans to make it.

CHAPTER TEN

Cost-Volume-Profit Analysis and Leverage

 COST-VOLUME-PROFIT ANALYSIS

Cost-volume-profit (CVP) analysis, together with cost behavior information, helps CFOs perform many useful analyses. CVP analysis deals with how profit and costs change with a change in volume. More specifically, it looks at the effects that changes in such factors as variable costs, fixed costs, selling prices, volume, and mix of products sold have on profits. By studying the relationships of costs, sales, and net income, the CFO is better able to cope with many planning decisions.

Break-even analysis, a branch of CVP analysis, determines the break-even sales. The break-even point—the financial crossover point at which revenues exactly match costs—does not show up in corporate earnings reports, but CFOs find it an extremely useful measurement in a variety of ways.

How can you use CVP analysis in solving business problems?

CVP analysis tries to answer these questions:

- What sales volume is required to break even?
- What sales volume is necessary to earn a desired profit?
- What profit can be expected on a given sales volume?
- How would changes in selling price, variable costs, fixed costs, and output affect profits?
- How would a change in the mix of products sold affect the break-even and target income volume and profit potential?

What does "contribution margin" mean?

For accurate CVP analysis, variable costs must be distinguished from fixed costs. Mixed costs must be separated into their variable and fixed components.

In order to compute the break-even point and perform various CVP analyses, note these important concepts.

- *Contribution margin (CM).* The contribution margin is the excess of sales (S) over the variable costs (VC) of the product or service. It is the amount of money available to cover fixed costs (FC) and to generate profit. Symbolically, $CM = S - VC$.
- *Unit CM.* The unit CM is the excess of the unit selling price (p) over the unit variable cost (v). Symbolically, unit $CM = p - v$.
- *CM ratio.* The CM ratio is the contribution margin as a percentage of sales, that is,

$$\text{CM ratio} = \frac{CM}{S} = \frac{S - VC}{S} = 1 - \frac{VC}{S}$$

The CM ratio can also be computed using per unit data as follows:

$$\text{CM ratio} = \frac{\text{Unit CM}}{p} = \frac{p - v}{p} = 1 - \frac{v}{p}$$

Note that the CM ratio is 1 minus the variable cost ratio. For example, if variable costs account for 70 percent of the price, the CM ratio is 30 percent.

Example 10.1

To illustrate the various concepts of CM, consider these data for Delta Toy Store:

	Total	Per Unit	Percentage
Sales (1,500 units)	$37,500	$25	100%
Less: Variable costs	15,000	10	40
Contribution margin	$22,500	$15	60%
Less: Fixed costs	15,000		
Net income	$ 7,500		

From the data listed, CM, unit CM, and the CM ratio are computed as:

$$CM = S - VC = \$37,500 - \$15,000 = \$22,500$$

$$\text{Unit CM} = p - v = \$25 - \$10 = \$15$$

$$\text{CM ratio} = \frac{CM}{S} = \frac{\$22,000}{\$37,500} = 0.6 - \frac{v}{p}$$

$$\frac{\text{Unit CM}}{p} = \frac{\$15}{\$25} = 0.6 = 60\%$$

How can the break-even sales be computed?

The break-even point represents the level of sales revenue that equals the total of the variable and fixed costs for a given volume of output at a particular capacity use rate. For example, you might want to ask the break-even occupancy rate (or vacancy rate) for a hotel or the break-even load rate for an airliner.

Generally, the lower the break-even point, the higher the profit and the less the operating risk, other things being equal. The break-even point also provides CFOs with insights into profit planning. It can be computed using these formulas:

$$\text{Break-even point in units} = \text{Fixed costs/Unit CM}$$

$$\text{Break-even point in dollars} = \text{Fixed costs/CM ratio}$$

Example 10.2

Using the same data given in Example 10.1, where unit CM = $25 – $10 = $15 and CM ratio = 60%, we get:

$$\text{Break-even point in units} = \$15,000/\$15 = 1,000 \text{ units}$$

$$\text{Break-even point in dollars} = \$15,000/0.6 = \$25,000$$

or, alternatively,

$$1,000 \text{ units} \times \$25 = \$25,000$$

How do you determine target income volume?

Besides determining the break-even point, CVP analysis determines the sales required to attain a target net income. The formula is:

$$\text{Target income sales volume} = \frac{\text{Fixed costs plus target income}}{\text{Unit CM}}$$

Example 10.3

Using the same data given in Example 10.1, assume that Delta Toy Store wishes to attain a target income of $15,000 before tax. Then the target income volume would be:

$$\frac{\$15,000 + \$15,000}{\$25 - 10} = \frac{\$30,000}{\$15} = 2,000$$

What is the impact of income taxes on target income volume?

If target income is given on an after-tax basis, the target income volume formula becomes:

$$\text{Target income volume} = \frac{\text{Fixed costs} + \dfrac{(\text{Target after-tax income})}{1 - \text{Tax rate}}}{\text{Unit CM}}$$

Example 10.4

Assume in Example 10.1 that Delta Toy Store wants to achieve an after-tax income of $6,000. The tax rate is 40 percent. Then:

$$\text{Target income volume} = \frac{\$15,000 + \dfrac{\$6,000}{1 - 0.4}}{\$15} = \frac{\$15,000 + \$10,000}{\$15}$$

$$= 1.667 \text{ units}$$

What is the cash break-even point?

If a company has a minimum of available cash or the opportunity cost of holding excess cash is too high, management may want to know the volume of sales that will cover all cash expenses during a period. This is known as the *cash break-even point*. Not all fixed operating costs involve cash payments. For example, depreciation expenses are noncash fixed charges. To find the cash break-even point, the noncash charges must be subtracted from fixed costs. Therefore, the cash break-even point is lower than the usual break-even point. The formula is:

$$\text{Cash break-even point} = \frac{\text{Fixed costs} - \text{Depreciation}}{\text{Unit CM}}$$

Example 10.5

Assume from Example 10.1 that the total fixed costs of $15,000 include depreciation of $1,500. Then the cash break-even point is:

$$\frac{\$15,000 - \$1,500}{\$25 - 10} = \frac{\$13,500}{\$15} = 900 \text{ units}$$

Delta Toy Store has to sell 900 units to cover only the fixed costs involving cash payments of $13,500 and to break even.

What is the use of margin of safety?

The *margin of safety* is a measure of difference between the actual sales and the break-even sales. It is the amount by which sales revenue may drop before losses begin, and it is expressed as a percentage of expected sales:

$$\text{Margin of safety} = \frac{\text{Expected sales} - \text{Break-even sales}}{\text{Expected sales}}$$

The margin of safety is used as a measure of operating risk. The larger the ratio, the safer the situation since there is less risk of reaching the break-even point.

Example 10.6

Assume Delta Toy Store projects sales of $35,000 with a break-even sales level of $25,000. The projected margin of safety is

$$\frac{\$35,000 - \$25,000}{\$35,000} = 28.57\%$$

 WHAT-IF ANALYSIS

The concepts of contribution margin and the contribution income statement have many applications in profit planning and short-term decision making. Many what-if scenarios can be evaluated using them as planning tools, especially utilizing a spreadsheet program such as Excel. Some applications are illustrated in Examples 10.7 to 10.11 using the same data as in Example 10.1.

Example 10.7

Recall from Example 10.1 that Delta Toy Store has a CM of 60 percent and fixed costs of $15,000 per period. Assume that the company expects sales to go up by $10,000 for the next period. How much will income increase?

Using the CM concepts, we can quickly compute the impact of a change in sales on profits. The formula for computing the impact is:

Change in net income = Dollar change in sales × CM ratio

Thus,

Increase in net income = $10,000 × 60% = $6,000

Therefore, the income will go up by $6,000, assuming there is no change in fixed costs.

If we are given a change in unit sales instead of dollars, then the formula becomes:

Change in net income = Change in unit sales × Unit CM

Example 10.8

Assume that the store expects sales to go up by 400 units. How much will income increase? From Example 10.1, the company's unit CM is $15. Again, assuming there is no change in fixed costs, the income will increase by $6,000.

$$400 \text{ units} \times \$15 = \$6,000$$

Example 10.9

What net income is expected on sales of $47,500?
   The answer is the difference between the CM and the fixed costs:

CM: $47,500 × 60%	$28,500
Less: Fixed costs	15,000
Net income	$13,500

Example 10.10

Delta Toy Store is considering increasing the advertising budget by $5,000, which would increase sales revenue by $8,000. Should the advertising budget be increased?
   The answer is no, since the increase in the CM is less than the increased cost:

Increase in CM: $8,000 × 60%	$4,800
Increase in advertising	5,000
Decrease in net income	$ (200)

Example 10.11

Consider the original data. Assume again that Delta Toy Store is currently selling 1,500 units per period. In an effort to increase sales, management is considering cutting its unit price by $5 and increasing the advertising budget by $1,000.
   If these two steps are taken, management feels that unit sales will go up by 60 percent. Should the two steps be taken?
   A $5 reduction in the selling price will cause the unit CM to decrease from $15 to $10. Thus,

Proposed CM: 2,400 units × $10	$24,000
Present CM: 1,500 units × $15	22,500
Increase in CM	$1,500
Increase in advertising outlay	1,000
Increase in net income	$500

The answer, therefore, is yes.

SALES-MIX ANALYSIS

Break-even and CVP analysis require some additional computations and assumptions when a company produces and sells more than one product. In multiproduct firms, sales mix is an important factor in calculating an overall company break-even point.

Different selling prices and different variable costs result in different unit CM and CM ratios. As a result, the break-even points and CVP relationships vary with the relative proportions of the products sold, called the *sales mix*.

In break-even and CVP analysis, it is necessary to predetermine the sales mix and then compute a weighted average unit CM. It is also necessary to assume that the sales mix does not change for a specified period. The break-even formula for the company as a whole is:

$$\text{Break-even sales in units (or in dollars)} = \frac{\text{Fixed costs}}{\text{Weighted average unit CM (or CM ratio)}}$$

Example 10.12

Assume that Knibex, Inc. produces cutlery sets of high-quality wood and steel. The company makes a deluxe cutlery set and a standard set that have the following unit CM data:

	Deluxe	Standard
Selling price	$15	$10
Variable cost per unit	12	5
Unit CM	$3	$5
Sales mix	60%	40%
Fixed costs	$76,000	

The weighted average unit CM = ($3)(0.6) + ($5)(0.4) = $3.80. Therefore, the company's break-even point in units is:

$$\$76,000/\$3.80 = 20,000 \text{ units}$$

which is divided as:

A:	20,000 units × 60% =	12,000 units
B:	20,000 units × 40% =	8,000
		20,000 units

Example 10.13

Assume that Dante, Inc. is a producer of recreational equipment. It expects to produce and sell three types of sleeping bags—the Economy, the Regular, and the Backpacker. Information on the bags is given in the accompanying table.

(continued)

Budgeted	Economy	Regular	Backpacker	Total
Sales	$30,000	$60,000	$10,000	$100,000
Sales mix	30%	60%	10%	100%
Less: VC	24,000	40,000	5,000	69,000
CM	$6,000	$20,000	$5,000	$31,000
CM ratio	20%	331/3%	50%	31%
Fixed costs				$18,600
Net income				$12,400

The CM ratio for Dante, Inc. is $31,000/$100,000 = 31\%$. Therefore, the break-even point in dollars is

$$\$18,000/0.31 = \$60,000$$

which will be split in the mix ratio of 3:6:1 to give us the following break-even points for the individual products:

Economy:	$60,000 \times 30\% =$	$18,000
Regular:	$60,000 \times 60\% =$	36,000
Backpacker:	$60,000 \times 10\% =$	6,000
		$60,000

One of the most important assumptions underlying CVP analysis in a multi-product firm is that the sales mix will not change during the planning period. But if the sales mix changes, the break-even point will also change.

Example 10.14

Assume that total sales from Example 10.13 was achieved at $100,000 but that an actual mix came out differently from the budgeted mix (i.e., for Regular, 60 to 30 percent, and for Backpacker, 10 to 40 percent).

	Actual			
	Economy	Regular	Backpacker	Total
Sales	$30,000	$30,000	$40,000	$100,000
Sales mix	30%	30%	40%	100%
Less: VC	24,000	20,000[a]	20,000[b]	64,000
CM	$6,000	$10,000	$20,000	$36,000
CM ratio	20%	331/3%	50%	36%
Fixed costs				$18,600
Net income				$17,400

[a] $20,000 = \$30,000 \times (100\% - 33\frac{1}{3}\%) = \$30,000 \times 66\frac{2}{3}\%$
[b] $20,000 = \$40,000 \times (100\% - 50\%) = \$40,000 \times 50\%$

The shift in sales mix toward the more profitable line C has caused the CM ratio for the company as a whole to go up from 31 to 36 percent.

The new break-even point will be:

$$\$51,667 = \$18,600/0.36$$

The break-even dollar volume has decreased from $60,000 to $51,667. The improvement in the mix caused net income to go up. It is important to note that, generally, the shift of emphasis from low-margin to high-margin products will increase the overall profits of the company.

 ## CVP ANALYSIS FOR NONPROFIT ORGANIZATIONS

CVP analysis and break-even analysis are not limited to profit firms. CVP is appropriately called cost-volume-*revenue* (CVR) analysis when it pertains to nonprofit organizations. The CVR model not only calculates the break-even service level but helps answer a variety of what-if decision questions.

Example 10.15

LMC, Inc., a Los Angeles county agency, has a $1.2 million lump-sum annual budget appropriation for an agency to help rehabilitate patients with mental illness. In addition, the agency charges each patient $600 a month for board and care. All of the appropriation and revenue must be spent. The variable costs for rehabilitation activity average $700 per patient per month. The agency's annual fixed costs are $800,000. The agency manager wishes to know how many patients can be served. Let x = number of patients to be served.

$$\text{Revenue} = \text{Total expenses}$$
$$\text{Lump-sum appropriation} + 600(12)x = \text{Variable expenses} + \text{Fixed costs}$$
$$\$1,200,000 + \$7,200x = \$8,400 \times x + \$800,000$$
$$(\$7,200 - \$8,400)x = \$800,000 - \$1,200,000$$
$$-\$1,200x = \$400,000$$
$$x = \$400,000/\$1,200$$
$$x = 33 \text{ patients}$$

We will investigate two what-if scenarios:

1. Suppose the manager of the agency is concerned that the total budget for the coming year will be cut by 10 percent to a new amount of $1,080,000. All other things remain unchanged. The manager wants to know how this budget cut affects the next year's service level.

$$\$1,080,000 + \$7,200x = \$8,400 \times x + \$800,000$$
$$(\$7,200 - \$8,400)x = \$800,000 - \$1,080,000$$
$$-\$1,200x = \$280,000$$

(continued)

$$x = \$280,000/\$1,200$$
$$x = 233 \text{ patients}$$

2. The manager does not reduce the number of patients served despite a budget cut of 10 percent. All other things remain unchanged. How much more does the manager have to charge patients for board and care? In this case, X = board and care charge per year

$$\$1,080,000 + 333x = \$8,400(333) + \$800,000$$
$$333x = \$2,797,200 + \$800,000 - \$1,080,000$$
$$333x = \$2,517,200$$
$$x = \$2,517,200/333 \text{ patients}$$
$$x = \$7,559$$

Thus, the monthly board and care charge must be increased to $630 ($7,559/12 months).

What are the assumptions underlying break-even and CVP analysis?

The basic break-even and CVP models are subject to a number of limiting assumptions, notably:

- The selling price per unit is constant throughout the entire relevant range of activity.
- All costs are classified as fixed or variable.
- The variable cost per unit is constant.
- There is only one product or a constant sales mix.
- Inventories do not change significantly from period to period.
- Volume is the only factor affecting variable costs.

LEVERAGE

Leverage is that portion of the fixed costs that represents a risk to the firm. "Operating leverage," a measure of operating risk, refers to the fixed operating costs found in the firm's income statement. "Financial leverage," a measure of financial risk, refers to financing a portion of the firm's assets, bearing fixed financing charges in hopes of increasing the return to the common stockholders. The higher the financial leverage, the higher the financial risk and the higher the cost of capital. Cost of capital rises because it costs more to raise funds for a risky business. Total leverage is a measure of total risk.

How do you measure operating leverage?

Operating leverage is a measure of operating risk and arises from fixed operating costs. A simple indication of operating leverage is the effect that a change in sales has on earnings.

The formula is:

$$\text{Operating leverage at a given level of sales } (x) = \frac{\text{Percentage change in EBIT}}{\text{Percentage change in sales}}$$

$$= \frac{\Delta\,\text{EBIT}/\text{EBIT}}{\Delta x/x} = \frac{(p-v)\,\Delta x/(p-v)x - \text{FC}}{\Delta x/x}$$

$$= \frac{(p-v)x}{(p-v)x - \text{FC}}$$

where EBIT = Earnings before interest and taxes = $(p-v)x - \text{FC}$

Example 10.16

The Peters Company manufactures and sells doors to home builders. The doors are sold for $25 each. Variable costs are $15 per door, and fixed operating costs total $50,000. Assume further that the Peters Company is currently selling 6,000 doors per year. Its operating leverage is:

$$\frac{(p-v)x}{(p-v)x - \text{FC}} = \frac{(\$25 - \$15)(6,000)}{(\$25 - \$15)(6,000) - \$50,000}$$

$$= \frac{\$60,000}{\$10,000} = 6$$

which means that if sales increase (decrease) by 1 percent, the company can expect net income to increase (decrease) by six times that amount, or 6 percent.

How do you calculate financial leverage?

Financial leverage is a measure of financial risk and arises from fixed financial costs. One way to measure financial leverage is to determine how earnings per share are affected by a change in EBIT (or operating income).

$$\text{Financial leverage at a given level of sales } (x) = \frac{\text{Percentage change in EPS}}{\text{Percentage change in EBIT}}$$

$$= \frac{(p-v)x - \text{FC}}{(p-v)x - \text{FC} - \text{IC}}$$

where
EPS = Earnings per share
   IC = Interest charges (i.e., interest expense or preferred stock dividends)

[Preferred stock dividend must be adjusted for taxes; i.e., preferred stock dividend/$(1-t)$, where t is the tax rate.]

Example 10.17

Using the data in Example 10.16, we see that the Peters Company has total financial charges of $2,000, half in interest expense and half in preferred stock dividend. Assume a corporate tax rate of 40 percent.

First, the fixed financial charges are:

$$IC = \$1,000 + \frac{\$1,000}{(1 - 0.4)} = \$1,000 + \$1,667 = \$2,667$$

Therefore, Peters's financial leverage is computed as follows:

$$\frac{(p - v)x - FC}{(p - v)x - FC - IC} = \frac{(\$25 - \$15)(6,000) - \$50,000}{(\$25 - \$15)(6,000) - \$50,00 - \$2,667}$$

$$= \frac{\$10,000}{\$7,333} = 1.36$$

which means that if EBIT increases (decreases) by 1 percent, Peters can expect its EPS to increase (decrease) by 1.36 times, or 1.36 percent.

How do you determine total leverage?

Total leverage is a measure of total risk. The way to measure total leverage is to determine how EPS is affected by a change in sales.

$$\text{Financial leverage at a given level of sales } (x) = \frac{\text{Percentage change in EPS}}{\text{Percentage change in sales}}$$

$$= \text{Operating leverage} \times \text{Financial leverage}$$

$$= \frac{(p - v)x}{(p - v)x - FC} \times \frac{(p - v)x - FC}{(p - v)x - FC - IC}$$

$$= \frac{(p - y)x}{(p - v)x - FC - IC}$$

Example 10.18

From Examples 10.16 and 10.17, we see that the total leverage for the Peters Company is:

Operating leverage × Financial leverage = 6 × 1.36 = 8.16

or

$$\frac{(p-v)x}{(p-v)x - FC - IC} = \frac{(\$25 - \$15)(6{,}000)}{(\$25 - \$15)(6{,}000) - \$50{,}000 - \$2{,}667}$$

$$= \frac{\$60{,}000}{\$7{,}333} = 8.18 \text{ (due to rounding error)}$$

which means that if sales increase (decrease) by 1 percent, Peters can expect its EPS to increase (decrease) by 8.18 percent.

CHAPTER ELEVEN

Short-Term Decisions

W HAT ARE THE typical short-term nonrecurring decisions that you face? When performing the manufacturing and selling functions, management constantly faces the problem of choosing between alternative courses of action. Typical questions to be answered include what to make, how to make it, where to sell the product, and what price to charge. The CFO faces many short-term, nonroutine decisions. In a short-term situation, fixed costs are generally irrelevant to the decision at hand. CFOs must recognize two important concepts as major decision tools: *relevant costs* and *contribution margin*.

 ## RELEVANT COSTS

In each short-term situation, the ultimate management decision rests on cost data analysis. Cost data are important in many decisions, since they are the basis for profit calculations. Cost data are classified by function, behavior patterns, and other criteria, as discussed previously.

However, not all costs are of equal importance in decision making, and CFOs must identify the costs that are relevant to a decision. Such costs are called *relevant costs*.

Which costs are relevant in a decision?

The relevant costs are the expected future costs (and also revenues) that differ between the decision alternatives. Therefore, the sunk costs (past and historical costs) are not considered relevant in the decision. What is relevant are the incremental or differential costs.

What is incremental analysis?

Under the concept of relevant costs, which may be called the incremental, differential, or relevant cost approach, decision making involves four steps:

1. Gather all costs associated with each alternative.
2. Drop the sunk costs.
3. Drop those costs that do not differ between alternatives.
4. Select the best alternative based on the remaining cost data.

When should a company accept special orders?

A company often receives a short-term, special order for its products at lower prices than usual. In normal times, the company may refuse such an order because it will not yield a satisfactory profit. If times are bad, however, such an order should be accepted if the incremental revenue obtained from it exceeds the incremental costs. The company is better off receiving some revenue, above its incremental costs, than receiving nothing at all.

A price lower than the regular price is called a *contribution price*. This approach to pricing is often called the contribution approach to pricing or the variable pricing model.

This approach is most appropriate under these three conditions:

1. When operating in a distress situation
2. When there is idle capacity
3. When faced with sharp competition or in a competitive bidding situation

Example 11.1

Assume that a company with 100,000-unit capacity is currently producing and selling only 90,000 units of product each year at a regular price of $2. If the variable cost per unit is $1 and the annual fixed cost is $45,000, the income statement looks like this:

Sales (90,000 units)	$180,000	$2.00
Less: Variable cost (90,000 units)	90,000	1.00
Contribution margin	$ 90,000	$1.00
Less: Fixed cost	45,000	0.50
Net income	$ 45,000	$0.50

The company has just received an order that calls for 10,000 units at $1.20 per unit, for a total of $12,000. The buyer will pay the shipping expenses. The acceptance of this order will not affect regular sales. The company's president is reluctant to accept the order, however, because the $1.20 price is below the $1.50 factory unit cost ($1.50 = $1.00 + $0.50). Should the company accept the order?

The answer is yes. The company can add to total profits by accepting this special order, even though the price offered is below the unit factory cost. At a price of $1.20, the order will contribute $0.20 per unit (contribution margin [CM] per unit = $1.20 − $1.00 = $0.20) toward fixed cost, and profit will increase by $2,000 (10,000 units × $0.20).

Using the contribution approach to pricing, the variable cost of $1.00 will be a better guide than the full unit cost of $1.50. Note that the fixed costs do not change because of the presence of idle capacity.

The same result can be seen in more detail, as shown next.

	Per Unit	Without Special Order (90,000 Units)	With Special Order (100,000 Units)	Difference
Sales	$2.00	$180,000	$192,000	$12,000
Less: Variable costs	1.00	90,000	100,000	10,000
CM	$1.00	$ 90,000	$ 92,000	$ 2,000
Less: Fixed cost	0.50	45,000	45,000	—
Net income	$0.50	$ 45,000	$ 47,000	$ 2,000

Example 11.2

The marketing manager has decided that for Product A, she wants a markup of 30 percent over cost. Particulars concerning a unit of Product A are:

Direct material	$ 4,000
Direct labor	10,000
Overhead	2,500
Total cost	$16,500
Markup on cost (30%)	4,950
Selling price	$21,450

Total direct labor for the year equals 1.2 million. Total overhead for the year equals 25 percent of direct labor ($300,000), of which 40 percent is fixed and 60 percent is variable. The customer offers to buy a unit of Product A for $18,000. Idle capacity exists.

You should accept the extra order because it provides an increased contribution margin, as indicated next.

Selling price		$18,000
Less: Variable costs		
Direct material	$ 4,000	
Direct labor	10,000	
Variable overhead ($10,000 × 15%)[a]	1,500	(15,500)
Contribution margin		$ 2,500
Less: Fixed overhead		(0)
Net income		$ 2,500

[a] Variable overhead equals 15% of direct labor, calculated as follows:
(Variable overhead/direct labor) = (60% × $300,000/$1,200,000) = ($180,000/$1,200,000) = 15%

How do you determine a bid price?

The relevant cost approach can be used to determine the bid price on a contract.

Example 11.3

Travis Company has received an order for 6,000 units. The CFO wants to know the minimum bid price that would produce a $14,000 increase in profit. The current income statement follows.

Income Statement		
Sales (30,000 units × $20)		$600,000
Less cost of sales		
Direct material	$ 60,000	
Direct labor	150,000	
Variable overhead (150,000 × 40%)	60,000	
Fixed overhead	80,000	(350,000)
Gross margin		$250,000
Less selling and administrative expenses		
Variable (includes transportation costs of $0.20 per unit)	15,000	
Fixed	85,000	(100,000)
Net income		$150,000

If the contract is taken, the cost patterns for the extra order will remain the same, with these exceptions:

- ▪ Transportation costs will be paid by the customer.
- ▪ Special tools costing $6,000 will be required for just this order and will not be reusable.
- ▪ Direct labor time for each unit under the order will be 10 percent longer.

The bid price is derived in this manner:

Current Cost Per Unit		
Selling price	$20.00	($600,000/30,000)
Direct material	$20.00	($60,000/30,000)
Direct labor	5.00	($150,000/30,000)
Variable overhead	40% of direct labor cost	($60,000/$150,000)
Variable selling and administrative expense	$0.50	($15,000/30,000)

As can be seen in the income statement that follows, the contract price for the 6,000 units should be $80,000 $($680,000 – $600,000), or $13.33 per unit ($80,000/6,000).

The contract price per unit of $13.33 is less than the $20 current selling price per unit. Note that by accepting the order, total fixed cost will remain the same except for the $6,000 cost of special tools.

What is a make-or-buy (outsource) decision?

Often companies purchase subcomponents used to make their products instead of making them in their in-house manufacturing facilities. Buying services, products, or components of products from outside vendors instead of producing them is called *outsourcing*. The decision whether to produce a subcomponent in-house or to buy it externally from an outside vendor is called a *make-or-buy (outsource) decision*. Examples include:

- Providing payroll processing in-house or outsourcing it to an outside service bureau
- Developing a training program in-house or sending employees outside for training
- Providing data processing and network services internally or buying them

Other strong candidates for outsourcing include managing fleets of vehicles, sales and marketing, e-commerce, information technology, and custodial services.

This decision involves both quantitative and qualitative factors. The qualitative factors include ensuring product quality and the necessity for long-run business relationships with the supplier. The quantitative factors deal with cost. The quantitative effects of the make-or-buy decision are best seen through the relevant cost approach.

The term "outsourcing" is often used interchangeably with "offshoring" and sometimes with "business process outsourcing" (BPO). "Outsourcing" requires more precise definition. When a company outsources the supply of products, services, or component parts, it delegates them to a third-party provider, either abroad or at home. BPO is a more specialized form of outsourcing in which an entire business process, such as accounting, procurement, or human resources, is handed to a third party. With offshoring, a company relocates processes or production to a lower-cost, foreign location in the form of subsidiaries or affiliates.

Reliable outsourcing requires:

- Beginning by outsourcing simple activities, such as data processing, and stepping up gradually to complex processes, such as financial services
- Checking among providers for any accreditation with internal standard setters
- Drawing up detailed terms and conditions for the contract, including how services should be delivered and providers' incentives for meeting targets

Example 11.4

Assume that a firm has prepared these cost estimates for the manufacture of a subassembly component based on an annual production of 8,000 units:

	Per Unit	Total
Direct materials	$ 5	$ 40,000
Direct labor	4	32,000
Variable factory overhead applied	4	32,000
Fixed factory overhead applied (150% of direct labor cost)	6	48,000
Total cost	$19	$152,000

(continued)

Income Statement

	Current (30,000)	Projected (36,000)	
Sales	$600,000	$680,000[a]	(Computed last)
Cost of sales			
Direct material	$ 60,000	$ 72,000	($2 × 36,000)
Direct labor	150,000	183,000	($150,000 + [6,000 × $5.50[b]])
Variable overhead	$ 60,000	$ 73,200	($183,000 × 40%)
Fixed overhead	80,000	86,000	($80,000 + $6,000)
Total	$350,000	$414,200	
Variable selling and administration costs	$ 15,000	$ 16,800	($15,000 + [6,000 × $0.30])[c]
Fixed selling and administrative costs	85,000	85,000	
Total	$100,000	$101,800	
Net income	$150,000	164,000[d]	

[a] Net income + Selling and administrative expensive + cost of sales = sales
$164,000 + $101,800 + $414,200 = $680,000
[b] $5 × 1.10 = $5.50
[c] $0.50 – $0.20 = $0.30
[d] $150,000 + $14,000 = $164,000

The supplier has offered to provide the subassembly at a price of $16 each. Two-thirds of fixed factory overhead, which represents executive salaries, rent, depreciation, and taxes, continues regardless of the decision. Should the company buy or make the product?

The key to the decision lies in the investigation of those relevant costs that change between the make-or-buy alternatives. Assuming that the productive capacity will be idle if not used to produce the subassembly, the analysis takes this form:

	Per Unit		Total of 8,000 Units	
	Make	Buy	Make	Buy
Purchase price		$16		$128,000
Direct materials	$5		$ 40,000	
Direct labor	4		32,000	
Variable overhead	4		32,000	
Fixed overhead that can be avoided by not making	2		16,000	
Total relevant costs	$15	$16	$120,000	$128,000
Difference in favor of making	$1		$8,000	

The make-or-buy decision must be investigated, along with the broader perspective of considering how best to utilize available facilities. There are three alternatives:

1. Leave facilities idle.
2. Buy the parts and rent out idle facilities.
3. Buy the parts and use idle facilities for other products.

What is a sell-or-process-further decision?

When two or more products are produced simultaneously from the same input by a joint process, these products are called *joint products*. The term "joint costs" is used to describe all the manufacturing costs incurred prior to the point where the joint products are identified as individual products, referred to as the *split-off point*. At the split-off point, some of the joint products are in final form and salable to the consumer, whereas others require additional processing.

In many cases, however, the company might have an option: It can sell the goods at the split-off point or process them further in the hope of obtaining additional revenue. In connection with this type of decision, called the *sell-or-process-further decision*, joint costs are considered irrelevant, since the joint costs have already been incurred at the time of the decision and therefore represent sunk costs. The decision will rely exclusively on additional revenue compared to the additional costs incurred due to further processing.

Example 11.5

The Gin Company produces three products, A, B, and C, from a joint process. Joint production costs for the year were $120,000. Product A may be sold at the split-off point or processed further. The additional processing requires no special facilities, and all additional processing costs are variable. Sales values and cost needed to evaluate the company's production policy regarding product A follow.

		Additional Cost and Sales Value After Further Processing	
Units Produced	Sales Value at Split-off	Sales	Costs
3,000	$60,000	$90,000	$25,000

Should product A be sold at the split-off point or processed further?

Incremental sales revenue	$30,000
Incremental costs, additional processing	25,000
Incremental gain	$ 5,000

In summary, product A should be processed as shown. Keep in mind that the joint production cost of $120,000 is not included in the analysis, since it is a sunk cost and, therefore, irrelevant to the decision.

How do you decide whether to keep or drop a product line?

The decision whether to keep or drop an old product line must take into account both qualitative and quantitative factors. However, any final decision should be based primarily on the impact the decision will have on CM or net income.

Example 11.6

The Beta grocery store has three major product lines: produce, meats, and canned food. The store is considering dropping the meat line because the income statement shows it is being sold at a loss. The income statement for these product lines is shown next.

	Canned Produce	Meats	Food	Total
Sales	$10,000	$15,000	$25,000	$50,000
Less:				
Variable costs	6,000	8,000	12,000	26,000
CM	$ 4,000	$ 7,000	$13,000	$24,000
Less: Fixed costs				
Direct	$ 2,000	$ 6,500	$ 4,000	$ 12,500
Allocated	1,000	1,500	2,500	5,000
Total	$ 3,000	$ 8,000	$ 6,500	$ 17,500
Net income	$ 1,000	$ (1,000)	$ 6,500	$ 6,500

In this example, direct fixed costs are those costs that are identified directly with each of the product lines, whereas allocated fixed costs are the amount of common fixed costs allocated to the product lines using some base such as space occupied. The amount of common fixed costs typically continues regardless of the decision and thus cannot be saved by dropping the product line to which it is distributed.

The next calculations show the effects on the company as a whole with and without the meat line:

	Keep Meats	Drop Meats	Difference
Sales	$50,000	$35,000	$(15,000)
Less: Variable cost	26,000	18,000	(8,000)
CM			
Less: Fixed cost	$24,000	$ 17,000	$ (7,000)
Direct	$ 12,500	$ 6,000	$ (6,500)
Allocated	5,000	5,000	—
Total	$ 17,500	$ 11,000	$ (6,500)
Net Income	$ 6,500	$ 6,000	$ (500)

Alternatively, the incremental approach would show the following:

If Meats Dropped		
Sales revenue lost		($15,000)
Gains:		
Variable cost avoided	$8,000	
Direct fixed costs avoided	6,500	14,500
Increase (decrease) in net income		$ (500)

From either of the two methods, we see that by dropping meats the store will lose an additional $500. Therefore, the meat product line should be kept. One of the dangers in allocating common fixed costs is that such allocations can make a product line look less profitable than it really is. Because of such an allocation, the meat line showed a loss of $1,000, but it in effect contributes $500 ($7,000 – $6,500) to the recovery of the company's common fixed costs.

BEST USE OF SCARCE RESOURCES

In general, the emphasis on products with higher contribution margin maximizes a firm's total net income, even though total sales may decrease. This is not true, however, where there are constraining factors and scarce resources. The constraining factor may be machine hours, labor hours, or cubic feet of warehouse space.

In the presence of these constraining factors, maximizing total profits depends on getting the highest contribution margin per unit of the factor (rather than the highest contribution margin per unit of product output).

Example 11.7

Assume that a company produces two products, A and B, with the following contribution margins per unit.

	A	B
Sales	$8	$24
Variable costs	6	20
CM	$2	$ 4
Annual fixed costs	$42,000	

As is indicated by CM per unit, B is more profitable than A since it contributes more to the company's total profits than A ($4 vs. $2). But let us assume that the firm has a limited capacity of 10,000 labor hours. Let us further assume that A requires two labor hours to produce and B requires 5 labor hours. One way to express this limited capacity is to determine the contribution margin per labor hour.

(continued)

	A	B
CM/unit	$2.00	$4.00
Labor hours required per unit	2	5
CM per labor hour	$1.00	$0.80

Since A returns the higher CM per labor hour, it should be produced and B should be dropped.

Exhibit 11.1 summarizes guidelines for typical short-term decisions.

 ## THEORY OF CONSTRAINTS

How does the theory of constraints handle limiting constraints?

A binding constraint can limit a company's profitability. For example, a manufacturing company may have a bottleneck operation, through which every unit of a product must pass before moving on to other operations. The *theory of constraints* calls for identifying such limiting constraints and seeking ways to relax them. Also referred to as *managing constraints*, this management approach can significantly improve an organization's level of goal attainment. Management can relax a constraint by expanding the capacity of a bottleneck operation in many ways, including:

EXHIBIT 11.1 Decision Guidelines

Decision	Description	Decision Guidelines
Special order	Should a discount-priced order be accepted when there is idle capacity?	If regular orders are not affected, accept order when the revenue from the order exceeds the incremental cost. Fixed costs are usually irrelevant.
Make-or-buy	Should a part be made or bought from a vendor?	Choose lower-cost option. Fixed costs are usually irrelevant. Often opportunity costs are present.
Close a segment	Should a segment be dropped?	Compare loss in contribution margin with savings in fixed costs.
Sell or process further	Should joint products be sold at split-off or processed further?	Ignore joint costs. Process further if incremental revenue exceeds incremental cost.
Scarce resources	Which products should be emphasized when capacity is limited?	Emphasize products with highest contribution margin per unit of scarce resource (e.g., CM per machine hour).

- *Outsourcing* (subcontracting) all or part of the bottleneck operation
- Investing in additional production equipment and employing *parallel processing*, in which multiple-product units undergo the same production operation simultaneously
- Working *overtime* at the bottleneck operation
- *Retaining* employees and shifting them to the bottleneck
- Eliminating any *non–value-added activities* at the bottleneck operation

CHAPTER TWELVE

Financial Forecasting, Planning, and Budgeting

 ## FINANCIAL FORECASTING: THE PERCENT-OF-SALES METHOD

What is financial forecasting and why is it done?

Financial forecasting, an essential element of planning, is the basis for budgeting activities. It is also needed when estimating future financing requirements. The company may look for financing either internally or externally. *Internal financing* refers to cash flow generated from the company's normal operating activities. *External financing* refers to funds provided by parties external to the company. You need to analyze how to estimate external financing requirements. Basically, forecasts of future sales and related expenses provide the firm with the information to project future external financing needs.

The four basic steps in projecting financing needs are:

1. Project the firm's sales. The sales forecast is the initial step. Most other forecasts (budgets) follow the sales forecast.
2. Project additional variables, such as expenses.
3. Estimate the level of investment in current and fixed assets to support the projected sales.
4. Calculate the firm's financing needs.

How does the percent-of-sales method work?

The most widely used method for projecting the company's financing needs is the *percent-of-sales method.* This method involves estimating the various expenses, assets, and liabilities for a future period as a percentage of the sales forecast and then using these percentages, together with the projected sales, to construct forecasted balance sheets. Example 12.1 illustrates how to develop a pro forma balance sheet and determine the amount of external financing needed.

Example 12.1

Assume that sales for 2X11 equal $20, projected sales for 2X12 equal $24, net income equals 5% of sales, and the dividend payout ratio is 40 percent. Exhibit 12.1 illustrates the method, step by step. All dollar amounts are in millions.

The five steps for the computations are:

1. Express those balance sheet items that vary directly with sales as a percentage of sales. Any item such as long-term debt that does not vary directly with sales is designated "n.a.," or "not applicable."
2. Multiply these percentages by the 2X12 projected sales of $24 to obtain the projected amounts as shown in the last column.
3. Insert figures for long-term debt, common stock, and paid-in capital from the 2X11 balance sheet.
4. Compute 2X12 retained earnings as shown in footnote a.
5. Sum the asset accounts, obtaining total projected assets of $7.20, and add the projected liabilities and equity to obtain $7.12, the total financing provided. Since liabilities and equity must total $7.20, but only $7.12 is projected, we have a shortfall of $0.08 "external financing needed."

EXHIBIT 12.1 Pro Forma Balance Sheet (in Millions of Dollars)

	Present (2X11)	% of Sales (2X11 Sales = $20)	Projected (2X12 Sales = $24)	
Assets				
Current assets	2	10	2.4	
Fixed assets	4	20	4.8	
Total assets	6		7.2	
Liabilities and Stockholders' Equity				
Current liabilities	2	10	2.4	
Long-term debt	2.5	n.a.	2.5	
Total liabilities	4.5		4.9	
Common stock	0.1	n.a.	0.1	
Paid-in capital	0.2	n.a.	0.2	
Retained earnings	1.2		1.92[a]	
Total equity	1.5		2.22	
Total liabilities and stockholders' equity	6		7.12	Total financing provided
			0.08[b]	External financing needed
			7.2	Total

[a] 2X12 retained earnings = 2X11 retained earnings + projected net income – cash dividends paid = $1.2 + 5%($24) – 40%[5%($24)] = $1.2 + $1.2 – $0.48 = $2.4 – $0.48 = $1.92.

[b] External financing needed = projected total assets – (projected total liabilities + projected equity) = $7.2 – ($4.9 + $2.22) = $7.2 – $7.12 = $0.08.

Although the forecast of additional funds required can be made by setting up pro forma balance sheets as described here, it is often easier to use the following formula:

External funds needed (EFN) = Required increase in assets − Spontaneous increase in liabilities − Increase in retained earnings

$$EFN = (A/S)\Delta S - (L/S)\Delta S - (PM)(PS)(1 - d)$$

where
A/S = Assets that increase spontaneously with sales as a percentage of sales
L/S = Liabilities that increase spontaneously with sales as a percentage of sales
DS = Change in sales
PM = Profit margin on sales
PS = Projected sales
 d = Dividend payout ratio

In this example,

A/S = $6/$20 = 30%
L/S = $2/$20 = 10%
DS = ($24 − $20) = $4
PM = 5% on sales
PS = $24
 d = 40%

Plugging these figures into the formula yields:

$$EFN = 0.3(\$4) - 0.1(\$4) - (0.05)(\$24)(1 - 0.4)$$

$$= \$1.20 - \$0.40 - \$0.72 = \$0.08$$

Thus, the amount of external financing needed is $800,000, which can be raised by issuing notes payable, bonds, stocks, or any combination of these financing sources.

The major advantage of the percent-of-sales method of financial forecasting is that it is simple and inexpensive to use. One important assumption behind the use of the method is that the firm is operating at full capacity. This means that the company has no sufficient productive capacity to absorb a projected increase in sales and thus requires additional investment in assets. Therefore, the method must be used with extreme caution if excess capacity exists in certain asset accounts.

 BUDGETING

What is a budget?

A *comprehensive (master) budget* is a formal statement of the CFO's expectation regarding sales, expenses, volume, and other financial transactions of an organization for the coming period. Simply put, a budget is a set of pro forma (projected or planned) financial statements. It consists basically of a pro forma income statement, pro forma balance sheet, and cash budget.

A budget is a tool for both planning and control. At the beginning of the period, the budget is a plan or standard; at the end of the period, it serves as a control device to help the CFO measure its performance against the plan so that future performance may be improved.

With the aid of computer technology, budgeting can be used as an effective device for evaluation of what-if scenarios. Such scenarios allow management to move toward finding the best course of action among various alternatives through simulation.

If management does not like what it sees on the budgeted financial statements in terms of various financial ratios such as liquidity, activity (turnover), leverage, profit margin, and market value ratios, it can always alter the contemplated decision and planning set.

What are the types of budgets?

The budget is classified broadly into two categories:

1. *Operating budget*, reflecting the results of operating decisions
2. *Financial budget*, reflecting the financial decisions of the firm

What is an operating budget?

The operating budget consists of:

- Sales budget
- Production budget
- Direct materials budget
- Direct labor budget
- Factory overhead budget
- Selling and administrative expense budget
- Pro forma income statement

What does the financial budget contain?

The financial budget consists of:

- Cash budget
- Pro forma balance sheet

How do you prepare a budget?

The five major steps in preparing the budget are:

1. Prepare a sales forecast.
2. Determine expected production volume.
3. Estimate manufacturing costs and operating expenses.

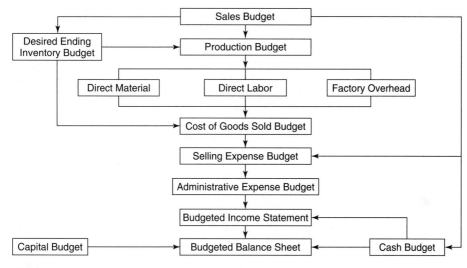

EXHIBIT 12.2 Comprehensive (Master) Budget

4. Determine cash flow and other financial effects.
5. Formulate projected financial statements.

Exhibit 12.2 shows a simplified diagram of the various parts of the comprehensive (master) budget, the master plan of the company.

To illustrate how all these budgets are developed, we focus on a manufacturing company called the Delta Company, which produces and markets a single product. We assume that the company develops the master budget in contribution format for 2X12 on a quarterly basis. Throughout the illustration, we highlight the variable cost–fixed cost breakdown.

Sales Budget

The sales budget is the starting point in preparing the master budget, since estimated sales volume influences nearly all other items appearing throughout the master budget. The sales budget ordinarily indicates the quantity of each product expected to be sold. After sales volume has been estimated, the sales budget is constructed by multiplying the expected sales in units by the expected unit sales price. Generally, the sales budget includes a computation of expected cash collections from credit sales, which will be used later for cash budgeting. The sales budget is illustrated in Exhibit 12.3.

Production Budget

After sales are budgeted, the production budget can be determined. The production budget sets forth the number of units expected to be manufactured to meet budgeted sales and inventory requirements. The expected volume of production is determined by subtracting the estimated inventory at the beginning of the period from the sum of the units expected to be sold and the desired inventory at the end of the period. The production budget is illustrated in Exhibit 12.4.

EXHIBIT 12.3 Delta Company Sales Budget for the Year Ending December 31, 2X12

	Quarter				
	1	2	3	4	Total
Expected sales in units	800	700	900	800	3,200
Unit sales price	× $80	× $80	× $80	× $80	× $80
Total sales	$64,000	$56,000	$72,000	$64,000	$256,000
Schedule of Expected Cash Collections					
Accounts receivable, 12/31/2X11	$9,500[a]				$9,500
1st-quarter sales ($64,000)	44,800[b]	$17,920[c]			62,720
2nd-quarter sales ($56,000)		39,200	$15,680		54,880
3rd-quarter sales ($72,000)			50,400	$20,160	70,560
4th-quarter sales ($64,000)				44,800	44,800
Total cash collections	$54,300	$57,120	$66,080	$64,960	$242,460

[a] All $9,500 accounts receivable balance is assumed to be collectible in the first quarter.
[b] 70% of a quarter's sales are collected in the quarter of sale.
[c] 28% of a quarter's sales are collected in the quarter following, and the remaining 2% are uncollectible.

Direct Material Budget

When the level of production has been computed, a direct material budget should be constructed to show how much material will be required for production and how much material must be purchased to meet this production requirement. See Exhibit 12.5.

EXHIBIT 12.4 Delta Company Production Budget for the Year Ending December 31, 2X12

	Quarter				
	1	2	3	4	Total
Planned sales	800	700	900	800	3,200
Desired ending inventory[a]	70	90	80	100[b]	100
Total needs	870	790	980	900	3,300
Less: Beginning inventory[c]	80	70	90	80	80
Units to be produced	790	720	890	820	3,220

[a] 10% of the next quarter's sales.
[b] Estimated.
[c] The same as the previous quarter's ending inventory.

EXHIBIT 12.5 Delta Company Direct Material Budget for the Year Ending December 31, 2X12

	Quarter				
	1	2	3	4	Total
Units to be produced	790	720	890	820	3,220
Material needs per unit (lb)	× 3	× 3	× 3	× 3	× 3
Material needs for production	2,370	2,160	2,670	2,460	9,660
Desired ending inventory of materials[a]	216	267	246	250[b]	250
Total needs	2,586	2,427	2,916	2,710	9,910
Less: Beginning inventory of materials[c]	237	216	267	246	237
Materials to be purchased	2,349	2,211	2,649	2,464	9,673
Unit price	× $2	× $2	× $2	× $2	× $2
Purchase cost	$4,698	$4,422	$5,298	$4,928	$19,346
Schedule of Expected Cash Disbursements					
Accounts payable, 12/31/2X11	$2,200				$2,200
1st-quarter purchases ($4,698)	2,349	$2,349[d]			4,698
2nd-quarter purchases ($4,422)		2,211	$2,211		4,422
3rd-quarter purchases ($5,298)			2,649	$2,649	5,298
4th-quarter purchases ($4,928)				2,464	2,464
Total disbursements	$4,549	$4,560	$4,860	$5,113	$19,082

[a] 10% of the next quarter's units needed for production.
[b] Estimated.
[c] The same as the prior quarter's ending inventory.
[d] 50% of a quarter's purchases are paid for in the quarter of purchase; the remainder are paid for in the following quarter.

The purchase will depend on both expected usage of materials and inventory levels. The formula for computation of the purchase is:

$$\text{Purchase in units} = \text{Usage} + \text{Desired ending material inventory units} - \text{Beginning inventory units}$$

The direct material budget is usually accompanied by a computation of expected cash payments for materials.

Direct Labor Budget

The production requirements as set forth in the production budget also provide the starting point for preparing the direct labor budget. To compute direct labor requirements, expected production volume for each period is multiplied by the number of direct labor hours required to produce a single unit. The direct labor hours to meet production requirements is then multiplied by the direct labor cost per hour to obtain budgeted total direct labor costs. See Exhibit 12.6.

EXHIBIT 12.6 Delta Company Direct Labor Budget for the Year Ending December 31, 2X12

	Quarter				
	1	2	3	4	Total
Units to be produced	790	720	890	820	3,220
Direct labor hours per unit	× 5	× 5	× 5	× 5	× 5
Total hours	3,950	3,600	4,450	4,100	16,100
Direct labor cost per hour	× $5	× $5	× $5	× $5	× $5
Total direct labor cost	$19,750	$18,000	$22,250	$20,500	$80,500

Factory Overhead Budget

The factory overhead budget should provide a schedule of all manufacturing costs other than direct materials and direct labor. Using the contribution approach to budgeting requires the development of a predetermined overhead rate for the variable portion of the factory overhead. In developing the cash budget, we must remember that depreciation does not entail a cash outlay and therefore must be deducted from the total factory overhead in computing cash disbursement for factory overhead. See Exhibit 12.7.

To illustrate the factory overhead budget, we assume that

- Total factory overhead budgeted = $6,000 fixed (per quarter), plus $2 per hour of direct labor.
- Depreciation expenses are $3,250 each quarter.
- All overhead costs involving cash outlays are paid for in the quarter incurred.

Ending Inventory Budget

The desired ending inventory budget provides us with the information required for constructing budgeted financial statements. Specifically, it will help compute the cost of goods

EXHIBIT 12.7 Delta Company Factory Overhead Budget for the Year Ending December 31, 2X12

	Quarter				
	1	2	3	4	Total
Budgeted direct labor hours	3,950	3,600	4,450	4,100	16,100
Variable overhead rate	× $2	× $2	× $2	× $2	× $2
Variable overhead budgeted	$7,900	$7,200	$8,900	$8,200	$32,200
Fixed overhead budgeted	6,000	6,000	6,000	6,000	24,000
Total budgeted overhead	$13,900	$13,200	$14,900	$14,200	$56,200
Less: Depreciation	3,250	3,250	3,250	3,250	13,000
Cash disbursement for overhead	$10,650	$9,950	$11,650	$10,950	$43,200

EXHIBIT 12.8 Delta Company Ending Inventory Budget for the Year Ending December 31, 2X12

	Ending Inventory Units	Unit Cost	Total
Direct materials	250 pounds	$2	$500
Finished goods	100 units	$41[a]	$4,100

[a] The unit variable cost of $41 is computed as shown next:

	Unit Cost	Units	Total
Direct materials	$2	3 pounds	$6
Direct labor	5	5 hours	25
Variable overhead	2	5 hours	10
Total variable manufacturing cost			$41

sold on the budgeted income statement. It will also give the dollar value of the ending materials and finished goods inventory to appear on the budgeted balance sheet. See Exhibit 12.8.

Selling and Administrative Expense Budget

The selling and administrative expense budget lists the operating expenses involved in selling the products and in managing the business. In order to complete the budgeted income statement in contribution format, variable selling and administrative expense per unit must be computed. See Exhibit 12.9.

EXHIBIT 12.9 Delta Company Selling and Administrative Expense Budget for the Year Ending December 31, 2X12

	Quarter				
	1	2	3	4	Total
Expected sales in units	$800	$700	$900	$800	$3,200
Variable selling and administrative expense per unit[a]	× $4	× $4	× $4	× $4	× $4
Budgeted variable expense	$3,200	$2,800	$3,600	$3,200	$12,800
Fixed selling and administrative expenses:					
Advertising	1,100	1,100	1,100	1,100	4,400
Insurance	2,800				2,800
Office salaries	8,500	8,500	8,500	8,500	34,000
Rent	350	350	350	350	1,400
Taxes			1,200		1,200
Total budgeted selling and administrative expenses[b]	$15,950	$12,750	$14,750	$13,150	$56,600

[a] Includes sales agents' commissions, shipping, and supplies.
[b] Paid for in the quarter incurred.

Cash Budget

The cash budget is prepared for the purpose of cash planning and control. It presents the expected cash inflow and outflow for a designated time period. The cash budget helps management keep cash balances in reasonable relationship to its needs. It aids in avoiding unnecessary idle cash and possible cash shortages. The cash budget typically consists of four major sections:

1. The *receipts* section, which is the beginning cash balance, cash collections from customers, and other receipts
2. The *disbursements* section, which comprises all cash payments made by purpose
3. The *cash surplus* or *deficit* section, which simply shows the difference between the cash receipts section and the cash disbursements section
4. The *financing* section, which provides a detailed account of the borrowings and repayments expected during the budgeting period

To illustrate, we make these assumptions:

- The company desires to maintain a $5,000 minimum cash balance at the end of each quarter.
- All borrowing and repayment must be in multiples of $500 at an interest rate of 10 percent per annum.
- Interest is computed and paid as the principal is repaid.
- Borrowing takes place at the beginning of each quarter and repayment at the end of each quarter.

An example cash budget is provided in Exhibit 12.10.

Budgeted Income Statement

The budgeted income statement summarizes the various component projections of revenue and expenses for the budgeting period. However, for control purposes, the budget can be divided into quarters or even months depending on the need. See Exhibit 12.11.

Budgeted Balance Sheet

The budgeted balance sheet is developed by beginning with the balance sheet for the year just ended and adjusting it, using all the activities that are expected to take place during the budgeting period. The budgeted balance sheet must be prepared for several reasons:

- It could disclose some unfavorable financial conditions that management might want to avoid.
- It serves as a final check on the mathematical accuracy of all the other schedules.
- It helps management perform a variety of ratio calculations.
- It highlights future resources and obligations.

To illustrate, we show the balance sheet for the year 2X11 in Exhibit 12.12 and the budgeted balance sheet for the year 2X12 in Exhibit 12.13.

EXHIBIT 12.10 Delta Company Cash Budget for the Year Ending December 31, 2X12

			Quarter			
		1	2	3	4	Total
Cash balance, beginning	Given	$10,000	$9,401	$5,461	$9,106	$10,000
Add: Receipts:						
Collection from customers		54,300	57,120	66,080	64,960	242,460
Total cash available		$64,300	$66,521	$71,541	$74,066	$252,460
Less:						
Disbursements:						
Direct materials		4,549	4,560	4,860	5,113	19,082
Direct labor		19,750	18,000	22,250	20,500	80,500
Factory overhead		10,650	9,950	11,650	10,950	43,200
Selling and administrative		15,950	12,750	14,750	13,150	56,600
Machinery purchase	Given	—	24,300	—	—	24,300
Income tax	Given	4,000	—	—	—	4,000
Total disbursements		54,899	69,560	53,510	49,713	227,682
Cash surplus (deficit)		9,401	(3,039)	18,031	24,353	24,778
Financing:						
Borrowing		—	8,500	—	—	8,500
Repayment		—	—	(8,500)	—	(8,500)
Interest		—	—	(425)	—	(425)
Total financing		—	8,500	(8,925)	—	(425)
Cash balance, ending		$9,401	$5,461	$9,106	$24,353	$24,353

EXHIBIT 12.11 Delta Company Budgeted Income Statement for the Year Ending December 31, 2X12

Sales (3,200 units @ $80)		$256,000
Less: Variable expenses		
Variable cost of goods sold (3,200 units @ $41)	$131,200	
Variable selling and admin.	12,800	144,000
Contribution margin		$112,000
Less: Fixed expenses		
Factory overhead	$24,000	
Selling and administration	43,800	67,800
Net operating income		$44,200
Less: Interest expense		425
Net income before taxes		$43,775
Less: Income taxes 20%		8,755
Net income		$35,020

Note: Data are derived from previous budgets.

EXHIBIT 12.12 Delta Company Balance Sheet December 31, 2X11

Assets		Liabilities and Stockholders' Equity	
Current Assets		**Current Liabilities**	
Cash	$10,000	Accounts payable	$2,200
Accounts receivable	9,500	Income tax payable	4,000
Material inventory	474	Total current liabilities	$6,200
Finished goods inventory	3,280		
Total current assets	$23,254		
Fixed Assets		**Stockholders' Equity**	
Land	$50,000	Common stock, no-par	$70,000
Building and equipment	100,000	Retained earnings	37,054
Accumulated depreciation	(60,000)	Total stockholders' equity	107,054
Total fixed assets	90,000		
		Total liabilities and	
Total assets	$113,254	stockholders' equity	$113,254

EXHIBIT 12.13 Delta Company Budgeted Balance Sheet December 31, 2X12

Assets		Liabilities and Stockholders' Equity	
Current Assets		**Current Liabilities**	
Cash	$ 24,353[a]	Accounts payable	$2,464[b]
Accounts receivable	23,040[c]	Income tax payable	8,755[d]
Material inventory	500[e]	Total current liabilities	$11,219
Finished goods inventory	4,100[f]		
Total current assets	$51,993		
Fixed Assets		**Stockholders' Equity**	
Land	$50,000[g]	Common stock, no-par	$70,000[h]
Building and equipment	124,300[i]	Retained earnings	72,074[j]
Accumulated depreciation	(73,000)[k]	Total stockholders' equity	142,074
Total fixed assets	101,300		
Total Assets	$153,293	Total liabilities and stockholders' equity	$153,293

[a] From cash budget.

[b] $2,200 + $19,346 − $19,082 = $2,464 (all accounts payable relate to material purchases), or 50% of 4th-quarter purchase = 50% ($4,928) = $2,464.

[c] $9,500 + $256,000 sales − $242,460 receipts = $23,040.

[d] From budgeted income statement.

[e] and [f] From Ending Inventory Budget.

[g] No change.

[h] No change.

[i] $100,000 + $24,300 = $124,300.

[j] $37,054 + $35,020 net income = $72,074.

[k] $60,000 + $13,000 = $73,000.

SOME FINANCIAL CALCULATIONS

To see what kind of financial condition the Delta Company is expected to be in for the budgeting year, a sample of financial ratio calculations is in order. (Assume 2X11 after-tax net income was $15,000.)

	2X11	2X12
Current ratio	$23,254/$6,200	$51,993/$11,219
(Current assets/Current liabilities)	= 3.75	= 4.63
Return on total assets	$15,000/$113,254	$35,020/$153,293
(Net income after taxes/Total assets)	= 13.24%	= 22.85%

Sample calculations indicate that the Delta Company is expected to have better liquidity as measured by the current ratio. Overall performance will be improved as measured by return on total assets. This could be an indication that the contemplated plan may work out well.

BUDGETING SOFTWARE

Much user-oriented software has been specifically designed for corporate planners, treasurers, budget preparers, managerial accountants, CFOs, and business analysts.

Spreadsheet software and computer-based financial modeling software are widely utilized for budgeting and planning in an effort to speed up the budgeting process and allow nonfinancial managers to investigate the effect of changes in budget assumptions and scenarios.

USING AN ELECTRONIC SPREADSHEET TO DEVELOP A BUDGET PLAN

This chapter shows a detailed procedure for formulating a master budget. However, in practice, a shortcut approach to budgeting is quite common using spreadsheet technology. For an illustration of a shortcut method, we show how to develop a projected income statement using Excel.

JKS Furniture Co., Inc., expects the following for the coming 12 months, 2X12:

- Sales for 1st month = $60,000
- Cost of sales = 60% of sales
- Operating expenses = $10,000 plus 5% of sales
- Income taxes = 25% of net income
- Sales increase by 5% each month

Based on this information, we develop a spreadsheet for the pro forma income statement for the next 12 months and in total, which is given in Exhibit 12.14. Using a

	1	2	3	4	5	6	7	8	9	10	11	12	TOTAL	PERCENT
Sales	$60,000	$63,000	$66,150	$69,458	$72,930	$76,577	$80,406	$84,426	$88,647	$93,080	$97,734	$102,620	$955,028	100%
Less: VC														
Cost of sales	$36,000	$37,800	$39,690	$41,675	$43,758	$45,946	$48,243	$50,656	$53,188	$55,848	$58,640	$61,572	$573,017	60%
Op. expenses	$3,000	$3,150	$3,308	$3,473	$3,647	$3,829	$4,020	$4,221	$4,432	$4,654	$4,887	$5,131	$47,751	5%
CM	$21,000	$22,050	$23,153	$24,310	$25,526	$26,802	$28,142	$29,549	$31,027	$32,578	$34,207	$35,917	$334,260	35%
Less: FC														
Op. expenses	$10,000	$10,000	$10,000	$10,000	$10,000	$10,000	$10,000	$10,000	$10,000	$10,000	$10,000	$10,000	$120,000	13%
Net income	$11,000	$12,050	$13,153	$14,310	$15,526	$16,802	$18,142	$19,549	$21,027	$22,578	$24,207	$25,917	$214,260	22%
Less: Tax	$2,750	$3,013	$3,288	$3,578	$3,881	$4,200	$4,536	$4,887	$5,257	$5,644	$6,052	$6,479	$53,565	6%
NI after tax	$8,250	$9,038	$9,864	$10,733	$11,644	$12,601	$13,607	$14,662	$15,770	$16,933	$18,155	$19,438	$160,695	17%

EXHIBIT 12.14 JKS Furniture Co., Inc., Pro Forma Income Statement for the Period Ending December 31, 2X12

spreadsheet program such as Excel, financial managers will be able to evaluate various what-if scenarios.

 ## LATEST GENERATION OF BUDGETING AND PLANNING SOFTWARE AND E-BUDGETING

While research shows that two-thirds of U.S. companies still rely on Microsoft Excel for their budgeting process, some companies are evolving to a more technologically advanced approach. As more and more companies operate globally, the Internet is playing an ever-greater role in the budgeting process. *E-budgeting* is an increasingly popular Internet- or intranet-based budgeting tool that can streamline and speed up an organization's budgeting process. The *e* in e-budgeting stands for both *electronic* and *enterprise wide*; employees throughout an organization, at all levels and around the globe, can submit and retrieve budget information electronically via the Internet. Budgeting software is utilized and made available on the Web (in a cloud computing environment), so that budget information electronically submitted from any location is in a consistent companywide format. Managers in organizations using e-budgeting have found that it greatly streamlines the entire budgeting process. In the past, these organizations have compiled their master budgets on hundreds of spreadsheets, which had to be collected and integrated by the corporate controller's office. One result of this cumbersome approach was that a disproportionate amount of time was spent compiling and verifying data from multiple sources. With e-budgeting, both the submission of budget information and its compilation are accomplished electronically by the Web-based budgeting software. Thus, e-budgeting is just one more area where the Internet has transformed how the workplace operates in the era of e-business.

The new budgeting and planning (B&P) software represents a giant step forward for accountants. Finance managers can use these robust, Web-enabled programs to scan a wide range of data, radically speed up the planning process, and identify managers who have failed to submit budgets. More often known as active financial planning software, this software includes applications and the new level of functionality that combine budgeting, forecasting analytics, business intelligence, and collaboration. Exhibit 12.15 lists popular B&P software.

The models help not only build a budget for profit planning but answer a variety of what-if scenarios. The resultant calculations provide a basis for choice among alternatives under conditions of uncertainty. Financial modeling can also be accomplished using spreadsheet programs such as Microsoft's Excel and Quattro Pro.

EXHIBIT 12.15 Popular Budgeting and Planning Software

Companies	Web Sites	Software
Microsoft	www.microsoft.com/en-us/dynamics/products/frx.aspx	Forecaster, Microsoft Dynamics
ActiveStrategy	www.activestrategy.com	ActiveStrategy Enterprise
Actuate	www.actuate.com	e.Reporting Suite
IBM Cognos	www.cognos.com	Cognos Finance, Cognos Visualizer, Cognos Enterprise, Business Intelligence
Rocket CorVu	www.rocketsoftware.com	CorPlanning, CorStrategy, CorBusiness, CorPortfolio
Epicor	www.epicor.com	Epicor e.Intelligence Suite
Infor	www.infor.com	Infor Smartstream Financials, Enterprise Solutions Expert Series, FRx
Lawson Software	www.lawson.com	Enterprise Budgeting SEA Applications— including E-Scorecard; Analytic Extensions
Oracle	www.oracle.com	Oracle Strategic Enterprise Management (SEM), Hyperion Planning
SAP	www.sap.com	SAP Strategic Enterprise Management (SEM), SAP Financial Analyzer Business Intelligence with mySAP.com
SAS Institute	www.sas.com	SAS Total Financial Management, Strategic Vision, SAS/Warehouse Administrator, SAS Enabling Technology (OLAP), SAS BusinessObjects Portfolio, Oros Products
Silvon	www.silvon.com	Stratum

CHAPTER THIRTEEN

Risk Management

THE NEWS DOMINATING the world's attention in recent years—terrorist attacks; corporate scandals; severe acute respiratory syndrome or *E. coli* outbreaks; natural disasters such as hurricanes, earthquakes, and tsunamis; and turbulent financial markets—has triggered a shift in corporate risk management practices. The calculation of risk has always been central to managerial decision making, but CEOs and CFOs are acutely aware of the need to deal proactively with uncertainties that can threaten their business.

With this in mind, larger firms have designated a chief risk officer (CRO), whose prime function is to make risk management a central part of the business. The CRO reports to the CFO, whereas the CFOs of smaller firms personally assume risk management responsibilities, known as *enterprise risk management* (ERM). Risks are often closely connected. Operational risks, for example, can quickly evolve into market risks if word gets out and the share price falls.

 ## ENTERPRISE RISK MANAGEMENT

ERM is widely used as a way to effectively manage the complex portfolio of risks that exist across an organization. Instead of relying on a traditional, "silo-based" strategy, where each area of the organization manages its own risk, ERM adopts a broader top-down view of risks that integrates and coordinates risk oversight across the entire enterprise. An effectively implemented ERM process should provide auditors important information about the client's most significant business risk exposures.

What is ERM intended to do?

ERM is a systematic way of understanding and managing the various risks a company faces. It involves identifying risk exposure, analyzing risk, measuring potential loss, determining the best insurance strategy (or whether to self-insure), making cost projections and control, and considering volatility of operations, timing of adverse events, claims adjustment, proper cost allocation, and the use of risk management software.

The risks that a business faces may negatively affect its reputation, bottom line, cost and availability of financing, credit rating, market price of stock, regulatory or legislative changes, and elimination of barriers to entry. The firm must make an evaluation of the trade-off between risk and return. A higher risk mandates a higher rate of return to justify taking the extra risk. A risk program must be in place and must have built-in flexibility for adjustment, as conditions require. The program must conform to the goals, objectives, and policies of the business. A well-managed ERM policy encourages a common language of risk among board members, managers, suppliers, customers, investors, and so on. It helps people at the front line who spot warning signals of potential problems to communicate them more quickly to those who can decide to take evasive action.

Do you see an increasing trend on broader focus on enterprise risk oversight?

Expectations that boards and audit committees are effectively overseeing an organization's risk management processes are at all-time highs. As the volume and complexity of risks increase due to highly volatile economic conditions, globalization, emerging technologies, and complex business transactions, key stakeholders are putting pressure on boards and senior executives to strengthen their approach to risk management. For example, the New York Stock Exchange Final Governance Rules require the audit committee to discuss management's guidelines and policies for risk oversight. Standard & Poor's evaluates an entity's enterprise-wide risk management as part of its credit rating analysis procedures. The Securities and Exchange Commission requires the board of directors to provide disclosures in proxy statements to stockholders that describe the board's involvement in risk oversight.

The recent financial crisis and natural disasters in Japan that crippled global production are leading to a renewed focus on how senior executives approach risk management, including the board's role in risk oversight. Companies exist to provide value for stakeholders but face uncertainty in their attempts to grow stakeholder value. A challenge for management is to determine how much uncertainty to accept and how to deal effectively with uncertainty and associated risks. Senior executives are working to strengthen risk oversight so that both management and the board are better informed about emerging risk exposures, particularly those impacting strategy.

A recent white paper by the Committee of Sponsoring Organizations of the Treadway Commission (COSO), *Strengthening Enterprise Risk Oversight for Strategic Advantage*, highlights four specific areas where senior management can work with its board to enhance the board's risk oversight capabilities:

1. *Discuss risk management philosophy and appetite.* Unless the board and management fully understand the level of risk that the organization is willing and able to take, it will be difficult for the board and management to oversee critical risk exposures effectively.

2. *Understand risk management practices.* For many organizations, the approach to risk management is ad hoc, informal, and implicit, leaving executives and boards with an incomplete view of key risks.
3. *Review the portfolio of risks in relation to risk appetite.* Ultimately, the goal is to evaluate whether existing risk exposures are in line with stakeholder appetite for risks.
4. *Be apprised of the most significant risks and related responses.* Because risks constantly evolve, management needs a process that provides timely and robust information about risks arising across the organization.

These four areas build off COSO's *Enterprise Risk Management—Integrated Framework*, which provides core principles for effective identification, assessment, and management of enterprise risks.

Why do companies need continuity planning?

An understanding of risk is essential in crisis management. Once a range of possible future crises has been established, contingency plans, such as continuity or recovery plans, can be put in place. Employees must be instructed what to do in such eventualities. Test runs should be practiced, and contingency plans must be updated periodically to incorporate new technologies, changing staff, and new areas of business activity. Areas of risk must be identified, and corrective action must be taken to reduce those risks. Unusually high risk will not only have negative effects on earnings but might also jeopardize the continuity of the operation.

Models and quantitative approaches including actuarial techniques may be used to appraise potential catastrophic losses, product/service liability, intellectual property losses, and business interruption. Probability distributions of expected losses should be arrived at based on the model or quantitative technique used.

AN APPROACH TO RISK MANAGEMENT

What steps do companies need to take in managing risks?

Firms often use this three-step process for managing risks.

1. Identify the risks faced by the firm.
2. Measure the potential impact of each risk. Some risks are so small as to be immaterial, whereas others have the potential for destroying the company. It is useful to segregate risks by potential impact and then to focus on the most serious threats.
3. Decide how each relevant risk should be handled. In most situations, risk exposure can be reduced through one of these techniques:
   ■ *Transfer the risk to an insurance company.* Often it is advantageous to insure against (hence transfer) a risk. However, insurability does not necessarily mean that a risk *should* be covered by insurance. In many instances, it might be better for the company to self-insure, which means bearing the risk directly rather than paying another party to bear it.

- *Transfer the function that produces the risk to a third party.* For example, suppose a furniture manufacturer is concerned about potential liabilities arising from its ownership of a fleet of trucks used to transfer products from its manufacturing plant to various points across the country. One way to eliminate this risk would be to contract with a trucking company to do the shipping, thus passing the risk to a third party.
- *Purchase derivative contracts to reduce risk.* Firms use derivatives to hedge risks. Commodity derivatives can be used to reduce input risks. For example, a cereal company may use corn or wheat futures to hedge against increases in grain prices. Similarly, financial derivatives can be used to reduce risks that arise from changes in interest rates and exchange rates.
- *Reduce the probability of occurrence of an adverse event.* The expected loss arising from any risk is a function of both the probability of occurrence and the dollar loss if the adverse event occurs. In some instances, it is possible to reduce the probability that an adverse event will occur. For example, the probability that a fire will occur can be reduced by instituting a fire prevention program, by replacing old electrical wiring, and by using fire-resistant materials in areas with the greatest fire potential.
- *Reduce the magnitude of the loss associated with an adverse event.* Continuing with the fire risk example, the dollar cost associated with a fire can be reduced by such actions as installing sprinkler systems, designing facilities with self-contained fire zones, and locating facilities close to a fire station.
- *Totally avoid the activity that gives rise to the risk.* For example, a company might discontinue a product or service line because the risks outweigh the rewards, as with the infamous decision by Dow-Corning to discontinue its manufacture of silicone breast implants.

A CLOSE LOOK AT RISK MANAGEMENT

Risk management includes the identification of risk exposure, evaluating risk, computing potential loss, setting the optimal insurance strategy (or self-insuring), instability in operations, claims adjustment, projecting costs, allocating costs, controlling risk, and corrective action.

Risks a company faces can have a negative impact on its reputation, market price of stock, costs, profitability, availability of financing, bond rating, and elimination of barriers to entry.

An appraisal must be made of the trade-off between risk and return. Taking on greater risk requires a higher return rate to justify being exposed to the higher risk.

A risk program must be instituted. This program must have built-in flexibility to adjust, as conditions mandate. The program must be consistent with the purposes, goals, and policies of the business entity.

There has to be a feasible contingency plan, such as a recovery plan. Workers must be informed what to do in various scenarios related to risk. Contingency plans should be updated to include staff changes and new technologies. Test runs should be practiced.

How is risk appraised?

The warning signs of excessive risk must be identified and controlled. These signs include poor communication, fragmentation, improper focus, hostile attitudes, failure to observe regulations, poor worker training and performance, lateness, and deficient planning.

When looking at a specific situation, appraise the risk profile, financial condition, and acceptable risk exposure. To what degree does the company's risk exceed preestablished maximum levels? What are the costs applicable to various risk types? There are various ways to reduce risk, including:

- Diversify operations, product/service lines, geographic areas, investments, market segments, and customer bases.
- Participate in joint ventures and partnerships with other companies.
- Add products/services with different seasonal demand.
- Have adequate insurance coverage (e.g., foreign risk protection).
- Vertically integrate to reduce the price and supply risk of raw materials.
- Sell low-priced merchandise as well as more expensive items to protect against inflationary and recessionary periods.
- Concentrate on a piggyback product base (similar merchandise associated with the same basic business).
- Sell to diversified industries to minimize cyclical economic turns.
- Change suppliers who are unreliable.

In appraising risk, ask and answer these questions:

- Who is responsible for risk management?
- What evaluation is being conducted of control aspects?
- What are the specific areas of risk susceptibility?
- Is risk being managed properly?
- What is the internal process to curtail risk?
- Are controls effective?
- Is financial and operational information being reported correctly?

What about using risk management software?

Software exists to appraise and control corporate risks. A risk management information system (RMIS) includes software and hardware elements. Here we consider just software implications and applications. The software chosen should provide an appropriate fit based on the business entity's circumstances and environment.

In selecting the most appropriate software, the CFO should take into account the firm's expectations and requirements, report-preparation needs, government regulations, communication levels, insurance coverage, legal liability issues, work flow, structure of organization, corporate culture, service/product line, worker experience and knowledge, claims processing and administration, corporate policies and procedures, nature of operations, and technological resources. The risk management and analysis software should include the ability for risk classifications.

Are the "right" managers being given suitable data in a timely way? What are the distribution and communication features of the software? Flexibility in software is desirable so that reports can be customized based on the information required and for whom. For example, a factory manager wants to know how many worker injuries took place and why. The accounting manager wants to know the financial impact of the accidents on the company's financial status and operating performance.

Software can be utilized to appraise safety statistical data by manager, responsibility unit, department, division, and geographic area. Prospective problems can be identified. An example of a risk management software application is generating a report on how many employee injuries took place by activity, operation, department, division, and geographic location. Is the company's incidence rate unusually high or low relative to competitors and within the industry? If it is, why?

In the event the company exchanges risk information with others (e.g., government agencies, investment bankers, insurance companies), software compatibility is required. A company can use its intranet to expand risk management throughout the company.

What is risk control?

Risk control includes alarm systems, inspections, and compliance. Physical and human aspects must be considered. Are the company's assets safe—for example, is machinery easy to operate and will not result in worker injury? The labeling of products should be clear and appropriate. Consumer dissatisfaction with the company's products or services should be noted.

The CFO should look at the business entity's contractual agreements, employment practices, and working conditions. Employee policies must be consistent and fair. Workers must be properly instructed on safety precautions.

What are risk modeling software applications?

Risk modeling assists the CFO in his or her decision making. Models can be used to evaluate risk by type along with impact on the company. Probable losses must be estimated. What will competitive reactions be? A contingency model can aid in planning a suitable strategy and response. A what-if analysis may be undertaken to look at the resulting impact of changing input variables and factors. The worst-case, best-case, and most-likely scenarios can be examined and reviewed. The software assists the CFO in determining the types, areas, and degree of risk facing the company. A maximum–minimum range of loss figures may be derived.

Risk modeling can be used to identify and define the type and amount of risks applicable to various exposures. A priority ranking based on risk may be prepared. Risk problem areas may be evaluated along with the suitable alternative responses.

Is there guidance for managing the business risk of fraud or fraud risk?

In 2008, the American Institute of CPAs (www.aicpa.org), the Institute of Internal Auditors (www.theiia.org), and the Association of Certified Fraud Examiners (www.acfe.com) jointly created *Managing the Business Risk of Fraud: A Practical Guide*, to assist boards, senior management, and internal auditors in their management of fraud risk within organizations. The guide defines five principles for fraud risk management:

> *Principle 1.* As part of an organization's governance structure, a fraud risk management program should be in place, including a written policy (or policies) to convey the expectations of the board of directors and senior management regarding managing fraud risk.
>
> *Principle 2.* Fraud risk exposure should be assessed periodically by the organization to identify specific potential schemes and events that the organization needs to mitigate.
>
> *Principle 3.* Prevention techniques to avoid potential key fraud risk events should be established, where feasible, to mitigate possible impacts on the organization.
>
> *Principle 4.* Detection techniques should be established to uncover fraud events when preventive measures fail or unmitigated risks are realized.
>
> *Principle 5.* A reporting process should be in place to solicit input on potential fraud, and a coordinated approach to investigation and corrective action should be used to help ensure that potential fraud is addressed appropriately and timely.

The guide describes how organizations of all sizes can establish their own fraud risk management programs and includes examples of key program components and resources that organizations can use as a starting point to develop an effective and efficient fraud risk management program.

 ## HOW TO REDUCE INVESTMENT RISK: DIVERSIFY

Diversification is usually an answer to reduction in risk. "Diversify" means "don't put all your eggs in one basket." With a diversified portfolio (e.g., stocks, bonds, real estate, and savings accounts), the value of all these investments will not increase or decrease at the same time or in the same magnitude. Thus, you can protect yourself against fluctuations. Your company may diversify into different lines of businesses that are not subject to the same economic and political influences and, in this way, protect itself against fluctuations in earnings.

What is portfolio theory?

The central theme of portfolio theory is that rational investors behave in a way that reflects their aversion to taking increased risk without being compensated by an adequate increase in expected return. In addition, for any given expected return, most investors will prefer a lower risk, and for any given level of risk, they will prefer a higher return to a lower return. Harry Markowitz showed how to calculate a set of "efficient" portfolios. An investor then will choose among a set of efficient portfolios that is consistent with his or her risk profile.

Most financial assets are not held in isolation but rather as part of a portfolio. Therefore, the risk-return analysis should not be confined to single assets only. It is important to look at portfolios and the gains from diversification. What is important is the return on the portfolio, not just the return on one asset, and the portfolio's risk.

How do you compute portfolio return?

The expected return on a portfolio (r_p) is simply the weighted average return of the individual sets in the portfolio, with the weights being the fraction of the total funds invested in each asset:

$$r_p = w_1 r_1 + w_2 r_2 + \ldots + w_n r_n = \sum_{j=1}^{n} w_j r_j$$

where
w_j = fraction for each respective asset investment
r_j = expected return on each individual asset
n = number of assets in the portfolio

$$\sum_{j=1}^{n} w_j r_j = 1.0$$

Example 13.1

A portfolio consists of assets A and B. Asset A makes up one-third of the portfolio and has an expected return of 18 percent. Asset B makes up the other two-thirds of the portfolio and is expected to earn 9 percent. The expected return on the portfolio is:

Asset	Return (r_j)	Fraction (w_j)	$w_j r_j$
A	18%	1/3	1/3 × 18% = 6%
B	9%	2/3	2/3 × 9% = 6%
			r_p = 12%

How do you calculate portfolio risk?

Unlike returns, the risk of a portfolio (σ_p) is not simply the weighted average of the standard deviations of the individual assets in the contribution; a portfolio's risk is also dependent on the correlation coefficients of its assets. The correlation coefficient (ρ) is a measure of the degree to which two variables move together. It has a numerical value that ranges from −1.0 to 1.0. In a two-asset (A and B) portfolio, the portfolio risk is defined as:

$$\sigma_p = \sqrt{w_A^2 \sigma_A^2 + w_B^2 \sigma_B^2 + 2\rho_{AB} w_A w_B \sigma_A \sigma_B}$$

where

σ_A and σ_B = Standard deviations of assets A and B, respectively

w_A and w_B = Weights, or fractions, of total funds invested in assets A and B

ρ_{AB} = Correlation coefficient between assets A and B

Incidentally, the correlation coefficient is the measurement of joint movement between two securities.

How do you diversify?

As can be seen in the preceding formula, the portfolio risk, measured in terms of σ, is not the weighted average of the individual asset risks in the portfolio. Note that in the formula, we have the third term, (ρ), which makes a significant contribution to the overall portfolio risk. The formula basically shows that portfolio risk can be minimized or completely eliminated by diversification. The degree of reduction in portfolio risk depends on the correlation between the assets being combined. Generally speaking, by combining two perfectly negatively correlated assets ($\rho = 1.0$), we can eliminate the risk completely. In the real world, however, most securities are negatively, but not perfectly, correlated; in fact, some assets are positively correlated. We could still reduce the portfolio risk by combining even positively correlated assets. An example of the latter might be ownership of two automobile stocks or two housing stocks.

Example 13.2

Assume:

Asset	Σ	w
A	20%	1/3
B	10%	2/3

The portfolio risk then is:

$$\sigma_p = \sqrt{w_A^2 \sigma_A^2 + w_B^2 \sigma_B^2 + 2\rho_{AB} w_A w_B \sigma_A \sigma_B}$$

$$= \sqrt{(1/3)^2 (0.2)^2 + (2/3)^2 (0.1)^2 + 2\rho_{AB}(1/3)(2/3)(0.2)(0.1)} = \sqrt{0.0089 + 0.0089\rho_{AB}}$$

1. Now assume that the correlation coefficient between A and B is +1 (a perfectly positive correlation). This means that when the value of asset A increases in response to market conditions, so does the value of asset B, and it does so at exactly the same rate as A. The portfolio risk when $\rho_{AB} = +1$ then becomes:

$$\sigma_p = \sqrt{0.0089 + 0.0089\,\rho_{AB}} = \sqrt{0.0089 + 0.0089(+1)} = \sqrt{0.0178} = 0.1334 = 13.34\%$$

2. If $\rho_{AB} = 0$, the assets lack correlation and the portfolio risk is simply the risk of the expected returns on the assets (i.e., the weighted average of the standard deviations of the individual assets in the portfolio). Therefore, when $\rho_{AB} = 0$, the portfolio risk for this example is:

(continued)

$$\sigma_p = \sqrt{0.0089+0.0089\rho_{AB}} = \sqrt{0.0089+0.0089(0)} = \sqrt{0.0089} = 0.0094 = 9.4\%$$

3. If $\rho_{AB} = -1$ (a perfectly negative correlation coefficient), then as the price of A rises, the price of B declines at the very same rate. In such a case, risk would be completely eliminated. Therefore, when $\rho_{AB} = -1$, the portfolio risk is

$$\sigma_p = \sqrt{0.0089+0.0089\rho_{AB}} = \sqrt{0.0089+0.0089(-1)} = \sqrt{0} = 0$$

When we compare the results of examples 1, 2, and 3, we see that a positive correlation between assets increases a portfolio's risk above the level found at zero correlation, whereas a perfectly negative correlation eliminates that risk.

Example 13.3

To illustrate the point of diversification, assume that the data on the next three securities are:

Year	Security X (%)	Security Y (%)	Security Z (%)
2X07	10	50	10
2X08	20	40	20
2X09	30	30	30
2X10	40	20	40
2X11	50	10	50
r_j	30	30	30
σ_j	14.14	14.14	14.14

Note here that securities X and Y have a perfectly negative correlation and that securities X and Z have a perfectly positive correlation. Notice what happens to the portfolio risk when X and Y and when X and Z are combined. Assume that funds are split equally between the two securities in each portfolio.

Year	Portfolio XY (50%–50%)	Portfolio XZ (50%–50%)
2X07	30	10
2X08	30	20
2X09	30	30
2X10	30	40
2X11	30	50
r_p	30	30
σ_p	0	14.14

Again, see that the two perfectly negative correlated securities (XY) result in a zero overall risk.

 BETA—THE CAPITAL ASSET PRICING MODEL

What is beta?

Many investors hold more than one financial asset. A portion of a security's risk (called *unsystematic risk*) can be controlled through diversification. This type of risk is unique to a given security. Business, liquidity, and default risks fall in this category. Nondiversifiable risk, more commonly referred to as *systematic risk*, results from forces outside of the firm's control and are therefore not unique to the given security. Purchasing power, interest rate, and market risks fall into this category. This type of risk is measured by *beta* (b).

Beta measures a security's volatility relative to an average security. A particular stock's beta is useful in predicting how much the security will go up or down, provided that you know which way the market will go. It helps you to figure out risk and expected return.

Most of the unsystematic risk affecting a security can be diversified away in an efficiently constructed portfolio. Therefore, this type of risk does not need to be compensated with a higher level of return. The only relevant risk is systematic risk, or beta risk, for which the investor can expect to receive compensation. You, as an investor, are compensated for taking this type of risk, which cannot be controlled.

Under the *capital asset pricing model* (CAPM), in general, there is a relationship between a stock's expected (or required return) and its beta. The next formula is helpful in determining a stock's expected return.

$$r_j = r_f + b(r_m - r_f)$$

In words,

$$\text{Expected return} = \text{Risk-free rate} + \text{Beta} \times \text{Market risk premium}$$

where

r_j = Expected (or required) return on security j
r_f = Risk-free rate on a security such as a Treasury bill
b = Beta, an index of systematic (nondiversifiable, noncontrollable) risk
r_m = Expected return on the market portfolio (such as Standard & Poor's 500 Stock Composite Index or Dow Jones 30 Industrials)

The market risk premium ($r_m - r_f$) equals the expected market return (rm) minus the risk-free rate (r_f). The market risk premium is the additional return above that which you could earn on, say a Treasury bill, to compensate for assuming a given level of risk (as measured by beta).

Thus, the formula shows that the required (expected) return on a given security is equal to the return required for securities that have no risk plus a risk premium required by the investor for assuming a given level of risk. The key idea behind the formula is that the relevant measure of risk is the risk of the individual security, or its beta. The higher the beta for a security, the greater the return expected (or demanded) by the investor.

Example 13.4

Assume that r_f = 6% and r_m = 10% If a stock has a beta of 2.0, its risk premium should be 8 percent.

$$b(r_m - r_f) = 2.0(10\% - 6\%) = 8\%$$

This means that you would expect (or demand) an extra 8 percent (risk premium) on this stock on top of the risk-free return of 6 percent. Therefore, the total expected (required) return on the stock should be 14 percent:

$$r_j = r_f + b(r_m - r_f)$$
$$6\% + 2.0(10\% - 6\%) = 6\% + 8\% = 14\%$$

Example 13.5

The higher a stock's beta, the greater the return expected (or demanded) by the investor, as shown here:

Stock	Beta	Required Return
ExxonMobil	0.85	6% + 0.85(12% − 6%) = 11.1%
Bristol-Meyers	1.0	6% + 1.0(12% − 6%) = 12%
Neiman-Marcus	1.65	6% + 1.65(12% − 6%) = 15.9%

How do you read beta?

Beta measures a security's volatility relative to an average security. To put it another way, it is a measure of a security's return over time to that of the overall market. For example, if your company's beta is 2.0, it means that if the stock market goes up 10 percent, your company's common stock goes up 20 percent; if the market goes down 10 percent, your company's stock price goes down 20 percent. Here is how to read betas:

Exhibit 13.1 shows examples of betas for selected stocks in October 2011.

EXHIBIT 13.1 Betas for Some Selected Corporations

Company	October 2011
Boeing (BA)	1.28
Google (GOOG)	1.11
Toyota (TM)	0.69
Nordstrom (JWN)	1.65
Intel (INTC)	1.07
Walmart (WMT)	0.31

Source: MSN Money Central Investor (http://money.msn.com/investing).

ARBITRAGE PRICING MODEL

What is the difference between the CAPM and the arbitrage pricing model?

The CAPM assumes that required rates of return depend only on one risk factor, the stock's beta. The arbitrage pricing model (APM) disputes this assumption and includes any number of risk factors:

$$r = r_f + b_1 RP_1 + b_2 RP_2 + \dots + b_n RP_n$$

where
   r = Expected return for a given stock or portfolio
   r_f = Risk-free rate
   b_i = Sensitivity (or reaction) of the returns of the stock to unexpected changes in economic forces ($i = 1, \dots n$)
   RP_i = Market risk premium associated with an unexpected change in the ith economic force ($i = 1, \dots n$)
   n = the number of relevant economic forces

Five economic forces are often suggested:

1. Changes in expected inflation
2. Unanticipated changes in inflation
3. Unanticipated changes in industrial production
4. Unanticipated changes in the yield differential between low- and high-grade bonds (the default-risk premium)
5. Unanticipated changes in the yield differential between long-term and short-term bonds (the term structure of interest rates)

Some analysts have documented the importance of industry factors, investor confidence, exchange rates, oil prices, and a host of other variables. It appears, however, that we are still a long way from being able to confidently describe the underlying reasons for cross-sectional differences in average returns.

Example 13.6

Suppose a three-factor APM holds and the risk-free rate is 6 percent. You are interested in two particular stocks, A and B. The returns on both stocks are related to factors 1 and 2 as shown:

$$r = 0.06 + b_1(0.09) - b_2(0.03) + b_3(0.04)$$

(continued)

The sensitivity coefficients for the two stocks are:

Stock	b_1	b_2	b_3
A	0.70	0.80	0.20
B	0.50	0.04	1.20

We can calculate the expected returns on both stocks as follows:

For stock A:

$r = 0.06 + (0.70)(0.09) - (0.80)(0.03) + (0.20)(0.04) = 10.70\%$

For stock B:

$r = 0.06 + (0.50)(0.09) - (0.04)(0.03) + (1.20)(0.04) = 14.10\%$

Stock B requires a higher return, indicating that it is the riskier of the two. Part of the reason is that its return is substantially more sensitive to the third economic force than that of stock A.

CHAPTER FOURTEEN

Capital Budgeting and Real Options

 ## WHAT IS CAPITAL BUDGETING?

Capital budgeting is the process of making long-term planning decisions for alternative investment opportunities. The company may have to make many investment decisions in order to grow. Examples of capital budgeting applications are selecting product line, keeping or selling a business segment, leasing or buying, and deciding which asset to invest in.

 ## WHAT ARE THE TYPES OF INVESTMENT PROJECTS?

There are typically two types of long-term investment decisions:

1. *Selection decisions* involve obtaining new facilities or expanding existing ones. Examples include:
   - Investments in property, plant, and equipment as well as other types of assets
   - Resource commitments in the form of new product development, market research, introduction of a computer, refunding of long-term debt, and so on
   - Mergers and acquisitions in the form of buying another company to add a new product line
2. *Replacement decisions* involve replacing existing facilities with new ones. Examples include replacing an old machine with a high-tech machine.

 ## WHAT ARE THE FEATURES OF INVESTMENT PROJECTS?

Long-term investments have three important features:

1. They typically involve a large amount of initial cash outlays, which tend to have a long-term impact on the firm's future profitability. Therefore, this initial cash outlay needs to be justified on a cost-benefit basis.

2. There are expected recurring cash inflows (e.g., increased revenues, savings in cash operating expenses, etc.) over the life of the investment project. This fact frequently requires considering the time value of money.
3. Income taxes could make a difference in the accept or reject decision. Therefore, income tax factors must be taken into account in every capital budgeting decision.

TIME VALUE FUNDAMENTALS

A dollar now is worth more than a dollar to be received later. This statement sums up an important principle: Money has a time value. This is not because inflation might make the dollar received at a later time worth less in buying power. The reason is that you could invest the dollar now and have more than a dollar at a specified later date.

Time value of money is a critical consideration in financial and investment decisions. For example, compound interest calculations are needed to determine future sums of money resulting from an investment. Discounting, or the calculation of present value, which is inversely related to compounding, is used to evaluate the future cash flow associated with capital budgeting projects. There are plenty of applications of time value of money in accounting and finance.

What is money worth in the future?

A dollar in hand today is worth more than a dollar to be received tomorrow because of the interest it could earn from putting it in a savings account or placing it in an investment account. Compounding interest means that interest earns interest. For the discussion of the concepts of compounding and time value, let us define:

F_n = Future value: the amount of money at the end of year n
P = Principal
i = Annual interest rate
n = Number of years

Then

F_1 = Amount of money at the end of year 1 = principal and interest
$= P + iP = P(1 + i)$

F_2 = Amount of money at the end of year 2 = $F_1(1 + i) = P(1 + i)(1 + i) = P(1 + i)^2$

The future value of an investment compounded annually at rate i for n years is

$$F_n = P(1 + i)^n = P \times T_1(i,n)$$

where $T_1(i,n)$ is the compound amount of $1 and can be found in Table A.1 in the Appendix.

What is the future value of an annuity?

An annuity is a series of payments (or receipts) of a fixed amount for a specified number of periods. Each payment is assumed to occur at the end of the period. The future value of

Example 14.1

You place $1,000 in a savings account earning 8 percent interest compounded annually. How much money will you have in the account at the end of four years?

$$F_n = P(1 + i)^n$$
$$F_4 = \$1,000(1 + 0.08)^4 = \$1,000\ T_1(8\%, 4\text{ years})$$

From Table A.1, the T_1 for four years at 8 percent is 1.361. Therefore,

$$F_4 = \$1,000(1.361) = \$1,361$$

Example 14.2

You invested a large sum of money in the stock of Delta Corporation. The company paid a $3 dividend per share. The dividend is expected to increase by 20 percent per year for the next three years. You wish to project the dividends for years 1 through 3.

$$F_n = P(1 + i)^n$$
$$F_1 = \$3(1 + 0.2)^1 = \$3\ T_1(20\%,1) = \$3(1.200) = \$3.60$$
$$F_2 = \$3(1 + 0.2)^2 = \$3\ T_1(20\%,2) = \$3(1.440) = \$4.32$$
$$F_3 = \$3(1 + 0.2)^3 = \$3\ T_1(20\%,3) = \$3(1.728) = \$5.18$$

an annuity is a compound annuity, which involves depositing or investing an equal sum of money at the end of each year for a certain number of years and allowing it to grow.

Let S_n = the future value on an n-year annuity and A = the amount of an annuity. Then we can write

$$S_n = A(1 + i)^{n-1} + A(1 + i)^{n-2} + \dots + A(1 + i)^0$$
$$= A[(1 + i)^{n-1} + (1 + i)^{n-2} + \dots + (1 + i)^0]$$

$$= A \times \sum_{t=0}^{n-1}(1+i)^t = A \times \frac{(1+i)^n - 1}{i} = A \times T_2(i,n)$$

where $T_2(i,n)$ represents the future value of an annuity of $1 for n years compounded at i percent and can be found in Table A.2 in the Appendix.

Example 14.3

You wish to determine the sum of money you will have in a savings account at the end of six years by depositing $1,000 at the end of each year for the next six years. The annual interest rate is 8 percent. The T_2 (8%, 6 years) is given in Table A.2 as 7.336. Therefore,

$$S_6 = \$1,000\ T_2(8\%,6) = \$1,000(7.336) = \$7,336$$

Example 14.4

You deposit $30,000 semiannually into a fund for 10 years. The annual interest rate is 8 percent. The amount accumulated at the end of the tenth year is calculated as:

$$S_n = A \times T_2(i,n)$$

where
$A = \$30,000$
$i = 8\%/2 = 4\%$
$n = 10 \times 2 = 20$

Therefore,

$S_{20} = \$30,000\ T_2(4\%,20)$
$= \$30,000(29.778) = \$893,340$

What is present value?

Present value is the present worth of future sums of money. The process of calculating present values, or discounting, is actually the opposite of finding the compounded future value. In connection with present value calculations, the interest rate *i* is called the *discount rate*. The discount rate we use is more commonly called the *cost of capital*, which is the minimum rate of return required by the investor.

Recall that $F_n = P(1 + i)^n$. Therefore,

$$P = \frac{F_n}{(1+i)^n} = F_n \frac{1}{(1+i)^n} = F_n \times T_3(i,n)$$

where $T_3(i,n)$ represents the present value of $1 and is given in Table A.3 in the Appendix.

Example 14.5

You have been given an opportunity to receive $20,000 six years from now. If you can earn 10 percent on your investments, what is the most you should pay for this opportunity? To answer this question, you must compute the present value of $20,000 to be received six years from now at a 10 percent rate of discount. F_6 is $20,000, *i* is 10 percent, and *n* is 6 years. T_3 (10%, 6 years) from Table A.3 is 0.564.

$$P = \$20,000[1/(1 + 0.1)^6] = \$20,000\ T_3(10\%,6)$$
$$= \$20,000(0.564) = \$11,280$$

This means that you can earn 10 percent on your investment, and you would be indifferent to receiving $11,280 now or $20,000 six years from today since the amounts are time equivalent. In other words, you could invest $11,300 today at 10 percent and have $20,000 in six years.

How do you compute mixed streams of cash flows?

The present value of a series of mixed payments (or receipts) is the sum of the present value of each individual payment. We know that the present value of each individual payment is the payment times the appropriate T_3 value.

Example 14.6

You are thinking of starting a new product line that initially costs $32,000. Your annual projected cash inflows are:

1	$10,000
2	$20,000
3	$5,000

If you must earn a minimum of 10 percent on your investment, should you undertake this new product line?

The present value of this series of mixed streams of cash inflows is calculated as follows:

Year	Cash Inflows	×	$T_3(10\%,n)$	Present Value
1	$10,000		0.909	$ 9,090
2	$20,000		0.826	$16,520
3	$5,000		0.751	$ 3,755
				$29,365

Since the present value of your projected cash inflows is less than the initial investment, you should not undertake this project.

What is the present value of an annuity?

Interest received from bonds, pension funds, and insurance obligations all involve annuities. To compare these financial instruments, we need to know the present value of each. The present value of an annuity (P_n) can be found by using this equation:

$$P_n = A \frac{1}{(1+i)^1} + A \frac{1}{(1+i)^2} + \cdots + A \frac{1}{(1+i)^2}$$

$$= A \left[\frac{1}{(1+i)^1} + \frac{1}{(1+i)^2} + \cdots + \frac{1}{(1+i)^2} \right]$$

$$= A \times \sum_{t=1}^{n} \frac{1}{(1+i)^t} = A \times \frac{1}{i} \left[1 - \frac{1}{(1+i)} \right] = A \times T_4(i, n)$$

Example 14.7

Assume that the cash inflows in Example 14.6 form an annuity of $10,000 for three years. Then the present value is

$$P_n = A \times T_4(i,n)$$
$$P_3 = \$10,000 \; T_4(10\%, \text{ 3 years})$$
$$= \$10,000(2.487) = \$24,870$$

where $T_4(i,n)$ represents the present value of an annuity of $1 discounted at i percent for n years and is found in Table A.4 in the Appendix.

Using Financial Calculators and Spreadsheet Programs

Many financial calculators, such as those made by Radio Shack, Hewlett-Packard, Sharpe, and Texas Instruments, contain preprogrammed formulas that perform many present value and future value applications. Spreadsheet software, such as Excel, has built-in financial functions that perform many such applications.

 POPULAR EVALUATION TECHNIQUES

Six methods of evaluating investment projects are:

1. Payback period
2. Discounted payback period
3. Accounting (simple) rate of return (ARR)
4. Net present value (NPV)
5. Internal rate of return (IRR) (or time-adjusted rate of return)
6. Profitability index (or present value index)

The NPV method and the IRR method are called *discounted cash flow* (DCF) methods. Each of these methods is discussed in the sections that follow.

Payback Period
How do you determine the payback period?

The payback period measures the length of time required to recover the amount of initial investment. It is computed by dividing the initial investment by the cash inflows through increased revenues or cost savings.

Decision rule: Choose the project with the shorter payback period. The rationale behind this choice is: The shorter the payback period, the less risky the project and the greater the liquidity.

Example 14.8

Assume cost of investment is $18,000 and annual after-tax cash savings is $3,000. Then the payback period is:

$$\text{Payback period} = \frac{\text{Initial investment}}{\text{Cost savings}} = \frac{\$18,000}{\$3,000} = 6 \text{ years}$$

What are the pros and cons of the payback period method?

The advantages of using the payback period method of evaluating an investment project are that it is simple to compute and easy to understand, and it handles investment risk effectively.

Example 14.9

Consider two projects whose after-tax cash inflows are not even. Assume each project costs $1,000.

	Cash Inflow	
Year	A($)	B($)
1	100	500
2	200	400
3	300	300
4	400	100
5	500	
6	600	

When cash inflows are not even, the payback period has to be found by trial and error. The payback period of project A is ($1,000 = $100 + $200 + $300 + $400) 4 years. The payback period of project B is ($1,000 = $500 + $400 + $100):

$$2 \text{ years} + (\$100/\$300) = 2\frac{1}{3} \text{ years}$$

Project B is the project of choice in this case, because it has the shorter payback period.

The shortcomings of this method are that it does not recognize the time value of money, and it ignores the impact of cash inflows received after the payback period. Essentially, cash flows after the payback period determine the profitability of an investment.

Discounted Payback Period

You can take into account the time value of money by using the discounted payback period. The payback period will be longer using the discounted method because money is worth less over time.

How do you determine the discounted payback period?

Discounted payback is computed by adding the present value of each year's cash inflows until they equal the initial investment.

$$\text{Discounted payback} = \frac{\text{Initial cash outlays}}{\text{Discounted annual cash inflows}}$$

Example 14.10

You invest $40,000 and receive the listed cash inflows. The discounted payback period is calculated as:

Year	Cash Inflows	T_1 Factor	Present Value	Accumulated Present Value
1	$15,000	0.9091	$13,637	13,637
2	20,000	0.8264	16,528	30,165
3	28,000	0.7513	21,036	51,201

Thus,

$$\$30,165 + \frac{\$40,000 - 30,165}{\$21,036} = 2 \text{ years} + 0.47 = 2.47$$

Accounting (Simple) Rate of Return

What is the accounting rate of return?

The *accounting rate of return* (ARR) measures profitability from the conventional accounting standpoint by relating the required investment—or sometimes the average investment—to the future annual net income.

Decision rule: Under the ARR method, choose the project with the higher rate of return.

Example 14.11

Consider this investment:

Initial investment	$6,500
Estimated life	20 years
Cash inflows per year	$1,000
Depreciation per year (using straight line)	$325

The accounting rate of return for this project is:

$$\text{ARR} = \frac{\text{Net income}}{\text{Investment}} = \frac{\$1,000 - \$325}{\$6,500} = 10.4\%$$

If average investment (usually assumed to be one-half of the original investment) is used, then:

$$\text{ARR} = \frac{\$1,000 - \$325}{\$3,250} = 20.8\%$$

What are the benefits and drawbacks of the ARR method?

The advantages of this method are that it is easily understood, simple to compute, and recognizes the profitability factor.

The shortcomings of this method are that it fails to recognize the time value of money, and it uses accounting data instead of cash flow data.

Net Present Value Method

What is net present value?

Net present value (NPV) is the excess of the present value (PV) of cash inflows generated by the project over the amount of the initial investment (*I*):

$$\text{NPV} = \text{PV} - I$$

The present value of future cash flows is computed using the so-called cost of capital (or minimum required rate of return) as the discount rate. When cash inflows are uniform, the PV would be

$$\text{PV} = A \times T_4(i,n)$$

where A is the amount of the annuity. The value of T_4 is found in Table A.4 of the Appendix.

Decision rule: If NPV is positive, accept the project; otherwise, reject it.

Example 14.12

Consider this investment:

Initial investment	$12,950
Estimated life	10 years
Annual cash inflows	$3,000
Cost of capital (minimum required rate of return)	12%

Present value of the cash inflows is:

$$\text{PV} = A \times T_4(i,n)$$

$$\text{PV} = \$3,000 \times T_4(12\%, \ 10 \ \text{years})$$

PV = $3,000 (5.650)	$16,950
Initial investment (*I*)	12,950
Net present value (NPV = PV − *I*)	$4,000

Since the NPV of the investment is positive, the investment should be accepted.

What are the pros and cons of the NPV method?

The advantages of the NPV method are that it obviously recognizes the time value of money, and it is easy to compute whether the cash flows form an annuity or vary from period to period.

Internal Rate of Return

What is internal rate of return?

Internal rate of return (IRR), also called *time-adjusted rate of return*, is defined as the rate of interest that equates I with the PV of future cash inflows. In other words, at IRR, I = PV or NPV = 0.

 Decision rule: Accept the project if the IRR exceeds the cost of capital; otherwise, reject it.

Example 14.13

Assume the same data given in Example 14.12, and set the following equality (*I* = PV):

$$\$12{,}950 = \$3{,}000 \times T_4(i, \text{ 10 years})$$

$$T_4(i, \text{ 10 years}) = \frac{\$12{,}950}{\$3{,}000} = 4.317$$

which stands somewhere between 18 and 20 percent in the 10-year line of Table A.4. The interpolation follows.

	PV of an Annuity of $1 Factor	
	$T_4(i, \text{ 10 years})$	
18%	4.494	4.494
IRR	4.317	
20%		4.192
Difference	0.177	0.302

Therefore,

$$IRR = 18\% + \frac{0.177}{0.302} \ (20\% - 18\%)$$

$$= 18\% + 0.586(2\%) = 18\% + 1.17\% = 19.17\%$$

 Since the IRR of the investment is greater than the cost of capital (12 percent), accept the project.

Can a computer help?

Spreadsheet programs can be used in making IRR calculations. For example, Excel has a function IRR (values, guess). Excel considers negative numbers as cash outflows, such as the initial investment, and positive numbers as cash inflows. Many financial calculators have similar features. As in Example 14.13, suppose you want to calculate the IRR of a $12,950 investment (the value $−12,950 entered in year 0 that is followed by 10 monthly cash inflows of 3000). Using a guess of 12 percent (the value of 0.12), which is in effect the cost of capital, your formula would be @ IRR(values, 0.12), and Excel would return 19.15 percent, as shown in the next table.

Year 0	1	2	3	4	5	6	7	8	9	10
−12,950	3,000	3,000	3,000	3,000	3,000	3,000	3,000	3,000	3,000	3,000
IRR = 19.15%										
NPV = $4,000.67										

Note

The Excel formula for NPV is NPV (discount rate, cash inflow values) + *I*, where *I* is given as a negative number. ▪

What are the benefits and drawbacks of the IRR method?

The advantage of using the IRR method is that it considers the time value of money and therefore is more exact and realistic than the ARR method.

The shortcomings of this method are that (1) it is time-consuming to compute, especially when the cash inflows are not even, although most financial calculators and personal computers have a key to calculate IRR; and (2) it fails to recognize the varying sizes of investment in competing projects.

Profitability Index (or Present Value Index)

What is the profitability index?

The *profitability index* is the ratio of the total PV of future cash inflows to the initial investment, that is, PV/I. This index is used as a means of ranking projects in descending order of attractiveness.

Decision rule: If the profitability index is greater than 1, accept the project.

Example 14.14

Using the data in Example 14.12, we find that the profitability index is

$$\frac{PV}{I} = \frac{\$16,950}{\$12,950} = 1.31$$

Since this project generates $1.31 for each dollar invested (i.e., its profitability index is greater than 1), accept the project.

The profitability index has the advantage of putting all projects on the same relative basis regardless of size.

 LIMITED FUNDS FOR CAPITAL SPENDING

How do you select the best mix of projects with a limited budget?

Many firms specify a limit on the overall budget for capital spending. Capital rationing is concerned with the problem of selecting the mix of acceptable projects that provides the highest overall NPV. The profitability index is used widely in ranking projects competing for limited funds.

Example 14.15

The Westmont Company has a fixed budget of $250,000. It needs to select a mix of acceptable projects from the following:

Projects	I($) (000s)	PV($) (000s)	NPV($) (000s)	Profitability Index	Ranking
A	70	112	42	1.6	1
B	100	145	45	1.45	2
C	110	126.5	16.5	1.15	5
D	60	79	19	1.32	3
E	40	38	-2	0.95	6
F	80	95	15	1.19	4

The ranking resulting from the profitability index shows that the company should select projects A, B, and D.

	I	PV
A	$70,000	$112,000
B	100,000	145,000
D	60,000	79,000
	$230,000	$336,000

Therefore,

$$\text{NPV} = \$336,000 - \$230,000 = \$106,000$$

A more general approach to solving capital rationing problems is the use of zero-one integer programming. Here the objective is to select the mix of projects that maximizes the NPV subject to a budget constraint.

Using the data given in Example 14.14, we can set up the problem as a zero-one programming problem such that

$$x_j = \begin{cases} 1 \text{ if project } j \text{ is selected} \\ 0 \text{ if project } j \text{ is not selected } (j = 1, 2, 3, 4, 5, 6) \end{cases}$$

The problem then can be formulated as follows.

Maximize

$\text{NPV} = \$42{,}000 \times x_1 + \$45{,}000 \times x_2 + \$16{,}000 \times x_3 + \$19{,}000 \times x_4 - \$2{,}000 \times x_5 + \$15{,}000 \times x_6$

subject to

$\$70{,}000 \times x_1 + \$100{,}000 \times x_2 + \$110{,}000 \times x_3 + \$60{,}000 \times x_4 + \$40{,}000 \times x_5 + \$80{,}000 \times x_6$

$\leq \$250{,}000$

$x_j = 0, 1 (j = 1, 2, \ldots, 6)$

Using the zero-one programming solution routine, we find that the solution to the problem is:

$$x_1 = A = 1, \, x_2 = B = 1, \, x_4 = D = 1$$

```
LINDO'S ZERO-ONE PROGRAMMING OUTPUT
: max  42000x1+45000x2+16500x3+19000x4=2000x5+15000x6
? st
? 70000x1+100000x2+110000x3+60000x4+40000x5+80000
? x6<250000
? x1+x=1
? end
: integer 6
: integer x1
: integer x2
: integer x3
: integer x4
: integer x5
: integer x6
: Go
```

```
                                OBJECTIVE FUNCTION VALUE
1)              106000.000      = NPV
VARIABLE        VALUE           REDUCED COST
x1                1.000000      -21500.000000    )         Note:
x2                1.000000      -30000.000000    )
x3                 .000000      -30000.000000    )         X1=1=A
x4                1.000000      -30000.000000    )         X2=1=B
x5                 .000000       -8000.000000    )         X4=1=D
x6                 .000000        3000.000000
                SLACK OR
ROW             SURPLUS         DUAL PRICES
2)               .000000            .150000
3)               .000000       10000.000000
NO. ITERATIONS=
BRANCHES=        0 DETERM=       11.00E 4
BOND ON OPTIMUM;  102000.0
ENUMERATION COMPLETE. BRANCHES=   0              PIVOTS=  2
LAST INTEGER SOLUTION IS THE BEST FOUND
RE-INSTALLING BEST SOLUTION...
```

and the NPV is \$106,000. Thus, projects A, B and D should be selected.

How do you choose between mutually exclusive investments?

Projects are said to be mutually exclusive if the acceptance of one project automatically excludes the acceptance of one or more other projects. In the case where one must choose between mutually exclusive investments, the NPV and IRR methods may result in contradictory indications. The three conditions under which contradictory rankings can occur are:

1. Projects that have different life expectancies
2. Projects that have different sizes of investment
3. Projects whose cash flows differ over time

For example, the cash flows of one project increase over time, while those of another decrease.

The contradictions result from two different assumptions with respect to the reinvestment rate on cash flows from the projects.

1. The NPV method discounts all cash flows at the cost of capital, thus implicitly assuming that these cash flows can be reinvested at this rate.
2. The IRR method implies a reinvestment rate at IRR. Thus, the implied reinvestment rate will differ from project to project.

The NPV method generally gives correct ranking, since the cost of capital is a more realistic reinvestment rate.

Example 14.16

Assume:

	Cash Flows					
	0	1	2	3	4	5
A	(100)	120				
B	(100)					201.14

Computing IRR and NPV at 10 percent gives the following different rankings:

	IRR	NPV at 10%
A	20%	9.01
B	15%	24.90

The NPVs plotted against the appropriate discount rates form a graph called a NPV profile (Exhibit 14.1).

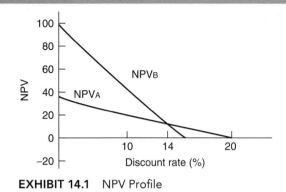

EXHIBIT 14.1 NPV Profile

At a discount rate larger than 14 percent, A has a higher NPV than B. Therefore, A should be selected. At a discount rate less than 14 percent, B has the higher NPV than A and thus should be selected. The correct decision is to select the project with the higher NPV, since the NPV method assumes a more realistic reinvestment rate (i.e., the cost of capital).

REAL OPTIONS

Almost all capital budgeting proposals can be viewed as *real options*. Also, projects and operations contain implicit options, such as the option as to when to take a project, the option to expand, the option to abandon, and the option to suspend or contract operations. Deciding when to take a project is called the *investment timing option*.

Example 14.17

A project costs $100 and has a single future cash flow. If we take it today, the cash flow will be $120 in one year. If we wait one year, the project will still cost $100, but the cash flow the following year (i.e., two years from now) will be $130 because the potential market is bigger. If these are only two options, and the relevant discount rate is 10 percent, what should we do?

To answer this question, we need to compute the two NPVs. If we take it today, the NPV is:

$$NPV = -\$100 + 120/1.1 = \$9.09$$

If we wait one year, the NPV at that time would be:

$$NPV = -\$100 + 130/1.1 = \$18.18$$

Thus, $18.18 is the NPV one year from now. We need the value today, so we discount back $18.18/1.1= $16.53.

If we wait, the NPV is $16.53 today compared to $9.09 if we start immediately, so the optimal time to begin the project is one year from now. The fact that we do not have to take a project immediately is often called the option to wait. In this example, the value of the option to wait is the difference in NPVs, $16.53 – 9.09 = $7.44. This $7.44 is the extra value created by deferring the start of the act as opposed to taking it today.

Example 14.18

A project costs $200 and has a future cash flow of $42 per year forever. If we wait one year, the project will cost $240 because of inflation, but the cash flows will be $48 per year forever. If these are the only two options, and the relevant discount rate is 12 percent, what should we do? What is the value of the option to wait?

In this case, the project is a simple perpetuity. If we take it today, the NPV is:

$$NPV = -\$200 + 42/1.12 = \$150$$

If we wait one year, the NFV at that time would be:

$$NPV = -\$240 + 48/1.12 = \$160$$

So, $160 is the NPV one year from now, but we need to know the value today. Discounting back one period, we get:

$$NPV = \$160/1.12 = \$142.86$$

If we wait, the NPV is $142.86 today compared to $150 if we start immediately, so the optimal time to begin the project is now. What is the value of the option to wait? It is not $142.86 – $150 = –$7.14. Because an option can never have a negative value, the option to wait has a zero value.

DISCOVERY-DRIVEN PLANNING

In conventional planning, the correctness of a plan is generally judged by how close projections come to outcomes. In *discovery-driven planning*, it is assumed that plan parameters may change because new information is revealed; therefore, the plan is subject to change. With conventional planning, it is considered appropriate to fund the entire project, as the expectation is that one can predict a positive outcome. With discovery-driven planning, funds are released based on the accomplishment of key milestones or checkpoints, at which point additional funding can be made available predicated on reasonable expectations for future success. Conventional project management tools, such as stage-gate models or the use of financial tools to assess innovation, have been found to be flawed in that they are not well suited for the uncertainty of innovation-oriented projects. Innovative growth that involves the development of an innovative new product or service can be attained by establishing and systematically testing project assumptions at progressively more challenging checkpoints, learning from the outcomes, and changing direction as appropriate. If the results live up to your assumptions, you release more funds until you get to the next checkpoint. If they don't, you implement changes to the project or cancel it. In the absence of such checkpoints, ego, corporate politics, and a desire to recoup some kind of return on investment almost guarantee that good money will be thrown after bad on unsuccessful projects. The key is to embed learning into the planning process.

EFFECT OF INCOME TAXES ON CAPITAL BUDGETING DECISIONS

How do income tax factors affect investment decisions?

Income taxes make a difference in many capital budgeting decisions. The project that is attractive on a before-tax basis may have to be rejected on an after-tax basis. Income taxes typically affect both the amount and the timing of cash flows. Since net income, not cash inflows, is subject to tax, after-tax cash inflows are not usually the same as after-tax net income.

Let us define:

S = Sales
E = Cash operating expenses
d = Depreciation
t = Tax rate

Then, before-tax cash inflows (or before-tax cash savings) = $S - E$ and net income = $S - E - d$. By definition,

After-tax cash inflows = Before-tax cash inflows − Taxes

$$= (S - E) - (S - E - d)(t)$$

Rearranging gives the shortcut formula:

$$\text{After-tax cash inflows} = (S - E)(1 - t) + (d)(t)$$

$$\text{or} = (S - E - d)(1 - t) + d$$

The deductibility of depreciation from sales in arriving at net income subject to taxes reduces income tax payments and thus serves as a tax shield.

$$\text{Tax shield} = \text{Tax savings on depreciation} = (d)(t)$$

Example 14.19

Assume:

S = $12,000
E = $10,000
d = $500 per year using the straight-line method
t = 30%

Then

$$\text{After-tax cash inflow} = (\$12{,}000 - \$10{,}000)(1 - 0.3) + (\$500)(0.3)$$
$$= (\$2{,}000)(0.7) + (\$500)(0.3)$$
$$= \$1{,}400 + \$150 = \$1{,}550$$
$$\text{Tax shield} = \text{Tax savings on depreciation} = (d)(t)$$
$$= (\$500)(0.3) = \$150$$

Since the tax shield is $d \times t$, the higher the depreciation deduction, the higher the tax savings on depreciation. Therefore, an accelerated depreciation method (such as double-declining balance) produces higher tax savings than the straight-line method. Accelerated methods produce higher present values for the tax savings, which may make a given investment more attractive.

Example 14.20

The Shalimar Company estimates that it can save $2,500 a year in cash operating costs for the next 10 years if it buys a special-purpose machine at a cost of $10,000. No salvage value is expected. Assume that the income tax rate is 30 percent and that the after-tax cost of capital (minimum required rate of return) is 10 percent. After-tax cash savings can be calculated as shown.

Note that depreciation by the straight-line method is $10,000/10 = $1,000 per year. Here before-tax cash savings = $(S - E)$ = $2,500. Thus,

$$\text{After-tax cash savings} = (S - E)(1 - t) + (d)(t)$$
$$= \$2,500(1 - 0.3) + \$1,000(0.3)$$
$$= \$1,750 + \$300 = \$2,050$$

To see if this machine should be purchased, the NPV can be calculated.

$$PV = \$2,050 \ T_4(10\%, 10 \text{ years}) = \$2,050(6.145)$$
$$= \$12,597.25$$

Thus, NPV = PV $- I$ = $12,597.25 $-$ $10,000 = $2,597.25. Since NPV is positive, the machine should be bought.

What is the effect of MACRS on investment decisions?

Although the traditional depreciation methods still can be used for computing depreciation for book purposes, 1981 saw a new way of computing depreciation deductions for tax purposes. The new rule is called the Modified Accelerated Cost Recovery System (MACRS) rule, as enacted by Congress in 1981 and then modified somewhat in 1986 under the Tax Reform Act of 1986. This rule is characterized in this way:

1. It abandons the concept of useful life and accelerates depreciation deductions by placing all depreciable assets into one of eight age property classes. It calculates deductions, based on an allowable percentage of the asset's original cost. (See Exhibits 14.2 and 14.3.) With a shorter life than useful life, the company would be able to deduct depreciation more quickly and save more in income taxes in the earlier years, thereby making an investment more attractive. The rationale behind the system is that this way the government encourages the company to invest in facilities and increase its productive capacity and efficiency. (Remember that the higher d, the larger the tax shield $d \times t$.)

2. Since the allowable percentages in Exhibit 14.2 add up to 100 percent, there is no need to consider the salvage value of an asset in computing depreciation.

3. The company may elect the straight-line method. The straight-line convention must follow what is called the *half-year convention*. This means that the company can deduct only half of the regular straight-line depreciation amount in the first year. The reason for electing to use the MACRS optional straight-line method is that some firms may prefer to stretch out depreciation deductions using the straight-line method rather than to accelerate them. Those firms are the ones that just start out or have little or no income and wish to show more income on their income statements.

4. If an asset is disposed of before the end of its class life, the half-year convention allows half the depreciation for that year (early disposal rule).

EXHIBIT 14.2 Modified Accelerated Cost Recovery System Classification of Assets

Year	3-Yr. (%)	5-Yr. (%)	7-Yr. (%)	10-Yr. (%)	15-Yr. (%)	20-Yr. (%)
	Property Class					
1	33.3	20.0	14.3	10.0	5.0	3.8
2	44.5	32.0	24.5	18.0	9.5	7.2
3	14.8[a]	19.2	17.5	14.4	8.6	6.7
4	7.4	11.5[a]	12.5	11.5	7.7	6.2
5		11.5	8.9[a]	9.2	6.9	5.7
6		5.8	8.9	7.4	6.2	5.3
7			8.9	6.6[a]	5.9[a]	4.9
8			4.5	6.6	5.9	4.5[a]
9				6.5	5.9	4.5
10				6.5	5.9	4.5
11				3.3	5.9	4.5
12					5.9	4.5
13					5.9	4.5
14					5.9	4.5
15					5.9	4.5
16					3.0	4.4
17						4.4
18						4.4
19						4.4
20						4.4
21						2.2
Total	100.0	100.0	100.0	100.0	100.0	100.0

[a] Denotes the year of changeover to straight-line depreciation.

EXHIBIT 14.3 MACRS Tables by Property Class

MACRS Property Class and Depreciation Method	Useful Life (ADR Midpoint Life[a])	Examples of Assets
3-year property 200% declining balance	4 years or less	Most small tools are included; the law specifically excludes autos and light trucks from this property class.
5-year property 200% declining balance	More than 4 years to less than 10 years	Autos and light trucks, computers, typewriters, copiers, duplicating equipment, heavy general-purpose trucks, and research and experimentation equipment are included. *(continued)*

EXHIBIT 14.3 *(continued)*

MACRS Property Class and Depreciation Method	Useful Life (ADR Midpoint Life[a])	Examples of Assets
7-year property 200% declining balance	10 years or more to less than 16 years	Office furniture and fixtures and most items of machinery and equipment used in production are included.
10-year property 200% declining balance	16 years or more to less than 20 years	Various machinery and equipment, such as that used in petroleum distilling and refining and in the milling of grain, are included.
15-year property 150% declining balance	20 years or more to less than 25 years	Sewage treatment plants, telephone and electrical distribution facilities, and land improvements are included.
20-year property 150% declining balance	25 years or more	Service stations and other real property with an ADR midpoint life of less than 27.5 years are included.
27.5-year property straight line	Not applicable	All residential rental property is included.
31.5-year property straight line	Not applicable	All nonresidential real property is included.

[a] *ADR* (asset depreciation range) *midpoint life* is the "useful life" of an asset in a business sense; the appropriate ADR midpoint lives for assets are designated in the tax regulations.

Example 14.21

Assume that a machine falls under a three-year property class under MACRS and costs $3,000 initially. The straight-line option under MACRS differs from the traditional straight-line method in that, under this method, the company would deduct only $500 depreciation in the first year and the fourth year ($3,000/3 years = $1,000; $1,000/2 = $500). The accompanying table compares the straight line with half-year convention with the MACRS deduction.

Year	Straight Line (half-year) Depreciation	Cost		MACRS%	MACRS Deduction
1	$ 500	$3,000	×	33.3	$ 999
2	1,000	3,000	×	44.5	1,335
3	1,000	3,000	×	14.8	444
4	500	3,000	×	7.4	222
	$3,000				$3,000

Example 14.22

A machine costs $10,000. Annual cash inflows are expected to be $5,000. The machine will be depreciated using the MACRS rule and will fall under the three-year property class. The cost of capital after taxes is 10 percent. The estimated life of the machine is five years. The salvage value of the machine at the end of the fifth year is expected to be $1,200. The tax rate is 30 percent. Should you buy the machine? Use the NPV method.

The formula for computing after-tax cash inflows $(S - E)(1 - t) + (d)(t)$ needs to be computed separately. The NPV analysis can be performed as follows:

					Present Value Factor @ 10%	Present Value
$(S - E)(1 - t)$:						
	$5,000 for 5 years	$5,000(1 − 0.3) = $3,500 for 5 years		$3,500	3.791[a]	$13,268.50
$(d)(t)$:						
Year	Cost	MACRS%	d	$(d)(t)$		
1	$10,000 ×	33.3%	$3,330	$999	0.909[b]	908.09
2	$10,000 ×	44.5	4,450	1,335	0.826[b]	1,102.71
3	$10,000 ×	14.8	1,480	444	0.751[b]	333.44
4	$10,000 ×	7.4	740	222	0.683[b]	151.63
Salvage value:[c]						
5:	$1,200	(1 − 0.3)	$840[c]	$840	0.621[b]	521.64
Present value (PV)						$16.286.01

[a] T_4 (10%, 4 years) = 3.170 (from Table A.4)
[b] T_3 values (year 1,2,3,4,5) obtained from Table A.3.
[c] Any salvage value received under the MACRS rules is a *taxable gain* (the excess of the selling price over book value, $1,200 in this example), since the book value will be zero at the end of the life of the machine. Thus, $1,200 × (1 − 0.3) = $840

Since NPV = PV − I = $16,286.01 = N − V $10,000 = $6,286.01 is positive, the machine should be bought.

CHAPTER FIFTEEN

The What and Why of Responsibility Accounting

 RESPONSIBILITY ACCOUNTING BASICS

What is responsibility accounting?

Responsibility accounting is the system for collecting and reporting revenue and cost information by areas of responsibility. It operates on the premise that managers should be held responsible for their performance, the performance of their subordinates, and all activities within their responsibility center.

What are the benefits of responsibility accounting?

Responsibility accounting, also called profitability accounting and activity accounting, has four advantages:

1. It facilitates delegation of decision making.
2. It helps management promote the concept of management by objective. In management by objective, managers agree on a set of goals. A manager's performance is then evaluated based on his or her attainment of these goals.
3. It provides a guide to the evaluation of performance and helps to establish standards of performance, which are then used for comparison purposes.
4. It permits effective use of the concept of management by exception, which means that the manager's attention is concentrated on the important deviations from standards and budgets.

What are the conditions for an effective responsibility accounting system?

Three basic conditions are necessary for an effective responsibility accounting system:

1. The organization structure must be well defined. Management responsibility and authority must go hand in hand at all levels and must be clearly established and understood.
2. Standards of performance in revenues, costs, and investments must be properly determined and well defined.
3. The responsibility accounting reports (or performance reports) should include only items that are controllable by the manager of the responsibility center. Also, they should highlight items calling for managerial attention.

What are the types of responsibility centers?

A well-designed responsibility accounting system establishes responsibility centers within the organization. A *responsibility center* is defined as a unit in the organization that has control over costs, revenues, and/or investment funds. Responsibility centers can be one of these types:

- *Cost center.* A cost center is the unit within the organization that is responsible only for costs. Examples include production and maintenance departments of a manufacturing company. *Variance analysis* based on standard costs and flexible budgets would be a typical performance measure of a cost center.
- *Profit center.* A profit center is the unit that is held responsible for the revenues earned and costs incurred in that center. Examples might include a sales office of a publishing company, an appliance department in a retail store, and an auto repair center in a department store. The contribution approach to cost allocation is widely used to measure the performance of a profit center.
- *Investment center.* An investment center is the unit within the organization that is held responsible for the costs, revenues, and related investments made in that center. The corporate headquarters or division in a large decentralized organization would be an example of an investment center.

Exhibit 15.1 illustrates the manner in which responsibility accounting can be used within an organization and highlights profit and cost centers.

 COST CENTER PERFORMANCE AND STANDARD COSTS

How do you measure the performance of a cost center?

One of the most important phases of responsibility accounting is establishing standard costs and evaluating performance by comparing actual costs with the standard costs. The difference between the actual costs and the standard costs, called the *variance*, is calculated for individual cost centers. Variance analysis is a key tool for measuring performance of a cost center.

Standard costs are costs that are established in advance to serve as targets to be met and, after the fact, to determine how well those targets were actually met. The standard

EXHIBIT 15.1 Organization Chart Company XYZ

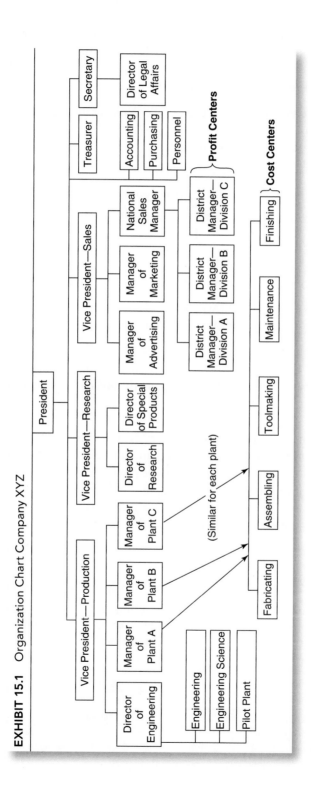

cost is based on physical and dollar measures. It is determined by multiplying the standard quantity of an input by its standard price.

Variance analysis based on standard costs and flexible budgets would be a typical tool for control of a cost center such as a production department.

General Model for Variance Analysis

Two general types of variances can be calculated for most cost items: a price variance and a quantity variance.

The price variance is calculated as:

$$\text{Price variance} = \text{Actual quantity} \times (\text{Actual price} - \text{Standard price})$$

$$= \text{AQ} \times (\text{AP} - \text{SP})$$
$$= \underset{(1)}{(\text{AQ} \times \text{AP})} - \underset{(2)}{(\text{AQ} \times \text{SP})}$$

The quantity variance is calculated as:

$$\text{Quantity variance} = (\text{Actual quantity} - \text{Standard quantity}) \times \text{Standard price}$$

$$= (\text{AQ} - \text{SQ}) \times \text{SP}$$
$$= \underset{(2)}{(\text{AQ} \times \text{SP})} - \underset{(3)}{(\text{SQ} \times \text{SP})}$$

Exhibit 15.2 shows a general model (three-column model) for variance analysis that incorporates items (1), (2), and (3) from the preceding equations. It is important to make four observations:

1. A price variance and a quantity variance can be calculated for all three variable cost items: direct materials, direct labor, and the variable portion of factory overhead. The variance is not called by the same name, however. For example, a price variance is called a materials price variance in the case of direct materials but a labor rate variance in the case of direct labor and a variable overhead spending variance in the case of variable factory overhead.

EXHIBIT 15.2 General Model for Variance Analysis of Variable Manufacturing Costs

Actual Quantity of Inputs, at Actual Price (AQ × AP)	Actual Quantity of Inputs, at Standard Price (AQ × SP)	Standard Quantity Allowed for Output, at Standard Price (SQ × SP)
(1)	(2)	(3)
Price Variance (1)–(2)	Quantity Variance (2)–(3)	
Total (Flexible Budget) Variance (1)–(3)		
■ Materials purchase price variance ■ Labor rate variance ■ Variable overhead spending variance	■ Materials quantity (usage) variance ■ Labor efficiency variance ■ Variable overhead efficiency variance	

2. A cost variance is unfavorable (U) if the actual price (AP) or actual quantity (AQ) exceeds the standard price (SP) or standard quantity (SQ); a variance is favorable (F) if the actual price or actual quantity is less than the standard price or standard quantity.

3. The standard quantity allowed for output—item (3)—is the key concept in variance analysis. This is the standard quantity that should have been used to produce actual output. It is computed by multiplying the actual output by the number of input units allowed.

4. Variances for fixed overhead are of questionable usefulness for control purposes, since these variances are usually beyond the control of the production department.

Next we illustrate the variance analysis for each of the variable manufacturing cost items.

How are material variances computed?

A materials purchase price variance is isolated at the time the material is purchased. It is computed based on the actual quantity purchased. The purchasing department is responsible for any materials price variance that might occur. The materials quantity (usage) variance is computed based on the actual quantity used. The production department is responsible for any materials quantity variance.

Unfavorable price variances may be caused by inaccurate standard prices, inflationary cost increases, scarcity in raw material supplies resulting in higher prices, and purchasing department inefficiencies. Unfavorable material quantity variances may be explained by poorly trained workers, improperly adjusted machines, or outright waste on the production line.

How are labor variances computed?

Labor variances are isolated when labor is used for production. They are computed in a manner similar to materials variances, except that in the three-column model, the terms

---

Example 15.1

Dallas Ewing Corporation uses a standard cost system. The standard variable costs for product J are:

Materials:	2 pounds at $3 per pound
Labor:	1 hour at $5 per hour
Variable overhead:	1 hour at $3 per hour

During March, 25,000 pounds of material were purchased for $74,750, and 20,750 pounds of material were used in producing 10,000 units of finished product. Direct labor costs incurred were $49,896 (10,080 direct labor hours), and variable overhead costs incurred were $34,776.

Using the general model (three-column model), the materials variances are shown in Exhibit 15.3

(continued)

EXHIBIT 15.3   Materials Variances

Actual Quantity of Inputs, at Actual Price (AQ × AP) (1)	Actual Quantity of Inputs, at Standard Price (AQ × SP) (2)	Standard Quantity Allowed for Output, at Standard Price (SQ × SP) (3)
25,000 lb × $2.99 = $74,750	25,000 lb × $3.00 = $75,000	20,000 lb × $3.00 = $60,000

Price Variance
= $250(F)

20,750 lb . $3.00 = $62,250

Quantity Variance
= $2,250 (U)

~10,000 units actually produced × 2 pounds allowed per unit
= 20,000 pounds.

It is important to note that the amount of materials purchased (25,000 pounds) differs from the amount of materials used in production (20,750 pounds). The materials purchase price variance was computed using 25,000 pounds purchased, whereas the materials quantity (usage) variance was computed using the 20,750 pounds used in production. A total variance cannot be computed because of the difference.

Alternatively, we can compute the materials variances as:

Materials purchase price variance = AQ(AP − SP)
= (AQ × AP) − (AQ × SP)
= (25,000 pounds)($2.99 − $3.00)
= $74,750 − $75,000
= $250 (F)

Materials quantity (usage) variance = (AQ − SQ)SP
= (20,750 pounds − 20,000 pounds)($3.00)
= $62,250 − $60,000
= $2,250 (U)

efficiency and *rate* are used in place of the terms *quantity* and *price*. The production department is responsible for both the prices paid for labor services and the quantity of labor services used. Therefore, the production department must explain why any labor variances occur.

Unfavorable rate variances may be explained by an increase in wages or the use of labor commanding higher wage rates than contemplated. Unfavorable efficiency variances may be explained by poor supervision, poor-quality workers, poor quality of materials requiring more labor time, or machine breakdowns.

Example 15.2

Using the same data given in Example 15.1, we can calculate the labor variances as shown in Exhibit 15.4.

EXHIBIT 15.4   Labor Variances

Actual Hours of Inputs, at Actual Rate (AH × AR) (1)	Actual Hours of Inputs, at Standard Rate (AH × SR) (2)	Standard Hours Allowed for Output, at Standard Rate (SH × SR) (3)
10,080h × $4.95 = $49,896	10,080h × $5.00 = $50,400	10,000h[a] × $5.00 = $50,000

Rate Variance (1) – (2) $504 (F)	Efficiency Variance (2) – (3) $400 (U)

Total Variance $104 (F)

[a] 10,000 units actually produced × 1 hour (h) allowed per unit = 10,000 hours.
Note: The symbols AQ, SQ, AP, and SP have been changed to AH, SH, AR, and SR to reflect the terms *hour* and *rate*.

Alternatively, we can calculate the labor variances as:

Labor rate variance = AH(AR − SR)
$$= (AH × AR) − (AH × SR)$$
$$= (10,080 \text{ hours})(\$4.95 − \$5.00)$$
$$= \$49,896 − \$50,400$$
$$= \$504 \text{ (F)}$$

Labor efficiency variance = (AH − SH)SR
$$= (10,080 \text{ hours} − 10,000 \text{ hours}) × \$5.00$$
$$= \$50,400 − \$50,000$$
$$= \$400 \text{ (U)}$$

How are variable overhead variances computed?

Variable overhead variances are computed in a way very similar to labor variances. The production department is usually responsible for any variable overhead variance.

Unfavorable variable overhead spending variances may be caused by many factors: These include acquiring supplies for a price different from the standard, using more supplies than expected, waste, and theft of supplies. Unfavorable variable overhead efficiency variances might be caused by such factors as poorly trained workers, poor-quality materials, faulty equipment, work interruptions, poor production scheduling, poor supervision, employee unrest, and so on.

When variable overhead is applied using direct labor hours, the efficiency variance will be caused by the same factors that cause the labor efficiency variance. However, when variable overhead is applied using machine hours, inefficiency in machinery will cause a variable overhead efficiency variance.

Example 15.3

Using the same data given in Example 15.1, we can compute the variable overhead variances as shown in Exhibit 15.5.

EXHIBIT 15.5 Variable Overhead Variances

Actual Hours of Inputs, at Actual Rate (AH × AR) (1)	Actual Hours of Inputs, at Standard Rate (AH × SR) (2)	Standard Hours Allowed for Output, at Standard Rate (SH × SR) (3)
10,080 h × $3.45 = $34,776	10,080 h × $3.00 = $30,240	10,000 h[a] × $3.00 = $30,000

Spending Variance   Efficiency Variance
(1) – (2)   (2) – (3)
$4,536 (U) $240 (U)

Total Variance $4,776 (U)

[a] 10,000 units actually produced × 1 hour (h) allowed per unit = 10,000 hours.

Alternatively, we can compute the variable overhead variances as

Variable overhead spending variance = AH(SR – SR)
= (AH × AR) – (AH × SR)
= (10,080 hours)($3.45 – $3.00)
= $34,776 – $30,240
= $4,536 (U)

Variable overhead efficiency variance = (AH – SH)SR
= (10,800 hours – 10,000 hours) × $3.00
= $30,240 – $30,000
= $240 (U)

 FLEXIBLE BUDGETS AND PERFORMANCE REPORTS

How is a flexible budget used?

A flexible budget is useful in cost control. In contrast to a static budget, the flexible budget is characterized in this way:

- It is geared toward a range of activity rather than a single level of activity.
- It is dynamic rather than static. By using the cost-volume formula (or flexible budget formula), a series of budgets can easily be developed for various levels of activity.

The static (fixed) budget is geared for only one level of activity and has problems in cost control. Flexible budgeting distinguishes between fixed and variable costs, thus allowing for a budget that can be automatically adjusted (via changes in variable cost totals) to the particular level of activity actually attained. Thus, variances between actual costs and budgeted costs are adjusted for volume ups and downs before differences due to price and quantity factors are computed.

The primary use of the flexible budget is to accurately measure performance by comparing actual costs for a given output with the budgeted costs for the same level of output.

Example 15.4

To illustrate the difference between the static budget and the flexible budget, assume that the Assembly Department of Jemco Industries, Inc., is budgeted to produce 6,000 units during June. Assume further that the company was able to produce only 5,800 units. The budget for direct labor and variable overhead costs is shown in Exhibit 15.6.

EXHIBIT 15.6   Jemco Industries, Inc., Direct Labor and Variable Overhead Budget Assembly Department for the Month of June

Budgeted production	6,000 units
Actual production	5,800 units
Direct labor	$39,000
Variable overhead costs:	
Indirect labor	6,000
Supplies	900
Repairs	300
	$46,200

If a static budget approach is used, the performance report will appear as shown in Exhibit 15.7. These cost variances are useless in that they are comparing oranges with apples. The problem is that the budget costs are based on an activity level of 6,000 units, whereas the actual costs were incurred at an activity level below this (5,800 units). From a control standpoint, it makes no sense to try to compare costs at one activity level with costs at a different activity level. Such comparisons would make a production manager look good as long as the actual production was less than the budgeted production. Using the cost-volume formula and generating the budget based on the 5,800 actual units gives the performance report in Exhibit 15.8. Notice that all cost variances are unfavorable (U), as compared to the favorable (F) cost variances on the performance report based on the static budget approach.

EXHIBIT 15.7   Jemco Industries, Inc., Direct Labor and Variable Overhead Budget Assembly Department for the Month of June

	Budget	Actual	Variance (U or F)[a]
Production in units	6,000	5,800	200 (U)
Direct labor	$39,000	$38,500	$500 (F)

(continued)

EXHIBIT 15.7 *(continued)*

Variable overhead costs

Indirect labor	6,000	5,950	50 (F)
Supplies	900	870	30 (F)
Repairs	300	295	5 (F)
	$46,200	$45,615	$585 (F)

[a] A variance represents the deviation of actual cost from the standard or budgeted cost. *U* and *F* stand for "unfavorable" and "favorable," respectively.

EXHIBIT 15.8 Jemco Industries, Inc., Performance Report Assembly Department for the Month of June

Budgeted production 6,000 units
Actual production 5,800 units

	Cost-Volume Formula[a]	Budget 5,800 Units	Actual 5,800 Units	Variance (U or F)
Direct labor	$6.50 per unit	$37,700	$38,500	$800 (U)
Variable overhead				
Indirect labor	1.00	5,800	5,950	150 (U)
Supplies	0.15	870	870	0
Repairs	0.05	290	295	5 (U)
	$7.70	$44,660	$45,615	$955(U)

[a] Assumed.

How are fixed overhead variances computed?

By definition, fixed overhead does not change over a relevant range of activity; the amount of fixed overhead per unit varies inversely with the level of production. In order to calculate variances for fixed overhead, it is necessary to determine a standard fixed overhead rate, which requires the selection of a predetermined (denominator) level of activity. This activity should be measured on the basis of standard inputs allowed. The formula is:

$$\text{Standard fixed overhead rate} = \frac{\text{Budgeted fixed overhead}}{\text{Budgeted level of activity}}$$

Total fixed overhead variance is simply under- or overapplied overhead. It is the difference between actual fixed overhead incurred and fixed overhead applied to production (generally, on the basis of standard direct labor hours allowed for actual production). Total fixed overhead variance combines fixed overhead spending (flexible-budget) variance and fixed overhead volume (capacity) variance, which are defined below.

- *Fixed overhead spending (flexible-budget) variance.* It is the difference between actual fixed overhead incurred and budgeted fixed overhead. This variance is not affected by the level of production. Fixed overhead, by definition, does not change with the level of activity. The spending (flexible-budget) variance is caused solely by events such as unexpected changes in prices and unforeseen repairs.
- *Fixed overhead volume (capacity) variance.* This variance results when the actual level of activity differs from the denominator activity used in determining the standard fixed overhead rate. Note that the denominator used in the formula is the expected annual activity level. Fixed overhead volume variance is a measure of the cost of failure to operate at the denominator (budgeted) activity level and may be caused by such factors as failure to meet sales targets, idleness due to poor scheduling, and machine breakdowns. The volume variance is calculated as shown:

Fixed overhead = Budgeted fixed overhead − Fixed overhead applied

or

= (Denominator activity − Standard hours allowed) × Standard fixed overhead rate

When denominator activity exceeds standard hours allowed, the volume variance is unfavorable because it is an index of less-than-denominator utilization of capacity.

There are no efficiency variances for fixed overhead. Fixed overhead does not change regardless of whether productive resources are used efficiently. For example, property taxes, insurance, and factory rents are not affected by whether production is being carried on efficiently.

Exhibit 15.9 illustrates the relationship between the various elements of fixed overhead and the possible variances.

EXHIBIT 15.9 Fixed Overhead Variances

Incurred: Actual Hours × Actual Rate (1)	Flexible Budget Based on Actual Hours (2)	Flexible Budget Based on Standard Hours Allowed (3)	Applied (4)
3-way Analysis	Spending Variance (1) − (2)	Efficiency Variance (Not Applicable)	Volume Variance (3) − (4)
2-way Analysis	Flexible Budget Variance (1) − (3)		Volume Variance (3) − (4)
	(1) − (4) Under- or Overapplied		

Example 15.5

The Geige Manufacturing Company has the following standard cost of factory overhead at a normal monthly production (denominator) volume of 1,300 direct labor hours:

Variable overhead (1 hour @ $2)

Fixed overhead (1 hour @ $5)

Fixed overhead budgeted is $6,500 per month. During the month of March, the following events occurred:

a. Actual overhead costs incurred (for 1,350 units of output) were:

Variable	Fixed
$2,053	$6,725

b. Standard hours allowed, 1,250 hours (1 hour × 1,250 units of output).

Note that:

a. Flexible budget formula:

Variable overhead rate	$2 per direct labor hour
Fixed overhead budgeted	$6,500

b. Standard overhead applied rates:

Variable	$2 per direct labor hour
Fixed	$5 per direct labor hour

Exhibit 15.10 shows all the variances for variable overhead as well as fixed overhead. Alternatively, fixed overhead volume variance can be calculated as:

Fixed overhead volume variance = (Denominator activity − Standard hours allowed) × Standard fixed overhead rate

= (1,300 hours − 1,250 hours) × $5

= 50 hours × $5 = $250 (U)

PRODUCTION MIX AND YIELD VARIANCES

What is the production mix variance?

The production mix variance is a cost variance that arises if the actual production mix deviates from the standard or budgeted mix. In a multiproduct, multi-input situation, the mix variances explain the portion of the quantity (usage, or efficiency) variance caused by using inputs (direct materials and direct labor) in ratios different from standard proportions, thus helping determine how efficiently mixing operations are performed.

The material mix variance indicates the impact the deviation from the budgeted mix has on material costs. The labor mix variance measures the impact of changes in the labor mix on labor costs.

$$\begin{matrix} \text{Material} \\ \text{mix} \\ \text{variance} \end{matrix} = \begin{pmatrix} \begin{matrix} \text{Actual units} \\ \text{used at} \\ \text{standard mix} \end{matrix} - \begin{matrix} \text{Actual units} \\ \text{used at} \\ \text{actual mix} \end{matrix} \end{pmatrix} \times \begin{matrix} \text{Standard} \\ \text{unit price} \end{matrix}$$

$$\begin{matrix} \text{Labor} \\ \text{mix} \\ \text{variance} \end{matrix} = \begin{pmatrix} \begin{matrix} \text{Actual units} \\ \text{used at} \\ \text{standard mix} \end{matrix} - \begin{matrix} \text{Actual units} \\ \text{used at} \\ \text{actual mix} \end{matrix} \end{pmatrix} \times \begin{matrix} \text{Standard} \\ \text{hourly rate} \end{matrix}$$

EXHIBIT 15.10 Variance Analysis for Variable Overhead and Fixed Overhead

Incurred: Actual Hours × Actual Rate (1,350 hrs) (1)	Based on Actual Hours (1,350 hrs) (2)	Flexible Budget Based on Standard Hours Allowed (1,250 hrs) (3)	Applied (1,250 hrs) (4)
V $2,853	$2,700 (1,350 × $2)	$2,500 (1,250 × $2)	$2,500
F 6,725	6,500	6,500	6,250
$9,578	$9,200	$9,000	$8,750

(3-way)	Spending Variance (1) – (2) V $153 (U) F 225 (U) $378 (U)	Efficiency Variance (Not Applicable) $200 (U) Not Applicable $200 (U)	Volume Variance (3) – (4) Not Applicable $250 (U) $250 (U)
(2-way)	Flexible Budget Variance (1) – (3) V $353 (U) + F $225 (U) = $578 (U)		Volume Variance (3) – (4) Not Applicable + F $250 (U) = $250 (U)
	Under- or Overapplied (1) – (4)c V $353 (U) + F $475 (U) = $828 (U)		

Example 15.6

J Company produces a compound composed of Materials Alpha and Beta, which are marketed in 20-lb bags. Material Alpha can be substituted for Material Beta. Standard cost and mix data have been determined as follows:

(continued)

Material	Unit Price	Standard Unit	Standard Mix Proportions
Alpha	$3	5 lb	25%
Beta	$4	15	75
		20 lb	100%

Processing each 20-lb bag of material requires 10 hours of labor. The company employs two types of labor, skilled and unskilled, working on two processes, assembly and finishing. The following standard labor cost has been set for a 20-lb bag:

	Standard Hours	Standard Wage Rate	Total	Standard Mix Proportions
Unskilled	4 hr	$2	$ 8	40%
Skilled	6	3	18	60
	10 hr	$2.60	$26	100%

At standard cost, labor averages $2.60 per unit. During the month of December, 100 20-lb bags were completed with these labor costs:

	Actual Hours	Actual Rate	Actual Wages
Unskilled	380 hr	$2.50	$ 950
Skilled	600	3.25	1,950
	980 hr	$2.96	$2,900

Material records show:

Material Alpha actually used, 700 lb @ $3.10

Material Beta actually used, 1,400 lb @ 3.90

Using the preceding formulas, the material mix variance and labor mix variance are computed as:

Material Mix Variance:

Material	Actual Units Used at Standard Mix[a]	Actual Units at Actual Mix	Diff	Standard Unit Price	Variance (U or F)
Alpha	525 lb	700 lb	175 (U)	$3	$525 (U)
Beta	1,575	1,400	175 (F)	$4	700 (F)
	2,100 lb	2,100 lb			$175 (F)

[a] This is the standard mix proportions of 25% and 75% applied to the actual material units used of 2,100 lb.

Labor Mix Variance:

	Actual Hrs Used at Standard Mix[a]	Actual Hrs. of Actual Mix	Diff	Standard Hourly Rate	Variance (U or F)
Unskilled	392 hr	380 hr	12 (F)	$2	$24 (F)
Skilled	588	600	12 (U)	3	36 (U)
	980 hr	980 hr			$12 (U)

[a] This is the standard mix proportion of 40% and 60% applied to the actual total labor hours used of 980.

Probable causes of unfavorable production mix variances are:

- Capacity restraints forcing substitution
- Poor production scheduling
- Lack of certain types of labor
- Short supply of certain materials

How do you compute the production yield variance?

The production yield variance is the difference between the actual yield and the standard yield. Yield is a measure of productivity. In other words, it is a measure of output from a given amount of input. For example, in the production of potato chips, we might expect a certain yield, such as 40 percent yield or 40 pounds of chips for 100 pounds of potatoes.

If the actual yield is less than the expected or standard yield for a given level of input, the yield variance is unfavorable. A yield variance is computed for labor as well as materials. A labor yield variance is considered the result of the quantity and/or the quality of labor used. The yield variance explains the remaining portion of the quantity variance and is caused by a yield of finished product that does not correspond with the quantity that actual inputs should have produced. When there is no mix variance, the yield variance equals the quantity variance.

$$\begin{matrix} \text{Material} \\ \text{yield} \\ \text{variance} \end{matrix} = \begin{pmatrix} \begin{matrix} \text{Actual units} \\ \text{used at} \\ \text{standard mix} \end{matrix} - \begin{matrix} \text{Actual output} \\ \text{units used at} \\ \text{standard mix} \end{matrix} \end{pmatrix} \times \begin{matrix} \text{Standard} \\ \text{unit} \\ \text{price} \end{matrix}$$

$$\begin{matrix} \text{Labor} \\ \text{yield} \\ \text{variance} \end{matrix} = \begin{pmatrix} \begin{matrix} \text{Actual hours} \\ \text{used at} \\ \text{standard mix} \end{matrix} - \begin{matrix} \text{Actual output} \\ \text{hours used at} \\ \text{standard mix} \end{matrix} \end{pmatrix} \times \begin{matrix} \text{Standard} \\ \text{hourly} \\ \text{rate} \end{matrix}$$

The four probable causes of unfavorable production yield variances are:

1. Use of low-quality materials and/or labor
2. Faulty equipment
3. Improper production methods
4. An improper or costly mix of materials and/or labor

Example 15.7

A company uses a standard cost system for its production of a chemical product. This chemical is produced by mixing three major raw materials, A, B, and C. The company has these standards:

36 lb of Material A @ 1.00	= $ 36.00
48 lb of Material B @ 2.00	= $ 96.00
36 lb of Material C @ 1.75	= $ 63.00
120 lb of standard mix @ 1.625	= $195.00

(continued)

The company should produce 100 lb of finished product at a standard cost of $1.625 per lb ($195/120 lb). Converting 120 lb of materials into 100 lb of finished chemical requires 400 direct labor hours at $3.50 per hour, or $14 per lb. During the month of December, the company completed 4,250 lb of output with the following labor: direct labor 15,250 hours @ $3.50. Material records show:

Material A	1,160 lb used
Material B	1,820
Material C	1,480

Material yield variance can be calculated as shown in the next table.

With a standard yield of 83.3 percent (100/120), 4,250 lb of completed output should have required 17,000 hours of direct labor (4,250 lb × 400 direct labor hours/100). Comparing the hours allowed for the actual input, 14,866.67 hours, with the hours allowed for actual output, 17,000 hours, we find a favorable labor yield variance of $7,466.66:

Labor Yield Variance:

Actual hours at expected output	$52,033.34
Actual output (4,250 lb × 400/100=17,000 hr @ $3.50 or 4,250 lb @ $14.00)	59,500.00
	$7,466.66 (F)

Material	Actual Input Units at Standard Mix	Actual Output Units Standard Mix[a]	Diff	Standard Unit Price	Variance (U or F)
A	1,338 lb	1,275 lb	63 U	$1.00	$ 63 (U)
B	1,784	1,700	84 F	2.00	168 (U)
C	1,338	1,275	63 U	1.75	110.25 (U)
	4,460 lb	4,250 lb			$341.25 (U)

[a] This is the standard mix proportions of 30%, 40%, and 30% applied to the actual output units used of 4,250 lb.

CHAPTER SIXTEEN

Control of Profit Centers

 HOW DO YOU EVALUATE PROFIT CENTERS?

Segmental reporting is the process of reporting the activities of profit centers such as divisions, product lines, or sales territories. The *contribution approach* is valuable for segmented reporting because it emphasizes the cost behavior patterns and the controllability of costs that are generally useful for the profitability analysis of various segments of an organization.

The contribution approach is based on the theses that:

- Fixed costs are much less controllable than variable costs.
- Direct fixed costs and common fixed costs must be clearly distinguished. Direct fixed costs are those fixed costs that can be identified directly with a particular segment of an organization, whereas common fixed costs are those costs that cannot be identified directly with the segment.
- Common fixed costs should be clearly identified as unallocated in the contribution income statement by segments. Any attempt to allocate these types of costs, on some arbitrary basis, to the segments of the organization can destroy the value of responsibility accounting. It would lead to unfair evaluation of performance and misleading managerial decisions.

These three concepts are highlighted in the contribution approach:

1. *Contribution margin:* Sales minus variable costs.
2. *Segment margin:* Contribution margin minus direct (traceable) fixed costs. Direct fixed costs include discretionary fixed costs, such as certain advertising, research and development, sales promotion, and engineering, as well as traceable and

committed fixed costs, such as depreciation, property taxes, insurance, and the segment managers' salaries.

3. *Net income:* Segment margin less unallocated common fixed costs. Segmental reporting can be made by division, product or product line, sales territory, service center, salesperson, store or branch office, or domestic or foreign operations.

Exhibit 16.1 illustrates two levels of segmental reporting: (1) by segments defined as divisions and (2) by segments defined as product lines of a division.

The segment margin is the best measure of the profitability of a segment. Unallocated fixed costs are common to the segments being evaluated and should be left unallocated in order not to distort the performance results of segments.

EXHIBIT 16.1   Segmental Income Statement

(1) Segments Defined as Divisions

		Segments	
	Total Company	Division 1	Division 2
Sales	$150,000	$90,000	$60,000
Less: Variable costs			
Manufacturing	40,000	30,000	10,000
Selling and admin.	20,000	14,000	6,000
Total variable costs	$ 60,000	$44,000	$ 16,000
Contribution margin	$ 90,000	$46,000	$44,000
Less: Direct fixed costs	70,000	43,000	27,000
Divisional segment margin	$ 20,000	$ 3,000	$ 17,000
Less: Unallocated common fixed costs	10,000		
Net income	$ 10,000		

(2) Segments Defined as Product Lines of Division 2

		Segments	
	Division 2	Deluxe Model	Regular Model
Sales	$60,000	$20,000	$40,000
Less: Variable costs			
Manufacturing	10,000	5,000	5,000
Selling and administrative	6,000	2,000	4,000
Total variable costs	$ 16,000	$ 7,000	$ 9,000
Contribution margin	$44,000	$13,000	$ 31,000
Less: Direct fixed costs	26,500	9,500	17,000
Product line margin	$ 17,500	$ 3,500	$ 14,000
Less: Unallocated common fixed costs	500		
Divisional segment margin	$ 17,000		

PROFIT VARIANCE ANALYSIS

How does profit variance analysis work?

Profit variance analysis, often called gross profit analysis, deals with how to analyze the profit variance that constitutes the departure between actual profit and the previous year's income or the budgeted figure. The primary goal of profit variance analysis is to improve performance and profitability in the future.

Profit, whether it is gross profit or contribution margin, is affected by at least three basic items: sales price, sales volume, and costs. In addition, in a multiproduct firm, if not all products are equally profitable, profit is affected by the mix of products sold.

The difference between budgeted and actual profits is due to one or more of these changes:

- Changes in unit sales price and cost, called sales price and cost price variances, respectively. The difference between sales price variance and cost price variance is often called a contribution-margin-per-unit variance or a gross-profit-per-unit variance, depending on what type of costing system is being referred to—that is, absorption costing or direct costing. Contribution margin, however, is considered a better measure of product profitability because it deducts from sales revenue only the variable costs that are controllable in terms of fixing responsibility. Gross profit does not reflect cost-volume-profit relationships. Nor does it consider directly traceable marketing costs.
- Changes in the volume of products sold summarized as the sales volume variance and the cost volume variance. The difference between the two is called the *total volume variance*.
- Changes in the volume of the more profitable or less profitable items referred to as the *sales mix variance*.

Detailed analysis is critical to management when multiple products exist. The volume variances may be used to measure a change in volume (while holding the mix constant), and the mix may be employed to evaluate the effect of a change in sales mix (while holding the quantity constant). This type of variance analysis is useful when the products are substituted for each other or when the products that are not necessarily substitutes for each other are marketed through the same channel.

What are the types of standards in profit variance analysis?

To determine the various causes for a favorable variance (an increase) or an unfavorable variance (a decrease) in profit, we need some kind of yardstick to compare against the actual results. The yardstick may be based on the prices and costs of the previous year or any year selected as the base period. Some companies summarize profit variance analysis data in their annual report by showing departures from the previous year's reported income. However, one can establish a more effective control and budgetary method rather than the previous year's data. Standard or budgeted mix can be determined using such sophisticated techniques as linear and goal programming.

How do you calculate profit variances for single-product firms?

Profit variance analysis is simplest in a single-product firm, for there is only one sales price, one set of costs (or cost price), and a unitary sales volume. An unfavorable profit variance can be broken down into four components: a sales price variance, a cost price variance, a sales volume variance, and a cost volume variance.

The sales price variance measures the impact on the firm's contribution margin (or gross profit) of changes in the unit selling price. It is computed as:

$$\text{Sales price variance} = (\text{Actual price} - \text{Budget price}) \times \text{Actual sales}$$

If the actual price is lower than the budgeted price, for example, this variance is unfavorable; it tends to reduce profit. The cost price variance, however, is simply the summary of price variances for materials, labor, and overhead. (This is the sum of material price, labor rate, and factory overhead spending variances.) It is computed as:

$$\text{Cost price variance} = (\text{Actual cost} - \text{Budget cost}) \times \text{Actual sales}$$

If the actual unit cost is lower than budgeted cost, for example, this variance is favorable; it tends to increase profit. We simplify the computation of price variances by taking the sales price variance less the cost price variance and call it the gross-profit-per-unit variance or contribution-margin-per-unit variance.

The sales volume variance indicates the impact on the firm's profit of changes in the unit sales volume. This is the amount by which sales would have varied from the budget if nothing but sales volume had changed. It is computed as:

$$\text{Sales volume variance} = (\text{Actual sales} - \text{Budget sales}) \times \text{Budget price}$$

If actual sales volume is greater than budgeted sales volume, this is favorable; it tends to increase profit. The cost volume variance has the same interpretation. It is:

$$(\text{Actual sales} - \text{Budget sales}) \times \text{Budget cost per unit}$$

The difference between the sales volume variance and the cost volume variance is called the *total volume variance*.

How do you calculate variances for multiproduct firms?

When a firm produces more than one product, there is a fourth component of the profit variance. This is the sales mix variance, the effect on profit of selling a different proportionate mix of products from that which has been budgeted. This variance arises when different products have different contribution margins. In a multiproduct firm, actual sales volume can differ from that budgeted in two ways. The total number of units sold could differ from the target aggregate sales. In addition, the mix of the products actually sold may not be proportionate to the target mix. Each of these two different types of changes in volume is reflected in a separate variance.

The total volume variance is divided into the two: the sales mix variance and the sales quantity variance. These two variances should be used to evaluate the marketing department of the firm. The sales mix variance shows how well the department has done in terms of selling the more profitable products, while the sales quantity variance measures how well the firm has done in terms of its overall sales volume. They are computed as:

$$\frac{\text{Sales mix}}{\text{variance}} = \left(\begin{array}{cc} \text{Actual sales at} & \text{Budget sales} \\ \text{budget mix} & \text{at budget mix} \end{array} \right)$$

$$\times \text{ Budget CM (or gross profit)/unit}$$

$$\frac{\text{Sales quantity}}{\text{variance}} = \left(\begin{array}{cc} \text{Actual sales at} & \text{Actual sales} \\ \text{budget mix} & \text{at budget mix} \end{array} \right)$$

$$\times \text{ Budget CM (or gross profit)/unit}$$

$$\frac{\text{Total volume}}{\text{variance}} = \left(\begin{array}{cc} \text{Actual sales at} & \text{Budget sales} \\ \text{actual mix} & \text{at budget mix} \end{array} \right)$$

$$\times \text{ Budget CM (or gross profit)/unit}$$

where CM = contribution margin

Example 16.1

The controller of the Royalla Publishing Company prepared the following comparative statement of operations for 2X11 and 2X12.

	2X11	2X12
Sales in units	97,500	110,000
Selling price	$ 9.00	$ 8.80
Sales revenue	$ 877,500	$ 968,000
Cost of goods sold	$ 585,000	$ 704,000
Gross profit	$ 292,500	$ 264,000

The controller was very pleased with the performance of the company in 2X11. Analyze the decline in gross profit between 2X11 and 2X12 by calculating:

■ Sales price variance

■ Cost price variance

■ Sales volume variance

■ Cost volume variance

■ Total volume variance (sales volume variance − cost volume variance) or (sales mix variance + sales quantity variance)

■ Sales mix variance

■ Sales quantity variance

(continued)

2X11 gross profit	$ 292,500
2X12 gross profit	264,000
Decrease in gross profit to be accounted for	$ 28,500

a. Sales price variance

2X12 actual sales revenue	$ 968,000
2X12 actual sales revenue at 2X11 price (110,000 @ $ 9)	$ 990,000
	$ 22,000 (U)

b. Cost price variance

2X12 actual	$ 704,000
2X12 actual at 2X11 cost per unit (110,000 @ $6[a])	660,000
	$ 44,000

[a] 2X11 cost per unit = $585,000/97,500 = $6

c. Sales volume variance

2X12 actual volume at 2X11 price	$990,000 (110,000 × $9)
2X11 actual volume at 2X11 price	877,500
2X12 actual – 2X11 actual) × 2X11 prices	$112,500 (F)

d. Cost volume variance

2X12 actual volume at 2X11 cost	$ 660,000 (110,000 × $6)
2X11 actual volume at 2X11 cost	585,000
(2X12 actual – 2X11 actual) × 2X11 cost	$ 75,000

e. Total volume variance = sales volume variance – cost volume variance = $112,500 (F) – $75,000 (U) = $37,500 (F), which is broken down into the sales mix variance and the sales quantity variance as shown in (f) and (g) below.

f. Sales mix variance = 0 since we have only one product in this problem.

g. Sales quantity variance.

2X12 Actual Volume	2X11 Budgeted Volume	Diff.	2X11 Gross Profit per Unit[b]	Variance ($)
110,000	97,500	12,500 (F)	$3	$ 37,500 (F)

[b] 2X11 gross profit per unit = 2X11 selling price–2X11 cost of goods sold = $9 – $6 = $3

The decline in gross profit of $28,500 can be explained as:

	Gains	Losses
Gain due to favorable sales volume variance	$112,500 (F)	
Losses due to:		
Unfavorable sales price variance		$ 22,000 (U)
Unfavorable cost price variance		44,000 (U)
Unfavorable cost volume variance		75,000 (U)
	$112,500 (F)	$141,000 (U)

The decrease in gross profit is thus accounted for:

$$141,000 \text{ (U)} - 112,500 \text{ (F)} = 28,500 \text{ (U)}$$

Example 16.2

The Lake Tahoe Ski Store sells two ski models—Model X and Model Y. For the years 2X11 and 2X12, the store realized a gross profit (GP) of $246,640 and $211,650, respectively. The owner of the store was astounded since the total sales volume in dollars and in units was higher for 2X12 than for 2X11 yet the gross profit achieved actually declined. Given below are the store's unaudited operating results for 2X11 and 2X12. No fixed costs were included in the cost of goods sold per unit.

Year	Selling Price	Model X Cost of Goods Sold per Unit	Sales (in Units)	Sales Revenue
1	$150	$110	2,800	$420,000
2	$160	$125	2,650	$424,000
Year	Selling Price	Model Y Cost of Goods Sold per Unit	Sales (in Units)	Sales Revenue
1	$172	$121	2,640	$454,080
2	$176	$135	2,900	$510,400

Explain why the gross profit declined by $34,990. Include a detailed variance analysis of price changes and changes in volume for both sales and cost. Also subdivide the total volume variance into changes in price and changes in quantity.

Sales price and sales volume variances measure the impact on the firm's CM (or GP) of changes in the unit selling price and sales volume. In computing these variances, all costs are held constant in order to stress changes in price and volume. Cost price and cost volume variances are computed in the same manner, holding price and volume constant. All these variances for the Lake Tahoe Ski Store are computed as follows.

(continued)

Sales Price Variance

Actual sales for 2X12:

Model X $2,650 × $160 = $424,000		
Model Y $2,900 × 176 = 510,400	$934,400	
Actual 2X12 sales at 2X11 prices:		
Model X 2,650 × $150 = $397,500		
Model Y 2,900 × 172 = 498,800	$896,300	
	$ 38,100	(F)

Sales Volume Variance

Actual 2X12 sales at 2X11 prices:	$896,300	
Actual 2X11 sales (at 2X11 prices):		
Model X 2,800 × $150 = $420,000		
Model Y 2,640 × 172 = 454,080	$874,080	
	$ 22,220	(F)

Cost Price Variance

Actual cost of goods sold for 2X12:		
Model X 2,650 × $125 = $331,250		
Model Y 2,900 × 135 = 391,500	$722,750	
Actual 2X12 sales at 2X11 costs:		
Model X 2,650 × $110 = $291,500		
Model Y 2,900 × 121 = 350,900	$642,400	
	$ 80,350	(U)

Cost Volume Variance

Actual 2X12 sales at 2X11 costs:	$642,400	
Actual 20 X 1 sales (at 2X11 costs):		
Model X 2,800 × $110 = $308,000		
Model Y 2,640 × 121 = 319,440	$627,440	
	$ 14,960	(U)

Total volume variance = sales volume variance – cost volume variance
$$= \$22,220 \text{ (F)} - \$15,960 \text{ (U)}$$
$$= \$7,260 \text{ (F)}$$

The total volume variance is computed as the sum of a sales mix variance and a sales quantity variance as follows.

SALES MIX VARIANCE

Model	2X12 Actual Sales at 2X11 Mix[a]	2X12 Actual Sales at 2X12 Mix	Diff.	2X11 Gross Profit per Unit	Variance $
X	2,857	2,650	207 (U)	$40	$ 8,280 (U)
Y	2,693	2,900	207 (F)	$51	10,557 (F)
	5,550	5,550			$ 2,277 (F)

[a] This is the 2X11 mix (used as standard or budget) proportions of 51.47% (2,800/5,440) and 48.53% (2,640/5,440) applied to the actual 2X12 sales figure of 5,550 units.

SALES QUANTITY VARIANCE

Model	2X12 Actual Sales at 2X11 Mix[b]	2X11 Actual Sales at 2X11 Mix	Diff.	2X11 Gross Profit per Unit	Variance $
X	2,857	2,800	57 (F)	$40	$2,280 (F)
Y	2,693	2,640	53 (F)	$51	2,703 (F)
	5,550	5,440			$4,983 (F)

[b] This is the 2X11 mix (used as standard or budget) proportions of 51.47% (2,800/5,440) and 48.53% (2,640/5,440) applied to the actual 2X12 sales figure of 5,550 units.

A favorable total volume variance is due to a favorable shift in the sales mix (i.e., from Model X to Model Y) and also to a favorable increase in sales volume (by 110 units), which is shown as:

Sales mix variance	$2,277 (F)
Sales quantity variance	$4,983 (F)
	$7,260 (F)

However, there remains the decrease in gross profit. The decrease in gross profit of $34,990 can be explained as:

	Gains	Losses
Gain due to increased sales price	$38,100 (F)	
Loss due to increased cost		$80,350 (U)
Gain due to increase in units sold	4,983 (F)	
Gain due to shift in sales mix	2,277 (F)	
	$45,360 (F)	$80,350 (U)

Hence, net decrease in gross profit = $80,350 − $45,360 = $34,990 (U).

Despite the increase in sales price and volume and the favorable shift in sales mix, the Lake Tahoe Ski Store ended up losing $34,990 compared to 2X11. The major reason for this comparative loss was the tremendous increase in cost of goods sold, as indicated by an unfavorable cost price variance of $80,350. The costs for both Model X and Model Y went up significantly over 2X11. The store has to take a close look at the cost picture. Even though only variable costs were included in cost of goods sold per unit, both variable and fixed costs should be analyzed in an effort to cut down on controllable costs. In doing that, it is essential that responsibility be clearly fixed to given individuals. In a retail business like the Lake Tahoe Ski Store, operating expenses such as advertising and payroll of store employees must also be closely scrutinized.

How do you improve sales mix?

Many product lines include a lower-margin price leader model and often a high-margin deluxe model. For example, the automobile industry includes in its product line low-margin, energy-efficient small cars and higher-margin deluxe models. In an attempt to increase overall profitability, management would wish to emphasize the higher-margin expensive items, but salespeople might find it easier to sell low-margin cheaper models. Thus, a salesman might meet his unit sales quota with each item at its budgeted price, but because of mix shifts, he could be far short of contributing his share of budgeted profit.

CFOs should realize that (1) greater proportions of more profitable products mean higher profits and (2) higher proportions of lower-margin sales reduce overall profit despite the increase in overall sales volume. That is, an unfavorable mix may easily offset a favorable increase in volume, and vice versa.

What should performance reports look like?

Profit variance analysis aids in fixing responsibility by separating the causes of the change in profit into price, volume, and mix factors. With responsibility resting in different places, the segregation of the total profit variance is essential. The performance reports based on the analysis of profit variances must be prepared for each responsibility center, indicating these six considerations:

1. Is it controllable?
2. Is it favorable or unfavorable?
3. If it is unfavorable, is it significant enough for further investigation?
4. Who is responsible for what portion of the total profit variance?
5. What are the causes for an unfavorable variance?
6. What is the remedial action to take?

The performance report must address these types of questions. The report is useful in two ways: (1) in focusing attention on situations in need of management action and (2) in increasing the precision of planning and control of sales and costs. The report should be produced as part of the overall responsibility accounting system.

CHAPTER SEVENTEEN

Performance of Investment Centers and Transfer Pricing

THE ABILITY TO measure performance is essential in developing management incentives and controlling the operation toward the achievement of organizational goals. A typical decentralized subunit is an investment center that is responsible for an organization's invested capital (operating assets) and the related operating income. There are two widely used measurements of performance for the investment center: the rate of return on investment (ROI) and residual income (RI).

 ## RATE OF RETURN ON INVESTMENT

How do you calculate ROI?

ROI relates a division's operating income to operating assets:

$$\text{ROI} = \frac{\text{Operating income}}{\text{Operating assets}}$$

Example 17.1

Consider the following financial data for a division:

Operating assets	$100,000
Operating income	$18,000

$$\text{ROI} = \frac{\$18,000}{\$100,000} = 18\%$$

RESIDUAL INCOME

What is residual income?

RI is another approach to measuring performance in an investment center. RI is the operating income that an investment center is able to earn above some minimum rate of return on its operating assets. RI, unlike ROI, is an absolute amount of income rather than a specific rate of return:

$$RI = \text{Operating income} - (\text{Minimum required rate of return} \times \text{operating assets})$$

Example 17.2

In Example 17.1, assume the minimum required rate of return is 13 percent. Then the residual income of the division is:

$$\$18,000 - (13\% \times \$100,000) = \$18,000 - \$13,000 = \$5,000$$

What are the benefits of RI?

When RI is used to evaluate divisional performance, the objective is to maximize the total amount of residual income, not to maximize the overall ROI figure. RI is regarded as a better measure of performance than ROI because it encourages investment in projects that would be rejected under ROI. A major disadvantage of RI, however, is that it cannot be used to compare divisions of different sizes. RI tends to favor the larger divisions owing to the larger amount of dollars involved.

 INVESTMENT DECISIONS UNDER ROI AND RI

How can you use ROI and RI?

The decision of whether to use ROI or RI as a measure of divisional performance affects CFOs' investment decisions. Under the ROI method, division managers tend to accept only the investments whose returns exceed the division's ROI; otherwise, the division's overall ROI would decrease. Under the RI method, however, division managers would accept an investment as long as it earns a rate in excess of the minimum required rate of return. The addition of such an investment will increase the division's overall RI.

Example 17.3

Consider the same data given in Examples 17.1 and 17.2:

Operating assets	$100,000
Operating income	$18,000
Minimum required rate of return	13%
ROI = 18% and RI = $5,000	

Assume that the division is presented with a project that would yield 15 percent on a $10,000 investment. The division manager would not accept this project under the ROI approach since the division is already earning 18 percent. Acquiring this project will bring down the present ROI to 17.73 percent:

	Present	New Project	Overall
Operating assets (a)	$100,000	$10,000	$110,000
Operating income (b)	18,000	1,500	19,500
ROI (b/a)	18%	15%	17.73%

Under the RI approach, the manager would accept the new project because it provides a higher rate than the minimum required rate of return (15 percent versus 13 percent). Accepting the new project will increase the overall residual income to $5,200:

	Present	New Project	Overall
Operating assets (a)	$100,000	$10,000	$110,000
Operating income (b)	18,000	1,500	19,500
Minimum required income at 13% (c)	13,000	1,300[a]	14,300
RI (b − c)	$ 5,000	$ 200	$ 5,200

[a] $10,000 × 13% = $1,300

RI is regarded as a better of measure of performance than ROI because it encourages investment in projects that would be rejected under ROI. A major disadvantage of RI, however, is that it cannot be used to compare divisions of different sizes. RI tends to favor the larger divisions owing to the larger amount of dollars involved.

Residual Income and Economic Value Added

RI is better known as *Economic Value Added* (EVA), which is discussed more fully in Chapter 18. Many firms are addressing the issue of aligning division managers' incentives with those of the firm by using EVA as a measure of performance. EVA encourages managers to focus on increasing the value of the company to shareholders because EVA is the value created by a company in excess of the cost of capital for the investment base. EVA can be improved in three ways:

1. Invest capital in high-performing projects.
2. Use less capital.
3. Increase profit without using more capital.

 ## TRANSFER PRICING

Why is transfer pricing important?

Goods and services are often exchanged between various divisions of a decentralized organization. The transfer price is the selling price credited to the selling division and the cost charged to the buying division for an internal transfer of a good or service. The choice of transfer prices does not only affect divisional performance; it also is important in decisions involving make or buy, whether to buy internally or outside, and choosing between production possibilities.

How are transfer prices determined?

Goods and services often are exchanged between various divisions of a decentralized organization. A major goal of transfer pricing is to enable divisions that exchange goods or services to act as independent businesses.

The question then is: What monetary values should be assigned to these exchanges or transfers? Market price? Some kind of cost? Some version of either? Unfortunately, no single transfer price will please everyone—that is, top management, the selling division, and the buying division—involved in the transfer. Various transfer pricing schemes are available, such as market price, cost-based price, or negotiated price.

The choice of a transfer pricing policy (i.e., which type of transfer price to use) is normally decided by top management. The decision will typically include consideration of these issues:

- *Goal congruence.* Will the transfer price promote the goals of the company as a whole? Will it harmonize the divisional goals with organizational goals?
- *Performance evaluation.* Will the selling division receive enough credit for its transfer of goods and services to the buying division? Will the transfer price hurt the performance of the selling division?
- *Autonomy.* Will the transfer price preserve autonomy; the freedom of the selling and buying division managers to operate their divisions as decentralized entities?
- *Other factors.* Other relevant factors include minimization of tariffs and income taxes and observance of legal restrictions.

What are alternative transfer pricing schemes?

Transfer prices can be based on:

- Market price
- Cost-based price—variable or full cost
- Negotiated price
- General formula, which is usually the sum of variable costs per unit and opportunity cost for the company as a whole (lost revenue per unit on outside sales)

How suitable is market price for transfers?

Market price is the best transfer price in the sense that it will maximize the profits of the company as a whole, if it meets these two conditions:

1. A competitive market price exists.
2. Divisions are independent of each other.

If either one of these conditions is violated, market price will not lead to an optimal economic decision for the company.

What are the pros and cons of cost-based prices?

Cost-based transfer price, another alternative transfer pricing scheme, is easy to understand and convenient to use. But there are some disadvantages, including:

- Inefficiencies of selling divisions are passed on to the buying divisions with little incentive to control costs. The use of standard costs is recommended in such a case.
- The cost-based method treats the divisions as cost centers rather than profit or investment centers. Therefore, measures such as ROI and RI cannot be used for evaluation purposes.

The variable-cost-based transfer price has an advantage over the full-cost method because, in the short run, it may tend to ensure the best utilization of the overall company's resources. The reason is that, in the short run, fixed costs do not change. Any use of facilities without the incurrence of additional fixed costs will increase the company's overall profits.

When is negotiated price used?

A negotiated price generally is used when there is no clear outside market. A negotiated price is a price agreed on between the buying and selling divisions that reflects unusual or mitigating circumstances. This method is widely used when no intermediate market price exists for the product transferred and the selling division is assured of a normal profit.

Example 17.4

Company X just purchased a small company that specializes in the manufacture of part no. 323. Company X is a decentralized organization and will treat the newly acquired company as an autonomous division called Division B with full profit responsibility.

Division B's fixed costs total $30,000 per month, and variable costs per unit are $18. Division B's operating capacity is 5,000 units. The selling price per unit is $30. Division A of company X is currently purchasing 2,500 units of part no. 323 per month from an outside supplier at $29 per unit, which represents the normal $30 price less a quantity discount.

Top management wants to decide what transfer price should be used. Five alternative prices are:

1. $30, market price
2. $29, the price that Division A is currently paying to the outside supplier
3. $23.50, negotiated price, which is $18 variable cost plus one-half of the benefits of an internal transfer [($29 − $18) × 1/2]
4. $24, full cost, which is $18 variable cost plus $6($30,000/5,000 units) fixed cost per unit
5. $18 variable cost

(continued)

We discuss each of these five prices.

1. $30 would not be an appropriate transfer price. Division B cannot charge a price higher than the price Division A is paying now ($29).
2. $29 would be an appropriate transfer price if top management wishes to treat the divisions as autonomous investment centers. This price would cause all of the benefits of internal transfers to accrue to the selling division, with the buying division's position remaining unchanged.
3. $23.50 would be an appropriate transfer price if top management wants to treat the divisions as investment centers but wants to share the benefits of an internal transfer equally between them, as follows:

Variable costs of Division B	$18.00
1/2 of the difference between the variable costs of Division B and the price Division A is paying ($29 – $18) × 1/2	5.50
Transfer price	$23.50

Note that $23.50 is just one example of a negotiated transfer price. The exact price depends on how the benefits are divided.

4. $24 [$24 = $18 + ($30,000/5,000 units)] would be an appropriate transfer price if top management treats divisions like cost centers with no profit responsibility. All benefits from both divisions will accrue to the buying division. This will maximize the profits of the company as a whole but adversely affect the performance of the selling division. Another disadvantage of this cost-based approach is that inefficiencies (if any) of the selling division are being passed on to the buying division.
5. $18 would be an appropriate transfer price for guiding top management in deciding whether transfers between the two divisions should take place. Since $18 is less than the outside purchase price of the buying division, and the selling division has excess capacity, the transfer should take place because it will maximize the profits of the company as a whole. However, if $18 is used as a transfer price, then all of the benefits of the internal transfer accrue to the buying division, and it will hurt the performance of the selling division.

When can you use a general formula for pricing transfers?

It is not easy to find a cure-all answer to the transfer pricing problem, since the three problems of goal congruence, performance evaluation, and autonomy must all be considered simultaneously. It is generally agreed, however, that some form of competitive market price is the best approach to the transfer pricing problem. The following formula would be helpful in this effort:

$$\frac{\text{Transfer}}{\text{price}} = \frac{\text{Variable costs}}{\text{per unit}} + \frac{\text{Opportunity costs per unit}}{\text{for the company as a whole}}$$

Opportunity costs are defined as net revenue forgone by the company as a whole if the goods and services are transferred internally. The reasoning behind this formula is that the selling division should be allowed to recover its variable costs plus opportunity cost (i.e., revenue that it could have made by selling to an outsider) of the transfer. The selling department should not have to suffer lost income by selling within the company.

Example 17.5

Company X has more than 50 divisions, including A, B, and K. Division A, the buying division, wants to buy a component for its final product and has an option to buy from Division B or from an outside supplier at the market price of $200. If Division A buys from the outside supplier, it will in turn buy selected raw materials from Division K for $40. This will increase its contribution to overall company profits by $30 ($40 revenue minus $10 variable costs). Division B, however, can sell its component to Division A or to an outside buyer at the same price. Division B, working at full capacity, incurs variable costs of $150. Exhibit 17.1 depicts the situation. Will the use of $200 as a transfer price lead to optimal decisions for the company as a whole?

The optimal decision from the viewpoint of Company X as a whole can be looked at in terms of its net cash outflow, as follows:

	Division A's Action	
	Buy from B	**Buy from Outsider**
Outflow to the company as a whole	$(150)	$(200)
Cash inflows	—	to B: $50 ($200 – $150)
		to K: $30 ($40 – $10)
Net cash outflow to the company as a whole	$(150)	$(120)

To maximize the profits of Company X, Division A should buy from an outside supplier. The transfer price that would force Division A to buy outside should be the sum of variable costs and opportunity costs, that is,

$$\$150 + \$50 + \$30 = \$230 \text{ per unit}$$

In other words, if Division B charges $230 to Division A, Division A will definitely buy from the outside source for $200.

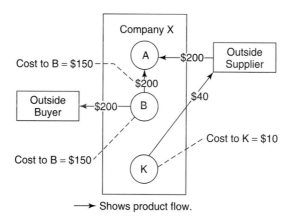

→ Shows product flow.

EXHIBIT 17.1 Transfer Pricing Situation

CHAPTER EIGHTEEN

How to Analyze and Improve Corporate Profitability and Shareholder Value

 MEASURES OF MANAGERIAL PERFORMANCE AND SHAREHOLDER RETURN

How do you measure managerial performance and the return to stockholders?

The ability to measure performance is essential in developing incentives and controlling operations toward the achievement of organizational goals. Perhaps the most widely used single measure of profitability of an organization is the *rate of return on investment* (ROI). Related is the return to stockholders, known as the *return on equity* (ROE).

An alternative measure that gained huge popularity is Economic Value Added (EVA™). A problem with just assessing performance with financial measures like ROI, ROE, and EVA is that the financial measures are backward looking. In other words, today's financial measures tell you about the accomplishments and failures of the past. An approach to performance measurement that also focuses on what managers are doing today to create future shareholder value is the *balanced scorecard*.

What is return on investment?

ROI relates net income to invested capital (total assets). It provides a standard for evaluating how efficiently management employs the average dollar invested in a firm's assets, whether that dollar came from owners or creditors. Furthermore, a better ROI can also translate directly into a higher return on the stockholders' equity. ROI is calculated as:

$$\text{ROI} = \frac{\text{Net profit after taxes}}{\text{Total assets}}$$

Example 18.1

Consider the following financial data:

Total assets	$100,000
Net profit after taxes	18,000

Then

$$\text{ROI} = \frac{\text{Net profit after taxes}}{\text{Total assets}} = \frac{\$18,000}{\$100,000} = 18\%$$

The problem with this formula is that it only tells you about how a company did and how well it fared in the industry. Other than that, it has very little value from the standpoint of profit planning.

What is the DuPont formula?

In the past, managers tended to focus on the margin earned and ignored the turnover of assets. It is important to realize that excessive funds tied up in assets can be just as much of a drag on profitability as excessive expenses. The DuPont Corporation was the first major company to recognize the importance of looking at both net profit margin and total asset turnover in assessing the performance of an organization. The ROI breakdown, known as the *DuPont formula*, is expressed as a product of these two factors, as shown next.

$$\text{ROI} = \frac{\text{Net profit after taxes}}{\text{Total assets}}$$

$$= \frac{\text{Net profit after taxes}}{\text{Sales}} \times \frac{\text{Sales}}{\text{Total assets}}$$

$$= \text{Net profit margin} \times \text{Total assets turnover}$$

The DuPont formula combines the income statement and balance sheet into this otherwise static measure of performance. Net profit margin is a measure of profitability or operating efficiency. It is the percentage of profit earned on sales. This percentage shows how many cents attach to each dollar of sales. Total asset turnover, however, measures how well a company manages its assets. It is the number of times by which the investment in assets turns over each year to generate sales.

The breakdown of ROI is based on the thesis that the profitability of a firm is directly related to management's ability to manage assets efficiently and to control expenses effectively.

Example 18.2

Assume the same data as in Example 18.1. Also assume sales of $200,000. Then

$$\text{ROI} = \frac{\text{Net profit after taxes}}{\text{Total assets}} = \frac{\$18,000}{\$100,000} = 18\%$$

Alternatively,

$$\text{Net profit margin} = \frac{\text{Net profit after taxes}}{\text{Total assets}} = \frac{\$18,000}{\$100,000} = 9\%$$

$$\text{Total asset turnover} = \frac{\text{Sales}}{\text{Total assets}} = \frac{\$200,000}{\$100,000} = 2 \text{ times}$$

Therefore,

$$\text{ROI} = \text{Net profit margin} \times \text{Total asset turnover} = 9\% \times 2 \text{ times} = 18\%$$

The breakdown provides a lot of insights to CFOs on how to improve the profitability of the company and investment strategy. (Note that net profit margin and total asset turnover are called hereafter *margin* and *turnover*, respectively, for short.) Specifically, it has at least four advantages over the original formula (i.e., net profit after taxes/total assets) for profit planning:

1. Focusing on the breakdown of ROI provides the basis for integrating many of the management concerns that influence a firm's overall performance. This will help managers gain an advantage in the competitive environment.
2. The breakdown emphasizes the importance of turnover as a key to overall ROI. In fact, turnover is just as important as profit margin in enhancing overall return.
3. It explicitly recognizes the importance of sales, which is not there in the original ROI formula.
4. The breakdown stresses the possibility of trading one off for the other in an attempt to improve a company's overall performance. The margin and turnover complement each other. In other words, a low turnover can be made up for by a high margin, and vice versa.

Example 18.3

The breakdown of ROI into its two components shows that a number of combinations of margin and turnover can yield the same rate of return, as shown next.

	Margin	×	Turnover	= ROI
(1)	9%	×	2 times	= 18%
(2)	6%	×	3 times	= 18%
(3)	3%	×	6 times	= 18%
(4)	2%	×	9 times	= 18%

The margin–turnover relationship and its resulting ROI is depicted in Exhibit 18.1.

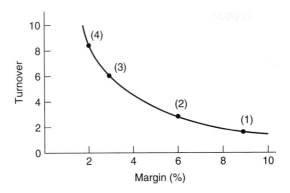

EXHIBIT 18.1 Margin–Turnover Relationship

Is there an optimal ROI?

Exhibit 18.1 can also be looked at as showing four companies that performed equally well (in terms of ROI) but with varying income statements and balance sheets. There is no ROI is satisfactory for all companies. Manufacturing firms in various industries will have low rates of return. Structure and size of the firm influence the rate considerably. A company with a diversified product line might have only a fair return rate when all products are pooled in the analysis. In such cases, it seems advisable to establish separate objectives for each line as well as for the total company.

Sound and successful operation must point toward the optimum combination of profits, sales, and capital employed. The combination will necessarily vary depending on the nature of the business and the characteristics of the product. An industry with products tailor-made to customers' specifications will have different margins and turnover ratios compared with industries that mass-produce highly competitive consumer goods. For example, combination (4) on the exhibit may describe a supermarket operation that inherently works with low margin and high turnover, while combination (1) may be a jewelry store that typically has a low turnover and high margin.

How do you use ROI for profit planning?

The breakdown of ROI into margin and turnover gives management insight into planning for profit improvement by revealing where weaknesses exist: margin or turnover, or both. Various actions can be taken to enhance ROI. Generally, management can employ three alternatives:

1. Improve margin.
2. Improve turnover.
3. Improve both.

Alternative 1 demonstrates a popular way of improving performance. Margins may be increased by reducing expenses, raising selling prices, or increasing sales faster than expenses. Some of the ways to reduce expenses are:

■ Use less costly inputs of materials.
■ Automate processes as much as possible to increase labor productivity.

- Bring the discretionary fixed costs under scrutiny, with various programs either curtailed or eliminated. Discretionary fixed costs arise from annual budgeting decisions by management. Examples include advertising, research and development, and management development programs. The cost-benefit analysis is called for in order to justify the budgeted amount of each discretionary program.

A company with pricing power can raise selling prices and retain profitability without losing business. *Pricing power* is the ability to raise prices even in poor economic times when unit sales volume may be flat and capacity may not be fully utilized. It is also the ability to pass on cost increases to consumers without attracting domestic and import competition, political opposition, regulation, new entrants, or threats of product substitution. The company with pricing power must have a unique economic position. Companies that offer unique, high-quality goods and services (where the service is more important than the cost) have this economic position.

Alternative 2 may be achieved by increasing sales while holding the investment in assets relatively constant, or by reducing assets. Some of the strategies to reduce assets are:

- Dispose of obsolete and redundant inventory. The computer has been extremely helpful in this regard, making perpetual inventory methods more feasible for inventory control.
- Devise various methods of speeding up the collection of receivables and also evaluate credit terms and policies.
- See if there are unused fixed assets.
- Use the converted assets obtained from use of the previous methods to repay outstanding debts or repurchase outstanding issues of stock. You may release them elsewhere to get more profit, which will improve margin as well as turnover.

Alternative 3 may be achieved by increasing sales or by any combinations of alternatives 1 and 2.

Exhibit 18.2 shows complete details of the relationship of ROI to the underlying ratios—margin and turnover—and their components. This will help identify more detailed strategies to improve margin, turnover, or both.

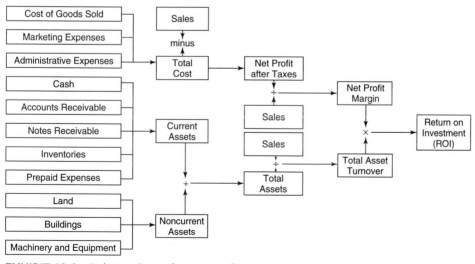

EXHIBIT 18.2 Relationships of Factors Influencing ROI

Example 18.4

Assume that management sets a 20 percent ROI as a profit target. It is currently making an 18 percent return on its investment.

$$\text{ROI} = \frac{\text{Net profit after taxes}}{\text{Total assets}} = \frac{\text{Net profit after taxes}}{\text{Sales}} \times \frac{\text{Sales}}{\text{Total assets}}$$

Present situation:

$$18\% = \frac{18{,}000}{200{,}000} \times \frac{200{,}000}{100{,}000}$$

The following alternatives are illustrative of the strategies that might be used. (Each strategy is independent of the others.)

Alternative 1: Increase the margin while holding turnover constant. Pursuing this strategy would involve leaving selling prices as they are and making every effort to increase efficiency so as to reduce expenses. By doing so, expenses might be reduced by $2,000 without affecting sales and investment to yield a 20 percent target ROI, as follows.

$$20\% = \frac{20{,}000}{200{,}000} \times \frac{200{,}000}{100{,}000}$$

Alternative 2: Increase turnover by reducing investment in assets while holding net profit and sales constant. Working capital might be reduced or some land might be sold, reducing investment in assets by $10,000 without affecting sales and net income to yield the 20 percent target ROI, as follows.

$$20\% = \frac{18{,}000}{200{,}000} \times \frac{200{,}000}{90{,}000}$$

Alternative 3: Increase both margin and turnover by disposing of obsolete and redundant inventories or through an active advertising campaign. For example, trimming down $5,000 worth of investment in inventories would also reduce the inventory holding charge by $1,000. This strategy would increase ROI to 20 percent.

$$20\% = \frac{19{,}000}{200{,}000} \times \frac{200{,}000}{95{,}000}$$

Excessive investment in assets is just as much of a drag on profitability as excessive expenses. In this case, cutting unnecessary inventories also helps cut down the expenses of carrying those inventories, so that both margin and turnover are improved at the same time. In practice, alternative 3 is much more common than alternative 1 or 2.

What is the relationship between ROI and return on equity?

Generally, a better management performance (i.e., a high or above-average ROI) produces a higher return to investors (equity holders). However, even a poorly managed company that suffers from a below-average performance can generate an above-average return on the stockholders' equity, simply called the *return on equity* (ROE). This is because borrowed funds can magnify the returns a company's profits represent to its stockholders.

Another version of the DuPont formula, called the *modified DuPont formula*, reflects this effect. The formula ties together the ROI and the degree of financial leverage (use of borrowed funds). The financial leverage is measured by the equity multiplier, which is the ratio of a company's total asset base to its equity investment, or, stated another way, the ratio of how many dollars of assets held per dollar of stockholders' equity. It is calculated by dividing total assets by stockholders' equity. This measurement gives an indication of how much of a company's assets are financed by stockholders' equity and how much with borrowed funds.

ROE is calculated as:

$$ROI = \frac{\text{Net profit after taxes}}{\text{Stockholders' equity}}$$

$$= \frac{\text{Net profit after taxes}}{\text{Total assets}} \times \frac{\text{Total assets}}{\text{Stockholders' equity}}$$

$$= ROI \times \text{Equity multiplier}$$

ROE measures the returns earned on the owners' (both preferred and common stockholders') investment. The use of the equity multiplier to convert the ROI to the ROE reflects the impact of the leverage (use of debt) on stockholders' return:

$$\text{The equity multiplier} = \frac{\text{Total assets}}{\text{Stockholders' equity}}$$

$$= \frac{1}{(1 - \text{Debt ratio})}$$

Exhibit 18.3 shows the relationship among ROI, ROE, and financial leverage.

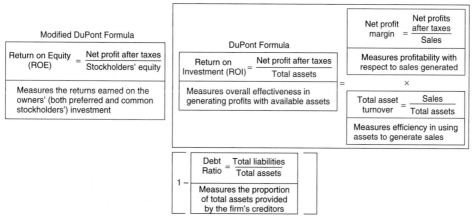

EXHIBIT 18.3   ROI, ROE, and Financial Leverage (Modified Du Pont Formula)

Example 18.5

In Example 18.1, assume stockholders' equity of $45,000. Then

$$\text{Equity multiplier} = \frac{\text{Total assets}}{\text{Stockholders' equity}}$$

$$= \frac{\$100,000}{\$45,000} = 2.22$$

$$= \frac{1}{(1 - \text{Debt ratio})} = \frac{1}{1 - 0.55} = \frac{1}{0.45} = 2.22$$

$$\text{ROE} = \frac{\text{Net profit after taxes}}{\text{Stockholders' equity}} = \frac{\$18,000}{\$45,000} = 40\%$$

$$\text{ROE} = \text{ROE} \times \text{Equity Multiplier} = 18\% \times 2.22 = 40\%$$

If the company used only equity, the 18 percent ROI would equal ROE. However, 55 percent of the firm's capital is supplied by creditors ($45,000/$100,000 = 45% is the equity-to-asset ratio; $55,000/$100,000 = 55% is the debt ratio). Since the 18 percent ROI all goes to stockholders, who put up only 45 percent of the capital, the ROE is higher than 18 percent. This example indicates that the company was using leverage (debt) favorably.

Example 18.6

To further demonstrate the interrelationship between a firm's financial structure and the return it generates on the stockholders' investments, let us compare two firms that generate $300,000 in operating income. Both firms employ $800,000 in total assets, but they have different capital structures. One firm employs no debt, whereas the other uses $400,000 in borrowed funds. The comparative capital structures are shown as:

	A	B
Total assets	$800,000	$800,000
Total liabilities	—	$400,000
Stockholders' equity (a)	800,000	400,000
Total liabilities and stockholders' equity	$800,000	$800,000

Firm B pays 10 percent interest for borrowed funds. The comparative income statements and ROEs for firms A and B would look like this:

	A	B
Operating income	$300,000	$300,000
Interest expense	—	(40,000)
Profit before taxes	$300,000	$260,000
Taxes (30% assumed)	(90,000)	(78,000)

Net profit after taxes (b)	$210,000	$182,000
ROE [(b)/(a)]	26.25%	45.5%

The absence of debt allows firm A to register higher profits after taxes. Yet the owners in firm B enjoy a significantly higher return on their investments. This provides an important view of the positive contribution debt can make to a business, but within a certain limit. Too much debt can increase the firm's financial risk and thus the cost of financing.

If the assets in which the funds are invested are able to earn a return greater than the fixed rate of return required by the creditors, the leverage is positive and the common stockholders benefit. The advantage of this formula is that it enables the company to break its ROE into a profit margin portion (net profit margin), an efficiency-of-asset-utilization portion (total asset turnover), and a use-of-leverage portion (equity multiplier). It shows that the company can raise shareholder return by employing leverage—taking on larger amounts of debt to help finance growth.

Since financial leverage affects net profit margin through the added interest costs, management must look at the various pieces of this ROE equation, within the context of the whole, to earn the highest return for stockholders. CFOs have the task of determining just what combination of asset return and leverage will work best in its competitive environment. Most companies try to keep at least a level equal to what is considered to be "normal" within the industry.

SUSTAINABLE RATE OF GROWTH

The sustainable rate of growth (g^*) represents the rate at which a firm's sales can grow if it wants to maintain its present financial ratios and does not want to resort to the sale of new equity shares. A simple formula can be derived for g^* where we assume that a firm's assets and liabilities all grow at the same rate as its sales, that is,

$$\text{Sustainable rate of growth } (g^*) = \text{ROE} (1 - b)$$

Recall that ROE is the firm's return on equity:

$$\text{ROE} = \frac{\text{Net profit after taxes}}{\text{Stockholders' equity}} = \frac{\text{Net profit after taxes}}{\text{Total assets}} \times \frac{\text{Total assets}}{\text{Stockholders' equity}}$$

$$= \text{ROI} \times \text{Equity multiplier}$$

and b is the firm's dividend payout ratio, that is,

$$\frac{\text{Dividends per share}}{\text{Earnings per share}}$$

The term $(1 - b)$ is sometimes referred to as the *plowback ratio* since it indicates the fraction of earnings that are reinvested, or plowed back, into the firm. Consequently, a firm's sustainable rate of growth is determined by its ROE (i.e., its anticipated net profit margin, asset turnover, and capital structure) as well as its dividend policy.

How do you calculate the sustainable rate of growth?

Consider three firms:

Firm	ROI	Equity Multiplier	Plowback Ratio	g*
A	10%	3.33	50%	16.65%
B	10%	3.33	100%	33.30%
C	10%	2.00	100%	20.00%

Comparing Firms A and B, we see that the only difference is that Firm A pays out half its earnings in common dividends (i.e., plows back half its earnings), whereas Firm B retains, or plows back, *all* of its earnings. The net result is that Firm B with its added source of internal equity financing can grow at twice the rate of Firm A (33.30 percent compared to 16.65 percent). Likewise, comparing Firms B and C, we note that they differ only in that Firm B finances only 30 percent (1/3.33) of its assets with equity, whereas Firm C finances 50 percent (1/2.00) of its assets with equity. The result is that Firm C's sustainable rate of growth is 20 percent compared to 33.30 percent for Firm B. This example indicates Firm B was using leverage (debt) favorably.

For this equation to depict a firm's sustainable rate of growth accurately, three assumptions must hold:

1. The firm's assets must vary as a constant percent of sales (i.e., even fixed assets expand and contract directly with the level of firm sales).
2. The firm's liabilities must all vary directly with firm sales. This means that the firm's management will expand its borrowing (both spontaneous and discretionary) in direct proportion with sales to maintain its present ratio of debt to assets.
3. The firm pays out a constant proportion of its earnings in common stock dividends regardless of the level of firm sales.

Since all three of these assumptions are only rough approximations to the way that firms actually behave, the equation provides crude approximation of the firm's actual sustainable rate of growth. However, an estimate of g^* using the equation can be a very useful first step in the firm's financial planning process.

 ECONOMIC VALUE ADDED

Why is EVA gaining popularity?

EVA is a concept similar to residual income but is often applied at the overall firm level as well as at the departmental level. It is a registered trademark of Stern Stewart & Co. (www.sternstewart.com), which developed the concept.

EVA is a measure of economic profit, but not the accounting profit we are accustomed to seeing in a corporate profit and loss statement. It is a measure of an operation's true profitability. The cost of debt capital (interest expense) is deducted when calculating net income, but no cost is deducted to account for the cost of common equity. Hence, in an economic sense, net income overstates "true" income. EVA overcomes this flaw in conventional accounting.

EVA is found by taking the net operating profit after taxes (NOPAT) for a particular period (such as a year) and subtracting the annual cost of all the capital a firm uses. EVA recognizes *all* capital costs, including the opportunity cost of the shareholder funds. It is a business's true economic profit. Such economic profits are the basis of shareholder value creation.

Note

The calculation of EVA can be complex because it makes various cost of capital and accounting principles adjustments.
The formula is:
EVA = NOPAT − After-tax cost of total capital

= Earnings before interest and taxes × (1 − tax rate) −
(Total capital × After-tax cost of capital) ■

Total capital used here is total assets *minus* current liabilities. Hence, it is long-term liabilities *plus* equity (preferred stock and common equity). Thus, EVA is an estimate of a business's true economic profit for the year, and it differs sharply from accounting profit. EVA represents the residual income that remains after the cost of *all* capital, including equity capital, has been deducted, whereas accounting profit is determined without imposing a charge for equity capital. Equity capital has a cost because funds provided by shareholders could have been invested elsewhere where they would have earned a return. In other words, shareholders give up the opportunity to invest funds elsewhere when they provide capital to the firm. The return they could earn elsewhere in investments of equal risk represents the cost of equity capital. This cost is an *opportunity cost* rather than an *accounting cost*, but it is quite real nevertheless.

Example 18.7 illustrates how an operation's economic profit differs from its accounting profit.

Example 18.7

A company with $100,000 in equity capital (stated at fair value) and $100,000 in 8 percent debt (also at fair value) had $60,000 in earnings before interest and taxes (EBIT). Assume also that $200,000 equals capital employed. The corporate tax rate is 40 percent. If that company's after-tax weighted-average cost of capital (WACC) is 14 percent, the EVA is $2,000, calculated as:

(continued)

EBIT	$60,000
Minus taxes (40% × $60,000)	(24,000)
NOPAT	$36,000
Capital charge (14% × $200,000)	(28,000)
EVA	$ 8,000

The company's traditional income statement reports income of $31,200, calculated as:

EBIT	$60,000
Minus interest (8% × $100,000)	(8,000)
Income before taxes	52,000
Income taxes (40% × $52,000)	(20,800)
Net income after taxes	$31,200

Initially, a 31.2 percent return on equity ($31,200 of net income/$100,000 of equity capital) seems favorable, but what is the cost of that equity capital? Given equal amounts of debt and equity, the cost of the equity capital must be 23.2 percent because the after-tax WACC was 14 percent and the after-tax cost of debt capital was 4.8% = 8% (1.0 − 40%).

Since 14% = (4.8%)(1/2) + ×(1/2), × = 23.2%

Thus, $23,200 of the $31,200 of net income is nothing more than the opportunity cost of equity capital. The $8,000 of EVA is the only portion of earnings that has created value for the shareholders. Accordingly, if income after taxes had been only $20,000 (a 20 percent return on equity), shareholder value would have been reduced because the cost of equity capital would have exceeded the return.

EVA and Value Creation

In the previous example, the $2,000 of EVA is the only portion of earnings that has created value for the shareholders. EVA provides a good measure of whether the firm has added to shareholder value. Therefore, if managers focus on EVA, this will help to ensure that they operate in a manner that is consistent with maximizing shareholder value. Note also that EVA can be determined for divisions—it is more often called *residual income*—as well as for the company as a whole, so it provides a useful basis for determining managerial compensation at all levels.

Although most companies adopt EVA for purposes of internal reporting and for calculating bonuses, some are publishing the results in corporate annual reports. For example, Eli Lilly reports EVA in the Financial Highlights section of the annual report. SPX stated clearly in its 2010 annual report: "EVA is the foundation of everything we do. . . . It is a common language, a mindset, and the way we do business."

More on NOPAT

Before computing NOPAT, analysts routinely adjust the company's reported earnings figures. These adjustments fall into three broad categories:

1. Isolate a company's sustainable operating profits by removing nonoperating or nonrecurring items from reported income.
2. Eliminate after-tax interest expense from the profit calculation so that profitability comparisons over time or across companies are not clouded by differences in financial structure.
3. Adjust for distortions related to as accounting quality concerns, which involve potential adjustments to both income and assets for items such as the off-balance sheet operating leases.

NOPAT is used to improve the comparability of EVA calculations. Otherwise, firms with different debt structures could have the same operating performance but different net incomes.

$$\text{NOPAT} = \text{Net income after taxes} + [\text{Charges and gains} \times (1 - \text{Tax rate}) + \text{Interest} \times (1 - \text{Tax rate})]$$

Example 18.8 illustrates the NOPAT computation.

Example 18.8

We are given the following income statement for years 2X11 and 2X12:

Comparative Income Statement		
	2X12	**2X11**
Sales	$5,199.0	$5,954.0
Cost of sales	(2,807.5)	(3,294.4)
Gross margin	2,391.5	2,659.6
Selling, general, and administrative expenses	(1,981.0)	(2,358.8)
Restructuring charges and gains	113.4	1,053.5
Interest expense	(106.8)	(131.6)
Other revenue and expenses	(1.5)	(2.2)
Before-tax income	415.6	1,220.5
Income taxes (40%)	(166.2)	(488.2)
Net income	$249.4	$732.3

NOPAT CALCULATIONS

	2X12	**2X11**
Net income as reported	$249.4	$732.3
Restructuring charges and gains after-tax	−68.04	−632.1
Interest expense after-tax	64.08	79.0
NOPAT	$245.4	$179.2

For example, for year 20X2,

$$\begin{aligned}\text{NOPAT} &= \text{Net income after taxes} + [\text{Charges and gains} \times (1 - \text{Tax rate}) + \\ &\quad \text{Interest} \times (1 - \text{Tax rate})] \\ &= \$247.90 - \$113.40(1 - 0.4) + \$106.80(1 - 0.4) \\ &= \$247.90 - \$68.04 + \$64.08 = \$254.40\end{aligned}$$

Capital Charge

The capital charge is the most distinctive and important aspect of EVA. Under conventional accounting, most companies appear profitable, but many in fact are not. The capital charge equals the after-tax WACC (calculated based on fair values of debt and equity) times the investment base or total capital employed (total assets minus current liabilities or the sum of long-term debt, preferred stock, and common equity).

Key Features of EVA

The main characteristics of EVA can be summarized in this way:

- For internal purposes, EVA is a better measure of profitability than ROI because a manager with a high ROI would be reluctant to invest in a new project with a lower ROI than is currently being earned, even though that return might be higher than the cost of capital. Thus, including a capital charge on departmental income statements helps managers to make decisions that will benefit the company.
- There is evidence of a direct correlation between EVA and increases in stock prices. For example, AT&T found an almost perfect correlation between its EVA and its stock price. In fact, many analysts have found that stock prices track EVA far more closely than other factors such as earnings per share, operating margin, or ROE. The argument is that simply having a continuing stream of income is not enough; that income must exceed the cost of capital for a stock to rise significantly in the stock market.
- EVA uses dollars instead of percentages to measure changes. For example, it is much more appealing to report that the company generated $1 million in shareholder value than to say that the ROI increased from 10 to 15 percent.
- EVA is the only financial management system that provides a common language for employees across all operating and staff functions and allows all management decisions to be modeled, monitored, communicated, and compensated in a single and consistent way—always in terms of the value added to shareholder investment.

What can value-driven managers do to improve EVA?

As a simplified form,

$$\text{EVA} = \text{NOPAT} - \text{After-tax WACC} \times \text{Net assets}$$

Another way to look at it is:

$$\text{EVA} = \left(\frac{\text{NOPAT}}{\text{Net assets} \times \text{Net assets}} \right)$$
$$- (\text{After-tax WACC} \times \text{Net assets})$$
$$= \left(\frac{\text{NOPAT}}{\text{Net assets}} - \text{After-tax WACC} \right) \times \text{Net assets}$$

$$= (\text{Return on net assets} - \text{After-tax WACC}) \times \text{Net assets}$$
$$= (\text{Return on net assets} - \text{WACC}) \times \text{Net assets}$$

Assuming other variables stay constant, EVA increases when return on net assets (RONA) increases, when WACC decreases, when net assets increase (assuming profitable growth), or when net assets decrease (in the case of money-losing assets).

Evidence from EVA adopters shows six ways to achieve improvements.

1. Increase asset turnover.
2. Dispose of unprofitable businesses.
3. Refurbish assets.
4. Structure deals that require less capital.
5. Increase leverage and use less equity finance.
6. Invest in profitable growth.

Note that three of these actions (increasing asset turnover, repairing assets, and structuring deals with less capital) increase EVA through improvement in RONA. Disposing of unprofitable businesses increases EVA, providing improvements in the spread between RONA and WACC are greater than the reduction in net assets. Increasing leverage increases EVA by reducing WACC, assuming that the company is underlevered when it begins taking on more debt. Investing is profitable and increases EVA, as long as the RONA on the investment exceeds the WACC.

EVA Compensation

EVA bonus plans do not just motivate managers to think about current EVA. If they did, managers would focus entirely on short-term performance at the expense of the future. Value-creating investments might be avoided because their immediate effects on EVA are negative. The solution is to give managers a direct economic state in future EVA, not just the current period. The performance evaluation will be more meaningful if the current EVA is compared to EVAs from previous periods, target EVAs, and EVAs from other operating units or companies.

A Caveat

EVA is no panacea, and it is no substitute for sound corporate strategies. But when EVA and management bonus systems are linked together, alignment between the interests of managers and shareholders improves. The effect is that when managers make important decisions, they are more likely to do so in ways that deliver superior returns for shareholders.

 ## BALANCED SCORECARD

How does a balanced scorecard to evaluate performance work?

A problem with assessing performance only with financial measures like ROI, ROE, and EVA is that the financial measures are backward looking. In other words, today's financial measures tell you about the accomplishments and failures of the past. An approach to performance measurement that also focuses on what managers are doing today to create future shareholder value is the balanced scorecard.

Essentially, a *balanced scorecard* is a set of performance measures constructed for four dimensions of performance. As indicated in Exhibit 18.4, the dimensions are financial, customer, internal processes, and learning and growth. Having financial measures is critical, even if they are backward looking. After all, they have a great effect on the evaluation of the company by shareholders and creditors. Customer measures examine the company's success in meeting customer expectations. Internal process measures examine the company's success in improving critical business processes. And learning and growth measures examine the company's success in improving its ability to adapt, innovate, and grow. The customer, internal processes, and learning and growth measures are generally thought to be predictive of future success (i.e., they are not backward looking).

EXHIBIT 18.4   Balanced Scorecard

		Measures
Financial	Is the company achieving its financial goals?	Operating income Return on assets Sales growth Cash flow from operations Reduction of administrative expense
Customer	Is the company meeting customer expectations?	Customer satisfaction Customer retention New customer acquisition Market share On-time delivery Time to fill orders
Internal Processes	Is the company improving critical internal processes?	Defect rate Lead time Number of suppliers Material turnover Percent of practical capacity
Learning and Growth	Is the company improving its ability to innovate?	Amount spent on employee training Employee satisfaction Employee retention Number of new products New product sales as a percent of total sales Number of patents

How is balance achieved in a balanced scorecard?

A variety of potential measures for each dimension of a balanced scorecard are indicated in Exhibit 18.4. After reviewing these measures, note how "balance" is achieved:

- Performance is assessed across a *balanced set of dimensions* (financial, customer, internal processes, and innovation).

- *Quantitative* measures (e.g., number of defects) are balanced with qualitative measures (e.g., ratings of customer satisfaction).
- There is a balance of *backward-looking* measures (e.g., financial measures like growth in sales) and *forward-looking* measures (e.g., number of new patents as an innovation measure).

Note: The balanced scorecard measures vary with a company's strategy and industry. Exhibit 18.5 lists examples of performance indicators for each balanced scorecard dimension across a wide range of industries.

EXHIBIT 18.5 Examples of Balanced Scorecard Measures by Industry

Industry	Financial Dimension	Customer Dimension	Internal Process Dimension	Learning and Growth Dimension
Airlines	Return on assets	Frequent flier program participation rates	Percentage of on-time takeoffs and arrivals	Labor contract length
Consumer retail banks	Ratio of assets to debt	Number of new accounts opened	Number of new branches	Hours of employee training completed
Accounting, consulting, and law firms	Profit margin	Client retention rate	Percentage of projects completed on time	Certification and education levels of professionals
Computer manufacturers	Sales growth from new products	Number of corporate customers	Number of product defects	Percentage of factory employees who completed quality control training
Supermarkets	Inventory turnover	Customer satisfaction	Product spoilage rates	Employee turnover rates

You can log on to numerous web resources to learn more about the balanced scorecard and performance evaluations. For example, managers frequently look to industry "best practices" or examples of successful implementations at other firms when developing measurement programs. The next list provides valuable resources for evaluating performance and business decision making across a wide range of industries.

- The Balanced Scorecard Institute (www.balancedscorecard.org). The Balanced Scorecard Institute is an independent educational institute that provides training and guidance to assist government agencies and companies in applying best practices in balanced scorecard and performance measurement for strategic management and transformation. Its web site provides background information about implementing the balanced scorecard and the proper selection of nonfinancial measures. It also provides several examples of past successes.

- American Productivity and Quality Center (www.apqc.org). The APQC, an internationally recognized nonprofit organization, provides expertise in benchmarking and best practices research. APQC helps organizations adapt to rapidly changing environments, build new and better ways to work, and succeed in a competitive marketplace. It has a membership of over 450 prestigious global firms including 3M, AT&T, Cisco Systems, and Ernst & Young. The objective of this collaborative center is to "Understand how innovative organizations create succession management programs to identify and cultivate potential leaders who will provide a sustainable business advantage." The Best Practices and Free Resources links lead to many useful resources.
- Management Help (www.managementhelp.org). This web site offers a robust library of decision-making tools and resources. The site offers many resources on such topics as strategic planning, performance measurement, employee development, and make-or-outsource decisions. It also includes online discussion groups, decision-making guidance, and free reference material.
- Performance Measurement Association (www.performanceportal.org). This web site, home to the United Kingdom's PMA, covers references to valuable articles, a free newsletter, and insight into current trends in performance measurement. It is representative of the types of professional associations that managers join to share ideas and continue the development of their personal and managerial skills.

Information Technology and IT Systems

NFORMATION TECHNOLOGY (IT) and IT systems are used in all business domains. For example, finance uses information to forecast revenues and maximize investment, make selections on stocks, and even predict bankruptcies. Accounting uses information systems to record transactions, prepare financial statements, manage cash flow, or predict profit or loss. In marketing, information systems are used to develop new merchandise and services and customer segmentation, determine the locations for production and distribution facilities (so that the cost can be reduced and more customers will be attracted), formulate price strategies (so they can maximize total profits), and even develop the promotion policies (so that advertising will be more efficient). In manufacturing, information systems are used to process customer orders, develop production schedules, design new products, and test the quality of products.

 COMPUTER TECHNOLOGIES AVAILABLE FOR BUSINESS

Network technologies allow users to share information and other resources. As a result, information retrieval can be more efficient and available. Current Internet technology provides businesses with a variety of external business information. Multimedia information transmissions (text, graphics, images, and video) are also available on the Internet. With the impact of the Internet, intranet becomes another new technology popular to business. Intranet is a small version of the Internet in one organization. It provides almost the same services as the Internet would do but with better security and privacy. E-commerce is a way of life. Artificial intelligence (AI) technologies are also applied to business functions. Neural networks have been used to predict the stock and bond markets. Expert systems are used to help managers with financial decisions.

Wireless networking is fast becoming a viable alternative for companies that can utilize its advantages of enhanced connectivity and flexibility. In the future, more intelligent agents will be used in the business environment to improve the quality of services and products.

ROLE OF INFORMATION SYSTEMS IN THE STRATEGIC PLAN

Strategic planning is the process of selecting the organization's long-term objectives and of setting the strategies for achieving those objectives. This planning process is the responsibility of strategic management and is concerned with the overriding issues facing the organization, such as product lines and profitability. Given the international, competitive, and dynamic environment confronted by organizations, strategic planning is crucial to their survival.

Information systems (IS) can play an important role in the development of the strategic plan and in monitoring ongoing operations to measure attainment of the plan. During the strategic planning process, data from the entity-wide database can be compared to data about the competition to determine an organization's relative strengths and weaknesses. For example, these data might include sales trends, gross margin on sales, age of capital assets, skills of existing personnel, debt/equity ratio, and so on. These data can be presented in reports from the existing information systems applications, such as sales/marketing, human resources management, fixed assets, finance and inventory, or via the models incorporated in the decision support system (DSS) and executive information system (EIS). Note that data from the environment can also be incorporated into the DSS and EIS output. Strategic planners can combine the environmental data with those obtained internally to assess the organization's competitive position. The demand for such information has been a major driver in the move to enterprise resource planning (ERP) systems, which bring all of the organization's information together into a single entity-wide database and generally provide the associated tools for strategic analysis and decision support.

In addition to assisting in the planning phase, the IS can be used to follow up by reporting certain performance indicators that illustrate the status of processes and critical success factors. For example, the number of franchises along with the level of sales and number of customer complaints for each should indicate the status of an organization's franchise network. Other performance indicators might be the number of new products, the cost to manufacture the products, and their selling price. If the entity-wide database is developed in light of the strategic plan, many of the data for the performance indicators should be readily available.

In addition to an organizational strategic planning process, there must be a strategic planning process for the IS function. That process must be coordinated with the organization's strategic planning process to ensure that the strategic plan is supported and that IT is used to its best advantage. For example, during the strategic planning process, organizations should seek to achieve strategic advantage over their competitors by utilizing available IT. This is particularly observable as companies ponder how to deal with the rapidly evolving world of e-business.

MANAGEMENT INFORMATION SYSTEMS

What is a management information system?

A management information system (MIS) comprises computer-based processing and/or manual procedures that provide useful, complete, and timely information. This information must support management decision making in a rapidly changing business environment. The MIS system must supply managers with information quickly, accurately, and completely. The MIS has many subsystems: accounting information system (AIS), marketing information system, financial information system, production/operations information system, and human resource information system. For example, an AIS is a subsystem of a MIS and processes financial and transactional data relevant to managerial decisions as well as financial accounting. *Note:* A manufacturer's AIS has well-defined reporting needs for routine information about purchasing and payables. Purchase requisitions document user department needs, and purchase orders provide evidence that purchase transactions were appropriately authorized. A formal receiving procedure segregates the purchasing and receiving functions and establishes the quantity, and timeliness of goods received. Vendor invoices establish the liability for payment and should be compared with the foregoing documents.

When do you use decision support systems?

DSSs are designed to help managers reach a decision by summarizing or comparing data from different resources. They are suitable for semistructured and unstructured problems. DSSs often include query languages, statistical analysis capabilities, spreadsheets, and graphics to help decision makers evaluate the decision. DSSs are a type of MIS expressly developed to support the decision-making process. DSSs facilitate a dialogue between the user, who is considering alternative problem solutions, and the systems, with its built-in models and accessible database. More advanced DSSs include capabilities that allow users to create a model of the variables affecting a decision. With a model, users can ask what-if questions by changing one or more of the variables and seeing what the projected results would be. A simple model for determining the best product price would include factors for the expected sales volume at each price level. Many people use electronic spreadsheets for simple modeling tasks. A DSS is sometimes combined with an EIS. DSS applications used in business include systems that estimate profitability, plan monthly operations, determine the source and application of funds, and schedule staff.

 WHO USES EXECUTIVE INFORMATION SYSTEMS?

An EIS is a DSS made specially for top managers and specifically supports strategic decision making. An EIS is also called an *executive support system* (ESS). The EIS is designed to generate information that is abstract enough to present the whole company operation in a simplified version to satisfy senior management. Characteristically, senior managers employ a great variety of informal sources of information, so that computerized information systems are able to provide only limited assistance. However, the CEO, senior and executive vice presidents, and the board of directors also need to be able to track the performance of their company and of its various units, assess the business environment, and develop strategic directions for the company's future. *Note:* An EIS focuses on strategic (long-range) objectives and gives immediate information about a firm's critical success factors. Information is typically supplied from nontraditional computer sources. However, an EIS program can be used on computers of all sizes. An EIS is not a program for providing top management with advice and answers from a knowledge-based (expert) system.

In particular, these executives need a great diversity of external information to compare their company's performance to that of its competition and to investigate the general trends of the economies in the many countries where the company may be doing business. EIS is therefore designed to address the information needs for senior management who may not be familiar working with computer systems. EIS also provides features that make them easier for executives to use. EIS provides a graphical user interface that can be mouse or touch screen oriented. EIS relies heavily on graphic presentation of both the menu options and data.

What are the basic concepts and applications of artificial intelligence and expert systems?

AI is the application of human reasoning techniques to machines. AI systems use sophisticated computer hardware and software to simulate the functions of the human mind. Expert systems are the most promising applications of AI and have received the most attention. Expert systems are computer programs exhibiting behavior characteristics of experts. These systems involve the creation of computer software that emulates the way people solve problems. Like a human expert, an expert system gives advice by drawing upon its own store of knowledge and by requesting information specific to the problem at hand. Expert systems are not exactly the same thing as DSSs.

A DSS is computer-based software that assists decision makers by providing data and models. It performs primarily semistructured tasks whereas an expert system is more appropriate for unstructured tasks. DSSs can be interactive just as expert systems are. But, because of the way DSSs process information, they typically cannot be used for unstructured decisions that involve nonquantitative data. Unlike expert systems, DSSs do not make decisions; they merely attempt to improve and enhance decisions by providing indirect support without automating the whole decision process.

Some general characteristics indicate whether a given business application is likely to be a good candidate for the development of an expert system. For example, application requires the use of expert knowledge, judgment, and experience. The business problem must have a heuristic nature and must be defined clearly. The area of expertise required for the application must be well defined and recognized professionally, and the organization developing the expert system must be able to recruit an expert who is willing to cooperate with the expert system's development team. The size and complexity of the application must be manageable in the context of organizational resources, available technical skills, and management support.

An expert system, sometimes called a *knowledge system*, is a set of computer programs that perform a task at the level of a human expert. Expert systems are created on the basis of knowledge collected on specific topics from human experts, and the systems imitate the reasoning process of a human being. There are six components to the expert system:

1. Knowledge base
2. Domain database
3. Database management system
4. Inference engine
5. User interface
6. Knowledge acquisition facility

The knowledge base contains the rules used when making decisions. Expert systems have emerged from the field of AI, which is the branch of computer science that is attempting to create computer systems that simulate human reasoning and sensation. User interface features online help facilities, debugging tools, and other tools designed to assist users.

Expert systems are used by management and nonmanagement personnel to solve specific problems, such as how to reduce production costs, improve workers' productivity, or reduce environmental impact. They are computer programs that come up with a solution to a problem in much the same way an expert would, by methodically using a narrowly defined domain of knowledge that is built into the program. The key to the definition is that the domain must be narrowly defined. At this time, an expert system cannot be developed to give useful answers about all questions; these systems are limited, just as a human expert is limited to a particular field. For example, one expert system would not tell the controller whether to lease or buy a piece of equipment based on the tax differences.

 ## VALUE CHAIN MANAGEMENT SOFTWARE

What are the software systems that impact value chain management?

Firms employ a wide variety of software systems to process information and improve the operation of the value chain. They are ERP systems, supply chain management (SCM) systems, and customer relationship management (CRM) systems.

Enterprise Resource Planning Systems

ERP systems grew out of material requirements planning (MRP) systems, which have been used for more than 20 years. MRP systems computerized inventory control and production planning. Key features included an ability to prepare a master production schedule and a bill of materials and generate purchase orders. ERP systems update MRP systems with better integration, relational databases, and graphical user interfaces. Features now encompass supporting accounting and finance, human resources, and various e-commerce applications, including SCM and CRM, which are explained next.

ERP Selection Criteria Checklist

Are you faced with the challenge of selecting an ERP application? It's a time-consuming process for IT/IS managers to assess application vendors, then compare what they are offering to what the organization needs. We have designed this checklist to expedite the process and to help ensure that you touch all the bases as your investigate each vendor.

Database and Network

- How many user licenses are required?
- Is the ERP designed to work with different relational database management systems (RDBMs), such as Oracle, Sybase, and Informix?
- Does the vendor have any built-in programs to handle integration?
- How will the data warehousing aspects be addressed?
- What is the maximum time it takes for uploading the remote data?
- What is the minimum time it takes for uploading the remote data?
- Does the software support distributed data processing?
- Does the software support a parallel processing option?
- Has the vendor had any problems in the past regarding concurrency?
- Does the software have an audit trail on key transactions?
- How many security layers have been incorporated into the software?
- What kind of networking protocols does the software support?
- Does the software support BLOB (binary large object) data types and others?
- What is the largest database the vendor has handled so far for the modules you are interested in?
- What is the smallest database size handled by the vendor so far for the modules you are interested in?

Implementation

- Has the vendor implemented sites in this region?
- Has the vendor implemented ERP in your industry segment?
- Has the vendor implemented the same modules that your organization needs?
- Will there be immediate delivery of the product?
- Does the vendor have a specific implementation plan?
- How long did it take for the vendor to implement the same modules elsewhere?
- How many years of experience does the vendor have with implementation?
- Does the vendor have good project plan initiatives?
- Does the vendor have a good implementation team with the required skills?
- Does the vendor have the Certification of Excellence given by other customers?
- What is the minimum implementation time for the modules you have chosen?
- What is the maximum implementation time for the modules you have chosen?

Business Processes

- Does the vendor promise any reduction in lead times of those business processes in which you have some interest?
- What is the minimum processing time for MRP?
- What is the maximum processing time for MRP?
- What is the minimum processing time for master production schedule (MPS)?
- What is the maximum processing time for MPS?
- Does the software optimize the business processes after implementation?
- Does the software use a built-in business process modeler?

Hardware and Software

- What kind of hardware support does the vendor offer?
- How many years of experience does the vendor have with the hardware/software that will be used for your project?
- Who are the alliance partners for the hardware support?
- What is the upgrade support for the software?
- Does the software have any interface to support the latest technology?
- How is the vendor maintaining the documentation for the software?
- Is the software Web enabled?
- Will the software be implemented in modules?
- Will the software be purchased in modules?
- Will the software accounting adhere to international standards and adhere to each country's standards?
- How many operating systems does the software support?
- Does the software allow posting of transaction both in batch mode and online?
- Does the software support multilingual operation?

Support

- What support will the vendor provide after implementation?
- If the vendor is out of country, how is support provided?
- How much time will the vendor devote to ERP training for end users?
- Describe the user interface (UI)/graphical user interface (GUI) package support and how each will give end users ease of operation.
- Did the vendor complete any customization at any previously implemented sites? (Describe by percentage and the modules.)
- How will the vendor complete the reports' customization?
- Does the software have any built-in programs to handle data conversions?
- Is the front-end application developed using proprietary software?
- Is the customization cost included in the ERP cost?
- Can the vendor give approval for accessing other customers' data?
- Does the vendor have any test data built into the software for proper training?
- If any bugs are found in the software during or after implementation, what is the replacement support?
- Is the vendor ready to work with third-party tools and software? ▪

Supply Chain Management Systems

SCM is the organization of activities between a company and its suppliers in an effort to provide for the profitable development, production, and delivery of goods to customers. By sharing information, production lead times and inventory holding costs have been reduced, while on-time deliveries to customers have been improved. SCM software systems support the planning of the best way to fill orders and help tracking of products and components among companies in the supply chain. Walmart and Procter & Gamble (P&G) are two companies that have become well known for their cooperation in the use of SCM. When P&G products are scanned at a Walmart store, P&G receives information on the sale via satellite and thus knows when to make more product and the specific Walmart stores to which the product should be shipped. Related cost savings are passed on, at least in part, to Walmart customers.

Customer Relationship Management Systems

CRM systems automate customer service and support. They also provide for customer data analysis and support e-commerce storefronts. While CRM systems are constantly evolving, they have already led to some remarkable changes in the way companies interact with customers. For example, FedEx allows customers to track their packages on the Web. This service is becoming commonplace, but it did not exist 10 years ago. Amazon.com uses CRM technology to make suggestions to customers based on their personal purchase histories. The ultimate development of CRM remains to be seen, but undoubtedly mobile communication will play a significant role. Many companies are already experimenting with systems to send messages to cell phone users offering them special discounts and buying opportunities.

EXTENSIBLE BUSINESS REPORTING LANGUAGE

What is the purpose of Extensible Business Reporting Language?

The existence of many data formats on the Internet prevents users from analyzing financial information without many labor-intensive conversions. Excessive time is devoted to extracting useful information from available accounting and financial data. Further, time is wasted rekeying the same information into a spreadsheet. For example, data in the Securities and Exchange Commission's (SEC) database (Electronic Data Gathering, Analysis, and Retrieval System, or EDGAR), cannot be imported directly into spreadsheets. EDGAR performs automated collection, validation, indexing, acceptance, and forwarding of submissions by companies and others that are required by law to file forms with the SEC. The comparison of numbers and ratios requires significant effort and very time-consuming rekeying.

Extensible Business Reporting Language (XBRL) makes available financial information in an easy-to-use format on the Internet. Formerly code-named XFRML, a freely available electronic language for financial reporting, it is an Extensible Markup

Language (XML)-based framework that provides the financial community a standards-based method to prepare, publish in a variety of formats, reliably extract, and automatically exchange financial statements of publicly held companies and the information they contain.

What are some major applications of XBRL?

There are many accounting, financial, and business applications of XBRL including:

- Automating business reporting.
- Financial statement preparation and analysis. For example, XBRL financial statements on a company's web site can go directly into Microsoft Excel so rekeying is not required.
- Auditing of financial statements.
- Managing and distributing accounting data.
- Consolidating and reporting data to regulatory bodies.
- Collecting and updating financial data on borrowers such as by accessing the borrower's web page.
- Assessing credit risk.
- Integrating investment information.
- Communicating financial performance to users of financial statements.
- Internal management reporting, such as cost control and analysis.

With an XBRL, companies are now able to measure their performance more accurately against their competitors. For regulators, the advantages of XBRL are clear. The ability to receive files via the Internet and read them with computers is a big attraction. Being able to manipulate the data automatically offers huge cost savings. Regulators can run instantaneous analyses of trends and ratios that might be indicative of underpayment of tax. They can divide tax returns into high risk and low risk to help inspectors decide where to focus resources and which companies might be eligible for a lighter touch.

 WEB 2.0

How does Web 2.0 compare with traditional processing?

Web 2.0 is a loose collection of capabilities, technologies, business models, and philosophies that characterizes the new and emerging business uses of the Internet. Software as a service (SaaS) is an example of Web 2.0. The web itself has evolved from a mere repository of passively consumed information to Web 2.0—a dynamic, interactive environment. Users are empowered, active participants who create content, review products, and edit and share information. Web 2.0 concepts have led to the development and evolution of web culture communities and hosted services, such as social networking sites, video sharing sites, wikis, and blogs. Exhibit 19.1 compares Web 2.0 with traditional processing. (For some reason, the term "Web 1.0" is not used.)

EXHIBIT 19.1 Comparison of Traditional Processing with Web 2.0

Traditional Processing	Web 2.0 Processing
Software as product	Software as service
Infrequent, controlled releases	Frequent releases of perpetual betas
Business model relies on sale of software licenses	Business model relies on advertising or other revenue from use
Extensive advertising	Viral marketing
Product value fixed	Product value increases with use and users
Publishing	Participation
Major winners: Microsoft, Oracle, SAP	Major winners: Google, Amazon.com, eBay

 ## CLOUD COMPUTING AND COMPARATIVE ADVANTAGE

Mobile communication and cloud computing are the two prevailing technological trends today. In many businesses, desktop computers are fast becoming obsolete with the advent of ever smaller laptops, netbooks, smartphones, and other compact mobile devices. Furthermore, virtual private networks (VPNs) offer secure access to company information from any location in the world that provides an Internet connection. If you use Flickr, Gmail, or Facebook, to name a few, you are already participating in cloud computing. Your photos and other data are stored in a remote location, and you can access them by using your personal computer (PC), laptop, netbook, smartphone, or PDA.

Most IT departments are forced to spend a significant portion of their time on frustrating implementation, maintenance, and upgrade projects that too often do not add significant value to the company's bottom line. Increasingly, IT teams are turning to cloud computing technology to minimize the time spent on lower-value activities and allow IT to focus on strategic activities with greater impact on the business. Cloud computing is a better way to run your business. With cloud computing, you are not managing hardware and software. The shared infrastructure means it works like a utility: You pay only for what you need, upgrades are automatic, and scaling up or down is easy.

Instead of running your apps yourself, they run on a shared data center. When you use any app that runs in remote network clusters, or "clouds," you just log in, customize it, and start using it. That is the power of cloud computing. Businesses are running all kinds of apps in the cloud these days, such as CRM, human resources, accounting, and custom-built apps. Cloud-based apps can be up and running in a few days, which is unheard of with traditional business software. They are more competitive and cost less, because you do not need to pay for all the people, products, and facilities to run them.

And it turns out cloud-based apps are more scalable, more secure, and more reliable than most apps. Plus, upgrades—always the latest versions—are taken care of for you, so your apps get security and performance enhancements and new features—automatically. Cloud computing is business computing run on a shared data center.

What are the rewards of the cloud?

Companies are lured to cloud computing by the promise of greater efficiency and higher profits. Avon, for example, hopes that its move to manage a sales force of 6 million reps worldwide with cloud computing will lead to greater effectiveness and higher sales. Blue Cross of Pennsylvania has enabled its 300,000 members to access medical histories and claims information with their smartphones. Like other tech companies, Serena Software has fully embraced the cloud, even using Facebook as the primary source of internal communication. Coca-Cola Enterprises has provided 40,000 sales reps, truck drivers, and other workers in the field with portable devices to connect with the home office instantly to respond to changing customer needs and problems on the road.

What opportunities and risks are offered by cloud computing?

Some see the shift from storing information on isolated machines to information sharing in digital and social networks as the largest growth opportunity since the Internet boom. The market for cloud products and services will likely soar. However, skeptics warn that caution about the risks of convenience is in order. For one thing, once the information leaves our computing device for the cloud, we do not know who can intercept it. In addition to data security, networks must be reliable, so that users can access them anytime. Google's recent software glitch allowed unauthorized access to a certain percentage of user files and left some Gmail customers unable to use their online applications. Cloud computing is flexible and cost efficient. But without proven public cloud protection and trusted compliance codes, security remains its largest hurdle.

Accountants Head to the Cloud

The American Institute of Certified Public Accountants (AICPA) has ramped up its endorsement of SaaS solutions for small and midsize businesses, citing lower costs and competitive advantages.

Unlike the development curve of many business trends, the use of cloud computing to lower accounting costs has gained an early foothold among smaller companies. There is practically limitless room for growth; what almost everyone regards as the most successful cloud software provider to date, salesforce.com, started out at the lower end but now continues to find a berth in larger and larger companies.

The AICPA is pushing to accelerate adoption of cloud solutions among its 350,000 members, focusing especially on small and midmarket companies as well as certified public accounting firms. The AICPA's first official endorsement of a cloud vendor, payroll-solutions provider Paychex, came several years ago. But the institute has rolled out more such partnerships with increasing frequency, including with bill.com for invoice management and payment in 2008, financial management and accounting software maker Intacct in 2010, and tax-automation supplier Copanion at year-end 2009.

In spring of 2011, another cloud vendor received the institute's stamp of approval, CPA2Biz, an AICPA subsidiary that provides the parent with technology and marketing services and advocates the use of accounting automation by small businesses.

The pitch is that the cloud offers a steep drop in IT costs, since applications are hosted by the vendors and provided on demand rather than via physical installations or seat licenses. It is extremely important for CFOs, controllers, and CPA firms to leverage this new way of doing business. Putting these solutions in place provides sustainable competitive advantages.

MOBILE COMPUTING (WIRELESS TECHNOLOGY)

What does "mobile computing" mean?

Mobile computing (wireless networking) is fast becoming a viable alternative for companies that can utilize the advantages it provides. It can provide enhanced connectivity and flexibility for companies seeking to expand a computer network or make their employees more mobile. Major technology companies are behind its standards, and the price and choice of products should only improve.

Two major developing technologies are changing the computer networking landscape: Wi-Fi (Wireless Fidelity) and Bluetooth. These two forms of wireless technology can change the entire infrastructure of business networks. Many new hardware and software products, produced by many big-name technology companies, are equipped for use with Bluetooth and Wi-Fi. The Bluetooth Special Interest Group (SIG; www.bluetooth.com) and the Wi-Fi Alliance (www.wi-fi.org) are groups formed to help effectively develop, integrate, and implement these wireless technologies globally. These two groups have created global standards for each technology, which must be met by any company producing hardware or software to operate with Bluetooth or Wi-Fi.

What does mobile computing mean for CEOs, CIOs, and users?

CEOs

Mobile working can dramatically boost productivity and improve an organization's responsiveness and flexibility, but it also poses challenges for the CEO. But as the trend toward mobile working gathers pace, these are issues that executives cannot afford to ignore. As wired and wireless network-enabled notebook PCs, tablets, and smartphones proliferate, mobile working is becoming a reality. This expansion has significant advantages—and risks—for corporate managements. On the positive side, mobile and remote access to corporate systems such as e-mail and enterprise portals and to applications such as contact management and CRM systems often provide a competitive edge for companies while improving both customer and employee satisfaction. But on the negative side, mobile technologies and services tend to come with premium price tags, pushing costs up at a time when CEOs are still under pressure to improve margins and show rapid returns on investments. Mobile systems are also notoriously difficult to manage and control and, perhaps most seriously, ad hoc arrangements can represent a real threat to enterprise system security. Balancing the risks and rewards of mobile working and establishing a corporate policy framework to cover, for example, remote access to corporate networks has become an important issue for CEOs—an issue that they ignore at their peril.

CEOs will want to ensure that they are getting value for money when they invest in mobile working infrastructure, so they probably will want to see estimates—and subsequently evidence—of productivity gains and other tangible improvements. They will also want to see investment return projections and probably will be involved in making choices about competing projects.

CIOs

Given the fast pace of change in the technology industry, particularly in the mobile device sector, it is also often a challenge for a CIO to keep up with hardware, software, and service developments and to provide the level of support—often with reduced resources—that users have come to expect. One way to minimize the support overhead is to standardize on a set of devices such as notebook PCs, PDAs, mobile phones, and communicators. However, often this delays deployment and can lead to end user frustration. Another option is to outsource the provision of devices and services. For example U.S.-based Aruba, which supplies secure Wi-Fi networks for corporate customers, says many of them also want it to manage the deployment and maintenance of the Wi-Fi system.

One of the fastest-growing areas in the mobile technology sector is security. Typically, larger companies will deploy VPNs to facilitate secure access for mobile and remote users, such as home office workers, to a corporate network. However, there are secure alternatives, including remote access programs such as LapLink and the GoToMyPC remote access service that can be rolled out across an enterprise or made available to a few users.

There is also a growing market for software and hardware such as mini-USB drives and biometric devices such as fingerprint readers designed to protect confidential or sensitive data stored on a portable PC.

Other vendors have developed systems designed to enable secure access to e-mail and other corporate services from Internet public access points such as hotels, conference centers or even Wi-Fi hot spots.

Most CIOs have already discovered that the trend toward mobile working is like a runaway steamroller—it is not about to stop. So while it makes sense to lay down guidelines about which mobile devices are supported and how they should be used, ultimately the CIO has to deal with the realities of mobile working.

Users

The rapid growth of mobile working and the proliferation of new hardware devices, software, and services designed to enable mobile workers to do their jobs from virtually anywhere poses both great opportunities and challenges. For many employees, the availability of basic tools like portable PCs, tablets, and smartphones gives them much greater freedom and flexibility. For example, salespeople can use mobile technologies to update customer profiles, download price quotes, and provide their audiences with dazzling multimedia presentations. Executives can send and receive email messages, peer into the corporate ERP system, or check share prices and competitors' web sites while traveling using Wi-Fi or wireless local area networks (WLAN).

HANDHELD DEVICE SECURITY AND CONTINGENCY PLANNING

While these mobile devices provide productivity benefits, they also pose new risks to an organization for the following reasons:

- Because of their small size and use outside the office, handheld devices can be easier to misplace or to have stolen than a laptop or notebook computer. If they do fall into the wrong hands, gaining access to the information they store or are able to access remotely can be relatively easy.
- Communications networks, desktop synchronization, and tainted storage media can be used to deliver malware to handheld devices. Malware is often disguised as a game, device patch, utility, or other useful third-party application available for download. Once installed, malware can initiate a wide range of attacks and spread itself onto other devices.
- Similar to desktop computers, smartphones are subject to spam, but this can include text messages and voice mail in addition to electronic mail. Besides the inconvenience of deleting spam, charges may apply for inbound activity. Spam can also be used for phishing—attempts to acquire sensitive information such as usernames, passwords, and credit card details.
- Electronic eavesdropping on phone calls, messages, and other wirelessly transmitted information is possible through various techniques. Installing spy software on a device to collect and forward data elsewhere, including capturing conversations via a built-in microphone, is perhaps the most direct means, but other components of a communications network, including the airwaves, are possible avenues for exploitation.

Handheld device security (also called mobile device security, wireless handheld device security, enterprise device security, handheld security, device security, and wireless data security) and the corresponding contingency plans must be addressed in the company's overall contingency planning. The National Institute of Standards and Technology (NIST) has issued two publications addressing this. The first one, *Guidelines on Cell Phone and PDA Security* (www.itbusinessedge.com/cm/docs/DOC-1371), provides an overview of cell phone and PDA devices in use today and offers insights into making informed information technology security decisions on their treatment. The document gives details about the threats and technology risks associated with the use of these devices and the available safeguards to mitigate them. Organizations can use this information to enhance security and reduce incidents involving cell phone and PDA devices.

The second document is *NIST Contingency Planning Guide for IT Systems* (www.itbusinessedge.com/cm/docs/DOC-1370). This in-depth guide provides instructions, recommendations, and considerations for government IT contingency planning. The term "contingency planning" refers to interim measures to recover IT services following an emergency or system disruption. Interim measures may include the relocation of IT systems and operations to an alternate site, the recovery of IT functions using alternate equipment, or the performance of IT functions using manual methods.

DISASTER RECOVERY AND BUSINESS CONTINUITY PLANNING

Hurricanes, tsunamis, earthquakes, fires, floods, criminal and terrorist acts, and human error can all severely damage an organization's computing resources and thus the health of the organization itself. Many companies, especially online e-commerce retailers and wholesalers, airlines, banks, and Internet service providers, for example, are crippled by losing even a few hours of computing power. That is why it is important for organizations to develop disaster recovery procedures and formalize them in a *disaster recovery plan.* Such a plan specifies which employees will participate in disaster recovery and what their duties will be; what hardware, software, and facilities will be used; and the priority of applications that will be processed. Arrangements with other companies for use of alternative facilities as a disaster recovery site and off-site storage of an organization's databases are also part of an effective recovery effort.

Your contingency plan should focus on the continuity of your business. Its primary purpose is to reduce the risk of financial loss and enhance your organization's ability to recover from a disruption promptly, at least cost. It should apply to all facets of your organization: staff, computer programs, data, workspace, production, and vital records. Contingency planning for your information systems should look at all critical areas including local and wide-area networks, distributed databases, and PCs.

The trend to run critical business applications, such as finance or CRM, over the Internet means that many companies are better protected—especially in a cloud environment. Measures such as outsourcing data centers or Web server operations also include an immediate degree of protection, while the growth in plentiful, reasonably cheap bandwidth makes hardware backup techniques, such as data mirroring to remote sites, viable for a wider range of businesses.

A common mistake in contingency planning is an excessive focus on *computer* recovery. You really need *business continuity planning* (BCP). Undue emphasis on the technology, rather than the business, is counterproductive. Quick recovery of computer technology is useless if your organization cannot recover its business. Excessive focus on computer technology results in committing too many resources to redundant processing facilities.

A contingency is an event that may or may not occur. The focus of computer security contingency planning is to provide options in case disruption strikes. Recovery from loss of key personnel is usually accomplished through succession planning and backup training. Computer facilities typically are covered by insurance policies, and businesses generally can recover their investment in computers and equipment. But losses in a disaster or catastrophe typically exceed what is recoverable through insurance policies. Some types of losses are uninsurable.

In formulating your disaster recovery plan, conduct a business impact analysis, determining the likely cost of each risk taken to a worst-case scenario. A business impact analysis considers how various threats and vulnerabilities might affect the continuity of your business. Incorporate into your plan recovery strategies for specific disasters, emphasizing your backup strategy, including the role of any off-site facilities that will be needed.

Checklist for a Comprehensive Plan

You may not be able to block every angle of attack, but here are a few steps and points that will help minimize your vulnerability.

- Develop a comprehensive plan that touches all parts and functions of your organization and all points of vulnerability.
- Evaluate, prioritize, and defend information appropriately.
- Put up good firewalls between the Internet and the strictly internal part of your network.
- Consider a VPN for essential lines, such as those carrying fund transfers.
- Assume an attack will come from those best able to launch it (i.e., insiders).
- Consider preventing outgoing e-mail from carrying attachments.
- Encrypt all data that goes over the Internet, especially if it relates to transfers of funds.
- Ensure physical security of computers, related paper files, disks, backup media, and the like.
- Establish and propagate a written policy on computer security.
- Educate all employees on how to comply with computer security policy.
- Keep and monitor an audit log of network traffic.
- Inform employees that the computer is monitored.
- Do background checks on all new employees. Know the people who have access to your system.
- Have the system vulnerability tested, ideally by a third party.
- Ensure password security by using unguessable words. Change passwords and log-ins often.
- Use the traditional kinds of checks and balances you use to prevent fraud.
- Use antivirus software at all levels of the network. Keep it updated.
- Back up all data. Keep the backup media safe.

CFO'S VIEW OF INFORMATION TECHNOLOGY: A CURRENT SURVEY

According to a 2010 joint survey conducted by Gartner and the Financial Executives Research Foundation, *"CFOs' Priorities for Technology Identified in the 2011 Gartner FEI Technology Study"* (www.gartner.com/it/page.jsp?id=1738314 and www.gartner.com/resId=1718414), more IT organizations report to the CFO than the CEO or any other executive. Forty-two percent of IT organizations surveyed said they reported to the CFO, and 53 percent of CFOs said that they would like to move to this reporting arrangement. In 41 percent of organizations, the senior financial executives (mostly CFOs) who responded to the survey viewed themselves as being the main decision maker for IT investments. This response occurred in most situations where IT reports to the CFO, but it also occurred in other reporting models. In another 34 percent, CFOs are among the key recommending/sponsoring executives. Thus, in 75 percent of firms, the CFO plays a vital role in determining IT investment. In addition, 20 percent of CFOs have a minor role by providing some input, and in only 5 percent of cases does the CFO not participate in IT decision making. In most organizations, the CFO and CIO work together daily to finance IT and provide information that supports financial processes, but there is also an opportunity for them to form a powerful alliance that generates more value for the enterprise.

The major findings of the study are summarized next.

1. *The CFO may have more influence in technology decisions than the CIO.* CFOs alone have authorized 26 percent of all IT investments, while CIOs alone have authorized only 5 percent of IT investments.
2. *CFOs see Web 2.0, Web-oriented software, cloud computing, and social networking as leading technologies.* For the second year in a row, Web-oriented software was seen as the top technology to affect the finance organization. Cloud computing came a close second. Social networking ranked third.
3. *CFOs view ERP projects as successful.* We often hear that ERP projects are costly and have not met objectives. However, the survey shows that ERP implementations have not been that disappointing, with 54 percent giving their completed ERP projects a successful rating.
4. *CFOs promote return-to-growth projects.* Of the organizations surveyed, 86 percent are willing to invest in technologies that can demonstrate competitive advantage; 70 percent are deferring some projects as a strategy to control costs in IT, while 21 percent have stopped projects in progress, and only 8 percent are halting all enhancement activity.
5. *CFOs prioritize data quality.* Problems with the quality of data often negate the benefits of investment in business intelligence and analytics, leading to poor decisions. Although 51 percent have no formal initiatives to improve data quality, almost all the respondents indicated they are pursuing one-time approaches to improve the integrity of their information
6. *CFOs do not see XBRL benefits.* XBRL is currently a requirement for all publicly traded companies in the United States. However, most companies have taken an outsourcing approach. Employing it for internal reporting could significantly improve results reporting. But 37 percent plan to use it for external reporting only, and just 5 percent plan to use it for internal reporting.
7. *CFOs in North America are not acting on IFRS.* Recently, the SEC announced a proposed move to *International Financial Reporting Standards* (IFRS), the standard used by more than 100 countries. However, 76 percent have not even begun planning for IFRS, despite a potential 2014–2016 requirement. Most respondents (80 percent) do not see any benefit from conversion to IFRS. Not surprisingly, only 8 percent have

engaged the IT organization in IFRS planning. This is a problem, because most organizations will need to do some work on their financial management systems.

8. *CFOs view profitability management as the top technological constrain.* Most organizations have difficulty understanding profitability as anything other than an aggregate corporate level. Twenty percent of respondents viewed measuring product and customer profitability as the top constraint.

9. *CFOs improve on business intelligence and corporate performance management in 2010.* Although most organizations (72 percent) consider management and financial information to be consistent, 27 percent believe there are significant issues that require manual intervention. This was an improvement over 2009, when the results were 62 and 38 percent.

10. *CFOs see outsourcing and shared services opportunities.* Outsourcing of accounting services will increase 24 percent in the next three to five years, while shared services will increase 23 percent in the same period. As finance seeks to transform itself to a more valued business partner from a transaction processor, CFOs should look to these opportunities to improve efficiency and free up resources. CFOs can use the results of this study to benchmark their organization and form a baseline for improvements to the CIO/CFO partnership.

Management of Assets and Liabilities

CHAPTER TWENTY

Working Capital and Cash Management

T HE ABILITY TO manage working capital will enhance the return and lower the risk of running short of cash. There are a number of ways to manage working capital and cash to result in optimal balances, including quantitative techniques. The amount invested in any current asset can change daily and requires close monitoring. Current assets are being improperly managed if funds tied up in them can be used more productively elsewhere.

 EVALUATING WORKING CAPITAL

How can working capital be managed to achieve the best results?

Working capital equals current assets less current liabilities. In optimally managing working capital, current assets and current liabilities have to be constantly regulated. A consideration must be given to how assets should be financed (e.g., short-term debt, long-term debt, or equity). There is a trade-off between return and risk that has to be taken into account. If funds move from fixed assets to current assets, there is a reduction in liquidity risk, greater ability to obtain short-term financing, and more flexibility, because the company can better adjust current assets to changes in sales volume. However, typically less of a return is earned on current assets than fixed assets. The advantage with using noncurrent debt relative to short-term debt is that it involves less liquidity risk. However, long-term debt usually has a higher cost than short-term debt arising from the uncertainty of the longer time period. The increased financing cost lowers profitability.

The hedging approach to finance should be used where assets are financed by liabilities of similar maturity. This results in sufficient funds to pay debt when it is due. For example, long-term assets should be financed with long-term debt rather than short-term borrowings.

Rule of thumb: The longer it takes to buy or manufacture goods, the more working capital is needed. Working capital is also affected by the volume of purchases and the unit cost. For example, if the company can receive a raw material in three weeks, it needs to hold less inventory than if there was a one-month lead time.

Tip: Buy material early if lower prices are available and if the material's cost savings exceed inventory carrying costs.

CASH MANAGEMENT

Without monitoring your cash—how to measure it, invest it, borrow it, and collect it—you can cheat yourself out of extra profits or even run into trouble with creditors and bankruptcy.

What should be done about cash balances?

A centralized cash management system minimizes idle cash and maximizes available cash. The cash management system should integrate all the cash flows into and out of the business, including domestic and international divisions and subsidiaries. A centralized system flags situations where one subsidiary is borrowing at high interest rates while another subsidiary has idle cash. A coordination of cash processes should exist such as investment, disbursement, and collection.

Cash should be made available to cash-using divisions from cash-generating ones to keep borrowing at a minimum. For example, foreign currency payments should be netted among divisions to eliminate currency conversion and reduce float time between operations. There should be an integration of foreign currency requirements between the parent and subsidiaries. A multinational company must use a bank known for *quality* international services, including networking, cash concentration, and clearing. The CFO should obtain competitive quotations before making a disbursement in a foreign country.

The objective of cash management is to invest excess cash for a return and at the same time have sufficient liquidity for future needs. The cash balance should neither be excessive nor deficient. For example, companies with many bank accounts may be accumulating excessive balances. Do you know how much cash you need, how much you have, where the cash is, what the sources of cash are, and where the cash will be used? This knowledge is especially crucial during recessions. Cash forecasting determines the best time to incur and pay back debt and the amount to transfer daily between accounts. A daily computerized listing of cash balances and transaction reporting should be prepared so that the CFO has up-to-date information in order to make decisions on how best to use funds. A listing of daily transactions identifies any problems so that immediate rectification may be made.

Recommendation: The CFO should establish, control, and report bank accounts, services, and activities. Are banking services cost effective? Analyze each bank account as to type, balance, and cost. What is the processing cost for checks, bank transfers, and direct debits? The adequacy of controls for intercompany transactions and transfers should be reviewed. When cash receipts and cash payments are synchronized and predictable, smaller cash balances may be maintained. If immediate liquidity is desired, one should invest in marketable securities.

General rule: Additional cash should be invested in income-producing securities with maturities structured to provide the necessary liquidity.

A financially strong company that is able to borrow at favorable interest rates even in difficult financial times may hold a lower cash balance than a highly leveraged company that is a poor credit risk.

A high-tech company may need more cash on hand to withstand unexpected eventualities and financial problems. A mature, established company may hold minimal cash with short-term cash requirements met through short-term debt.

How much cash should be held?

The minimum cash to hold is the greater of (1) compensating balances (a deposit held by a bank to compensate it for providing services) or (2) precautionary balances (money held in cash for an emergency) plus transaction balances (money to cover uncleared checks). The company needs sufficient cash to satisfy daily requirements.

The longer the time period between cash payment to cash receipt, the higher the cash balance should be. A declining trend in cash may mean a looming cash crisis. If collections are not received in a timely fashion, you may be unable to make payments to suppliers and for operating expenses. Major capital expenditures should be timed for when cash is plentiful. Factors in determining the amount of cash to hold include:

- Overdraft protection.
- Instability in business activity.
- Length of the planning period.
- Overall financial strength and liquidity.
- Ability to borrow on favorable terms.
- Payment dates of debt.
- Expected future cash flows, taking into account the probabilities of different cash flows under alternative circumstances. Since cash forecasting may result in errors, there should be excess cash on hand or short-term debt capacity to cover such eventuality.
- Overall business risks.
- Likelihood of unexpected problems (e.g., customer defaults).
- Rate of return.

Less cash is needed on hand when a company can borrow quickly from a bank, such as under a line of credit agreement, which allows a firm to borrow immediately up to a predetermined maximum amount. Check to see the commitment fee, if any, on the unused portion of the line.

Watch the amount of the compensating balance, since the portion of a loan that serves as collateral is restricted and unavailable for use. Are compensating balances too costly? Is cash unnecessarily tied up in other accounts (e.g., loans to employees, insurance deposits)? *Warning:* Liquid asset holdings are needed during a downturn in a company's cycle, when funds from operations decline.

The CFO should invest excess cash in marketable securities for a return. The marketable securities may then be sold when funds are needed. For example, a seasonal company may buy marketable securities when it has excess funds and then sell the securities when cash deficits occur. A firm may also invest in marketable securities when funds are held temporarily in anticipation of short-term capital expansion. In selecting an investment portfolio, consider return, marketability, default risk, and maturity date.

Coupon and security collection assures that any interest the company is entitled to is received and that securities maturing or sold are properly collected and deposited.

Recommendation: Do not fund peak seasonal cash requirements internally. Rather, borrow on a short-term basis to enable internal funds to be used more profitably throughout the year, such as by investing in plant and equipment.

The thrust of cash management is to accelerate cash receipts and delay cash payments.

Acceleration of Cash Inflow

You should appraise the reasons and take corrective steps to rectify any delays in receiving and depositing cash. Ascertain how and where cash receipts come, how cash is transferred from outlying accounts to the main corporate account, banking policy on fund availability, and time lag between receiving a check and depositing it.

What is the float time?

The types of delays in processing checks are:

- *Mail float:* The time it takes for a check to move from customer to the company
- *Processing float:* The time it takes for the company to record the payment in the books
- *Deposit collection float:* The time for a check to clear

The CFO should evaluate the causes and take corrective measures for delays in having cash receipts deposited. One should ascertain how and where the cash receipts come, how cash is transferred to the bank account, banking policy regarding availability of funds, and time lag between receiving a check and depositing it.

What does the amount of float depend on?

The amount of float depends on both the time lag and the dollars involved. Float may be determined in dollar-days multiplying the lag in days by the dollar amount delayed. The cost of float is the interest lost because the money was not available for investment or the interest paid because money had to be borrowed during the lag period. The cost of float is computed by multiplying the average daily float by the cost of capital (opportunity cost) for the time period involved.

$$\text{Average daily float} = \frac{\$200,000}{30} = \$6,667$$

$$\text{Average daily receipts} = \frac{\$60,000}{30} = \$2,000$$

$$\text{Average daily float} = \$2,000 \times 3.333 = \$6,667$$

$$\text{Average cost of float} = \$6,667 \times 0.09 = \$600$$

How can cash be received sooner?

There are many ways to accelerate cash receipts, as described next:

- Set up a lockbox arrangement with collection points situated closer to customers. Customer payments are mailed to strategic post office boxes to speed mailing and depositing time. Banks collect from these boxes several times a day and make deposits to the corporate account. Furthermore, weekend deposits into the lockbox should be acceptable. Companies that use lockboxes receive a computer listing of payments received by account and a daily total.

  Recommendation: Undertake a cost-benefit analysis to ensure that the lockbox arrangement results in net savings. Determine the average face value of checks received, cost of operations eliminated, reducible processing overhead, and reduction in mail float days. Because per-item processing cost is usually significant, it is beneficial to use a lockbox with low-volume, high-dollar collections. However, lockboxes are becoming available to companies with high-volume, low-dollar receipts as technological advances (such as machine-readable documents) lower the per-item cost. *Tip:* Compare the return earned on freed cash to the cost of the lockbox. A wholesale lockbox is used for checks received from other *companies*. The average cash receipt is large, and the number of cash receipts is small. The bank prepares an electronic list of payments received and transmits the information to the company. A wholesale lockbox strengthens internal control because there is a separation between billing and receivables processing. Many wholesale lockboxes result in mail time reductions of no more than one business day and check-clearing time reductions of only a few tenths of one day. Wholesale lockboxes are cost effective for companies having gross revenues of at least several million dollars. They work best when large checks are received from distant customers. A *retail lockbox* is used for a company dealing with the public (retail consumers as distinguished from companies). Retail lockboxes usually have numerous transactions of a nominal amount. The lockbox reduces float and transfers workload from the company to the bank. The bottom line should be more cash flow and fewer expenses.
- Identify and monitor changes in collection patterns. The reasons for delays should be ascertained, and the underlying problems should be corrected.

- On the return envelope for customer remission, use bar codes, nine-digit code numbers, and post office box numbers.

> ## Note
> Accelerated Reply Mail (ARM) is the assignment of a unique "truncating" ZIP code to payments, such as lockbox receivables. The coded remittances are removed from the postal system and processed by banks or third parties. ■

- Send customers preaddressed, stamped envelopes. Include an "Attention" line on the return envelope to speed delivery within the company. Return envelopes reduce customers' errors in addressing and accelerating mail handling.
- Obtain permission from a customer to have a preauthorized debit (PAD) charged to the customer's bank account automatically for recurring charges. An example is an insurance company that has PADs charged to its policy holders for insurance premiums. These debits take the form of paper preauthorized checks or paperless automatic clearing house entries. PADs result in cost savings because they avoid the process of billing a customer, receiving and processing a payment, and depositing a check.

> ## Note
> Variable payments are not as efficient as fixed payments because the amount of the PAD must be changed each period, and usually customers must be notified by mail of the amount of the debit. PADs are suggested for constant, relatively nominal, periodic (e.g., monthly, semiweekly) payments. ■

- Transfer funds between banks by wire transfers or depository transfer checks (DTCs). Wire transfers can be used for intracompany transactions. They can be made by computer terminal and telephone. A wire transfer allows for the same-day transfer of funds. It should be made only for significant dollar amounts since transfer fees are charged by both the originating bank and the receiving bank. Examples include making transfers to and from investments, placing funds in an account the day checks are expected to clear, and placing funds in any other account that requires immediate fund availability. Two types of wire transfers are preformatted (recurring) and free-form (nonrepetitive). Extensive authorization is not required for preformatted wire transfers. This type is appropriate for usual transfers such as for investments and other company accounts. The company specifies an issuing bank and a receiving bank along with the account number. There is greater control for nonrecurring transfers. The control includes written confirmation rather than confirmation by telephone or computer terminal. Wire transfers may also be used to fund other types of checking accounts, such as payroll accounts. In order to control balances in the account, the account may be funded on a staggered basis. However, to guard against an overdraft, balances should be maintained in another account at the bank.

Paper or paperless DTCs can be used to transfer funds between the company's bank accounts. Although no signature is required on DTCs, the check is still payable to the bank for credit to the company's account. However, controls must be in place so an employee does not use DTCs to transfer money from an account on which he or she does not have signature authorization to an account in which he or she does. DTCs usually clear in one day. If *manual* DTCs are used, preprinted checks include all information except the amount and date. Manual preparation is suggested if there are only a few checks prepared daily. If there are *automated* DTCs, they are printed as needed.

Tip: It is typically cheaper to use the bank's printer than for the company to buy its own. Automatic check preparation is suggested when many transfer checks are prepared daily.

- Encourage customers to use a purchase order with payment voucher attached. The payment voucher is a blank draft that the seller fills out, detaches, and then deposits. It is usually for amounts less than $1,000. Buyers will deal only with sellers they trust to make this arrangement.
- Accelerate billing. Send out bills to customers immediately when the order is shipped. Also, send out individual invoices rather than only a monthly statement. Correct invoice errors immediately.
- Require deposits on large or custom orders or progress billings as the work progresses.
- Promptly correct invoice errors. Customers should be encouraged to call an 800 telephone number if discrepancies exist.
- Charge interest on delinquent accounts receivable.
- Offer discounts for early payment.
- Have postdated checks from customers.
- Provide cash-on-delivery terms.
- Deposit checks immediately.
- Make repeated collection calls and visits.

Example 20.1

The CFO is considering whether to start a lockbox arrangement that will cost $150,000 annually. The daily average collections are $700,000. The system will reduce mailing and processing time by two days. The rate of return is 14 percent.

Return on freed cash (14% × 2 × $700,000)	$196,000
Annual cost	150,000
Net advantage of lockbox system	$ 46,000

Example 20.2

You currently have a lockbox arrangement with Bank X in which it handles $5 million a day in return for an $800,000 compensating balance. You are considering canceling this arrangement and further dividing your western region by entering into contracts with two other banks. Bank Y will handle $3 million a day in collections with a compensating balance of $700,000, and Bank Z will handle $2 million a day with a compensating balance of $600,000. Collections will be half a day faster than at present. The rate of return is 12 percent.

Accelerated cash receipts ($5 million per day × 0.5 day)	$2,500,000
Increased compensating balance	500,000
Improved cash flow	$2,000,000
Rate of return	× 0.12
Net annual savings	$ 240,000

How can cash payments be delayed to earn a greater return?

An evaluation should be made of who the payees are and to what degree time limits may be stretched.

Approaches to delay cash payments include:

▪ Centralize the payables operation so that debt may be paid at the most opportune time and so that the amount of disbursement float may be determined. Never pay vendors early.

▪ Establish zero-balance accounts (ZBAs) for all disbursing units. These accounts are in the same concentration bank. Checks are drawn against these accounts, with the balance in each account never exceeding $0. Divisional disbursing authority is maintained at the local management level. The benefits of ZBAs are enhanced control over cash payments, reduction in excess cash balances maintained in regional banks, and a possible increase in disbursing float. Under the ZBA arrangement, the company deposits funds into its payroll and payables checking accounts only when it anticipates checks will clear. This strategy is aggressive. *Caution:* Be on guard against overdrafts and service charges. In a ZBA arrangement, the bank automatically transfers money from a master (concentration) account as checks are presented against the payroll and payables accounts. Hence, payroll and payable accounts are retained at zero balances. Under ZBA, the CFO does not have to anticipate clearing times on each account.

▪ Use controlled disbursing in which checks are drawn against a bank that has the capability to inform the issuer early enough each day to allow funding in an exact amount the same day.

▪ Make partial payments and/or postdate checks.

▪ Request additional information about an invoice before paying it.

■ Use payment drafts, where payment is not made on demand. Instead, the draft is presented for collection to the bank, which in turn goes to the issuer to accept it. A draft may be used to allow for inspection before payment. When approved, the company deposits the funds. The net result is that less of a checking balance is required.

> **Note**
>
> The use of drafts involves bank charges (e.g., fixed monthly fee) and the inconveniences of always having to formally approve the draft before paying it. ■

■ Draw checks on remote banks (e.g., a New York company using a Texas bank).
■ Mail from post offices with limited service or where mail has to go through numerous handling points. *Tip:* If you use float properly, you can maintain higher bank balances than the actual lower book balances. For example, if you write checks averaging $200,000 each day and three days are needed for them to clear, your checking balance will be $600,000 less than the bank's records indicate.
■ Use remote mailing—that is, mailing checks from a location far removed from both the payee and drawee bank. A company having a centralized processing of accounts payable can install remote check printers in their plants and offices around the country. The central computer determines from which banks to draw the check and which check printer to use to maximize delay time.
■ Use probability analysis to determine the expected date for checks to clear. *Suggestion:* Have separate checking accounts (e.g., payroll, dividends) and monitor check clearing dates. Payroll checks are not all cashed on the payroll date, so funds can be deposited later to earn a return.
■ Use a computer terminal to transfer funds between various bank accounts at opportune times.
■ Use a charge account to lengthen the time between buying goods and paying for them.
■ Stretch payments as long as there is no associated finance charge or impairment in credit. Prepare a priority list of who should get paid first and who should get paid last.
■ Do not pay bills before they are due.
■ Avoid making prepaid expenses. For example, if you are going to prepay insurance, do it for one year, not three years.
■ Compensate others with noncash consideration, such as stock or notes.
■ Delay the frequency of payments to employees (e.g., expense account reimbursements, payrolls). Avoid giving employees cash advances, such as for travel and entertainment or loans. Have a monthly payroll rather than a weekly payroll. In a recession, the employer may eliminate or delay payroll payments to employees. Employees may be asked to take furloughs (e.g., two weeks off without pay) or give up current pay to be paid at a later date (e.g., postponing one week's pay to a later year or at retirement).
■ Pay commissions on sales when the receivables are collected instead of when the sales are made.

EXHIBIT 20.1 Cash Management System

Acceleration of Cash Receipts	Delay of Cash Payments
Lockbox system	Pay by draft
Concentration banking	Requisition more frequently
Preauthorized checks	Disbursing float
Preaddressed stamped envelopes	Make partial payments
Obtain deposits on large orders	Use charge accounts
Charge interest on overdue receivables	Delay frequency of paying employees

- Mail payments late in the day or on Fridays.
- Engage in barter arrangements to avoid a cash payment. However, barter transactions are reportable for tax purposes based on the fair market value of what has been exchanged.

A cash management system is shown in Exhibit 20.1.

Example 20.3

Every two weeks, the company issues checks that average $500,000 and take three days to clear. The CFO wants to find out how much money can be saved annually if the transfer of funds is delayed from an interest-bearing account that pays 0.0384 percent per day (annual rate of 14%) for those three days:

$$\$500,000 \times (0.000384 \times 3) = \$576$$

The savings per year is $576 × 26 (yearly payrolls) = $14,976.

Cash Flow Software

Computer software allows for day-to-day cash management, determining cash balances, planning and analyzing cash flows, finding cash shortages, and investing cash surpluses. Spreadsheet software such as Excel can assist in developing cash projections and answering what-if questions.

CASH MANAGEMENT MODELS

How do you use cash models to determine the optimal cash balance?

William Baumol developed a model (Exhibit 20.2) to determine the optimum amount of transaction cash under conditions of certainty. The objective is to minimize the sum of

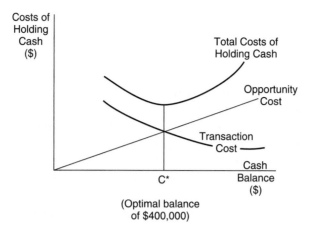

(Optimal balance
of $400,000)

EXHIBIT 20.2 William Baumol's Cash Model

the fixed costs of transactions *and* the opportunity cost of holding cash balances. These costs are expressed as:

$$F \times \frac{T}{C} + i\frac{C}{2}$$

where
F = Fixed cost of a transaction
T = Total cash needed for the time period involved
C = Cash balance
i = Interest rate on marketable securities

Example 20.4

You estimate a cash need for $4 million over a one-month period where the cash account is expected to be disbursed at a constant rate. The opportunity interest rate is 6 percent per annum, or 0.5 percent for a one-month period. The transaction cost each time you borrow or withdraw is $100.

The optimal transaction size (the optimal borrowing or withdrawal lot size) and the number of transactions you should make during the month follow.

$$C^* = \sqrt{\frac{2FT}{i}} = \sqrt{\frac{2(100)(4,000,000)}{0.005}} = \$400,000$$

The optimal transaction size is $400,000. The average cash balance is:

$$\frac{C^*}{2} = \frac{\$400,000}{2} = \$200,000$$

The number of transactions required is:

$4,000,000/$400,000 = 10 transactions during the month

The optimal level of cash (C^*) is determined using the following formula:

$$C^* = \sqrt{\frac{2FT}{i}}$$

You can use a stochastic model for cash management where uncertainty exists for cash payments. The Miller-Orr model places an upper and lower limit for cash balances. When the upper limit is reached, a transfer of cash to marketable securities is made. When the lower limit is reached, a transfer from securities to cash occurs. A transaction will not occur as long as the cash balance falls within the limits.

The Miller-Orr model takes into account the fixed costs of a securities transaction (F), which is assumed to be the same for buying as well as selling, the daily interest rate on marketable securities (i), and the variance of daily net cash flows (σ^2). The purpose is to satisfy cash requirements at the least cost. A major assumption is the randomness of cash flows. The two control limits in the Miller-Orr model may be specified as d dollars as an upper limit and zero dollars at the lower limit. When the cash balance reaches the upper level, d less z dollars of securities are bought and the new balance becomes z dollars. When the cash balance equals zero, z dollars of securities are sold and the new balance again reaches z. Of course, practically speaking, the minimum cash balance is established at an amount greater than zero due to delays in transfer as well as to having a safety buffer.

The optimal cash balance z is computed as:

$$z = \sqrt[3]{\frac{3F\sigma^2}{4i}}$$

Example 20.5

You wish to use the Miller-Orr model. The following information is supplied:

Fixed cost of a securities transaction	$10
Variance of daily net cash flows	$50
Daily interest rate on securities (10.8%/360)	0.0003

The optimal cash balance, the upper limit of cash needed, and the average cash balance are:

$$z = \sqrt[3]{\frac{3(10)(50)}{4(0.0003)}} = \sqrt[3]{\frac{1,500}{0.0012}} = \sqrt[3]{1,250,000} = \$102$$

The optimal cash balance is $102. The upper limit is $306 (3 × $102). The average cash balance is

$$\$136 = \frac{\$102 + \$306}{3}$$

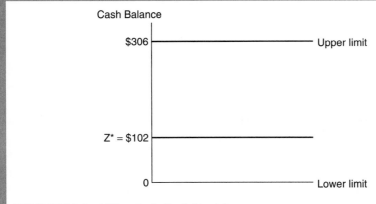

EXHIBIT 20.3 Miller-Orr's Cash Model

A brief elaboration on these findings is needed for clarification. When the upper limit of $306 is reached, $204 of securities ($306 – $102) will be purchased to bring you to the optimal cash balance of $102. When the lower limit of zero dollars is reached, $102 of securities will be sold to again bring you to the optimal cash balance of $102. See Exhibit 20.3.

The optimal value for d is computed as $3z$. The average cash balance will approximate $(z + d)/3$.

BANKING RELATIONSHIPS

How should you deal with banks?

The company may want to restrict the maximum total deposit at a bank experiencing financial difficulties to the amount federally insured.

> ### Note
>
> With a checking account, the maximum deposit may be exceeded on the bank's records but not on the company's books because of the clearing time for checks and concentration entries. ▪

A maximum deposit that exceeds the insurance limit should be determined to keep at specific banks. Deposits of unlimited amounts should be authorized at financial institutions.

Some banks offer better services than others in meeting company needs. In selecting a bank, consider:

- Location (affects lockboxes and disbursement points)
- Type and cost of services
- Fund availability

The financial strength of the bank should be determined. Reference may be made to ratings provided by services tracking banks.

Each bank account should be analyzed by comparing the value of the company balance kept at the bank to the service charges. Although the bank will provide such analysis for you, it is biased and must be carefully evaluated.

A balance reporting system can be used where the lead bank gathers information for all other banks. The information can then be transferred to the company through telecommunications. The cost effectiveness of the system should be appraised periodically.

Most checks clear in one business day. Clearing time of three or more business days is unusual. Ask the financial institution to give same-day credit on a deposit received before a specified cutoff time. However, if the deposit is made over the counter with a letter, those funds may not be immediately available. If the deposit is made early enough, particularly through a lockbox, immediate fund availability may be achieved.

Typically it is financially better to pay a higher deposited-item charge in return for accelerated fund availability.

In performing an account reconciliation, the bank sorts checks into serial number order, lists all checks cleared, and matches issued checks provided by the company to paid checks so as to list outstanding checks and exception items. One objective is to reconcile the cash balances on deposit at various banks for control purposes. The services are cost effective only when many checks are involved.

A bank reconciliation is prepared of each bank account to ensure that the balance per books equals the balance per bank after adjusting for reconciling items. The bank reconciliation serves as an internal control measure.

 ## INTERNATIONAL CASH MANAGEMENT

How should cash be managed when international dealings are involved?

International cash management minimizes the exposure of foreign-located funds to exchange rate risks and minimizes governmental restrictions on the movement of funds among countries. Will the foreign country delay or block payments? For example, exchange control regulations may result in long delays in getting funds out of the country, or civil disturbances may interfere with payment. You must analyze the political and economic trends in the foreign country. For example, cash held in a socially depressed country is subject to risk.

Cash can be accelerated by having bank accounts in each country. In many countries, customers pay their bills by requesting their bank to deduct the amount owed from their account and to transfer the funds to another firm's account.

Multinational commercial banks, particularly those with branches or affiliates in many countries, can be helpful to multinational firms. Some of the larger U.S. multinational commercial banks have foreign departments whose only purpose is to help multinational companies solve international cash management problems. An international bank can hasten funds flow and thus reduce the multinational company's exposure to foreign exchange rate risk. The bank can recommend the best route for the transfer of funds and the national currency to be used. The time for foreign transactions can be as long as two weeks, and such delays can tie up significant funds. Multinational commercial banks aid in reducing this delay because they can transfer funds between countries on the same day, provided there are affiliated branches in the two countries. We assume here that government restrictions on the remission of funds do *not* exist.

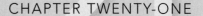

CHAPTER TWENTY-ONE

Management of Accounts Receivable

A CCOUNTS RECEIVABLE MANAGEMENT directly affects corporate profitability and cash flow. For example, too much money tied up in accounts receivable would be a drag on earnings. The CFO must consider discount policy, whether to grant credit to marginal customers, how to hasten collections and reduce uncollectible accounts, and how to establish credit terms.

 ## MANAGING RECEIVABLES

How should accounts receivable be handled?

The order entry, billing, and accounts receivable activities should be evaluated to ensure that proper procedures and controls exist from the day an order is received until collection is made. What is the average time lag between completing the sales transaction and invoicing the customer? If it is excessive, why?

There are two kinds of float in accounts receivable management—invoicing and mail. *Invoicing float* is the days between the time goods are shipped to the customer and the time the invoice is rendered. Invoices should be timely processed. Mail float is the time between the preparation of an invoice and the time it is received by the customer. *Mail float* can be reduced by:

- Decentralizing invoicing and mailing
- Coordinating outgoing mail with post office schedules
- Using express mail services for large invoices
- Enforcing due dates
- Offering discounts

In managing accounts receivable, the CFO should take into account the opportunity cost of holding receivables. The opportunity cost is tying up money in accounts receivable that could be invested elsewhere for a return. Therefore, ways to analyze and hasten collections should be undertaken.

An important consideration is the amount and credit terms given to customers, since this will impact sales volume and collections. For example, a longer credit term will likely increase sales. The credit terms have a direct bearing on the costs and revenue derived from receivables. If credit terms are stringent, there will be less investment in accounts receivable and less bad debts. However, this will result in lower sales, reduced profits, and adverse customer reaction. If credit terms are lax, there will be higher sales and gross profit. This will result in greater bad debts and a higher opportunity cost of carrying the investment in accounts receivable because marginal customers take longer to pay. Receivable terms should be liberalized when you want to dispose of excessive inventory or obsolete items. Longer receivable terms are recommended for industries in which products are sold before retail seasons (e.g., swimsuits). In the case of perishable goods, short receivable terms or even payment on delivery is advised.

In appraising a prospective customer's ability to pay, take into account the customer's honesty, financial strength, and pledged security. A customer's creditworthiness may be evaluated by using quantitative techniques, such as regression analysis. These models are useful when there are many small customers. Bad debt losses can be accurately forecasted when a company sells to many customers and when its credit policies have remained static.

The CFO has to consider the costs of granting credit, including administrative costs of the credit department, computer services, fees to rating agencies, and periodic field investigations.

What credit reporting agencies supply information?

Reference can be made to retail credit bureaus and credit reference services in evaluating a customer's ability to pay. One service is Dun and Bradstreet (D&B), which rates companies. D&B reports contain information about a company's nature of business, financial status, prior payment history as reported by suppliers, amounts currently owed and past due, lawsuits, insurance coverage, audit opinion, leases, number of employees, terms of sale, banking relationships and account information (e.g., current bank loans), location of business, criminal proceedings, and seasonality characteristics.

What standards should be used in accounts receivable operations?

To monitor and improve accounts receivable activities, unit credit standards may be established. For invoice preparation, a cost per invoice, order, or item may be set. For credit investigation and approval, unit cost standards may include cost per account, sales order, or credit sales transaction. In examining credit correspondence records, cost per sales order, account sold, or letter may be used. In preparing customer statements, unit cost standards may be cost per statement or account sold. The standard for the computation of commissions on cash collections may be based on cost per remittance.

How can accounts receivable be managed to maximize earnings?

There are many ways to optimize profitability from accounts receivable and keep losses to a minimum. These include:

- Minimize billing float, which refers to the amount of time between the time of shipment, when a bill or invoice could have been rendered, to the time a bill or invoice is actually mailed. Billing may be accelerated through electronic data interchange rather than using the mails.
- "Cycle bill" for uniformity in the billing process.
- Mail customer statements within 24 hours of the end of the accounting period.
- Mail an invoice to customers when the order is processed at the warehouse rather than when merchandise is shipped.
- Bill for services periodically when work is performed or charge a retainer. *Tip*: Bill large sales immediately.
- Use seasonal datings. When business is slow, sell to customers with delayed payment terms to stimulate demand from those who cannot pay until later in the season. Compare profitability on incremental sales plus the reduction in inventory carrying costs, which have to exceed the opportunity cost on the additional investment in average accounts receivable.
- Carefully evaluate customer financial statements before granting credit. Ratings should be obtained from financial advisory services.
- Avoid high-risk receivables (e.g., customers in a financially depressed industry or locality). Be careful of accounts in business less than one year. (About 50 percent of businesses fail within the first two years.)
- Note that customer receivables have greater default risk than corporate accounts.
- Adjust credit limits based on changes in customer's financial soundness.
- Accelerate collections from customers having financial difficulties. Also, withhold products or services until payment is received.
- Request collateral for questionable accounts. *Tip*: The collateral value should equal or exceed the account balance.
- Age accounts receivable to identify delinquent customers. Interest should be charged on such accounts. Aged receivables can be compared to previous years, industry standards, and competition. Prepare bad-debt loss reports showing cumulative bad debt losses detailed by customer, size of account, and terms of sale. These reports should be summarized by department, product line, and type of customer (e.g., industry).

Note

Bad debt losses are usually higher for smaller companies than for larger ones. The company should charge back to the salesperson the commission already paid on an uncollectible account. ■

- Use outside collection agencies when net savings result.
- Factor accounts receivable when immediate funds are needed. However, confidential information may have to be disclosed.
- Have credit insurance to guard against unusual bad debt losses. *What to consider*: In deciding whether to obtain this insurance, consider expected average bad debt losses, financial soundness of your firm to withstand the losses, and the insurance cost.
- Consider marketing factors, since a tight credit policy may mean less business.
- Monitor customer complaints about order item and invoice errors and orders not filled on time.
- Identify customers taking cash discounts who have not paid within the discount period.
- Look at the relationship of credit department costs to credit sales.

The collection period for accounts receivable partly depends on corporate policy and conditions. In granting trade credit, competition and economic conditions have to be considered. In a recession, the CFO may liberalize the credit policy to obtain additional business. For example, the company might not rebill customers who take a cash discount even after the discount period expires. In times of short supply, however, credit policy may be tightened because the seller has the upper hand.

What are the attributes of a good credit system?

A credit system should be:

- Clear, fast, and consistent
- Careful of customer's privacy
- Inexpensive (e.g., credit analysis and decision making is centralized).
- Based on prior experience, attentive to account characteristics of good, questionable, and bad accounts.

Tip: Determine the correlation between customer characteristics and future uncollectibility.

 INVESTMENT IN ACCOUNTS RECEIVABLE

The CFO must determine the dollar investment tied up in accounts receivable. The accounts receivable balance depends on many factors, including terms of sale, financial soundness of customers, product quality, interest rates, and economic conditions.

Example 21.1

A company sells on terms of net/30. The accounts are on average 20 days past due. Annual credit sales are $600,000. The investment in accounts receivable is:

$$50/360 \times \$600,000 = \$83,333.28$$

Example 21.2

The cost of a product is 30 percent of selling price, and the cost of capital is 10 percent of selling price. On average, accounts are paid four months after sale. Average sales are $70,000 per month.

The investment in accounts receivable from this product is:

Accounts receivable	
(4 months × $70,000)	$280,000
Investment in accounts receivable	
[$280,000 × (0.30 + 0.10)]	$112,000

Example 21.3

You have accounts receivable of $700,000. The average manufacturing cost is 40 percent of the sales price. The before-tax profit margin is 10 percent. The carrying cost of inventory is 3 percent of selling price. The sales commission is 8 percent of sales. The investment in accounts receivable is:

$$\$700,000(0.40 + 0.03 + 0.08) = \$700,000(0.51) = \$357,000$$

Should customers be offered a discount for the early payment of account balances?

The CFO has to compare the return on freed cash resulting from customers paying earlier to the cost of the discount.

Example 21.4

The following data are provided:

Current annual credit sales	$14,000,000
Collection period	3 months
Terms	Net/30
Minimum rate of return	15%

The company is considering offering a 3/10, net/30 discount. We expect 25 percent of the customers to take advantage of it. The collection period will decline to two months.

The discount should be offered, as indicated in the following calculations:

(continued)

Advantage

Increased profitability:

Average accounts receivable balance before a change in policy

$$\frac{\text{Credit sales}}{\text{Account receivable turnover}} = \frac{\$14,000,000}{4} = \$3,500,000$$

Average accounts receivable balance after change in policy

$$\frac{\text{Credit sales}}{\text{Account receivable turnover}} = \frac{\$14,000,000}{6} = \$2,333,333$$

Reduction in average accounts receivable balance	$1,116,667
Rate of return	× 0.15
Return	$ 175,000
Disadvantage	
Cost of the discount	
0.30 × 0.25 × $14,000,000	$ 105,000
Net advantage of discount	$ 70,000

Should the company give credit to marginal customers?

In granting credit to marginal customers, compare the profit on sales to the added cost of the receivables.

Note

If idle capacity exists, the additional profit is the contribution margin on the sales because fixed costs are constant. The additional cost on the additional receivables results from the increased number of bad debts and the opportunity cost of tying up funds in receivables for more days. ■

Example 21.5

Sales price per unit	$120
Variable cost per unit	$80
Fixed cost per unit	$15
Annual credit sales	$600,000
Collection period	1 month
Minimum return	16%

If you relax the credit policy, you estimate that

- Sales will increase by 40 percent.
- The collection period on total accounts will be two months.
- Bad debts on the increased sales will be 5 percent.

Preliminary calculations:

Current units ($600,000/$120)	5,000
Additional units (5,000 × 0.4)	2,000

The new average unit cost is now calculated:

	Units	×	Unit cost	=	Total cost
Current units	5,000	×	$95		$475,000
Additional units	2,000	×	$80		160,000
Total	7,000				$635,000

$$\text{New average unit cost} = \frac{\text{Total cost}}{\text{Units}} = \frac{\$635,000}{7,000} = \$90.71$$

Since at idle capacity fixed cost remains constant, the incremental cost is only the variable cost of $80 per unit. This will result in a decline in the new average unit cost.

Advantage	
Additional profitability:	
Incremental sales volume units	2,000
× Contribution margin per unit (Selling price – variable cost) $120 – $80	× $40
Incremental profitability	$ 80,000
Disadvantage	
Incremental bad debts:	
Incremental units × Selling price 2,000 × $120	$240,000
Bad debt percentage	× 0.05
Additional bad debts	$ 12,000

Opportunity cost of funds tied up in accounts receivable:
Average investment in accounts receivable after change in policy:

$$\frac{\text{Credit sales}}{\text{Account receivable turnover}} \times \frac{\text{Unit cost}}{\text{Selling price}}$$

$$\frac{\$840,000 \, @}{6} \times \frac{\$90.71}{\$120} = \$105,828$$

@ 7,000 units × $120 = $840,000
Current average investment in accounts receivable:

(continued)

$$\frac{\$600,000}{12} \times \frac{\$95}{\$120}$$

Additional investment in accounts receivable	$ 66,245
Minimum return	× 0.16
Opportunity cost of funds tied up	$ 10,599

Net advantage of relaxation in credit standards:

Additional earnings		$ 80,000
Less:		
Additional bad debt losses	$12,000	
Opportunity cost	10,599	22,599
Net savings		$ 57,401

The company may have to decide whether to extend full credit to presently limited credit customers or no-credit customers. Full credit should be given only if net profitability occurs.

Example 21.6

Category	Bad Debt Percentage	Collection Period	Credit Policy	Increase in Annual Sales if Credit Restrictions Are Relaxed
X	2%	30 days	Unlimited	$80,000
Y	5%	40 days	Restricted	600,000
Z	30%	80 days	No credit	850,000

Gross profit is 25 percent of sales. The minimum return on investment is 12 percent. The solution to this problem is presented in the following table.

	Category Y		Category Z	
Gross profit				
$600,000 × 0.25		$150,000		
$850,000 × 0.25				212,500
Less bad debts				
$600,000 × 0.05		−30,000		−255,000
$850,000 × 0.30				
Incremental average investment in accounts receivable				
40/360 × (0.75 × $600,000)		$50,000		
80/360 × (0.75 × $850,000)			$141,667	
Opportunity cost of incremental investment in accounts receivable	× 0.12	−6,000	× 0.12	−17,000
Net earnings		$114,000		$(−59,500)

Credit should be extended to category Y.

Example 21.7

You are considering liberalizing the credit policy to encourage more customers to purchase on credit. Currently, 80 percent of sales are on credit and there is a gross margin of 30 percent. Other relevant data are:

	Currently	Proposal
Sales	$300,000	$450,000
Credit sales	240,000	360,000
Collection expenses	4% of credit sales	5% of credit sales
Accounts receivable turnover	4.5	3

An analysis of the proposal yields the following results:

Average accounts receivable balance	
(credit sales/accounts receivable turnover)	
Expected average accounts receivable $360,000/3	$120,000
Current average accounts receivable $240,000/4.5	53,333
Increase	$ 65,667
Gross profit:	
Expected increase in credit sales ($360,000 − $240,000)	$120,000
Gross profit rate	× 0.30
Increase	$ 36,000
Collection expenses:	
Expected collection expenses 0.05 × $360,000	$ 18,000
Current collection expenses 0.04 × $240,000	9,600
Increase	$ 8,400

A more liberal credit policy should be instituted.

Example 21.8

The company is planning a sales campaign in which it will offer credit terms of 3/10, net/45. We expect the collection period to increase from 60 days to 80 days. Relevant data for the contemplated campaign follow.

	Without Sales Campaign		With Sales Campaign	
Gross margin (0.3 × $8,000,000)		$2,400,000	0.3 × $10,000,000	$3,000,000
Sales subject to discount				
0.65 × $8,000,000	$5,200,000			
0.85 × $10,000,000			$ 8,500,000	
Sales discount	× 0.03	−156,000	× 0.03	−255,000
Investment in average accounts receivable				*(continued)*

	Without Sales Campaign		With Sales Campaign	
60/360 × $8,000,000 × 0.7	$ 933,333			
80/360 × $10,000,000 × 0.7			$1,555,555	
Return rate	× 0.14	−130,667	× 0.14	−217,778
Net profit		$2,113,333		$2,527,222

	Percent of Sales	Percent of Sales
	Before Campaign	During Campaign
Cash sales	40	30
Payment from		
1–10	25	55
11–100	35	15

The proposed sales strategy will probably increase sales from $8 million to $10 million. There is a gross margin rate of 30 percent. The rate of return is 14 percent. Sales discounts are given on cash sales.

The company should undertake the sales campaign, because earnings will increase by $413,889 ($2,527,222 – $2,113,333).

Refer to the table on the previous page for the numerical calculations.

How are your receivable records excluding those for customers?

Some receivable transactions other than regular sales may result in losses. Examples include insurance and freight claims. The CFO should formulate a plan to handle these transactions. Unfortunately, some companies lack the needed record keeping. In fact, some firms only retain pieces of correspondence.

CHAPTER TWENTY-TWO

Inventory Management

T HE OBJECTIVE OF inventory management is to formulate policies that will result in an optimal inventory investment. The optimal inventory level varies among industries and among companies in a given industry. The successful management of inventory minimizes inventory at all manufacturing stages while retaining cost-efficient production volume. This improves corporate earnings and cash flow. By operating with minimum inventory and with short production lead times, the company increases its flexibility. This flexibility immediately responds to changing market conditions.

 INVENTORY RECORDING AND CONTROL

What inventory records should be kept?

Inventory files should contain records of balance on hand, quantity committed, and inventory location. The inventory balance must be adequate to maintain production schedules, properly utilize machines, and meet customer orders. Some inventory must be kept at the different manufacturing stages as hedges against the variabilities of supply and demand as well as to hedge against the possibility of problems arising during the manufacturing process. A sales forecast is the beginning step for effective inventory management since expected sales determines how much inventory is required.

Inventory records should provide information to meet the needs of the financial, production, sales, and purchasing managers. Inventory information may include the following by major type:

- Unit cost
- Quantity on order

- Historical usage
- Minimum–maximum quantities
- Quantities in transit
- Scheduling dates
- Delivery times
- Quantities set aside for specific customers, production orders, and contracts

With regard to minimum–maximum quantities, such a procedure is practical when the rate of sale or use of the product is *stable* and when the order time is short. The minimum is a cushion in case of an emergency. The maximum is the ceiling desired inventory. The reorder point is between the minimum and maximum.

A master item file should exist containing identification, description, and specifications of the item's raw material, component parts, and assembly relationship. An item specification should include current information about the part, the uses of the item, possible substitutions, the production process, demand information, overall supply, and competitive factors. Information can also be provided about suppliers, and the availability and price of the item.

What inventory balance should be kept?

The inventory balance depends on many variables, including sales, production cycle, cyclicality, perishability and obsolescence, inventory financing, liquidity, and markdowns in the industry. The objective is to maximize sales with minimum inventory. Therefore, inventory levels should be closely correlated to the selling cycle. A poor inventory management system may be indicated by the failure to achieve production plans, manufacturing bottlenecks, downtime, slow-moving or obsolete merchandise, expediting of parts, rush jobs, poor customer service, poor forecasts and inadequate performance reporting, and internal conflicts between members of the organization such as production and marketing.

An advantage of a bloated inventory is the reduction in manufacturing costs from larger production runs. A bloated inventory also provides a safety buffer if there is a nondelivery of raw materials or the previous department's manufacturing process breaks down.

Accurate sales forecasting is essential because a high sales estimate can result in high inventory levels, obsolescence, markdowns, and inventory write-offs. A low sales estimate can result in low inventory and lost sales.

Suppliers should be appraised in terms of fair pricing, meeting delivery dates, quality of goods shipped (e.g., consistent with product specifications), and ability to meet rush orders.

What inventory management policies should be practiced?

There are many benefits to sound inventory management. It:

- Reduces waste and cost from excess storage, handling, and obsolescence
- Reduces manufacturing delays because sufficient raw material balances are maintained, which results in lower production costs and longer runs

- Reduces the chance of inventory theft
- Improves customer service because materials are available

Following are some suggestions for inventory management policies:

- Evaluate the adequacy of raw materials, which depends on expected production, condition of equipment, supplier reliability, and seasonality. Raw material requirements can be projected using such techniques as statistical analysis of historical trends and cycles, econometric models, and Delphi methods. Use material management guidelines to specify what and how much should be stored. The manufacturing process requires an appropriate balance of parts to produce an end item. Watch for a situation in which you have two of three components because this results in having two excess inventories when there is a stockout of the third.
- Forecast future movements in raw material prices, so that if prices are expected to increase, additional materials are purchased at lower prices.
- Discard slow-moving merchandise to reduce inventory carrying costs and improve cash flow.
- Stock items with higher profit margins.
- Guard against inventory buildup because of carrying and opportunity costs.
- Minimize inventory when there are liquidity and/or inventory financing difficulties.
- Plan for a stock balance that will guard against and cushion the possible loss of business from a shortage in materials. The timing of an order also depends on seasonality factors.
- Ensure that inventory is received when needed for smooth production. Compare vendor and production receipts to promised delivery dates.
- Stock additional merchandise for a long sales order-entry process.
- Try to convince customers to retain higher stock levels to reduce the company's inventory of finished goods.
- Examine the quality of merchandise received. The ratio of purchase returns to purchases should be examined. A sharp increase in the ratio indicates that a new supplier may be needed. A performance measurement and evaluation system should exist to appraise vendor quality and reliability. If the vendor is unreliable, problems will occur in production scheduling, imbalances in work in process, and rush purchase orders.
- Keep a careful record of back orders. A high back-order level indicates that less inventory is required because back orders can be used as an indicator of the production required, resulting in improved manufacturing planning and procurement. The trend in the ratio of the dollar amount of back orders to the average per-day sales is enlightening.
- Evaluate the purchase and inventory control functions. Any problems must be identified and solved. If controls are deficient, inventory balances should be minimized.
- Accuracy is needed in order for the bills of materials to indicate the parts and quantities received to produce an end product. Conduct audits on the production floor when the parts are assembled.
- Have accurate inventory records and assign inventory responsibilities to managers. For example, assign to the engineering manager responsibility for the bills of material. Do you have the necessary inventory measurement tools (e.g., scales)?
- Closely supervise warehouse and materials handling staff to guard against theft and to maximize efficiency.

- Frequently review stock lines for poor earnings.
- Minimize the lead time in the acquisition, manufacturing, and distribution functions. (The lead time is how long it takes to receive merchandise from suppliers after an order is placed.) Depending on lead times, an increase in inventory stocking may be required or the purchasing pattern may have to be altered. Calculate the ratio of the value of outstanding orders to average daily purchases to indicate the lead time for receiving orders from suppliers. The ratio indicates whether the inventory balance should be increased or buying patterns should be changed. Are vendors keeping their promises?
- Examine the time between raw material input and the completion of production to determine whether production and engineering techniques can be instituted to speed the production process.
- Appraise the degree of and reasons for spoilage, and take corrective measures.
- Prepare an inventory analysis report presenting the number of months of insurance coverage. The report should highlight items with excess inventory coverage resulting from such causes as changes in customer demand or poor inventory practices.
- Maintain adequate inventory control, such as by applying computer techniques. For example, a retail business may use a point-of-sale computerized electronic register. The register updates inventory for sales and purchases, facilitating the computation of reorder points and quantity per order.
- Examine the trend in unit cost. The causes for variations should be studied to determine whether they arise from factors within or beyond management control (e.g, increase in oil prices, financial management deficiencies).
- Have economies in production run size to reduce setup costs and idle time.
- Have vendors consign inventory to you and invoice it as it is used.
- Use computer techniques and operations research to control inventory. For example, statistical forecasting techniques can be used to compute inventory levels related to a predetermined acceptability level.

How can the purchasing department help?

The purchasing department can aid in inventory management in a number of ways. It can:

- Determine a price for raw materials that will protect the business in unstable markets.
- Gradually increase the purchase order as you get to know the supplier better.
- Have blanket orders for operating supplies.
- Utilize stringent control over subcontracted operations.
- Schedule delivery of raw materials using statistical and just-in-time techniques.

What are the signs of inventory problems?

The symptoms of inventory management problems are:

- Inventory write-downs
- Differing rates of turnover among inventory items within the same inventory class
- Material shortages

- Uneven production and downtime
- Order cancellations
- Periodic extension of back orders
- Lack of storage facilities
- Frequent layoffs and rehirings

What inventory control measures can be taken?

Internal controls over inventory guard against theft and other irregularities. A periodic surprise count will confirm agreement between the book inventory and physical inventory. There should be controlled audit groups of work in process moving through the manufacturing stages to ensure that work in process is properly documented.

Shortages can occur and go unnoticed for a long time if controls are deficient. Controls are required in the acquisition and handling phases. There should be segregation in the purchasing, receiving, storing, and shipping of inventories.

An inventory control system should achieve these objectives:

- Proper record keeping
- Aiding in forecasting usage and needs
- Reporting exceptions
- Maintaining safeguards against misuse
- Implementing inventory decision models

How can you appraise and evaluate inventory?

Inventory analysis considers these issues:

- Inventory months' supply on hand by period for each major product
- Customer order backlog relative to the inventory balance
- Customer order backlog in weeks as a percentage of the production process cycle (lead time)
- Safety stock and slow-moving (obsolete) goods as a percentage of cost of sales and of the inventory balance
- Inventory carrying cost by month, quarter, and year

Work in process should be completed in a timely manner to realize sales and cash flow.

The marketing department should be held responsible for obsolete and slow-moving merchandise that it originally recommended. Before a product design is altered at the suggestion of marketing, it should be carefully studied.

Inventory items vary in profitability and the amount of space occupied. Inventory management involves a trade-off between the costs of keeping inventory compared to the benefits of holding it. Higher inventory balances result in increased costs from storage, spoilage, theft and casualty insurance, higher property taxes for larger facilities, increased manpower requirements, and interest on borrowed funds to finance inventory purchase. However, an increase in inventory lowers the possibility of lost sales from stockouts and the incidence of production slowdowns. Furthermore, large-volume purchases will result in greater purchase discounts. Inventory levels are also affected by short-term interest rates. For example, as short-term interest rates increase, the optimum level of holding inventory decreases.

How can handling costs be reduced?

To reduce costs of handling inventory:

- Minimize seasonal stocking.
- Decrease the time between filling an order and replacing the stock sold.
- Consolidate the number of inventory storage locations and/or warehouses.
- Avoid shutting down the plant, such as by having varying vacations.
- Simplify and standardize the product.
- Stop supplying "old" service parts; rather, give customers blueprints so they can internally produce parts.
- Speed routing reproduction by using standardized forms.
- Keep materials at subassemblies, not final assemblies.
- Use several assembly lines and move crews to the next line that has already been set up.

What influences inventory balances?

The inventory balance depends on:

- Reliability in estimating customer needs. Consideration should be given to the forecasting error.
- Accuracy of manufacturing documents (e.g., bill of materials, route sheets).
- Vertical integration of the product line as indicated by manufactured versus purchased parts.

The inventory of raw materials depends on the anticipated level and seasonality of production and the reliability of supply sources.

Work in progress usually varies the most and depends on the timing of the production run, stages in the manufacturing cycle, quality problems, lead time, and lot-sizing.

Work in progress is a liability to inventory managers because it takes away production capacity and cash while increasing the obsolescence and shrinkage risk. While machine utilization is good, a buildup of work in progress is bad.

The CFO may have to decide whether it is more profitable to sell inventory as is or to sell it after further processing. Assume inventory can be sold as is for $600,000 or sold for $800,000 if it is put into further processing costing $30,000. The latter should be chosen because further processing results in $770,000 profit compared to $600,000 for the current sale.

There should be periodic counts of inventory to check it on an ongoing basis as well as to reconcile the book and physical amounts. *Recommendation:* Standardized labeling and quantity markings will reduce counting time and result in orderly warehouse stocking. *Tip:* The count should be during nonworking hours. Alternatively, warehouse pickers could carefully enter daily movement when the cycle count occurs. The advantages to cyclic counting are that it:

- Does not require a plant shutdown, as does a year-end count
- Enables the timely detection and correction of the causes of inventory error
- Allows the efficient use of a few full-time experienced counters throughout the year
- Facilitates the modification of computer inventory programs

 INVENTORY COSTS

What are the costs associated with inventory?

Inventory carrying costs include handling, warehousing, insurance, and property taxes. There is also an opportunity cost of holding inventory. A provisional cost for spoilage and obsolescence should also be included. Carrying cost increases as the size of the inventory increases. Carrying cost equals:

$$\text{Carrying cost} = \frac{Q}{2} \times C$$

where
Q = quantity ordered
C = carrying cost per unit

Inventory ordering costs are the costs of placing an order and receiving the goods. They include freight and the clerical costs to place the order. The ordering costs can be reduced by placing fewer orders. In the case of manufactured items, ordering cost includes the scheduling cost. Ordering cost equals:

$$\text{Ordering cost} = \frac{S}{Q} \times P$$

where
S = total usage
Q = quantity per order
P = cost of placing an order

The total inventory cost is therefore:

$$\frac{QC}{2} + \frac{SP}{C}$$

There is a trade-off between ordering and carrying costs. A greater order quantity will increase carrying costs but lower ordering costs.

ECONOMIC ORDER QUANTITY

The economic order quantity (EOQ) is the optimum amount of goods to order each time so that total inventory costs are minimized. The EOQ should be determined for each major product:

$$EOQ = \sqrt{\frac{2SP}{C}}$$

Assumptions underlying the EOQ model are:

- Demand is constant and known.
- No discount is given for quantity purchases.
- Depletion of stock is linear and constant.
- *Lead time*, which is the time between placing an order and receiving delivery, is a constant; that is, stockout is not possible.

The number of orders for a period is the usage (*S*) divided by the EOQ.

Example 22.1

You want to know how often to place orders. This information exists:

$$S = 500 \text{ units per month}$$
$$P = \$40 \text{ per order}$$
$$C = \$4 \text{ per unit}$$

$$EOQ = \sqrt{\frac{2SP}{C}} = \sqrt{\frac{2(500)(40)}{4}} = \sqrt{10,000} = 100 \text{ units}$$

The number of orders each month is:

$$S/EOQ = 500/100 = 5$$

Therefore, an order should be placed about every six days (31/5).

Example 22.2

You want to determine how often to place an order for product X. The purchase price is $15. The annual carrying cost is $200. The ordering cost is $10. You expect to sell 50 units per month. The desired average inventory is 40 units.

$$S = 50 \times 12 = 600$$
$$P = \$10$$

$$C = \frac{\text{Purchase price} \times \text{Carrying cost}}{\text{Average investment}} = \frac{\$15 \times \$20}{40 \times \$15} = 5$$

$$EOQ = \sqrt{\frac{2SP}{C}} = \sqrt{\frac{2(600)(10)}{5}} = \sqrt{\frac{12,000}{5}} = \sqrt{2,400} = 49 \text{ (rounded)}$$

The number of orders per year is:

$$\frac{S}{EOQ} = \frac{600}{49} = 12 \text{ orders (rounded)}$$

You should place an order approximately every 30 days (365/12).

REORDER POINT

The reorder point (ROP) is the inventory level at which to place an order. However, the ROP requires knowledge of the lead time from placing to receiving an order. The ROP may be affected by the months of supply or total dollar ceilings on inventory to be held or to be ordered.

Reorder point equals:

Lead time × Average usage per unit of time

This reveals the inventory level at which a new order should be placed. If a safety stock is needed, then add this amount to the ROP.

The larger the *vendor's* backlog, the greater will be the work in process. This results in a longer and more inaccurate lead time. If a product is made to a customer's order, the lead time is the procurement time, run time, queue time, move time, and setup time for raw material.

Example 22.3

A company needs 6,400 units evenly throughout the year. There is a lead time of 1 week. There are 50 working weeks in the year. The reorder point is:

$$1 \text{ week} \times \frac{6,400}{50 \text{ weeks}} = 1 \times 128 = 12$$

When the inventory level drops to 128 units, a new order should be placed.

An optimal inventory level can be based on comparing the incremental profitability resulting from having more merchandise to the opportunity cost of carrying the higher inventory balances.

Example 22.4

The current inventory turnover is 12 times. Variable costs are 60 percent of sales. An increase in inventory balances is expected to prevent stockouts, thus increasing sales. Minimum rate of return is 18 percent. Relevant data follow.

Sales	Turnover
$800,000	12
890,000	10
940,000	8
980,000	7

(1)	(2)	(3)
Sales	Turnover	[(1)/(2)] Average Inventory Balance
$800,000	12	$66,667
890,000	10	89,000
940,000	8	117,500
980,000	7	140,000

(4) Opportunity Cost of Carrying Incremental Inventory[a]	(5) Increased Profitability[b]	(6) [(5)–(4)] Net Savings
—	—	—
$4,020	$36,000	$31,980
5,130	20,000	14,870
4,050	16,000	11,950

[a] Increased inventory × 0.18.

[b] Increased sales × 0.40.

The optimal inventory level is $89,000, because it results in the highest net savings.

How are stockouts avoided?

The stockout of raw materials or work in process can cause a production slowdown. A safety stock should be held to avoid a stockout situation. Safety stock is the minimum inventory for an item based on anticipated usage (demand) and delivery (lead) time of materials. A safety stock guards against unusual product demand or unexpected delivery problems. The variability in demand of the item can be measured by the standard deviation or mean absolute deviation. The standard deviation measures the degree to which the actual level at the end of the cycle differs from the normal level. The trend period in computing standard deviations should consider market characteristics, product maturity, and demand volatility. A large standard deviation indicates significant inventory variation. Therefore, the probability of being out of stock at various times during the year is high if there is no safety stock. Safety stock prevents the potential damage to customer relations and to future sales that can occur when there is a lack of inventory to fill an order. A safety stock increases the inventory balance. In effect, safety stock requires a balancing of expected costs of stockouts against the costs of carrying the additional inventory. *Rule of thumb:* A typical inventory management system uses a 5 percent stockout factor.

Example 22.5

An order is placed when the inventory level reaches 210 units rather than 180 units. The safety stock is thus 30 units. In other words, you expect to be stocked with 30 units when the new order is received.

The optimum safety stock is the point where the increased carrying cost equals the opportunity cost of a potential stockout. The increased carrying cost equals the carrying cost per unit multiplied by the safety stock.

$$\text{Stockout cost} = \text{Number of orders}\left(\frac{\text{Usage}}{\text{Order Quantity}}\right) \times \text{Stockout units}$$
$$\times \text{Units stockout cost} \times \text{Probability of a stockout}$$

Example 22.6

A company uses 100,000 units annually. Each order is for 10,000 units. Stockout is 1,000 units; this amount is the difference between the maximum daily usage during the lead time less the reorder point, ignoring a safety stock factor. The acceptable stockout probability is 30 percent. The per unit stockout cost is $2.30. The carrying cost per unit is $5.00.

The stockout cost is:

$$\frac{100,000}{10,000} \times 1,000 \times \$2.30 \times 0.3 = \$6,900$$

To calculate the amount of safety stock:

$$\text{Let } X = \text{Safety stock}$$
$$\text{Stockout cost} = \text{Carrying cost of safety stock}$$
$$\$6,900 = \$5X$$
$$1,380 \text{ units} = X$$

Example 22.7

A company uses 250,000 units per year. Each order is for 25,000 units. Stockout is 4,000 units. The tolerable stockout probability is 25 percent. The per unit stockout cost is $4.00. The carrying cost per unit is $8.00.

(continued)

$$\text{Stockout cost} = \frac{250{,}000}{25{,}000} \times 4{,}000 \times \$4.00 \times 0.25 = \$40{,}000$$

$$\text{Amount of safety stock needed} = \frac{\text{Stockout cost}}{\text{Carrying cost per unit}} = \frac{\$40{,}000}{8} = 5{,}000 \text{ units}$$

HOW TO FIND THE OPTIMAL SAFETY STOCK SIZE

Service level can be defined as the probability that demand will not exceed supply during lead time. Thus, a service level of 80 percent implies a probability of 80 percent that demand will not exceed supply. To determine the optimal level of safety stock size, ascertain the costs of not having enough inventory (stockout costs). Here are three cases for computing the safety stock. The first two do not recognize stockout costs; the third case does.

Case 1: Variable Usage Rate, Constant Lead Time

$$\text{ROP} = \text{Expected usage during lead time} + \text{safety stock}$$

$$= \bar{\mu} \, LT + zLT(\sigma_\mu)$$

where

μ = Average usage rate
LT = Lead time
σ_μ = Standard deviation of usage rate
z = Standard normal variable as defined in Exhibit 22.1

For a normal distribution, a given service level amounts to the shaded area under the curve to the left of ROP in Exhibit 22.2.

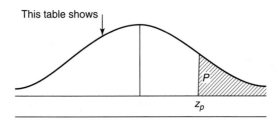

EXHIBIT 22.1   Values of z_p for Specified Probabilities P

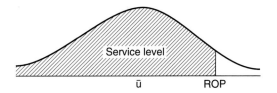

EXHIBIT 22.2 Service Level

Example 22.8

A company uses large cases of a product at an average rate of 50 units per day. Usage can be approximated by a normal distribution with a standard deviation of 5 units per day. Lead time is 4 days. Thus:

$$\bar{\mu} = 50 \text{ units per day}$$

$$\sigma_\mu = 5 \text{ units}$$

$$LT = 4 \text{ days}$$

For a service level of 99 percent (see Exhibit 22.3), $z = 2.33$ (from Exhibit 22.1). Thus:

$$\text{Sefety stock} = 2.33\sqrt{4}\,(5) = 23.3 \text{ cans}$$

$$ROP = 50(4) + 23.3 = 223.3 \text{ cans}$$

Case 2: Constant Usage Rate, Variable Lead Time

For constant usage with variable lead time, the reorder point is:

$$ROP = \text{Expected usage during lead time} + \text{Safety stock}$$

$$= \bar{\mu}\,LT + z\mu\sigma_{LT}$$

where
μ = Constant usage rate
LT = Average lead time
σ_{LT} = Standard deviation of lead time

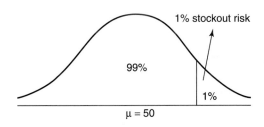

EXHIBIT 22.3 Service Level = 99%

Example 22.9

A company uses 10 gallons of product X per day. Lead time is normally distributed with a mean of 6 days and a standard deviation of 2 days. Thus,

$$\mu = 10 \text{ gallons per day}$$
$$\overline{LT} = 6 \text{ days}$$
$$\sigma_{LT} = 2 \text{ days}$$

$$\text{Safety stock} = 2.33(10)(2) = 46.6 \text{ gallons}$$
$$\text{ROP} = 10(6) + 46.6 = 106.6$$

Exhibit 22.4 shows the changes in level of inventory over time.

The product generating the highest contribution margin per square foot should usually have the most priority in allocating space.

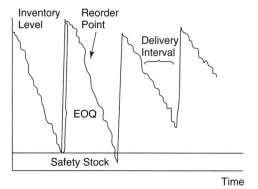

EXHIBIT 22.4   Changes in Level of Inventory

Example 22.10

The following information pertains to product X:

Sales price	$15
Variable cost per unit	5
Contribution margin per unit	$10
Contribution margin per dozen	$120
Storage space per dozen	2 cubic feet
Contribution margin per cubic foot	$60
Number of units sold per period	4
Expected contribution margin per cubic foot	$240

ABC INVENTORY CONTROL

ABC analysis concentrates on the most important items considering gross profitability, sensitive price or demand patterns, and supply excesses or shortages. The ABC method involves the classification of inventory into one of four categories, A, B, C, or D. The grouping is based on the potential savings associated with a proper level of control.

Perpetual inventory records should be kept for group A items because of the required accuracy and frequent attention, often daily. Group A items usually refer to 1 out of every 10 items in inventory typically representing 70 percent of the dollar value of inventory. Group B items are less expensive but are still important and require intermediate control. Group B items usually account for 20 percent of the number of inventory items and 20 percent of the dollar value. Group C items constitute most of the inventory. Since they are usually less expensive and used less, less attention is paid to them. There is typically a high safety stock level for C items. There should be blanket purchase orders for A items and only spot buys for Bs and Cs. Group D items are the losers. There has been no usage of D items for an extended time period (e.g., six months). Group D items should not be reordered without special authorization. Items may be reclassified as needed. For example, a fragile item or one being stolen can be reclassified from C to A.

The higher the value of the inventory items, the more control required. For example, in looking at group A items, carefully examine records, bills of materials, customer orders, open purchase orders, and open manufacturing orders.

The five steps in ABC are:

1. Segregate inventory into components.
2. Compute annual dollar usage by inventory type.
3. Rank inventory according to dollar usage ranging from high to low (e.g., As in top 30 percent, Bs in next 50 percent, and Cs in last 20 percent).
4. Tag inventory with the appropriate classification so proper attention can be given to it.
5. Record classifications in the inventory records.

SERVICE BUSINESS

How should a service business handle inventory?

In a service business, inventories are less tangible than durable goods, and they are perishable by nature. Examples of inventory in a service business include empty seats in an airplane, empty hotel rooms, and empty tables in a restaurant. In these instances, inventory is lost as time passes and the "empty" condition continues. Inventory also includes service parts.

Inventory in a service business consists of two levels:

1. *Primary level.* This level represents the capacity of the facility or equipment to provide the service.
2. *Secondary level.* This level is the variable capacity used at different time periods to deliver the service.

Marginal pricing may be used to obtain income from otherwise lost opportunities. Examples are hotels offering weekend specials and airlines with off-peak fares. The aim is to divert minimal income from the normal service customer by attracting lower-margin business. The profit of the service business is influenced by the perishability of the service inventory.

The labor force should be such that labor costs are matched with the ability to sell the product.

CHAPTER TWENTY-THREE

Management of Payables

THE CFO MUST ensure that a well-managed accounts payable system is in operation. Any warning signs of problems with payables must be identified and solved.

 ## ACCOUNTS PAYABLE SYSTEM

Controlling the cash that leaves the company is as important as controlling the cash that comes in. To achieve control, payables must be aggressively managed in accordance with the company's financial position and goals. Payment of bills must not be simply made but planned. Above all, payables must be viewed as a flexible system that the CFO can manipulate in response to other factors, such as sales decreases or slowdowns in collections.

A well-managed accounts payable system should:

- *Evaluate cash flow.* Every accounts payable strategy should be rooted in the realities of the company's cash flow status. For example, if it takes 90 days to collect from customers, it is financially self-destructive to pay bills within 45 days. How long does it take dollars spent to be replaced? The CFO should monitor the cash-to-cash cycle representing the length of time elapsing from the expenditure of dollars on inventory to the receipt of cash from sales. Take, for instance, a retailer who buys a product on January 1 and pays for it on January 30; it takes the retailer 60 days from that point to sell that product (which brings the retailer to March 31) and 45 days after that to collect the cash (May 15). The cash-to-cash cycle adds up to 105 days, which is the length of time the retailer is behind after expending the cash.
- *Set goals.* Once cash flow has been appraised, establish written payment goals so there can be no confusion among bill payers. Avoid a situation in which staff

members make the decisions about which bills are to be paid and when—usually suppliers who complain the most are paid first, regardless of overall benefit to the business. The payment of bills should be timed to coordinate exactly with formal disbursement goals. This means checks should be dated no earlier than the dates on which payments are due (and suppliers should receive checks no more than a day or two earlier than the due date). The goal should be to hold cash in interest-bearing accounts until the last possible minute in which payments must be made and still maintain good relations with suppliers.

- *Establish payment priorities.* It is advisable to establish a two-tiered list of payment priorities, which then becomes part of the formal payment strategy. Tier 1, the group that should be paid at all costs and at whatever terms have been agreed on, should include major vendors and service suppliers, bankers, and the state and federal tax authorities. Tier 2, which offers more room for short-term maneuvering during cash flow crunches, should consist of minor suppliers whose goodwill is less vital to the overall well-being of the company. Payment priorities should be in writing.

- *Aggressively negotiate payment.* Granted, there is not much room for negotiation with bankers or tax collectors, but once they are taken care of, everything else on the payables front is open for discussion. The CFO has leverage to negotiate better-than-usual terms from major suppliers, especially during recessionary times, when vendors are afraid of losing business. Determine the optimal payment terms (using the cash-to-cash or other cash flow information as a guide) and then, when orders are placed—not when bills become due or overdue—negotiate to achieve those terms.

- *Forecast cash needs.* The CFO should predict how much cash is needed—and when— to fulfill the payables obligations. That forecast becomes an important tool in averting cash flow problems. Will funds be available at the right time from bank accounts or bank credit lines? If funds will not be available, take precautionary measures, such as stepping up customer collection efforts.

- *Keep good payables records.* Payable records include weekly updates about the aging of every outstanding bill; documentation that matches each bill paid with its original sales order, delivery records, and payment invoice; and total cost records, including interest penalties paid on each bill. The last is important because it may not be evident how much interest penalties add to the cost of doing business when the company winds up having to pay charges to finance late payables.

- *Review payables records regularly.* Payables reports are as important as other cash flow documents and must be evaluated. Review payables—aging schedules— weekly; cost records can be appraised monthly.

- *Recognize warning signs.* Since cash flow cycles vary, there may be periods when payables get stretched without any long-term risk. But it is essential to spot indications of more serious problems. One approach is to draw up a "payables problems" checklist, which breaks down average bill age, promptness of tax payments, any interest charges, and other warning factors.

- *Pay the right amount.* Make payments in accordance with purchase order terms, and take discounts where allowed. Payments should be made only against the original invoice to prevent a duplicate payment against a photocopy or summary statement. Match all vendor invoices against receiving reports and purchase orders.

MANAGING PAYABLES

In managing payables, what must be considered?

Sound management of accounts payables requires the following actions:

- *Prioritize.* Financial obligations fall into three categories: bills to be paid as soon as they are due (wages and salaries, bank loans, and taxes), bills to be paid within 15 days (to important contractors for services already performed), and bills you try to pay within 30 days (all others). As your business begins to feel the recessionary pinch, try to stretch that third category out longer. In looking at cash flow, accounts payable are something that the CFO has some control over—and suppliers can be "played with" if needed.
- *Negotiate.* Negotiate longer payment terms in advance, although the process can be time consuming. Contact major vendors to ask when they absolutely have to have their money. Then record this information in each vendor's accounts payable file. It sets the guidelines for payment of all major outstanding obligations. With smaller suppliers, however, there may not be much potential payoff from stretching out payments.
- *Monitor payables closely.* Each week, analyze an accounts payable aging schedule along with other cash flow documents. As a last resort, the company should use its credit line to make payments if cash collections from customers are behind schedule.
- *Demonstrate good faith.* When money does not come in, the company is in a jam. One possible solution: Pay only *absolute essentials*, such as salaries, rent, taxes, and loans. These expenditures cannot be delayed. Suppliers are more tolerant and flexible since they need the business. However, try to pay more to the demanding vendors and less to those more likely to wait. A partial payment shows vendors that the company is trying to pay them. Do not just send the money—get on the phone and explain what is happening and why and set up an informal payment schedule. Let the vendors know when they can expect to receive the balance due. A follow-up letter should confirm the telephone conversation.

Is your business heading for accounts payable problems?

Some typical symptoms of accounts payable problems are:

- *Aged payables.* Chances are that the company is heading for trouble when bills start becoming, on average, 45 to 60 days past due. (The only exception: bills whose issuers have approved late payment terms without interest penalties, at the time of order.)
- *Interest penalties.* Do not box yourself in by paying interest charges on overdue bills—unless there are clear financial benefits from using funds elsewhere. Once the company is paying penalties to even a few vendors on a regular monthly basis, it is in trouble. Instead, approach creditors with a plan that will reduce or perhaps eliminate interest charges.
- *Hassles from creditors.* Make it a habit to communicate informally with creditors whenever a cash crunch is developing. Creditors typically are understanding if the company has good intentions and is honest.

What information should you obtain from vendors?

Money can be saved by getting to know the policies of vendors and suppliers. Probe them for the best prices and terms. Ask open-ended questions, such as "What else can you do for me?" Ask vendors to complete an information sheet that forces them to write down the terms and conditions of their sales plans. With this form, their verbal promises become written ones. A list of useful information follows.

- Vendor's name, address, and phone number (Will the vendor accept collect calls? Is there an 800 number?)
- Sales representative's name, phone number, and qualifications
- Amount of minimum purchase
- Quantity discounts available
- Advertising/promotion allowances
- Availability of extended payment terms
- Financing charge on overdue accounts
- Delivery terms
- Service policies
- Return privileges for damaged goods (who pays the freight?)
- Credit terms (how flexible is the company?)

PART FIVE

V

Financing the Business

CHAPTER TWENTY-FOUR

Short-Term and Intermediate-Term Financing

THIS CHAPTER PROVIDES information about short-term and intermediate-term financing sources. Short-term financing is typically used to meet seasonal and temporary fluctuations in funds position. For example, short-term financing can provide working capital, finance current assets (such as receivables and inventory), or furnish interim financing for a long-term project or capital asset until long-term financing can be issued. Long-term financing may not be currently suitable because of long-term credit risk or unusually high cost. Intermediate-term financing is primarily obtained from banks and lessors.

 SHORT-TERM FINANCING

Before deciding on how much short-term financing is needed, the CFO should check the company's cash flow on a monthly or even weekly basis, taking into account economic conditions, timing of receipts and payments, and seasonality.

How does short-term financing stack up compared to long-term financing?

Short-term financing has several beneficial aspects, including being easier to arrange, being less costly, and having greater flexibility. The drawbacks of short-term financing are that interest rates fluctuate more often, refinancing is usually needed, and the risk of inability to pay along with its associated consequences (e.g., credit rating).

What sources of short-term financing may be tapped?

The CFO may decide to use trade credit, bank loans, bankers' acceptances, finance company loans, commercial paper, receivable financing, and inventory financing. A particular source may be more appropriate in a specific situation. Some sources are more beneficial than others depending upon interest rates and collateral requirements.

What variables have to be taken into account when deciding which short-term financing source to use?

The factors influencing the selection of a particular financing source include:

- *Cost*, including interest rate and front-end fees (e.g., legal fees, points)
- *Prepayment penalties*
- *Impact on financial ratios*
- *Effect on credit rating.* Some sources of short-term financing may negatively impact the company's credit rating, such as factoring accounts receivable.
- *Risk.* Consider the reliability of the source of funds for future borrowing. If the company is significantly affected by external factors, it will need more stability and reliability in financing.
- *Restrictions.* Certain creditors may impose limitations, such as requiring a minimum working capital.
- *Flexibility.* Certain lenders are more willing to accommodate the company, for example, to periodically adjust the amount of funds needed.
- *Anticipated money market conditions* (e.g., future interest rates) and availability of future financing
- *Inflation rate*
- *Profitability and liquidity positions*
- *Stability and maturity of operations*
- *Tax rate*

If the firm will be short of cash during certain periods, the CFO should arrange for financing (such as a line of credit) in advance rather than waiting for a crisis.

How can trade credit best be used?

Trade credit is a spontaneous (recurring) financing source since it comes from normal operations. It is the least costly way to finance inventory. The benefits of trade credit are:

- It is readily available from suppliers.
- There is no collateral requirement.
- Interest is usually nonexistent.
- It is convenient.
- Trade creditors are generally tolerant if the company gets into financial straits.

If the business has liquidity problems, it may be able to stretch accounts payable. However, among the disadvantages of doing so are the giving up of any cash discount offered and the probability of lowering the company's credit rating. The CFO may prepare a report evaluating accounts payable in terms of lost discounts, aged unpaid invoices, and days to pay.

Should creditors be paid earlier to obtain a cash discount?

It is usually best to take advantage of a cash discount on the early payment of accounts payable because the failure to do so results in a high opportunity cost. The cost of not taking a discount equals:

$$\frac{\text{Discount lost}}{\substack{\text{Dollar proceed you have use of by not} \\ \text{taking the discount}}} \times \frac{360}{\substack{\text{Number of days you have use of the} \\ \text{money by not taking the discount}}}$$

Example 24.1

The company buys $100,000 in raw materials on terms of 2/10, net/30. The company fails to take the discount and pays the bill on the 30th day. The cost of the discount is:

$$\frac{\$20,000}{\$980,000} \times \frac{360}{20} = 36.7\%$$

The company is advised to take the discount because the opportunity cost is 36.7 percent, even if it has to borrow the funds from the bank. The interest rate on a bank loan would be much less than 36.7 percent.

When are bank loans advisable?

Banks give the business the ability to operate with minimal cash and still be confident of planning activities even in light of uncertainty.

Bank loans are not spontaneous financing like trade credit. One example is a self-liquidating (seasonal) loan used to pay for a temporary increase in accounts receivable or inventory. As soon as the assets realize cash, the loan is repaid.

Bank financing may take these forms: unsecured loans, secured loans, lines of credit, and installment loans.

How do unsecured loans work?

Most short-term unsecured (no collateral) loans are self-liquidating. This kind of loan is suggested if the company has an excellent credit rating. It is typically used to finance projects with fast cash flows. It is advisable when the company has immediate cash and can either repay the loan in the near term or quickly obtain longer-term financing. Seasonal cash shortfalls and desired inventory buildups are reasons to use an unsecured loan. The disadvantages of such a loan are that, because it is made for the short term, it has a higher interest rate than a secured loan and payment in a lump sum is required.

When is a collateralized loan necessary?

If the company's credit rating is poor, the bank may require security. Collateral may be in the form of inventory, marketable securities, or fixed assets. *Tip:* Even if the company can obtain an unsecured loan, it can still give security to get a lower interest rate.

How much line of credit can the company get?

Under a line of credit, the bank contracts to lend money on a recurring basis up to a given amount. Credit lines are usually for one year and are renewable. The CFO should determine whether the line of credit is sufficient for current and future needs.

The advantages of a line of credit are the easy and quick availability of funds during credit crunches and the ability to borrow only as much as needed and repay when adequate cash is available. *Recommendation:* Use a line of credit if the company is working on large long-term projects when receipts are minimal or nonexistent until job completion. The disadvantages of a credit line are the collateral requirements and the additional financial disclosure that must be furnished to the bank. Furthermore, the bank may place restrictions on the company, such as a ceiling on fixed asset acquisitions or the maintenance of a minimum working capital. The bank often imposes a commitment fee on the amount of the unused credit line.

A line of credit agreement may require the company to maintain a compensating balance with the bank. The compensating balance is stated as a percentage of the loan and increases the effective interest rate.

Example 24.2

The company borrows $200,000 and must keep a 12 percent compensating balance. It also has an unused credit line of $100,000, for which there is a 10 percent compensating balance. The minimum balance to maintain is:

$$(\$200,000 \times 0.12) + (\$100,000 \times 0.10) = \$24,000 + \$10,000 = \$34,000$$

The bank may test the company's financial soundness by requiring it to repay the loan for a brief time during the year (e.g., for one month). If the company is unable to do so, it should probably finance long term. The payment shows the bank that the loan is actually seasonal instead of permanent.

Why would a letter of credit be used?

A letter of credit is a conditional bank commitment on behalf of the firm to pay a third party based on specified terms. A payment is made on presentation of proof of shipment or other performance. The advantages of a letter of credit are that the company does not have to pay cash before shipment and funds can be used elsewhere for a return. Banks impose a fee and a rate for bankers' acceptances arising after shipment that approximates the prime interest rate.

What is the benefit of a revolving credit agreement?

A revolving credit arrangement involves short-term notes (usually 90 days). The loan may be renewed or additional funds may be borrowed up to a maximum amount. The advantages of revolving credit are readily available, and there are fewer restrictions compared to the line-of-credit arrangement.

Is an installment loan advisable?

In an installment loan, there are monthly payments. When the principal on the loan decreases sufficiently, refinancing can occur at a lower interest rate. This loan may be tailored to meet the company's seasonal financing needs.

What is the real cost of borrowing?

Interest on a loan may be paid either at maturity (ordinary interest) or in advance (discounting the loan). When interest is paid in advance, the loan proceeds are reduced and the effective (true) interest cost is increased.

Example 24.3

The company borrows $300,000 at 16 percent interest per annum on a discount basis. The loan is repaid one year later. The effective interest rate is:

$$\text{Interest} = \$300,000 \times 0.16 = \$48,000$$
$$\text{Proceeds} = \$300,000 - \$48,000 = \$252,000$$

$$\text{Effective interest rate} = \frac{\text{Interest}}{\text{Proceeds}} = \frac{\$48,000}{\$252,000} = 19\%$$

A compensating balance increases the effective interest rate.

Example 24.4

The effective interest rate for a one-year, $600,000 loan that has a nominal interest rate of 19 percent, with interest due at maturity and requiring a 15 percent compensating balance, follows. Effective interest rate (with compensating balance) equals:

$$\frac{\text{Interest rate} \times \text{Principal}}{\text{Proceeds (\%)} \times \text{Principal}} = \frac{0.19 \times \$600,000}{(1.00 - 0.15) \times \$600,000} = \frac{\$114,000}{\$510,000} = 22.4\%$$

Example 24.5

Assume the same facts as in the previous example, except that the loan is discounted. The effective interest rate (with discount) equals:

$$\frac{\text{Interest rate} \times \text{Principal}}{(\text{Proceeds (\%)} \times \text{Principal}) - \text{Interest}}$$

$$\frac{0.19 \times \$600,000}{(0.85 \times \$600,000) - \$114,000} = \frac{\$114,000}{\$396,000} = 28.8\%$$

Example 24.6

The company has a credit line of $400,000 but must keep a compensating balance of 13 percent on outstanding loans and a compensating balance of 10 percent on the unused credit. The interest rate on the loan is 18 percent. The company borrows $275,000. The effective interest rate is computed as follows. The compensating balance is:

$$
\begin{array}{ll}
0.13 \times \$275,000 & \$35,750 \\
0.10 \times \$125,000 & \underline{12,500} \\
& \underline{\underline{\$48,250}}
\end{array}
$$

Effective interest rate (with line of credit) equals:

$$\frac{\text{Interest rate (on loan)} \times \text{Principal}}{\text{Principal} - \text{Compensating balance}}$$

$$\frac{0.18 \times \$275,000}{\$275,000 - \$48,250} = \frac{\$49,500}{\$226,750} = 21.8\%$$

The effective interest rate associated with an installment loan is illustrated in the next example. Assume a one-year loan due in equal monthly installments. The effective rate will be based on the average amount outstanding for the year. The interest is computed on the face amount of the loan.

Example 24.7

The company borrows $400,000 at an interest rate of 10 percent to be paid in 12 monthly installments. The average loan balance is $400,000/2 = $200,000. The effective interest rate is $40,000/$200,000 = 20%.

Example 24.8

Assume the same information as in Example 24.7 except that the loan is discounted. The interest of $40,000 is deducted in advance so the proceeds received are $400,000 – $40,000 = $360,000. The average loan balance is $360,000/2 = $180,000. The effective interest rate is $40,000/$180,000 = 22.2%.

The effective interest cost computation may be more complicated when there are differing installment payments. The true interest cost of an installment loan is the internal rate of return of the applicable cash flows converted on an annual basis (if desired).

Example 24.9

The company borrows $100,000 and will repay it in three monthly installments of $25,000, $25,000, and $50,000. The interest rate is 12 percent.

Amount of borrowing equals:

Installment loan	$100,000
Less: Interest on first installment ($100,000 × 0.25 × 0.12)	3,000
Balance	$ 97,000

Effective interest cost of installment loan equals:

$$0 = -\$97,000 + \frac{\$25,000\%}{(1+\text{Cost})} + \frac{\$25,000\%}{(1+\text{Cost})^2} + \frac{\$50,000\%}{(1+\text{Cost})^3}$$

$= 1.37\%$ on monthly basis

$= 1.37\% \times 12 = 16.44\%$ on annual basis

Interest rate hedging can be accomplished with swaps, caps, and collars. These products protect the company from rising interest rates. In a swap, the borrower substitutes a variable interest rate loan for a fixed rate loan. In a cap, the borrower for an up-front fee puts a limit on how high a floating interest rate may go. A collar puts a cap or rising interest rates and a floor on decreasing interest rates. The collar has a lower up-front charge than a cap because of the advantage of falling interest rates to the borrower. The benefits of interest rate hedging are: the company locks in a maximum financing cost; there is more flexibility; and interest rates are known in advance, reducing the speculative risk of changing interest rates. These strategies are especially appealing to seasonal borrowers.

What is a banker's acceptance?

A *banker's acceptance* is a short-term, non–interest-bearing draft (up to six months), drawn by the company and accepted by a bank, that orders payment to a third party at a future date. It is usually issued up to $1 million on a discount basis. The creditworthiness of the draft is of good quality because it has the backing of the bank, not the drawer. It is, in effect, a debt instrument arising from a self-liquidating transaction. Bankers' acceptances are often used to finance the shipment and handling of both domestic and foreign goods. Acceptances typically have maturities of less than 180 days.

Is the company forced to take out a commercial finance loan?

When bank credit is not available, the company may need to contact a commercial finance company. The finance company loan has a higher interest rate than a bank loan and typically is secured. The amount of collateral generally will be more than the balance of the loan. Commercial finance companies also finance the installment purchases of industrial equipment.

Is the company financially strong enough to issue commercial paper?

Commercial paper can be issued only if the company has a strong credit rating. Therefore, the interest rate is below that of a bank loan, usually ½ percent less than the prime interest rate. Commercial paper is unsecured and sold at a discount (below face value). The maturity date is typically less than 270 days; otherwise Securities and Exchange Commission registration is required. Since the note is issued at a discount, the interest is immediately deducted from the face of the note by the creditor, but the company will pay the full face value. Commercial paper can be issued through a dealer or placed directly to an institutional investor.

The advantages of commercial paper are the absence of collateral and a lower interest rate. The disadvantage is that commercial paper can be issued only by large, financially secure companies.

Example 24.10

A company's balance sheet appears as:

ASSETS	
Current assets	$ 540,000
Fixed assets	800,000
Total assets	$1,340,000
LIABILITIES AND STOCKHOLDERS' EQUITY	
Current liabilities:	
Notes payable to banks	$ 100,000
Commercial paper	650,000
Total current liabilities	$ 750,000
Long-term liabilities	260,000
Total liabilities	$1,010,000
Stockholders' equity	330,000
Total liabilities and stockholders' equity	$1,340,000

The company has issued a high percentage of commercial paper relative to both its current liabilities, 86.7 percent ($650,000/$750,000), and its total liabilities, 64.4 percent ($650,000/$1,010,000). The company probably should do more bank borrowing because in a money market squeeze it is advantageous to have a working relationship with a bank.

Example 24.11

The company needs $300,000 for the month of November. It has two options:

1. A one-year line of credit for $300,000 with a bank. The commitment fee is 0.5 percent, and the interest charge on the used funds is 12 percent.
2. Issue two-month commercial paper at 10 percent interest. Because the funds are needed for only one month, the excess funds ($300,000) can be invested in 8 percent marketable securities for December. The total transaction fee for the marketable securities is 0.3 percent.

The line of credit costs:

Commitment fee for unused period (0.005)(300,000)(11/12)	$1,375
Interest for one month (0.12)(300,000)(1/12)	3,000
Total cost	$4,375

The commercial paper costs:

Interest charge (0.10)(300,000)(2/12)	$5,000
Transaction fee (0.003)(300,000)	900
Less interest earned on marketable securities (0.08)(300,000)(1/12)	(2,000)
Total cost	$3,900

The commercial paper arrangement is less costly.

Should receivables be used for financing?

In accounts receivable financing, the accounts receivable are the collateral for the loan as well as the source of repayment.

Receivable financing avoids the need for long-term financing and generates recurring cash flow. However, there are high administrative costs when many small accounts exist.

Accounts receivable may be financed under either a factoring or assignment (pledging) arrangement. *Factoring* is the sale of accounts receivable to a finance company *without recourse*. The purchaser assumes all credit and collection risks. The amount received equals the face value of the receivables less the commission charge, which is usually 2 to 4 percent higher than the prime interest rate. The cost of factoring is the factor's commission for credit investigation, interest on the unpaid balance of advanced funds, and a discount from the face value of the receivables where high credit risk exists. Customer payments are made directly to the factor.

The advantages of factoring are immediate availability of money, reduction in overhead since the credit examination activity is no longer needed, obtaining financial advice, receipt of seasonal advances, and strengthening of the balance sheet position.

The disadvantages of factoring are the high cost and the customer's negative impression because of the change in ownership of the receivables. Furthermore, factors may antagonize customers by their demanding collection methods of delinquent accounts.

In an *assignment* (pledging), there is no transfer of the ownership of the accounts receivable. Receivables are given to a finance company *with recourse*. The finance company typically advances between 50 and 85 percent of the face value of the receivables in cash. The company incurs a service charge, interest on the advance, and bad debt losses. Customer remissions continue to be made directly to the company.

The assignment of accounts receivable has the advantages of immediate availability of cash, cash advances available on a seasonal basis, and avoidance of negative customer reaction. The disadvantages include the high cost, the continuance of clerical work on the accounts receivable, and the bearing of all credit risk.

The CFO has to recognize the impact of a change in accounts receivable policy on the cost of financing receivables. The cost of financing may rise or fall under different conditions; for example, when credit standards are eased, costs rise; when recourse for defaults is given to the finance company, costs decrease; and when the minimum invoice amount of a credit sale is increased, costs decline.

Example 24.12

A factor will purchase the company's $120,000 per month accounts receivable. The factor will advance up to 80 percent of the receivables for an annual charge of 14 percent, and a 1.5 percent fee on receivables purchased. The cost of this factoring arrangement is:

Factor fee [0.015 × ($120,000 × 12)]	$21,600
Cost of borrowing [0.14 × ($120,000 × 0.8)]	13,440
Total cost	$35,040

Example 24.13

A factor charges a 3 percent fee per month. The factor lends the company up to 75 percent of receivables purchased for an additional 1 percent per month. Credit sales are $400,000 per month. As a result of the factoring arrangement, the company saves $6,500 per month in credit costs and a bad debt expense of 2 percent of credit sales.

XYZ Bank has offered an arrangement to lend the company up to 75 percent of the receivables. The bank will charge 2 percent per month interest plus a 4 percent processing charge on receivable lending.

The collection period is 30 days. If the company borrows the maximum per month, should it stay with the factor or switch to XYZ Bank?

Cost of factor:	
Purchased receivables (0.03 × $400,000)	$12,000
Lending fee (0.01 × $300,000)	3,000
Total cost	$15,000
Cost of bank financing:	
Interest (0.02 × $300,000)	$6,000
Processing charge (0.04 × $300,000)	12,000
Additional cost of not using the factor:	
Credit costs	6,500
Bad debts (0.02 × $400,000)	8,000
Total cost	$32,500

The company should stay with the factor.

Example 24.14

A company needs $250,000 and is considering the alternatives of arranging a bank loan or going to a factor. The bank loan terms are 18 percent interest, discounted, with a compensating balance of 20 percent. The factor will charge a 4 percent commission on invoices purchased monthly, and the interest rate on the purchased invoices is 12 percent, deducted in advance. By using a factor, the company will save $1,000 monthly credit department costs, and uncollectible accounts estimated at 3 percent of the factored accounts receivable will not occur. Which is the better option?

The bank loan that will net the company its desired $250,000 in proceeds is:

$$\frac{\text{Proceeds}}{(100\% - \text{Proceeds deducted})} = \frac{\$250,000}{100\% - (18\% + 20\%)}$$

$$\frac{\$250,000}{1.00 - 0.38} = \frac{\$250,000}{0.62} = \$403,226$$

The effective interest rate of the bank loan is:

$$\text{Effective interest} = \frac{\text{Interest rate}}{\text{Proceeds (\%)}} = \frac{0.18}{0.62} = 29.0\%$$

(continued)

The amount of accounts receivable that should be factored to net the firm $250,000 is:

$$\frac{\$250,000}{1.0 - 0.16} = \frac{\$250,000}{0.84} = \$297,619$$

The total annual cost of the bank arrangement is:

Interest ($250,000 × 0.29)	$72,500
Additional cost of not using a factor:	
Credit costs ($1,000 × 12)	12,000
Uncollectible accounts ($297,619 × 0.03)	8,929
Total cost	$93,429

The effective interest rate associated with factoring accounts receivable is:

$$\text{Effective interest rate} = \frac{\text{Interest rate}}{\text{Proceeds (\%)}}$$

$$= \frac{12\%}{100\% - (12\% + 4\%)} = \frac{0.12}{0.84} = 14.3\%$$

The total annual cost of the factoring alternative is:

Interest ($250,000 × 0.143)	$35,750
Factoring ($297,619 × 0.04)	11,905
Total cost	$47,655

The factoring arrangement should be selected because it costs almost half as much as the bank loan.

Example 24.15

A company is examining a factoring arrangement. The company's sales are $2.7 million, accounts receivable turnover is nine times, and a 17 percent reserve on accounts receivable is required. The factor's commission charge on average accounts receivable payable at the point of receivable purchase is 2.0 percent. The factor's interest charge is 16 percent of receivables after subtracting the commission charge and reserve. The interest charge reduces the advance. The annual effective cost under the factoring arrangement is computed next.

$$\text{Average accounts receivable} = \frac{\text{Credit sales}}{\text{Turnover}}$$

$$= \frac{\$2,700,000}{9} = \$300,000$$

The company will receive the following amount by factoring its accounts receivable:

Average accounts receivable	$300,000
Less: Reserve ($300,000 × 0.17)	−51,000
Commission ($300,000 × 0.02)	−6,000
Net prior to interest	$243,000
Less: Interest ($243,000 × 16%/9)	4,320
Proceeds received	$238,680

The annual cost of the factoring arrangement is:

Commission ($300,000 × 0.02)	$ 6,000
Interest ($243,000 × (16%/9)	4,320
Cost each 40 days (360/9)	$ 10,320
Turnover	× 9
Total annual cost	$92,880

The annual effective cost under the factoring arrangement based on the amount received is:

$$\frac{\text{Annual cost}}{\text{Average amount received}} = \frac{\$92,880}{\$238,680} = 38.9\%$$

Should inventories be used for financing?

Inventory can be financed when the company has fully exhausted its borrowing capacity on receivables. Inventory financing requires marketable, nonperishable, and standardized merchandise with a fast turnover. The goods should not be susceptible to rapid obsolescence. Inventory is of better collateral if it can be marketed apart from the company's marketing organization. Inventory financing should take into account the price stability of the product and its selling costs.

The advance is high when marketable inventory exists. In general, the financing of raw materials and finished goods is about 75 percent of their value. The interest rate approximates 3 to 5 points over the prime interest rate.

The drawbacks to inventory financing include the high interest rate and the inventory restrictions.

The types of inventory financing include a floating (blanket) lien, warehouse receipt, and trust receipt. A *floating lien* has the creditor's security in the aggregate inventory rather than in its components. Even though the company sells and restocks, the lender's security interest continues. A *warehouse receipt* has the lender obtain an interest in the inventory stored at a public warehouse; however, the fixed costs of this arrangement are high. In a field warehouse arrangement, the warehouser provides a secured area at the company's location. The company has access to the goods but must account for them. In a trust *receipt* loan, the creditor has title to the goods but releases them to the company to sell on the creditor's behalf. As merchandise is sold, the company remits the funds to the lender. An example of trust receipt use is automobile dealer financing. The drawback of the trust receipt arrangement is that it only applies to specific items.

A collateral certificate can be issued by a third party to the lender guaranteeing the existence of pledged inventory. The advantage of a collateral certificate is flexibility because merchandise does not have to be segregated or possessed by the lender.

Example 24.16

The company wants to finance $500,000 of inventory. Funds are required for three months. A warehouse receipt loan may be taken at 16 percent with a 90 percent advance against the inventory's value. The warehousing cost is $4,000 for the three-month period. The cost of financing the inventory is:

Interest [0.16 × 0.90 × $500,000 × (3/12)]	$18,000
Warehousing cost	4,000
Total cost	$22,000

Example 24.17

The company experiences growth in operations but is having liquidity problems. Six large, financially strong companies are customers, responsible for 75 percent of sales. On the basis of the financial information for 20X1, should the company borrow on receivables or inventory? (See Exhibit 24.1.)

EXHIBIT 24.1 Balance Sheet

ASSETS		
Current assets		
Cash	$ 27,000	
Receivables	380,000	
Inventory (consisting of 55% of work in process)	320,000	
Total current assets		$727,000
Fixed assets		250,000
Total assets		$977,000
LIABILITIES AND STOCKHOLDERS' EQUITY		
Current liabilities		
Accounts payable	$260,000	
Loans payable	200,000	

(continued)

EXHIBIT 24.1 *(continued)*

Accrued expenses	35,000	
Total current liabilities		$495,000
Noncurrent liabilities		
Bonds payable		110,000
Total liabilities		$605,000
Stockholders' equity		
Common stock	$250,000	
Retained earnings	122,000	
Total stockholders' equity		372,000
Total liabilities and stockholders' equity		$977,000

Selected income statement information follows.

Sales	$1,800,000
Net income	130,000

Receivable financing should be used since a high percentage of sales are made to only six large financially strong companies. Receivables appear collectible. It is easier to control a few large customer accounts.

Inventory financing is not likely because of the high percentage of partially completed items. Lenders are reluctant to finance inventory when there is a large work-in-process balance because the goods will be difficult to process and sell by lenders.

What other assets can be used for financing?

Assets other than inventory and receivables, such as real estate, plant and equipment, cash surrender value of life insurance, and securities, can be used as collateral for short-term bank loans. Lenders are usually receptive to advance a high percentage of the market value of bonds. Furthermore, loans may be made based on a guaranty of a third party. Major features of short-term financing sources are presented in Exhibit 24.2.

How is short-term financing different from long-term financing?

Short-term financing is easier to obtain, has lower cost, and is more flexible than long-term financing. However, short-term financing makes the borrower susceptible to interest rate fluctuations, requires earlier refinancing, and is more difficult to repay. *Recommendation:* Use short-term financing as additional working capital, to finance short-lived assets, or as interim financing on long-term projects. Long-term financing is suitable to finance long-term assets or construction projects.

EXHIBIT 24.2 Summary of Major Short-Term Financing Sources

Type of Financing	Source	Cost or Terms	Features
A. Spontaneous Sources			
Accounts payable	Suppliers	No explicit cost, but there is an opportunity cost if cash discount for early payment is not taken. Companies should take advantage of discount offered.	Main source of short-term financing typically on terms of 0 to 120 days.
Accrued expenses	Employees and tax agencies	None	Expenses incurred but not yet paid (e.g., accrued wages payable, accrued taxes payable).
B. Unsecured Sources			
Bank loans			
Single-payment note	Commercial banks	Prime interest rate plus risk premium. Interest rate may be fixed or variable. Unsecured loans are less costly than secured loans.	Single-payment loan to satisfy a funds shortage to last a short time period.
Lines of credit	Commercial banks	Prime interest rate plus risk premium. Interest rate may be fixed or variable. A compensating balance typically is required. Line of credit must be cleaned up periodically.	Agreed-on borrowing limit for funds to satisfy seasonal needs.
Commercial paper	Commercial banks, insurance companies, other financial institutions, and other companies	A little less than prime interest rate.	Unsecured, short-term note of financially strong companies.
C. Secured Sources			
Accounts receivable as collateral			
Pledging	Commercial banks and finance companies	2–5% above prime plus fees (usually 2–3%). Low administrative costs. Advances typically ranging from 60–85%.	Qualified accounts receivable accounts serve as collateral. Upon collection of the account, borrower remits to lender. Customers are not notified of arrangement, with recourse, meaning that company bears risk of nonpayment.

(continued)

EXHIBIT 24.2 *(continued)*

Type of Financing	Source	Cost or Terms	Features
Factoring	Factors, commercial banks, and commercial finance companies	Typically a 2–3% discount from face value of factored receivables. Interest on advances of almost 3% over prime. Interest on surplus balances held by factor of about ½% per month. Costs with factoring are higher than with pledging.	Certain accounts receivable are sold on a discount basis without recourse. Customers are notified of arrangement. The factor provides more services than is the case with pledging.
Inventory collateral Floating liens	Commercial banks and commercial finance companies	About 4% above prime. Advance is about 40% of collateral value.	Collateral is the entire inventory. There should be a stable inventory with many inexpensive items.
Trust receipts (floor planning)	Commercial banks and commercial finance companies	About 3% above prime. Advances ranging from 80% to 100% of collateral value.	Collateral is specific inventory that is typically expensive. Borrower retains collateral. Borrower remits proceeds to lender upon sale of inventory.
Warehouse receipts	Commercial banks and commercial finance companies	About 4% above prime plus about a 2% warehouse fee. Advance of about 80% of collateral value.	Collateralized inventory is controlled by lender. Warehousing company issues a warehouse receipt held by lender. Warehousing company acts as lender's agent.

INTERMEDIATE-TERM FINANCING

Should you take out an intermediate-term bank loan?

Intermediate-term loans mature in more than one year. They are suitable when short-term unsecured loans are not, such as when a business is bought, capital assets are purchased, and long-term debt is retired. If a company wants to issue long-term debt or equity securities but market conditions are unfavorable, it may take an intermediate loan to bridge the gap until long-term financing can be arranged on favorable terms. A firm can employ extendable debt when there is a continuing financing need. This reduces the time and cost of many debt issuances.

The interest rate on an intermediate-term loan is usually more than on a short-term loan because of the longer maturity. The interest rate may be either fixed or variable (e.g., based on changes in the prime interest rate). The cost of an intermediate-term loan depends on the amount of the loan and the company's financial standing.

Ordinary intermediate-term loans are due in periodic equal installments except for the last payment, which may be higher (referred to as a balloon payment). The schedule of loan payments should be based on the company's cash flow status. The periodic payment equals:

$$\text{Periodic payment} = \frac{\text{Amount of loan}}{\text{Present value factor}}$$

Example 24.18

The company contracts to repay a term loan in five equal year-end installments. The amount of the loan is $150,000 and the interest rate is 10 percent. The payment each year is:

$$\frac{\$150,000}{3.7908} = \$39,569.48$$

where 3.7908 is the present value of an annuity for five years at 10%
The total interest on the loan is:

Total payments (5 × $39,569.48)	$ 197,847.40
Principal	150,000.00
Interest	$ 47,847.40

Example 24.19

The company takes out a term loan in 20 year-end annual installments of $2,000 each. The interest rate is 12 percent. The amount of the loan is:

$$\$2,000 = \frac{\text{Amount of loan}}{7.4694}$$

where 7.4694 is the present value of an annuity for 20 years at 12%

$$\text{Amount of loan} = \$2,000 \times 7.4694 = \$14,939.80$$

The amortization schedule for the first two years is:

Year	Payment	Interest[a]	Principal	Balance
0				$14,938.80
1	$2,000	$1,792.66	$207.34	14,731.46
2	2,000	1,767.78	232.22	14,499.24

[a] 12% times the balance of the loan at the beginning of the year.

What restrictions does the company face?

Restrictive provisions that the lender may insist on in an intermediate-term loan are:

- *General provisions used in most agreements that vary based on the company's financial position.* Examples are current ratio and debt–equity ratio.
- *Routine (uniform) provisions that are used universally in most agreements.* Examples are the payment of taxes and the maintenance of insurance to ensure maximum lender protection.
- *Specific provisions tailored to a particular situation.* Examples are the placing of limits on future loans and the carrying of adequate life insurance for executives.

What are the advantages and disadvantages of intermediate-term loans?

The advantages of intermediate-term loans are:

- Flexibility in that the terms may be changed as the company's financing requirements change.
- Financial information is kept confidential because there is no public issuance.
- The loan may be arranged quickly compared to a public offering.
- The possible nonrenewal of a short-term loan is avoided.
- There are no public flotation costs.

  The disadvantages of intermediate-term loans are:

- Collateral and possible restrictive covenants are required, as opposed to none for commercial paper and unsecured short-term bank loans.
- Budgets and financial statements may have to be submitted routinely to the lender.
- The bank sometimes asks for sweeteners, such as stock warrants or a share of the profits.

What is a revolving credit agreement?

Revolving credit, typically used for seasonal financing, may have a three-year maturity, but the notes are short term, usually 90 days. The advantages of revolving credit are flexibility and ready availability. The company may renew a loan or enter into additional financing up to a maximum amount. A revolving credit agreement usually has fewer restrictions than a line of credit, but there is a slightly higher interest rate.

How can an insurance company term loan be used?

Insurance companies and other institutional lenders may extend intermediate-term loans. Insurance companies usually accept loan maturity dates exceeding 10 years, but their rate of interest is often higher than that of bank loans. Insurance companies do not require compensating balances, but usually there is a prepayment penalty, which is often not the case with a bank loan. A company may take out an insurance company loan when it wants a longer maturity period.

How does equipment financing work?

Equipment can serve as security for a loan. An advance is made against the market value of the equipment. The more marketable the equipment is, the higher the advance will be. The cost of selling the equipment is also relevant. The repayment schedule is structured so that the market value of the equipment at any time exceeds the unpaid loan principal.

Equipment financing can be obtained from banks, finance companies, and equipment manufacturers. Equipment loans may be collateralized by a chattel mortgage or a conditional sales contract. A *chattel mortgage* is a lien on property except for real estate. In a *conditional sales contract*, the seller of the equipment keeps title to it until the buyer has met the terms; otherwise the seller repossesses the equipment. The buyer makes periodic payments over a given time period. A conditional sales contract is often used by a small company with poor credit standing.

Equipment trust certificates can be issued to finance the acquisition of readily salable equipment. Preferably, the equipment should be general purpose and movable. A trust is formed to buy the equipment and lease it to the user. The trust issues the certificates to finance about 80 percent of the purchase price and holds title to the equipment until all the certificates have been repaid at which time the title passes to the lessee.

Are you better off leasing?

The lessee uses property in exchange for making rental payments. The advantages of leasing include:

- Immediate cash payment is not required.
- It provides for *temporary* equipment need and flexibility in operations.
- A purchase option may exist, allowing the company to obtain the property at a bargain price at the termination date of the lease. This provides the flexibility to make the purchase decision based on the value of the property at the expiration date.
- The lessor's service capability is used.
- There are usually fewer financing restrictions (e.g., limitations on dividends) by the lessor compared to a lender.
- The obligation for future rental payment does not have to be reported as a liability on the balance sheet for an operating lease.
- It permits the company, in effect, to depreciate land, which is not allowed if land is bought.
- In bankruptcy or reorganization, the maximum claim of lessors is three years of rental payments. With debt, creditors have a claim for the entire balance.
- It eliminates equipment disposal.

Leasing may be better than buying when a company cannot use all of the tax deductions and tax credits associated with the assets in a timely fashion.

The drawbacks to leasing are:

▪ Leasing has a higher cost than if the asset is bought. The lessee is not building equity.

▪ The interest cost of leasing is usually higher than the interest cost on debt.

▪ If the property reverts to the lessor at the end of the lease, the lessee must either sign a new lease or buy the property at higher current prices. Furthermore, the lessor realizes the salvage value of the property.

▪ The lessor may have to keep property no longer desired (i.e., obsolete equipment).

▪ Improvements cannot be made to the leased property without the lessor's consent.

Example 24.20

The company enters into a lease for a $100,000 machine. It is to make 10 equal annual payments at year-end. The interest rate on the lease is 14 percent. The periodic payment equals:

$$\frac{\$100,000}{5.2161} = \$19,171$$

where 5.2161 is the present value of an ordinary annuity factor for $n = 10$, $i = 14\%$ (from Table A.4)

Example 24.21

Assume the same facts as in Example 24.20, except that now the annual payments are to be made at the beginning of each year. The periodic payment equals:

Year	Factor
0	1.0
1–9	4.9464
	5.9464

$$\frac{100,000}{5.9464} = \$16,817$$

The interest rate on a lease can be computed. Divide the value of the leased property by the annual payment to obtain the factor, then use the factor to find the interest rate with the aid of an annuity table.

Example 24.22

The company leased $300,000 of property and is to make equal annual payments at year-end of $40,000 for 11 years. The interest rate on the lease agreement is:

$$\frac{\$300,000}{\$40,000} = 7.5$$

Going to the present value of annuity table and looking across 11 years to a factor nearest to 7.5, we find 7.4987 at a 7 percent interest rate. Thus, the interest rate in the lease agreement is 7 percent.

The capitalized value of a lease can be found by dividing the annual lease payment by an appropriate present value of annuity factor.

Example 24.23

Property is to be leased for eight years at an annual rental payment of $140,000 payable at the beginning of each year. The capitalization rate is 12 percent. The capitalized value of the lease is:

$$\frac{\text{Annual lease payment}}{\text{Present value factor}} = \frac{\$140,000}{1+4.5638} = \$25,163$$

Is it cheaper to buy or lease an asset?

A decision may have to be made whether it is cheaper to buy an asset or lease it. Present value analysis may be used for this purpose (see Chapter 14).

CHAPTER TWENTY-FIVE

Long-Term Financing

L ONG-TERM FINANCING IS for more than five years. The CFO should be familiar with the what, why, and how of equity and long-term debt financing. Equity financing consists of issuing preferred stock and common stock, whereas long-term debt financing consists primarily of issuing bonds. Long-term financing is often used to finance long-lived assets (e.g., plant) or construction projects. A capital-intensive business will have greater reliance on long-term debt and equity. This chapter presents a comparison of public versus private placement of securities and discusses the advantages and disadvantages of issuing long-term debt, preferred stock, and common stock as well as the financing strategy most appropriate under a set of circumstances. The financing policies should be in response to the overall strategic direction of the company.

A company's mix of long-term funds is referred to as the *capital structure*. The ideal capital structure maximizes the total value of the company and minimizes the overall cost of capital. The formulation of an appropriate capital structure takes into account the nature of the business and industry, the corporate business plan, the current and historical capital structure, and the planned growth rate.

Should securities be publicly or privately placed?

Equity and debt securities may be issued either publicly or privately. A consideration in determining whether to issue securities to the public or privately is the type and amount of required financing.

In a public issuance, the shares are bought by the general public. In a private placement, the company issues securities directly to either one or a few large institutional investors.

Private placement has these advantages relative to a public issuance:

- The flotation cost is less. *Flotation cost* is the expense of registering and selling the stock issue. The flotation cost for common stock exceeds that for preferred stock. The flotation cost expressed as a percentage of gross proceeds is higher for smaller issues than for larger ones.
- It avoids Securities and Exchange Commission filing requirements.
- It avoids the disclosure of information to the public.
- There is less time involved in obtaining funds.
- There is greater flexibility.
  Private placement has these drawbacks relative to a public issuance:
- There is a higher interest rate due to less liquidity of a debt issue relative to public issuance.
- There is typically a shorter maturity period than for a public issue.
- It is more difficult to obtain significant amounts of money privately than publicly.
- Large investors typically use stringent credit standards, which require the company to be in strong financial condition. In addition, there are more restrictive terms.
- Large institutional investors may watch the company's activities more closely than smaller investors in a public issue.
- Large institutional investors are more capable of obtaining voting control of the company.

TYPES OF LONG-TERM DEBT AND WHEN EACH SHOULD BE USED

We now discuss the characteristics, advantages, and disadvantages of long-term debt financing. In addition to the various types of debt instruments, the circumstances in which a particular type of debt is most appropriate are considered. Sources of long-term debt include mortgages and bonds. The amount of debt a company may have depends largely on its available collateral. Bond refunding is also discussed.

What should you know about mortgages?

Mortgages are notes payable that have as collateral real assets and require periodic payments. Mortgages can be undertaken to finance the purchase of assets, construction of plant, and modernization of facilities. The bank will require that the value of the property exceed the mortgage on that property. Most mortgage loans are for between 70 percent and 90 percent of the value of the collateral. Mortgages can be obtained from a financial institution, typically a bank. It is easier to obtain mortgage loans for multiple-use real assets than for single-use ones.

There are two types of mortgages: a *senior* mortgage, which has first claim on assets and earnings, and a *junior* mortgage, which has a subordinate lien.

A mortgage may have a closed-end provision that prevents the company from issuing additional debt of the same priority against the specific property. If the mortgage is open-ended, the company can issue additional first-mortgage bonds against the property.

Mortgages have a number of advantages, including favorable interest rates, less financing restrictions, extended maturity date, and availability. A drawback is the collateral requirement.

When should bonds be issued?

The *indenture* describes the features of the bond issue. It may provide for certain restrictions on the company, such as a limitation on dividends and minimum working capital requirements. If a provision of the indenture is violated, the bonds are in default. The indenture may have a negative pledge clause, which precludes the issuance of new debt taking priority over existing debt. The clause can apply to currently held and future assets.

The price of a bond depends on several factors, such as maturity date, interest rate, and collateral. In selecting a maturity date, consider the debt repayment schedule, which should not be overloaded at one time. Furthermore, if the company's credit rating is expected to improve in the near term, short-term debt should be issued because the company will be able to refinance at a lower interest rate.

Bond prices and market interest rates are inversely related. For example, as market interest rates increase, the price of the existing bond falls because investors can invest in new bonds paying higher interest rates.

What types of bonds can be issued?

The various types of bonds are:

- *Debentures.* Because debentures are unsecured (no collateral) debt, they can be issued only by large, financially strong companies with excellent credit ratings.
- *Subordinated debentures.* The claims of the holders of these bonds are subordinated to those of senior creditors. Debt having a prior claim over the subordinated debentures is set forth in the bond indenture. Typically, in liquidation, subordinated debentures come after short-term debt.
- *Mortgage bonds.* These are bonds secured by real assets. The first-mortgage claim must be met before a distribution is made to a second-mortgage claim. There may be several mortgages for the same property (e.g., building).
- *Collateral trust bonds.* The collateral for these bonds is the company's security investments in other companies (bonds or stocks), which are given to a trustee for safekeeping.
- *Convertible bonds.* These may be converted to stock at a later date based on a specified conversion ratio. The *conversion ratio* equals the par value of the convertible security divided by the conversion price. Convertible bonds are typically issued in the form of subordinated debentures. Convertible bonds are more marketable and are typically issued at a lower interest rate than are regular bonds because they offer the conversion right to common stock. Of course, if bonds are converted to stock, debt repayment is not involved. A convertible bond is a quasi-equity security because its market value is tied to its value if converted rather than as a bond.

- *Income bonds.* These bonds pay interest only if there is a profit. The interest may be cumulative or noncumulative. If cumulative, the interest accumulates regardless of earnings and, if bypassed, must be paid in a later year when adequate earnings exist. Income bonds are appropriate for companies with large fixed capital investments and large fluctuations in earnings or for emerging companies with the expectation of low earnings in the early years.
- *Guaranteed bonds.* These are debt issued by one party with payment guaranteed by another.
- *Serial bonds.* A portion of these bonds comes due each year. At the time serial bonds are issued, a schedule shows the yields, interest rates, and prices for each maturity. The interest rate on the shorter maturities is lower than the interest rate on the longer maturities because less uncertainty exists regarding the future.
- *Deep discount bonds.* These bonds have very low interest rates and thus are issued at substantial discounts from face value. The return to the holder comes primarily from appreciation in price rather than from interest payments. The bonds are volatile in price. Since these bonds are typically callable at par, the refunding flexibility of the issuer is reduced.
- *Zero coupon bonds.* These bonds do not provide for interest. The return to the holder is in the form of appreciation in price. Lower interest rates may be available for zero coupon bonds (and deep discount bonds) because of the lack of callability and possible foreign tax laws.
- *Variable rate bonds.* The interest rates on the bonds are adjusted periodically to changes in money market conditions (e.g., prime interest rate). These bonds are popular when there is uncertainty of future interest rates and inflation.
- *Deferred interest bonds.* These are bonds in which the periodic interest payments are fully or partially deferred in the first few years (usually three to seven years). In another version, the bond payments lower coupons during the deferred years and higher (stepped-up) coupons in later years. They may be used in a buyout or financial restructuring arrangement. The deferred period allows the issuer to improve operations, sell off assets, and refinance. The bonds typically are subordinated, have a call feature, and provide a conversion option. In deciding whether this type of bond is suitable, the issuer should consider anticipated future interest rates, current debt position, and expected future cash flows.
- *Eurobonds.* These bonds are issued outside the country in whose currency the bonds are denominated. Eurobonds cannot be issued to U.S. investors, only to foreign investors, because they are not registered with the Securities and Exchange Commission. The bonds are typically in bearer form. *Tip:* Check to see if the Eurodollar market will give the company a lower-cost option than the U.S. market. These bonds usually can be issued only by high-quality borrowers.

Exhibit 25.1 summarizes the characteristics and priority claims of bonds.

If the company is small and emerging with an unproven track record, it may have to issue junk bonds (high-yielding risky bonds).

EXHIBIT 25.1 Summary of Characteristics and Priority Claims of Bonds

Bond Type	Characteristics	Priority of Lender's Claim
Debentures	Available only to financially strong companies. Convertible bonds are typically debentures.	General creditor.
Subordinated debentures	Comes after senior debt holders.	General creditor.
Mortgage bonds	Collateral is real property or buildings.	Paid from proceeds from sale of the mortgaged assets. If any deficiency exists, general creditor status applies.
Collateral trust bonds	Secured by stock and (or) bonds owned by issuer. Collateral value is usually 30% more than bond value.	Paid from proceeds of stock and (or) bond that is collateralized. If there is a deficiency, general creditor status applies.
Income bonds	Interest is paid only if there is net income. Often issued when company is in reorganization because of financial problems.	General creditor.
Deep discount (and zero coupon) bonds	Issued at very low or no (zero) coupon rates. Issued at prices significantly below face value. Usually callable at par value.	Unsecured or secured status may apply, depending on issue features.
Variable rate bonds	Coupon rate changes within limits based on changes in money or capital market rates. Appropriate when uncertainty exists regarding inflation and future interest rates. Because of automatic adjustment to changing market conditions, these bonds sell near face value.	Unsecured or secured status may apply, depending on issue features.

What are the advantages and disadvantages of debt financing?

The advantages of issuing long-term debt include:

- Interest is tax-deductible but dividends are not.
- Bondholders do not share in superior earnings of the company.
- The repayment of debt is in cheaper dollars during inflation.
- There is no dilution of company control.
- Financing flexibility can be accomplished by including a call provision in the bond indenture that allows the company to retire the debt before maturity.
- It may safeguard the company's financial stability (e.g., in tight money markets when short-term loans are not available).

The disadvantages of issuing long-term debt include:

- Interest must be paid even if profits are low or there are losses.
- Debt must be repaid at maturity.
- Higher debt indicates financial risk, which may increase the interest cost.

- Indenture provisions may place stringent restrictions on the company.
- Overcommitments may arise because of forecasting errors.

How does issuing debt compare with issuing equity securities?

The advantages of issuing debt instead of equity are:

- Interest is tax deductible whereas dividends are not.
- During inflation the payback will be in cheaper dollars.
- There is no dilution of voting control.
- Flexibility in financing is possible by including a call provision in the bond indenture.

The disadvantages of issuing debt rather than equity are:

- Interest and principal must be paid regardless of the company's cash flow.
- Indenture restrictions often exist.

The mixture of long-term debt to equity depends on company policy, credit availability, and after-tax cost of financing. When debt is high, the company should minimize other corporate risks (e.g., product risk). The amount of leverage in the capital structure depends on the company's inclination toward risk and the debt levels at competing companies.

When should long-term debt be issued?

Debt financing is appropriate when:

- The interest rate on debt is below the rate of return earned on the money borrowed. By using other people's money, corporate after-tax profit will increase.
- There is stability in revenue and earnings so that the company will be able to pay interest and principal in both good and bad years. However, cyclicality should not prevent a company from having any debt. The important thing is to accumulate no more interest and principal obligations than you can handle in bad times.
- The profit margin is satisfactory so that earnings are sufficient to meet debt obligations.
- The company's cash flow and liquidity are adequate.
- The debt–equity ratio is low so the company can absorb additional obligations.
- There is a low risk level.
- Stock prices are depressed so that it is not advisable to issue common stock at the current time.
- There is a concern that if common stock was issued, greater control might fall in the wrong hands.
- The company is mature.
- Inflation is expected so that debt can be paid back in cheaper dollars.
- There is a lack of competition (such as barriers to entry into the industry).
- The company is growing.
- There is a high tax rate, making the deductibility of interest attractive.

- Bond indenture restrictions are not excessive.
- Money market trends are favorable to obtain financing.

What if there are financing problems?

Your company may want to refinance short-term debt on a long-term basis (such as by extending the maturity dates of loans) to alleviate current liquidity and cash flow problems.

As the default risk of your company becomes higher, so will the interest rate to compensate for the greater risk.

The threat of financial distress or even bankruptcy is the ultimate limitation on leverage. Beyond a debt limit, the tax savings on interest expense will be offset by an increased interest rate demanded by creditors for the greater risk. Excessive debt may lower the market price of stock because of the greater risk associated with it.

Should bonds be refunded?

An issuer may refund bonds prior to maturity either by issuing a serial bond or by exercising a call privilege on a straight bond. The issuance of serial bonds permits the company to refund the debt over the life of the issue. A call feature allows the company to retire a bond before the expiration date.

If future interest rates are expected to decrease, a call provision is advisable since the company can buy back the higher-interest bond and issue a lower-interest bond. The timing for the refunding depends on expected future interest rates. A call price usually is established above the face value of the bond. The resulting call premium equals the difference between the call price and the maturity value. The company pays the premium to the bondholder in order to acquire the outstanding bonds before the maturity date. The call premium is typically equal to one year's interest if the bond is called in the first year, and it declines at a constant rate each subsequent year.

A callable bond usually has a lower offering price and will be issued at an interest rate higher than one without the call provision.

Example 25.1

Your company has a $20 million, 10 percent bond issue outstanding that has 10 years to maturity. The call premium is 7 percent of face value. The company can issue 10-year bonds in the amount of $20 million at an 8 percent interest rate. The flotation costs of the new issue are $600,000.

There should be refunding of the original bond issue as shown next:

Old interest payments ($20,000,000 × 0.10)	$2,000,000
New interest payments ($20,000,000 × 0.08)	1,600,000
Annual savings	$400,000
Call premium ($20,000,000 × 0.07)	$1,400,000
Flotation cost	600,000
Total cost	$2,000,000

(continued)

Year	Calculation	Present Value
0	−$2,000,000 × 1	−$2,000,000
1–10	$400,000 × 6.71[a]	2,684,000
Net present value		$684,000

[a] Present value of annuity factor for $i = 8\%$, $n = 10$.

Example 25.2

Your company is considering calling a $10 million, 20-year bond that was issued 5 years ago at a nominal interest rate of 10 percent. The call price on the bonds is 105. The bonds were initially sold at 90. The discount on bonds payable at the time of sale was, therefore, $1 million, and the net proceeds received were $9 million. The initial flotation cost was $100,000. The firm is considering issuing $10 million, 8 percent, 15-year bonds and using the net proceeds to retire the old bonds. The new bonds will be issued at face value. The flotation cost for the new issue is $150,000. The company's tax rate is 46 percent. The after-tax cost of new debt, ignoring flotation costs, is 4.32 percent (8% × 54%). With the flotation cost, the after-tax cost of new debt is estimated at 5 percent. There is an overlap period of three months in which interest must be paid on the old and new bonds.

The initial cash outlay is:

Cost to call old bonds ($10,000,000 × 105%)	$10,500,000
Cost to issue new bond	150,000
Interest on old bonds for overlap period	
($10,000,000 × 10% × 3/12)	250,000
Initial cash outlay	$10,900,000

The initial cash inflow is:

Proceeds from selling new bond		$10,000,000
Tax-deductible items		
Call premium	$500,000	
Unamortized discount ($1,000,000 × 15/20)	750,000	
Overlap in interest ($10,000,000 × 10% × 3/12)	250,000	
Unamortized issue cost of old bond ($100,000 × 15/20)	75,000	
Total tax-deductible items	$ 1,575,000	
Tax rate	× 0.46	

Tax savings		724,500
Initial cash inflow		$ 10,724,500

The *net* initial cash outlay is therefore:

Initial cash outlay	$ 10,900,000
Initial cash inflow	10,724,500
Net initial cash outlay	$175,500

The annual cash flow for the old bond is:

Interest (10% × $10,000,000)		$1,000,000
Less: Tax-deductible items		
Interest	$ 1,000,000	
Amortization of discount ($1,000,000/20 years)	50,000	
Amortization of issue cost ($100,000/20 years)	5,000	
Total tax-deductible items	$1,055,000	
Tax rate	× 0.46	
Tax savings		485,300
Annual cash outflow with old bond		$514,700

The annual cash flow for the new bond is:

Interest		$800,000
Less: Tax-deductible items		
Interest	$800,000	
Amortization of issue cost ($150,000/15 years)	10,000	
Total tax-deductible items	$810,000	
Tax rate	× 0.46	
Tax savings		372,600
Annual cash outflow with new bond		$427,400

The net annual cash savings with the new bond compared to the old bond is:

Annual cash outflow with old bond	$514,700
Annual cash outflow with new bond	427,400
Net annual cash savings	$87,300

The net present value associated with the refunding is:

	Calculation	Present Value
Year 0	−$175,500 × 1	−$175,500
Years 1–15	$87,300 × 10.38[a]	+906,174
Net present value		$730,674

[a] Present value of annuity factor for i = 5%, n = 15.

Since a positive net present value exists, the old bond should be refunded.

What are variable notes?

Variable coupon renewable notes are long-term financing instruments with the potential of significant cost savings. They are usually for 50 years and contain a put feature allowing note holders to accept a reduced coupon spread for the last three payments. The coupon is changed weekly based on a spread over the rates for three-month Treasury bills. Interest is paid quarterly. The issuer may use this as a long-term financing source while paying short-term interest rates.

 ISSUANCE OF EQUITY SECURITIES

The sources of equity financing consist of preferred stock and common stock. The advantages and disadvantages of issuing preferred and common are discussed, along with the various circumstances in which either financing source is most suited. Stock rights are also described.

When should preferred stock be issued?

Preferred stock is a hybrid of bonds and common stock. Preferred stock comes after debt but before common stock in liquidation and in the distribution of earnings. Preferred stock may be issued when the cost of common stock is high. The best time to issue preferred stock is when the company has excessive debt and an issue of common stock might cause control problems. Preferred stock is a more expensive way to raise funds than a bond issue because the dividend payment is not tax deductible.

Preferred stock may be cumulative or noncumulative. *Cumulative* preferred stock means that if any prior years' dividend payments have been missed, they must be paid before dividends can be paid to common stockholders. If preferred dividends are in arrears for a long time, the company may find it difficult to resume its dividend payments to common stockholders. With *noncumulative* preferred stock, the company need not pay missed preferred dividends. Preferred stock dividends are limited to the rate specified, which is based on the total par value of the outstanding shares. Most preferred stock is cumulative.

Participating preferred stock means that if declared dividends exceed the amount typically given to preferred stockholders and common stockholders, the preferred and common stockholders will participate in the excess dividends. Unless stated otherwise, the distribution of the excess dividends will be based on the relative total par values. Nonparticipating preferred stock does *not* participate with common stock in excess dividends. Most preferred stock is nonparticipating.

Preferred stock may be callable. The call provision is beneficial when interest rates decline because the company has the option of discontinuing payment of dividends at a rate that has become excessive by buying back preferred stock that was issued when bond interest rates were high. Unlike bonds, preferred stock *rarely* has a maturity date. However, if preferred stock has a sinking fund provision, this establishes a maturity date for repayment.

There are different types of preferred stock. Limited life preferred stock has a maturity date or can be redeemed at the holder's option. Perpetual preferred stock automatically converts to common stock at a specified date. There is also preferred stock with floating rate dividends so as to keep the preferred stock at par by changing the dividend rate.

The cost of preferred stock typically is tied to changes in interest rates. The cost of preferred stock will most likely be low when interest rates are low. When the cost of common stock is high, preferred stock issuance may be at a lower cost.

What are the advantages and disadvantages of issuing preferred stock?

A preferred stock issue has these advantages:

- Preferred dividends do not have to be paid (important in times of financial problems), whereas interest on debt must be paid.
- Preferred stockholders cannot force the company into bankruptcy.
- Preferred shareholders do not share in unusually high earnings because the common stockholders are the real owners of the business.
- A growth company can earn better profits for its original owners by issuing preferred stock having a fixed dividend rate than by issuing common stock.
- Preferred stock issuance does not dilute the ownership interest of common stockholders in terms of earnings participation and voting rights.
- The company does not have to use assets, as security as might be the case with issuing debt.
- There is an improvement in the debt–equity ratio.
  A preferred stock issue has these disadvantages:
- Preferred stock requires a higher yield than bonds because of increased risk.
- Preferred dividends are not deductible on the tax return.
- There are higher flotation costs than with bonds.

How does preferred stock compare to bonds and common stock?

Preferred stock has these advantages over bonds:

- The company can omit a dividend readily
- No maturity date exists.
- No sinking fund is required.

Disadvantages of preferred stock issuance compared to bonds are:

- It requires a higher yield than debt because it is more risky to the holder.
- Dividends are not tax deductible.

The advantages of preferred stock over common stock are that preferred stock avoids both dilution of control and the equal participation in profits that are afforded to common stockholders.

When is the issuance of common stock advised?

Common stock is the residual equity ownership in the business. Common stockholders have voting power but come after preferred stockholders in receiving dividends and in liquidation. Common stock does not involve fixed charges, maturity dates, or sinking fund requirements.

In timing a public issuance of common stock, follow this guidance:

- Do not offer shares near the expiration date for options on the company's stock since the option related transaction may impact share price.
- Offer higher-yielding common stock just prior to the ex-dividend date to attract investors.
- Issue common stock when there is little competition of share issuance by other companies in the industry.
- Issue shares in bull markets and refrain from issuing them in bear markets.

How is market price of stock estimated?

The estimated market price per share for a company can be determined as:

$$\frac{\text{Expected dividend}}{\text{Cost of capital} - \text{Growth rate in dividends}}$$

Example 25.3

Your company expected the dividend for the year to be $10 a share. The cost of capital is 13 percent. The growth rate in dividends is expected to be constant at 8 percent. The price per share is:

$$\text{Price per share} = \frac{\text{Expected dividend}}{\text{Cost of capital} - \text{Growth rate in dividends}}$$

$$= \frac{\$10}{0.13 - 0.08 = 0.05} = \$200$$

The price/earnings (P/E) ratio is another way to price the share of stock of a company.

Example 25.4

Your company's earnings per share is $7. It is expected that the company's stock should sell at eight times its earnings. The market price per share is therefore:

P/E = Market price per share/Earnings per share
Market price per share = P/E multiple × Earnings per share
= 8 × $7 = $56

You may want to determine the market value of your company's stock. There are a number of ways to do this.

Example 25.5

Assuming an indefinite stream of future dividends of $300,000 and a required return rate of 14 percent, the market value of the stock equals:

$$\text{Market value} = \frac{\text{Expected dividends}}{\text{Rate of return}}$$

$$= \frac{\$300,000}{0.14} = 2,142,857$$

If there are 200,000 shares, the market price per share is:

$$\text{Market value} = \frac{\$2,142,857}{200,000} = \$10.71$$

Example 25.6

Your company is considering a public issue of its securities. The average price/earnings multiple in the industry is 15. The company's earnings are $400,000. There will be 100,000 shares outstanding after the issuance of the stock. The expected price per share is:

$$\text{Total market value} = \text{Net income} \times \text{P/E multiple}$$
$$= \$400,000 \times 15 = \$6,000$$

$$\text{Price per share} = \frac{\text{Market value}}{\text{Shares}}$$

$$= \frac{\$6,000,000}{100,000} = \$60$$

Example 25.7

Your company issues 400,000 new shares of common stock to current stockholders at a $25 price per share. The price per share before the new issue was $29. Currently there are 500,000 outstanding shares. The expected price per share after the new issue is:

Value of outstanding shares (500,000 × $29)	$14,500,000
Value of newly issued shares (400,000 × $25)	10,000,000
Value of entire issue	$24,500,000

$$\text{Value per share} = \frac{\text{Value of entire share}}{\text{Total number of shares}}$$

$$= \frac{\$24,500,00}{900,000} = \$27.22$$

Example 25.8

Your company is considering constructing a new plant. The firm usually distributes all its earnings in dividends. Capital expansion has been financed through the issue of common stock. The firm has no preferred stock or debt.

These expectations exist:

Net income	$23,000,000
Shares outstanding	5,000,000
Construction cost of new plant	$16,000,000

Incremental annual earnings expected because of the new plant is $2 million. The rate of return expected by stockholders is 12 percent per annum. The total market value of the firm if the plant is financed through the issuance of common stock is:

$$\frac{\text{Total net income}}{\text{Rate of return}} = \frac{\$25,000,000}{0.12} = \$208,330,000$$

The CFO may want to compute the company's P/E ratio and required rate of return.

Example 25.9

Your company has experienced an 8 percent growth rate in earnings and dividends. Next year it anticipates earnings per share of $4.00 and dividends per share of $2.50. The company will be having its first public issue of common stock. The stock will be issued at $50.00 per share.

The price-earnings ratio is:

$$\frac{\text{Market price per share}}{\text{Earnings per share}} = \frac{\$50}{\$4} = 12.5 \text{ Times}$$

The required rate of return on the stock is:

$$\frac{\text{Dividends per share}}{\text{Market price per share}} + \text{Growth rate in dividends}$$

$$\frac{\$2.50}{\$50.00} + 0.08 = 0.13$$

If your company has *significant* debt, it would be better off financing with an equity issue to lower overall financial risk.

What are the advantages and disadvantages of issuing common stock?

The issuance of common stock has these advantages:

- There is no requirement to pay fixed charges, such as interest or dividends.
- There is no repayment date or sinking fund stipulation.
- A common stock issue improves the company's credit rating compared to the issuance of debt. For example, the debt–equity ratio is improved.

The issuance of common stock has these disadvantages:

- Dividends are not tax deductible.
- Ownership interest is diluted. The additional voting rights could vote to take control away from the current ownership group.
- Earnings and dividends are spread over more shares outstanding.
- The flotation costs of a common stock issue are higher than with preferred stock and debt financing.

It is less costly to finance operations from internally generated funds because financing out of retained earnings involves no flotation costs. Retained earnings can be used as equity funding if the company believes its stock price is lower than the real value of its assets. Retained earnings is also preferred if transaction costs are high for external financing.

The company can use dividend reinvestment plans and employee stock option plans to raise financing and thus avoid issuance costs and the market effect of a public offering.

A summary comparison of bonds and common stocks is presented in Exhibit 25.2.

EXHIBIT 25.2 Summary Comparison of Bonds and Common Stock

Bonds	Common Stock
Bondholders are creditors.	Stockholders are owners.
No voting rights exist.	Voting rights exist.
There is a maturity date.	There is no maturity date.
Bondholders have prior claims on profits and assets in bankruptcy.	Stockholders have residual claims on profits and assets in bankruptcy.
Interest payments represent fixed charges.	Dividend payments do not constitute fixed charges.
Interest payments are deductible on the tax return.	There is no tax deductibility for dividend payments.
The rate of return required by bondholders is typically lower than what stockholders require.	The rate of return required by stockholders is typically greater than what bondholders require.

Example 25.10

Your company has 500,000 shares of common stock outstanding and is planning to issue another 100,000 shares through stock rights. Each current stockholder will receive one right per share. Each right permits the stockholder to buy one-fifth of a share of new common stock (100,000 shares/500,000 shares). Hence, five rights are needed to buy one share of stock. A shareholder holding 10,000 shares would therefore be able to buy 2,000 new shares (10,000 × 1/5). By exercising his or her right, the stockholder would now have a total of 12,000 shares, representing a 2 percent interest (12,000/600,000) in the total shares outstanding. This is the same 2 percent ownership (10,000/500,000) the stockholder held prior to the rights offering.

How many rights are needed to buy one share?

Once the subscription price has been decided on, the number of rights needed to purchase a share of stock can be determined as:

$$\text{Shares to be sold} = \frac{\text{Amount of funds to be obtained}}{\text{Subscription price}}$$

The number of rights needed to acquire one share equals:

$$\text{Rights per share} = \frac{\text{Total shares outstanding}}{\text{Shares to be sold}}$$

Example 25.11

Your company wants to obtain $800,000 by a rights offering. There are presently 100,000 shares outstanding. The subscription price is $40 a share. The shares to be sold equal:

$$\text{Shares to be sold} = \frac{\text{Amount of funds to be obtained}}{\text{Subscription price}}$$

$$= \frac{\$800,000}{\$40} = 20,000 \text{ shares}$$

The number of rights needed to acquire one share equals:

$$\text{Right per share} = \frac{\text{Total shares outstanding}}{\text{Shares to be sold}}$$

$$= \frac{100,000}{20,000} = 5$$

> **Note**
>
> Thus, five rights will be required to buy each new share at $40. Each right enables the holder to buy one-fifth of a share of stock. ■

How do you determine what a right is worth?

The value of a right should, theoretically, be the same whether the stock is selling with rights on or with ex rights (no right attached).

When stock is selling with rights on, the value of a right equals:

$$\frac{\text{Market value of stock with rights on} - \text{Subscription price}}{\text{Number of rights needed to buy one share} + 1}$$

Example 25.12

Your company's common stock sells for $55 a share with rights on. Each stock-holder is given the right to buy one new share at $35 for every four shares held. The value of each right is:

$$\frac{\$55 - \$35}{4 + 1} = \frac{\$20}{5} = \$4$$

When stock is traded ex rights, the market price is expected to decline by the value of the right. The market value of stock trading ex rights should theoretically equal:

$$\text{Market value of stock with rights on} - \text{Value of a right when stock is selling rights on}$$

The value of a right when stock is selling ex rights equals:

$$\frac{\text{Market value of shock trading ex rights} - \text{Subscription price}}{\text{Number of rights needed to buy one new share}}$$

Example 25.13

Assuming the same information as in Example 25.12, the value of the company's stock trading ex rights should equal:

Market value of stock with rights on – value of a right when stock is selling rights on:

$$\$55 - \$4 = \$51$$

(continued)

The value of a right when stock is selling ex rights is therefore:

$$\frac{\text{Market value of stock trading ex rights} - \text{Subscription price}}{\text{Number of rights needed to buy one new share}}$$

$$\frac{\$51 - \$35}{4} = \frac{\$16}{4} = \$4$$

Note

The theoretical value of the right is identical when the stock is selling rights on or ex rights. ■

What are stock rights?

Stock rights are options to buy securities at a given price at a future date. They are a good source of common stock financing. The preemptive right means existing stockholders have the first option to buy additional shares to maintain their ownership percentage.

The CFO may participate in deciding on the life of the right (typically about two months), its price (usually below the current market price), and the number of shares required to buy a share.

 FINANCING STRATEGY

Some companies obtain most of their funds from issuing stock and from earnings retained in the business. Other companies borrow to the limit and obtain additional money from stockholders only when they can no longer borrow. Most companies are somewhere in between.

The CFO must select the best source of financing based on the situation. He or she has to consider the various circumstances to determine the best mix of financing.

In formulating a financing strategy in terms of source and amount, the CFO should take into account these points:

- *The cost and risk of alternative financing sources.*
- *The trend in market conditions and how they will affect the future availability of funds and interest rates.* For example, if interest rates are expected to increase, the company would be advised to finance with long-term debt at the currently lower interest rates. If stock prices are high, equity issuance may be preferred over debt.
- *The current debt–equity ratio.* An excessive ratio, for example, reflects financial risk indicating that further financing should be from equity sources.
- *The maturity dates of debt.* For example, the company should refrain from having all debt expire at one time because in an economic crisis, the company may not have sufficient cash to make payment.

▪ *The restrictions in loan agreements.* For example, a restriction may place a limit on the debt–equity ratio.

▪ *The type and amount of security demanded by long-term creditors.*

▪ *The ability to modify financing strategy to meet the changing economic climate.* For example, a company susceptible to cyclical variations should have less debt so as to meet principal and interest at the trough of the cycle. If profits are unstable and/or there is strong competition, greater reliance should be on equity financing.

▪ *The amount, nature, and stability of internally generated funds.* If there is adequacy and stability in earnings, the company can tolerate more debt.

▪ *The adequacy of credit lines to meet present and future needs.*

▪ *The inflation rate.* Paying debt will be in cheaper dollars.

▪ *The corporate earning power and liquidity.* For example, a liquid business is able to repay debt.

▪ *The type and riskiness of assets.* Poor-quality assets lack cash realizability to meet debt payments.

▪ *The nature of the product line.* A company that has technological obsolescence risk in its product line (e.g., computers) should use less debt.

▪ *The uncertainty of large expenditures.* If major cash outlays may be needed (e.g., lawsuit), there should be unused debt capacity available.

▪ *The tax rate.* A higher tax rate makes debt more attractive because of the tax deductibility of interest.

▪ *Foreign operations.* If operations are in high-risk foreign areas and foreign competition is keen, or if the exchange rate vacillates widely, a conservative debt posture is warranted.

What financing situations does the company face, and what is it doing about it?

Let us select the best possible source of financing based on the facts of each situation in the following examples.

Example 25.14

Your company is considering issuing either debt or preferred stock to finance the purchase of a plant costing $1.3 million. The interest rate on the debt is 15 percent; the dividend rate on the preferred stock is 10 percent; the tax rate is 34 percent.

The annual interest payment on the debt is:

$$15\% \times \$1,300,000 = \$195,000$$

The annual dividend on the preferred stock is:

$$10\% \times \$1,300,000 = \$130,000$$

The required earnings before interest and taxes to meet the dividend payment is:

$$\frac{\$130,000}{(1-0.34)} = \$196,970$$

If your company anticipates earning $196,970 without a problem, it should issue the preferred stock.

Example 25.15

Your company has sales of $30 million a year. It needs $6 million in financing for capital expansion. The debt–equity ratio is 68 percent. Your company is in a risky industry, and net income is not stable. The common stock is selling at a high P/E ratio compared to competition. Under consideration is either the issuance of common stock or debt.

Because your company is in a high-risk industry and has a high debt–equity ratio and unstable earnings, issuing debt would be costly, restrictive, and potentially dangerous to future financial health. The issuance of common stock is recommended.

Example 25.16

Your company is a mature one in its industry. There is limited ownership. The company has vacillating sales and earnings. Your firm's debt–equity ratio is 70 percent relative to the industry standard of 55 percent. The after-tax rate of return is 16 percent. Since your company is a seasonal business, there are certain times during the year when its liquidity position is inadequate. Your company is unsure about the best way to finance.

Preferred stock is one possible means of financing. Debt financing is not recommended due to the already high debt–equity ratio, the fluctuation in profit, the seasonal nature of the business, and the deficient liquidity posture. Because of the limited ownership, common stock financing may not be appropriate because this would dilute the ownership.

Example 25.17

A new company is established, and it plans to raise $15 million in funds. The company expects that it will obtain contracts that will provide $1.2 million a year in before-tax profits. The firm is considering whether to issue bonds only or an equal amount of bonds and preferred stock. The interest rate on AA corporate bonds is 12 percent. The tax rate is 50 percent.

The company will probably have difficulty issuing $15 million of AA bonds because the interest cost of $1.8 million (12% × $15,000,000) associated with these bonds is greater than the estimated earnings before interest and taxes. The issuance of debt by a new company is a risky alternative.

Financing with $7.5 million in debt and $7.5 million in preferred stock is also not recommended. Although some debt may be issued, it is not practical to finance the balance with preferred stock. In the case that $7.5 million of AA bonds were issued at the 12 percent rate, the company would be required to pay $900,000 in interest. In this event, a forecasted income statement would look as follows:

Earnings before interest and taxes	$1,200,000
Interest	900,000
Taxable income	$ 300,000
Taxes	150,000
Net income	$ 150,000

The amount available for the payment of preferred dividends is only $150,000. Hence, the maximum rate of return that could be paid on $7.5 million of preferred stock is 0.02 ($150,000/$7,500,000).

Stockholders would not invest in preferred stock that offers only a 2 percent rate of return.

The company should consider financing with common stock.

Example 25.18

Your company wants to construct a plant that will take about 1½ years to construct. The plant will be used to produce a new product line, for which your company expects a high demand. The new plant will materially increase corporate size. The following costs are expected:

Cost to build plant	$800,000
Funds needed for contingencies	$100,000
Annual operating costs	$175,000

The asset, debt, and equity positions of your company are similar to industry standards. The market price of the company's stock is less than it should be, taking into account the future earning power of the new product line. What would be an appropriate means to finance the construction?

Since the market price of stock is less than it should be and considering the potential of the product line, convertible bonds and installment bank loans might be appropriate means of financing, since interest expense is tax deductible. In addition, the issuance of convertible bonds might not require repayment, since the bonds are likely to be converted to common stock because of the company's profitability. Installment bank loans can be paid off gradually as the new product generates cash inflow. Funds needed for contingencies can be in the form of open bank lines of credit.

If the market price of the stock was not at a depressed level, financing through equity would be an alternative financing strategy.

Example 25.19

Your company wants to acquire another business but has not determined an optimal means to finance the acquisition. The current debt–equity position is within the industry guidelines. In prior years, financing has been achieved through the issuance of short-term debt.

Profit has shown vacillation, and as a result the market price of the stock has fluctuated. Currently, however, the market price of stock is strong. Your company's tax bracket is low.

The purchase should be financed through the issuance of equity securities for these reasons:

- The market price of stock is currently at a high level.
- The issuance of long-term debt will cause greater instability in earnings because of the high fixed interest charges. In consequence, there will be more instability in stock price.
- The issuance of debt will result in a higher debt–equity ratio relative to the industry norm. This will negatively impact the company's cost of capital and availability of financing.
- Because it will take a long time to derive the funds needed for the purchase price, short-term debt should not be issued. If short-term debt is issued, the debt would have to be paid before the receipt of the return from the acquired business.

Example 25.20

Breakstone Corporation wants to undertake a capital expansion program and must, therefore, obtain $7 million in financing. The company has a good credit rating. The current market price of its common stock is $60. The interest rate for long-term debt is 18 percent. The dividend rate associated with preferred stock is 16 percent, and Breakstone's tax rate is 46 percent.

Relevant ratios for the industry and the company are:

	Industry	Breakstone
Net income to total assets	13%	22%
Long-term debt to total assets	31%	29%
Total liabilities to total assets	47%	45%
Preferred stock to total assets	3%	0
Current ratio	2.6	3.2
Net income plus interest to interest	8	17

Dividends per share is $8, the dividend growth rate is 7 percent, no sinking fund provisions exist, the trend in earnings shows stability, and the present ownership group wishes to retain control. The cost of common stock is:

$$\frac{\text{Dividends per share}}{\text{Market price per share}} + \text{Dividend growth rate}$$

$$\frac{\$8}{\$60} + 0.07 = 20.3\%$$

The after-tax cost of long-term debt is 9.7 percent (18% × 54%). The cost of preferred stock is 16 percent. How should Breakstone finance its expansion? The issuance of long-term debt is more appropriate for seven reasons:

1. Its after-tax cost is the lowest.
2. The company's ratios of long-term debt to total assets and total liabilities to total assets are less than the industry average, pointing to the company's ability to issue additional debt.
3. Corporate liquidity is satisfactory based on the favorable current ratio relative to the industry standard.
4. Fixed interest charges can be met, taking into account the stability in earnings, the earning power of the firm, and the very favorable times-interest-earned ratio. Additional interest charges should be met without difficulty.
5. The firm's credit rating is satisfactory.
6. There are no required sinking fund provisions.
7. The leveraging effect can take place to further improve earnings.

In the case that the firm does not want to finance through further debt, preferred stock would be the next best financing alternative, since its cost is lower than that associated with common stock and no dilution in the ownership interest will take place.

Example 25.21

Harris Corporation has experienced growth in sales and net income but is in a weak liquidity position. The inflation rate is high. At the end of 2X12, the company needs $600,000 for these reasons:

New equipment	$175,000
Research and development	95,000
Paying overdue accounts payable	215,000
Paying accrued liabilities	60,000
Desired increase in cash balance	55,000
	$600,000

Exhibit 25.3 is the financial statement for 2X12.

(continued)

EXHIBIT 25.3 Harris Corporation Balance Sheet, December 31, 2X12

ASSETS

Current assets		
Cash	$ 12,000	
Accounts receivable	140,000	
Notes receivable	25,000	
Inventory	165,000	
Office supplies	20,000	
Total current assets		$362,000
Fixed assets		468,000
Total assets		$830,000
LIABILITIES AND STOCKHOLDERS' EQUITY		
Current liabilities		
Loans payable	$ 74,000	
Accounts payable	360,000	
Accrued liabilities	55,000	
Total current liabilities		$489,000
Long-term debt		61,000
Total liabilities		$550,000
Stockholders' equity		
Common stock	$200,000	
Retained earnings	80,000	
Total stockholders' equity		280,000
Total liabilities and stockholders' equity		$830,000

Harris Corporation
Income Statement
For the Year Ended Dec. 31, 2X12

Sales	$1,400,000
Cost of sales	750,000
Gross margin	$650,000
Operating expenses	480,000
Income before tax	$170,000
Tax	68,000
Net income	$102,000

It is anticipated that sales will increase on a yearly basis by 22 percent and that net income will increase by 17 percent. What time of financing is best suited for Harris Corporation?

The most suitable type of financing is long-term. A company in a growth stage needs a large investment in equipment, and research and development expenditure. With regard to 2X12, $270,000 of the $600,000 is required for this purpose. A growth company also needs funds to satisfy working capital requirements. Here, 45.8 percent of financing is necessary to pay overdue accounts payable and accrued liabilities. The firm also needs sufficient cash to capitalize on lucrative opportunities. The present cash balance to total assets is at a low 1.4 percent.

Long-term debt financing is recommended for these reasons:

SOLUTION

1. The ratio of long-term debt to stockholders' equity is a low 21.8 percent. The additional issuance of long-term debt will not impair the overall capital structure.
2. The company has been profitable, and there is an expectation of future growth in earnings. Internally generated funds should therefore ensue, enabling the payment of fixed interest charges.
3. During inflation, the issuance of long-term debt generates purchasing power gains because the firm will be repaying creditors in cheaper dollars.
4. Interest expense is tax deductible.

Example 25.22

On average over the past 10 years, Tektronix's return on equity has not been sufficient to finance growth of the business; thus, an infusion of new capital from outside sources has been required. Most of the additional capital has been in the form of long-term debt, which represented 13 percent of total capital in fiscal 2X05 and 21 percent of total capital in fiscal 2X09.

With expansion of the business expected to accelerate in the next few years after the current lull, but, with return on equity likely to remain somewhat depressed because of competitive factors and costs associated with "preparing for the 2X10s," a need for additional capital is developing. Also, of the $146 million of long-term debt outstanding at the fiscal 2X09 year-end, nearly $65 million matures in the fiscal 2X10 to fiscal 2X12 period. Thus, it is possible that as much as $100 million of capital may have to be raised to meet all requirements.

In anticipation of capital needs, Tektronix in fiscal 2X09 borrowed funds in the commercial paper market, and the company intends to replace these commercial paper borrowings at some future time with long-term financing.

Given the foregoing circumstances, and also given that Tektronix common stock currently is quoted on the New York Stock Exchange at 160 percent of book value and that the current interest rate on newly issued triple-A industrial bonds of long maturity is 14 percent, evaluate on an immediate and longer-term basis each of the following options. Include economic and capital market assumptions.

(a) Tektronix is selling 2 million shares of common stock at $50 per share.
(b) Tektronix is selling a $100 million straight debenture issue maturing in 20 years.
(c) Tektronix is selling a $100 million bond issue convertible into common stock and maturing in 20 years.

1. From the timing viewpoint, selling equity is attractive considering price-to-book rates (160 percent) and comparatively modest dilution (2 million shares represents 11 percent of currently outstanding shares, less impact of after-tax cost of borrowing to be retired). However, price soon could move higher given a better economic environment, earnings recovery, and resultant stronger general stock market. Long-term, selling equity is expensive, as continuing dividend service is with after-tax dollars. Also, immediate return on equity capital will diminish with reduced leverage as debt matures.

(continued)

2. Increasing debt, net of maturities, to a larger part of total capital is tolerable by most standards. According to the data provided, debt of about $146 million would increase to around $181 million ($146 + $100 – $65), and by 2X12 this sum presumably would not represent much more than the current 21 percent subject to earnings retention during the interim. However, this would be an appealing option only if interest rate assumptions indicate other than a rather meaningful decline over the next year or two, and if pro forma interest charge coverage and/or the current lull in the business do not seriously impact the rating and issue price of the bonds. The after-tax cost of debt service will be comparatively low, and so would be the net cost of capital. Another consideration will be sinking fund requirements and call restrictions and price.
3. A convertible bond issue has certain disadvantages but it also has advantages:
    a. It can be sold at a lower interest cost than a straight debt.
    b. The potential dilution is less than an issue of common reflecting the premium over the common market.

This case has been adapted from the Chartered Financial Analysts (CFA) exam.

CHAPTER TWENTY-SIX

Warrants and Convertibles

WARRANTS AND CONVERTIBLES are unique compared to other types of securities because they may be converted into common stock. The CFO needs to have a good understanding of warrants and convertibles along with their valuation, their advantages and disadvantages, and when their issuance is recommended.

 ## WARRANTS

A *warrant* is the option given stockholders to buy a predetermined number of shares of stock at a given price. Warrants may be detachable or nondetachable. A *detachable* warrant may be sold separately from the bond with which it is associated. Thus, the holder may exercise the warrant but not redeem the bond. Your company may issue bonds with detachable warrants to purchase additional bonds so as to hedge the risk of adverse future interest rate movements, since the warrant is convertible into a bond at a fixed interest rate. If interest rates increase, the warrant will be worthless, and the issue price of the warrant will partially offset the higher interest cost of the future debt issue. A *nondetachable* warrant is sold with its bond to be exercised by the bond owner simultaneously with the convertible bond.

Your company may sell warrants separately (e.g., American Express) or in combination with other securities (e.g., MGM).

To obtain common stock, the warrant must be given up along with the payment of cash, called the *exercise price*. Although warrants usually mature on a specified date, some are perpetual. A holder of a warrant may exercise it by purchasing the stock, sell it on the market to other investors, or continue to hold it. The company cannot force the exercise of a warrant.

If desired, the company can have the exercise price of the warrant change over time (e.g., increase each year).

If a stock split or stock dividend is issued before the warrant is exercised, the option price of the warrant will be adjusted for it.

Warrants may be issued to obtain additional funds. When a bond is issued with a warrant, the warrant price is usually established between 10 and 20 percent above the stock's market price. If the company's stock price increases above the option price, the warrants will be exercised at the option price. The closer the warrants are to their maturity date, the greater is the likelihood that they will be exercised.

What is a warrant worth?

The theoretical value of a warrant is computed by a formula. The formula value is typically less than the market price of the warrant because the speculative appeal of a warrant allows the investor to obtain personal leverage:

Value of warrant = (Market price per share − Exercise price)
× Number of shares that may be bought

Example 26.1

A warrant for XYZ Company's stock gives the owner the right to buy one share of common stock at $25 a share. The market price of the common stock is $53. The formula price of the warrant is $28 (($53 − $25) × 1).

If the owner had the right to buy three shares of common stock with one warrant, the theoretical value of the warrant would be $84 (($53 − $25) × 3).

If the stock is selling for an amount below the option price, there will be a negative value. Since this is illogical, a zero value is assigned.

Example 26.2

Assume the same facts as in, except that the stock is selling at $21 a share. The formula amount is ($21 − $25) × 1 = −$4. However, zero will be assigned.

Warrants do not have an investment value because there are *no* interest, dividends, or voting rights. Therefore, the market value of a warrant is attributable only to its convertibility feature into common stock. However, the market price of a warrant is typically more than its theoretical value, which is referred to as the *premium* on the warrant. The lowest amount that a warrant will sell for is its theoretical value.

The value of a warrant depends on the remaining life of the option, dividend payments on the common stock, the fluctuation in price of the common stock, whether the warrant is listed on the exchange, and the investor's opportunity. There is a higher price for a warrant when its life is long, the dividend payment on common stock is small, the stock price is volatile, it is listed on the exchange, and the value of funds to the investor is great (because the warrant requires a lesser investment).

Example 26.3

ABC stock has a market value of $50. The exercise price of the warrant is also $50. Thus, the theoretical value of the warrant is $0. However, the warrant will sell at a premium (positive price) if there is the possibility that the market price of the common stock will exceed $50 prior to the expiration date of the warrant. The more distant the expiration date, the greater will be the premium, since there is a longer period for possible price appreciation. The lower the market price relative to the exercise price, the less the premium will be.

Example 26.4

Assume the same facts as in Example 26.3, except that the current market price of the stock is $35. In this case, the warrant's premium will be much lower since it would take longer for the stock's price to increase above $50 a share. If investors expect that the stock price would not increase above $50 at a later date, the value of the warrant would be $0.

If the market price of ABC stock rises above $50, the market price of the warrant will increase, and the premium will decrease. In other words, when the stock price exceeds the exercise price, the market price of the warrant approximately equals the theoretical value so that the premium disappears. The reduction in the premium arises because of the lessening of the advantage of owning the warrant compared to exercising it.

Should you issue a warrant?

The advantages of issuing warrants are:

- They serve as sweeteners for an issue of debt or preferred stock.
- They permit the issuance of debt at a low interest rate.
- They allow for balanced financing between debt and equity.
- Funds are received when the warrants are exercised.

The disadvantages of issuing warrants are:

- When exercised, they will result in a dilution of common stock, which in turn lowers the market price of stock.
- They may be exercised when the business has no need for additional capital.

 ## CONVERTIBLE SECURITIES

What is a convertible security, and when should it be issued?

A *convertible security* can be exchanged for common stock by the holder, and in some cases the issuer, according to specified terms. Examples are convertible bonds and convertible preferred stock. Common shares are issued when the convertible security is exchanged. The conversion ratio equals:

$$\text{Conversion ratio} = \frac{\text{Par value of convertible security}}{\text{Conversion price}}$$

The *conversion price* is the price the holder pays for the common stock when the conversion is made. The conversion price and the conversion ratio are established at the date the convertible security is issued. The conversion price should be tied to the growth prospects of the company. The greater the potential, the greater the conversion price.

Example 26.5

A $1,000 bond is convertible into 30 shares of stock. The conversion price is $33.33 ($1,000/30 shares).

Example 26.6

A share of convertible preferred stock with a par value of $50 is convertible into four shares of common stock. The conversion price is $12.50 ($50/4).

Example 26.7

A $1,000 convertible bond is issued that allows the holder to convert the bond into 10 shares of common stock. Thus, the conversion ratio is 10 shares for 1 bond. Since the face value of the bond is $1,000, the holder is tendering this amount upon conversion. The conversion price equals $100 per share ($1,000/10 shares).

Example 26.8

Y Company issued a $1,000 convertible bond at par. The conversion price is $40. The conversion ratio is:

$$\text{Conversion ratio} = \frac{\text{Par value of convertible security}}{\text{Conversion price}} = \frac{\$1,000}{\$40} = 25$$

The conversion value of a security is computed as:

$$\text{Conversion value} = \text{Common stock price} \times \text{Conversion ratio}$$

When a convertible security is issued, it is priced higher than its conversion value. The difference is the conversion premium. The percentage conversion premium is computed as:

$$\text{Percentage conversion premium} = \frac{\text{Market value} - \text{Conversion value}}{\text{Conversion value}}$$

A convertible bond is a quasi-equity security because its market value is keyed to its value if converted instead of as a bond. The convertible bond may be deemed a delayed issue of common stock at a price above the current level.

Example 26.9

LA Corporation issued a $1,000 convertible bond at par. The market price of the common stock at the date of issue was $48. The conversion price is $55.

$$\text{Conversion ratio} = \frac{\text{Par value of convertible security}}{\text{Conversion price}} = \frac{\$1,000}{\$55} = 18.18$$

Conversion value of the bond equals:

$$\text{Common stock price} \times \text{Conversion ratio} = \$48 \times 18.18 = \$872$$

The difference between the conversion value of $872 and the issue price of $1,000 is the conversion premium of $128. The conversion premium may also be expressed as a percentage of the conversion value. The percent in this case is:
Percentage conversion premium equals:

$$\frac{\text{Market value} - \text{Conversion value}}{\text{Conversion value}} = \frac{\$1,000 - \$872}{\$872} = \frac{\$128}{\$872} = 14.7\%$$

The conversion terms may increase in steps over specified time periods. As time elapses, fewer common shares are exchanged for the bond. In some cases, after a specified time period, the conversion option may expire.

A convertible security usually includes a clause that protects it from dilution caused by stock dividends, stock splits, and stock rights. The clause typically prevents the issuance of common stock at a price lower than the conversion price. The conversion price is adjusted for a stock split or stock dividend, enabling the common shareholder to retain his or her percentage interest.

Example 26.10

A 3-for-1 stock split requires a tripling of the conversion ratio. A 20 percent stock dividend necessitates a 20 percent increase in the conversion ratio.

The voluntary conversion of a security by the holder depends on the relationship of the interest on the bond compared to the dividend on the stock, the risk preference of the holder (stock has a greater risk than a bond), and the current and expected market price of the stock.

What is the value of a convertible security?

A convertible security is a hybrid security because it has attributes similar to common stock and bonds. It is expected that the holder eventually will receive both interest yield and capital gain. Interest yield is the coupon interest relative to the amount invested.

The capital gain yield applies to the difference between the conversion price and the stock price at the issuance date and the expected growth rate in stock price.

The investment value of a convertible security is the value of the security, assuming it was not convertible but had all other attributes. For a convertible bond, its investment value equals the present value of future interest payments plus the present value of the maturity amount. For preferred stock, the investment value equals the present value of future dividend payments plus the present value of expected selling price.

Conversion value is the value of the stock received upon converting the bond. As the price of the stock increases, so will its conversion value.

Example 26.11

A $1,000 bond is convertible into 18 shares of common stock with a market value of $52 per share. The conversion value of the bond equals:

$$\$52 \times 18 \text{ shares} = \$936$$

Example 26.12

At the date a $100,000 convertible bond is issued, the market price of the stock is $18 a share. Each $1,000 bond is convertible into 50 shares of stock. The conversion ratio is thus 50. The number of shares the bond is convertible into is:

$$(\$100,000/\$1,000) = 100 \text{ bonds}$$

$$100 \text{ bonds} \times 50 \text{ shares} = 5,000 \text{ shares}$$

The conversion value is $90,000 ($18 × 5,000 shares).

If the stock price is anticipated to grow at 6 percent per year, the conversion value at the end of the first year is:

Shares	5,000
Stock price ($18 × 1.06)	$19.08
Conversion value	$95,400.00

A convertible security will not sell at less than its value as straight debt (nonconvertible security). This is because the conversion privilege has to have some value in terms of its potential convertibility to common stock and in terms of reducing the holder's risk exposure to a declining bond price. (Convertible bonds fall off less in price than straight debt issues.) Market value will equal investment value only when the conversion privilege is worthless because of a low market price of the common stock relative to the conversion price.

When convertible bonds are issued, the business expects that the value of common stock will appreciate and that the bonds will eventually be converted. If conversion does occur, the company could then issue another convertible bond referred to as *leapfrog financing*.

If the market price of common stock decreases instead of increasing, the holder will not convert the debt into equity. In this case, the convertible security remains as debt and is called a "hung" convertible.

A convertible security holder may prefer, for two reasons, to hold the security rather than converting it even though the conversion value exceeds the investment cost. First, as the price of the common stock increases, so will the price of the convertible security. Second, the holder receives regular interest payments or preferred dividends. To force conversion, companies issuing convertibles often have a call price. The call price is above the face value of the bond (about 10 to 20 percent higher). This forces the conversion of stock, provided the stock price exceeds the conversion price. The holder would prefer a higher-value common stock than a lower call price for the bond.

The issuing company may force conversion of its convertible bond to common stock when financially advantageous, such as when the market price of the stock has declined or when the interest rate on the convertible debt is currently higher than the going market interest rates. United Technologies is an example of a company that has had a conversion of its convertible bond when the market price of its stock was low.

Example 26.13

The conversion price on a $1,000 debenture is $40, and the call price is $1,100. In order for the conversion value of the bond to equal the call price, the market price of the stock would have to be $44 ($1,100/25). If the conversion value of the bond is 15 percent higher than the call price, the approximate market price of common stock would be $51 (1.15 × $44). At a $51 price, conversion is assured because if the investor did not convert, he or she would experience an opportunity loss.

Example 26.14

ABC Company's convertible bond has a conversion price of $80. The conversion ratio is 10. The market price of the stock is $140. The call price is $1,100. The bondholder would prefer to convert to common stock with a market value of $1,400 ($140 × 10) rather than have his or her convertible bond redeemed at $1,100. In this situation, the call provision forces the conversion when the bondholder might be inclined to wait longer.

Does it pay to issue a convertible security?

The advantages of issuing convertible securities are:

- Convertibility is a sweetener in a debt offering by giving the investor an opportunity to share in the price appreciation of common stock.
- The issuance of convertible debt allows for a lower interest rate on the financing compared to issuing straight debt.

- There are fewer financing restrictions with a convertible security.
- Convertibles provide a means of issuing equity at prices higher than the current market price.
- A convertible security may be issued in a tight money market, when it is difficult for a creditworthy company to issue a straight bond or preferred stock.
- The call provision enables the company to force conversion whenever the market price of the stock exceeds the conversion price.
- If the company issued straight debt now and common stock later to meet the debt, it would incur flotation costs twice, whereas with convertible debt, flotation costs would occur only once, with the initial issuance of the convertible bonds.

The disadvantages of issuing convertible securities are:

- If the company's stock price appreciably increases, it would have been better off financing through a regular issuance of common stock by waiting to issue it at the higher price rather than allowing conversion at the lower price.
- The company has to pay the convertible debt if the stock price does not appreciate.

What should the financing policy be?

When a company's stock price is depressed, convertible debt rather than common stock issuance may be advisable if the price of stock is expected to increase. A conversion price above the current market price of stock will involve the issuance of fewer shares when the bonds are converted relative to selling the shares at a current lower price. Furthermore, there is less share dilution. The conversion will take place only if the price of the stock rises above the conversion price. The drawback is that if the stock price does not increase and conversion does not occur, an additional debt burden is placed on the firm.

The issuance of convertible debt is recommended when the company wants to leverage itself in the short term but does not want to pay interest and principal on the convertible debt in the long term (due to its conversion).

A convertible issue is a good financing instrument for a growth company with a low dividend yield on stock. The higher the growth rate, the earlier the conversion. For example, a convertible bond may be a temporary source of funds in a construction period. It is a relatively inexpensive source for financing growth. A convertible issuance is not recommended for a company with a modest growth rate since it would take a long time to force conversion. During such a time, the company will not be able to issue additional financing easily. A long conversion period may imply to investors that the stock has not done as well as expected. The growth rate of the firm is an important factor in determining whether convertibles should be issued.

Your company can also issue bonds exchangeable for the common stock of other companies. Your company may do this if it owns a sizable stake in another company's stock and it wants to raise cash. There is an intention to sell shares at a later date because of an expectation of share price appreciation.

In conclusion, a convertible bond is a delayed common equity financing. The issuer expects stock price to rise in the future (e.g., two to four years) to stimulate conversion. Convertible bonds may be appropriate for smaller, rapidly growing companies.

> **Note**
>
> If your company has an uncertain future tax position, it may issue convertible preferred stock exchangeable at the option of the company (i.e., when it becomes a taxpayer) into convertible debt of the company. ■

How do convertibles compare with warrants?

The differences between convertibles and warrants are:

- Exercising convertibles does not usually generate additional funds to the company, whereas the exercise of warrants does.
- When conversion takes place, the debt ratio is reduced. However, the exercise of warrants adds to the equity position with debt still remaining.
- Because of the call feature, the company has more control over the timing of the capital structure with convertibles than with warrants.

CHAPTER TWENTY-SEVEN

Cost of Capital and Capital Structure Decisions

THE *COST OF CAPITAL* is defined as the rate of return that is necessary to maintain the market value of the firm (or price of the firm's stock). CFOs must know the cost of capital (the minimum required rate of return) when making capital budgeting decisions, helping to establish the optimal capital structure, and making decisions about issues such as leasing, bond refunding, and working capital management. The cost of capital is used either as a discount rate under the net present value (NPV) method or as a hurdle rate under the internal rate of return (IRR) method. The cost of capital is computed as a weighted average of the various capital components, which are items on the right-hand side of the balance sheet such as debt, preferred stock, common stock, and retained earnings.

 ## INDIVIDUAL COSTS OF CAPITAL

The elements of capital have component costs, identified as follows:

k_i = before-tax cost of debt
$k_d = k_i (1 - t)$ = after-tax cost of debt, where t = tax rate
k_p = cost of preferred stock
k_s = cost of retained earnings (or internal equity)
k_e = cost of external equity, or cost of issuing new common stock
k_o = firm's overall cost of capital, or a weighted average cost of capital

475

Cost of Debt

The before-tax cost of debt can be found by determining the IRR (or yield to maturity; YTM) on the bond cash flows.

However, the following shortcut formula can be used for approximating the YTM on a bond:

$$k_i = \frac{I + (M - V)/n}{(M + V)/2}$$

where
I = annual interest payments in dollars
M = par or face value, usually $1,000 per bond
V = market value or net proceeds from the sale of a bond
n = years

Since the interest payments are tax deductible, the cost of debt must be stated on an after-tax basis. The after-tax cost of debt is:

$$k_d = k_i(1 - t)$$

where t is the tax rate.

Cost of Preferred Stock

The cost of preferred stock, k_p, is found by dividing the annual preferred stock dividend, d_p, by the net proceeds from the sale of the preferred stock, p, as follows.

$$k_p = \frac{d_p}{p}$$

Since preferred stock dividends are not a tax-deductible expense, these dividends are paid after taxes. Consequently, no tax adjustment is required.

Example 27.1

Assume that the Carter Company issues a $1,000, 8 percent, 20-year bond whose net proceeds are $940. The tax rate is 40 percent. The before-tax cost of debt, k_i, is:

$$k_i = \frac{I + (M - V)/n}{(M - V)/2} = \frac{\$80 + (\$1,000 - \$940)/20}{(\$1,000 + \$940)} = \frac{\$83}{\$970} = 8.56\%$$

Therefore, the after-tax cost of debt is:

$$k_d = k_i(1 - t) = 8.56\%(1 - 0.4) = 5.14\%$$

Example 27.2

Suppose that the Carter Company has preferred stock that pays a $13 dividend per share and sells for $100 per share in the market. The flotation (or underwriting) cost is 3 percent, or $3 per share. Then the cost of preferred stock is:

$$K_p = \frac{d_p}{p} = \frac{\$13}{\$97} = 13.4\%$$

Cost of Equity Capital

The cost of common stock, k_e, is generally viewed as the rate of return investors require on a firm's common stock. Two techniques for measuring the cost of common stock equity capital are widely used: Gordon's growth model and the capital asset pricing model (CAPM) approach.

Gordon's growth model is:

$$P_0 = \frac{d_1}{r - g}$$

where

P_0 = value (or market price) of common stock
d_1 = dividend to be received in one year
r = investor's required rate of return
g = rate of growth (assumed to be constant over time)

Solving the model for r results in the formula for the cost of common stock:

$$r = \frac{d_1}{P_0} + g \text{ or } k_e = \frac{d_1}{P_0} + g$$

Note that the symbol r is changed to k_e to show that it is used for the computation of cost of capital.

Capital Asset Pricing Model Approach

An alternative approach to measuring the cost of common stock is to use the CAPM, which involves these four steps:

1. Estimate the risk-free rate, r_f, generally taken to be the U.S. Treasury bill rate.
2. Estimate the stock's beta coefficient, b, which is an index of systematic (or nondiversifiable market) risk.

3. Estimate the rate of return on the market portfolio, rm, such as the Standard & Poor's 500 Stock Composite Index or Dow Jones 30 Industrials.
4. Estimate the required rate of return on the firm's stock, using the CAPM equation:

$$k_e = r_f + b(r_m - r_f)$$

Again, note that the symbol r_j is changed to k_e.

Example 27.3

Assume that the market price of the Carter Company's stock is $40. The dividend to be paid at the end of the coming year is $4 per share and is expected to grow at a constant annual rate of 6 percent. Then the cost of this common stock is:

$$k_e = \frac{D_1}{P_0} + g = \frac{\$4}{\$40} + 6\% = 16\%$$

The cost of new common stock, or external equity capital, is higher than the cost of existing common stock because of the *flotation costs* involved in selling the new common stock. Flotation costs, sometimes called *issuance costs,* are the total costs of issuing and selling a security that include printing and engraving, legal fees, and accounting fees.

If f is flotation cost in percent, the formula for the cost of new common stock is:

$$k_e = \frac{D_1}{P_0(1-f)} + g$$

Cost of Retained Earnings

The cost of retained earnings, k_s, is closely related to the cost of existing common stock, since the cost of equity obtained by retained earnings is the same as the rate of return investors require on the firm's common stock. Therefore,

$$k_e = k_s$$

Example 27.4

Assume the same data as in Example 27.3, except the firm is trying to sell new issues of stock A and its flotation cost is 10 percent. Then:

$$k_e = \frac{D_1}{P_0(1-f)} + g = \frac{\$4}{\$40(1-0.1)} + 6\% = \frac{\$4}{\$36} + 6\%$$

$$= 11.11\% + 6\% = 17.11\%$$

Example 27.5

Assuming that r_f is 7 percent, b is 1.5, and r_m is 13 percent, then:

$$k_e = r_f + b(r_m - r_f) = 7\% + 1.5(13\% - 7\%) = 16\%$$

This 16 percent cost of common stock can be viewed as consisting of a 7 percent risk-free rate plus a 9 percent risk premium, which indicates that the firm's stock price is 1.5 times more volatile than the market portfolio to the factors affecting nondiversifiable, or systematic, risk.

Overall Cost of Capital

The firm's overall cost of capital is the weighted average of the individual capital costs, with the weights being the proportions of each type of capital used. Let k_o be the overall cost of capital.

$k_o = \Sigma$ (percentage of the total capital structure supplied by each source of capital
$\times$ cost of capital for each source)

$$= \sum w_d k_d + w_p k_p + w_e k_e + w_s k_s$$

where
w_d = % of total capital supplied by debts
w_p = % of total capital supplied by preferred stock
w_e = % of total capital supplied by external equity
w_s = % of total capital supplied by retained earnings (or internal equity)

WEIGHTS

The weights can be historical (book-value or market-value), target, or marginal.

Historical Weights

Historical weights are based on a firm's existing capital structure. The use of these weights is based on the assumption that the firm's existing capital structure is optimal and therefore should be maintained in the future. Two types of historical weights can be used: book-value weights and market-value weights.

Book-Value Weights

The use of book-value weights in calculating the firm's weighted cost of capital assumes that new financing will be raised employing the same method the firm used for its present capital structure. The weights are determined by dividing the book value of each capital component by the sum of the book values of all the long-term capital sources. The computation of overall cost of capital is illustrated in Example 27.6.

Market-Value Weights

Market-value weights are determined by dividing the market value of each source by the sum of the market values of all sources. The use of market-value weights for computing a firm's weighted average cost of capital is theoretically more appealing than the use of book-value weights because the market values of the securities closely approximate the actual dollars to be received from their sale.

Target Weights

If the firm has a target capital structure (desired debt-equity mix) that is maintained over the long term, then that capital structure and associated weights can be used in calculating the firm's weighted cost of capital.

Marginal Weights

Marginal weights involve use of the *actual* financial mix used in financing the proposed investments. In using target weights, the firm is concerned with what it believes to

---

Example 27.6

Assume the following capital structure and cost of each source of financing for the Carter Company:

Source		Cost
Mortgage bonds ($1,000 par)	$20,000,000	5.14% (Example 27.1)
Preferred stock ($100 par)	5,000,000	13.40% (Example 27.2)
Common stock ($40 par)	20,000,000	17.11% (Example 27.3)
Retained earnings	5,000,000	16.00% (Example 27.4)
	$50,000,000	

The book value weights and the overall cost of capital are computed as:

Source	Book Value	Weights	Cost	Weighted Cost
Debt	$20,000,000	40%[a]	5.14%	2.06%[b]
Preferred stock	5,000,000	10	13.40%	1.34
Common stock	20,000,000	40	17.11%	6.84
Retained earnings	5,000,000	10	16.00%	1.60
	$50,000,000	100%		11.84

Overall cost of capital = k_o = 11.84%

[a] $20,000,000/$50,000,000 = 0.40 = 40%
[b] 5.14% × 40% = 2.06%

Example 27.7

In addition to the data from Example 27.6, assume that the security market prices are:

$$
\begin{aligned}
\text{Mortgage bond} &= \$1{,}100 \text{ per bond} \\
\text{Preferred stock} &= \$90 \text{ per share} \\
\text{Common stock} &= \$80 \text{ per share}
\end{aligned}
$$

The firm's number of securities in each category is:

$$
\text{Mortgage bonds} = \frac{\$20{,}000{,}000}{\$1{,}000} = \$20{,}000
$$

$$
\text{Preferred stock} = \frac{\$5{,}000{,}000}{\$100} = \$50{,}000
$$

$$
\text{Common stock} = \frac{\$2{,}000{,}000}{\$40} = \$500{,}000
$$

Therefore, the market-value weights are:

Source	Number of Securities	Price	Market Value
Debt	20,000	$1,100	$22,000,000
Preferred stock	50,000	$ 90	4,500,000
Common stock	500,000	$ 80	40,000,000
			$66,500,000

The $40 million common stock value must be split in the ratio of 4 to 1 (the $20 million common stock versus the $5 million retained earnings in the original capital structure), since the market value of the retained earnings has been impounded into the common stock.

The firm's cost of capital is:

Source	Market Value	Weights	Cost	Weighted Average
Debt	$22,000,000	33.08%	5.14%	1.70%
Preferred stock	4,500,000	6.77	13.40%	0.91
Common stock	32,000,000	48.12	17.11%	8.23
Retained earnings	8,000,000	12.03	16.00%	1.92
	$66,500,000	100.00%		12.76%

Overall cost of capital = k_o = 12.76%

be the optimal capital structure or target percentage. In using marginal weights, the firm is concerned with the actual dollar amounts of each type of financing to be needed for a given investment project. This approach, though attractive, presents a problem. The cost of capital for the individual sources depends on the firm's financial risk, which is affected by the firm's financial mix. If the company alters its present capital structure, the individual costs will change, which makes it more difficult to

Example 27.8

The Carter Company is considering raising $8 million for plant expansion. The CFO estimates using the following mix for financing this project:

Debt	$4,000,000	50%
Common stock	2,000,000	25%
Retained earnings	2,000,000	25%
	$8,000,000	100%

The company's cost of capital is computed as:

Source	Marginal Weights	Cost	Weighted Cost
Debt	50%	5.14%	2.57%
Common stock	25	17.11%	4.28
Retained earnings	25	16.00%	4.00
	100%		10.85%

Overall cost of capital = k_o = 10.85%

compute the weighted cost of capital. The important assumption needed is that the firm's financial mix is relatively stable and that these weights will closely approximate future financing practice.

How do you determine the firm's optimal capital structure?

The concepts to be covered in this chapter relate closely to the cost of capital and also to the crucial problem of determining the firm's optimal capital structure. We cover three methods that show how to build an appropriate financing mix.

 EBIT–EPS APPROACH TO CAPITAL STRUCTURE DECISIONS

This analysis is a practical tool that enables the CFO to evaluate alternative financing plans by investigating their effect on earnings per share (EPS) over a range of earnings before interest and taxes (EBIT) levels. Its primary objective is to determine the EBIT breakeven, or indifference, points between the various alternative financing plans. The indifference point identifies the EBIT level at which the EPS will be the same regardless of the financing plan chosen by the CFO.

This indifference point has major implications for capital structure decisions. At EBIT amounts in excess of the EBIT indifference level, the more heavily levered financing plan will generate a higher EPS. At EBIT amounts below the EBIT indifference level, the financing plan

Example 27.9

Assume that ABC Company, with long-term capitalization consisting entirely of $5 million in stock, wants to raise $2 million for the acquisition of special equipment by (1) selling 40,000 shares of common stock at $50 each, (2) selling bonds at 10 percent interest, or (3) issuing preferred stock with an 8 percent dividend. The present EBIT is $800,000, the income tax rate is 50 percent, and 100,000 shares of common stock are now outstanding. To compute the indifference points, we begin by calculating EPS at a projected EBIT level of $1 million.

	All Common	All Debt	All Preferred
EBIT	$1,000,000	$1,000,000	$1,000,000
Interest		200,000	
Earnings before taxes (EBT)	$1,000,000	$800,000	$1,000,000
Taxes	500,000	400,000	500,000
Earnings after taxes (EAT)	$500,000	$400,000	$500,000
Preferred stock dividend			160,000
Earnings available to common stockholders	$500,000	$400,000	$340,000
Number of shares	140,000	100,000	100,000
EPS	$3.57	$4.00	$3.40

Now connect the EPSs at the level of EBIT of $1 million with the EBITs for each financing alternative on the horizontal axis to obtain the EBIT–EPS graphs. We plot the EBIT necessary to cover all fixed financial costs for each financing alternative on the horizontal axis. For the common stock plan, there are no fixed costs, so the intercept on the horizontal axis is zero. For the debt plan, there must be an EBIT of $200,000 to cover interest charges. For the preferred stock plan, there must be an EBIT of $320,000 (i.e.,$160,000/(1 − 0.5)) to cover $160,000 in preferred stock dividends at a 50 percent income tax rate; thus, $320,000 becomes the horizontal axis intercept. (See Exhibit 27.1.) In this example, the indifference point between all common and all debt is:

$$\frac{(EBIT - I)\,(1 - t) - PD}{S_1} = \frac{(EBIT - I)\,(1 - t) - PD}{S_2}$$

$$\frac{(EBIT - 0)\,(1 - 0.5) - 0}{140,000} = \frac{(EBIT - 200,000)\,(1 - 0.5) - 0}{100,000}$$

involving less leverage will generate a higher EPS. Therefore, it is of critical importance for the CFO to know the EBIT indifference level. The indifference points between any two methods of financing can be determined by solving for EBIT in this equality:

$$\frac{(\text{EBIT} - I)(1 - t) - PD}{S_1} = \frac{(\text{EBIT} - I)(1 - t) - PD}{S_2}$$

where

t = tax rate

PD = preferred stock dividends

S_1 and S_2 = number of shares of common stock outstanding after financing for plan 1 and plan 2, respectively

A Word of Caution

It is important to realize that financial leverage is a double-edged sword. It can magnify profits, but it can also increase losses. The EBIT–EPS approach helps the CFO examine

EXHIBIT 27.1 EBIT–EPS Graph

Rearranging yields:

$$0.5(\text{EBIT})(100,000) = 0.5(\text{EBIT})(140,000) - 0.5(200,000)(140,000)$$
$$20,000(\text{EBIT}) = 14,000,000,000$$
$$\text{EBIT} = \$700,000$$

Similarly, the indifference point between all common and all preferred would be:

$$\frac{(\text{EBIT} - I)(1 - t) - PD}{S_1} = \frac{(\text{EBIT} - I)(1 - t) - PD}{S_2}$$

$$\frac{(\text{EBIT} - 0)(1 - 0.5) - 0}{140,000} = \frac{(\text{EBIT} - 0)(1 - 0.5) - 160,000}{100,000}$$

Rearranging yields:

$$0.5(\text{EBIT})(100,000) = 0.5(\text{EBIT})(140,000) - 160,000(140,000)$$
$$20,000(\text{EBIT}) = 22,400,000,000$$
$$\text{EBIT} = \$1,120,000$$

Based on these computations and observing Exhibit 27.1, we can draw three conclusions:

1. At any level of EBIT, debt is better than preferred stock, since it gives a higher EPS.
2. At a level of EBIT above $700,000, debt is better than common stock. If EBIT is below $700,000, the reverse is true.
3. At a level of EBIT above $1,120,000, preferred stock is better than common. At or below that point, the reverse is true.

the impact of financial leverage as a financing method. Investment performance is crucial to the successful application of any leveraging strategy.

 ## ANALYSIS OF CORPORATE CASH FLOWS

A second tool of capital structure management involves the *analysis of cash flows*. When considering the appropriate capital structure, it is important to analyze the cash flow ability of the firm to service fixed charges, among other things. The greater the dollar amount of debt and/or preferred stock the firm issues and the shorter its maturity, the greater the fixed charges of the firm. These charges include principal and interest payments on debt, lease payments, and preferred stock dividends. Before assuming additional fixed charges, the firm should analyze its expected future cash flows, for fixed charges must be met with cash. The inability to meet these charges, with the exception of preferred stock dividends, may result in insolvency. The greater and more stable the expected future cash flows of the firm, the greater the debt capacity of the company.

 ## COVERAGE RATIOS

A third tool is the calculation of comparative coverage ratios. Among the ways we can gain insight into the debt capacity of a firm is through the use of coverage ratios. In the computation of these ratios, a CFO typically uses EBIT as a rough measure of the cash flow available to cover debt-servicing obligations. Perhaps the most widely used coverage ratio is times interest earned, which is simply:

$$\text{Times interest earned} = \frac{\text{EBIT}}{\text{Interest on debt}}$$

Assume that the most recent annual EBIT for a company was \$4 million and that interest payments on all debt obligations were \$1 million. Therefore, times interest earned would be four times. This tells us that EBIT can drop by as much as 75 percent and the firm still will be able to cover its interest payments out of earnings.

However, a coverage ratio of only 1.0 indicates that earnings are just sufficient to satisfy the interest burden. Although it is difficult to generalize what is an appropriate interest coverage ratio, a CFO usually is concerned when the ratio gets much below 3 to 1. However, it all depends. In a highly stable industry, a relatively low times-interest-earned ratio may be appropriate, whereas it is not appropriate in a highly cyclical one.

Unfortunately, the times-interest-earned ratio tells us nothing about the ability of the firm to meet principal payments on its debt. The inability to meet a principal payment constitutes the same legal default as failure to meet an interest payment. Therefore, it is useful to compute the coverage ratio for the full debt-service burden. This ratio is:

$$\text{Debt-service coverage} = \frac{\text{EBIT}}{\text{Interest} + \dfrac{\text{Principal payments}}{1 - \text{Tax rate}}}$$

Here principal payments are adjusted upward for the tax effect. The reason is that EBIT represents earnings *before* taxes. Because principal payments are not tax deductible, they must be paid out of after-tax earnings. Therefore, we must adjust principal payments so that they are consistent with EBIT. If principal payments in our previous example were $1.5 million per annum and the tax rate were 34 percent, the debt-service coverage ratio would be:

$$\text{Debt-service coverage} = \frac{\$4 \text{ million}}{\$1 \text{ million} + \dfrac{\$1.5 \text{ million}}{1 - 0.34}} = 1.22$$

A coverage ratio of 1.22 means that EBIT can fall by only 22 percent before earnings coverage is insufficient to service the debt. The closer the ratio is to 1.0, the worse things are, all other things being equal. However, even with a coverage ratio of less than 1.0, a company may still meet its obligations if it can renew some of its debt when it comes due.

The financial risk associated with leverage should be analyzed on the basis of the firm's ability to service total fixed charges. Although lease financing is not debt per se, its impact on cash flows is exactly the same as the payment of interest and principal on a debt obligation. Therefore, annual lease payments should be added to the denominator of the formula in order to properly reflect the total cash flow burden associated with financing.

Two types of comparison should be undertaken with a coverage ratio.

1. Compare the coverage ratio with past and expected future ratios of the same company. The idea behind *trend analysis* is to determine whether there has been an improvement or a deterioration in coverage over time.
2. Evaluate the capital structure of other companies having similar business risk. Companies used in this comparison may be those in the same industry. If the firm is contemplating a capital structure significantly out of line with that of similar companies, it is conspicuous to the marketplace.

This is not to say, however, that the firm is wrong; other companies in the industry may be too conservative with respect to the use of debt. The optimal capital structure for all companies in the industry might call for a higher proportion of debt to equity than the industry average. As a result, the firm may well be able to justify more debt than the industry average. Because investment analysts and creditors tend to evaluate companies by industry, however, the firm should be able to justify its position if its capital structure is noticeably out of line in either direction.

Ultimately, a CFO wants to make generalizations about the appropriate amount of debt (and leases) for a firm to have in its capital structure. It is clear that over the long term, the source to service debt for a going concern is earnings. Therefore, coverage ratios are an important analytical tool. However, coverage ratios are but one tool by which a CFO is able to reach conclusions with respect to the company's best capital structure. Coverage ratios are subject to certain limitations and, consequently, cannot be used as the only means of determining the capital structure. For one thing, the fact that EBIT falls below the debt-service burden does not spell immediate doom for the company. Often alternative sources of funds, including renewal of a loan, are available, and these sources must be considered.

CAPITAL STRUCTURE DECISIONS

How do companies decide in practice which route to go in raising capital? It is a complex decision, related to a company's balance sheet, market conditions, outstanding obligations, and a host of other factors.

Many CFOs believe that these six factors influence capital structure:

1. Growth rate and stability of future sales
2. Competitive structure in the industry
3. Asset makeup of the individual firm
4. The business risk to which the firm is exposed
5. Control status of owners and management
6. Lenders' attitudes toward the industry and the company

Surveys indicate that the majority of CFOs of large firms believe in the concept of an optimal capital structure. The optimal capital structure is approximated by the identification of target debt ratios. The factor most frequently mentioned by CFOs that affects the level of the target debt ratio is the company's ability to service fixed financing costs. Other factors identified as affecting the target are maintaining a desired bond rating, providing an adequate borrowing reserve, and exploiting the advantages of financial leverage.

CHAPTER TWENTY-EIGHT

Dividend Policy

YOUR COMPANY'S DIVIDEND policy is important for these reasons:

- It impacts the financing program and capital budget.
- It affects cash flow. A company experiencing liquidity problems may be forced to restrict its dividend payments.
- It influences investor attitudes. For example, stockholders do not like dividends cut because they associate it with corporate financial problems. Furthermore, in formulating a dividend policy, the CFO must determine and fulfill the stockowners' objectives. Otherwise, the stockholders may sell their shares, which in turn may lower the market price of the stock. Stockholder dissatisfaction raises the possibility that an outside group may acquire control of the company.
- It lowers stockholders' equity since dividends reduce retained earnings and so results in a higher debt–equity ratio.

If your company's cash flows and investment requirements are unstable, the CFO should not recommend a high regular dividend. It would be better to establish a low regular dividend that can be met even in bad years.

TYPES OF DIVIDEND POLICIES

What dividend policy is best for your company?

The company's dividend policy should maximize owner wealth while providing adequate financing for the business. When the company's profitability increases, the CFO does not automatically raise the dividend. Generally, there is a time lag between increased earnings and the payment of a higher dividend. The CFO should be optimistic that the increased earnings will be sustained before he or she increases the dividend. If dividends are increased, they should continue to be paid at the higher rate. The CFO can choose from at least four different types of dividend policies:

1. *Stable dividend-per-share policy.* Many companies use this policy because it is looked upon favorably by investors. A stable dividend implies a low-risk company. If the dividend is maintained even in loss years, the shareholders are more apt perceive the losses as temporary. Furthermore, some stockholders rely on the receipt of stable dividends for income. A stable dividend policy is also necessary for a company to be placed on a list of securities in which financial institutions (pension funds, insurance companies) invest. The inclusion on the list provides greater marketability for corporate shares.

2. *Constant dividend-payout ratio (dividends per share/earnings per share).* Under this policy, a constant percentage of earnings is paid out in dividends. Because net income fluctuates, dividends paid will also vary using this policy. A problem arises if the company's earnings fall drastically or if there is a loss; in such a case, the dividends paid will be significantly reduced or nonexistent. This policy will not maximize market price per share since most stockholders do not want variability in their dividend receipts.

3. *Compromise policy.* A compromise between the policies of a stable dollar amount and a percentage amount of dividends is for a company to pay a lower dollar amount per share plus a percentage increment in good years. Although this policy provides flexibility, it also results in uncertainty in the minds of investors as to the amount of dividends they are likely to receive. Stockholders typically do not like such uncertainty. However, this policy may be suitable when earnings vary considerably over the years. The percentage, or extra, portion of the dividend should not be paid regularly; otherwise, it becomes meaningless.

4. *Residual-dividend policy.* When a company's investment opportunities are not stable, the CFO may wish to consider a vacillating dividend policy. The amount of earnings retained depends on the availability of investment opportunities. Dividends represent the residual amount from earnings after the company's investment needs are satisfied.

In theory, how much should be paid in dividends?

Theoretically, the company should retain earnings rather than distribute them when the corporate return exceeds the return investors can obtain on their money elsewhere. Furthermore, if the company obtains a return on its profits that exceeds the cost of

Example 28.1

Company A and company B are identical except for their dividend policies. Company A pays out a constant percentage of its net income (40 percent dividends), while company B pays out a constant dollar dividend. Company B's market price per share is higher than that of company A because the stock market looks favorably upon stable dollar dividends, which imply less uncertainty.

Example 28.2

Hayes Manufacturing Company had a net income of $800,000 in 2X11. Earnings have grown at an 8 percent annual rate. Dividends in 2X11 were $300,000. In 2X12, the net income was $1.1 million. This was much higher than the typical 8 percent annual growth rate. It is anticipated that profits will be back to the 8 percent rate in future years. The investment in 2X12 was $700,000.

Assuming a stable dividend payout ratio of 25 percent, the dividends to be paid in 2X12 will be $275,000 ($1,100,000 × 25%).

If a stable dollar dividend policy is maintained, the 2X12 dividend payment will be $324,000 ($300,000 × 1.08).

Assuming a residual dividend policy is maintained and 40 percent of the 2X12 investment is financed with debt, the 2X12 dividend will be:

$$Equity\ needed = \$700,000 \times 60\% = \$420,000$$

Since net income exceeds the equity needed, all of the $420,000 of equity investment will be derived from net income.

$$Dividend = \$1,100,000 - \$420,000 = \$680,000$$

If the investment for 2X12 is to be financed with 80 percent debt and 20 percent retained earnings, and any net income not invested is paid out in dividends, then the dividends will be:

$$Earnings\ retained = \$700,000 \times 20\% = \$140,000$$
$$Dividend = Net\ income - Earnings\ retained$$
$$\$960,000 = \$1,100,000 - \$140,000$$

capital, the market price of its stock will be maximized. However, theoretically the company should not keep funds for investment if it earns less of a return than what the investors can earn elsewhere. If the owners have better investment opportunities outside the company, the firm should pay a high dividend.

Although theoretical considerations from a financial perspective should be taken into account when establishing dividend policy, the *practicality* of the situation is that investors expect to be paid dividends. Psychological factors that may adversely impact the market price of the stock of a company that does not pay dividends come into play.

 ## VARIABLES TO BE CONSIDERED

What are the important variables in establishing dividend policy?

A company's dividend policy depends on many variables, some of which have already been mentioned. Other factors to be considered are:

- *Profitability.* Dividend distribution is tied to earnings.
- *Earnings stability.* A company with stable earnings is better able to distribute a higher percentage of its profit than one with unstable earnings.

- *Tax penalties.* The tax penalties for excess accumulation of retained earnings may result in high-dividend payouts.
- *Financial leverage.* A company with a high debt–equity ratio is more likely to retain profits so that it will have the funds to pay interest and principal on debt when due.
- *Restrictive covenants.* There may be a restriction in a loan agreement limiting the dividend payments.
- *Growth rate.* A rapidly growing company, even if profitable, may have to cut back on dividends to keep funds within the business for growth.
- *Uncertainty.* The payment of dividends reduces the uncertainty in stockholders' minds about the firm's financial condition.
- *Ability to finance externally.* A company that is able to obtain outside financing can afford to have a higher dividend payout ratio. When external sources of funds are limited, more earnings will be retained for planned financial needs.
- *Age and size.* An older, established, large company is usually better able to maintain dividend payments.
- *Maintenance of control.* Management that is reluctant to issue additional common stock because it does not want to dilute control of the firm will retain a higher percentage of its earnings. Internal financing enables management to keep control within the company.

How does stock repurchase benefit or hinder the company?

The purchase of treasury stock is an alternative to paying dividends. Since outstanding shares will be fewer after stock has been repurchased, earnings per share will increase (assuming net income is held constant). The increase in earnings per share may result in a higher market price per share.

Example 28.3

A company earned $2.5 million in 2X12. Of this amount, it decided that 20 percent would be used to buy treasury stock. Currently, there are 400,000 shares outstanding. Market price per share is $18. The company can use $500,000 (20% × $2.5 million) to buy back 25,000 shares through a tender offer of $20 per share. The offer price of $20 is higher than the current market price of $18 because the company feels its buyback will drive up the price of existing shares due to the demand/supply relationship.

Current earnings per share (EPS) is:

$$\text{EPS} = \frac{\text{Net income}}{\text{Out standing shares}} = \frac{\$2,500,000}{400,000} = \$6.25$$

The current price/earnings (P/E) multiple is:

$$\frac{\text{Market price per share}}{\text{EPS}} = \frac{\$18}{\$6.25} = 2.88 \text{ times}$$

Earnings per share after treasury stock is acquired becomes:

$$\frac{\$2,500,000}{400,000 - 25,000} = \frac{\$2,500,000}{375,000} = \$6.67$$

The expected market price, assuming the P/E ratio (multiple) remains the same, is:

$$\text{P/E multiple} \times \text{New EPS} = \text{Expected market price}$$
$$2.88 \times \$6.67 = \$19.21$$

The benefits from a stock repurchase include:

- Treasury stock can be resold if additional funds are needed. If the treasury stock was acquired for a price less than the current market price, the excess increases paid-in capital.
- If there is temporary excess cash, the CFO may prefer to repurchase stock than to pay a higher dividend that he or she believes cannot be maintained.
- Treasury stock can be used for stock options or future acquisitions.
- If management is holding stock, they will favor a stock repurchase rather than a dividend because of the favorable tax treatment.

The disadvantages of treasury stock acquisition include:

- If investors believe that the company is engaging in a repurchase plan because there are no alternative good investment prospects, a decline in the market price of stock may occur. However, there are instances when this has not happened, such as when General Electric announced a plan of periodic reacquisition of stock because of a lack of more attractive investment opportunities.
- If the reacquisition of stock appears to be manipulation, the Securities and Exchange Commission may investigate. Furthermore, if the Internal Revenue Service concludes that the repurchase is designed to avoid the payment of tax on dividends, tax penalties may be imposed because of the improper accumulation of earnings.

CHAPTER TWENTY-NINE

Financial Management of Multinational Corporations

MANY COMPANIES ARE multinational corporations (MNCs) that have significant foreign operations and derive a high percentage of their sales from overseas. The CFOs of MNCs need to understand the complexities of international finance to make sound financial and investment decisions. International finance involves consideration of managing working capital, financing the business, control of foreign exchange and political risks, and foreign direct investments. Most important, the CFO has to consider the value of the U.S. dollar relative to the value of the currency of the foreign country in which business activities are being conducted. Currency exchange rates may materially affect receivables and payables as well as imports and exports of the U.S. company in its multinational operations. The effect is more pronounced with increasing activities abroad.

FINANCIAL MANAGEMENT ESSENTIALS FOR MNCs

Financial management of MNCs has unique characteristics. They are:

- *Multiple-currency problem.* Sales revenues may be collected in one currency, assets denominated in another, and profits measured in a third.
- *Various legal, institutional, and economic constraints.* There are variations in such things as tax laws, labor practices, balance-of-payment policies, and government controls with respect to the types and sizes of investments, types and amount of capital raised, and repatriation of profits.
- *Internal control problem.* When the parent office of a MNC and its affiliates are widely located, internal organizational difficulties arise.

What are popular financial goals of MNCs?

A survey of CFOs of MNCs lists the financial goals of MNCs in the following order of importance:

1. Maximize growth in corporate earnings, whether total earnings, earnings before interest and taxes (EBIT), or earnings per share.
2. Maximize return on equity.
3. Guarantee that funds are always available when needed.

What types of foreign operations are right for you?

When strong competition exists in the United States, a company may look to enter or expand its foreign base. However, if a company is unsuccessful in the domestic market, it is likely to have problems overseas as well. Furthermore, the CFO must be cognizant of local customs and risks in the international markets.

A large, well-established company with much international experience may eventually have wholly owned subsidiaries. However, a small company with limited foreign experience operating in risky areas may be restricted to export and import activity.

If the company's sales force has minimal experience in export sales, it is advisable to use foreign brokers when specialized knowledge of foreign markets is needed. When sufficient volume exists, the company may establish a foreign branch sales office including salespeople and technical service staff. As the operation matures, production facilities may be located in the foreign market. However, some foreign countries require licensing before foreign sales and production can take place. In this case, a foreign licensee sells and produces the product. A problem with this situation is that confidential information and knowledge are passed on to the licensees, who can then become competitors at the expiration of the agreement.

A joint venture with a foreign company is another way to proceed internationally and share the risk. To allow foreign companies to operate in their countries, some governments require joint ventures. The foreign company may have local goodwill that can help ensure success. Potential drawbacks are less control over activities and conflict of interests.

In evaluating the impact that foreign operations have on the entity's financial health, the CFO should consider the extent of international transactions, foreign restrictions and laws, tax structure of the foreign country, and the economic and political stability of the country. If a subsidiary is operating in a high-tax country with a double-tax agreement, dividend payments are not subject to further U.S. taxes. One way to transfer income from high-tax areas to low-tax areas is to levy royalties or management fees on the subsidiaries.

 ## FOREIGN EXCHANGE MARKET

What is the foreign exchange market?

There is no central marketplace for the foreign exchange market. Rather, business is carried out over telephone, wire service, or cable. The major dealers are large banks. A company that wants to buy or sell currency typically uses a commercial bank. International transactions and investments involve more than one currency. For example, when a U.S. company sells merchandise to a Japanese firm, the American firm wants to be paid in dollars but the Japanese company typically expects to receive yen. Because of the foreign exchange market, the buyer may pay in one currency while the seller may receive payment in another currency.

What are spot and forward foreign exchange rates?

An exchange rate is the ratio of one unit of currency to another. An exchange rate is established between the different currencies. The conversion rate between currencies depends on the demand/supply relationship. Because of the change in exchange rates, companies are susceptible to exchange rate fluctuation risks due to a net asset or net liability position in a foreign currency. (See Exhibit 29.1.)

EXHIBIT 29.1 Sample Foreign Exchange Rates, August 5, 2X12

Country	Contract	U.S. Dollar Equivalent	Currency per U.S.$
Britain	Spot	1.6124	0.6202
(pound; £)	30-day future	1.6091	0.6215
	90-day future	1.6030	0.6238
	180-day future	1.5934	0.6276
Japan	Spot	0.008341	119.89
(yen; ¥)	30-day future	0.008349	119.77
	90-day future	0.008366	119.53
	180-day future	0.008394	119.13

Exchange rates may be in terms of dollars per foreign currency unit (called a *direct quote*) or units of foreign currency per dollar (called an indirect quote). Therefore, an indirect quote is the reciprocal of a direct quote and vice versa:

$$\text{Indirect quote} = 1/\text{Direct quote}$$

$$£/\$ = 1/(\$/£)$$

Example 29.1

A rate of $1.6124/£1 means each £1 costs the U.S. company $1.6124. In other words, the U.S. company gets $1/1.6124 = £0.6202$ for each dollar.

The *spot rate* is the exchange rate for immediate delivery of currencies exchanged, whereas the *forward rate* is the exchange rate for later delivery of currencies exchanged. For example, there may be a 90-day exchange rate. The forward exchange rate of a currency will be slightly different from the spot rate at the current date because of future expectations and uncertainties.

Forward rates may be greater than the current spot rate (premium) or less than the current spot rate (discount).

What are cross rates?

A cross rate is the indirect calculation of the exchange rate of one currency from the exchange rates of two other currencies.

Example 29.2

The dollar per pound and the yen per dollar rates are given in Exhibit 29.1. From this information, you could determine the yen per pound (or pound per yen) exchange rates. For example, you see that:

$$(\$/£) \times (¥/\$) = (¥/£)$$

$$1.6124 \times 119.89 = 193.31$$

Thus, the pound per yen exchange rate is

$$1/193.31 = £0.00517 \text{ pound per } ¥1$$

Example 29.3

On February 1, 2X12, forward rates on the British pound were at a premium in relation to the spot rate, while the forward rates for the Japanese yen were at a discount from the spot rate. This means that participants in the foreign exchange market anticipated that the British pound would appreciate relative to the U.S. dollar in the future but the Japanese yen would depreciate against the dollar.

The percentage discount or premium is computed as follows. Forward premium (or discount) equals:

$$\frac{\text{Forward rate} - \text{Spot rate}}{\text{Spot rate}} \times \frac{12}{\text{Length of forward contract in months}} \times 100$$

where if the forward rate is greater than the spot rate, the result is the annualized premium in percent; otherwise, it is the annualized discount in percent.

Because most currencies are quoted against the dollar, it may be necessary to work out the cross rates (see Exhibit 29.2) for currencies other than the dollar. The cross rate is needed to consummate financial transactions between two countries.

EXHIBIT 29.2 Example of Key Currency Cross Rates

	British £	Euro €	Japanese ¥	U.S. $
British £	—	0.7054	0.00517	0.62020
Euro €	1.4176	—	0.00733	0.87920
Japanese ¥	193.31	136.36	—	119.89
U.S. $	1.6124	1.1374	0.00834	—

On August 5, 2X12, a 30-day forward contract in Japanese yen (see Exhibit 29.1) was selling at a 1.15 percent premium:

$$\frac{0.008349 - 0.008341}{0.008341} \times \frac{12 \text{ months}}{1 \text{ month}} \times 100 = 1.15\%$$

How do you control foreign exchange risk?

Foreign exchange rate risk exists when the contract is written in terms of the foreign currency or denominated in foreign currency. Exchange rate fluctuations increase the riskiness of the investment and incur cash losses. CFOs must not only seek the highest return on temporary investments but must also be concerned about the changing values of the currencies invested. CFOs do not necessarily eliminate foreign exchange risk; they can only try to contain it.

FINANCIAL STRATEGIES

In countries where currency values are likely to drop, CFOs of the subsidiaries should:

- Avoid paying advances on purchase orders unless the seller pays interest on the advances sufficient to cover the loss of purchasing power.
- Not have excess idle cash. Excess cash can be used to buy inventory or other real assets.
- Buy materials and supplies on credit in the country in which the foreign subsidiary is operating, extending the final payment date as long as possible.
- Avoid giving excessive trade credit. If accounts receivable balances are outstanding for an extended time period, interest should be charged to absorb the loss in purchasing power.
- Borrow local currency funds when the interest rate charged does not exceed U.S. rates after taking into account expected devaluation in the foreign country.

TYPES OF FOREIGN EXCHANGE EXPOSURE

What are three different types of foreign exchange exposure?

The CFOs of MNCs are faced with the dilemma of three different types of foreign exchange risk.

1. *Translation exposure*, often called *accounting exposure*, measures the impact of an exchange rate change on the firm's financial statements. An example would be the impact of a euro devaluation on a U.S. firm's reported income statement and balance sheet.
2. *Operating exposure*, often called *economic exposure*, is the potential for the change in the present value of future cash flows due to an unexpected change in the exchange rate.
3. *Transaction exposure* measures potential gains or losses on the future settlement of outstanding obligations that are denominated in a foreign currency. An example would be a U.S. dollar loss after the euro devalues on payment received for an export invoiced in euros before that devaluation.

Translation Exposure

A major purpose of translation is to provide data of expected impacts of rate changes on cash flow and equity. In the translation of foreign subsidiaries' financial statements into the U.S. parent's financial statements, the foreign currency is translated into U.S. dollars. Balance sheet accounts are translated using the current exchange rate at the balance sheet date. If a current exchange rate is not available at the balance sheet date, use the first exchange rate available after that date. Income statement accounts are translated using the weighted-average exchange rate for the period.

Accounting Standards Codification No. 830-10-15, *Foreign Currency Matters: Overall* (Financial Accounting Standards No. 52, *Foreign Currency Translation*) requires translation by the current rate method. Under the current rate method:

- All balance sheet assets and liabilities are translated at the current rate of exchange in effect on the balance sheet date.
- Income statement items are usually translated at an average exchange rate for the reporting period.
- All equity accounts are translated at the historical exchange rates that were in effect at the time the accounts first entered the balance sheet.
- Translation gains and losses are reported as a separate item in the stockholders' equity section of the balance sheet. Translation gains and losses are included in net income only when there is a sale or liquidation of the entire investment in a foreign entity.

Operating Exposure

Operating (economic) exposure is the possibility that an unexpected change in exchange rates will cause a change in the future cash flows of a firm and its market value. It differs from translation and transaction exposures in that it is subjective and thus not easily quantified.

Note

The best strategy to control operating exposure is to diversify operations and financing internationally. ■

Transaction Exposure

Foreign currency transactions may result in receivables or payables fixed in terms of the amount of foreign currency to be received or paid. Transaction gains and losses are reported in the income statement.

Foreign currency transactions are those transactions whose terms are denominated in a currency other than the entity's functional currency. Foreign currency transactions take place when a business:

- Buys or sells on credit goods or services the prices of which are denominated in foreign currencies
- Borrows or lends funds, and the amounts payable or receivable are denominated in a foreign currency
- Is a party to an unperformed forward exchange contract
- Acquires or disposes of assets, or incurs or settles liabilities denominated in foreign currencies

Note

Transaction losses differ from translation losses, which do not influence taxable income. ■

What is long versus short position?

When a devaluation of the dollar takes place, foreign assets and income in strong-currency countries are worth more dollars as long as foreign liabilities do not offset this beneficial effect.

Foreign exchange risk can be analyzed by examining expected receipts or obligations in foreign currency units. A company expecting receipts in foreign currency units (*long* position in the foreign currency units) has the risk that the value of the foreign currency units will drop. This results in devaluing the foreign currency relative to the dollar. If a company is expecting to have obligations in foreign currency units (*short* position in the foreign currency units), there is risk that the value of the foreign currency will rise and the company will need to buy the currency at a higher price.

If net claims are greater than liabilities in a foreign currency, the company has a long position since it will benefit if the value of the foreign currency rises. If net liabilities exceed claims with respect to foreign currencies, the company is in a short position because it will gain if the foreign currency drops in value.

What is your monetary position?

Monetary balance is avoiding either a net receivable or a net payable position. Monetary assets and liabilities do not change in value with devaluation or revaluation in foreign currencies.

A company with a long position in a foreign currency will be receiving more funds in the foreign currency. It will have a net monetary asset position (monetary assets exceed monetary liabilities) in that currency.

A company with net receipts is a net monetary creditor. Its foreign exchange rate risk exposure has a net receipts position in a foreign currency that is susceptible to a drop in value.

A company with a future net obligation in foreign currency has a net monetary debtor position. It faces a foreign exchange risk of the possibility of an increase in the value of the foreign currency.

How can foreign exchange risk be neutralized?

Foreign exchange risk can be neutralized or hedged by a change in the asset and liability position in the foreign currency. Here are some ways to control exchange risk.

- *Entering a hedge.* Here the exposed position in a foreign currency is offset by borrowing or lending in the money market.

Example 29.4

XYZ, an American importer, enters into a contract with a British supplier to buy merchandise for £4,000. The amount is payable on the delivery of the good, 30 days from today. The company knows the exact amount of its pound liability in 30 days. However, it does not know the payable in dollars. Assume that the 30-day money-market rates for both lending and borrowing in the United States and United Kingdom are 0.5 percent and 1 percent, respectively. Assume further that today's foreign exchange rate is $1.50 per £1.

In a money-market hedge, XYZ can take these steps:

1. Buy a one-month U.K. money market security worth £4,000/(1 + 0.005) = £3,980. This investment will compound to exactly £4,000 in one month.
2. Exchange dollars on today's spot (cash) market to obtain the £3,980. The dollar amount needed today is £3,980 × $1.7350 per £1 = $6,905.30.
3. If XYZ does not have this amount, it can borrow it from the U.S. money market at the going rate of 1 percent. In 30 days, XYZ will need to repay $6,905.30 × (1 + 0.1) = $7,595.83.

Note

XYZ need not wait for the future exchange rate to be available. On today's date, the future dollar amount of the contract is known with certainty. The British supplier will receive £4,000, and the cost to XYZ to make the payment is $7,595.83. ■

- *Hedging by purchasing forward (or futures) exchange contracts.* The forward exchange contract is a commitment to buy or sell, at a specified future date, one currency for a specified amount of another currency (at a specified exchange rate). This can be a hedge against changes in exchange rates during a period of contract or exposure to risk from such changes. More specifically, you first buy foreign exchange forward contracts to cover payables denominated in a foreign currency, and then sell foreign exchange forward contracts to cover receivables denominated in a foreign currency. This way, any gain or loss on the foreign receivables or payables due to changes in exchange rates is offset by the gain or loss on the forward exchange contract.

Example 29.5

In the previous example, assume that the 30-day forward exchange rate is $1.7272. XYZ may take the following steps to cover its payable.

1. Buy a forward contract today to purchase £4,000 in 30 days.
2. On the 30th day, pay the foreign exchange dealer £4,000 × $1.7272 per £1 = $6,908.80 and collect £4,000. Pay this amount to the British supplier.

Note

Using the forward contract, XYZ knows the exact worth of the future payment in dollars ($6,908.80). ▪

Note

The basic difference between futures contracts and forward contracts is that futures contracts are for specified amounts and maturities, whereas forward contracts are for any size and maturity desired. ▪

▪ *Hedging by foreign currency options.* Foreign currency options can be purchased or sold in three different types of markets: (1) options on the physical currency, purchased on the over-the-counter (interbank) market; (2) options on the physical currency on organized exchanges, such as the Philadelphia Stock Exchange and the Chicago Mercantile Exchange; and (3) options on futures contracts, purchased on the International Monetary Market of the Chicago Mercantile Exchange.

Note

The difference between using a futures contract and using an option on a futures contract is that with a futures contract, the company must deliver one currency against another or reverse the contract on the exchange; with an option, the company may abandon the option and use the spot (cash) market if that is more advantageous. ▪

- *Repositioning cash by leading and lagging the time at which an MNC makes operational or financial payments.* Often, money- and forward-market hedges are not available to eliminate exchange risk. Under such circumstances, leading (accelerating) and lagging (decelerating) can be used to *reduce* risk.

Note

A net asset position (i.e., assets minus liabilities) is not desirable in a weak or potentially depreciating currency. In this case, you should expedite the disposal of the asset. By the same token, you should lag or delay the collection against a net asset position in a strong currency. ▪

- *Maintaining a balance between receivables and payables denominated in a foreign currency.* MNCs typically set up multilateral netting centers as special departments to settle the outstanding balances of affiliates of an MNC with each other on a net basis. It is the development of a clearinghouse for payments by the firm's affiliates. If there are amounts due among affiliates, they are offset insofar as possible. The net amount would be paid in the currency of the transaction. The total amounts owed need not be paid in the currency of the transaction; thus, a much lower quantity of the currency must be acquired.

Note

The major advantage of the system is a reduction of the costs associated with a large number of separate foreign exchange transactions. ▪

- *Positioning of funds through transfer pricing.* A transfer price is the price at which an MNC sells goods and services to its foreign affiliates or, alternatively, the price at which an affiliate sells to the parent. For example, a parent that wishes to transfer funds from an affiliate in a depreciating-currency country may charge a higher price on the goods and services sold to this affiliate by the parent or by affiliates from strong-currency countries. Transfer pricing affects not only transfer of funds from one entity to another but also the income taxes paid by both entities.

What are some key questions to ask that help to identify foreign exchange risk?

A systematic approach to identifying an MNC's exposure to foreign exchange risk is to ask a series of questions regarding the net effects on profits of changes in foreign currency revenues and costs. The questions are:

- Where is the MNC selling? (domestic versus foreign sales share)
- Who are the firm's major competitors? (domestic versus foreign)

- Where is the firm producing? (domestic versus foreign)
- Where are the firm's inputs coming from? (domestic versus foreign)
- How sensitive is quantity demanded to price? (elastic versus inelastic)
- How are the firm's inputs or outputs priced? (priced in a domestic market or a global market; the currency of denomination)

Can you forecast foreign exchange rates?

The forecasting of foreign exchange rates is a formidable task. Most MNCs rely primarily on bank and bank services for assistance and information in preparing exchange rate projections. These economic indicators are considered to be the most important for the forecasting process:

- Recent rate movements
- Relative inflation rates
- Balance of payments and trade
- Money supply growth
- Interest rate differentials

 INTEREST RATE PARITY

Interest rates have an important influence on exchange rates. In fact, there is an important economic relationship between any two nations' spot rates, forward rates, and interest rates. This relationship is called the interest rate parity theorem (IRPT). This theorem states that the ratio of the forward and spot rates is directly related to the two interest rates.

Specifically, the premium (P) or discount (D) should be:

$$P(\text{or } D) = \frac{r_f - r_d}{1 + r_f}$$

where
r_f = foreign interest rate
r_d = domestic interest rate

When interest rates are relatively low, this equation can be approximated as P (or $D) = -(r_f - r_d)$.

The IRPT implies that the P (or D) calculated by the equation should be the same as the P (or D) calculated by:

$$P(\text{or } D) = \frac{F - S}{S} = \frac{12 \text{ months}}{n} \times 100$$

where
F = forward exchange rate (e.g., $/foreign currency)
S = spot exchange rate (e.g., $/foreign currency)
n = length of forward contract in months

Example 29.6

On August 5, 2X12, a 30-day forward contract in the Japanese yen (see Exhibit 29.1) was selling at a 1.15 percent premium:

$$\frac{0.008349 - 0.008341}{0.008341} \times \frac{12 \text{ months}}{1 \text{ month}} \times 100 = 1.15\%$$

The 30-day U.S. T-bill rate is 8 percent annualized. What is the 30-day Japanese rate?
Using the equation:

$$P(\text{or } D) = \frac{r_f - r_d}{1 + r_f}$$

$$0.0115 = \frac{r_f - 0.08}{1 + r_f}$$

$$0.0115(1 + r_f) = r_f - 0.08$$
$$0.0115 + 0.0115\, r_f = r_f - 0.08$$
$$0.09115 = 0.9885\, r_f$$
$$r_f = 0.0922$$

The 30-day Japanese rate should be 9.22 percent.

 ## PURCHASING POWER PARITY

Inflation, which is a change in price levels, also affects future exchange rates. The mathematical relationship that links changes in exchange rates and changes in price level is called the *purchasing power parity theorem* (PPPT). The PPPT states that the ratio of the forward and spot rates is directly related to the two inflation rates:

$$\frac{F}{S} = \frac{1 + p_d}{1 + p_f}$$

where
p_d = domestic inflation rate
p_f = foreign inflation rate

Example 29.7

Assume the following data for the United States and the United Kingdom:

Expected U.S. inflation rate = 5%
Expected U.K. inflation rate = 10%

Then

$$S = \$1.6124/£1$$

$$\frac{F}{1.6124} = \frac{1.05}{1.10}$$

so

$$F = \$1.5391/£1$$

If the U.K. has the higher inflation rate, then the purchasing power of the pound is declining faster than that of the dollar. This will lead to a forward discount on the pound relative to the dollar.

APPRAISING FOREIGN INVESTMENTS

How do you analyze foreign investments?

Foreign investment decisions are basically capital budgeting decisions at the international level. The decision requires two major components:

1. Estimation of the relevant future cash flows. Cash flows are the dividends and possible future sales price of the investment. The estimation depends on the sales forecast, the effects on exchange rate changes, the risk in cash flows, and the actions of foreign governments.
2. Choice of the proper discount rate (cost of capital). The cost of capital in foreign investment projects is higher due to the increases in:

   ▪ Currency risk (or foreign exchange risk)—changes in exchange rates. This risk may adversely affect sales by making competing imported goods cheaper.
   ▪ Political risk (or sovereignty risk)—possibility of nationalization or other restrictions with net losses to the parent company. Examples of political risks include:

     ▪ Expropriation of plants and equipment without compensation or with minimal compensation that is below actual market value
     ▪ Nonconvertibility of the affiliate's foreign earnings into the parent's currency—the problem of "blocked funds"
     ▪ Substantial changes in the laws governing taxation
     ▪ Government controls in the host country regarding wages, compensation of personnel, hiring of personnel, sales price of the product, transfer payments to the parent, and local borrowing

How do you measure political risk?

Many MNCs and banks have attempted to measure political risks in their businesses. They even hire or maintain a group of political risk analysts. Several independent services provide political risk and country risk ratings.

▪ *Euromoney* magazine publishes an annual *Country Risk Rating*, which is based on a measure of different countries' access to international credit, trade finance, political risk, and its payment record. The rankings are generally confirmed by political risk insurers and top syndicate managers in the Euromarkets.

■ *The Economist Intelligence Unit*, a New York–based subsidiary of the *Economist Group*, London, provides ratings based on such factors as external debt and trends in the current account, the consistency of government policy, foreign exchange reserves, and the quality of economic management.

■ *International Country Risk Guide* is published by the PRS Group (www.prsgroup.com) and offers a composite risk rating as well as individual ratings for political, financial, and economic risk for 161 countries. The political variable—which makes up half of the composite index—includes factors such as government corruption and how economic expectations diverge from reality. The financial rating looks at such things as the likelihood of losses from exchange controls and loan defaults. Finally, economic ratings consider such factors as inflation and debt-service costs. (See Exhibit 29.3.)

EXHIBIT 29.3 Country Risk, Ranked by Composite Risk Rating, July 2008 versus August 2009

Rank in 07/08	Country	Composite Risk Rating 07/08	Composite Risk Rating 08/09	07/08 versus 08/09	Rank in 09/08
1	Norway	91.8	92.3	−0.5	1
2	Luxembourg	89.3	89.5	−0.3	3
3	Brunei	88.5	88.5	0.0	4
3	Switzerland	88.5	89.8	−1.3	2
5	Finland	87.5	88.5	−1.0	4
6	Singapore	87.0	88.0	−1.0	6
6	Sweden	87.0	87.8	−0.8	7
8	Denmark	86.0	87.0	−1.0	7
8	Germany	86.0	85.8	0.3	10
10	Netherlands	85.5	85.8	−0.3	10
11	Canada	85.0	83.8	1.3	17
11	Hong Kong	85.0	85.8	−0.8	10
11	Kuwait	85.0	86.0	−1.0	9
14	Austria	84.8	82.0	2.8	23
15	Botswana	84.0	85.0	−1.0	13
16	Taiwan	83.8	81.0	2.8	25
16	United Arab Emirates	83.8	84.3	−0.5	15
18	Belgium	83.3	82.5	0.8	20
18	Ireland	83.3	85.0	−1.8	13
20	Oman	82.5	84.3	−1.8	15

Source: Extract from *International Country Risk Guide*, Copyright, 1984–Present, The PRS Group, Inc. (www.prsgroup.com).

What are the methods for dealing with political risk?

To the extent that forecasting political risks is a formidable task, what can an MNC do to cope with them? Several methods have been suggested.

- *Avoidance.* Try to avoid political risk by minimizing activities in or with countries that are considered to be of high risk. Use a higher discount rate for projects in riskier countries.
- *Adaptation.* Try to reduce such risk by adapting the activities (e.g., by using hedging techniques discussed previously).
- *Diversification.* Diversify across national borders, so that problems in one country do not risk the company.
- *Risk transfer.* Buy insurance policies for political risks.

Example 29.8

Most developed nations offer insurance for political risk to their exporters. These policies cover risks such as currency inconvertibility, civil or foreign war damages, or expropriation. Examples of organizations offering such policies include:

- In the United States, the Export-Import Bank of the United States (which offers policies to exporters) and the Overseas Private Investment Corporation (which offers policies to U.S. organizations making foreign investments).
- In the United Kingdom, the Export Credit Guarantee Department
- In Canada, the Export Development Council
- In Germany, an agency called Hermes

 FINANCING

What are international sources of financing?

A company may finance its activities abroad, especially in countries where it is operating. A successful company in domestic markets is more likely to be able to attract financing for international expansion.

The most important international sources of funds are the Eurocurrency market and the Eurobond market. Also, MNCs often have access to national capital markets in which their subsidiaries are located. (See Exhibit 29.4.)

EXHIBIT 29.4   International Financial Markets

Market	Instruments	Participants	Regulator
International monetary system	Special drawing rights; gold; foreign exchange	Central banks; International Monetary Fund	International Monetary Fund

(continued)

EXHIBIT 29.4 *(continued)*

Market	Instruments	Participants	Regulator
Foreign exchange markets	Bank deposits; currency; futures and forward contracts	Commercial and central banks; firms; individuals	Central bank in each country
National money markets (short term)	Bank deposits and loans; short-term government securities; commercial paper	Banks; firms; individuals; government agencies	Central bank; other government agencies
National capital markets (long term)	Bonds; long-term bank deposits and loans; stocks; long-term government securities	Banks; firms; individuals; government agencies	Central bank; other government agencies
Eurocurrency market	Bank deposits; bank loans; eurocommercial paper	Commercial banks; firms; government agencies	Substantially unregulated
Eurobond market	Bonds	Banks; firms; individuals; government agencies	Substantially unregulated

The Eurocurrency market is a largely short-term (usually less than one year of maturity) market for bank deposits and loans denominated in any currency except the currency of the country where the market is located. For example, in London, the Eurocurrency market is a market for bank deposits and loans denominated in dollars, yen, euros, and any other currency except British pounds. The main instruments used in this market are certificates of deposit, time deposits, and bank loans.

Note

The term "market" in this context does not mean a physical marketplace but a set of bank deposits and loans. ■

The Eurobond market is a long-term market for bonds denominated in any currency except the currency of the country where the market is located. Eurobonds may be of different types, such as straight, convertible, and with warrants. Although most Eurobonds are fixed rate, variable-rate bonds also exist. Maturities vary, but 10 to 12 years is typical.

Although Eurobonds are issued in many currencies, a stable, fully convertible, and actively traded currency should be selected. In some cases, if a Eurobond is denominated in a weak currency, the holder has the option of requesting payment in another currency.

Sometimes large MNCs establish wholly owned offshore finance subsidiaries. These subsidiaries issue Eurobond debt, and the proceeds are given to the parent or to overseas operating subsidiaries. Debt service goes back to bondholders through the finance subsidiaries.

If the Eurobond was issued by the parent directly, the United States would require a withholding tax on interest. There may also be an estate tax when the bondholder dies.

These tax problems do not arise when a bond is issued by a finance subsidiary incorporated in a tax haven. Hence, the subsidiary may borrow at less cost than the parent.

In summary, the Euromarkets offers borrowers and investors in one country the opportunity to deal with borrowers and investors from many other countries, buying and selling bank deposits, bonds, and loans denominated in many currencies.

Exhibit 29.5 provides a list of funding sources available to a foreign affiliate of an MNC (debt and equity).

EXHIBIT 29.5   International Sources of Credit

Borrowing	Domestic inside the Firm	Domestic Market	Foreign inside the Firm	Foreign Market	Euromarket
Direct, short term	Intrafirm loans, transfer pricing, royalties, fees, service charges	Commercial paper	International intrafirm loans, international transfer pricing, dividends, royalties, fees		Eurocommercial paper
Intermediated short term		Short-term bank loans, discounted receivables	International back-to-back loans	Short-term bank loans, discounted receivables	Euro short-term loans
Direct, long term	Intrafirm loans, invested in affiliates	Stock issue, bond issue	International intrafirm long-term loans, foreign direct investment	Stock issue, bond issue	Eurobonds
Intermediated, long term		Long-term bank loans	International back-to-back loans	Long-term bank loans	Euro long-term loans

ANALYSIS OF FOREIGN INVESTMENTS

How do you make foreign investment decisions?

Foreign investment decisions are basically capital budgeting decisions at the international level. Capital budgeting analysis for foreign as compared to domestic investment introduces at least six complications:

1. Cash flows to a project and to the parent must be differentiated.
2. National differences in tax systems, financial institutions, and financial norms and in constraints on financial flows must be recognized.
3. Different inflation rates can affect profitability and the competitive position of an affiliate.
4. Foreign exchange rate changes can alter the competitive position of a foreign affiliate and the value of cash flows between the affiliate and the parent.
5. Segmented capital markets create opportunities for financial gains, or they may cause additional costs.
6. Political risk can significantly change the value of a foreign investment.

The methods of evaluating multinational capital budgeting decisions include net present value (NPV), adjusted present value, and internal rate of return (IRR).

Example 29.9

Here we illustrate a case of multinational capital budgeting by analyzing a hypothetical foreign investment project in Korea by a U.S. manufacturing firm (called Am-tel). The analysis is based on the following data gathered by a project team.

- *Product.* The company (hereafter Ko-tel) is expected to be a wholly owned Korean manufacturer of customized integrated circuits for use in computers, automobiles, and robots. Ko-tel's products would be sold primarily in Korea, and all sales would be denominated in Korean won (₩).
- *Sales.* Sales in the first year are forecasted to be ₩26 billion. Sales are expected to grow at 10 percent per year for the foreseeable future.
- *Working capital.* Ko-tel needs gross working capital (i.e., cash, receivables, and inventory) equal to 25 percent of sales. Half of gross working capital can be financed by local payables, but the other half must be financed by Ko-tel or Am-tel.
- *Parent-supplied components.* Components sold to Ko-tel by Am-tel have a direct cost to Am-tel equal to 95 percent of their sales price. The margin is therefore 5 percent.
- *Depreciation.* Plant and equipment will be depreciated on a straight-line basis for both accounting and tax purposes over an expected life of 10 years. No salvage value is anticipated.
- *License fees.* Ko-tel will pay a license fee of 2.5 percent of sales revenue to Am-tel. This fee is tax deductible in Korea but provides taxable income to Am-tel.
- *Taxes.* The Korean corporate income tax rate is 35 percent, and the U.S. rate is 38 percent. Korea has no withholding tax on dividends, interest, or fees paid to foreign residents.

- *Cost of capital.* The cost of capital (or minimum required return) used in Korea by companies of comparable risk is 22 percent. Am-tel also uses 22 percent as a discount rate for its investments.
- *Inflation.* Prices are expected to increase as follows:

  Korean general price level: + 9% per year

  Ko-tel average sales price: + 9% per year

  Korean raw material costs: + 3% per year

  Korean labor costs: + 12% per year

  U.S. general price level: + 5% per year

- *Exchange rates.* In the year in which the initial investment takes place, the exchange rate is ₩950 to $1. Am-tel forecasts the won to appreciate relative to the dollar at 1 percent per annum.
- *Dividend policy.* Ko-tel will pay 70 percent of accounting net income to Am-tel as an annual cash dividend. Ko-tel and Am-tel estimate that over a five-year period, the other 30 percent of net income must be reinvested to finance working capital growth.
- *Financing.* Ko-tel will be financed by Am-tel with an $11 million purchase of ₩8.25 billion of common stock, all to be owned by Am-tel.

In order to develop the normal cash flow projections, Am-tel has made six assumptions:

1. Sales revenue in the first year of operations is expected to be ₩26 billion. Won sales revenue will increase annually at 10 percent because of physical growth and at an additional 9 percent because of price increases. Consequently, sales revenue will grow at (1.1)(1.09) = 1.20, or 20 percent per year.
2. Korean raw material costs in the first year are budgeted at ₩4 billion. Korean raw material costs are expected to increase at 10 percent per year because of physical growth and at an additional 3 percent because of price increases. Consequently, raw material cost will grow at (1.1)(1.03) = 1.13, or 13 percent per year.
3. Parent-supplied component costs in the first year are budgeted at 9 billion. Parent-supplied component costs are expected to increase annually at 10 percent because of physical growth, plus an additional 5 percent because of U.S. inflation, plus another 1 percent in won terms because of the expected appreciation of the won relative to the dollar. Consequently, the won cost of parent-supplied imports will increase at (1.1)(1.05)(0.99) = 1.14 or 14 percent per year.
4. Direct labor costs and overhead in the first year are budgeted at 5,000 million won. Korean direct labor costs and overhead are expected to increase at 10 percent per year because of physical growth and at an additional 12 percent because of an increase in Korean wage rates. Consequently, Korean direct labor and overhead will increase at (1.1)(1.12) = 1.232, or 23.2 percent per year.
5. Marketing and general and administrative expenses are budgeted at ₩4 billion, fixed plus 4 percent of sales.
6. Liquidation value. At the end of five years, the project (including working capital) is expected to be sold on a going-concern basis to Korean investors for ₩9 billion, equal to about $10 million at the expected exchange rate of ₩903.44 /$1. This sales price is free of all Korean and U.S. taxes, and will be used as a terminal value.

Given the facts and stated assumptions, the beginning balance sheet presented in Exhibit 29.6 shows revenue and cost projections for Ko-tel over the expected five-year life of the project. Exhibit 29.7 shows sales and cost data.

EXHIBIT 29.6   Beginning Balance Sheet

	Millions of Won	Thousands of Dollars
Assets		
1 Cash balance	650	684
2 Accounts receivable	-	-
3 Inventory	1,050	1,105
4 Net plant and equipment	7,000	7,368
5 Total	8,700	9,158
Liabilities and Net Worth		
6 Accounts payable	700	737
7 Common stock equity	8,000	8,421
8 Total	8,700	9,158

Won/$=	950
Pro. Cost	-11,000
Liq. Value	9,000,000

EXHIBIT 29.7   Sales and Cost Data

Item	1	2	3	4	5
1 Total sales revenue	26,000	31,174	37,378	44,816	53,734
2 Korean raw material	4,000	4,532	5,135	5,818	6,591
3 Components purchases from Am-tel	9,000	10,291	11,767	13,455	15,385
4 Korean labor and overhead	5,000	6,160	7,589	9,350	11,519
5 Depreciation	700	700	700	700	700
6 Cost of sales [(2)+(3)+(4)+(5)]	18,700	21,683	25,191	29,323	34,196
7 Gross margin [(1)-(6)]	7,300	9,491	12,186	15,493	19,538
8 License fee [2.5% of (1)]	650	779	934	1,120	1,343
9 Marketing and general & administrative	5,040	5,247	5,495	5,793	6,149
10 EBIT* [(7)-(8)-(9)]	1,610	3,465	5,757	8,580	12,046
11 Korean income taxes (35%)	564	1,213	2,015	3,003	4,216
12 Net income after Korean taxes [(10)-(11)]	1,047	2,252	3,742	5,577	7,830
13 Cash dividend [70% of (12)]	733	1,576	2,619	3,904	5,481

*EBIT= earnings before interest and taxes

Exhibit 29.8 shows how the annual increase in working capital investment is calculated. According to the facts, half of gross working capital must be financed by Ko-tel or Am-tel.

Exhibit 29.13 Depicts a NPV graph of various scenarios.

EXHIBIT 29.8   Working Capital Calculation

			Year		
Item	1	2	3	4	5
1 Total revenue	26,000	31,174	37,378	44,816	53,734
2 Net working capital needs at year-end [25% of (1)]	6,500	7,794	9,344	11,204	13,434
3 Less year-beginning working capital	1,700	6,500	7,794	9,344	11,204
4 Required addition to working capital	4,800	1,294	1,551	1,860	2,230
5 Less working capital financed in Korean by payables	2,400	647	775	930	1,115
6 Net new investment in working capital	2,400	647	775	930	1,115

Therefore, half of any annual increase in working capital would represent an additional required capital investment. Exhibit 29.9 forecasts project cash flows from the viewpoint of Ko-tel. Thanks to healthy liquidation value, the project has a positive NPV and an IRR greater than the 22 percent local (Korean) cost of capital for projects of similar risk. Therefore, Ko-tel passes the first of the two tests of required rate of return.

EXHIBIT 29.9 Cash Flow Projection, NPV, and IRR for Ko-tel

Item	0	1	Year 2	3	4	5
1 EBIT [Exhibit 29-7, (10)]		1,610	3,465	5,757	8,580	12,046
2 Korean income taxes (35%)		564	1,213	2,015	3,003	4,216
3 Net income, all equity basis		1,047	2,252	3,742	5,577	7,830
4 Depreciation		700	700	700	700	700
5 Liquidation value						9,000
6 Half of addition to working capital		2,400	647	775	930	1,115
7 Cost of project	(8,000)					
8 Net cash flow	(8,000)	(654)	2,305	3,667	5,347	16,415
12 IRR			33.09%		▪	
13 NPV = PV (at 22%) - I			$3,519.54			

Exhibit 29.9 Cash Flow Projection - NPV and IRR for Ko-Tel

Does Ko-tel also pass the second test? That is, does it show at least a 22 percent required rate of return from the viewpoint of Am-tel? Exhibit 29.10 shows the calculation for expected after-tax dividends from Ko-tel to be received by Am-tel. For purposes of this example, note that Am-tel must pay regular U.S. corporate income taxes (38 percent rate) on dividends received from Ko-tel.

EXHIBIT 29.10 After-Tax Dividend Received by Am-tel

Item	0	1	Year 2	3	4	5
In Millions of Won						
1 Cash dividend paid [Exhibit 29-4, (13)]		733	1,576	2,619	3,904	5,481
2 A 70% of Korean income tax						
[Exhibit 29-7, (11)]		394	849	1,410	2,102	2,951
3 Grossed-up dividend [(1) + (2)]		1,127	2,425	4,030	6,006	8,432
4 Exchange-rate (won/$)	950	941	931	922	913	903
In Thousands of Dollars						
5 Grossed-up dividend [(3)/(4) x 1000]		1,198	2,605	4,372	6,581	9,333
6 U.S. tax (38%)		455	990	1,661	2,501	3,547
7 Credit for Korean taxes [(2)/(4) x 1000]		419	912	1,530	2,303	3,267
8 Additional U.S. Tax due						
[(6)-(7), if (6) is larger]		36	78	131	197	280
9 Excess U.S. tax credit						
[(7)-(6), if (7) is larger]		-	-	-	-	-
10 Dividend received by Am-tel						
after all taxes [(1)/(4) x 1000-(8)]		743	1,615	2,711	4,080	5,787

However, the U.S. tax law allows Am-tel to claim a tax credit for income taxes paid to Korea on the Korean income that generated the dividend. The process of calculating the regional income in Korea is called "grossing up" and is illustrated in Exhibit 29.10, lines (1), (2), and (3).

This imputed Korean won income is converted from won to dollars in lines (4) and (5). Then the U.S. income tax is calculated at 38 percent in line (6). A tax credit is given for the Korean income taxes paid, as calculated in line (7). Line (8) then shows the net additional U.S. tax due, and line (10) shows the net dividend received by Am-tel after the additional U.S. tax is paid. Finally, Exhibit 29.11 calculates the rate of return on cash flows from Ko-tel from the viewpoint of Am-tel. Ko-tel passes the test because it has a positive NPV and an IRR above the 22 percent rate of return required by Am-tel.

EXHIBIT 29.11   NPV and IRR for Am-tel

Item	0	1	2	3	4	5
			Year			
In Million of Won						
1 License fee from Ko-tel (2.5%) [Exhibit 29-7, (7)]		650	779	934	1,120	1,343
2 Margin on exports to Ko-tel [5% of (3) in Exhibit 29-4]		450	515	588	673	769
3 Total receipts		1,100	1,294	1,523	1,793	2,113
4 Exchange rate (won/$)	950	941	931	922	913	903
In thousands of Dollars						
5 Pre-tax receipts [(3)/(4) x 1000]		1,170	1,390	1,652	1,965	2,338
6 U.S. taxes (38%)		444	528	628	747	889
7 License fees and export profits, after tax		725	862	1,024	1,218	1,450
8 After-tax dividend [Exhibit 5, (10)]		743	1,615	2,711	4,080	5,787
9 Project cost	(11,000)					
10 Liquidation value						9,962
11 Net cash flow	(11,000)	1,468	2,477	3,735	5,299	17,198
12 IRR		29.30%				
13 NPV = PV (at 22%) - I		$2,679.17				

So far the project investigation team has used a set of most likely assumptions to forecast rates of return. It is now time to subject the most likely outcome to sensitivity analyses. One can test sensitivity to political and foreign exchange risk by simulating what would happen to net present value and earnings under a variety of what-if discount rate scenarios. Spreadsheet programs such as Excel can be utilized to test various scenarios (see Exhibit 29.12).

EXHIBIT 29.12 NPV Profiles for Ko-tel and Am-tel: Sensitivity Analysis

Discount rate (%)	0	4	8	12	16	20	22	24	28	32	36	40
Project pt of view (Ko-Tel)	$ 19,080.30	$ 14,825.10	$ 11,383.91	$ 8,576.47	$ 6,267.33	$ 4,353.58	$ 3,519.54	$ 2,756.24	$ 1,414.14	$ 279.48	$ (685.41)	$ (1,510.43)
Parent pt of view (Parent)	$ 19,176.35	$ 14,686.58	$ 11,046.90	$ 8,069.58	$ 5,613.51	$ 3,571.45	$ 2,679.17	$ 1,861.10	$ 418.65	$ (805.77)	########	$ (2,749.72)

EXHIBIT 29.13 Profiles for Ko-tel and Am-tel: Sensitivity Analysis

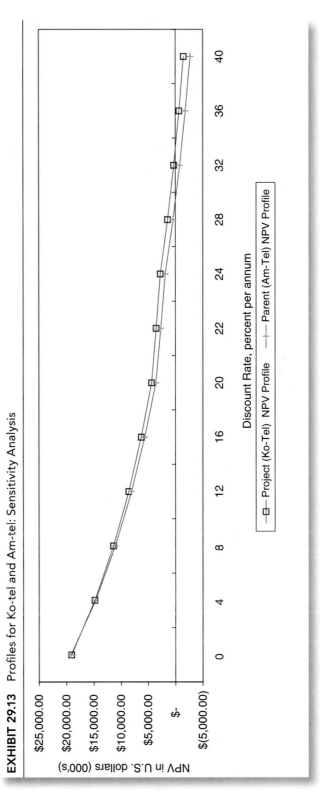

Financial Analysis, Insurance and Legal Considerations, and Economics

CHAPTER THIRTY

Financial Statement Analysis

FINANCIAL STATEMENT ANALYSIS examines a company's historical financial performance and its future prospects. It appraises the health and operating performance of the business. This chapter covers analytical techniques in appraising the balance sheet, analyzing the income statement, and evaluating the financial structure. CFOs analyze the financial statements to see how the company looks to the financial community and what corrective actions can be taken to minimize and solve financial problems. Areas of risk are identified. Means to efficiently utilize assets and earn greater returns are emphasized. Financial statement analysis aids in determining the appropriateness of mergers and acquisitions.

A company's financial condition influences its price/earnings (P/E) ratio, bond rating, cost of financing, and availability of financing.

FINANCIAL ANALYSIS ESSENTIALS

To see how the company fares in the industry or how it is doing over time, a comparison with the benchmark is essential. Tools such as horizontal and vertical analyses can unveil areas needing attention.

What kind of financial comparisons should CFOs make?

To obtain worthwhile conclusions from financial ratios, the CFO has to make two comparisons.

1. *Industry comparison.* The CFO should compare the company's ratios to those of competing companies in the industry or with industry standards. Industry norms can be obtained from such services as Standard & Poor's and Moody's.

- In analyzing the company, the CFO should appraise the trends in the industry. What is the pattern of growth or decline? The profit dollar is worth more if earned in a healthy, expanding industry than in a declining one.
- The CFO should make certain that the financial data of competitors are comparable to his or her company. For example, the CFO will have difficulty comparing the profitability of his or her company if it uses first-in, first-out with a competitor that uses last-in, first-out (LIFO) for inventory valuation. In this case, the CFO should restate the earnings of both companies on a comparative basis.

2. *Trend analysis.* A company's ratio can be compared over several years to identify direction of financial position and operating performance. An attempt should be made to uncover the reasons for the change.

What are some tips for doing financial analysis?

The optimum value for any ratio varies across industry lines, through time, and within different companies in the same industry. In other words, a ratio deemed optimum for one company may be inadequate for another. A ratio is typically deemed optimum within a given range of values. An increase or decrease beyond this range points to something unusual requiring investigation. *Example:* Whereas a low current ratio may indicate deficient liquidity, a very high current ratio may reflect inefficient utilization of assets (e.g., excessive inventory) or inability to use short-term credit to the firm's advantage.

For a seasonal business, the CFO may find that year-end financial data are not representative. Thus, quarterly or monthly averages may be used to level out seasonality effects.

When computing ratios for analytical purposes, the CFO may also want to use the realistic values for balance sheet accounts instead of historical amounts. For example, land recorded at $4 million may have a market value of $4.8 million.

A distorted trend indicates a problem mandating management attention. However, a lack of change does not always infer normalcy. For example, manpower growth may have increased, but production/sales may be constant or decreasing. Thus, manpower costs may be disproportionate to operational activity.

What is the difference between horizontal and vertical analysis?

Horizontal analysis looks at the trend in accounts over years and assists in spotting areas of wide divergence requiring additional attention. Horizontal analysis can also be presented by showing trends relative to a base year.

In *vertical analysis*, a significant item on a financial statement is used as a base value, and all other items on the financial statement are compared to it. In performing vertical analysis for the balance sheet, total assets is assigned 100 percent. Each asset is expressed as a percentage of total assets. Total liabilities and stockholders' equity is also assigned 100 percent. Each liability and stockholders' equity account is then expressed as a percentage of total liabilities and stockholders' equity. In the income statement, net sales is given the value of 100 percent, and all other accounts are appraised in comparison to net sales. The resulting figures are then given in a common-size statement.

Vertical analysis is helpful in disclosing the internal structure of the business and potential problem areas. It reveals the relationship between each income statement account and revenue. It indicates the mix of assets that generate income and the mix of the sources of financing, whether by current or noncurrent liabilities or by equity. Besides making internal evaluation possible, vertical analysis may be used to appraise the company's relative position in the industry. Horizontal and vertical analysis point to possible problem areas to be evaluated by the CFO.

 BALANCE SHEET ANALYSIS

A CFO can analyze asset and liability accounts, evaluate liquidity, appraise solvency, and look to signs of possible business failure. The CFO is concerned with the realizability of assets, turnover, and earning potential. Besides analyzing financial health, the CFO will want to make recommendations for improvement so that financial problems are rectified. Also, the CFO should identify strengths that may be further tapped.

Are assets of high or low quality?

Asset quality relates to the certainty of the amount and timing of the realization of the assets in cash. Therefore, assets should be categorized by risk category.

What to do: Calculate the high-risk assets to total assets ratio and the high-risk assets to sales ratio. If high risk exists in assets, future write-offs may occur. For example, the realization of goodwill is more doubtful than that of equipment. The risk of each major asset category should also be appraised. For example, receivables from an economically unstable government (e.g., Brazil) have greater risks than receivables from General Electric.

> ### Note
> Single-purpose assets have greater risk than multipurpose ones. ■

What to watch for: Look out for assets with no separable value that cannot be sold easily, such as intangibles and works in process. Marketable securities, however, are readily salable.

In evaluating realization risk, the impact of changing government policies on the entity has to be considered. Risk may exist with chemicals and other products deemed hazardous to health. Huge inventory losses may arise.

We now analyze each of the major assets.

What should be considered in evaluating the cash account?

The CFO should determine how much of the cash balance is unavailable or restricted. Examples are a compensating balance and cash held in a foreign country when remission restrictions exist.

Note

Foreign currency holdings generally are stated at year-end exchange rates but may change rapidly. ■

The CFO should determine the ratio of sales to cash. A high turnover rate may indicate a deficient cash position leading to financial problems if additional financing is not available at reasonable interest rates. A low turnover ratio may indicate excessive cash being retained.

Example 30.1

	2X11	2X12
Cash	$500,000	$400,000
Sales	8,000,000	9,000,000
Industry norm for cash turnover rate	15.8 times	16.2 times

The turnover of cash is 16 ($8,000/$500,000) in 2X11 and 22.5 ($9,000/$400,000) in 2X12. The company has a cash deficiency in 2X12, which implies a possible liquidity problem.

The CFO should distinguish between two types of cash: that needed for operating purposes and that required for capital expenditures. Whereas the first type must be paid, the second is postponable.

How is an analysis of accounts receivable useful?

Realization risk in receivables can be appraised by studying the nature of the receivable balance. Examples of high-risk receivables include amounts from economically unstable foreign countries, receivables subject to offset provisions, and receivables due from a company experiencing severe financial problems. Furthermore, companies dependent on a few customers have greater risk than those with a large number of important accounts. Receivables due from industry are typically safer than receivables arising from consumers. Fair trade laws are more protective of consumers.

Accounts receivable ratios include the accounts receivable turnover and the average collection period. The accounts receivable turnover ratio indicates the number of times accounts receivable is collected during the period. It equals net sales divided by average accounts receivable. A higher turnover rate reveals faster collections. An excessively high ratio, however, may point to a tight credit policy, with the company not tapping the potential for profit through sales to customers in higher-risk categories. In changing its credit policy, though. the company must consider the profit potential against the risk in selling to more marginal customers.

The average collection period (day's sales in receivables) is the number of days it takes to collect receivables. It equals 365 days divided by the accounts receivable turnover.

Collection periods can be calculated by type of customer, product line, and market territory.

An increase in collection days may indicate customer balances becoming uncollectible. One reason for an increase may be that the company is now selling to highly marginal customers. An aging schedule is helpful in detecting patterns of cash collection from customers.

The quality of receivables can also be appraised by referring to customer ratings issued by credit agencies.

The CFO should look for a buildup in the ratios of (1) accounts receivable to total assets and (2) accounts receivable to sales as indicative of a collection problem. Receivables outstanding in excess of the expected payment date and relative to industry norm implies a higher probability of uncollectibility.

The trend in sales returns and allowances is a reflection of the quality of merchandise sold.

What are important concerns when analyzing inventories?

An inventory buildup may mean realization problems. The buildup may be at the plant, wholesaler, or retailer. A sign of a buildup is when inventory increases at a much faster rate than the increase in sales. *What to watch for:* A decline in raw materials coupled with a rise in work in process and finished goods could point to a future production slowdown.

If the company is holding excess inventory, there is an opportunity cost of tying up money in inventory. Furthermore, there is a high carrying cost for storing merchandise. Why are certain types of merchandise not selling well? Calculate turnover rates for each inventory category and by department. Possible reasons for a low turnover rate are overstocking, obsolescence, product line deficiencies, or poor marketing efforts. There are cases where a low inventory rate is appropriate. *Examples:* A higher inventory level may arise because of expected future increases in price or when a new product has been introduced but the advertising efforts have not been felt yet.

Note

The turnover rate may be unrepresentatively high when the business uses a natural year-end because at that time the inventory balance will be exceptionally low. ■

What to do: Compute the number of days inventory is held and compare it to the industry norm and previous years.

$$\text{Inventory turnover} = \frac{\text{Cost of goods sold}}{\text{Average inventory}}$$

$$\text{Age of inventory} = \frac{365}{\text{Turnover}}$$

Also look at the trend in inventory to sales. A high turnover rate may point to inadequate inventory, possibly leading to a loss in business.

What to watch for: Beware of merchandise that is susceptible to price variability, faddish, specialized, perishable, technological, or luxury goods. On the contrary, standardized, staple, and necessity items have low realization risk.

Note

Raw material inventory is safer than finished goods or work in process since raw material has more universal and varied uses. ▪

Questions to ask:

- Is inventory collateralized against a loan? If so, creditors can retain it in the event of nonpayment of the obligation.
- Is there adequate insurance? There is a particular problem when insurance cannot be obtained for the item because of high risk (e.g., geographic location of inventory is in a high-crime area or there is susceptibility to floods).
- Is inventory subject to political risk (e.g., big cars during an oil crisis)?

Look for inventory that is overstated owing to mistakes in quantities, costing, pricing, and valuation.

Warning: The more technical a product and the more dependent the valuation on internally developed cost records, the more susceptible to error cost estimates are.

In gauging manufacturing efficiency, you should look at the relationship between indirect labor and direct labor since constant levels of both are needed to efficiently run the organization.

Example 30.2

A company presents this makeup of inventory:

	2X11	2X12
Raw materials	$89,000	$ 78,000
Work in process	67,000	120,000
Finished goods	16,000	31,000

The CFO's analysis of inventory shows there was a material divergence in the inventory components between 2X11 and 2X12. There was a reduction in raw material by 12.4 percent ($11,000/ $89,000), while work in process rose by 79.1 percent ($53,000/$67,000) and finished goods rose by 93.8 percent ($15,000/$16,000). The lack of consistency in the trend between raw materials relative to work in process and finished goods may imply a forthcoming cutback in production. An obsolescence problem may also exist applicable to work in process and finished goods due to the sizable buildup.

The company's operating cycle—which equals the average collection period plus the average age of inventory—should be determined. A short operating cycle is desired so that cash flow is expedited.

What are the key areas to look at in the investment portfolio?

An indication of the fair value of investments may be the revenue, such as dividend income or interest income received from those investments. Have decreases in portfolio market values been recognized in the accounts? Higher realization risk exists where there is a declining trend in the percentage of earnings derived from investments to their carrying value. Also check for unrealized losses in the portfolio occurring after year-end.

Example 30.3

Company X presents this information:

	2X11	2X12
Investments	$50,000	$60,000
Investment income	$ 7,000	$ 5,000

The percent of investment income to total investments decreased from 14 percent in 2X11 to 8.3 percent in 2X12, pointing to higher realization risk in the portfolio.

If a company is buying securities in other companies for diversification purposes, this will reduce overall risk. Risk in an investment portfolio can be ascertained by computing the standard deviation of its rate of return.

An investment portfolio of securities fluctuating widely in price is of higher realization risk than a portfolio that is diversified by industry and economic sector. But the former portfolio will show greater profitability in a bull market.

Recommendations: Appraise the extent of diversification and stability of the investment portfolio. There is less risk when securities are negatively correlated (price goes in opposite directions) or not correlated compared to a portfolio of positively correlated securities (price goes in same direction). Is the portfolio of poor-quality securities, such as junk bonds?

Note cases in which held-to-maturity securities have an unamortized cost in excess of market value.

In evaluating fixed assets, what should be considered?

Is there sufficient maintenance of productive assets to ensure current and future earning power? Lessened operational efficiency and breakdowns occur when obsolete assets have not been replaced and/or required repairs made.

What to do: Determine the age and condition of each major asset category as well as the cost to replace old assets. Determine output levels, downtime, and temporary discontinuances. Inactive and unproductive assets are a drain on the firm. Are the fixed assets specialized or risky, making them susceptible to obsolescence?

> ## Note
> Pollution-causing equipment may require replacement or modification to satisfy governmental environmental standards. ■

Ratio trends to be calculated are:

- Fixed asset acquisitions to total assets. The trend is particularly revealing for a technological company that has to keep up-to-date. A decrease in the trend points to the failure to replace older assets on a timely basis.
- Repairs and maintenance to fixed assets.
- Repairs and maintenance to sales.
- Sales to fixed assets.
- Net income to fixed assets.

The fixed asset turnover ratio (net sales to average fixed assets) aids in appraising a company's ability to use its asset base efficiently to obtain revenue. A low ratio may mean that investment in fixed assets is excessive relative to the output generated.

A high ratio of sales to floor space indicates the efficient utilization of space.

A company having specialized or risky fixed assets has greater vulnerability to asset obsolescence. Examples include machinery used to manufacture specialized products and fad items.

When a company's rate of return on assets (e.g., net income to fixed assets) is poor, the firm may be justified in not maintaining fixed assets. If the industry is declining, fixed asset replacement and repairs may have been restricted.

It is better for a company when assets are mobile and/or can easily be modified since it affords the firm greater flexibility. If the assets are easily accessible, it will also be easier to repair them. The location of the assets is also important since that may affect their condition and security. The location will also affect property taxes, so a company may be able to save on taxes by having the plant located in a low-tax area.

What to watch for: A material decline in sales coupled with a significant increase in capital expenditures may be inconsistent. It may point to overexpansion.

Example 30.4

Company T presents this information regarding its fixed assets:

	2X11	2X12
Fixed assets	$120,000	$105,000
Repairs and maintenance	6,000	4,500
Replacement cost	205,000	250,000

The company has inadequately maintained its assets, as indicated by:

▪ The reduction in the ratio of repairs and maintenance to fixed assets from 5 percent in 2X11 to 4.3 percent in 2X12.
▪ The material variation between replacement cost and historical cost.
▪ The reduction in fixed assets over the year.

How should property, plant, and equipment be managed and controlled?

Fixed assets should meet the operational needs of the business with maximum productivity at minimum cost. These long-term expenditures are significant in amount and can result in great loss to the company if fixed assets are improperly managed. Capital investments result in a higher break-even point, owing to the resulting costs associated with them, including depreciation, insurance, and property taxes.

A new company requires greater capital expansion for growth. An established, mature company with strong market share has less need for additional capital facilities.

For control purposes, unique control numbers should be securely affixed to fixed assets. There should be periodic appraisals of the adequacy of insurance coverage.

The company should not buy elaborate manufacturing facilities for a new product until it has shown success in the market. In the beginning stages, production may be subcontracted. With an established product, productivity is achieved through internal capital expansion. In appraising production facilities, scrap, rejects, cost per unit, and malfunctioning time should be considered.

The CFO is concerned with these issues in managing fixed assets:

▪ Purchasing the right equipment for the company's needs
▪ Proper timing of capital expenditures
▪ Keeping capital expenditures within the financial capabilities of the business
▪ Physical care and security of property

What are concerns with appraising intangibles?

Realization risk is indicated when there is a high ratio of intangible assets to total assets. The amounts recorded for intangibles may be overstated relative to their market value or to their future income-generating capacity.

What to do: Calculate trends in these ratios:

- Intangible assets to total assets
- Intangible assets to stockholders' equity
- Intangible assets to sales
- Intangible assets to net income
- Dubious intangible assets (e.g., goodwill) to total assets

Watch for leasehold improvements, because they have no cash realizability.

Note

In some cases, intangibles may be undervalued, such as a successful patented product. However, can the patented product be infringed on by minor alteration? What is the financial strength of the company to defend itself against those infringing on its patented product? What are the expiration dates of patents, and are new products being developed? ■

A company's goodwill account should be appraised to ascertain whether the firm acquired has superior earning potential to justify the excess of cost over fair market value of net assets paid for it. If the acquired company does not have superior profit potential, the goodwill has no value because excess earnings do not exist relative to other companies in the industry. However, internally developed goodwill is expensed and not capitalized. It represents an undervalued asset, such as the good reputation of McDonald's.

Are the company's assets being properly utilized?

Asset utilization can be measured by the total asset turnover (net sales/average total assets). The ratio is useful in appraising an entity's ability to use its asset base efficiently to generate revenue. A low ratio may be caused from numerous factors, and it is essential to identify the causes. For example, it must be determined if the investment in assets is excessive relative to production. If so, the business may wish to consolidate its present operation, perhaps by selling some of its assets and investing the funds for a higher return or using them to expand into a more profitable area.

The operating assets ratio (total operating assets to total assets) concentrates on those assets *actively employed in current operations.* Such assets exclude past-oriented assets and future-oriented assets. Past-oriented assets arise from prior errors, inefficiencies, or losses because of competitive factors or changes in business plans. These assets have not yet been formally recognized in the accounts. Examples are obsolete goods, idle plants, receivables under litigation, delinquent receivables, and nonperforming loans (no interest being recognized). Future-oriented assets are acquired for corporate growth or for generating future sales. Examples are land held for speculation and factories under construction. Nonoperating assets reduce profits and return on investment because no benefit to current operations occurs. They neither generate sales nor reduce costs. Rather, they are a drain on the company and may require financing.

What is the nature of the assets?

Are any of the current assets used to secure long-term debt or contingent liabilities as pledges or guarantees?

Even though current assets are about the same or slightly above current liabilities, the company may still experience liquidity difficulties if the maturity schedule of the liabilities is ahead of the expected cash realization of the assets. For example, the payment schedule of the debts may be concentrated toward the beginning of the year, but the cash realization of the assets may be evenly disbursed throughout the year. If this occurs, the company may be forced to discount its receivables or quickly liquidate inventory at lower prices. Although doing this will generate immediate cash, it dilutes the realizable value of the current assets. In effect, the actual value of the assets becomes less than the fair value of the liabilities.

Assets that are interdependent create a financial disadvantage. For example, the sale of equipment on the assembly line may adversely affect the remaining equipment. However, one marketable security can be sold without affecting the others.

Wide variability in the price of assets is a negative sign because the company may be forced to sell an asset at a time of financial need at significant loss (i.e., market value is materially below book value).

There is more liquidity risk with noncurrent assets than with current assets because of the greater disposition difficulty.

The CFO should determine whether off-balance sheet assets exist. Examples are a tax loss carryforward benefit, expected rebates, and a purchase commitment to acquire an item at a price lower than the prevailing one. The CFO should also identify assets reflected on the balance sheet at an amount substantially less than their real value. Examples are patents recorded at cost, even though the present value of future benefits substantially exceeds it, and land that does not reflect its appreciated value.

ASC No. 715-20, *Compensation—Retirement Benefits—General* (Financial Accounting Standards Board Statement No. 87, *Employers' Accounting for Pensions*), on pension plans does not allow the recognition of a minimum asset for the excess of the fair value of pension plan assets less the accumulated benefit obligation. For analytical purposes, such a minimum asset should be considered as an unrecorded asset for the excess of fair value of plan assets over the projected benefit obligation.

Recommendation: Note the existence of unrecorded assets representing resources of the business or items expected to have future economic benefit.

What should be taken into account when evaluating liabilities?

The CFO should calculate the trends in the ratios of:

- Current liabilities to total liabilities
- Current liabilities to stockholders' equity
- Current liabilities to sales

Increasing trends point to liquidity difficulty.

Note

Stretching short-term payables is not a good sign. ■

The CFO should determine the trend in "patient" (e.g., supplier) to "pressing" (e.g., bank, Internal Revenue Service) liabilities. When liquidity problems exist, the company is better off with patient creditors that will work with it. Thus, a high ratio of pressing liabilities to total liabilities is unfavorable.

Example 30.5

A company presents this information:

	2X11	2X12
Current Liabilities		
Trade payables	$ 33,000	$28,000
Bank loans	51,000	78,000
Commercial paper	35,000	62,000
Taxes payable	8,000	12,000
Total current liabilities	$ 127,000	$ 180,000
Total noncurrent liabilities	$ 310,000	$ 315,000
Total liabilities	$ 437,000	$ 495,000
Total revenue	$1,100,000	$1,150,000

Relevant ratios are

Current liabilities to total revenue	11.5%	15.7%
Current liabilities to total liabilities	29.1%	36.4%
Pressing current liabilities to patient current liabilities	2.85%	5.43%

There is more liquidity risk in 2X12, as reflected by the higher ratios. In fact, the number of pressing liabilities has risen significantly in terms of percentage.

Certain liabilities should not be considered obligations for analytical purposes because they may not require future payment. Examples are:

■ The deferred tax credit account, if it applies to a temporary difference that will keep recurring (e.g., depreciation as long as capital expansion occurs)

- Unearned revenue related to passive income sources, such as rents
- Convertible bonds with attractive conversion features

Corporate obligations that are not recorded in the balance sheet must be considered when evaluating the entity's going-concern potential. Examples are lawsuits, disputes under a government contract, operating leases, commitments for future loans to a troubled company, guarantees of future performance, and bonus payment obligations.

The minimum liability for the pension plan equals the accumulated benefit obligation less the fair value of pension plan assets. However, the projected benefit obligation (based on anticipated future salaries) is a better measure of the plan's obligation than the accumulated benefit obligation (based on current salaries). Therefore, the CFO should consider as an unrecorded liability the excess of the projected benefit obligation over the accumulated benefit obligation.

Example 30.6

Accumulated benefit obligation	$50,000,000
Less: Fair value of plan assets	40,000,000
Minimum (booked) liability	$10,000,000

If the projected benefit obligation is $58 million, the unrecorded liability is $8 million ($58 million less $50 million).

An equity account may be in essence a liability, such as preferred stock with a maturity date or subject to sinking fund requirements.

How easily can the company obtain financing?

The company's ability to obtain financing at reasonable rates is affected by external considerations (e.g., Federal Reserve policy) and internal considerations (e.g., degree of existing debt).

The extent of loan restrictions on the company should be examined. How close is the company to violating a given restriction, which may in turn call the loan?

Can the company issue commercial paper and short-term bank debt? If there is a loan, has the collateral value of the loan diminished relative to the balance of the loan? If so, additional security may be required. Also examine the trend in the effective interest rate and compensating balance requirement relative to competition. Does the weighted-average debt significantly exceed the year-end debt balance?

How should liabilities be managed and controlled?

In managing liabilities, a major concern is whether the business has adequate resources to meet maturing debt. Otherwise, the company will be in financial difficulty. The debt structure affects both the short-term and long-term financial status of the enterprise.

The CFO must be assured that all financial obligations are presented and disclosed in the financial statements. Furthermore, the liability position and related ratios must be in compliance with any restrictions in loan agreements. The company must borrow money when needed in a timely fashion and at a reasonable interest rate.

Liability management involves the proper planning of all types of obligations. The CFO must know current balances of, say, accounts payable and accrued expenses, and how far they can be stretched. Are liabilities within acceptable industry norms? Can the company withstand periods of adversity? How does the overall economic picture look, and what effect does it have on the business?

The CFO should prepare a number of reports to analyze the actual status of liabilities and to properly plan the debt structure. Some useful reports include:

- Periodic reports (e.g., quarterly, monthly) on the status of material liabilities, such as pensions, leases, and healthcare
- Periodic reports comparing actual liabilities to allowable amounts in credit agreements
- Comparisons of budgeted liabilities to actual liabilities
- Listing and status of contingent liabilities and their amounts
- Aging of accounts payable

How is an analysis of stockholders' equity useful?

If management reduces or omits its dividends, it may imply that the company has financial difficulties. Management is better off varying its dividends rather than paying constant dividends so it can more easily reduce dividends in troubled times. If stockholders are accustomed to receiving constant dividends, it will be more difficult for management to lower its dividends without upsetting stockholders.

A loan agreement that places restrictions on the company, such as its ability to pay dividends, inhibits management's freedom of action and is a negative sign.

If treasury stock is acquired, the market price of the company's stock will rise because fewer shares will be on the market. If a company had previously purchased treasury stock at a cost that is significantly below the current market price, it is sitting on a significant potential increase in cash flow and paid-in capital.

If a company issues preferred stock for the first time or if it substantially issues preferred stock in the current year, it may mean the company had problems with issuing its common stock. This is a negative sign since the investing public may view its common stock as risky.

If convertible bonds or convertible preferred stock are converted to common stock, that means that bondholders or preferred stockholders are optimistic about the company. However, this will result in a drop in the market price of common stock as more shares are issued. On the plus side, the company does not have to pay the interest payment on bonds and the dividend payment on preferred stock.

A high ratio of retained earnings to stockholders' equity is a good sign; it indicates that capital financing is being achieved internally.

Stockholders are interested in dividends and prefer high ratios for dividend yield (dividends per share/market price per share) and dividend payout (dividends per share/ earnings per share [EPS]). A decline in these ratios may cause concern among stock-holders.

Is the company liquid?

Liquidity is the company's ability to convert noncash assets into cash or to obtain cash to pay current debt. The CFO has to examine the stock and flow of liquid resources. The timing of the cash inflows and outflows also has to be considered.

Liquidity is crucial in carrying out business activity, particularly in times of adversity, such as when a business is shut down by a strike or when operating losses result from a recession or a significant rise in raw material prices. If liquidity is inadequate to cushion such losses, serious financial difficulties may result.

Liquidity is affected by the company's ability to obtain financing (e.g., lines of credit) and to postpone cash payments. The mixture of current assets and current liabilities is also relevant. How "near to cash" are assets and liabilities? A deficient liquidity position may render a company unable to make timely interest and principal payments on debt.

Liquidity ratios are static at year-end. Thus, it is important for the CFO to analyze expected future cash flows. If future cash outflows are much more than cash inflows, there will be a deteriorating liquidity position.

What to watch for: If your business is seasonal, year-end financial data are not representative. In this case, use averages based on quarterly or monthly data to level out seasonal effects.

A seasonal business that is a net borrower should use long-term financing as a precautionary measure. Furthermore, a company with financial difficulties should have debts mature during the peak rather than the trough of the season.

Can you modify unexpected difficulties by changing the amount and timing of future cash flows? Doing this involves consideration of the closeness of assets to cash, ability to obtain financing, amount of nonoperating assets that can be sold, ability to alter operating and investing activities, and payback periods on projects.

What ratios can be used to appraise liquidity?

Some important funds flow ratios are:

▪ *Current ratio.*

$$\text{Current ratio} \ = \frac{\text{Current assests}}{\text{Current liabilities}}$$

Seasonal variability affects this ratio. The current ratio appraises the company's ability to pay current debt out of current assets. A high ratio is needed if the company has a problem borrowing quickly and if there are troubling business conditions, among other reasons. A limitation of this ratio is that it may increase just before financial distress because of a company's attempt to improve its cash position by selling fixed assets. Such dispositions have a negative impact on productive

> ## Note
>
> Current assets that are pledged to secure long-term liabilities are not available to pay current debt. If these current assets are included in the calculation, a distorted ratio arises. ■

capacity. Another limitation of the ratio is that it will be higher when inventory is carried on a LIFO basis.

- *Quick ratio.*

$$\text{Quick ratio} = \frac{\text{Cash} + \text{Marketable securities} + \text{Accounts receivable}}{\text{Current liablities}}$$

This is a more stringent test of liquidity than the current ratio because it excludes inventories and prepaid expenses.

- *Working capital.*

$$\text{Working capital} = \text{Current assets} - \text{Current liabilities}$$

A high working capital helps when the company has difficulty borrowing on short notice. However, an excess working capital may be bad because funds could be invested in noncurrent assets for a greater return. Compare working capital to other financial statement items such as sales and total assets. For example, working capital to sales indicates if the company is optimally using its liquid resources. To identify changes in the composition of working capital, the CFO should determine the trend in the percentage of each current asset to total current assets. A movement from cash to inventory, for example, indicates less liquidity.

- *Working capital to long-term debt.* This ratio indicates if there is adequate working capital to pay long-term debt.
- *Working capital to current liabilities.* A low ratio reveals deficient liquidity since liquid funds are inadequate to meet current debt.
- *Specific current asset to total current assets.* For example, a shift of cash to inventory means less liquidity.
- *Sales to current assets.* A high ratio indicates inadequate working capital. Current liabilities may be due before inventories and receivables turn over to cash.
- *Working capital provided from operations to net income.* A high ratio is desirable because it indicates earnings are backed up by liquid funds.
- *Working capital provided from operations/Total liabilities.* This ratio reveals how much internally generated working capital can meet obligations.

- *Cash + marketable securities to current liabilities.* This ratio reveals the cash available to pay short-term debt.
- *Cost of sales, operating expenses, and taxes to average total current assets.* This ratio indicates the adequacy of current assets in meeting ongoing expenses.
- *Quick assets to year's cash expenses.* This tells how many days of expenses the highly liquid assets could support.
- *Sales to short-term trade liabilities.* This ratio indicates if the business could partly finance operations with cost-free funds. If the company can obtain trade credit easily, this is a positive sign. A decline in trade credit means creditors have less faith in the financial soundness of the business.
- *Net income to sales.* This ratio indicates the profitability generated from revenue and is an important measure of operating performance. It also provides clues to a company's pricing, cost structure, and manufacturing efficiency. If the ratio declines, loan repayment problems may exist because a lack in earnings spells financial distress.
- *Fixed assets to short-term debt.* If you finance long-term assets with current debt, there may be a problem in paying the debt because the return and proceeds from the fixed asset will not be realized before the maturity dates of the current debt.
- *Short-term debt to long-term debt.* A high ratio means greater liquidity risk. The company is susceptible in a money-market squeeze.
- *Accounts payable/Average daily purchases.* This ratio is the number of days needed for the company to pay creditors. Is the company meeting its payables commitment? Accounts payable payment period (in days) is equal to 365/Accounts payable turnover. (The accounts payable turnover equals purchases divided by accounts payable.)
- *Current liabilities to total liabilities.* A high ratio means less liquidity because there is a greater proportion of current debt.
- *(Accounts receivable + Inventory) − (Accounts payable + Accrued expenses payable).* Some banks look at this figure as an indication of a company's liquid position because it concentrates on the major current accounts.
- *Liquidity index.* This is the number of days current assets are removed from cash. A shorter period is preferred.

Example 30.7

	Amount		Days Removed from Cash	Total
Cash	$ 10,000	×	—	—
Accounts receivable	40,000	×	25	$1,000,000
Inventory	60,000	×	40	2,400,000
	$110,000			$3,400,000

$$\text{Index} = \frac{\$3,400,000}{\$110,000} = 30.9 \text{ days}$$

Example 30.8

Company B provides this financial information:

Current assets	$400,000
Fixed assets	800,000
Current liabilities	500,000
Noncurrent liabilities	600,000
Sales	5,000,000
Working capital provided from operations	100,000
Industry norms are:	
Fixed assets to current liabilities	4.0 times
Current liabilities to noncurrent liabilities	45.0%
Sales to current assets	8.3 times
Working capital provided from operations to total liabilities	30.5%
Company B's ratios are:	
Fixed assets to current liabilities	1.6 times
Current liabilities to noncurrent liabilities	83.3%
Sales to current assets	12.5 times
Working capital provided from operations to total liabilities	9.1%

Company B's liquidity ratios are all unfavorable relative to industry standards. High short-term debt and deficient current assets are high, and there is inadequate working capital provided from operations to meet total debt.

What is the trade-off between liquidity risk and return?

Liquidity risk is reduced by holding greater current assets than noncurrent assets. However, the return rate will decrease because the return on current assets (e.g., marketable securities) is typically less than the rate earned on productive fixed assets. Furthermore, excessively high liquidity may mean that management has not aggressively sought out desirable capital investment opportunities. A proper balance between liquidity and return is crucial to the overall financial standing of the business.

Is the company solvent?

Solvency is a company's ability to pay long-term debt payments (principal and interest). The CFO should consider the long-term financial and operating structure of the business. An evaluation is made of the magnitude of noncurrent debt and the realization risk in noncurrent assets. A high ratio of long-term assets to long-term liabilities is desirable. Solvency depends on earning power because a company will not be able to pay obligations unless it is profitable.

When practical, the CFO should use the market value of assets rather than book value in ratio computations because the former is more representative of fair value.

What ratios can be used to evaluate solvency?

A stable earnings and cash flow from operations enhances confidence in the company's ability to pay debt. Long-term debt ratios to be computed are:

- *Total liabilities to total assets.* This ratio indicates the percentage of total funds obtained from creditors. If the company owes too much, it may have difficulty in repaying the debt. At the optimum debt/assets ratio, the weighted-average cost of capital is less than at any other debt to asset level.
- *Long-term debt to stockholders' equity.* High leverage indicates risk because it may be difficult for the company to meet interest and principal payments as well as obtain reasonable financing. The problem is acute when cash problems exist. Excessive debt means less financial flexibility because the company will have a problem in obtaining funds during a tight money market. A desirable debt/equity ratio depends on many factors, including the rates of other firms in the industry, the access to debt financing, and stability in earnings.
- *Cash flow from operations to long-term debt.* This ratio shows whether internally generated funds are sufficient to meet noncurrent liabilities.
- *Interest coverage (Net income + Interest + Taxes/Interest).* A high ratio indicates that earnings are adequate to meet interest charges. It is a safety margin indicator showing how much of a decline in profit the company can tolerate.
- *Cash flow generated from operations plus interest to interest.* This ratio indicates available cash to meet interest charges. Unlike profit, cash pays interest. A higher ratio is needed for a cyclical business.
- *Net income before taxes and fixed charges to fixed charges.* This ratio helps evaluate the company's ability to meet fixed costs. A low ratio points to risk because when corporate activity falls, the company is unable to pay fixed charges.
- *Cash flow from operations plus fixed charges to fixed charges.* A high ratio indicates the company's ability to meet fixed charges. Furthermore, a company with stable operations is more apt to handle fixed costs.
- *Noncurrent assets to noncurrent liabilities.* Long-term debt is eventually paid from long-term assets. A high ratio affords more protection for long-term creditors.
- *Retained earnings to total assets.* The trend in this ratio reflects the company's profitability over the years.
- *Total liabilities to sales.* This ratio indicates the amount of sales financed by creditors.
- *Stockholders' equity to sales.* This ratio indicates the proportion of sales financed by stockholders' equity. It is generally safer for sales to be financed by equity than debt. A review of the ratio reveals if the owners are investing too much or too little relative to the sales volume. Is owners' equity being employed effectively?

 ## POTENTIAL FOR BUSINESS FAILURE

Bankruptcy occurs when the company cannot pay maturing financial obligations. We are particularly interested in predicting cash flow. Financial problems affect the P/E ratio, bond rating, and cost of capital.

Example 30.9

The following partial balance sheet and income statement data are provided for Company D.

Long-term assets	$700,000
Long-term liabilities	500,000
Stockholders' equity	300,000
Net income before tax	80,000
Cash flow provided from operations	100,000
Interest expense	20,000
Average norms taken from competitors:	
Long-term assets to long-term liabilities	2.0
Long-term debt to stockholders' equity	0.8
Cash flow to long-term liabilities	0.3
Net income before tax plus interest to interest	7.0
Company D's ratios are:	
Long-term assets to long-term liabilities	1.4
Long-term debt to stockholders' equity	1.67
Cash flow to long-term liabilities	0.2
Net income before tax plus interest to interest	5.0

After comparing the company's ratios with the industry averages, it appears that the company's solvency is worse than its competition, as evidenced by the greater long-term liabilities in the capital structure and lower interest coverage.

A quantitative indicator in predicting failure is *Altman's Z-score*. The Z-score is about 90 percent accurate in predicting failure one year in advance and about 80 percent reliable in forecasting it two years in advance. For a detailed discussion of Z-score, see Edward I. Altman, "Financial Ratios, Discriminant Analysis, and the Prediction of Corporate Bankruptcy," *Journal of Finance* (September 1968).

The Z-score equals:

$$\frac{\text{Working capital}}{\text{Total assets}} \times 1.2 + \frac{\text{Retained earnings}}{\text{Total assets}} \times 1.4 + \frac{\text{Operating income}}{\text{Total assets}}$$

$$\times 3.3 + \frac{\text{Market value of common and prefered}}{\text{Total assets}} \times 0.6$$

$$+ \frac{\text{Sales}}{\text{Total assets}} \times 0.999$$

The scores and the probability of short-term illiquidity follow.

Score	Probability of Illiquidity
1.80 or less	Very high
1.81 to 2.99	Not sure
3.0 or greater	Not likely

Example 30.10

A company presents this information:

Working capital	$280,000
Total assets	875,000
Total liabilities	320,000
Retained earnings	215,000
Sales	950,000
Operating income	130,000
Common stock	
Book value	220,000
Market value	310,000
Preferred stock	
Book value	115,000
Market value	170,000

The Z-score equals:

$$\frac{\$280,000}{\$875,000} \times 1.2 + \frac{\$215,000}{\$875,000} \times 1.4 + \frac{\$130,000}{\$875,000} \times 3.3 + \frac{\$480,000}{\$320,000} \times 0.6 + \frac{\$950,000}{\$875,000} \times 0.999$$

$$= 0.384 + 0.344 + 0.490 + 0.9 + 1.0857 = \underline{3.2037}$$

The probability of failure is not likely.

There are updated versions of Altman's model. You may refer to *Altman's Corporate Financial Distress* (New York: John Wiley & Sons, 1983). For more on this and other prediction models, see Chapter 38.

The liquidation value of a company may be estimated by using J. Wilcox's gambler's ruin prediction formula:

Cash + (Marketable securities at market value) + (79% of inventory, accounts receivable, and prepaid expenses) + (50% of other assets) – (Current liabilities + Long-term liabilities)

What warning signs exist as to future corporate failure?

The CFO should note these quantitative factors in predicting corporate failure:

- Low cash flow to total liabilities
- High debt-to-equity and high debt to total assets
- Low return on investment
- Low profit margin
- Low retained earnings to total assets
- Low working capital to total assets and low working capital to sales
- Low fixed assets to noncurrent liabilities
- Inadequate interest coverage
- Instability in earnings
- Small-size company in terms of sales and/or total assets
- Sharp decline in price of stock, bond price, and earnings
- A significant increase in beta (the fluctuation in the price of the company's stock compared to a market index)
- Market price per share materially below book value per share
- Cutback in dividends
- A significant increase in the weighted-average cost of capital
- High fixed cost to total cost structure (high operating leverage)
- Failure to maintain capital assets (e.g., a decline in the ratio of repairs to fixed assets)

The CFO should note these qualitative factors in predicting failure:

- Inability to control costs
- New company
- Declining industry
- High degree of competition
- Inability to obtain suitable financing and, when obtained, significant loan restrictions
- Inability to meet past-due obligations
- Moving into new areas in which expertise is lacking
- Failure to keep up to date, such as in a technologically oriented business
- High business risk (e.g., positive correlation in the product line; vulnerability to strikes)
- Inadequate insurance
- Cyclicality in business operations
- Inability to adjust production to meet consumption needs
- Susceptibility to stringent governmental regulation (e.g., companies in the real estate industry)

- Susceptibility to unreliable suppliers and energy shortages
- Renegotiation of debt and/or lease agreements

What can be done to avoid business failure?

If the CFO can predict with reasonable accuracy that the company is developing financial distress, he or she can recommend corrective actions.

The CFO can use these financial/quantitative factors to minimize the potential for failure:

- Avoid heavy debt. If liabilities are excessive, finance with equity.
- Dispose of unprofitable divisions and product lines.
- Manage assets for maximum return at the least practical risk.
- Stagger and extend the maturity dates of debt.
- Use quantitative techniques, such as multiple regression analysis, to compute the correlation between variables and the possibility of business failure.
- Ensure that a safety buffer exists between actual status and compliance requirements (e.g., working capital) in loan agreements.
- Have a negative correlation between products and investments.
- Lower dividend payouts.

The CFO can recommend these nonfinancial factors that minimize the potential for failure:

- Vertically and horizontally diversify the product line and operations.
- Diversify geographically.
- Finance assets with liabilities of similar maturity (hedging).
- Have adequate insurance.
- Enhance marketing efforts (e.g., advertise in the right place).
- Implement cost-reduction programs.
- Improve productivity.
- Minimize the adverse impact of inflation and recession on the business (e.g., price on a next-in, first-out basis).
- Invest in multipurpose, rather than single-purpose, assets, because of their lower risks.
- Reconsider entering industries with a high rate of failure.
- Have many projects, rather than only a few, that significantly affect operations.
- Consider introducing product lines that are the least affected by the business cycle and have stable demand.
- Avoid going from a labor-intensive to a capital-intensive business because the latter has a high degree of operating leverage.
- Avoid long-term fixed-fee contracts to customers. Incorporate inflation adjustment and energy-cost indices in contracts.
- Avoid entering markets on the downturn or that are highly competitive.
- Adjust to changes in technology.

INCOME STATEMENT ANALYSIS

What should be considered in analyzing the income statement?

Analysis of the income statement indicates a company's earning power, earnings quality, and operating performance. The CFO should be familiar with the important factors in appraising the income statement. Net income backed up by cash is essential for corporate liquidity. The accounting policies should be realistic in reflecting the substance of the transactions. Accounting changes should be made for legitimate reasons only. Furthermore, a high degree of estimation in the income measurement process results in uncertainty in reported figures. Earnings stability enhances the predictability of future results based on currently reported profits.

In analyzing the income statement, the CFO should look at quantitative (e.g., ratio analysis) and qualitative factors (e.g., pending litigation).

Earnings potential and earnings quality affect the P/E ratio, bond rating, effective interest rate, compensating balance requirement, availability of financing, and desirability of the firm as either an acquirer or acquiree.

Why are discretionary costs important to look at?

Discretionary costs can be changed at will. They can be decreased when a company is having problems. *What to do:* Exami ne current discretionary costs relative to previous years and to future requirements. An index number may be used to compare the current year discretionary cost to the base amount. A reduction in discretionary costs (e.g., advertising, research, repairs) is undesirable if their absence will have a negative effect on the future.

Example 30.11

These data are supplied:

	2X09	2X10	2X11
Sales	$95,000	$125,000	$84,000
Research	9,000	14,000	3,000

The most representative year (base year) is 2X09. After 2X12, the CFO believes that research is essential for the company's success because of the technological nature of the industry.

	2X09	2X10	2X11
Research to sales	9.5%	11.2%	3.6%

Looking in base dollars, 2X09, represents 100. 2X10 is 156 ($14,000/$9,000). 2X11 has an index of 33 ($3,000/$9,000).

A red flag is posted for 2X11. Research is lower than in previous years. There should have been a boost in research considering the technological updating needed for 2X12.

Example 30.12

This information on plant assets applies for a company:

	2X11	2X12
Equipment	$4,500	$4,800
Less: Accumulated depreciation	3,000	3,200
Book value	$1,500	$1,600
Repairs	400	320
Replacement cost of equipment	6,800	7,700
Consumer Price Index value of equipment	7,400	8,500
Revenue	48,000	53,000
Working capital	2,900	2,600
Cash	1,100	970
Debt–equity ratio	42%	71%
Equipment downtime	2%	5%

Finance company loans have increased relative to bank loans over the year. The CFO wants to analyze equipment and repairs.

Repairs to gross equipment decreased from 8.9 percent in 2X11 ($400/$4,500) to 6.7 percent in 2X12 ($320/$4,800). In a similar vein, repairs to revenue went from 0.83 percent in 2X11 ($400/$48,000) to 0.6 percent in 2X12 ($320/$53,000).

Over the year, there was a greater variation between replacement cost and book value and Consumer Price Index value and book value, indicating that equipment is aging.

The increased downtime means there is more equipment malfunctioning. Equipment purchased over the year was minimal, 6.7 percent ($300/$4,500).

The company's capital maintenance is inadequate. Repairs to fixed assets and repairs to revenue are down, and there are insufficient replacements. Perhaps these are the reasons for the increased downtime.

The company may have a problem purchasing fixed assets when needed because of a deteriorating liquidity position. Financial leverage has increased significantly over the year. It is difficult for the company to obtain adequate financing at reasonable interest rates, as evidenced by the need to borrow from finance companies.

Recommendation: Analyze the trend in the discretionary costs to sales ratio and the discretionary costs to assets ratio. If a cost-reduction program produces substantial cuts in discretionary costs, future profitability will suffer. However, cost control is justified when (1) in previous years, discretionary expenditures were excessive because of deficient and ill-conceived corporate strategy, or (2) competition has decreased. A material increase in discretionary costs may have a significant positive impact on corporate earning power and future growth.

How much of the earnings is supported by cash?

Cash flow from operations equals net income plus noncash expenses less noncash revenue. The CFO should examine the trend in the ratio of cash flow from operations to net income. A high ratio is warranted because it means that earnings are backed up by cash.

In evaluating cash adequacy, compute:

- Cash flow generated from operations before interest expense
- Cash flow generated from operations less cash payments to meet debt principal, dividends, and capital expenditures

What tax factors have to be considered in appraising earnings?

Earnings are not really available if a high percentage of foreign profits will not be repatriated back to the United States for an extended time period.

It is better if the company's earnings and growth do not rely on a lowered tax rate that is susceptible to a future change in the tax law or that places restrictions on the firm.

Of what value is residual income?

Residual income is an economic income considering the opportunity cost of placing funds in the business. An increasing trend in residual income to net income indicates strong corporate profitability because the company is earning enough to meet its imputed cost of capital.

Residual income equals:

Net income
Less: Minimum return (cost of capital) × Total assets
Residual income

Example 30.13

A company's net income is $800,000, total assets are $4.6 million, and cost of capital is 13.40 percent.

Residual income equals:

Net income	$800,000
Less: Minimum return × Total assets 13.40% × $4,600,000	616,400
Residual income	$183,600

The ratio of residual income to net income is 23 percent ($183,600/$800,000). (Residual income is discussed in more detail in Chapter 17.)

Are accounting policies realistic?

Accounting policies should be realistic in reflecting the economic substance of the company's transactions. The underlying business and financial realities of the company and industry have to be considered. For example, the depreciation method should most approximately measure the decline in service potential of the asset. Examples of realistic accounting policies are cited in *AICPA Industry Audit Guides*.

How certain are the earnings?

The more subjective the accounting estimates in the income measurement process, the greater is the uncertainty associated with net income. *What to do:* Examine the difference between actual experience and the estimates used. A wide difference implies uncertain earnings.

Example 30.14

This information applies to a company:

	2X11	2X12
Cash and near-cash revenue	$98,000	$107,000
Noncash revenue items	143,000	195,000
Total revenue	$241,000	$302,000
Cash and near-cash expenses	$37,000	$58,000
Noncash expenses	67,000	112,000
Total expenses	$104,000	$170,000
Net income	$137,000	$132,000

Estimation-related ratios can now be calculated.

	2X11	2X12
Estimated revenue to total revenue	59%	65%
Estimated revenue to net income	104%	148%
Estimated expenses to total expenses	64%	66%
Estimated expenses to total revenue	28%	37%
Estimated expenses to net income	49%	85%

In each case, there was greater estimation in the income measurement process in 2X12 compared to 2X11. A high degree of estimation results in uncertain profits.

Examine the trend in these ratios:

- High estimation assets (e.g., fixed assets) to total assets
- Cash expenses to revenue
- Estimated expenses to revenue
- Cash revenue to revenue
- Estimated revenue to revenue
- Estimated expenses to net income
- Estimated revenue to net income

What is the significance of discontinued operations?

Income from discontinued operations is typically of a one-time nature and should be ignored when predicting future earnings. Furthermore, a discontinued operation implies that the company is in a state of decline or that a poor management decision is the reason for the firm's entering the discontinued line of business initially.

What are some useful profitability ratios?

A sign of good financial health and how effectively the company is managed is its ability to generate earnings and return on investment. Absolute dollar profit is of minimal significance unless it is compared to the assets generating it.

A company's profit margin (net income to sales) indicates how well it is managed and provides clues to a company's pricing, cost structure, and manufacturing efficiency. A high gross profit percent (gross profit to sales) is favorable because it indicates that the company can control its production costs.

Return on investment is how much profit is achieved from the investment. Two key ratios of return on investment are return on total assets and return on owners' equity.

The *return on total assets* (net income/average total assets) indicates the efficiency with which management has used its resources to obtain revenue. Furthermore, a decline in the ratio may stem from a productivity problem.

The *return on common equity* (earnings available to common stock/average stockholders' equity) measures the rate of return on the common stockholders' investment. (Return on investment is fully discussed in Chapter 17.)

An increase in the gross profit margin (gross profit to sales) may mean that the company was able to increase its sales volume or selling price or to reduce its cost of sales. Manufacturers typically have higher gross profit rates than merchandisers.

The net operating profit ratio (net operating profit to sales) may be used to evaluate operating managers. The analysis is before considering interest expense since financing is usually arranged by the finance managers.

A high ratio of sales to working capital indicates efficient utilization of liquid funds. The sales backlog should be used to monitor sales status and planning. Compute the days of sales in backlog equal to:

$$\frac{\text{Backlog balance}}{\text{Sales volume/Days in period}}$$

Is the backlog for long-term delivery (e.g., five years from now), or is it on a recurring basis to maintain continuing stability?

Some other ratios reflective of operations are:

- *Revenue to number of employees; revenue to employee salaries.* Higher ratios are reflective of better employee productivity.
- *Average yearly wage per employee; average hourly wage rate.* These ratios examine the ability to control labor costs.
- *Average fixed assets per employee.* This shows the productivity of using fixed assets by employees.
- *Indirect labor to direct labor.* A low ratio is reflective of controlling the labor component of overhead.
- *Purchase discounts to purchases.* A high ratio indicates effective management of purchases.
- *General and administrative (G&A) expenses to selling expense.* This ratio indicates control of G&A expenses. G&A expenses relative to selling expenses should decline with increased sales volume. If the ratio increases, inadequate controls over administrative activities exist.

How is the growth rate computed?

A company's growth rate should be compared to that of competitors and industry averages. Measures of growth rate include:

$$\frac{\text{Change in retained earnings}}{\text{Stockholders' equity at beginning of year}}$$

$$\frac{\text{EPS at end of year} - \text{EPS at beginning of year}}{\text{EPS at beginning of year}}$$

The growth rate in sales, dividends, total assets, and the like may be computed in a similar fashion.

MARKET VALUE RATIOS

What are some important market value ratios?

Market value ratios apply to a comparison of the company's stock price relative to its earnings (or book value) per share. The dividend-related ratios are also considered. The ratios include:

- *EPS* (net income divided by outstanding shares)
- *P/E ratio* (market price per share divided by earnings per share)
- *Book value per share*, which is computed as:

$$\frac{\text{Total stockholders' equity} - (\text{Liquidation of preferred stock} + \text{Preferred dividends in arrears})}{\text{Common stock outstanding}}$$

A comparison of book value per share to market price per share indicates how investors feel about the company.

- *Dividend yield* (dividends per share divided by market price per share)
- *Dividend payout* (dividends per share divided by EPS)

Investors look unfavorably on lower dividends, since dividend payout is a sign of the financial health of the business.

ANALYZING THE FINANCIAL STRUCTURE OF THE FIRM

Quantitative measures can be used to evaluate the company's stability. Comparisons should be made to prior years of the firm, competing companies, and industry norms. Types of stability measurements include:

- *Trend in average reported earnings.* Average earnings over a long time period (such as five years) will level out abnormal and erratic income statement components as well as cyclical factors.
- *Average pessimistic earnings.* This represents the average earnings based on the worst possible scenario for the company's operational activities. The average minimum earnings is useful in appraising a company having high risk operations.
- *Standard deviation (SD).*

$$SD = \sqrt{\frac{\sum(y - \bar{y})^2}{n}}$$

where
y = net income for period t

$\bar{y}$ = average net income

n = number of periods

- *Coefficient of variation (CV).*

$$CV = \frac{SD}{\bar{y}}$$

The coefficient of variation is a relative measure of instability to facilitate a comparison between competing companies. The higher the coefficient, the greater the risk.

- *Instability index of earnings (I).*

$$I = \sqrt{\frac{\sum(y - y^t)^2}{n}}$$

where y^t = trend earnings for period t and is determined as:

$$y^t = a + b^t$$

where
a = dollar intercept
b = slope of trend line
t = time period

■ *Beta.* Beta is computed by a computer run based on this equation:

$$r_{jt} = a_j + b_j r_{mt} + E_{jt}$$

where
r_{jt} = return of security j for period t
a_j = constant for security j
b_j = beta for security j
r_m = return on a market index, such as the New York Stock Exchange Index
E_{jt} = error term

Beta measures the systematic risk of a stock. A beta greater than 1 indicates that the company's market price of stock fluctuates more than the change in the market index, indicating a risky security. A fluctuation in stock price infers greater business risk and instability. For example, a beta of 1.4 means the company's stock price rises or falls 40 percent faster than the market. A beta of 1 means the company's stock price moves the same as the market index. A beta of less than 1 indicates the company's stock price fluctuates less than the stock market index, indicating lower corporate risk. Of course, a company's beta may change over time. The betas for individual companies can be obtained from various sources, such as Standard & Poor's.

Example 30.15

A company shows this trend in reported earnings:

2X08	$100,000
2X09	110,000
2X10	80,000
2X11	120,000
2X12	140,000

$$SD = \sqrt{\frac{\Sigma(y - \bar{y})^2}{n}}$$

(continued)

$$\bar{y} = \frac{\Sigma y}{n} = \frac{100{,}000 + 110{,}000 + 80{,}000 + 120{,}000 + 140{,}000}{5}$$

$$= \frac{550{,}000}{5} = 110{,}000$$

Year	(y – y)	(y – y)²
2X08	–10,000	100,000,000
2X09	0	0
2X10	–30,000	900,000,000
2X11	+10,000	100,000,000
2X12	+30,000	900,000,000
		2,000,000,000

$$SD = \sqrt{\frac{2{,}000{,}000{,}000}{5}} = \sqrt{400{,}000{,}000} = 20{,}000$$

$$CV = \frac{SD}{\bar{y}} = \frac{20{,}000}{110{,}000} = 18.2\%$$

Note

An increase in (1) and (2) or a decrease in (3) indicates greater earnings instability because of the high fixed costs. ■

Are costs highly leveraged?

Operating leverage is the degree to which fixed charges exist in a company's cost structure. Measures of operating leverage are:

1. Fixed costs to total costs
2. Percentage change in operating income to the percentage change in sales volume
3. Net income to fixed costs

   A high percentage of variable costs to total costs indicates greater earnings stability. Variable costs can be adjusted more readily than fixed costs to meet declining product demand.

   A high-break-even company is vulnerable to economic declines.

What is the nature of the product line?

A company's product line affects its overall stability and profitability. Where possible, product risk should be minimized, such as by moving toward negative correlation among products.

Product Line Measures

The degree of correlation between products is evident from a correlation matrix determined by a computer run.

Product demand elasticity is determined as:

$$\frac{\text{Percent change in quantity}}{\text{Percent change in price}}$$

If > 1 Elastic demand

If = 1 Unitary demand

If < 1 Inelastic demand

Red flag. Products that are positively correlated and have elastic demands have high risk. Companies with product lines that have negative correlations and inelastic demand (e.g., healthcare products) are stable. Products with different seasonal peaks can be added to stabilize production and marketing operations.

Example 30.16

The correlation matrix of a product line follows.

Product	A	B	C	D	E	F
A	1.0	0.13	−0.02	−0.01	−0.07	0.22
B	0.13	1.0	−0.02	−0.07	0.00	0.00
C	−0.02	−0.02	1.0	0.01	0.48	0.13
D	−0.01	−0.07	0.01	1.0	0.01	−0.02
E	−0.07	0.00	0.48	0.01	1.0	0.45
F	0.22	0.00	0.13	−0.02	0.45	1.0

Perfect correlation exists with the same product. For instance, the correlation between product F and product F is 1.0.

High positive correlation exists between products E and C (0.48) and products E and F (0.45). Because these products are tightly interwoven, risk exists.

Low negative correlation exists between products A and D (−0.01) and products A and C (−0.02).

No correlation is present between products B and E (0.00) and products B and F (0.00).

It would be better if some products had significant negative correlations (e.g., −0.7), but this is not the case.

Example 30.17

Data for products X and Y follow.

	X	Y
Selling price	$10.00	$8.00
Unit sales	10,000	13,000

If the selling price of product X is increased to $11.00, it is predicted that sales volume will decrease by 500 units. If the selling price of product Y is raised to $9.50, sales volume is anticipated to fall by 4,000 units.

Product demand elasticity equals:

$$\frac{\text{Percent change in quantity}}{\text{Percent change in price}}$$

Inelastic demand exists with product X:

$$\frac{500/10,000}{\$1.00/\$10.00} = \frac{0.05}{0.10} = 0.5$$

Elastic demand occurs with product Y:

$$\frac{4,000/13,000}{\$1.50/\$8.00} = \frac{0.307}{0.188} = 1.63$$

What are some financial measures of marketing effectiveness?

The CFO may evaluate marketing effectiveness in these ways:

- Appraise product warranty complaints and their dispositions.
- Calculate revenue, cost, and profit by product line, customer, industry segment, geographic area, distribution channel, type of marketing effort, and average order size.
- Evaluate new products in terms of risk and profitability.
- Appraise strengths and weaknesses of competition as well as their reactions to the company's promotion efforts.
- Determine revenue; marketing costs; and profits before, during, and after promotion programs.
- Appraise sales generated by different types of selling efforts (e.g., direct mail, television, newspaper).
- Analyze sales force effectiveness by determining the profit generated by salespeople, call frequency, sales incentives, sales personnel costs (e.g., auto), and dollar value of orders obtained per hour spent.
- Determine sales and/or net income per employee.
- Examine the trend in the ratio of marketing costs to sales.

How can risk be appraised?

In appraising risk, the CFO should compare the company's risk exposure to the competition and to past trends of the firm. Uncertainty makes it difficult to predict future performance. The major risks faced by the company are:

- *Corporate risk*, such as the underinsurance of assets (e.g., declining trend in insurance expense to fixed assets, unusual casualty losses). Diversification is a way to reduce corporate risk.
- *Industry risk*, such as an industry under public and governmental scrutiny (e.g., real estate industry). An approach to diminish industry risk is to move toward a variable cost–oriented business.
- *Economic risk*, such as the effect of a recession on product demand. This risk may be curtailed by having a low-priced product substitute for a high-priced item (e.g., cereal for meat).
- *Political risk*, such as the need for lobbying efforts. Avoid operations in highly regulated areas.
- *Social risk*, such as a company experiencing customer boycotts or bias suits. A way to reduce this risk is community involvement.
- *Environmental risk*, such as a product line or service exposed to the weather. A way to lower this risk is to have counterseasonal products.

What is the nature of your industry?

Labor-intensive businesses typically have greater stability than capital-intensive ones since the former have a higher percentage of variable costs, whereas the latter have a higher percentage of fixed costs. Capital-intensive industries are susceptible to cyclicality. Companies in a consumer product industry have greater stability because of inelastic product demand.

A company may have variability because of an industry cycle. An example is the steel industry, which has a 5- to 10-year cycle because of the refurbishing of steel furnaces.

 INDUSTRY CHARACTERISTICS INDICATIVE OF GREATER RISK

Risk is affected by the characteristics of the industry in which the company is operating. Industry-specific characteristics are:

- Competition—difficulty of entry, price wars, cheaper imports
- Technological changes (e.g., computers) causing obsolescence risk and difficulty in keeping up to date
- Governmental regulation, such as by a utility regulatory commission.
- Susceptibility to cyclical effects
- High-risk product lines without adequate insurance coverage

If you have difficulty obtaining insurance in your industry, try to pool risks by setting up mutual insurance companies.

Are you vulnerable to political uncertainties?

Political risk refers to foreign operations and governmental regulation. Multinational companies with foreign exposure have uncertainties in repatriation of funds, currency fluctuations, and local customs and regulations. Operations in politically and economically unstable foreign regions mean instability. The following ratios may be examined to help determine what risks the company faces.

- Questionable foreign revenue to total revenue
- Questionable foreign earnings to net income
- Total export revenue to total revenue
- Total export earnings to net income
- Total assets in questionable foreign countries to total assets
- Total assets in foreign countries to total assets

 ## CONSIDERATIONS IN FOREIGN OPERATIONS

Foreign operations are characterized by the following factors.

- *Foreign exchange rates.* Watch out for vacillating foreign exchange rates, which can be measured by the percentage change over time and/or its standard deviation. The trend in cumulative foreign translation gains and losses (reported in the stockholders' equity section) should be examined. When foreign assets are balanced against foreign liabilities, you are better insulated from changes in exchange rates. Evaluate your exposed position for each major foreign country. When the dollar is devalued, net foreign assets and income in countries with strong currencies are worth more dollars. Forward exchange contracts should be viewed positively because the company is minimizing its foreign currency exposure by hedging against exchange risk from foreign currency transactions.
- *Foreign country's tax rate and duties.* Companies dependent on government contracts have more instability because government spending is vulnerable to political whims of legislators and war-threatening situations. *Suggestion:* Determine the percentage of earnings from government contract work and the extent to which such work is recurring. Look at government regulation over the company because it influences the bottom line (e.g., utility rate increases are less than those that have been asked for). *Recommendation:* Examine current and future effects of governmental interference on the company by studying current and proposed governmental laws and regulations. The sources of such information include legislative hearings, trade journals, and newspapers. Stringent environmental and safety regulations eat into profits. Analyze the effect of present and proposed tax legislation and determine the areas of IRS scrutiny.

CHAPTER THIRTY-ONE

Analysis, Evaluation, and Control of Revenue and Costs

A COMPANY CAN IMPROVE its bottom line and overall operations by analyzing, planning, monitoring, and controlling revenue and costs. Control reports help in this process. This chapter provides some benchmarks in this evaluation and control process.

CONTROL REPORTS

Control reports are issued to highlight poor performance so that timely corrective action can be taken. The reports should be frequent and detailed, and should look at each important operational level.

Summary reports should present performance over a long time period (e.g., monthly) and provide an overview of performance.

The form and content of the control report varies depending on the functions and responsibilities of the executives receiving it. The reports may be narrative, tabular, or graphic. A lower-level manager is more concerned with details. A higher-level manager is more interested in summaries, trends, and relationships. The reports may be in both financial and nonfinancial terms.

How can revenue be controlled?

Important questions needing answering in sales analysis are: What was sold? Where was it sold? Who sold it? What was the profit?

Sales and profitability analysis involves these considerations:

- *Customer:* Industry or retail, corporate or governmental, domestic or foreign
- *Product:* Type of commodity, size, price, quality, and color

- *Distribution channel:* Wholesaler, retailer, agent, broker
- *Sales effort:* Personal visit, direct mail, coupon, ad (e.g., newspaper, magazine), media (television, radio)
- *Territory:* Country, state, city, suburb
- *Order size:* Normal purchase, volume purchase
- *Organization:* Department, branch
- *Salesperson:* Group, individual
- *Terms of sale:* Cash purchase, cash on delivery, charge account, installment purchase

Profitability can be determined by territory, product, customer, channel of distribution, salespeople, method of sale, organization, and operating division. In deciding on a product line, economies of production have to be considered.

The CFO should watch out for significant changes in sales trends in terms of profit margin and distribution channels. How do actual sales conform to sales goals and budgets? In analyzing the trend in sales, the CFO may see the need to redirect sales effort and/or change the product. The types and sizes of desirable accounts and orders should be determined. Volume selling price breaks may be given for different order sizes.

In appraising sales volume and prices, the CFO should not ignore the possibility that unfavorable variances have arisen from salespeople having excessive authority in establishing selling prices.

Pricing should be reviewed periodically after considering relevant factors, such as increasing costs. All types of costs must be considered including total costs, marginal costs, and out-of-pocket costs.

The CFO should compare the profit margins on alternative products in deciding which ones to emphasize. He or she should also consider the probable effect of volume on the profit margin and the importance of changes in composition, manufacturing processes, and quality on the costs to produce and distribute the product.

The CFO should determine:

- The least cost geographic location for warehouses
- The minimum acceptable order
- How best to serve particular accounts, such as by mail order, telephone, jobber, and so on

The CFO may find that most sales are concentrated in a few products. In fact, a few customers may represent a significant portion of company sales. The CFO may be able to reduce selling costs by concentrating sales effort on major customers and products. Perhaps salesperson assignments should be modified, such as concentrating on only a few territories. Perhaps a simplification of the product line is needed.

The CFO should provide the alternative costs for the varying methods of sale. For example, how should samples be distributed to result in the best effect on sales at minimum cost?

In evaluating sales effort, the CFO should consider the success of business development expense (e.g., promotion and entertainment) by customer, territory, or salesperson.

How can customers be analyzed?

Customer analysis should indicate the number of accounts and dollar sales by customer volume bracket and average order size. A small order size may result in unprofitable sales because of such factors as high distribution costs and high order costs. In this case, the CFO should analyze distribution costs by size of order in order to bring the problem under control and take appropriate corrective action.

It may cost more to sell to certain types of customers than to others among different classes as well as within a particular class. For example, a particular customer may require greater services than typical, such as delivery and warehousing. A particular customer may demand a different price, such as for volume purchases. Profitability analysis by customer should be made so as to see where to place salespeople's time, what selling price to establish, where to control distribution costs, and what customer classes to discontinue. A determination should also be made as to which customers have increasing or decreasing sales volume. Sales effort may be curtailed on large-volume accounts that only buy low-profit margin items and on low-volume accounts that are at best marginally profitable.

From a sales and profitability perspective, it may not pay to carry all varieties, sizes, and colors. The company should emphasize the profitable products, which may not be the odd items (e.g., unusual colors, odd sizes).

What analysis can be made of sales?

Sales that have not been realized should be listed and analyzed, particularly with regard to any problems that may have been experienced. Such analysis considers:

- Orders received
- Unfilled orders
- Lost sales
- Cancellations

> **Note**
>
> The analysis of orders is particularly crucial when goods are made to order. ■

Sales deductions should be analyzed to indicate problems that could lead to deficient profits. Problems may be indicated when excessive discounts, allowances, and freight costs exist. What are the extent of and reasons for returns, price adjustments, freight allowances, and so on? A determination should be made of who is responsible. A defective product is the responsibility of manufacturing. An excessive freight cost or wrong delay is the responsibility of traffic.

Sales should be analyzed in terms of both price and volume to identify unfavorable trends, weaknesses, and positive directions.

CONTROL OF COSTS

Cost control must be exercised over manufacturing and nonmanufacturing costs. Costs should be incurred only for necessary business expenditures that will provide revenue benefit to the firm.

How can manufacturing costs be controlled?

The purpose of cost control is to obtain an optimum product consistent with quality standards from the various input factors, including material, labor, and facilities. The input–output relationship is crucial. In other words, the best result should be forthcoming at the least cost. The office should be shut down when the factory is not in operation. Since most costs are controllable by someone within the organization, responsibility should be assigned.

Changes in standard prices for material, labor, and overhead should be noted along with their effects on the unit standard cost of the product. Perhaps there is a need for material substitutions or modifications in specifications or processes.

Labor control should be jointly developed between staff and management. Line supervisors have prime responsibility to control labor costs. Actual performance of labor should be compared against a realistic yardstick. Unfavorable discrepancies should be followed up.

The CFO may assist in controlling labor costs in these ways:

- Prepare an analysis of overtime hours and cost. Make sure overtime is approved in advance.
- Prepare a report on labor turnover, training cost, and years of service.
- Determine the standard work hours for the production program.
- Establish procedures to limit the number of employees placed on the payroll to that called for by the production plan.
- Make sure that an employee is performing services per his or her job description. Are high-paid employees doing menial work?
- Consider overtime hours and cost, turnover rate, output per worker, and relationship between indirect labor and direct labor.
- Improve working conditions to enhance productivity.
- Analyze machinery to ensure it is up-to-date.

Because most overhead items are small in amount, proper control may be neglected. Of course, in the aggregate, overhead may be substantial. Areas to look at include the personal use of supplies and photocopying, and the use of customized forms when standardized ones would suffice.

In order to control overhead, standards must be established and compared against actual performance. Periodic reports of budget and actual overhead costs should be prepared to identify problem areas. Overhead costs can be preplanned, such as planning indirect labor staff (e.g., maintenance), to avoid excessive hours. The preplanning approach may be beneficial when significant dollar cost is involved, such as in the purchase of repair materials and supplies. A record of purchases by responsibility unit may be helpful. Purchase requirements should be properly approved.

The cost of idle equipment should be determined to gauge whether facilities are being utilized properly. What is the degree of plant utilization relative to what is normal?

What can be done to minimize manufacturing costs?

The control of distribution costs is a much more difficult problem than the control of manufacturing costs. In distribution, we have to consider the varying nature of the personality of seller and buyer. Competitive factors must be taken into account. In production, however, the worker is the only human element. In marketing, there are more methods and greater flexibility relative to production. Several distribution channels may be used. Because of the greater possibility for variability, distribution processes are more difficult to standardize than production activities. If distribution costs are excessive, who and where does the responsibility lie? Is it a problem territory? Is the salesperson doing a poor job?

Distribution costs and effort must be planned, controlled, and monitored. Distribution costs can be analyzed by functional operation, nature of expense, and application of distribution effort.

In functional operation, distribution costs are analyzed in terms of individual responsibility. This is a particularly useful approach in large companies. Functional operations requiring measurement are identified. Examples of such operations might be circular mailing, warehouse shipments, and salesperson calls on customers.

In looking at the nature of the expense, costs are segregated by month, and trends in distribution costs are examined. The ratio of distribution costs to sales over time should be enlightening. A comparison to industry norms is recommended.

In looking at the manner of application, distribution costs must be segregated into direct costs, indirect costs, and semidirect costs.

Direct costs are specifically identifiable to a particular segment. Examples of direct costs assignable to a salesperson are salary, commission, and travel and entertainment expense. But these same costs may be indirect or semidirect if attributable to product analysis. An expense that is direct in one application may not be in another.

Indirect costs are general corporate costs and must be allocated to segments (e.g., territory, product) on a rational basis. Examples are corporate advertising and salaries of general sales executives. Advertising may be allocated based on sales. General sales executives' salaries may be allocated based on time spent by territory or product. Here a time log may be kept.

Semidirect costs are related in some measurable way to particular segments. Such costs may be distributed in accordance with the services required. For example, the variable factor for warehousing may be weight handled. Order handling costs may be in terms of the number of orders. The allocation base is considerably less arbitrary than with indirect costs.

A comparison should be made between actual and budgeted figures for salesperson salaries, bonuses, and expenses. The salary structure in the industry may serve as a good reference point.

An examination should be made as to the effect of advertising on sales. Perhaps a change in media is needed.

Telephone expense may be controlled in these ways:

- Requiring prior approval for long-distance calls
- Using controls to restrict personal use of the telephone, such as a key lock
- Discarding or returning unnecessary equipment

The trend in warehouse expense to sales should be analyzed. Increasing trends may have to be investigated.

To reduce dues and subscription expenses, a control is necessary, such as having a card record of each publication by subscribed to, by whom, and why. If another employee must use that publication, he or she knows where to go.

There should be centralized control over contributions, perhaps in the hands of a committee of senior management. A general policy must be established as to amount and for what purposes.

PERFORMANCE MEASURES

Performance appraisal must take into account the trend in a measure over time within the company, compared to competition, and compared to industry benchmarks. Performance measures may be appraised by customer, sales territory, contract, job, service, product, division, department, and manager.

What performance measures may be used?

Performance measures include the:

- Number of skills per worker
- Output per labor-hour
- Lead time
- Setup time compared to total manufacturing time
- Backup of orders
- Non–value-added cost to total cost
- Rework costs on manufactured goods
- Number and duration of production delays
- Time per business process
- Repeat sales to customers
- Production costs to total costs
- Production costs to total sales
- Number of complaints and warranty services required

- Time between order placement and receipt
- Time between receipt of an order and delivery
- Number and length of breakdowns in machinery

The CFO should formulate with manufacturing managers optimum production volume that minimizes carrying and setup costs.

Quality

The *cost of quality* (COQ) is the cost to correct poor quality or to improve good quality. It considers the costs to guard against product defects (e.g., proper machine maintenance, employee training), appraisal costs (e.g., inspecting, training), and cost of the failure to have quality (e.g., rework, warranties). Problems must be identified and corrected in a timely way. Compute the trend in the following ratios: COQ to sales, and COQ to total operating costs. The CFO's objective is to minimize COQ subject to the restraints of production limitations, customer requirements, and company policy.

Productivity

Productivity is enhanced by minimizing direct labor cost. An attempt should be made to reduce indirect labor costs relative to direct labor costs. Greater and more efficient productivity may be derived by consolidating facilities and equipment. A productivity measure is the relationship of the time, cost, and quality of an "input" to the quality and units generated for the output. There should be a proper input-output balance. Resource utilization should be optimized.

Personnel Performance

In looking at personnel performance, consider sales dollars and volume relative to the number of employees. Compute the following ratios:

- Labor costs to sales, profit, and total costs
- Revenue to number of workers
- Sales volume to number of workers
- Revenue to wages
- Employee turnover rate

Sales Efforts

Salesperson effectiveness should be evaluated, such as by reviewing salesperson incentives, call frequency, dollar value of orders obtained per hour spent, cost per salesperson, and revenue generated by salesperson.

An appraisal of promotional and advertising effectiveness can be made by analyzing the profit prior to and after promotion, dollar expenditure by media compared to sales generated, marketing costs to sales, and media measures. A test market analysis should also be undertaken comparing the industry versus the consumer markets. An activity analysis may also be performed looking at sales and marketing, order management, and customer support.

Space Utilization

In analyzing space utilization, consider:

- Production per square foot = Units manufactured/Square feet of space for equipment
- Customer space = Number of customers/Square feet of space
- Expense per square foot for owned property = Expenses of owning property/Square feet of space
- Revenue per square foot = Net sales/Square feet of space
- Sales per square foot of equipment = Net sales/Square feet of space for equipment
- Rent per square foot = Rent expense/Square feet of space
- Profit per square foot = Net income/Square feet of space
- Employee space = Square feet of space/Number of employees

BUSINESS PROCESSES

A *business process* is an activity, function, or operation that crosses departments and divisions of a company to produce the good or perform the service. By emphasizing a process, it is easier to comprehend the complexities and interrelationships among organizational units, and assist in improved communication as to where each responsibility unit fits in. Emphasizing and improving the business process results in improved effectiveness and efficiency.

When evaluating business processes, take into account:

- The quality of the process
- Whether all steps in the process are necessary
- Work flow
- What the process costs and how long it takes
- Problems or bottlenecks in the process

Are there redundant steps? Are the steps too costly, time consuming, or complex? Can the steps be simplified and more time efficient? The CFO should look into what processes can be dropped, curtailed, added, or expanded. A modification of a process may be needed periodically depending on changing circumstances.

How can processes be improved?

The following actions can be taken to improve a business process:

- Prioritize strategies.
- Reduce cycle time.
- Use up-to-date technology.
- Improve operational sequence.
- Reorganize procedures.

- Reduce the number of employees or functions in the process.
- Clarify job descriptions and instructions.
- Improve training.
- Upgrade machinery.

A "value-added appraisal" should be performed for each responsibility unit, activity, function, or operation. Is the value added sufficient to justify that activity or business segment? If not, what can be done to improve the situation?

A business process analysis is especially called for when profitability of product lines or services is shrinking, market share is declining significantly, service quality is deteriorating, and customer response time is becoming prohibitive.

Operational audits should be conducted to examine corporate policies and procedures and ensure that they are functioning properly.

CHAPTER THIRTY-TWO

Insurance and Legal Considerations

THE CFO SHOULD be familiar with insurance and law. Insurance coverage protects against fire and theft losses, product liability, and contract repudiation. Federal and state laws deal with the relationship between the employer and employee.

 INSURANCE PROTECTION

In a large company, a risk manager position should exist to handle insurance issues. The risk manager should report directly to the CFO. In a smaller company, the CFO may be responsible for insurance matters him- or herself.

Insurance protection minimizes the risk of loss. Insurance may be mandated by law, such as workers' compensation. Insurance coverage may be required by contract, such as fire insurance in order to adhere to the provisions of a loan agreement. The CFO must understand insurance requirements and procedures, and must monitor and control insurance costs while maintaining sufficient insurance coverage. The CFO has to consider the limits for risk assumption or retention, self-insurance, and uninsurable risks. Furthermore, suitable documentation of insurance procedures is needed.

What are your duties in the insurance area?

The CFO has many responsibilities in insurance protection, including:

- Identifying and appraising risks
- Monitoring changes in the corporate environment as it affects insurance
- Estimating the probability of loss
- Maintaining insurance records

- Keeping abreast of new developments in insurance
- Ensuring compliance with federal and local regulatory laws

In evaluating insurable hazards, the CFO should examine properties and related contractual obligations (e.g., leases, mortgages) in detail. Each structure should be listed along with its condition, safety, location, and replacement cost.

In insignificant risk areas, deductibles should be established to satisfy company needs and result in premium savings. *Tip:* A new business should have higher deductibles until experience of loss incidences and their financial effect is gained.

Insurance policies should be reviewed periodically to avoid uninsured losses. As the company changes in size, products, geographic areas, and so on, it may have to alter the type and amount of insurance. There may have to be a revision in policy limits and deductibles based on the company's current situation. If the deductible is increased, the premium will be decreased. When reviewing insurance, the CFO has to consider new risks, trends in litigation, changes in inventory policy, sale or purchase of fixed assets, switch in distribution channels, and fair market value of property.

Note

Insurance is not needed for everything. In some nonessential areas, self-insurance may be enough. In deciding whether to insure against a risk, the CFO must weigh the probable loss against the insurance premium. If the difference is negligible, it may not pay to insure the item. *General rule:* Insure against potential catastrophes that would significantly impair ongoing operations. ■

What insurance records are needed?

Many insurance records should be maintained, including:

- Records of premiums, losses, and settlements. The ratio of premiums to losses should be computed.
- Expense distribution records, including information about payments, refunds, accruals, write-offs, and allocation amounts and bases to segments.
- Claim records, including the names of claim representatives, claim procedures, documentation, claim information (e.g., date), and status of the claim.
- Records of the values of insured items.
- Binder records of *pending* insurance.
- Location records of insured items.
- Transportation logs for corporate vehicles, including delivery trucks and automobiles. Information includes miles driven and to be driven, condition, and location.
- Other files, including due dates for premiums, notice of hearings, and inspections.

An insurance manual should be kept detailing the procedures to be followed on all aspects of insurance coverage by type, including obtaining insurance, filing claims, financial reporting and presentation, allocation bases to allocate premiums to reporting units, and settlement issues.

All insurable losses must be reported and documented immediately. The CFO must know what types of losses have occurred, where, and of what magnitude. The damaged items must be segregated until the adjuster has made a review. The CFO should determine the reason for the loss and recommend remedial steps.

At year-end, an insurance report should be prepared containing a description of the types of insurance and coverage, premiums paid, self-insured items, and the adequacy of established reserves.

The insurance record (Exhibit 32.1) lists the insurance policies, policy dates, annual premium, and coverage.

The CFO should keep records of the use and sale of property. Insurance claim information should be maintained for such items as cash, securities, inventory, and fixed assets. The CFO should check the track record, support, and documentation for all claims.

EXHIBIT 32.1 Insurance Record

Insurance Company	Broker	Identifying Number of Policy	Amount of Policy	Term	Expiration Date	Annual Premium	Coverage	Exclusions

How do you know what insurance broker to use?

In choosing an insurance broker, these points should be considered:

- Insurer's financial condition
- Types of coverage, insurance products available, and rates
- Timely and full resolution of insurance claims
- Services provided and expertise of staff

TYPES OF INSURANCE

The types of business insurance include product liability, commercial property, umbrella excess policy, marine, contingent business interruption, automobile, and aircraft.

To what extent are you affected by product liability?

Insurance coverage is needed for losses arising from damages suffered by other parties because of defects in the company's products, services, operations, or employee actions. An evaluation should be conducted of contracts, leases, and sales orders. What federal and state product liability statutes apply? What is the probability of loss, the degree, and the frequency?

What is covered under commercial property insurance?

The commercial property policy is a comprehensive one insuring inventory on the premises, warehouses, and in transit. It also covers property damage, personal injuries, product liability, advertising liability, fire damage on rental premises, flood and earthquake losses, and loss of valuable records. The coverage *excludes* certain items, such as cash and securities, property sold under installments, precious metals, aircraft, and imports or exports. These are covered under other types of policies.

The commercial property policy is the prime "all-risk" policy of the company. Losses exceeding policy limits are recoverable under the umbrella policy.

How do you determine the insurance reimbursement?

Casualty insurance covers such items as fire loss and water damage. The premiums are typically paid in advance and debited to Prepaid Insurance, which is then amortized over the policy period. Casualty insurance reimburses the holder for the fair market value of lost property. Insurance companies usually have a coinsurance provision so that the insured bears a portion of the loss. The insurance reimbursement formula follows (assumes an 80 percent coinsurance clause):

$$\frac{\text{Face value of policy}}{0.8 \times \text{Fair market value of insured property}} \times \text{Fair market value of loss}$$

$$= \text{Possible reimbursement} \frac{1}{2}$$

Insurance reimbursement is based on the lower of the face of the policy, fair market value of loss, or possible reimbursement.

Example 32.1

Case	Face of Policy	Fair Market Value of Property	Fair Market Value of Loss
A	$4,000	$10,000	$6,000
B	6,000	10,000	10,000
C	10,000	10,000	4,000

Insurance reimbursement follows:

Case A: $\dfrac{\$4,000}{0.8 \times \$10,000} \times \$\ 6,000 = \$3,000$

Case B: $\dfrac{\$6,000}{0.8 \times \$10,000} \times \$10,000 = \$7,500$

Case C: $\dfrac{\$10,000}{0.8 \times \$10,000} \times \$\ 4,000 = \$5,000$

A blanket policy covers several items of property. The face of the policy is allocated based on the fair market values of the insured assets.

Example 32.2

A blanket policy of $15,000 applies to equipment I and equipment II. The fair values of equipment I and II are $30,000 and $15,000, respectively. Equipment II is partially destroyed, resulting in a fire loss of $3,000.

The policy allocation to equipment II is computed as:

	Fair Market Value	Policy
Equipment I	$30,000	$10,000
Equipment II	15,000	5,000
	$45,000	$15,000

The insurance reimbursement is:

$$\frac{\$5,000}{0.8 \times \$15,000} \times \$3,000 = \$1,500$$

When there is a fire loss, the destroyed asset must be removed from the books. Fire loss is charged for the book value of the property. The insurance reimbursement reduces the fire loss. The fire loss is an extraordinary item shown net of tax.

Example 32.3

Merchandise costing $5,000 is fully destroyed. There is no insurance for it. Furniture costing $10,000 with accumulated depreciation of $1,000 and having a fair market value of $7,000 is fully destroyed. The policy is for $10,000. Building costing $30,000 with accumulated depreciation of $3,000 and having a fair market value of $20,000 is 50 percent destroyed. The face of the policy is $15,000. The journal entries to record the fire loss on the books follow.

(continued)

| Fire loss | 5,000 | |
| Inventory | | 5,000 |

Fire loss	9,000	
Accumulated depreciation	1,000	
Furniture		10,000

Fire loss	13,500	
Accumulated depreciation	1,500	
Building		15,000

Insurance reimbursement totals $16,375, computed as:
Furniture:

$$\frac{\$10,000}{0.8 \times \$7,000} \times \$7,000 = \$12,500$$

Building:

$$\frac{\$15,000}{0.8 \times \$20,000} \times \$10,000 = \$9,375$$

The journal entry for the insurance reimbursement is:

| Cash | 16,375 | |
| Fire loss | | 16,375 |

The net fire loss is $11,125 ($27,500 − $16,375).

What is boiler explosion insurance?

Boiler explosion insurance covers losses of property arising from an explosion.

What is an umbrella policy?

The umbrella policy insures against all risks not covered under another policy. For example, if the commercial property policy covers up to $15 million, the umbrella policy would provide coverage in excess of $15 million but not to exceed $40 million. It is an "excess coverage" policy taking effect after another policy has paid its limit. The umbrella policy is essential in a comprehensive insurance program.

How does marine insurance work?

Marine insurance applies to the importing of merchandise on terms of FOB (free-on-board) shipping point. The policy covers goods in transit. Insurance coverage is required because the company obtains title when the goods are shipped. Each shipment is covered separately, and the premium is based on the value of that shipment. The marine coverage should be to the receiving warehouse dock. Once at the warehouse, the commercial property policy is in effect.

> ## Note
>
> A general term bond for entry of merchandise should also be taken out covering landed merchandise while it passes through customs and brokers' hands. ■

What is business interruption insurance?

Business interruption insurance applies when operations are disturbed or cease because of an unforeseen or infrequent event, such as fire, flood, tornado, earthquake, and vandalism. This policy covers the loss in profit during the shutdown, continuing fixed costs, incremental costs to replace equipment, overtime, or the cost of having the product produced elsewhere. There may also be coverage for losses arising from a supplier's inability to deliver goods due to an unexpected occurrence.

What does insurance on vehicles involve?

Insurance on vehicles applies to a company's owned vehicles. The insurance for corporate planes includes normal property damage and liability insurance to insured parties.

How are insurance bonds helpful?

There are several kinds of insurance bonds, including comprehensive, miscellaneous, and performance. A comprehensive bond is fidelity coverage for employees due to theft of cash or property. If your company sells to a municipality, it may be required to have miscellaneous bid and performance bonds. The bid bond is usually in place of a certified check, which has to accompany government bonds. The performance bond insures against the company's failure to perform under the government contract.

MEDICAL AND CATASTROPHE COVERAGE

Many employers provide medical and catastrophe insurance for current and retired employees.

What is Workers' Compensation?

Workers' Compensation reimburses the employer for liability arising from occupational health hazards falling under state law. It usually covers the employer's liability for employee lawsuits alleging personal injuries. The premium is based on the total dollar payroll. The Department of Labor's Office of Workers' Compensation Programs

(OWCP) administers four major disability compensation programs that provide wage replacement benefits, medical treatment, vocational rehabilitation, and other benefits to federal workers or their dependents who are injured at work or acquire an occupation-related disease.

Does the state require disability insurance?

Some states require that employees be covered for accidents and disabilities occurring off the job. The premium is dictated by state law and paid for by the employee. The employer may opt to pay the entire premium as a fringe benefit. If a state does not have a disability law, private insurance may be carried.

How does life insurance work?

The lives of key executives may be insured. The insurance may provide cash to buy the deceased's common stock.

Note

If the company is the beneficiary of life insurance, the premiums are not tax deductible. However, they are expensed for financial reporting purposes. The proceeds received upon death are not taxable income. ■

The cash surrender value of life insurance is the sum payable upon cancellation of the policy by the insured; the insured will of course receive less than the premium paid. Cash surrender value is classified under long-term investments. It applies to ordinary life and limited payment policies. Typically it is not applicable to term insurance. The insurance premium consists of two elements: expense and cash surrender value.

Example 32.4

A premium of $6,000 is paid that increases the cash surrender value by $2,000. The appropriate entry is:

Life insurance expense	4,000	
Cash surrender value of life insurance	2,000	
Cash		6,000

The gain on a life insurance policy typically is not considered an extraordinary item since it is in the ordinary course of business.

LIABILITY INSURANCE COVERAGE FOR CFOs

In today's litigious environment, CFOs need coverage for their activities, which could result in losses to investors and creditors. Liability exposure exists for corporate financial problems due to the default of junk bonds, failure of an initial public offering, governmental action (e.g., by the Securities and Exchange Commission), and so on.

 ## BUSINESS LAW

A brief discussion of business law follows. The CFO should consult with legal counsel about all legal issues.

Laws involving the employer–employee relationship include:

- *Federal Insurance Contribution Act (FICA)*, commonly referred to as Social Security, requires a FICA tax to be withheld from each employee's salary with an equal matching contribution by the employer.
- *Fair Labor Standards Act (FLSA)* deals with wages and hours. A minimum wage is specified, and employees must receive equal pay for equal work. Thus, wage discrimination is prohibited due to race, sex, age, and so on. Certain employees must receive time and one-half for overtime. An employer cannot hire a child below a certain age, typically 16.
- *Occupational Safety and Health Act (OSHA)* mandates that the employer provide a safe and healthy working environment.
- *Employee Retirement Income Security Act (ERISA)* requires pension plans to be in conformity with specified requirements including vesting, funding, participation, and disclosure.
- *Workers' Compensation* applies to on-the-job injuries. The employer pays a specified amount into an insurance fund.
- *Title VII of the Civil Rights Act of 1964* prohibits discrimination based on color, gender, national origin, pregnancy, race, religion, and sex, including sexual harassment.
- *Age Discrimination in Employment Act (ADEA)* protects employees who are 40 years of age or older from discrimination on the basis of age.
- Antitrust laws exist regarding restraints of trade and monopoly

The following agreements are illegal:

- Price fixing
- Division of markets
- Requiring the customer to buy a second product if he or she orders a first one
- Sale of product to retailer only if the retailer contracts not to resell the product below a certain price
- Group boycott of a customer

The CFO who files a registration statement for a public offering of equity and debt securities must have some familiarity with security laws and regulations.

The legal ramifications of a manufacturer's potential liability cause the CFO to assume responsibility for risk assessment in contracts. A major consideration is controlling payments and receipts when contracts are canceled and in estimating liquidated or consequential damages for product failure.

Environmental laws must be conformed to; otherwise substantial fines may be assessed. Environmental obligations may include cleanup costs, civil and/or criminal litigation over injury and damage claims, constraints on future operations, and uninsurable accidents. Reference should be made to the regulations of the Environmental Protection Agency and proper insurance carried. The CFO may have to prepare annual reports under the Superfund Amendments and Reauthorization Act. The CFO continually must appraise the company's internal procedures to monitor and conform to federal, state, and local dictates. Besides complying with existing regulations, why not plan ways to comply with proposed regulations? *Tip:* Undertake an environmental audit to measure the company's environmental performance against internal company policies and procedures and external environmental requirements. Such an audit is also of assistance in valuing a potential targeted company.

CHAPTER THIRTY-THREE

Reading Economic Indicators

T HE CFO SHOULD have an understanding of economics and the economy's
effect on the company. He or she should know how to read and interpret various
economic indices and statistics that are vital to the success of the business in a
dynamic, ever-changing economic environment. This knowledge will enable better
financial and investment decisions.

 ## HOW CAN YOU KEEP TRACK OF THE ECONOMY WITH ECONOMIC AND MONETARY INDICATORS?

To sort out the confusing mix of statistics that flow almost daily from the government
and to help you keep track of what is going on in the economy, we examine various
economic and monetary indicators.

Economic and monetary indicators reflect where the economy seems to be headed
and where it has been. Each month government agencies, including the Federal Reserve
Board, and several economic institutions publish various indicators. These can be broken down into five broad categories:

- Measures of Overall Economic Performance
- Price Indices
- Indices of Labor Market Conditions
- Money and Credit Market Indicators
- Measures for Major Product Markets

Measures of Overall Economic Performance

These measures include gross national and domestic products, industrial production,
personal income, housing starts, unemployment rate, and retail sales.

Gross Domestic Product

Gross domestic product (GDP) measures the value of all goods and services produced by the economy within its boundaries, and is the nation's broadest gauge of economic health. This measure is normally stated in annual terms, although data are compiled and released quarterly. The Department of Commerce compiles GDP. It is reported as a "real" figure; that is, economic growth minus the impact of inflation. The figure is tabulated on a quarterly basis, coming out in the month after a quarter has ended. It is then revised at least twice, with those revisions being reported once in each of the months following the original release.

GDP reports appear in most daily newspapers and online at services. They are also available on the Federal Government Statistics Web site at www.fedstats.gov. GDP is often a measure of the state of the economy. For example, many economists speak of recession when there has been a decline in GDP for two consecutive quarters. The GDP in dollar and real terms is a useful economic indicator. An expected growth rate of 3 percent in real terms would be very attractive for long-term investment and would affect the stock market positively. Since inflation and price increases are detrimental to equity prices, a real growth of GDP without inflation is favorable and desirable.

A series of events leading from a rising GDP to higher security prices can be shown as:

GDP up → Corporate profits up → Dividends up → Security prices up

A word of caution: GDP fails the timely release criterion for useful economic indicators. Unfortunately, there is no way of measuring whether we are in a recession or prosperity currently based on the current GDP measure. Only after the quarter is over can it be determined whether there was growth or decline. Experts examine other measures, such as unemployment rate, industrial production, durable orders, corporate profits, retail sales, and housing activity, to look for a sign of recession.

Industrial Production

This index shows changes in the output of U.S. plants, mines, and utilities. Detailed breakdowns of the index provide a reading on how individual industries are faring. The index is issued monthly by the Federal Reserve Board.

Personal Income

This index shows the before-tax income received by individuals and unincorporated businesses, such as wages and salaries, rents, and interest and dividends, and other payments, such as unemployment and Social Security. It represents consumers' spending power. When personal income rises, it usually means that consumers will increase their purchases, which will in turn favorably affect the economic climate.

Note

Consumer spending makes a major contribution (67 percent) to the nation's GDP. Personal Income data are released monthly by the Commerce Department. ▪

Housing Starts

Housing Starts is an important economic indicator that offers an estimate of the number of dwelling units on which construction has begun. The figures are issued monthly by the Bureau of the Census. When an economy is going to take a downturn, the housing sector (and companies within it) is the first to decline. This index indicates the future strength of the housing sector of the economy. At the same time, it is closely related to interest rates and other basic economic factors.

Unemployment Rate, Initial Jobless Claims, and Help-Wanted Index

Unemployment is the nonavailability of jobs for people able and willing to work at the prevailing wage rate. It is an important measure of economic health, since full employment is generally construed as a desired goal. When the various economic indicators are mixed, many analysts look to the unemployment rate as being the most important. Weekly initial claims for unemployment benefits are another closely watched indicator along with the unemployment rate to judge the jobless situation in the economy.

The help-wanted advertising index tracks employers' advertisements for job openings in the classified section of newspapers in 50 or so labor market areas. The index represents job vacancies resulting from turnover in exiting positions, such as workers changing jobs or retiring and from the creation of new jobs. The help-wanted figures are seasonally adjusted.

The *unemployment rate* is the number of unemployed workers divided by total employed and unemployed who constitute the labor force. Both statistics are released by the Department of Labor. The help-wanted advertising figures are obtained from classified advertisements in newspapers in major labor markets.

These figures are frequently reported in daily newspapers, business dailies, business TV shows, and through online services. Labor Department releases can be found at www.stats.bls.gov. The effect of unemployment on the economy is summarized next.

- *Less tax revenue.* Fewer jobs means less income tax to the state and nation, which means a bigger U.S government deficit and forces states to make cuts in programs to balance their budgets.
- *Higher government costs.* When people lose jobs, they often must turn to the government for benefits.
- *Less consumer spending.* Without a job, an individual cannot afford to buy a car, computer, house, or vacation.
- *Empty stores.* Retailers and homebuilders cannot absorb lower sales for long. Soon they have to lay off workers and, and in more serious shortfalls, file for bankruptcy.
- *Manufacturing cuts.* The companies that make consumer products or housing materials are also forced to cut jobs as sales of their goods fall.
- *Real estate pain.* As companies fail and as individuals struggle, mortgages and other bank loans go unpaid. That causes real estate values to go down and pummels lenders.

A word of caution: No one economic indicator is able to point to the direction in which an economy is heading. It is common that many indicators give mixed signals regarding, for example, the possibility of a recession.

But perhaps the best example of economic theory being turned on its head is the fact that low unemployment figures in 1998 did not create inflationary pressures. Both investors and shoppers can thank increased productivity and cheap foreign goods for that change.

Retail Sales

Retail sales is the estimate of total sales at the retail level. The index includes everything from groceries to durable goods. It is used as a measure of future economic conditions: A long slowdown in sales could spell cuts in production. Retail sales are a major concern because they represent about half of overall consumer spending.

> **Note**
>
> The amount of retail sales depends heavily on consumer confidence. The data are issued monthly by the Commerce Department. ▪

Price Indices

Price indices are designed to measure the rate of inflation. Various price indices are used to measure living costs, price level changes, and inflation. They are:

Consumer Price Index (CPI)

The Consumer Price Index (CPI) is the best-known inflation gauge. The CPI measures the cost of buying a fixed bundle of goods (some 400 consumer goods and services), representative of the purchases of the typical working-class urban family. The fixed basket is divided into these categories: food and beverages, housing, apparel, transportation, medical care, entertainment, and other. Generally referred to as a cost-of-living index, it is published by the Bureau of Labor Statistics (BLS) of the U.S. Department of Labor. The CPI is widely used for escalation clauses. The base year for the CPI index was 1982 to 1984, at which time it was assigned 100. A chain of events leading from lower rates of inflation to increased consumer spending and possibly the up security market can be shown as:

CPI down → Real personal income up → Consumer confidence up → Consumer spending up (Retail sales up + Housing starts up + Auto sales up) → Security market up

Producer Price Index

Like the CPI, the Producer Price Index (PPI) is a measure of the cost of a given basket of goods priced in wholesale markets, including raw materials, semifinished goods, and finished goods at the early stage of the distribution system.

The PPI is published monthly by the BLS of the Department of Commerce. The PPI signals changes in the general price level, or the CPI, some time before they actually materialize. (Since the PPI does not include services, caution should be exercised when the principal cause of inflation is service prices.) For this reason, the PPI and especially some of its subindexes, such as the Index of Sensitive Materials, serve as one of the leading indicators that are closely watched by policy makers. It is the one that signals changes in the general price level, or the CPI, some time before they actually materialize.

GDP Deflator

The GDP Deflator (Implicit Price Index) is the third index of inflation that is used to separate price changes in GDP calculations from real changes in economic activity. The GDP Deflator is a weighted average of the price indices used to deflate the components of GDP. Thus, it reflects price changes for goods and services bought by consumers, businesses, and governments. The GDP Deflator is found by dividing current GDP in a given year by constant (real) GDP. Because it covers a broader group of goods and services than the CPI and PPI, the GDP Deflator is a widely used price index that is frequently used to measure inflation. Unlike the CPI and PPI, which are available monthly, the GDP Deflator is available only quarterly. It is published by the U.S. Department of Commerce.

Employment Cost Index

The Employment Cost Index (ECI) is the most comprehensive and refined measure of underlying trends in employee compensation as a cost of production. It measures the cost of labor, and it includes changes in wages and salaries and employer costs for employee benefits. The ECI tracks wages and bonuses, sick and vacation pay, plus benefits such as insurance, pensions and Social Security, and unemployment taxes from a survey of 18,300 occupations at 4,500 sample establishments in private industry and 4,200 occupations within about 800 state and local governments.

Note

Indices get major coverage in daily newspapers and business dailies, on business TV programs such as Bloomberg and CNBC, and on Internet financial news services. The government web sites www.stats.bls.gov and www.census.gov/econ also provide these data. ▪

Check to see whether the inflation rate has been rising—a negative, or bearish, sign for stock and bond investors—or falling, which is bullish.

Rising prices are public enemy No. 1 for stocks and bonds. Inflation usually hurts stock prices because higher consumer prices lessen the value of future corporate earnings, which make shares of those companies less appealing to investors. By contrast, when prices rocket ahead, investors often flock to long-term inflation hedges, such as real estate. A chain of events leading from lower rates of inflation to increased consumer spending and, possibly, an up stock market can be shown as:

Inflation down $\rightarrow$ Real personal income up $\rightarrow$ Consumer confidence up $\rightarrow$ Consumer spending up $\rightarrow$ Retail sales up $\rightarrow$ Housing starts up as auto sales jump $\rightarrow$ Stock market up

Note

Former Federal Reserve chairman Alan Greenspan regards the ECI as a good measure to determine whether wage pressures are sparking inflation. ■

Indices of Labor Market Conditions

Indicators covering labor market conditions are unemployment rate, average production worker workweek, applications for unemployment compensation, and hourly wage rates.

Money and Credit Market Indicators

The most widely reported indicators in the media are money supply, consumer credit, the Dow Jones Industrial Average, and the Treasury bill rate.

Measures for Major Product Markets

These measures are designed to be indicators for segments of the economy, such as housing, retail sales, steel, and automobile. Examples are 10-day auto sales, advance retail sales, housing starts, and construction permits.

HOUSING-RELATED MEASURES

House-related indicators involve home affordability, home sales, and home prices. Important housing-related measures are presented next.

NAHB–Wells Fargo Housing Opportunity Index

The Housing Opportunity Index (HOI) for a given area (available at www.nahb.org/reference_list.aspx?sectionID=135) is defined as the share of homes sold in that area that would have been affordable to a family earning the local median income based on standard mortgage underwriting criteria. It is an index calculated quarterly by the National Association of Home Builders (NAHB) that compares the median income in a locality with the median home price. The index is stated as the percent of the population with the median income in the area that would be able to afford the median-priced house. For example, in 2000, 81 percent of median-income households in Indianapolis (with a median income of $57,700) would be able to afford the median-priced home (which cost $122,000). In comparison, San Francisco, with a median income of $74,900 and a median house price of $464,000, had a HOI of 10.3 percent. Therefore, there are really two major components: income and housing cost. For income, NAHB uses the annual median family income estimates for metropolitan areas published by the Department of Housing and Urban Development. NAHB assumes that a family can afford to spend 28 percent of its gross income on housing; this is a conventional assumption in the lending industry. That share of median income is then divided by 12 to arrive at a monthly figure. On the cost side, NAHB receives every month an electronic record of sales transactions from First American Real Estate Solutions (formerly, TRW). The data include information on state, county, date of sale, and sales price of homes sold.

S&P/Case-Shiller National Home Price Index

S&P/Case-Shiller national home price index is a closely watched gauge of U.S. home prices. It measures the residential housing market, tracking changes in the value of the residential real estate market in 20 metropolitan regions across the United States. Options and futures based on Case-Shiller index are traded on Chicago Mercantile Exchange.

Note

Indicators are only signals, telling the CFO something about the economic conditions in the country, a particular area, or an industry and, over time, the trends that seem to be shaping up. ▪

INDICES OF LEADING, COINCIDENT, AND LAGGING ECONOMIC INDICATORS

The Index of Leading Indicators is the economic series of indicators that tends to predict future changes in economic activity. This index was designed to reveal the direction of the economy in the next six to nine months. By melding 10 economic yardsticks, an index is created that has shown a tendency to change before the economy makes a major turn—hence the term "leading indicators." The index is designed to forecast economic activity six to nine months ahead.

This series, calculated and published monthly by the Conference Board, consists of 10 components:

1. *Average weekly hours for U.S. manufacturing workers.* Employers find it a lot easier to increase the number of hours worked in a week than to hire more employees.
2. *Average weekly initial claims for unemployment insurance.* The number of people who sign up for unemployment benefits signals changes in present and future economic activity.
3. *Manufacturers' new orders, consumer goods, and materials.* New orders mean more workers hired, more materials and supplies purchased, and increased output. Gains in this series usually lead recoveries by as much as four months.

4. *Vendor performance, slower deliveries diffusion index.* This index represents the percentage of companies reporting slower deliveries. As the economy grows, firms have more trouble filling orders.
5. *Manufacturers' new orders, nondefense capital goods.* Factories will employ more as demand for big-ticket items, especially those not bought by the government, stay strong.
6. *Building permits, new private housing units.* Optimistic builders are often a good sign for the economy.
7. *Stock prices, 500 common stocks.* Stock market advances usually precede business upturns by three to eight months.
8. *Money supply, M2.* A rising money supply means easy money that sparks brisk economic activity. This usually leads recoveries by as much as 14 months.
9. *Interest rate spread, 10-year Treasury bonds minus federal funds rate.* A steep yield curve, when long rates are much higher than short ones, is a sign of a healthy economic outlook.
10. *Consumer Confidence Index.* Consumer spending buys two-thirds of GDP (all goods and services produced in the economy), so any sharp change could be an important factor in an overall turnaround.

The monthly report is well covered by daily business publications, major newspapers, business TV shows, and on the Internet. You can also check the Conference Board's web site at www.conference-board.com. If the index is consistently rising, even only slightly, the economy is chugging along and a setback is unlikely. If the indicator drops for three or more consecutive months, you can look for an economic slowdown and possibly a recession in the next year or so. A rising (consecutive percentage increases in) indicator is bullish for the economy and the stock market, and vice versa. Falling index results could be good news for bondholders looking to make capital gains from falling interest rates. The Conference Board points out that although the press often states that three consecutive downward movements in the leading index signal a recession, the board does not endorse the use of such a simple, inflexible rule. Its studies show that a 1 percent decline (2 percent when annualized) in the leading index, coupled with declines in a majority of the 10 components, provides a reliable, but not perfect, recession signal.

Note

The composite figure is designed to tell only in which direction business will go. It is not intended to forecast the magnitude of future ups and downs. The index has also given some false warning signals in recent years. ■

What are coincident indicators?

Coincident indicators are the types of economic indicator series that tend to move up and down in line with the aggregate economy and therefore are measures of current economic activity. They are intended to gauge current economic conditions. Examples are gross national product, employment, retail sales, and industrial production.

What are lagging indicators?

Lagging indicators are the ones that follow or trail behind aggregate economic activity. Currently the government publishes six lagging indicators: unemployment rate, labor cost per unit, loans outstanding, average prime rate charged by banks, ratio of consumer installment credit outstanding to personal income, and ratio of manufacturing and trade inventories to sales.

 ## OTHER IMPORTANT ECONOMIC INDICES

The CFO should also be familiar with other important indices. This section describes some widely watched indices.

What is the Forbes Index?

Forbes magazine publishes the Forbes Index. This index (1976 = 100) is a measure of U.S. economic activity composed of eight equally weighted elements: total industrial production, new claims for unemployment, cost of services relative to all consumer prices, housing starts, retail sales, level of new orders for durable goods compared with manufactures' inventories, personal income, and total consumer installment credit.

What is the Purchasing Index?

The National Association of Purchasing Management releases its monthly Purchasing Index, which tells about the buying intentions of corporate purchasing agents.

What is the Institute for Supply Management's Index?

This index, based on a survey of 375 companies in 17 industries, measures new orders, inventories, exports, and employment in the service sector. Services account for five-sixths of the $10 trillion U.S. economy and include industries such as entertainment, utilities, health care, farming, insurance, retail sector, restaurants, and zoos.

What are the two major consumer confidence indices?

The Conference Board's Consumer Confidence Index (www.conference-board.org/data /consumerdata.cfm) measures consumer optimism and pessimism about general business conditions, jobs, and total family income.

The Index of Consumer Sentiment is compiled by the University of Michigan Survey Research Center. It measures consumers' personal financial circumstances and their outlook for the future. The survey is compiled through a telephone survey of 500 households. The index is used by the Commerce Department in its monthly Index of

Leading Economic Indicators and is regularly charted in the Department's *Business Conditions Digest.*

What is the Optimism Index?

The National Federation of Independent Business, a Washington-based advocacy group, publishes the Optimism Index, which is based on small-business owners' expectations for the economy. The benchmark year is 1978.

 ## MONETARY INDICATORS AND HOW THEY IMPACT THE ECONOMY

What are monetary indicators?

Monetary indicators are statistical indicators of the effect that the money supply has on the economy. Examples include stock market prices, Treasury Bill rates, and credit market conditions. These indicators are of particular importance to CFOs because they greatly impact firms in terms of the costs of debt and equity financing and security prices. They involve long-term interest rates, which are important because bond yields compete with stock yields. Monetary and credit indicators are often the first signs of market direction. If monetary indicators move favorably, this is an indication that a decline in stock prices may be over. A stock market top may be ready for a contraction if the Federal Reserve tightens credit, making consumer buying and corporate expansion more costly and difficult.

Monetary indicators that are regularly watched are:

- Dow Jones 20-bond index
- Dow Jones utility average
- New York Stock Exchange utility average
- Treasury bill yield
- 30-year Treasury bond yield

Bonds and utilities are yield instruments and therefore are money-sensitive. They are impacted by changing interest rates. If the listed monetary indicators are active and pointing higher, it is a sign that the stock market will start to take off. In other words, an upward movement in these indicators takes place in advance of a stock market increase.

A brief description of monetary and economic variables that CFOs should watch carefully follows.

What is the money supply?

The *money supply* is the level of funds available at a given time for conducting transactions in an economy, as reported by the Federal Reserve Board. The Federal Reserve System can influence the money supply through its monetary policy measures. There are several definitions of the money supply: M1 (which is currency in circulation, demand deposits, traveler's checks, and those in interest-bearing Negotiable Order of Withdrawal [NOW] accounts), M2 (which is the most widely followed measure, equal to M1 plus savings deposits, money market deposit accounts, and money market funds), and M3 (which is M2 plus large Certificates of Deposit). Moderate growth is thought to have a positive impact on the economy. Rapid growth is viewed as inflationary; in contrast, a sharp drop in the money supply is considered recessionary.

What are interest rates?

Interest rates represent the costs to borrow money, and they come in many forms. There are long-term and short-term interest rates, depending on the length of the loan; there are interest rates on super-safe securities (such as U.S. Treasury bills), and there are interest rates on junk bonds of financially troubled companies; there are nominal (coupon) interest rates, real (inflation-adjusted) or risk-adjusted interest rates, and effective interest rates (or yields). Interest rates depend on the maturity of the security. The longer the period, the higher will be the interest rate because of the greater uncertainty.

Some of the more important interest rates are briefly explained next.

- *Prime rate.* This is the rate banks charge their best customers for short-term loans. It is a bellwether rate in that it is construed as a sign of rising or falling loan demand and economic activity. When the prime rate is climbing, it means companies are borrowing heavily and the economy is still on an upward swing.
- *Federal funds rate.* This is the rate on short-term loans among commercial banks for overnight use. The Fed influences this rate by conducting open market operations and by changing banks' required reserve.
- *Discount rate.* This is the charge on loans to depository institutions by the Federal Reserve Board. A change in the discount rate is considered a major economic event and is expected to have an impact on security prices, especially bonds. A change in the prime rate usually follows the change in the discount rate.
- *90-day Treasury bills.* The yield of these bills represents the direction of short-term rates and is a closely watched indicator. When yields on 90-day bills rise sharply, this may signal a resurgence of inflation. Subsequently, the economy could slow down.
- *10-year Treasury bonds.* The security known as the *T-bond* has the most widely watched interest rate in the world. This bond is seen as the daily barometer of how the bond market is performing. The 10-year T-bond bond is a fixed-rate direct obligation of the U.S. government. There are no call provisions on T-bonds. Traders watch the price of the U.S. Treasury's most recently issued 10-year bond, often called the bellwether. The price is decided by a series of dealers who own the exclusive right to make markets in the bonds in U.S. markets. (The bonds trade around the clock in foreign markets.) Bond yields are derived from the current trading price and the bond's nominal coupon rate. Because of their long-term nature, T-bonds are extra sensitive to inflation that could ravage the buying power of their fixed-rate payouts. Thus, the T-bond market also is watched as an indicator of where inflation

may be headed. In addition, T-bond rates somewhat impact fixed-rate mortgages. The T-bond yield is also seen as a barometer for the housing industry, a key leading indicator for the economy.

Interest rates are controlled by the Fed's monetary policy. The Fed's monetary policy tools involve: (1) changes in the required reserve ratio, (2) changes in the discount rate, and (3) open market operations—that is, purchase and sale of government securities. Cuts in the discount rate are aimed at stimulating the economy—a positive development for stocks. A summary of the effect of cutting the discount rate on the economy follows.

Effects of Lowering the Discount Rate

The discount rate is what the Federal Reserve charges on short-term loans to member banks. A cut in the discount rate will yield a series of impacts on the economy. When the Fed cuts the discount rate, it means banks can get cash cheaper and thus charge less on loans. The following effects are felt through the economy.

- *Effect 1.* Within a few days of a cut in the discount rate, banks are likely to start passing on the discounts by cutting their prime rate, which is what banks charge on loans to their best corporate customers.
- *Effect 2.* When the prime rate is cut, businesses are more likely to borrow. Adjustable consumer loans, such as credit card rates, are tied to the prime. These loans become cheaper, stimulating spending.
- *Effect 3.* Within a few weeks, rates on mortgage, auto, and construction loans drop.
- *Effect 4.* The lower rates go, the more investors move their cash to stocks, creating new wealth.

The goal is to kick-start the economy. If lower interest rates cause businesses to start growing again, laid-off workers get jobs, retailers start selling, and the economy starts to roll again.

The impact of open market operations on the money supply, level of interest rates, and loan demand can be summarized in this way:

Fed sells securities → Bank reserve down → Bank lending down → Money supply down → Interest rates up → Loan demand down → Inflation → Fed raises discount rate → Interest rates up → Demand for money down → Demand for products down → Prices down

What is inflation?

Inflation is the general rise in prices of consumer goods and services. The federal government measures inflation by comparing prices today—measured in terms of the CPI, PPI, GDP Deflator, and/or ECI—to the base period, 1982 to 1984. As prices increase, lenders and investors will demand greater returns to compensate for the decline in purchasing power. Companies may reduce borrowing because of higher interest rates. This leads to less capital expenditures for property, plant, and equipment. As a result, output may decrease, resulting in employee layoffs. During inflation, selling prices may increase to keep pace with rising price levels, but the company's sales in real dollars remain the same. You still lose out since your company's tax liability will increase.

In such cases, most likely the Federal Reserve will tighten the money supply and raise interest rates (such as discount rate or federal fund rate). It becomes too expensive to borrow money. Therefore, there is less demand for products, which in turn pushes prices down. Inflation affects the prices of products in this way:

Easy Money Policy

Fed buys securities → Bank reserve up → Bank lending up → Money supply up → Interest rates down → Loan demand up

Tight Money Policy

Fed sells securities → Bank reserve down → Bank lending down → Money supply down → Interest rates up → Loan demand down

Interest rates are no more than a reflection of what expectations are for inflation. Inflation therefore means higher interest rates and thus higher borrowing cost to the company.

Is deflation desirable?

Deflation often has had the side effect of increasing unemployment in an economy, for the process leads to a lower level of demand in the economy. Other downside effects include possible pay cuts and more expensive repayment of consumer debts. Falling prices do have an upside: Mild deflation would assure working people (at least those who fend off pay cuts) of steadily rising real wages.

What is productivity and how does it affect unit labor costs?

Productivity is a measure of the efficiency of production, a ratio of output to what is required to produce it. Economists consider productivity the key to prosperity. Sizable gains mean companies can pay workers more, hold the line on prices, and still earn the kind of profits that keep stock prices rising. Increased productivity, or getting more worker output per hour on the job, is considered vital to increasing the nation's standard of living without inflation. Productivity measures the relationship between real output and the labor time involved in its production, or output per hour of work. The Labor Department compiles productivity figures from its own job surveys that produce unemployment reports and from the Commerce Department's work that creates GDP figures. Only business sector output—GDP minus government and not-for-profit organizations—is used in the productivity calculation.

Productivity measures reflect the joint effects of many influences, including changes in technology; capital investment; level of output; utilization of capacity, energy, and materials; the organization of production; managerial skill; and the characteristics and effort of the work force. The data are published in press releases, in BLS journals, and at the BLS web site, www.stats.bls.gov.

Real GDP increases when resource inputs and their productivity increase. Thus, to the extent that real GDP depends on labor inputs, real GDP equals total worker hours (labor input) times labor productivity (real output per worker per hour).

Data on productivity and unit labor costs are released by the Labor Department. Increased productivity, or getting more worker output per hour on the job, is considered vital to increasing the nation's standard of living without inflation. Meanwhile, unit labor cost is a key gauge of future price inflation along with the CPI, PPI, GDP Deflator, and ECI.

What is recession?

Recession means a sinking economy. Unfortunately, there is no consensus definition or measure of recession. Three or more straight monthly drops of the Index of Leading Economic Indicators are generally considered a sign of recession, as are two consecutive quarterly drops of GDP, or consecutive monthly drops in durable goods orders, which most likely result in less production and increasing layoffs in the factory sector. Recession tends to dampen the spirits of consumers and thus depress the prices of products and services.

To kick-start the economy, the Fed will loosen the money supply and lower interest rates, such as the discount rate. When the Fed cuts the discount rate, banks can get cash cheaper and thus charge less on loans.

Note that the size of the cut is a critical consideration. For example, a half-point discount rate cut by itself is not strong enough to get the economy moving fast. External political conditions (such as a crisis in the Middle East), the federal deficit, and problems in the bank and savings and loan industry would make companies hesitant to start expanding again and also make consumers nervous for a longer time than the Fed would anticipate.

What is the federal deficit?

The national debt is the sum of all money the government has borrowed to finance budget deficits. The only way for a government to reduce its debt is to run a budget surplus, obtaining more money than it spends. The surplus must then be used to pay off maturing debt (bonds, notes, etc.) rather than replacing them (rolling them over) with more debt. This federal deficit affects the economy as a whole.

Economists generally believe that larger federal deficits result in higher interest rates for two reasons: (1) Increased budget deficits raise the demand for the loanable funds, resulting in higher interest rates; and (2) larger deficits are apt to lead to higher inflation. This may be true either because the sources of the increased deficits—larger government spending and/or lower taxes—result in greater pressure for loan demand and hence inflation, or because the deficit will induce the Fed to expand the money supply to help finance the deficit, thus causing inflation. In any case, if the increased deficit elevates the public's expectation of inflation, it will tend to raise the level of interest rates. Furthermore, the financing of the deficit by issuance of government debt securities will compete with private sector companies and will deter economic expansion. It also forces companies to borrow at higher interest rates. This is called the *crowding-out effect.*

What is the balance of payments?

The *balance of payments* is a systematic record of a country's receipts from, or payments to, other countries. The *balance of trade* usually refers to goods within the goods and services category. It is also known as merchandise or "visible" trade because it consists of tangibles, such as foodstuffs, manufactured goods, and raw materials. "Services," the other part of the goods and services category, is known as "invisible" trade and consists of intangibles such as interest or dividends, technology transfers, services (e.g., insurance, transportation, financial), and so forth.

When the net result of both the current account and the capital account yields more credits than debits, the country is said to have a surplus in its balance of payments. When there are more debits than credits, the country has a deficit in the balance of payments.

Note

Persistent deficits generally depress the value of the dollar and can boost inflation. The reason for this is that a weak dollar makes foreign goods relatively expensive, often allowing U.S. makers of similar products to raise prices as well. ▪

What is better, a strong dollar (appreciation in foreign exchange rate) or a weak dollar (depreciation in foreign exchange rate)?

The answer is, unfortunately, it depends.

Note

The value of a dollar is a matter of concern particularly to the CFOs of multinational corporations. A strong dollar makes Americans' cash go farther overseas and reduces import prices—generally good for U.S. consumers and for foreign manufacturers. If the dollar is overvalued, U.S. products are harder to sell abroad and at home, where they compete with low-cost imports. ▪

A weak dollar can restore competitiveness to American products by making foreign goods comparatively more expensive. But too weak a dollar can spawn inflation, first through higher import prices and then through spiraling prices for all goods. Even worse, a falling dollar can drive foreign investors away from U.S. securities, which lose value along with the dollar. A strong dollar can be induced by interest rates. Interest rates that are relatively higher domestically than abroad will attract dollar-denominated investments, which will raise the value of the dollar. Exhibit 33.1 summarizes the impacts of changes in foreign exchange rates on the company's products and services.

EXHIBIT 33.1   Impacts of Changes in Foreign Exchange Rates

	Weak Currency (Depreciation/Devaluation)	Strong Currency (Appreciation/Revaluation)
Imports	More expensive	Cheaper
Exports	Cheaper	More expensive
Payables	More expensive	Cheaper
Receivables	Cheaper	More expensive
Inflation	Fuel inflation by making imports more costly	Low inflation
Foreign investment	Discourage foreign investment. Lower return on investment by international investors	High interest rates could attract foreign investors.
Effect	Raising interests could slow down the economy	Reduced exports could trigger a trade deficit

 ## UNDERSTANDING ECONOMIC DATA AND INDICATORS

CFOs must keep abreast of the economic trend and direction and attempt to see how they affect their businesses. Investors have to cut through all the economic indicators and statistical data so that they can make informed investment decisions. Unfortunately, there are too many economic indicators and variables to be analyzed.

Each variable has its own significance. In many cases, these variables could give mixed signals about the future of the economy.

Various government agencies and private firms tabulate the appropriate economic data and calculate various indices. Sources for these indicators are easily subscribed to at an affordable price or can be found in local public and college libraries. They include daily local newspapers and national newspapers such as *USA Today*, the *Wall Street Journal, Investor's Business Daily, Los Angeles Times*, and *New York Times* and periodicals such as *Business Week, Forbes, Fortune, Money, Worth, Barron's, Smart Money, Nation's Business*, and *U.S. News & World Report*. Internet users can look at the White House web site's Economic Statistics Briefing Room, which provides easy access to current federal economic indicators. The Briefing Room is at http://www.whitehouse.gov /briefing-room. Haver Analytics (www.haver.com) provides database and software products for economic analysis and business decision making. Haver Analytics maintains more than 150 economic and financial databases from over 550 government and private sources. Databases cover U.S. states, metropolitan areas, and counties, as well as Canada, Europe, Japan, Australia, New Zealand, China, and other emerging markets. Haver Analytics also maintains key third-party data including forecast and specialized databases covering the world economies.

ECONOMIC INDICATORS AND STOCKS AND BUSINESSES

The next chart summarizes the types of economic variables and their probable effect on the security market and the economy in general.

Economic Variables	Impact on Security Market and Businesses
Real growth in GDP	Positive (without inflation) for stocks and businesses.
Industrial production	Consecutive drops are a sign of recession. Bad for stocks and businesses.
Inflation	Detrimental to stocks and businesses.
Capacity utilization	A high percentage is positive, but full capacity is inflationary.
Durable goods orders	Consecutive drops are a sign of recession. Very bad for stocks and businesses in cyclical industries.
Increase in business investment, consumer confidence, personal income, etc.	Positive for businesses, especially retailing. Worrisome for utility companies.
Leading indicators	Rise is bullish for the economy and businesses; drops are a sign of bad times ahead.
Housing starts	Rise is positive for housing businesses.
Corporate profits	Strong corporate earnings are positive for businesses; corporate bonds also fare well.
Unemployment	Upward trend unfavorable for businesses and economy.
Increase in business inventories	Positive for those fearful of inflation; negative for those looking for growing economy.
Lower federal deficit	Lowers interest rates, good for many businesses. Potential negative for depressed economy.
Deficit in trade and balance of payments	Negative for economy and businesses of companies facing stiff import competition.
Weak dollar	Negative for economy; good for companies with stiff foreign competition.
Interest rates	Rising rates can choke off investment in new plants and lure skittish investors from businesses.

The chart merely serves as a handy guide and should not be construed as an accurate predictor in all cases. Many times the anticipation of good or bad news is built into the market, and when the news comes out, the reverse move happens. That is because traders are unwinding the positions they took to profit from that news.

 ## ECONOMIC INDICATORS AND BOND YIELDS

The bond investor analyzes the economy primarily to determine his or her investment strategy. It is not necessary for the investor to formulate his or her own economic forecasts. The next chart provides a concise and brief list of the significant economic indicators and how they affect bond yields. This table serves merely as a guide and should not be construed as accurate at all times.

Indicators	Effects on Bond Yields[a]	Reasons
Business Activity		
GDP and industrial production falls	Fall	As economy slows, Fed may ease credit by allowing rates to fall.
Unemployment rises	Fall	High unemployment indicates lack of economic expansion. Fed may loosen credit.
Inventories rise	Fall	Inventory levels are good indicators of duration of economic slowdown.
Trade deficit rises	Fall	Dollar weakens. That is inflationary.
Leading indicators	Rise	Advance signals about economic rise health; Fed may tighten credit.
Housing starts rise	Rise	Growing economy due to increased new housing demand; Fed may tighten credit; mortgage rates rise.
Personal income rises	Rise	Higher income means higher consumer spending, thus inflationary; Fed may tighten credit.
Inflation		
Consumer Price Index	Rise	Inflation rises.
Producer Price Index	Rise	Early signal for inflation increase.
Monetary Policy		
Money supply rises	Rise	Excess growth in money supply is inflationary; Fed may tighten credit.
Fed funds rate rises	Rise	Increase in business and consumer loan rates; used by Fed to slow economic growth and inflation.
Fed buys (sells) bills	Rise (fall)	Adds (deducts) money to the economy; interest rates may go down (up).
Required reserve rises	Rise	Depresses bank lending.

Note: The effects are based on yield and are therefore opposite of how bond prices will be affected.
[a] A fall in any of these indicators will have the opposite effect on yields.

Liquidity and Treasury

CHAPTER THIRTY-FOUR

Corporate Investments in Securities

T HIS CHAPTER COVERS how to manage a company's surplus liquidity funds. A firm's surplus funds or idle cash is usually considered only temporary. The funds should be made available to cover a shortfall in cash flow or working capital or to serve as a reservoir for capital spending and acquisition. Many companies flush with cash have been redeploying surplus cash—not only in increased dividends and mergers and acquisitions (M&A) activity but also in share buybacks, debt payouts, and in some capital expenditures.

 ## CASH AND LIQUIDITY MANAGEMENT

Cash is king in businesses. Without cash and liquidity management, businesses will not survive one day. Most CFOs are conservative (not speculative) when considering investing idle cash in financial securities since they believe the money should be on hand without loss in value of the funds when needed.

How is this surplus cash used?

Generally, there are five choices:

1. Investing in marketable securities
2. Reducing outstanding debt
3. Increasing compensating balances at banks
4. Buying back own stock
5. Paying cash dividends

What are the investment practices?

Here are some new insights on the investment tendencies of corporate investment officers, based on the Fortune 1000 list of large industrial firms. Respondents were asked to describe their own approach to cash management as aggressive, moderate, or passive. We focus on two types—aggressive and moderate. Respondents were asked to identify the percentage of their short-term portfolios invested in the typical marketable securities. The five most popular vehicles and the respective percentages are presented in Exhibit 34.1.

EXHIBIT 34.1 Investment Practices by Cash Managers

Type of Security	Aggressive Manager	Moderate Manager
Treasury securities	5.55%	8.82%
Commercial paper	18.16	17.53
Domestic certificates of deposit (CDs)	11.45	6.87
Eurodollar CDs	36.77	24.28
Repurchase agreements (repos)	11.27	18.99

Source: A. W. Frankle and J. M. Collins, "Investment Practices of the Domestic Cash Managers," *Journal of Cash Management* (May 1987).

The survey indicates that Eurodollar CDs are preferred by aggressive cash managers, with commercial paper being ranked second and domestic CDs ranked third.

The moderate cash managers also preferred Eurodollar CDs, with repos ranked second and commercial paper third.

As for the question on which investment attributes shaped their ultimate investment decisions, the aggressive cash managers ranked *yield* first, *risk of default* second, and *maturity* third, while the moderate managers ranked *risk of default* first, *yield* second, and *maturity* third.

What are the types of securities?

Securities cover a broad range of investment instruments, including common stocks, preferred stocks, bonds, and options. Two broad categories of securities are available to corporate investors: equity securities, which represent ownership of a company, and debt (or fixed income) securities, which represent a loan from the investor to a company or government. Fixed income securities generally stress current fixed income and offer little or no opportunity for appreciation in value. They are usually liquid and bear less market risk than other types of investments. This type of investment performs well during stable economic conditions and lower inflation. Examples of fixed income securities include corporate bonds, government securities, mortgage-backed securities, preferred stocks, and short-term debt securities.

Each type of security has not only distinct characteristics but also advantages and disadvantages. This chapter focuses on investing in fixed income (debt) securities—especially those with short- and intermediate-term maturity—normally utilized by corporate investors.

What are the factors to be considered in investment decisions?

Consideration should be given to safety of principal, yield and risk, stability of income, and marketability and liquidity.

- *Security of principal.* This is the degree of risk involved in a particular investment. The company will not want to lose part or all of the initial investment.
- *Yield and risk.* The primary purpose of investing is to earn a return on invested money in the form of interest, dividends, rental income, and capital appreciation. However, increasing total returns would entail greater investment risks. Thus, yield and degree of risk are directly related. Greater risk also means sacrificing security of principal. A CFO has to choose the priority that fits the corporation's financial circumstances and objectives.
- *Stability of income.* When steady income is the most important consideration, bond interest or preferred stock dividends should be emphasized. This might be the situation if the company needs to supplement its earned income on a regular basis with income from its outside investment.
- *Marketability and liquidity.* This is the ability to find a ready market to dispose of the investment at the right price.
- *Tax factors.* Corporate investors in high tax brackets will have different investment objectives from those in lower brackets. If the company is in a high tax bracket, it may prefer municipal bonds (interest is not taxable) or investments that provide tax credits or tax shelters, such as those in oil and gas.

In addition, many other factors need to be considered, including:

- Current and future income needs
- Hedging against inflation
- Ability to withstand financial losses
- Ease of management
- Amount of investment
- Diversification
- Long-term versus short-term potential

What are the questions to be asked?

In developing the corporation's investment strategy, it will be advisable to ask these questions:

- What proportions of funds does the company want safe and liquid?
- Is the company willing to invest for higher return but greater risk?
- How long of a maturity period is the company willing to take on its investment?
- What should be the mix of its investments for diversification?
- Does the company need to invest in tax-free securities?

What are the types of fixed income investment instruments?

A CFO can choose from many fixed income securities. They can be categorized into short-term and long-term investments:

Short-Term Vehicles

- U.S. Treasury bills
- CDs

- Banker's acceptances (BAs)
- Commercial paper
- Repos
- Money market funds
- Eurodollar time deposits

Long-Term Vehicles

- U.S. Treasury notes and bonds
- Corporate bonds
- Mortgage-backed securities
- Municipal bonds
- Preferred stock, fixed or adjustable
- Bond funds
- Unit investment trusts

What are the advantages and disadvantages of owning bonds?

A *bond* is a certificate or security showing the corporate investor lent funds to an issuing company or to a government in return for fixed future interest and repayment of principal. Bonds have these advantages:

- There is fixed interest income each year.
- Bonds are safer than equity securities such as common stock. This is because bondholders come before common stockholders in the event of corporate bankruptcy.

Bonds suffer from these disadvantages:

- They do not participate in incremental profitability.
- There are no voting rights associated with them.

 TERMS AND FEATURES OF BONDS

A corporate investment officer should be familiar with certain terms and features of bonds, including:

- *Par value.* The par value of a bond is the face value, usually $1,000.
- *Coupon rate.* The coupon rate is the nominal interest rate that determines the actual interest to be received on a bond. It is an annual interest per par value. For example, if a corporate investor owns an $11 million bond having a coupon rate of 10 percent, the annual interest to be received will be $100,000.
- *Maturity date.* It is the final date on which repayment of the bond principal is due.
- *Indenture.* The bond indenture is the lengthy, legal agreement detailing the issuer's obligations pertaining to a bond issue. It contains the terms and conditions of the bond issue as well as any restrictive provisions placed on the firm, known as restrictive covenants. The indenture is administered by an independent trustee.

A restrictive covenant includes maintenance of (1) required levels of working capital, (2) a particular current ratio, and (3) a specified debt ratio.
- *Trustee.* The trustee is the third party with whom the indenture is made. The trustee's job is to see that the terms of the indenture are actually carried out.
- *Yield.* The yield is different from the coupon interest rate. It is the effective interest rate the corporate investor earns on the bond investment. If a bond is bought below its face value (i.e., purchased at a discount), the yield is higher than the coupon rate. If a bond is acquired above its face value (i.e., bought at a premium), the yield is below the coupon rate.
- *Call provision.* A call provision entitles the issuing corporation to repurchase, or "call," the bond from holders at stated prices over specified periods.
- *Sinking fund.* In a sinking fund bond, money is put aside by the issuing company periodically for the repayment of debt, thus reducing the total amount of debt outstanding. This particular provision may be included in the bond indenture to protect investors.

What are the types of bonds?

Among the types of bonds available for investment are:

- *Mortgage bonds.* Mortgage bonds are secured by physical property. In case of default, bondholders may foreclose on the secured property and sell it to satisfy their claims.
- *Debentures.* Debentures are unsecured bonds. They are protected by the general credit of the issuing corporation. Credit ratings are very important for this type of bond. Federal, state, and municipal government issues are debentures. Subordinated debentures are junior issues ranking after other unsecured debt as a result of explicit provisions in the indenture. Finance companies have made extensive use of these types of bonds.
- *Convertible bonds.* Convertible bonds are subordinated debentures that may be converted, at the investor's option, into a specified amount of other securities (usually common stock) at a fixed price. They are hybrid securities having characteristics of both bonds and common stock in that they provide fixed interest income and potential appreciation through participation in future price increases of the underlying common stock.
- *Income bonds.* In income bonds, interest is paid only if earned. Such bonds are often called reorganization bonds.
- *Tax-exempt bonds.* Tax-exempt bonds are usually municipal bonds where interest income is not subject to federal tax, although the Tax Reform Act of 1986 imposed restrictions on the issuance of tax-exempt municipal bonds. Municipal bonds may carry a lower interest rate than taxable bonds of similar quality and safety. However, after-tax yield from these bonds are usually more than of bonds with a higher rate of taxable interest. Note that municipal bonds are subject to two principal risks: interest rate and default.
- *U.S. government and agency securities.* They include Treasury bills, notes, bonds, and mortgage-backed securities, such as Ginnie Maes. Treasury bills

represent short-term government financing and mature in 12 months or less. U.S. Treasury notes have a maturity of 1 to 10 years, whereas U.S. Treasury bonds have a maturity of 10 to 25 years and can be purchased in denominations as low as $1,000. All these types of U.S. government securities are subject to federal income taxes but not subject to state and local income taxes. "Ginnie Maes" represent pools of 25- to 30-year Federal Housing Administration or Veterans Administration mortgages guaranteed by the Government National Mortgage Association.

- *Zero coupon bonds.* With zero coupon bonds, instead of being paid out directly, the interest is added to the principal semiannually, and both the principal and accumulated interest are paid at maturity. *Tip:* This compounding factor results in the investor receiving higher returns on the original investment at maturity. Zero coupon bonds are not fixed income securities in the historical sense, because they provide no periodic income. The interest on the bond is paid at maturity. However, accrued interest, though not received, is taxable yearly as ordinary income. Zero coupon bonds have two basic advantages over regular coupon-bearing bonds: (1) A relatively small investment is required to buy these bonds; and (2) the investor is assured of a specific yield throughout the term of the investment.

- *Junk bonds.* Junk bonds, or high-yield bonds, are bonds with a speculative credit rating of Baa or lower by Moody's and BBB or lower by Standard & Poor's rating systems. Coupon rates on junk bonds are considerably higher than those of better-quality issues. Note that junk bonds are issued by companies without track records of sales and earnings, and therefore are subject to high default risk. Today, many non–mortgage-backed bonds issued by corporations are junk. Often a large number of junk bonds are used as part of corporate mergers or takeovers. Junk bonds are known for their high yields and high risk. Many risk-oriented corporate investors, including banks, specialize in trading them. However, the bonds may be defaulted on. During the periods of recession and high interest rates, where servicing debts is very difficult, junk bonds can pose a serious default risk to corporate investors.

How do you select a bond?

When selecting a bond, corporate investors should consider five basic factors:

1. Investment quality—bond ratings
2. Length of maturity—short term (0–5 years); medium term (6–15 years); long term (over 15 years)
3. Features of bonds—call or conversion features
4. Tax status
5. Yield to maturity

These factors are further described next.

- *Investment quality—bond ratings.* The investment quality of a bond is measured by its bond rating, which reflects the probability that a bond issue will go into default. The rating should influence the investor's perception of risk and therefore have an impact on the interest rate the investor is willing to accept, the price the investor is willing to pay, and the maturity period of the bond the investor is willing to accept. Bond investors tend to place more emphasis on independent analysis of quality than do common stock investors. Bond analysis and ratings are done, among others, by Standard & Poor's and Moody's. Exhibit 34.2 is a listing of the designations used by these well-known independent agencies. Descriptions on ratings are summarized. For original versions of descriptions, see Moody's *Bond Record* and Standard & Poor's *Bond Guide*.

EXHIBIT 34.2 Description of Bond Ratings[a]

Quality Indication	Moody's	Standard & Poor's
Highest quality	Aaa	AAA
High quality	Aa	AA
Upper medium grade	A	A
Medium grade	Baa	BBB
Contains speculative elements	Ba	BB
Outright speculative	B	B
Default definitely possible	Caa	CCC and CC
Default, only partial recovery likely	Ca	C
Default, little recovery likely	C	D

[a] Ratings may also have + or − signs to show relative standings in each class.

Corporate investors should pay careful attention to ratings because they can affect not only potential market behavior but relative yields as well. Specifically, the higher the rating, the lower the yield of a bond, other things being equal. It should be noted that the ratings do change over time, and the rating agencies have "credit watch lists" of various types. Corporate investment policy should specify this point: For example, the company is allowed to invest in only those bonds rated Baa or above by Moody's or BBB or above by Standard & Poor's, even though doing so means giving up about three quarters of a percentage point in yield.

- *Length of maturity.* In addition to the ratings, an investment officer can control the risk element through maturities. The maturity indicates how much the company stands to lose if interest rates rise. The longer a bond's maturity, the more volatile its price. There is a trade-off: Shorter maturities usually mean lower yields. A conservative corporate investor, which is typical, may select bonds with shorter maturities.
- *Features of bonds.* Check to see whether a bond has a call provision, which allows the issuing company to redeem its bonds after a certain date if it chooses to, rather than at maturity. The investor is generally paid a small premium over par if an issue is called, but not as much as the investor would have received if the bond was held until maturity. That is because bonds are usually called only if their interest rates are higher than the going market rate. Try to avoid bonds of companies that have a call provision and may be involved in event risk (M&A, leveraged buyouts, etc.). Also check to see if a bond has a convertible feature. Convertible bonds can be

converted into common stock at a later date. They provide fixed income in the form of interest. The corporate investor also can benefit from the appreciation value of common stock.

■ *Tax status.* If the investing company is in a high-tax bracket, it may want to consider tax-exempt bonds. Most municipal bonds are rated A or above, making them a good grade risk. They can also be bought in mutual funds.

■ *Yield to maturity.* Yield has a lot to do with the rating of a bond. How to calculate various yield measures is discussed next.

How do you calculate yield (effective rate of return) on a bond?

Bonds are evaluated on many different types of returns, including current yield, yield to maturity, yield to call (YTC), and realized yield.

■ *Current yield.* The current yield is the annual interest payment divided by the current price of the bond. This is reported in the *Wall Street Journal*, among others. The current yield is:

$$\frac{\text{Annual interest payment}}{\text{Current price}}$$

Example 34.1

Assume a 12 percent coupon rate $1,000 par value bond selling for $960. The current yield = $120/$960 = 12.5%.

The problem with this measure of return is that it does not take into account the maturity date of the bond. A bond with 1 year to run and another with 15 years to run would have the same current yield quote if interest payments were $120 and the price were $960. Clearly, the one-year bond would be preferable under this circumstance because you would not only get $120 in interest but also a gain of $40 ($1,000 – $960) with a one-year time period, and this amount could be reinvested.

■ *Yield to maturity (YTM).* The YTM takes into account the maturity date of the bond. It is the real return the investor would receive from interest income plus capital gain assuming the bond is held to maturity. The exact way of calculating this measure is somewhat complicated and not presented here. But the approximate method is:

$$\text{Yield} = \frac{I + (\$1,000 - V)/n}{(\$1,000 + V)/n}$$

where
I = dollars of interest paid per year
V = market value of the bond
n = number of years to maturity

Example 34.2

An investor bought a 10-year, 8 percent coupon, $1,000 par value bond at a price of $877.60. The rate of return (yield) on the bond if held to maturity is:

$$\text{Yield} = \frac{\$80 + (\$1,000 - \$877.60)/10}{(\$1,000 - \$877.60)/2} = \frac{\$80 + \$12.24}{\$938.80} = \frac{\$92.24}{\$938.80} = 9.8\%$$

As can be seen, since the bond was bought at a discount, the yield (9.8 percent) came out greater than the coupon rate of 8 percent.

▪ *Yield to call.* Not all bonds are held to maturity. If the bond can be called prior to maturity, the YTM formula will have the call price in place of the par value of $1,000.

Example 34.3

Assume a 20-year bond was initially bought at a 13.5 percent coupon rate, and after two years, rates have dropped. Assume further that the bond is currently selling for $1,180, the YTM on the bond is 11.15 percent, and the bond can be called in five years after issue at $1,090. Thus, if the investor buys the bond two years after issue, the bond can be called back after three more years at $1,090. The YTC can be calculated as:

$$\frac{\$135 + (\$1,090 - \$1,180)/3}{(\$1,090 + \$1,180)/2} = \frac{\$135 + (-\$90/3)}{\$1,135} = \frac{\$105}{\$1,135} = 9.25\%$$

The YTC figure of 9.25 percent is 1.9 percent (or 190 basis points, in bond terminology) less than the YTM of 11.15 percent. Clearly, you need to be aware of the differential because a lower return is earned.

▪ *Realized yield.* The investor may trade in and out of a bond long before it matures. The investor obviously needs a measure of return to evaluate the investment appeal of any bonds that are intended to be bought and quickly sold. Realized yield is used for this purpose. This measure is simply a variation of YTM, as only two variables are changed in the YTM formula. Future price is used in place of par value ($1,000), and the length of the holding period is substituted for the number of years to maturity.

Example 34.4

In Example 34.3, assume that the investor anticipates holding the bond only three years and that the investor has estimated interest rates will change in the future so that the price of the bond will move to about $925 from its present level of $877.70. Thus, the investor will buy the bond today at a market price of $877.70 and sell the issue three years later at a price of $925. Given these assumptions, the realized yield of this bond would be:

$$\text{Realized yield} = \frac{\$80 + (\$925 - \$877.70)/3}{(\$925 + \$877.70)/2} = \frac{\$80 + \$15.77}{\$901.35}$$

$$= \frac{\$95.77}{\$901.35} = 10.63\%$$

Use a bond table to find the value for various yield measures. A source is *Thorndike Encyclopedia of Banking and Financial Tables* (Warren, Gorham, and Lamont, 2002).

▪ *Equivalent before-tax yield.* Yield on a municipal bond needs to be looked at on an equivalent before-tax yield basis because the interest received is not subject to federal income taxes. The formula used to equate interest on municipals to other investments is:

$$\text{Tax equivalent yield} = \text{Tax-exempt yield}/(1 - \text{tax rate})$$

Example 34.5

If a company has a marginal tax rate of 34 percent and is evaluating a municipal bond paying 10 percent interest, the equivalent before-tax yield on a taxable investment will be:

$$\frac{10\%}{(1 - 0.34)} = 15.15\%$$

Thus, the company could choose between a taxable investment paying 15.15 percent and a tax-exempt bond paying 10 percent and be indifferent between the two.

How is interest rate risk determined?

Interest rate risk can be determined in two ways. One way is to look at the term structure of a debt security by measuring its average term to maturity—a duration. The other way is to measure the sensitivity of changes in a debt security's price associated with changes in its YTM. We discuss two measurement approaches: Macaulay's duration coefficient and interest rate elasticity.

▪ *Macaulay's duration coefficient.* Macaulay's duration (MD) is an attempt to measure risk in a bond. It is defined as the weighted average number of years required to

Example 34.6

A bond pays a 7 percent coupon rate annually on its $1,000 face value that has three years until its maturity and has a YTM of 6 percent. The computation of Macaulay's duration coefficient involves these three steps:

1. Calculate the present value of the bond for each year.
2. Express present values as proportions of the price of the bond.
3. Multiply proportions by years' digits to obtain the weighted average time.

(1) Year	(2) Cash Flow	(3) PV Factor @ 6%	(Step 1) (4) PV of Cash Flow	(Step 2) (5) PV as Proportion of Price of Bond	(Step 3) (6) Column (1) × Column (5)
1	$70	0.9434	$ 66.04	0.0643	0.0643
2	70	0.8900	62.30	0.0607	0.1214
3	1,070	0.8369	898.39	0.8750	2.6250
			$1,026.73	1.0000	2.8107

This three-year bond's duration is a little over 2.8 years. In all cases, a bond's duration is less than or equal to its term to maturity. Only a pure discount bond—that is, one with no coupon or sinking-fund payments—has duration equal to the maturity.

The higher the MD value, the greater the interest rate risk, since it implies a longer recovery period.

recover principal and all interest payments. Example 34.6 illustrates the duration calculations.

■ *Interest rate elasticity.* A bond's interest rate elasticity (E) is defined as

$$E = \frac{\text{Percentage change in bond price}}{\text{Percentage change in YTM}}$$

Since bond prices and YTMs always move inversely, elasticity will always be a negative number. Any bond's elasticity can be determined directly with the formula just given. Knowing the duration coefficient (MD), we can calculate the E using this simple formula:

$$-1E = MD\frac{YTM}{1+YTM}$$

Example 34.7

Using the same data in Example 34.6, the elasticity is calculated as:

$$-1E = 2.8107(0.6/1.06) = 0.1586$$

How do you invest in a bond fund?

A corporate investor may decide to invest in a bond fund. Three key facts about the bonds in any portfolio follow.

1. *Quality.* Check the credit rating of the typical bond in the fund. Ratings by Standard & Poor's and Moody's show the relative danger that an issuer will default on interest or principal payments. AAA is the best grade. A rating of BB or lower signifies a junk bond.
2. *Maturity.* The average maturity of a fund's bonds indicates how much a corporate investor stands to lose if interest rates rise. The longer the term of the bonds, the more volatile is the price. For example, a 20-year bond may fluctuate in price four times as much as a four-year issue.
3. *Premium or discount.* Some funds with high current yields hold bonds that trade for more than their face value, or at a premium. Such funds are less vulnerable to losses if rates go up. Funds that hold bonds trading at a discount to face value can lose the most.

Corporate investors must keep in mind these guidelines:

▪ *Rising interest rates drive down the value of all bond funds.* For this reason, rather than focusing only on current yield, the investor should look primarily at total return (yield plus capital gains from falling interest rates or minus capital losses if rates climb).
▪ *All bond funds do not benefit equally from tumbling interest rates.* If corporate investment officers think interest rates will decline and they want to increase total return, they should buy funds that invest in U.S. Treasuries or top-rated corporate bonds. Investment officers should consider high-yield corporate bonds (junk bonds) if they believe interest rates are stabilizing and are willing to take risk.
▪ *Unlike bonds, bond funds do not allow the corporate investor to lock in a yield.* A mutual fund with a constantly changing portfolio is not like an individual bond, which can be kept to maturity. If the investor wants steady, secure income over several years or more, he or she should consider, as alternatives to funds, buying individual top-quality bonds or investing in a municipal bond unit trust, which maintains a fixed portfolio.

Should you consider unit investment trusts?

Like a mutual fund, a unit investment trust offers investors the advantages of a large, professionally selected and diversified portfolio. Unlike a mutual fund, however, its portfolio is fixed; once structured, it is not actively managed. Unit investment trusts are available of tax-exempt bonds, money market securities, corporate bonds of different grades, mortgage-backed securities, preferred stocks, utility common stocks, and other investments. Unit trusts are most suitable for corporate investors who need a fixed income and a guaranteed return of capital. They disband and pay off investors after the majority of their investments have been redeemed.

Collateralized mortgage obligations (CMOs) are mortgage-backed securities that separate mortgage pools into short-, medium-, and long-term portions. Corporate investors can choose between short-term pools (such as 5-year pools) and long-term pools (such as 20-year pools).

Mortgage-backed securities enjoy liquidity and a high degree of safety because they are either government-sponsored or otherwise insured.

 ## OTHER FIXED INCOME INVESTMENTS

What are other short-term fixed income securities?

Besides bonds and mortgage-backed securities, there are other significant forms of debt instruments from which corporate investors can choose that are primarily short term in nature.

- *CDs.* These safe instruments are issued by commercial banks and thrift institutions and have traditionally been in amounts of $10,000 or $100,000 (jumbo CDs). CDs have a fixed maturity period varying from several months to many years. However, there is a penalty for cashing in the certificate prior to the maturity date.
- *Repos.* The repurchase agreement is a form of loan in which the borrower sells securities (such as government securities and other marketable securities) to the lender but simultaneously contracts to repurchase the same securities either on call or on a specified date at a price that will produce an agreed yield. For example, a corporate investment officer agrees to buy a 90-day Treasury bill from a bank at a price to yield 7 percent with a contract to buy the bills back one day later. Repos are attractive to corporate investors because, unlike demand deposits, repos pay explicit interest, and it may be difficult to locate a one-day-maturity government security. Although repos can be a sound investment, it will cost to buy them (for bank safekeeping fees, legal fees, and paperwork).
- *BAs.* A banker's acceptance is a draft drawn on a bank by a corporation to pay for merchandise. The draft promises payment of a certain sum of money to its holder at some future date. What makes BAs unique is that, by prearrangement, a bank accepts them, thereby guaranteeing their payment at the stated time. Most BAs arise in foreign trade transactions. The most common maturity for BAs is 3 months, although they can have maturities of up to 270 days. Their typical denominations are $500,000 and $1 million. BAs offer these advantages as a corporate investment vehicle:
  - Safety
  - Negotiability
  - Liquidity since an active secondary market for instruments of $1 million or more exists
  - Yield spreads that are several basis points higher than those of T-bills
  - Smaller investment amount producing a yield similar to that of a CD with a comparable face value
- *Commercial paper.* Commercial paper is issued by large corporations to the public. It usually comes in minimum denominations of $25,000 and represents an unsecured promissory note. It usually carries a higher yield than small CDs. The maturity is usually 30, 60, and 90 days. The degree of risk depends on the company's credit rating.

- *Treasury bills.* T-bills have a maximum maturity of 1 year and common maturities of 91 and 182 days. They trade in minimum units of $10,000. They do not pay interest in the traditional sense; they are sold at a discount and redeemed when the maturity date comes around, at face value. T-bills are extremely liquid in that there is an active secondary or resale market for these securities. T-bills have an extremely low risk because they are backed by the U.S. government.
- Yields on discount securities like T-bills are calculated using the formula:

$$\frac{P_1 - P_0}{P_0} \times \frac{52}{n}$$

where
P_1 = redemption price
P_0 = purchase price
n = maturity in weeks

Example 34.8

Assume that P_1 = $10,000, P_0 = $9,800, and n = 13 weeks. Then the T-bill yield is:

$$\frac{\$10,000 - \$9,800}{\$9,800} \times \frac{52}{13} = \frac{\$200}{\$9,800} \times 4 = 0.0816 = 8.16\%$$

- *Eurodollar time deposits and CDs.* Eurodollar time deposits are essentially nonnegotiable, full-liability, U.S. dollar–denominated time deposits in an offshore branch of a U.S. or foreign bank. Hence, these time deposits are not liquid or marketable. Eurodollar CDs, however, are negotiable and typically offer a higher return than domestic CDs because of their exposure to sovereign risk.
- *Student Loan Marketing Association (Sallie Mae) securities.* Sallie Mae purchases loans made by financial institutions under a variety of federal and state loan programs. Sallie Mae securities are not guaranteed but are generally insured by the federal government and its agencies. These securities include floating-rate and fixed-rate obligations with maturities of five years or more as well as discount notes with maturities from a few days to 360 days.

How do you choose money market funds?

Money market funds are a special form of mutual funds. Investors with a small amount to invest can own a portfolio of high-yielding CDs, T-bills, and similar securities of short-term nature. There is a great deal of liquidity and flexibility in withdrawing funds through check-writing privileges. Money market funds are considered very conservative because most of the securities purchased by the funds are quite safe.

Money market mutual funds invest in short-term government securities, commercial paper, and CDs. They provide more safety of principal than other mutual funds since net asset value never fluctuates. Each share has a net asset value of $1. The yield, however, fluctuates daily. The advantages are:

- Money market funds are no-load (they have no commission).
- There may be a low deposit in these funds.
- The fund is a form of checking account, allowing a firm to write checks against its balance in the account.

Disadvantage: The deposit in these funds is not insured, as it is in a money market account or other federally insured deposit in banks.

Exhibit 34.3 ranks various short-term investment vehicles in terms of their default risk.

EXHIBIT 34.3   Default Risk Among Short-Term Investment Vehicles

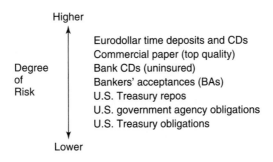

Higher

Degree
of
Risk

Eurodollar time deposits and CDs
Commercial paper (top quality)
Bank CDs (uninsured)
Bankers' acceptances (BAs)
U.S. Treasury repos
U.S. government agency obligations
U.S. Treasury obligations

Lower

Is investing in preferred stock desirable?

Preferred stock carries a fixed dividend that is paid quarterly. The dividend is stated in dollar terms per share or as a percentage of par (stated) value of the stock. Preferred stock is considered a hybrid security because it possesses features of both common stock and a corporate bond. It is like common stock in that:

- It represents equity ownership and is issued without stated maturity dates.
- It pays dividends.

Preferred stock is also like a corporate bond in that:

- It provides for prior claims on earnings and assets.
- Its dividend is fixed for the life of the issue.
- It can carry call and convertible features and sinking fund provisions.

Since preferred stocks are traded on the basis of the yield offered to investors, they are in effect viewed as fixed income securities and, as a result, are in competition with bonds in the marketplace.

Note

Corporate bonds, however, occupy a position senior to preferred stocks. ▪

Advantages of owning preferred stocks include:

▪ Their high current income, which is highly predictable
▪ Safety
▪ Lower unit cost ($10 to $25 per share)

Disadvantages are:

▪ Their susceptibility to inflation and high interest rates
▪ Their lack of substantial capital gains potential

Preferred Stock Ratings

Like bond ratings, Standard & Poor's and Moody's have long rated the investment quality of preferred stocks. Standard & Poor's uses basically the same rating system as it does with bonds, except that triple-A ratings are not given to preferred stocks. Moody's uses a slightly different system, which is shown in Exhibit 34.4.

EXHIBIT 34.4   Moody's Preferred Stock Rating System

Rating Symbol	Definition
Aaa	Top quality
Aa	High grade
A	Upper medium grade
Baa	Lower medium grade
Ba	Speculative type
B	Little assurance of future dividends
Caa	Likely to be already in arrears

These ratings are intended to provide an indication of the quality of the issue and are based largely on an assessment of the firm's ability to pay preferred dividends in a prompt and timely fashion.

Note

Preferred stock ratings should not be compared with bond ratings as they are not equivalent; preferred stocks occupy a position junior to bonds. ▪

How do you calculate expected return from preferred stock?

The expected return from preferred stock is calculated in a manner similar to the expected return on bonds. The calculations depend on whether the preferred stock is issued in perpetuity or if it has a call that is likely to be exercised.

▪ *In perpetuity.* Since preferred stock usually has no maturity date when the company must redeem it, you cannot calculate a yield to maturity. You can calculate a current yield as:

$$\text{Current yield} = D/P$$

where
D = annual dividend
P = market price of the preferred stock

Example 34.9

A preferred stock paying $4.00 a year in dividends and having a market price of $25 would have a current yield of 16 percent ($4/$25).

▪ *Yield to call.* If a call is likely, a more appropriate return measure is YTC. Theoretically, YTC is the rate that equates the present value of the future dividends and the call price with the current market price of the preferred stock. Example 34.10 presents two preferreds.

Example 34.10

Consider these two preferred stocks:

Preferreds	Market Price	Call Price	Dividends	Term to Call	YTC
A	$8/share	$9	$1/year	3 years	16.06%
B	$10/share	$9	$1/year	3 years	6.89%

▪ *Comparison to bond yields.* The example shows that yields on straight preferreds are closely correlated to bond yields, since both are fixed income securities. However, yields on preferreds are often below bond yields, which seems unusual because preferreds have a position junior to bonds. The reason is that corporate investors favor preferreds over bonds because of a dividend exclusion allowed in determining corporate taxable income, which will be explained next.

Should you consider adjustable rate preferred stock?

CFOs with excess funds can make short-term investments in long-term securities, such as long-term bonds and common and preferred stocks. They may be naturally adverse to the price volatility of long-term bonds, especially when they put money aside for a specific payment such as income taxes. Perhaps for a similar reason, common and preferred stocks would be equally unattractive for short-term investments. But this is not quite true, because these securities provide an interesting tax advantage for corporations. For example, if the company invests its surplus funds in a short- or long-term debt, it must pay tax on the interest received. Thus, for $1 of interest, a corporation in a 46 percent marginal tax bracket ends up with only $0.54. However, companies pay tax on only 20 percent of dividends received from investments in stocks. (Under current tax laws, corporations are allowed to exclude 50 percent of the dividends they receive from a stock—either common or preferred—from their taxable income.) Thus, for $1 of dividends received, the firm winds up with $1 − (0.250 × 0.46) = $0.23. The effective tax rate is only 9.1 percent.

The problem with preferred stocks is that since preferred dividends are fixed, the prices of preferred shares change when long-term interest rates change. Many corporate money managers are reluctant to buy straight preferred stocks because of their interest risk. To encourage corporate investments in preferred shares, a new type of preferred stock was introduced in May 1982 by Chemical New York Corporation. These securities—the so-called *adjustable rate (floating-rate) preferreds* (ARPs)—pay dividends that go up and down with the general level of interest rates. The prices of these securities are therefore less volatile than fixed-dividend preferreds, and they are a safer haven for the corporation's excess cash. Yields obtained from preferreds may be lower than the debt issue. Corporations buying preferreds would be happy with the lower yield because 50 percent of the dividends they receive escape tax.

MONEY MARKET PREFERRED STOCK

Money market preferred stock (MMPS), also known as auction-rate preferred stock, is the newest and most popular member of the preferred stock group attractive to corporate investors because it offers these advantages:

- Low market risk in the event of price decline
- Competitive yield
- Liquidity

MMPSs pay dividends and adjust rates up or down, depending on the current market, every seven weeks. Unlike other adjustable preferreds, the market, not the issuer, sets the rate at the auction. If no bids are placed for a stock, the dividend rate of MMPSs is automatically set at the 60-day AA commercial paper rate quoted by the Federal Reserve Bank. There is a possibility, however, of a failed auction if no buyers show up. Corporate investors must take into account the credit quality of a money market preferred stock. Money market preferreds include:

- Short-Term Auction Rate Stock (STARS)
- Dutch-Auction Rate Transferable Securities (DARTS)

- Market-Auction Preferred Stock (MAPS)
- Auction-Market Preferred Stock (AMPS)
- Cumulative Auction-Market Preferred Stock (CAMPS)

 PRIVATE EQUITY

Private equity is an asset class consisting of equity securities in operating companies that are not publicly traded on a stock exchange. Private equities are generally illiquid and thought of as long-term investments. Private equity investments are not subject to the same high level of government regulation as stock offerings to the general public. Private equity is also far less liquid than publicly traded stock.

What are some types of private equity?

- *Venture capital. Venture capital* refers to equity investments made, typically in companies in their early stages, to launch, develop, and/or expand a new business. Venture capital investment is often associated with new ideas or products that have not yet been tested. The earlier the investment stage, the greater the risk/return characteristics for the investor. In other words, investing at the very beginning of what may become a profitable technology could offer substantial returns if successful, but the probability of success may not be high. Waiting until a business or idea has begun and just investing in the expansion of that business may provide a lower return, but the investor has a higher probability of success when comparing to the start-up investor.
- *Leveraged buyouts (LBOs).* At its most basic level, an LBO is a method of acquiring a company with money that is nearly all borrowed. This allows investors to make a large acquisition without committing a lot of capital. The acquirers of the target company often attempt to sell or take the target company public after 5 or 10 years in the hopes of making sizable profits. Doing an LBO can be expensive and complex, but if successful can provide considerable returns. One of the most famous LBOs was the $25 billion takeover of RJR Nabisco by private equity firm Kohlberg Kravis Roberts in 1989.
- *Distressed or special situations.* This is a broad category referring to investments in equity or debt securities of financially stressed companies. Since this area focuses on investing in entities that are in default, under bankruptcy protection, or headed in that direction, investors must evaluate not only the ability for the entity to make a comeback but also which class of securities might be more beneficial to hold during a restructuring process.
- *Mezzanine capital.* Mezzanine capital deals typically are structured as either a subordinate debt or preferred stock investment with claims below that of the other debt issued by the entity but above that of the common stock holders. Entities that obtain financing in this manner must pay a higher cost due to the investor's junior position.
- *Other private equity strategies.* Other strategies may include investing in real estate, energy and power, merchant banking, or infrastructure.

CURRENT TRENDS IN LIQUIDITY MANAGEMENT STRATEGY

The current business, economic, and regulatory environments offer both opportunities and challenges for cash managers seeking to optimize their cash positions. Coupled with the aftermath of the Sarbanes-Oxley Act of 2002, which enforced stricter regulations around transparency and fiduciary oversight, institutional investors face a challenging environment that calls for a proactive approach to cash management. Given this environment, maintaining an optimal cash position is essential for CFOs, controllers, and treasurers, who have the opportunity to improve their companies' balance sheets through sound, flexible cash management strategies. Some of the key questions they are asking include:

- Given the current conditions, which vehicles are best for short-term investment of cash?
- What is the best overall liquidity plan and strategy for my organization?
- What are the trade-offs between outsourcing liquidity management and keeping it in-house?

This section addresses how companies are answering these questions, provides insight on key trends in liquidity management, and offers strategies for maximizing cash management.

Classifying Investments on the Balance Sheet

With the increased scrutiny and accounting changes that are occurring today, companies must be very careful about how they classify investments on their balance sheets. In the past, when a company classified assets on the balance sheet, they were classified as "cash and cash equivalents" and "short-term marketable securities." The Financial Accounting Standards Board is dropping "cash and cash equivalents" and redefining what "cash" means. Anything that is not considered "cash" now becomes a "short-term marketable security," effectively eliminating the classification of "cash equivalent." International Financial Reporting Standards (International Accounting Standards No. 7) provides the following definitions.

- *Cash:* Comprises cash on hand and demand deposits with banks
- *Cash equivalents:* Short-term, highly liquid investments that are readily convertible into known amounts of cash and that are subject to an insignificant amount of risk of changes in value

Companies Flush with Cash

Many companies flush with cash have been redeploying surplus cash—not only in increased dividends and M&A activity, but also in stock buybacks and in some capital expenditures.

Cash-Investment Policies Gain Popularity

A number of developments in recent years—including the enactment of Sarbanes-Oxley—have prompted many companies to adopt stricter liquidity management policies as part of improving financial controls. One of the obvious reasons for developing a written policy is that these companies have a fiduciary responsibility to their shareholders. Clearly delineating cash investment policies helps address today's more stringent transparency mandates and at the same time provides better controls for the company.

Diversification Not Fully Realized

While the policies of many organizations allow for the use of a significant variety of investment vehicles for short-term investments, relatively few of those companies embrace the opportunity to fully diversify. The number of different investments in a company's short-term portfolio is often a function of an organization's relative level of sophistication and resources. For example, companies with fewer resources or limited internal expertise may not have the ability to perform credit research. They may lean toward "plain vanilla" or more conservative investments, thereby making use of only a small portion of the market. To achieve a much fuller range of diversification, many more organizations are enlisting an outside professional investment manager to administer at least some of their short-term portfolios.

Expanding Allowable Investments

One category of short-term investments that could provide additional return, but that companies are not turning to in very large numbers, includes investment-grade securities at the lower end of the ratings scale. Companies' investment policies often dictate the levels of investment quality that are required in order to invest in various corporate-debt or municipal-debt vehicles, and some policies ignore the potential viability of BBB- or even A-rated investments. These ratings may not be the highest, but the investments they represent actually can offer excellent risk/reward characteristics. In effect, policies may establish credit-quality requirements that could be described as too conservative in certain instances. For instance, a policy that forbids investment in BBB-rated municipal bonds might impose an unnecessary opportunity cost, when you consider that such bonds have had lower historical default rates than some AAA-rated corporate debt.

"Cash plus funds" could offer a similar opportunity for higher returns, but relatively few liquidity managers are including them in their portfolios. "Cash plus" indicates something beyond a simple money market fund, such as ultra-short bond funds with fluctuating net asset values or even what are sometimes called "enhanced-cash" funds.

Investing Offshore

Another growing trend is for companies to invest cash outside the United States. Companies invest offshore for many reasons, such as to avoid certain U.S. taxes or to domicile an offshore insurance captive. Of course, companies must assess the foreign tax implications of maintaining cash offshore before making substantial investments.

Taking Control with Electronic Trading Portals

Another trend is the choice made by many businesses to use an electronic, multi-family fund trading portal to execute at least some of their short-term investment transactions, including money market mutual funds. This "self-service" approach is more common among large corporations with dedicated teams that trade frequently and therefore can more readily realize economic gains from an electronic trading portal. Frequently, companies that use an electronic, multifamily trading portal complement this approach by having a professional investment manager oversee a core portion of their portfolios. The way some companies approach liquidity management is to make "overnight" or money market investments—representing their primary liquidity—through the electronic, multifamily trading portal. They then outsource to a professional investment manager the responsibility of investing the other core cash balances in longer-term instruments.

Outsourcing on the Rise

One way to achieve sound investment management is through outsourcing. Recently more and more companies have been looking for advice and guidance from professional money managers. Outside money managers can provide companies with the market knowledge and insight needed to more effectively diversify their short-term investments while seeking to capture opportunities for higher returns than they currently achieve. You should expect a liquidity investment manager to provide key ongoing services:

- Strategic consulting
- Investment policy development
- Delivery of consistent, informative and timely reports
- In-person investment reviews with you or other staff members

VIII

PART EIGHT

Taxation

CHAPTER THIRTY-FIVE

Tax Factors in Financial Decision Making

THERE ARE MANY taxing agencies, including federal, state, and local, to which your company pays tax. If your company is operating internationally, it has the additional problem of applying tax laws of foreign countries. Taxes may be levied on income, sales, and property. The federal corporate income tax (filed on Form 1120) is the most important because it often represents the largest tax liability. Thus, it can have a major effect on your financial decisions.

 ## WHAT SHOULD YOU KNOW ABOUT TAXES?

To make sound financial and investment decisions, you must have an understanding of the basic concepts underlying the U.S. tax structure and how they affect your decisions. This section discusses first the general structure of the corporate income tax, such as taxable income, capital gains and losses, deductible expenses, operating loss carrybacks and carryforwards, tax rates, and tax prepayments and credits. Then it reviews various tax planning strategies to minimize your company's income tax liability in the current year and postpone the payment of taxes to later years. The advantages of electing S corporation status also are discussed.

The general tax formula for corporations is:

> Gross income
> Less: Deductions
> = Taxable income
> × Tax rates
> = Gross tax
> Less: Tax credits and prepayments
> = Tax due (or Refund)

A brief review of the various elements of this tax formula will provide a general understanding needed for effective tax planning.

 GROSS INCOME

What does gross income consist of?

Corporate gross income is of two types:

1. *Ordinary income,* which includes income from normal business operations as well as miscellaneous incomes, such as rents, interest, and dividends. Ordinary income is fully taxable; however, the corporation has a special exclusion for dividends received from taxable domestic corporations. Generally, 70 percent of the dividends received can be excluded from the corporation's gross income. For example, if a $100 dividend is received by the corporation, $70 can be excluded, and only $30 of the dividend is included in taxable income. This 70 percent exclusion can be increased to 80 percent if the corporation receiving the dividend owns at least 20 percent but less than 80 percent of the dividend-paying corporation's stock. And for ownership exceeding 80 percent of the dividend-paying corporation, the dividend received deduction will be 100 percent.
2. *Capital gains or losses,* resulting from the sale of capital assets. In general, assets bought and sold in the ordinary course of a company's business, such as inventory, receivables, and depreciable assets, generate ordinary income. The sale or exchange of all other assets, such as stocks, bonds, and real estate investments, generate capital gains or losses.

Capital gains and losses are classified as long term or short term. A long-term capital gain is a gain from the sale of assets held for more than one year. The highest tax rate on capital gains is 15 percent.

What are the allowable tax deductions?

All of a regular corporation's activities are considered to be connected with the conduct of a trade or business. Therefore, all the ordinary and necessary expenses paid or incurred during the year by your business are tax deductible.

Business meals and entertainment expenses are 80 percent deductible. The meal must have a direct relationship to carrying out your business activities. Business must be discussed before, during, and after the meal. The meal or beverage cannot be "lavish or extravagant." Transportation to and from the restaurant is 100 percent deductible. However, parking at a sports arena is only 80 percent deductible.

Generally, food- and entertainment-related employee benefits are fully deductible. Examples are departmental and office parties.

Example 35.1

You took a customer out to dinner and drinks, and it costs $125. The business meal is limited in terms of tax deductibility to $125 × 80% = $100. In addition, the taxi fare to the restaurant was $20. This is fully deductible.

Promotional items for public distribution are fully deductible (e.g., samples). Deductions for business gifts are limited to $25 per individual customer, client, or other business contact. Items clearly of an advertising nature that cost $4 or less and are imprinted with the company's name (e.g., pens, calendars, etc.) do not have to be included in the $25 limitation.

Example 35.2

You gave business gifts to 17 customers. These gifts, which were not of an advertising nature, had this fair market value: 4 @ $10, 4 @ $25, 4 @ $50, and 5 @ $100. These gifts are deductible as business expenses for $365 computed as:

4 @ $10	$ 40
13 @ $25	325
Total	$365

All bad debts incurred by the corporation are business related and can be used to offset the corporation's ordinary income. Corporations can no longer use the reserve method, which allows deductions for estimated bad debts. Instead, it must use the direct write-off method, which allows a bad debt deduction only at the time the debt actually becomes partially or totally worthless.

A charitable contribution made in cash or property is deductible. For contributions of inventory used to care for the ill, the needy, or infants and contributions of scientific property to an educational institution to be used for research, the amount of deduction is the cost of the property plus one-half of the potential profit (but not exceeding two times the cost). The deduction generally is limited to 10 percent of taxable income computed by excluding the charitable contribution itself, the dividends-received exclusion, and the net operating loss and capital loss carrybacks. Any charitable contribution in excess of the limitation may be carried forward and deducted in any of the five succeeding years.

With life insurance premiums, there are some circumstances in which a corporation may claim a deduction. These include premiums paid for "key man" life insurance (i.e., life insurance for any officer or employee who may have a financial interest in the company) and for group-term life insurance when the company is not the beneficiary. "Key man" life insurance premiums are deductible only if (1) the premium payments are an ordinary business expense as additional compensation to the key employee, and (2) the total amount of all compensation paid to that employee is not unreasonable.

As for group-term insurance, the premiums paid for coverage of up to $50,000 per employee are a deductible expense for the corporation and are not taxable income to the employee. For coverage above $50,000, the employee must include in income an amount equivalent to the cost of the additional protection. The group-term insurance policy must be nondiscriminatory; that is, it must provide coverage for all employees with only few permitted exceptions, such as those who work part time, who are under age 21, or who have not been employed for at least six months.

Other deductible expenses include interest, professional fees (e.g., independent accountants, outside attorneys), casualty and theft losses, and bad debts when a specific amount is deemed uncollectible. Nondeductible expenses include fines, penalties, and illegal payments.

 ## DEPRECIATION

How much of depreciation is tax deductible?

Your company has the choice of depreciating tangible assets under the straight-line method or the modified accelerated cost recovery (MACRS) method. The basis for determining depreciation is the cost of the assets and improvements. If land and building are purchased together, the purchase price must be apportioned between the land and the building because only the building cost is depreciable. The portion allocated to the land cannot be depreciated because land is considered to have unlimited useful life.

ACRS depreciation lowers taxes in the early years of an asset's life, thus improving corporate cash flow and making funds available for investment. The faster the cash flow, the greater the rate of return earned on the investment.

Your company may elect to deduct immediately part or all of the cost of a depreciable asset in the year of purchase rather than depreciating it over its useful life. This provision relates to personal property qualifying under ACRS and acquired for trade or business use. However, the maximum amount that may be expensed is $100,000 per year.

 ## AMORTIZATION

Some types of intangible assets may be amortized (i.e., written off systematically over their estimated useful lives) for tax purposes. For instance, a new company's organization costs may be amortized over a period of not less than 60 months.

What do you do about losses in the current year?

If a company has a net operating loss, the loss may be applied against income in other years. The loss can be carried back 2 years and then forward 20 years. Note that the taxpayer must first apply the loss against the taxable income in the 2 prior years. If the loss is not completely absorbed by the profits in these 2 years, it may be carried forward to each of the following 20 years. The taxpayer has the option of forgoing the carryback and can elect to carry the loss forward only. After the 20 years, any loss remaining may no longer be used as a tax deduction.

What tax rates apply?

The federal income tax rate is graduated, meaning that as additional profits are earned, the tax rate on the incremental earnings increases.

The federal corporate tax rates for 2011 are:

Taxable Income	Tax Rate
0–$50,000	15%
$50,001–$75,000	25%
$75,001–$100,000	34%
$100,001-$335,000	39%

Exception: A personal service corporation is subject to a fixed 35 percent tax rate.

The highest tax rate used in computing your company's total tax obligation is referred to as the *marginal tax rate*, which is the tax rate applicable to the next dollar of income. In addition to the marginal tax rate, the average (effective) tax rate is the one applicable to all taxable income. It is computed as:

$$\text{Effective tax rate} = \frac{\text{Total tax liability}}{\text{Taxable income}}$$

Besides the federal tax rate, companies have state and local income taxes that typically are based on federal taxable income. As a result, the effective tax rate a company pays is generally higher.

Because you are concerned with the tax obligation on the additional profit, the marginal tax rate must be considered when making financial decisions.

Were your tax prepayments adequate?

Under our tax system's principle of pay as you go, the corporation must prepay (1) 90 percent of its tax liability, or (2) 100 percent of the tax for the preceding year. The quarterly estimated payments are to be made on April 15, June 15, September 15, and December 15 for calendar-year taxpayers.

Are you entitled to a tax credit?

A tax credit reduces dollar for dollar the amount of tax otherwise payable. A foreign tax credit is allowed for income taxes paid to a foreign country. However, the foreign tax credit cannot be used to reduce the U.S. tax liability on income from U.S. sources. The allowable credit is calculated in this way:

$$\text{Foreign tax credit} = \frac{\text{Foreign source income}}{\text{Worldwide income}} \times \text{U.S. tax liability}$$

Example 35.3

In 2X12, your company had worldwide taxable income of $675,000 and tentative U.S. income tax of $270,000. The company's taxable income from business operations in Country X was $300,000, and foreign income taxes charged were $135,000 stated in U.S. dollars. The credit for foreign income taxes that can be claimed on the U.S. tax return for 2X12 is:

$$\text{Foreign tax credit} = \frac{\$300,000}{\$675,000} \times \$270,000 = \$120,000$$

 ## TAX PLANNING

How can tax planning reduce your taxes?

You have to analyze the tax consequences of alternative approaches in financial decision making. Ignoring the effect of income taxes will cause an overstatement in estimated income. An otherwise positive cash flow from an investment may become negative when the tax is taken into consideration. As a result, an investment alternative may be chosen that does not sufficiently generate the needed return for the risk exposure taken.

Tax planning includes the minimization of tax payments by attempting to eliminate the tax entirely or providing for taxation at lower tax rates. But often it is not possible to reduce the tax ultimately payable. As an alternative, much tax planning is concerned with *deferring* tax payments from the current year to a future tax year. Tax deferrals can contribute a great deal to the efficient use of resources available to the company.

A deferral is equivalent to an interest-free loan from the taxing authority. In addition, the business earns a return for another year on the funds that would have had to be paid to the federal and local taxing authorities; future tax payments will be made with "cheaper" dollars; and eventually there may be no tax payment (e.g., new tax laws). Thus, corporate taxes should be deferred when there will be a lower tax bracket in a future year or when the firm lacks the funds to meet the current tax obligation.

In tax planning, income and expenses should be shifted into tax years that will result in the least tax liability. In general, income should be deferred to future years and expenses should be accelerated into the current year.

How can income be deferred for tax purposes?

A good tax strategy is to defer income into a year in which it will be taxed at a lower rate. For example, if you expect tax rates to drop next year, you can reduce the tax obligation by deferring income into the next year. Thus, instead of selling an asset outright, the corporation can exchange that asset for a like-kind asset, and the gain on the exchange will be tax deferred. For example, a tangible asset, such as equipment, machinery, or an auto, held for productive use in business or for investment can be exchanged tax free for another tangible asset. Similarly, realty such as land, building, and warehouse, can be exchanged tax free for another piece of real property.

Another method to defer income is to report the gain from an asset sale under the installment method. This method can be used when the sale price is collected over more than one year. The company must determine a gross profit ratio for an installment sale and then apply this ratio to the cash collections each year to determine the amount of gain that is taxable in that year.

Can you obtain tax-exempt income?

The company should try to convert income to less taxed or even tax-exempt sources. For example, a change from investing in corporate bonds into investing in state and local obligations can convert taxable interest income into tax-exempt income. Interest earned on municipal bonds is not subject to federal taxes and is exempt from tax of the state in which the bond is issued. Of course, the market value of the bond changes with changes in the going interest rate.

Tax-free income is worth much more than taxable income. That is why tax-free bonds almost always have lower pretax yields. You can determine the equivalent taxable return in this way:

$$\text{Equivalent taxable return} = \frac{\text{Tax-free return}}{1 - \text{Marginal tax rate}}$$

Example 35.4

A municipal bond pays interest at the rate of 6 percent. The company's marginal tax rate is 34 percent. The equivalent rate on a taxable instrument is:

$$\frac{0.06}{1 - 0.34} = \frac{0.06}{0.66} = 9.1\%$$

When should you accelerate expenses?

Pay tax-deductible expenses in a year in which you will receive the most benefit. Accelerate expenses that will no longer be deductible or will be restricted in the future. Also, accelerate deductions into the current year if you anticipate lower tax rates in the next period. For example, if your company is a cash-basis taxpayer, prepay your future tax obligations, such as property taxes and estimated income taxes, to bring the deductible expenses into the current year. Also, selling a loss asset prior to year-end can accelerate a tax loss into the current year.

The company can donate property instead of cash. By donating appreciated property to a charity, the business can deduct the full market value and avoid paying tax on the gain.

Is a small business better off filing as an S corporation?

A small business corporation having 35 or fewer stockholders and only one class of stock may elect to be taxed as a Subchapter S corporation (more commonly known as an S corporation). An S corporation is taxed like a partnership. There is no tax at the corporate level, and all corporate income and losses are passed through to the stockholders. Income is allocated and taxed directly to the stockholders regardless of whether they actually receive it. An S corporation files an information tax return on Form 1120S and attaches a Schedule K-1 for each stockholder, showing his or her portion of taxable income or loss for the year. The corporate income is taxed only once to the stockholders at their individual tax rates.

The election to be taxed as an S corporation may be made by a qualified corporation at any time during the preceding taxable year or in the first 75 days of the year during which it applies. For the election to be valid, all stockholders must consent to the election in a signed statement.

An S corporation is advantageous because there is no tax at the corporate level and because the maximum tax rate to individuals is lower than that of the corporation. Thus, stockholders still obtain the benefits of a corporation, such as limited liability, while escaping the double taxation typically associated with the distribution of corporate profits. However, certain tax advantages that companies obtain do not go to S corporations. For example, fringe benefits paid to shareholders owning more than 2 percent of the stock are treated as distributions to the shareholders and are not deductible by the corporation. In addition, items that would be subject to special limitations on the shareholders' individual returns, such as interest, dividends, capital gains and losses, and charitable contributions, cannot be netted against the S corporation's income; instead they must be allocated to the shareholders' directly.

Mergers and Acquisitions, Divestitures, Failure, and Reorganization

CHAPTER THIRTY-SIX

Mergers and Acquisitions

A CQUISITIONS ARE MADE for a variety of reasons:

- To realize economies of scale and scope
- To access resources, such as technology, products, and distribution channels
- To build critical mass in growth industries
- To remove excess capacity and consolidate a mature industry
- To change the rules of competition as deregulation and technological change trigger convergence across industries

However, unless each transaction is assessed for the unique value creation potential of the combination, it is unlikely to generate competitive advantage for the acquiring company. Operationally, this amounts to managers asking what the key resources of the target company are in each transaction and how they will generate value when combined with the resources of the acquirer.

 ## VALUATION

How do you value a targeted company?

In a merger, we have to value the targeted company. As a starting point in valuation, the key financial data, including historical financial statements, forecasted financial statements, and tax returns, must be accumulated and analyzed. The assumptions of the valuation must be clearly spelled out.

The valuation approaches can be profit or asset oriented. Adjusted earnings can be capitalized at an appropriate multiple. Future adjusted cash earnings can be discounted by the rate of return that may be earned. Assets can be valued at fair market value, for example, through appraisal. Comparative values of similar companies can serve as benchmarks. Commercial software programs are available to do merger analysis.

How do you do a comparison with industry averages?

Valid comparisons can be made between the entity being valued and others in the same industry. Industry norms should be noted. General sources of comparative industry data found in financial advisory services include Standard & Poor's, Moody's, Value Line, Dun and Bradstreet, and Risk Management Association (RMA). Publicly available information on the targeted company includes the annual report; Securities and Exchange Commission (SEC) Forms 10-K, 10-Q, and 8-K; interim shareholder reports; proxy statements; press releases; and offering prospectuses.

In this chapter, we look at the various approaches to business valuation, including capitalization of earnings, capitalization of excess earnings, capitalization of cash flow, present value (discounted) of future cash flows, book value of net assets, tangible net worth, economic net worth, fair market value of net assets, gross revenue multiplier, profit margin/capitalization rate, price/earnings factor, comparative value of similar going concerns, and recent sales of stock. A combination of approaches can be used to obtain a representative value.

Capitalization of Earnings

How does capitalization of earnings influence value?

Primary consideration should be given to earnings when valuing a company. Historical earnings are typically the beginning point in applying a capitalization method to most business valuations. In general, historical earnings are a reliable predictor of future earnings. According to IRS Revenue Ruling 59-60, 1959-1, C.B. 237, the greatest emphasis should be placed on profitability when looking at a "going concern."

The value of the business may be based on its adjusted earnings times a multiplier for what the business sells for in the industry.

How is net income adjusted?

Net income should be adjusted for unusual and nonrecurring revenue and expense items. In adjusting net income of the business, we should add back the portion of the following items if they are personal rather than business related: auto expense, travel expense, and promotion and entertainment expense. Interest expense should also be added back to net income because it is the cost to borrow funds to buy assets or obtain working capital, and as such it is not relevant in determining the operating profit of the business. In the event lease payments arise from a low-cost lease, earnings should be adjusted to arrive at a fair rental charge. Extraordinary items (e.g., gain on the sale of land) should be removed from earnings to obtain typical earnings. If business assets are being depreciated at an accelerated rate, we should adjust net income upward. Therefore, the difference between the straight-line method and an accelerated depreciation method should be added back.

We should add back expenses for a closely held business solely for fringe benefits, health plan, pension plan, and life insurance. In addition, we should add back excessive salary representing the difference between the owner's salary and what a reasonable salary would be if we hired someone to do the job. All compensation should be considered including perks. Thus, if the owner gets a salary of $300,000 and a competent worker would get $80,000, the addback to net income is $220,000.

A tax provision (if none exists) should be made in arriving at the adjusted net income. The tax provision should be based on the current rates for each of the years.

If the company has a significant amount of investment income (e.g., dividend income, interest income, rental income from nonoperating property), net income may be reduced for the investment income with taxes being adjusted accordingly. We are concerned primarily with the income from operations.

What multiplier of earnings should be used?

The adjusted (restated) earnings results in a quality of earnings figure. The restated earnings are then multiplied by a multiplier to determine the value of a business. The multiplier should be higher for a low-risk business but generally not more than 10. The multiplier should be lower for a high-risk business, often only 1 or 2. An average multiplier, such as 5, is used when average risk exists. The price/earnings (P/E) ratio for a comparable company would be a good benchmark.

In valuation, some investment bankers use a multiple of the latest year's earnings or the annual rate of earnings of a current interim period (if representative). Example 36.1 is based on a multiplier of one-year profits.

Typically, a five-year average adjusted historical earnings figure is used. The five years' earnings up to the valuation date demonstrates past earning power. Note that for

Example 36.1

Adjusted net income for the current year	$ 400,000
× Multiplier	× 4
Valuation	$1,600,000

The adjusted net income is computed next.

Reported net income	$325,000
Adjustments:	
Personal expenses (e.g., promotion and entertainment)	50,000
Extraordinary or nonrecurring gain	(60,000)
Owners fringe benefits (e.g., pension plan)	40,000

(continued)

Excessive owners salary relative to a reasonable salary	30,000
Interest expense	20,000
Dividend revenue	(10,000)
Low-cost rental payments relative to a fair rental charge	(5,000)
Excess depreciation from using an accelerated method	10,000
Restated net income	$400,000

SEC registration and reporting purposes, a five-year period is used. Assuming a simple average is used, the computation is:

$$\text{Simple average adjusted earnings over 5 years} \times \text{Multiplier (Capitalizaton factor, P/E Ratio) of 5 (based on industry standard)} = \text{Value of business}$$

Example 36.2

Assume these net incomes:

2X12	$120,000
2X11	$100,000
2X10	$110,000
2X09	$ 90,000
2X08	$115,000

The multiplier is 4.

$$\text{Simple average earning} = \frac{\$120{,}000 + \$100{,}000 + \$110{,}000 + \$90{,}000 + \$115{,}000}{5}$$

$$= \frac{\$535{,}000}{5} = \$107{,}000$$

Simple average adjusted earnings over 5 years	$107,000
× Multiplier	× 4
Value of business	$428,000

Instead of a simple average, a weighted-average adjusted historical earnings figure is recommended. This gives more weight to the most recent years, which reflects higher current prices and recent business performance. If a five-year weighted average is used, the current year is given a weight of 5, while the first year is assigned a weight of 1. The multiplier is then applied to the weighted-average five-year adjusted earnings to get the value of the business.

Example 36.3

Year	Net Income (000s)	×	Weight	=	Total (000s)
2X12	$120	×	5	=	$ 600
2X11	100	×	4	=	400
2X10	110	×	3	=	330
2X09	90	×	2	=	180
2X08	115		1	=	115
			15		$1,625

Weighted-average 5-year earnings:

$$\$1,625,000/15 = \$108,333$$

Weighted-average 5-year earnings	$108,333
× Capitalization factor	× 4
Capitalization-of-earnings valuation	$433,332

The capitalization factor should be based on such factors as risk, stability of earnings, expected future earnings, and liquidity.

Has the owner of a closely held company failed to record cash sales to hide income? One way of determining this is to take purchases and add a typical profit markup in the industry. To verify reported profit, you can multiply the sales by the profit margin in the industry. If reported earnings is significantly below what the earnings should be based on the industry standard, there may be some hidden income.

Capitalization of Excess Earnings

How do we treat excess earnings?

The best way to treat excess earnings is to capitalize them by subtracting the normal rate of return on the weighted-average net tangible assets from the weighted-average adjusted earnings to determine excess earnings. It is suggested that the weighting be based on a five-year period. The excess earnings are then capitalized to determine the value of the intangibles (primarily goodwill). The addition of the value of the intangibles and the fair market value of the net tangible assets equals the total valuation. As per IRS Revenue Ruling 68-609, 1968-2 C.B. 327, the IRS recommends this method to value a business for tax purposes. The Revenue Ruling states that the return on average net tangible assets should be the percentage prevailing in the industry. If an industry percentage is not available, an 8 to 10 percent rate can be used. An 8 percent return rate is used for a business with a small risk factor and stable earnings, while a 10 percent rate of return is used for a business having a high risk factor and unstable earnings. The capitalization rate for excess earnings should be 15 percent (multiple of 6.67) for a business with a small risk factor and stable earnings; a 20 percent capitalization rate (multiple of 5) should be used for a business having a high risk factor and unstable earnings. Thus, the suggested return rate range is between 8 and 10 percent. The range for the capitalization rate may be between 15 and 20 percent.

Example 36.4

Weighted average net tangible assets are computed as:

Year	Amount (000s)	×	Weight	=	Total (000s)
2X08	$ 950	×	1		$ 950
2X09	1,000	×	2		2,000
2X10	1,200	×	3		3,600
2X11	1,400	×	4		5,600
2X12	1,500	×	5		7,500
			15		$19,650

Weighted average net tangible assets:

$$\$19,650,000/15 = \$1,310,000$$

Weighted average adjusted net income (5 years) – assumed	$ 600,000
Reasonable rate of return on weighted-average tangible net assets ($1,310,000 × 10%)	131,000
Excess earnings	$ 469,000
Capitalization rate (20%)	× 5
Value of intangibles	$2,345,000
Fair market value of net tangible assets	3,000,000
Capitalization-of-excess-earnings valuation	$5,345,000

Capitalization of Cash Flow

The adjusted cash earnings may be capitalized in arriving at a value for the firm. This method may be suitable for a service business.

Example 36.5

Adjusted cash earnings	$100,000
× Capitalization factor (25%)	× 4
Capitalization of cash flow	$400,000
Less liabilities assumed	50,000
Capitalization-of-cash-flow earnings	$350,000

Present Value of Future Cash Flows

What steps are involved in discounting?

A business is worth the discounted value of future cash earnings plus the discounted value of the expected selling price. Cash flow may be a more valid criterion of value than book profits because cash flow can be used for reinvestment. The growth rate in earnings may be based on past growth, future expectations, and the inflation rate. This approach is suggested in a third-party sale situation. We also have more confidence in it when the company is strong in the industry and has solid earnings growth. The problem with the method is that many estimates are required of future events. It probably should not be used when there has been an inconsistent trend in earnings. The steps are as follows:

Step 1. *Present value of cash earnings.* The earnings should be estimated over future years using an estimated growth rate. A common time frame for a cash flow valuation is 10 years. Once the future earnings are determined, they should be discounted. Future earnings may be based on the prior years' earnings and the current profit margin applied to sales. Cash earnings equals net income plus noncash expense adjustments such as depreciation.

Step 2. *Present value of sales price.* The present value of the expected selling price of the business at the date of sale should be determined. This residual value may be based on a multiple of earnings or cash flow, expected market value, and so on.

We can use as the discount rate the minimum acceptable return to the buyer for investing in the target company. The discount rate can take into account the usual return rate for money, inflation rate, a risk premium (based on such factors as local market conditions, earnings instability, and level of debt), and perhaps a premium for the illiquidity of the investment. If the risk-free interest rate is 7 percent (on government bonds), the risk premium is 8 percent, and the illiquidity premium is 7 percent, the capitalization (discount) rate will be 22 percent. The risk premium may range from 5 to 10 percent while the illiquidity premium may range from 5 to 15 percent. Some evaluators simply use as the discount rate the market interest rate of a low-risk asset investment.

Assuming one expects to hold the business for 14 years, and anticipates a 12 percent rate of return and constant earnings each year, the value of the business is based on:

For cash earnings: Present value of an ordinary annuity for $n = 14$, $i = 12\%$.
For selling price: Present value of $1 for $n = 14$, $i = 12\%$.

If earnings grow at an 8 percent rate, Table A.3 in the Appendix would be used to discount the annual earnings that would change each year.

Example 36.6

In 2X08, the net income is $200,000. Earnings are expected to grow at 8 percent per year. The discount rate is 10 percent. You estimate that the business is worth the discounted value of future earnings. The valuation equals:

Year	Net Income (Based on an 8% Growth Rate)	PV of $1 Factor (at 10% Interest)[a]	Present Value
2X08	$200,000	× 0.909	$181,800
2X09	208,000	× 0.826	171,808
2X10	224,600	× 0.751	168,675
2X11	242,568	× 0.683	165,674
2X12	261,973	× 0.621	162,685
Present Value of Future Earnings			$850,642

[a] See Table A.3 in the Appendix.

If the expected selling price at the end of year 2X12 is $600,000, the valuation of the business equals:

Present value of earnings	$850,642
Selling price in 2X12 $600,000 × 0.621	372,600
Valuation	$1,223,242

Operating Cash Flow

Some businesses may be valued at a multiple of operating cash flow. For example, radio and TV stations often sell for 8 to 12 times the operating cash flow.

Book Value

How do asset approaches work?

The business may be valued based on the book value of the net assets (assets less liabilities) at the most recent balance sheet date. This method is unrealistic because it does not take into account current values. It may be appropriate only when it is impossible to determine fair value of net assets and/or goodwill. However, book value may be adjusted for obvious understatements such as excess depreciation, last-in, first-out reserve, favorable leases, and low debt (e.g., low rental payments or unfunded pension and postretirement benefits). Unfortunately, it may be difficult for a buying company to have access to information regarding these adjustments.

Tangible Net Worth

The valuation of the company is its tangible net worth for the current year equal to:

> Stockholders' equity
> Less: Intangible assets
> Tangible net worth
> Economic net worth (adjusted book value)

Economic net worth equals:

> Fair market value of net assets
> Plus: Goodwill (as per agreement)
> Economic net worth

 ## FAIR MARKET VALUE OF NET ASSETS

The fair market value of the net tangible assets of the business may be determined through independent appraisal. To it, we add the value of the goodwill (if any). Note that goodwill applies to such aspects as reputation of the company, customer base, and high-quality merchandise. IRS Appeals and Review Memoranda Nos. 34 and 38 present formula methods to value goodwill. In the case of a small business, a business broker may be retained to do the appraisal of property, plant, and equipment. Business brokers are experienced because they put together the purchase of small businesses. According to Equitable Business Brokers, about 25 percent of businesses changing hands are sold through business brokers. Typically, the fair value of the net tangible assets (assets less liabilities) is higher than book value.

The general practice is to value inventory at a maximum value of cost. IRS Revenue Procedure 77-12 provides acceptable ways to allocate a lump-sum purchase price to inventories.

Unrecognized and unrecorded liabilities should be considered when determining the fair market value of net assets. For example, one company had both an unrecorded liability for liquidated damages for nonunion contracts of $3.1 million and an unrecorded liability for $4.9 million related to the estimated employer final withdrawal liability. As a result of unrecorded liabilities, the value of a business will be reduced further.

A tax liability may also exist that has not been recognized in the accounts. For example, the company's tax position may be adjusted by the IRS, which is currently auditing the tax return. This contingent liability should be considered in valuing the business.

Note

IRS Revenue Ruling 65-193 approves only those approaches where valuations can be determined separately for tangible and intangible assets. ▪

Similarly, unrecorded and undervalued assets, such as customer lists, patents, and licensing agreements, should be considered because they increase the value of the business.

Liquidation Value

Liquidation value is a conservative figure of value because it does not take into account the earning power of the business. Liquidation value is a floor price in negotiations. It is the estimated value of the company's assets, assuming their conversion into cash in a short time period. All liabilities and the costs of liquidating the business (e.g., appraisal fees, real estate fees, legal and accounting fees, recapture taxes) are subtracted from the total cash to obtain net liquidation value.

Liquidation value may be computed based on an orderly liquidation or a forced (rapid) liquidation. In the case of the latter, there will obviously be a lower value.

Replacement Value

What is replacement cost?

Replacement cost ("new") is the cost of duplicating from scratch the business's assets on an "as-if-new" basis. It typically will result in a higher figure than book value or fair market value of existing assets. Replacement cost provides a meaningful basis of comparison with other methods but should not be used as the acquisition value. A more accurate indicator of value is replacement cost adjusted for relevant depreciation and obsolescence.

Secured-Loan Value

What is the secured-loan value?

The secured-loan value reflects the borrowing power of the sellers' assets. Typically, banks will lend up to 90 percent of accounts receivable and 10 to 60 percent of the value of inventory, depending on how much represents finished goods, work in process, and raw materials. The least percentage amount will be work in process because of its greater realization risk and difficulty of sale. Turnover rates also are considered.

CAPITALIZATION OF REVENUE

How is revenue capitalized?

The value of the business may be determined by multiplying the revenue by the gross revenue multiplier common in the industry. The industry standard gross revenue

Example 36.7

If revenue is $14 million and the multiplier is 0.2, the valuation is:

$$\$14,000,000 \times 0.2 = \$2,800,000$$

multiplier is based on the average ratio of market price to sales prevalent in the industry. This approach may be used when earnings are questionable.

Similarly, insurance agencies often sell for about 150 percent of annual commissions.

Profit Margin/Capitalization Rate

The profit margin divided by the capitalization rate provides a multiplier, which is then applied to revenue. A multiplier of revenue that a company would sell at is the company's profit margin. The profit margin may be based on the industry average. The formula is:

$$\frac{\text{Profit margin}}{\text{Capitalization rate}} = \frac{\text{Net income/sales}}{\text{Capitalization rate}} = \text{Multiplier}$$

Example 36.8

Assume sales of $14 million, a profit margin of 5 percent, and a capitalization rate of 20 percent. The multiplier is 25 percent (5 percent/20 percent). The valuation is:

$$\text{Sales} \times 25\%$$
$$\$14,000,000 \times 25\% = \$3,500,000$$

The capitalization rate in earnings is the return demanded by investors. In arriving at a capitalization rate, the prime interest rate may be taken into account. The multiplier is what the buyer is willing to pay.

The IRS and the courts have considered recent sales as an important factor.

PRICE/EARNINGS RATIO

Can we use the price/earnings multiplier?

The value of a business may be based on the P/E factor applied to current (or expected) earnings per share. For publicly traded companies, the P/E ratio is known. Valuation for a privately held company is more difficult. Historical earnings must be adjusted for a closely held company to be consistent with the reported earnings of a public company. After suitable adjustments have been made, the average P/E ratio for the industry or for several comparable public companies is used to arrive at a value. Typically, a premium is added to the value estimate to incorporate uncertainty and additional risk and lack of marketability associated with private companies. A variation of the P/E method may also be used. Assuming an expected earnings growth rate of the seller and a desired return on investment (ROI), the acquirer determines an earnings multiple he or she would pay to achieve the ROI goal. Under this approach, the buyer determines the price he or she would be willing to pay instead of using a stock market–related price.

Example 36.9

Net income	$ 800,000
Outstanding shares	÷ 100,000
Earnings per share	$ 8
P/E ratio	× 10
Market price per share	$ 80
× Number of shares outstanding	× 100,000
Price/earnings valuation	$8,000,000

SIMILAR BUSINESSES

What are other businesses worth?

What would someone pay for this business? Reference may be made to the market price of similar publicly traded companies. Under this approach, you obtain the market prices of companies in the industry similar in nature to the one being examined. Recent sale prices of similar businesses may be used, and an average may be taken. Upward or downward adjustments to this average will be made depending on the particular circumstances of the company being valued.

There are two ways to arrive at an adjusted averaged value for a company based on comparable transactions. Under the equivalency adjustment method, you make an adjustment to each transaction before averaging based on such factors as size, profitability, earnings stability, and transactions structure. Transactions are adjusted downward if you deem a higher price was paid than would be appropriate for the target company, and vice versa. The average of the adjusted comparables approximates the estimated value of the target company.

With the simple averaging method, you determine a simple average of the comparable transactions, after excluding noncomparable cases, and adjust the target company's price insofar as it differs from the average features of the companies purchased in comparable transactions. The former approach is suggested where extensive data are available on the comparable transactions and where they differ substantially in their features. The latter approach is preferable where the comparable transactions are broadly similar or where many comparable transactions have occurred.

Although a perfect match is not possible, the companies should be reasonably similar (e.g., size, product, structure, geographic locations, diversity). The comparable transactions value will often be higher than the market value of the target's stock price. Several sources of industry information are Standard & Poor's, Dow Jones-Irwin, online

Example 36.10

A competing company has just been sold for $6 million. We believe the company is worth 90 percent of the competing business. Therefore, the valuation is $5.4 million.

information services (e.g., Compustat), and trade association reports. Extensive databases aid in the analysis of merger-market history.

 ## SALES OF STOCK

Can value be based on sales of stock?

The value of the business may be based on the outstanding shares times the market price of the stock. For an actively traded stock, the stock price provides an important benchmark. For a thinly traded stock, the stock price may not reflect an informed market consensus. Typically, the market price of the stock should be based on a discounted amount from the current market price since if all the shares are being sold, the market price per share may drop somewhat based on the demand/supply relationship. Furthermore, market value of stock is of use only in planning the actual strategy of acquiring a target company since the stock may be overvalued or undervalued relative to the worth of the target company to the acquirer.

 ## COMBINATION OF METHODS

The value of the business can be approximated by determining the average value of the results given by two or more methods.

Example 36.11

Assume that the fair market value of the net assets approach gives a value of $2.1 million while the capitalization of excess earnings method provides a value of $2.5 million. The value of the business would then be the average of these two methods, or $2,300,000 ([$2,100,000 + $2,500,000]/2).

Some courts have found a combination of methods supportable as long as greater weight is given to the earnings methods. The most weight should be placed on the earnings approaches and less on the asset approaches.

Example 36.12

Using the same information as the prior example, if a 2 weight was assigned to the earnings approach and a 1 weight was assigned to the fair market value of net assets method, the valuation would be:

Method	Amount	×	Weight	=	Total
Fair market value of net assets	$2,100,000	×	1		$2,100,000
Capitalization-of-excess earnings	2,500,000	×	2		5,000,000
			3		$7,100,000
					÷ 3
Valuation					$2,366,667

Accounting Adjustments

Material accounting adjustments should be made to the acquired company's figures to place them on a comparable basis to those of the acquirer. Adjustments should be made, where practical, for savings in administrative, technical, sales, plant, and clerical personnel costs resulting from the combination. These savings arise from the elimination of duplicate personnel, plant, office, and warehouse facilities. Savings in freight may result from the combination by shifting production to plants closer to markets.

SUCCESSFUL STRATEGY FOR MERGERS AND ACQUISITIONS

When a merger or acquisition fails, shareholder value is destroyed, and the productive resources in the target are destroyed or underused. CFOs can improve their prospects of success in five ways:

1. Establish a value range for the target that accounts for incomplete knowledge and guards against bias in making decisions
2. Undertake a transaction as a business process with such defined stages as target selection, valuation and negotiation, due diligence, implementation, and evaluation
3. Develop and retain skills and expertise in mergers and acquisitions
4. Be aware of the dangers of ignoring warning signs that emerge during negotiation
5. Understand when to walk away from a deal

As understanding of the processes increases, the success rates of these transactions should escalate.

CHAPTER THIRTY-SEVEN

Divestiture

THE DIVESTITURE OF business segments by corporations has become an accepted strategy for growth rather than diversification. Divestiture involves the partial or complete conversion, disposition, and reallocation of people, money, inventories, plants, equipment, and products. It is the process of eliminating a portion of the enterprise for subsequent use of the freed resources for some other purpose. A divestment may involve a manufacturing, marketing, research, or other business function.

WHY DIVEST?

A business segment may be subject to divestiture if:

- It does not produce an acceptable return on invested capital.
- It does not generate sufficient cash flow.
- It fits in with the overall corporate strategy.
- The worth of the pieces is greater than that of the whole.

Resource allocation becomes an important consideration in a diversified business. These resources include not only capital but also management talent. If management finds itself spending an excessive amount of time and energy on one segment of the corporation, that segment may be a candidate for divestiture. Then those resources can be redirected to the growing segments of the business. However, this operation also requires the attention of management.

What are the objectives and types of divestitures?

The usual objectives behind divestiture are to reposition the company in a market, raise cash, and reduce losses. The other alternatives to divestiture are liquidation and bankruptcy. There are four primary types of divestitures:

1. Sale of an operating unit to another firm
2. Sale of the managers of the unit being divested
3. Setting up the business to be divested as a separate corporation and then giving (or spinning off) its stock to the divesting firm's stockholders on a pro rata basis
4. Outright liquidation of assets

When the divestiture is in the form of a sale to another firm, it usually involves an entire division or unit and is generally for cash but sometimes for stock of the acquiring firm. In a managerial buyout, the division managers themselves purchase the division, often through a leveraged buyout (LBO), and reorganize it as a closely held firm. In a spinoff, the firm's existing stockholders are given new stock representing separate ownership in the company that was divested. The new company establishes its own board of directors and officers and operates as a separate entity. In a liquidation, the assets of the divested unit are sold off separately instead of as a whole.

What are the reasons for divestiture?

Prior to formulating a divestiture strategy and determining which segments should be divested, the reasons for divestiture need to be listed. The reasons given by management for divesting segments of their business include:

- Poor performance
- Changes in plans
- Excessive resource needs
- Operational constraints
- Source of funds
- Antitrust considerations

How do you determine what areas/units should be sold?

When trying to determine which areas or units of the company to sell, CFOs should follow these simple guidelines:

- The sum of a division's parts may be greater in value than the whole division.
- Simple components of a division may be sold more easily than the whole division itself.
- The disposal of a corporate division is a major marketing operation.
- Planning should include an evaluation from the viewpoint of the potential buyer.
- A spinoff should be considered if the division is large enough and may be potentially publicly traded.

In addition, the CFO must review existing operations and identify those divisions that do not relate to the primary focus of the company or do not meet internal financial and performance standards. The special strength of each division must also be considered. Does a division provide a unique service, have a special marketing, distribution system, or production facilities that may be of more value to another company? Also, the financial aspects must be considered. The historical and projected return on investment need to be calculated and tabulated for each division.

Using these guidelines and the information determined above, the CFO can focus on three topics: (1) the attractiveness and value to others versus the arguments for keeping the division; (2) what corrective action is needed to make the division a keeper; and (3) the current value of the division to the company. Only after considering all of these factors can a divestiture decision be made for a division.

How do you value and appraise divestiture?

Valuation of a division is not an exact science, and in the final analysis, the value of a division is in the eye of the purchaser. Here valuation methods will be broken down into asset valuation methods, those based on sales and income and those based on market comparisons. Although these methods vary in their applicability and depend on certain facts and circumstances, they can be used to determine a range of values for a division.

Methods of valuation or appraisal include: (1) asset valuation methods, (2) profitability methods, (3) market comparison methods, and (4) discounted cash flow methods.

ASSET VALUATION METHODS

Asset valuation methods are based on the asset value of a business segment. Four popular methods are described next.

1. *Adjusted net book value.* One of the most conservative methods of valuation is the adjusted net book value, because it determines the value based on historical (book) value and not on market value. This value can be further adjusted by adding to compensate for the shortage by adding in such items as favorable lease arrangements and other intangible items, including customer lists, patents, and goodwill.
2. *Replacement cost.* Another method is the replacement cost technique. It asks, "What would it cost to purchase the division's assets new?" This method will give a higher division value than the adjusted net book value method and is therefore good for adjusting the book value to account for new costs. This figure can also be used as a basis for determining the liquidation value of the division's assets. The most reasonable value comes from adjusting the replacement value for depreciation and obsolescence of equipment.
3. *Liquidation value.* The liquidation value is also a conservative estimate of a division's value since it does not consider the division's ongoing earning power. The liquidation value does provide the seller with a bottom-line figure as to how low the price can be. The liquidation value is determined by estimating the cash value of assets,

assuming that they are to be sold in a short period of time. All the liabilities, real and estimated, are then deducted from the cash that was raised to determine the net liquidation value. Liquidation value can be determined based on fire sale prices or on a longer term sales price. The fire sale value would be lower.

4. *Secured-loan value.* The secured-loan value technique is based on the borrowing power of the division's assets. Banks will usually lend up to 90 percent of the value of accounts receivable and anywhere from 10 to 60 percent on the value of inventory, depending on the quantity of the inventory in the conversion process.

PROFITABILITY METHODS

How are sales and income factors used?

Using sales and/or income figures as the basis for valuation can be made in two different ways.

1. *Price/earnings (P/E) ratios.* The P/E ratio for publicly held companies is known, and therefore valuation is made easy. The division's value can be determined by multiplying the P/E ratio by the expected earnings for the division. This will give a derived price that all suitors can readily understand. The earnings can be estimated from quarterly or annual reports published by the company. For privately held companies, however, it is difficult to determine a P/E ratio, as the stock of the company is not traded and the earnings are rarely disclosed. However, the earnings can be estimated, and an industry average P/E ratio can be used in the calculation to estimate the private company's sales value.

2. *Sales or earnings multiples.* Many rules of thumb can be used when estimating a division's value based on a multiple of sales or earnings. For example, insurance agencies sell for 200 percent of annual commissions; liquor stores sell for 10 times monthly sales. Another example would be radio stations selling for 8 times earnings or cash flow. These rules are fast and dirty, and may result in a completely erroneous estimate of a division's value. Most business brokers will know these rule of thumb values to assist the CFO in estimating the value of a division.

MARKET-BASED COMPARISONS

Every day that a public company is traded on the stock market, a new value is assigned to it by the traders. Thus, the stock price can be compared to equivalent companies, in terms of products, size of operations, and average P/E ratios. From these P/E ratios, an estimated sales price can be estimated, as described earlier.

In the case of private companies, it is difficult for buyers to determine the earnings of the company. However, they can compare the company to other companies that are publicly traded. Comparison to publicly traded companies is necessary as the sales price typically is disclosed in the sale or acquisition announcement.

DISCOUNTED CASH FLOW ANALYSIS

Another method of determining the value of a business segment is to use discounted cash flow (DCF) analysis. This method bases the value of the segment on the current value of its projected cash flow. In theory, this method should result in a division's value being equal to that determined by one of the P/E ratio calculations, since both reflect the current worth of the company's earnings. In actuality, DCF bases the value of the company on actual forecasted cash flows, whereas the stock market bases the stock price on other things, including the market's perception of the company and its potential cash flow.

The DCF method requires information on

- Forecasted actual cash flows
- Assumed terminal (residual) value of the division at the end of the forecast period (book value, zero, or a multiple of earnings are frequently used)
- Discount rate

Choosing the right discount rate is the key to the successful use of the DCF technique. It must take into account these factors:

- Purchaser's expected return on investment (ROI)
- Purchaser's assessment of risk
- Cost of capital
- Projected inflation rates
- Current interest rates

Whichever method of evaluation is chosen, it is wise to check that resulting value with at least one other method to see if it is a reasonable figure. We have to be careful of excessively high or low figures. It is also a good idea to determine the liquidation value of the company or division, for this will set a floor for negotiations.

Illustration: Discounted Cash Flow Analysis

The CFO will choose to divest a segment of the business if he or she perceives that the action will increase the wealth of the stockholders, as reflected in the price of the firm's stock. The price of the firm's stock will react favorably to a divestiture if the market perceives the new present value of the transaction to be positive.

Should a profitable business segment be retained and not divested, it would generate annual cash inflows for a particular or infinite number of years. DCF analysis involves a comparison of initial incoming cash flows resulting from the sale of a business unit with the present value of the forgone future cash inflows given up by the firm. The term *forgone future cash flows* refer to the cash flows that the business unit is anticipated to generate and will do so for the acquiring firm. The divesting firm gives up these cash inflows in exchange for the selling price of the business segment. For divestiture analysis to be of any value, the forgone future cash flow must be estimated accurately. The present value of these future inflows is found by discounting them at the firm's weighted average cost of capital, k.

Example 37.1

Exhibit 37.1 shows estimated cash inflows and outflows for a fictitious divestment candidate (FDC) over the next five years. The cash flows represent the CFO's best estimates of FDC's parent company, and he or she further believes that FDC will be able to be sold at its residual value of $58.7 million in five years. The firm's cost of capital is assumed to be known and is 15 percent.

EXHIBIT 37.1 FDC's Cash Flow Projections (in millions)

	1	2	3	4	5
Cash Inflows					
Net operating profit	$ 3.1	$ 3.6	$ 4.0	$ 5.1	$ 6.0
Depreciation	2.1	2.4	1.8	2.3	2.1
Residual value					58.7
Total	$ 5.2	$ 6.0	$ 5.8	$ 7.4	$ 66.8
Cash Outflows					
Capital expenditure	$ 1.7	$ 1.3	$ 0.8	$ 2.1	$ 1.7
Increase (decrease) in working capital	(6.3)	1.3	2.6	(0.5)	2.2
Total	$ (4.6)	$ 2.6	$ 3.4	$ 1.6	$ 3.9
Net cash inflow (NCF)	$ 9.8	$ 3.4	$ 2.4	$ 5.8	$ 62.9
PVIF (T3)[a]	× 0.8696	× 0.7561	× 0.6575	× 0.5718	× 0.4972
Net present value (NPV)	$ 8.5	$ 2.6	$ 1.6	$ 3.3	$ 31.3
Total NPV	$ 47.3				

[a] Present value of $1.00 at 15%. From Table A.3 in the Appendix.

The NPV of the future cash inflows of FDC is $47.3 million. If FDC were to be divested, the CFO of its parent company should only consider selling prices greater than this amount. This logic also assumes that the $47.3 million can be reinvested at a 15 percent rate of return.

Another way of looking at this valuing task makes use of the following equation for divestiture net present value (DNPV):

$$DNPV = P - \sum \frac{NCF_t}{(1+k)^t}$$

where

P = the selling price of the business unit
NCF_t = net cash flow in period t

$$DNPV = 50 - \frac{9.8}{1.15} + \frac{3.4}{(1.15)^2} + \frac{2.4}{(1.15)^3} + \frac{5.8}{(1.15)^4} + \frac{62.9}{(1.15)^5} = 50 - 47.3 = \$2.7 \text{ million}$$

From a financial point of view, this divestment is acceptable.

If the divestment candidate has an unlimited life, such as a division in a healthy industry, then cash flows must be forecasted to infinity. This task is made simple by treating the cash flows similarly to a constant growth stock and valuing accordingly. If the cash inflows are expected to remain constant (zero growth) to infinity, then the present value of the NCF can be determined in the same manner as for a preferred stock, or perpetuity. In this case, the DNPV will be:

$$DNPV = P - \frac{NCF}{k}$$

For future cash flows that are expected to grow at an after-tax rate of g, the present value of those flows can be found using the constant growth valuation model. In this case, the DNPV will be:

$$DNPV = P - \sum \frac{NCF_1}{k - g}$$

where
NCF_1 = expected NCF in the next period

A final situation often encountered when evaluating divestiture candidates is the case where the NCFs are expected to be uneven for a number of years followed by even growth. In this case, the DNPV can be found as:

$$DNPV = P - \frac{NCF_1}{1+k} + \frac{NCF_2}{(1+k)^2} + \ldots + \frac{NCF_{c-1}}{k-g} \times \frac{1}{1+k}$$

where
NCF_1 and NCF_2 = forgone cash flows in periods 1 and 2
c = first year in which constant growth applies

Firms should divest of assets only with positive DNPVs. Doing so will increase the value of the firm and subsequently the price of its stock. If two different candidates are mutually exclusive, the one with the highest DNPV should be divested since this will increase the value of the firm the most. If divestiture is forced by the government, for example, and the firm has a choice of candidates, all with negative DNPVs, it should divest the one whose DNPV is closest to zero, since this will reduce the value of the firm the least.

DIVESTITURE WITH UNCERTAINTY

Because of the difficulty in predicting the NCFs and also in knowing what kinds of prices will be offered for the divestment candidate, the divestment's NPV is normally uncertain.

For situations involving an unknown selling price (due to a lack of offers), the parent firm can either elect not to divest of the candidate or set its asking price such that the

DNPV will equal zero. This should be the minimum the parent is willing to accept. The firm can also look for other divestment candidates that offer promising DNPVs.

Adjusting for uncertain NCFs is much more difficult. Although there is no generally accepted method for accounting for this risk, a number of useful techniques borrowed from capital budgeting can be used here.

Risk-Adjusted Discount Rate

A risk-adjusted discount rate is one technique that can be used to account for the uncertainty of the expected NCFs. In the previous examples, the firm's weighted average cost of capital was used to discount the NCFs to their present value. This is an appropriate choice when the divestiture candidate is as risky as the firm itself. When it is more risky, a higher discount rate can be used for adjustment. This will reduce the present values of the cash flows and increase the DNPV. This is logical since a relatively risky divestment candidate with uncertain cash flows will be of less value to the firm, in present dollars. The added benefit of divesting such a candidate will be reflected in the increased DNPV. However, when the NCFs are more certain than those of the rest of the firm, the discount rate should be lowered. This lowers the DNPV and makes the divestiture less attractive. The first equation can be rewritten as:

$$DNPV = P - E\frac{NCF_t}{(1+k')^t}$$

where all terms are the same except for k', which is the adjusted rate to be used for discounting the cash flows. Using data from Exhibit 37.1 and assuming that the divestment candidate is less risky than the firm as a whole (lowering k from 0.15 to 0.14) shows:

$$DNPV = 50 - \frac{9.8}{1.14} + \frac{3.4}{(1.14)^2} + \frac{2.4}{(1.14)^3} + \frac{5.8}{(1.14)^4} + \frac{62.9}{(1.14)^5} = 50 - 48.9 = \$1.1 \text{ million}$$

Using a lower discount rate lessened the DNPV by $1.6 million ($2.7 million − $1.1 million). This is reasonable in that the attractiveness of a divestment candidate at a certain selling price will be lessened as the candidate is found to be less risky.

Sensitivity Analysis

Sensitivity analysis is another technique that can be used in making divestiture decisions. In sensitivity analysis, the parent company evaluates the effect that certain factors have on the NCFs. For example, a divestment candidate's NCFs might be largely influenced by the price of copper, the U.S. Navy defense budget, and upcoming union contract talks.

For these three influencing factors, a number of different scenarios, or forecasts, can be projected, each with its expected NCFs. For instance, the expected NCFs would be highest in the scenario where all three influencing factors are favorable. Having evaluated the NCFs and DNPVs for different scenarios, the parent firm has a better understanding of the range that the NCFs might fall in and also what factors influence them the most.

If the probability of the scenarios can be forecasted, statistical techniques can be used to give the probability of realizing a negative DNPV, the expected DNPV and the standard deviation, and coefficient of variation of DNPVs. This information would be very useful in making divestment decisions. It should be noted that the NCFs using sensitivity analysis are discounted at the firm's weighted average cost of capital.

Simulation

Simulation is a third technique used to account for the uncertainty of future cash flows. It is similar to but more sophisticated than the sensitivity analysis previously discussed. In simulation, the parent firm's CFO first identifies key factors that he or she believes are likely to influence the NCFs of a divestment candidate. Next the CFO creates a probability distribution describing the future outcome of each key factor. The CFO finally specifies the impact of each key variable on the NCFs and ultimately the DNPVs. The firm's cost of capital is again used to discount the NCFs. Computer programs are available to assist CFOs in the simulation analysis. After the data have been input and the program run, the computer will estimate NCFs and corresponding DNPVs over the whole range of probabilities. From this distribution, the CFO can determine the expected DNPV and the probability that the actual DNPV will be above or below some critical value. The uncertainty associated with the DNPV can also be determined, as measured by the dispersion of possible DNPV values. It is important to note that this technique is only as good as the input it receives from CFOs, and, even then, it cannot make a firm's divestment decision. It does, however, provide a comprehensive evaluation of the divestiture proposal.

CHAPTER THIRTY-EIGHT

Forecasting Corporate Financial Distress

THERE HAVE BEEN an increasing number of bankruptcies in recent years. Will your company be one? Will your major customers or suppliers go bankrupt? What warning signs exist, and what can be done to avoid corporate failure?

Bankruptcy is the final declaration of a company's inability to sustain current operations given current debt obligations. The majority of firms require loans and therefore increase their liabilities during their operations in order to expand, improve, or even just survive. Current debt in excess of assets is the most common factor in bankruptcy.

If you can recognize ahead of time that your company is developing financial distress, you can better protect yourself and your company. The CFO can reap significant rewards and benefits from a predictive model. For example, a predictive model is useful for:

- *Merger analysis.* The predictive model can help identify potential problems with a merger candidate.
- *Legal analysis.* Those investing or giving credit to your company may sue for losses incurred. The model can help in your company's defense.

CFOs have to try to build early warning systems to detect the likelihood of bankruptcy. Although financial ratio analysis is useful in predicting failure, it is limited because the methodology is basically univariate. Each ratio is examined in isolation, and the CFO must use professional judgment to determine whether a set of financial ratios are developing into a meaningful analysis.

In order to overcome the shortcomings of financial ratio analysis, mutually exclusive ratios are combined into groups to develop a meaningful predictive model. *Regression analysis* and *multiple discriminant analysis* (MDA) are two statistical techniques that have been used to predict the financial strength of a company.

PREDICTION MODELS

How can you use three different models?

Three predictive bankruptcy models are illustrated, with the aid of a spreadsheet program. They are the Z-score model, the degree of relative liquidity model, and the lambda index model.

The *Z-score model* evaluates a combination of several financial ratios to predict the likelihood of future bankruptcy. The model, developed by Edward Altman, uses multiple discriminant analysis to give a relative prediction of whether a firm will go bankrupt within five years. The *degree of relative liquidity model* evaluates a firm's ability to meet its short-term obligations. This model also uses discriminant analysis by combining several ratios to derive a percentage figure that indicates the firm's ability to meet short-term obligations. The lambda index model evaluates a firm's ability to generate or obtain cash on a short-term basis to meet current obligations and therefore predict solvency.

These models are outlined and described in detail below. Spreadsheet models have been developed to calculate the prediction of bankruptcy using data extracted from 10-K annual reports on file with the Securities and Exchange Commission (http://investing. money.msn.com/investments/sec-filings/?symbol=nav).

 Z-SCORE MODEL

What is the Z-score model?

Using a blend of the traditional financial ratios and multiple discriminant analysis, Altman developed a bankruptcy prediction model that produces a Z score as follows:

$$Z = 1.2 \times X1 + 1.4 \times X2 + 3.3 \times X3 + 0.6 \times X4 + 0.999 \times X5$$

where
X1 = Working capital/Total assets
X2 = Retained earnings/Total assets
X3 = Earnings before interest and taxes (EBIT)/Total assets
X4 = Market value of equity/Book value of debt
X5 = Sales/Total assets

Altman established these guidelines for classifying firms:

Z Score	Probability of Short-Term Illiquidity
1.8 or less	Very high
1.81 to 2.99	Not sure
3.0 or higher	Unlikely

The Z score is about 90 percent accurate in forecasting business failure one year in the future and about 80 percent accurate in forecasting it two years in the future. With the many important changes in reporting standards since the late 1960s, the

Z-score model is somewhat out of date. A second-generation model known as *zeta analysis* adjusts for these changes, primarily the capitalization of financial leases. The resulting zeta discriminant model is extremely accurate for up to five years before failure. This analysis is proprietary, so the exact weights for the model's seven variables cannot be specified here. The new study resulted in these variables explaining corporate failure:

X1 = Return on assets. Earnings before interest and taxes to total assets.
X2 = Stability of earnings. Measure by the "normalized measure of the standard error of estimate around a 10-year trend in X1."
X3 = Debt service. Earnings before interest and taxes to total interest payments.
X4 = Cumulative profitability. Retained earnings to total assets.
X5 = Liquidity. Current assets to current liabilities.
X6 = Capitalization. Equity to total capital.
X7 = Size measured by the firm's total assets.

APPLICATIONS

Two companies—Navistar International, which continues to struggle in the heavy and medium truck industry, and Best Products, Inc., which declared bankruptcy in January 1991—have been selected for our study. Financial data have been collected for the period 1979 to 1990 for Best and for the period 1981 to 2010 for Navistar.

Navistar International (formerly International Harvester), the maker of heavy-duty trucks, diesel engines, and school buses, continues to struggle. Exhibit 38.1 shows the 30-year financial history and the Z scores of Navistar. Exhibit 38.2 presents the corresponding graph.

Exhibit 38.2 shows that Navistar International performed at the edge of the ignorance zone ("unsure area"), for the year 1981. Since 1982, however, the company started signaling a sign of failure. However, by selling stock and assets, the firm managed to survive. After 1985, the company showed an improvement in its Z scores, although the firm continually scored on the danger zone. Note that the 1991 to 2010 Z scores were in the high-probability range of <1.81, except for the year 1999.

Best Products, Inc. has had a Z score in the 2.44 to 2.98 range from 1984 to 1988. The strong decline in 1989 may have correctly indicated the pending bankruptcy of Best in January 1991. (See Exhibits 38.3 and 38.4.)

How does the degree of relative liquidity model work?

The degree of relative liquidity (DRL) has been proposed as an alternative method for measuring the liquidity of a small firm and can have significant applications for larger companies. It has been compared to the two common liquidity ratios, the current and acid-test (or quick) ratios, which are often used to evaluate the liquidity of a firm. However, under certain circumstances these two ratios can provide incomplete and often misleading indications of a firm's ability to meet its short-term obligations and may be opposite to the trend at hand. A logical approach to evaluating several liquidity

EXHIBIT 38.1 Navistar International—NAV (New York Stock Exchange) Z Score—Prediction of Financial Distress

	Balance Sheet				Income Statement				Stock Data	Calculations						Misc Graph Value	
Year	Current Assets (CA)	Total Assets (TA)	Current Liabilities (CL)	Total Liablity (TL)	Retained Earnings (RE)	Working Capital (WC)	SALES	EBIT	Market Value or Net worth (MKT-NW)	WC/ TA (X1)	RE/ TA (X2)	EBIT/ TA (X3)	MKT-NW/ TL (X4)	SALES/ TA (X5)	Z Score	TOP GRAY	BOTTOM GRAY
1981	2672	5346	1808	3864	600	864	7018	-16	376	0.16	0.11	-0.00	0.10	1.31	1.71	2.99	1.81
1982	1656	3699	1135	3665	-1078	521	4322	-1274	151	0.14	-0.29	-0.34	0.04	1.17	-0.18	2.99	1.81
1983	1388	3362	1367	3119	-1487	21	3600	-231	835	0.01	-0.44	-0.07	0.27	1.07	0.39	2.99	1.81
1984	1412	3249	1257	2947	-1537	155	4861	120	575	0.05	-0.47	0.04	0.20	1.50	1.13	2.99	1.81
1985	1101	2406	988	2364	-1894	113	3508	247	570	0.05	-0.79	0.10	0.24	1.46	0.89	2.99	1.81
1986	698	1925	797	1809	-1889	-99	3357	163	441	-0.05	-0.98	0.08	0.24	1.74	0.73	2.99	1.81
1987	785	1902	836	1259	-1743	-51	3530	219	1011	-0.03	-0.92	0.12	0.80	1.86	1.40	2.99	1.81
1988	1280	4037	1126	1580	150	154	4082	451	1016	0.04	0.04	0.11	0.64	1.01	1.86	2.99	1.81
1989	986	3609	761	1257	175	225	4241	303	1269	0.06	0.05	0.08	1.01	1.18	2.20	2.99	1.81
1990	2663	3795	1579	2980	81	1084	3854	111	563	0.29	0.02	0.03	0.19	1.02	1.60	2.99	1.81
1991	2286	3443	1145	2866	332	1141	3259	232	667	0.33	0.10	0.07	0.23	0.95	1.84	2.99	1.81
1992	2472	3627	1152	3289	93	1320	3875	-145	572	0.36	0.03	-0.04	0.17	1.07	1.51	2.99	1.81
1993	2672	5060	1338	4285	-1588	1334	4696	-441	1765	0.26	-0.31	-0.09	0.41	0.93	0.76	2.99	1.81
1994	2870	5056	1810	4239	-1538	1060	5337	233	1469	0.21	-0.30	0.05	0.35	1.06	1.24	2.99	1.81
1995	3310	5566	1111	4696	-1478	2199	6342	349	966	0.40	-0.27	0.06	0.21	1.14	1.57	2.99	1.81
1996	2999	5326	820	4410	-1431	2179	5754	188	738	0.41	-0.27	0.04	0.17	1.08	1.41	2.99	1.81
1997	3203	5516	2416	4496	-1301	787	6371	316	1374	0.14	-0.24	0.06	0.31	1.16	1.37	2.99	1.81
1998	3715	6178	3395	5409	-1160	320	7885	515	1995	0.05	-0.19	0.08	0.37	1.28	1.57	2.99	1.81
1999	3203	5516	2416	4496	-1301	787	8642	726	2494	0.14	-0.24	0.13	0.55	1.57	2.17	2.99	1.81
2000	2374	6851	2315	5409	-143	59	8451	370	2257	0.01	-0.02	0.05	0.42	1.23	1.64	2.99	1.81
2001	2778	7164	2273	6037	-170	505	6739	162	2139	0.07	-0.02	0.02	0.35	0.94	1.28	2.99	1.81
2002	2607	6957	2407	6706	-721	200	7021	-85	1867	0.03	-0.10	-0.01	0.28	1.01	1.02	2.99	1.81
2003	2419	6929	2272	6637	-883	147	7585	91	2965	0.02	-0.13	0.01	0.45	1.09	1.25	2.99	1.81
2004	3167	7592	3250	7061	-604	-83	9724	438	2872	-0.01	-0.08	0.06	0.41	1.28	1.59	2.99	1.81
2005	4852	10786	4688	12485	-2699	164	12124	453	1991	0.02	-0.25	0.04	0.16	1.12	1.03	2.99	1.81
2006	6368	12830	5048	13944	-2399	1320	14200	826	2245	0.10	-0.19	0.06	0.16	1.11	1.28	2.99	1.81
2007	5445	11448	3991	12182	-2519	1454	12295	429	3185	0.13	-0.22	0.04	0.26	1.07	1.20	2.99	1.81
2008	5535	10390	3875	11742	-2392	1660	14724	660	2425	0.16	-0.23	0.06	0.21	1.42	1.62	2.99	1.81
2009	5748	10028	4185	11702	-2101	1563	11569	610	2163	0.16	-0.21	0.06	0.18	1.15	1.36	2.99	1.81
2010	5835	9730	3589	10654	-1878	2246	12145	543	3632	0.23	-0.19	0.06	0.34	1.25	1.64	2.99	1.81

Note: (1) To calculate "Z" score for private firms, enter Net Worth in the MKT-NW column. (For public-held companies, enter Markey Value of equity).
(2) EBIT = Earnings before Interest and Taxes

EXHIBIT 38.2 Z-Score Graph (Navistar)

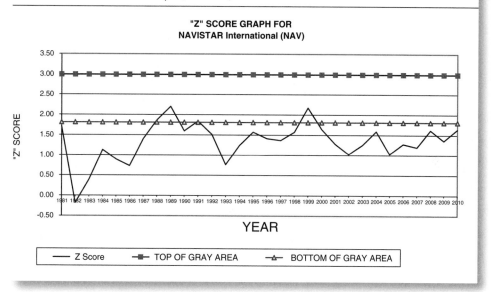

EXHIBIT 38.3 Best Products, Inc., Z-Score Data

				Balance Sheet			
Year	Current Assets (CA)	Total Assets (TA)	Current Liability (CL)	Total Liability (TL)	Retained Earnings (RE)	Net Worth (NW)	Working Capital (WC)
1984	745228	1202138	468590	787135	186486	415003	276638
1985	723684	1178424	443752	759278	193568	419146	279932
1986	840686	1331975	529690	916579	189306	415396	310996
1987	816853	1265637	400403	878479	160455	387158	416450
1988	811314	1239860	426065	836956	190960	402904	385249
1989	877937	1735595	738837	1646302	39293	89293	139100
1990	583773	1438208	412732	1366974	−14516	71234	171041

Income Statement	Stock Data		Calculations				Misc. Graph Values		
Sales	EBIT	Market Value (MKT)	WC/TA	RE/TA	EBIT/TA	MKT/ TA	SALES/ TA	Z Score	TOP GRAY	BOTTOM GRAY	Year
2081328	106952	319048	0.2301	0.1551	0.0890	0.4053	1.7314	2.76	2.99	1.81	1984
2252656	66705	407604	0.2375	0.1643	0.0566	0.5368	1.9116	2.93	2.99	1.81	1985
2234768	47271	253041	0.2335	0.1421	0.0355	0.2761	1.6778	2.44	2.99	1.81	1986
2142118	25372	202988	0.3290	0.1268	0.0200	0.2311	1.6925	2.47	2.99	1.81	1987
2066589	93226	672300	0.3107	0.1540	0.0752	0.8033	1.6668	2.98	2.99	1.81	1988
809457	96440	672300	0.0801	0.0226	0.0556	0.4084	0.4664	1.02	2.99	1.81	1989
2094570	73512	672300	0.1189	−0.0101	0.0511	0.4918	1.4564	2.05	2.99	1.81	1990

EXHIBIT 38.4 Z Score

measures simultaneously is to consider how appropriately each measure responds to changes relative to direction and degree of sensitivity. For example, an obsolete or slow-moving inventory and uncollectable accounts receivable may distort the current ratio. Uncollectible receivables and the exclusion of inventories can provide an incomplete picture for acid-test ratios.

The DRL represents the percentage of a firm's cash expenditure requirements that could be secured from beginning working capital and from cash generated through the normal operating process. An emphasis is placed on the availability of cash sources relative to cash needs, omitting sources and uses of cash such as:

- Capital expenditures and sale of fixed assets
- Sale and extinguishment of capital stock
- Receipt and repayment of long-term borrowings
- Investments and liquidations in marketable securities and bonds

The DRL is calculated by dividing the total cash potential by the expected cash expenditures. In equation form:

$$DRL = \frac{TCP}{E} \text{ or } \frac{WC + (OT \times SV)}{NSV - NI + NON + WCC}$$

where
TCP = Total cash potential
E = Cash expenditures for normal operations
WC = Beginning working capital (Beginning current assets – Beginning current liabilities)

OT = Operating turnover, or Sales/(Accounts receivable + Inventory × Sales/
    Cost of sales)
SVI = Sales value of inventory (Inventory at cost × Sales/Cost of sales)
NSV = Net sales values
NI = Net income
NON = Noncash expenditures (such as depreciation and amortization)
WCC = Change in working capital

If the DRL ratio is greater than 1.00 (or 100 percent), the firm can meet its current obligations for the period and have some net working capital available at the end of the period. If the DRL is less than 1.00, the firm should seek outside working capital financing before the end of the period.

The DRL can be derived by dividing the total cash potential by expected cash expenditures in the operating period. The TCP is the sum of initial cash potential and the cash potential from normal operations. The initial cash potential is reflected in the beginning working capital, assuming reported values can be realized in cash. The cash potential from operations can be determined by multiplying the operating turnover rate by the sales of value of existing finished goods inventory. The operating turnover rate reflects the number of times the sales value of finished goods inventory (at retail) and accounts receivables (net of uncollectables) is converted into cash in an operating period. The sales value of finished goods inventory is the adjustment of inventory at cost to retail value.

Application

Best Products, Inc., has had a DRL that has remained above 1.000 since 1985, peaking at 1.194 in 1987. (See Exhibits 38.5 and 38.6.) However, its DRL has been dropping since 1987 and took a significant plunge in 1990 down to 1.039. Although that DRL is above 1.000, the significant drop may have indicated a worsening situation for Best and predicted its January 1991 bankruptcy.

Based on this case, the DRL appears to have shown that the change in relative liquidity is more relevant than the absolute measure in predicting corporate bankruptcy.

What is the lambda index?

The *lambda index* is a ratio that focuses on two relevant components of liquidity—short-term cash balances and available credit—to gauge the probability that a firm will become insolvent. The index measures the probability of a company going bankrupt, and it includes the key aspect of uncertainty in cash flow measurement by utilizing a sample standard deviation. In consequence, it can be used like a z value from the standard normal distribution table.

For a given period, lambda is the sum of a company's initial liquid reserve and net flow of funds divided by the uncertainty associated with the flows:

$$\frac{\text{Initial liquid reserve} + \text{Total anticipated net cash flow during analysis horizon}}{\text{Uncertainty about net cash flow during analysis horizon}}$$

EXHIBIT 38.5 Best Products, Inc., DRL Data

	Balance Sheet						**Income Statement**			
Year	Accounts. Receivable	Inventory	Current Assets	Current Liability	Ending WC	Beginning WC	NSV	Cost of Sales	Net Income	Noncash expenses
1985	46746	658880	723684	443752	279932	276638	2252656	1692568	13609	65764
1986	45050	757051	840686	529690	310996	279932	2234768	1685198	2223	67341
1987	29670	649162	816853	400403	416450	310996	2142118	1592984	−25593	66647
1988	28571	670236	811314	426065	385249	416450	2066589	1499641	30527	38544
1989	32614	579651	877937	738837	139100	385249	809457	575467	39297	13216
1990	32213	509617	583773	412732	171041	139100	2094570	1529598	−53809	56008

	Calculations					**Graph Values**	
Operating Turnover	Sales Value of Inventory	Operations Cash Potential	Change Working Capital	Total Cash Potential	Expenditures	Degree of Relative Liquidity	Base
2.4	876910	2138650	3294	2415288	2169989	1.113	1.000
2.1	1003937	2138793	31064	2418725	2134140	1.133	1.000
2.4	872941	2071704	105454	2382700	1995610	1.194	1.000
2.2	923623	2004580	−31201	2421030	2028719	1.193	1.000
1.0	815342	778324	−246149	1163573	1003093	1.160	1.000
2.9	697849	2002150	31941	2141250	2060430	1.039	1.000

EXHIBIT 38.6 DRL Graph

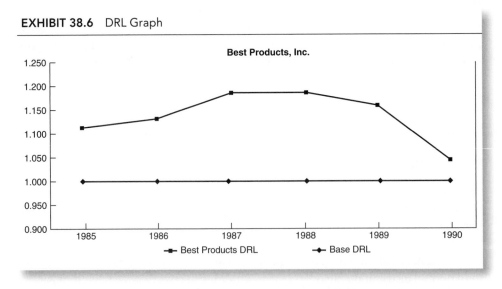

Unused lines of credit, short-term investments, and cash balances make up the initial liquid reserve. Net cash flow is the balance of cash receipts less cash outlays. The uncertainty is based on the standard deviation of net cash flow. In order to calculate and utilize the lambda index, a cash forecast should be used.

A worksheet can be prepared to contain 11 line items in the following order from top to bottom:

1. Short-term line of credit
2. Beginning liquid assets
3. Adjustments
4. Initial liquid reserve
5. Total sources of funds
6. Total uses of funds
7. Ending liquid assets
8. Ending liquid reserve
9. Standard deviation
10. Lambda index
11. Additional cash required to maintain a lambda of 3

A firm's short-term line of credit may not change during the course of the forecast (i.e., one year), which simplifies calculations. Liquid assets, by definition, include marketable securities and cash at the start of the forecast summary. By having an adjustments line item, you can see the result of decreasing or increasing the cash level. The initial liquid reserve is the total short-term line of credit with any adjustments. The total sources and uses of funds are forecasts by company management, resulting in a positive or negative net cash flow. The lambda value should rise if a firm's short-term line of credit does not change and it has a positive net cash flow. Ending liquid assets is the sum of three values: beginning liquid assets, adjustments, and net cash flow. Ending liquid reserve is the sum of two values: short-term line of credit and ending liquid assets. The standard deviation is drawn from the net cash flows from period to period. Next, the lambda index is calculated by dividing the ending liquid reserve by the standard deviation.

And finally, the last line item is additional cash needed to hold a lambda of 3. A negative number here indicates a lambda value of greater than 3 and, hence, a safer firm financially. A high negative value here, assuming that management is confident of its forecasts, may point out that those funds could be better utilized somewhere else.

Once an index value has been determined using the equation, the pertinent odds can be found by referencing a standard normal distribution table (see Exhibit 38.7). For example, a lambda of 2.33 has a value of .9901 from the table, which says that there is a 99 percent chance that problems will not occur and a 1 percent chance that they will.

Generally, a firm with a lambda value of 9 or higher is financially healthy, and firms with a lambda of 15 or more are considered very safe. A lambda value of 3 translates to 1 chance in 1,000 that necessary cash outlays will exceed available cash on hand. A lambda value of 3.9 puts the probability at 1 in 20,000. A low lambda of 1.64 is equivalent to a 1 in 20 chance of required disbursements exceeding available cash on hand. A worksheet that keeps a running tally of lambda shows how changes in the financial picture affect future cash balances.

There are a number of positive aspects to using the lambda index. The lambda index focuses on the key factors of liquidity, available unused credit and cash flows, which by contrast are ignored by standard cash forecasts. Furthermore, by including

EXHIBIT 38.7   Standard Normal Distribution Table

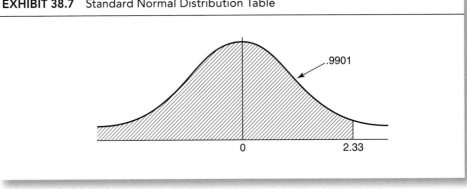

the standard deviation of cash flows, lambda penalizes irregular cash flows. The result of higher changes in cash flows would be a lower lambda.

A drawback to lambda, however, is the fact that it is significantly tied to revenue forecasts, which at times can be suspect depending on the time horizon and the industry involved. A strong lambda does not carry much weight if a firm is not confident about its forecast.

Application

Best Product's lambda index was a low of 2.39 in 1986 and a high of 4.52 in 1989. Its lambda index also dropped in 1990, reaching a level of 0.80. This is not surprising, since in January of 1991, Best filed for bankruptcy protection. (See Exhibits 38.8 and 38.9.)

Exhibit 38.10 summarizes guidelines for classifying firms under the three models.

A word of caution: Different people may use the Z score in varying ways. The Z score offers an excellent measure of the probability of a firm's insolvency, but, like any tool, it must used be with care and skill. The Z score should be studied over a number of years and should not be the sole basis of evaluation.

The Z score can also be used to compare the stability of different firms. Care should be exercised when the Z score is used for this purpose. The firms must be in the same market offering very similar, if not the same, products. In addition, the measure must be taken across the same period of years. These similarities are requirements in order to eliminate external environmental factors that would be reflected in the score.

The DRL is a more comprehensive measure of liquidity than the current ratio or the acid-test ratio. However, like those ratios, the DRL is a relative measure and should be used only in relation to either the firm's own historical DRL or to those of other businesses. Since the DRL does not incorporate the timing and variances in cash flows, comparing the DRL of two dissimilar firms is hazardous. It is important to note that the DRL does correctly identify an improved or deteriorated liquidity position; however, it does not suggest explicit causes of change. The DRL provides a basis from which to pursue an analysis and interpretation of those causes of change because the derivation of the DRL requires input for all factors that are relevant to liquidity position.

EXHIBIT 38.8 Best Products, Inc. Lambda Index

Year	1985	1986	1987	1988	1989	1990
Short-term line of credit	$100,000	$100,000	$100,000	$100,000	$100,000	$100,000
Beginning liquid assets	62,933	4,915	15,126	103,197	110,243	253,278
Adjustments						
Initial liquid reserve	162,933	10,4915	115,126	203,197	210,243	353,278
Total sources of funds	−58,018	10,211	88,071	7,046	143,035	−244,843
Total uses of funds						
Net cash flow	−58,018	10,211	88,071	7,046	143,035	−244,843
Ending liquid assets, short-term debt, and adjustments (net)	4,915	15,126	103,197	110,243	253,278	8,435
Ending liquid reserve	104,915	115,126	203,197	210,243	353,278	108,435
Standard deviation	NA	48,245	73,097	59,769	78,245	135,047
Calculated lambda index	NA	2.39	2.78	3.52	4.52	0.80
Additional cash required (remaining) to maintain lambda of 3.0	NA	29,610	16,095	−30,936	−118,542	296,706
Very safe		15.00	15.00	15.00	15.00	15.00
Healthy		9.00	9.00	9.00	9.00	9.00
Slight—1 in 20,000		3.90	3.90	3.90	3.90	3.90
Low—1 in 20		1.64	1.64	1.64	1.64	1.64

EXHIBIT 38.9 Lambda Index

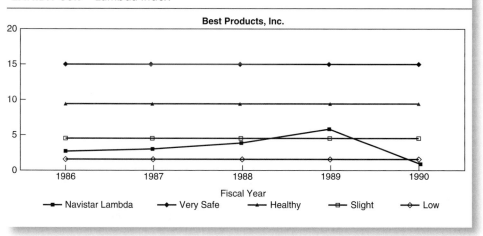

EXHIBIT 38.10 Classifying Guidelines under the Three Models

Model	Guidelines
Z-score Model	
Z Score	**Probability of Short-Term Illiquidity**
1.8 or less	Very high
1.81 to 2.99	Not sure
3.0 or higher	Unlikely
Degree of Relative Liquidity (DRL) Model	
DRL Score	**Probability of Short-Term Illiquidity**
Less than 1.00	Very high
Higher than 1.00	Unlikely
Lambda Index	
Lambda Score	**Probability of Short-Term Illiquidity**
1.64	1 in 20
3.90	1 in 20,000
9.00 or higher	Unlikely

As with DRL, the lambda index is a method for gauging a firm's liquidity, but you should consider a firm's historical background and always use common sense in evaluating any calculated value. A weak point of this model is that in order to calculate the index, forecasted figures must be used, making the final lambda value somewhat suspect in some cases.

39

Failure and Reorganization

W HEN A COMPANY fails, it can be either reorganized or dissolved. Business failure can occur in a number of ways, including a poor rate of return, technical insolvency, or bankruptcy.

 BUSINESS FAILURE

According to law, failure of a company can be technical insolvency, bankruptcy, or deficient rate of return. Creditors have recourse against the company's assets. Some reasons for business failure include poor management, lawsuit, overexpansion, an economic downturn affecting the company and/or industry, and catastrophe. The types of business failure are defined next.

- *Technical insolvency. Technical insolvency* means that the company cannot satisfy current obligations when due even if total assets exceed total liabilities.
- *Bankruptcy.* In bankruptcy, liabilities exceed the fair market value of assets. There is a negative real net worth.
- *Deficient rate of return.* A company may fail if its rate of return is negative or very low. If operating losses exist, the company may not be able to pay its debt. A negative return will cause a decline in the market price of stock. If a company's return is less than its cost of capital, it is losing money. However, a poor return in and of itself does not constitute legal evidence of failure.

How does a voluntary settlement work?

By voluntarily settling out of court with creditors, the company saves the costs associated with bankruptcy. The settlement allows the company either to continue or to be liquidated and is initiated to enable the debtor firm to recover some of its investment.

A creditor committee may opt to allow the business to operate if it is expected that the company will recover. Creditors may also keep doing business with the firm. In sustaining the company's existence, there may be:

- An extension
- A composition
- Creditor control
- Integration of each of the above

What is an extension?

In an *extension*, creditors will receive the amounts owed to them but over an extended time period. Purchases are made with cash. Creditors may agree not only to extend the payment date but also to subordinate their claims to current debt for suppliers giving credit in the extension period. The creditors are hopeful that the debtor will be able to resolve some of its problems.

The creditor committee may insist on certain controls, such as legal control over the company's assets or common stock, obtaining collateral, and approving all cash payments.

If certain creditors dissent to the agreement, they may be paid off to prevent them from declaring the firm bankrupt.

How does a composition come about?

In a *composition*, a voluntary reduction of the balance the debtor owes the creditor is made. The creditor receives a percentage of the obligation in full satisfaction of the debt. The arrangement allows the debtor to remain in business. The creditor may work with the debtor in resolving the company's financial problems, since a stable customer may ensue. The advantages of a composition are the elimination of court costs and the stigma of a bankrupt company.

If there are dissenting stockholders, they may be paid in full, or they may be permitted to recover a higher percentage so that they do not force the business to close.

An extension or composition is feasible if the creditors expect that the debtor will recover.

What is creditor control?

A committee of creditors may take control of the company if they are not satisfied with management. They will operate the business until they are paid. Once paid, the creditors may recommend that new management replace the old before further credit is granted.

How does integration work?

In an *integration*, the company and its creditors negotiate a plan involving a combination of extension, composition, and creditor control. For example, the agreement may stipulate a 20 percent cash payment of the balance owed, plus five future payments of 10 percent each, typically in notes. Therefore, the total payment is 70 percent.

The advantages of negotiated settlements are:

- They are easier to implement and less formal than bankruptcy proceedings.
- They cost less, especially in attorney fees.

The disadvantages of negotiated settlements are:

- If the troubled debtor continues to control its affairs, there may be a further decline in asset values. However, creditor controls can provide some protection.
- Unrealistic small creditors may drain the negotiating process.

REORGANIZATION

What is involved in a reorganization?

If a voluntary settlement does not occur, the company may be placed into bankruptcy by its creditors. The bankruptcy proceeding may either reorganize or liquidate the business.

Bankruptcy occurs when the company is unable to pay its bills or when liabilities exceed the fair market value of its assets. In such a situation, legal bankruptcy may be declared. A company may file for reorganization under which it will formulate a plan for continued existence.

Chapter 7 of the Bankruptcy Reform Act of 1978 outlines the procedures in liquidation. This chapter applies when reorganization is not feasible. Chapter 11 provides the steps of reorganizing a failed business.

The two types of reorganization petitions are:

1. *Voluntary.* The company requests its own reorganization. It does not have to be insolvent to file for it.
2. *Involuntary.* Creditors file for an involuntary reorganization of the company. An involuntary petition must set forth either that the debtor firm is not paying debts when due or that a creditor or another party has taken custody or other control over the debtor's assets. In general, most of the creditors or claims must support the petition.

The five steps in a reorganization are:

1. A reorganization petition is filed under Chapter 11 in court.
2. A judge approves the petition and either appoints a trustee or permits the creditors to elect one to handle the sale of the assets.
3. The trustee specifies a fair plan of reorganization to the court.
4. The plan is given to the creditors and stockholders to approve.
5. The debtor pays the expenses associated with the reorganization proceedings.

The trustee in a reorganization values the business, recapitalizes the company, and exchanges outstanding debts for new securities.

What is involved in valuing the company?

In valuing the business, the trustee estimates its liquidation value and compares it to its value as a going concern. Liquidation is suggested when the liquidation value exceeds the continuity value. If the company is more valuable when operating, reorganization is justified. The value of the reorganized business must take into account expected future earnings. The going-concern value represents the discounted value of future earnings.

Example 39.1

A company's petition for reorganization was filed under Chapter 11. The trustee computed the firm's liquidation value net of expenses as $4.5 million. The trustee estimated that the reorganized business will throw off $530,000 in annual earnings. The cost of capital is 10 percent. Assuming the earnings continue indefinitely, the value of the business as a going concern is:

$$\$530,000/0.10 = \$5,300,000$$

Since the company's value as a going concern ($5.3 million) exceeds its liquidation value ($4.5 million), reorganization is recommended.

What is recapitalization about?

If the trustee recommends reorganization, a plan must be drawn up. The obligations may be extended, or equity securities may be issued in substitution of the debt. Income bonds may be given for the debentures. Income bonds pay interest only if the company has a profit. Recapitalization is the process of exchanging liabilities for other types of liabilities or equity securities. The purpose of recapitalization is to have a mixture of debt and equity that will permit the company to pay its debts and provide a reasonable profit for the owners.

Example 39.2

The current capital structure of Y Corporation is:

Debentures	$1,500,000
Collateral bonds	3,000,000
Preferred stock	800,000
Common stock	2,500,000
Total	$7,800,000

There exists high financial leverage:

$$\frac{\text{Debt}}{\text{Equity}} = \frac{\$4,500,000}{\$3,300,000} = 1.36$$

Assuming the company is deemed to be worth $5 million as a going concern, the trustee can develop a less leveraged capital structure having a total capital of $5 million as:

Debentures	$1,000,000
Collateral bonds	1,000,000
Income bonds	1,500,000
Preferred stock	500,000
Common stock	1,000,000
Total	$5,000,000

The income bond of $1.5 million is similar to equity in appraising financial leverage, since interest is not paid unless there is income. The new debt/equity ratio is safer:

$$\frac{\text{Debt} + \text{Collateral bonds}}{\text{Incomebonds} + \text{Preferred stock} + \text{Common stock}} = \frac{\$2,000,000}{\$3,000,000} = 0.67$$

What is the procedure for exchanging obligations?

In exchanging obligations to derive an optimal capital structure, priorities are followed. Senior claims come before junior ones. Senior debt holders receive a claim on new capital equal to their previous claims. The last priority goes to common stockholders in receiving new securities. A debt holder usually receives a combination of different securities. Preferred and common stockholders may receive nothing. Typically, they retain some small ownership. After the exchange, the debt holders may become the company's new owners.

What is liquidation due to bankruptcy?

When a company becomes bankrupt, it may be liquidated under Chapter 7 of the Bankruptcy Reform Act of 1978. The major elements of liquidation are legal considerations, claim priority, and dissolution.

What legal aspects exist in bankruptcy?

When a company is declared bankrupt, creditors have to meet between 10 and 30 days after that declaration. A judge or referee presides over the meeting, and creditors show evidence of their claims. A trustee is appointed by the creditors. The trustee handles the property, liquidates the business, makes payments, keeps records, evaluates the creditors' claims, and provides information on the liquidation process.

Who gets paid first in bankruptcy?

Some claims come before others in bankruptcy. The following ranking order exists:

1. *Secured claims.* Secured creditors receive the value of the pledged assets. If the value of the secured assets does not fully satisfy the claims, the balance reverts to general creditor status.

2. *Bankruptcy administrative costs.* The costs of handling bankruptcy include legal and trustee expenses.
3. *Unsecured salaries and commissions.* These claims are limited to a maximum specified amount per individual and must have been incurred within 90 days of the bankruptcy petition.
4. *Unsecured customer deposit claims.* These claims are limited to a nominal amount.
5. *Taxes.* Unpaid taxes are owed to federal, state, and local governments.
6. *General creditor claims.* General creditors do not have specific collateral to support their claims. For example, debentures and accounts payable are unsecured.
7. *Preferred stockholders.*
8. *Common stockholders.*

How is the business dissolved?

After claims have been paid and an accounting of the proceedings made, an application may be filed to discharge the bankrupt business. In a discharge, the court releases the company from legitimate debts in bankruptcy, with the exception of debts that are immune to discharge. As long as a debtor has not been discharged within the previous six years and was not bankrupt because of fraud, the debtor may start a new business.

Example 39.3

The balance sheet of Ace Corporation for the year ended December 31, 2X12, follows.

Balance Sheet

Assets	
Current assets	$400,000
Fixed assets	410,000
Total assets	$810,000
Liabilities	
Current liabilities	$475,000
Long-term liabilities	250,000
Common stock	175,000
Retained earnings	(90,000)
Total liabilities and stockholders' equity	$810,000

The company's liquidation value is $625,000. Rather than liquidate, the company could reorganize with an investment of an additional $320,000. The reorganization is expected to generate earnings of $115,000 per year. A multiplier of 7.5 is appropriate. If the $320,000 is obtained, long-term debt holders will receive 40 percent of the common stock in the reorganized business in substitution for their current claims.

If $320,000 of further investment is made, the firm's going-concern value is $862,500 (7.5 × $115,000). The liquidation value is given at $625,000. Since the reorganization value exceeds the liquidation value, reorganization is called for.

Example 39.4

Fixed assets with a book value of $1.5 million were sold for $1.3 million. There are mortgage bonds on the fixed assets amounting to $1.8 million. The proceeds from the collateral sale are insufficient to pay the secured claim. The unsatisfied portion of $500,000 ($1,800,000 − $1,300,000) becomes a general creditor claim.

Example 39.5

Land having a book value of $1.2 million was sold for $800,000. Mortgage bonds on the land are $600,000. The excess of $200,000 will be returned to the trustee to pay other creditors.

Example 39.6

Charles Company is bankrupt. The book and liquidation values follow.

	Book Value	Liquidation Value
Cash	$ 600,000	$ 600,000
Accounts receivable	1,900,000	1,500,000
Inventory	3,700,000	2,100,000
Land	5,000,000	3,200,000
Building	7,800,000	5,300,000
Equipment	6,700,000	2,800,000
Total assets	$25,700,000	$15,500,000

The liabilities and stockholders' equity at the date of liquidation are:

Current Liabilities		
Accounts payable		$ 1,800,000
Notes payable	900,000	
Accrued taxes	650,000	
Accrued salaries[a]	$ 450,000	
Total current liabilities		$3,800,000
Long-term Liabilities		
Mortgage on land	$3,200,000	
First mortgage—building	2,800,000	
Second mortgage—building	2,500,000	
Subordinated debentures	4,800,000	
Total long-term liabilities		13,300,000
Total liabilities		$17,100,000

(continued)

Stockholders' Equity

Preferred stock	$4,700,000	
Common stock	6,800,000	
Retained earnings	(2,900,000)	
Total stockholders' equity		8,600,000
Total liabilities and stockholders' equity		$25,700,000

ª The salary owed to each worker is below the specified amount and was incurred within 90 days of the bankruptcy petition.

Expenses of the liquidation including legal costs were 15 percent of the proceeds. The debentures are subordinated only with regard to the two first-mortgage bonds.

The distribution of the proceeds follows.

Proceeds		$15,500,000
Mortgage on land	$3,200,000	
First mortgage—building	2,800,000	
Second mortgage—building	2,500,000	
Liquidation expenses (15% × $15,500,000)	2,325,000	
Accrued salaries	450,000	
Accrued taxes	650,000	
Total		11,925,000
Balance		$3,575,000

The percent to be paid to general creditors is:

$$\frac{\text{Proceeds balance}}{\text{Total owed}} = \frac{\$3,575,000}{\$7,500,000} = 47.66667\%$$

The balance due general creditors follows.

General Creditors	Owed	Paid
Accounts payable	$4,800,000	$858,000
Notes payable	900,000	429,000
Subordinated debentures	4,800,000	2,288,000
Total	$7,500,000	3,575,000

Example 39.7

The balance sheet of the Oakhurst Company is presented below.

Assets

Current assets

Cash	$9,000	
Marketable securities	6,000	
Receivables	1,100,000	
Inventory	3,000,000	
Prepaid expenses		$4,000

Total current assets			$ 4,119,000
Noncurrent assets			
Land	$1,800,000		
Fixed assets		2,000,000	
Total noncurrent assets			$3,800,000
Total assets			$ 7,919,000
Liabilities and Stockholders' Equity			
Current liabilities			
Accounts payable	$180,000		
Bank loan payable	900,000		
Accrued salaries	300,000[a]		
Employee benefits payable	70,000[b]		
Customer claims— unsecured	80,000[c]		
Taxes payable		$350,000	
Total current liabilities			$1,880,000
Noncurrent liabilities			
First mortgage payable	$1,600,000		
Second mortgage payable	1,100,000		
Subordinated debentures		700,000	
Total noncurrent liabilities			$3,400,000
Total liabilities			$5,280,000
Stockholders' equity			
Preferred stock (3,500 shares)	$350,000		
Common stock (8,000 shares)	480,000		
Paid-in-capital	1,600,000		
Retained earnings		209,000	
Total stockholders' equity			2,639,000
Total liabilities and stockholders' equity			$ 7,919,000

[a] The salary owed to each worker is below the specified amount and was incurred within 90 days of the bankruptcy petition.
[b] Employee benefits payable have the same limitations as unsecured wages and satisfy for eligibility in bankruptcy distribution.
[c] No customer claim is greater than the nominal amount.

    Additional data are:

1. The mortgages apply to the company's total noncurrent assets.
2. The subordinated debentures are subordinated to the bank loan payable. Therefore, they come after the bank loan payable in liquidation.
3. The trustee has sold the company's current assets for $2.1 million and the noncurrent assets for $1.9 million. Therefore, a total of $4 million was received.
4. The business is bankrupt, since the total liabilities of $5.28 million are greater than the $4 million of the fair value of the assets.

(continued)

Assume that the administration expense for handling the bankrupt company is $900,000. This liability is not reflected in the preceding balance sheet. The allocation of the $4 million to the creditors follows.

Proceeds		$4,000,000
Available to secured creditors		
First mortgage—payable from $1,900,000 proceeds of noncurrent assets	$1,600,000	
Second mortgage—payable from balance of proceeds of noncurrent assets	300,000	1,900,000
Balance after secured creditors		$2,100,000
Next priority		
Administrative expenses	$900,000	
Accrued salaries	300,000	
Employee benefits payable	70,000	
Customer claims—unsecured	80,000	
Taxes payable	350,000	1,700,000
Proceeds available to general creditors		$ 400,000

Now that the claims on the proceeds from liquidation have been met, general creditors receive the balance on a pro rata basis. The distribution of the $400,000 follows.

General Creditor	Amount	Pro Rata Allocation for Balance to Be Paid
Second-mortgage balance ($1,100,000 – $300,000)	$ 800,000	$ 124,031
Accounts payable	180,000	27,907
Bank loan payable	900,000	248,062[a]
Subordinated debentures	700,000	0
Total	$2,580,000	$400,000

[a] The salary owed to each worker is below the specified amount and was incurred within 90 days of the bankruptcy petition.

Example 39.8

Nolan Company is having severe financial problems. Jefferson Bank holds a first mortgage on the plant and has an $800,000 unsecured loan that is already delinquent. The Alto Insurance Company holds $4.7 million of the company's subordinated debentures to the notes payable. Nolan is deciding whether to reorganize the business or declare bankruptcy.

Another company is considering acquiring Nolan Company by offering to take over the mortgage of $7.5 million, pay the past due taxes, and pay $4.38 million for the firm.

Nolan's balance sheet follows.

Assets	
Current assets	$ 2,800,000
Plant assets	11,700,000
Other assets	3,000,000
Total assets	$17,500,000

Liabilities and Stockholders' Equity		
Current liabilities		
Accounts payable	$ 1,800,000	
Taxes payable	170,000	
Bank note payable	260,000	
Other current liabilities	1,400,000	
Total current liabilities		$ 3,630,000
Noncurrent liabilities		
Mortgage payable	$ 7,500,000	
Subordinated debentures	5,300,000	
Total noncurrent liabilities		12,800,000
Total liabilities		$16,430,000
Stockholders' equity		
Common stock	$ 1,000,000	
Premium on common stock	2,300,000	
Retained earnings	(2,230,000)	
Total stockholders' equity		$ 1,070,000
Total liabilities and stockholders' equity		$17,500,000

The impact of the proposed reorganization on creditor claims is indicated below.

Outstanding obligations		$16,430,000
Claims met through the reorganization		
Mortgage payable	$ 7,500,000	
Taxes payable	170,000	
Total		7,670,000
Balance of claims		$ 8,760,000

The cash arising from reorganization is given as $4.38 million, which is 50 percent ($4,380,000/$8,760,000) of the unsatisfied claims.

The distribution to general creditors follows.

General Creditor	Liability Due	50%	Adjusted for Subordination
Bank note payable	$260,000	$130,000	$260,000[a]
Subordinated debenture	5,300,000	2,650,000	2,520,000
Other creditors (accounts payable + other current liabilities)	3,200,000	1,600,000	1,600,000
Total	$8,760,000	$4,380,000	$4,380,000

[a] The bank note payable is paid in subordinated debenture.

CHAPTER FORTY

Valuation of Bonds and Stocks

V ALUATION IS THE process of determining the worth (or value) of an asset. Just like a company's investors, the company's financial managers must have a good understanding of how to value its stocks, bonds, and other securities to judge whether they are good buys or not. The failure to understand the concepts and computational procedures in valuing a security may preclude sound financial decisions. This fact is evident in the company's objective of maximizing the value of its common stock.

In this chapter, we use the concept of the time value of money to analyze the values of bonds and stocks. Basic bond valuation and stock valuation models under varying assumptions are discussed. In all cases, bond and stock values are found to be the present value of the future cash flows expected from the security.

 HOW TO VALUE A SECURITY

The process of determining security valuation involves finding the present value of an asset's expected future cash flows using the investor's required rate of return. Thus, the basic security valuation model can be defined mathematically as:

$$V = \sum_{t=1}^{n} \frac{C_t}{(1+r)^t}$$

where

V = intrinsic value or present value of a security
n = number of periods
C_t = expected future cash flows in period $t = 1, \ldots, n$
r = investor's required rate of return

HOW TO VALUE BONDS

A *bond* is a certificate or security showing funds loaned to a company in return for fixed future interest and repayment of principal. There are certain terms and features of bonds you should be familiar with, including:

- *Par value* (of a bond): The face value (maturity value), usually $1,000.
- *Coupon rate:* The nominal interest rate that determines the actual interest to be received on a bond. It is an annual interest based on par value. For example, if you own a $1,000 bond having a coupon rate of 6 percent, the annual interest payment you will receive is $60.
- *Maturity date:* The final date on which repayment of the bond principal is due.
- *Yield:* The effective interest rate you are earning on the bond investment. The yield is different from the coupon interest rate. If a bond is bought below its face value (i.e., purchased at a discount), the yield is higher than the coupon rate. If a bond is acquired above face value (i.e., bought at a premium), the yield is below the coupon rate.

The valuation process for a bond requires a knowledge of three basic elements:

1. The amount of the cash flows to be received by the investor, which is equal to the periodic interest to be received and the par value to be paid at maturity
2. The maturity date of the loan
3. The investor's required rate of return

Incidentally, the periodic interest can be received annually or semiannually. The value of a bond is simply the present value of these cash flows. Two versions of the bond valuation model are presented next:

If the interest payments are made annually, then

$$V = \sum_{t=1}^{n} \frac{1}{(1+r)^t} + \frac{M}{(1+r)^n} = I \times T_4(r, n) + M \times T_3(r, n)$$

where

V = intrinsic value or present value of a security
n = number of years to maturity
I = interest payment each year = coupon interest rate × par value
M = par value, or maturity value, typically $1,000
T_4 = present value interest factor of an annuity of $1 (which can be found in Table A.4 in the Appendix)
r = investor's required rate of return
T_3 = present value interest factor of $1 (which can be found in Table A.3 in the Appendix) (Both T_4 and T_3 were discussed in detail in Chapter 14.)

Example 40.1

Consider a bond, maturing in 10 years and having a coupon rate of 8 percent. The par value is $1,000. Investors consider 10 percent to be an appropriate required rate of return in view of the risk level associated with this bond. The annual interest payment is $80(8% × $1,000). The present value of this bond is:

$$V = \sum_{t=1}^{n} \frac{1}{(1+r)^t} + \frac{M}{(1+r)^n} = I \times T_4(r,n) + M \times T_3(r,n)$$

$$= \sum_{t=1}^{10} \frac{\$80}{(1+0.1)^t} + \frac{\$1,000}{(1+0.1)^{10}}$$

$$= \$80 \times T_4(10\%, 10) + \$1,000 \times T_3(10\%, 10)$$
$$= \$80(6.145) + \$1,000(0.386) = \$491.60 + \$386.00$$
$$= \$877.60$$

If the interest is paid semiannually, then

$$V = \sum_{t=1}^{2n} \frac{1/2}{(1+2/r)^t} + \frac{M}{(1+r/2)^{2n}} = \frac{1}{2} \times T_4\left(\frac{r}{2}, 2n\right) + M \times T_3\left(\frac{r}{2}, 2n\right)$$

Example 40.2

Assume the same data as in Example 40.1, except the interest is paid semiannually.

$$V = \sum_{t=1}^{2n} \frac{1/2}{(1+2/r)^t} + \frac{M}{(1+r/2)^{2n}} = \frac{1}{2} \times T_4\left(\frac{r}{2}, 2n\right) + M \times T_3\left(\frac{r}{2}, 2n\right)$$

$$= \sum_{t=1}^{20} \frac{\$40}{(1+0.05)^t} + \frac{\$1,000}{(1+0.05)^{20}}$$

$$= \$40 \times T_4(5\%, 20) + \$1,000 \times T_3(5\%, 20)$$
$$= \$40(12.462) + \$1,000(0.377) = \$498.48 + \$377.00$$
$$= \$875.48$$

How do you calculate yield (effective rate of return) on a bond?

Bonds are evaluated on many different types of returns, including current yield and yield to maturity, which are defined as follows:

Current yield. The current yield is the annual interest payment divided by the current price of the bond. This is reported in the *Wall Street Journal*, among others.
Yield to maturity. The expected rate of return on a bond, better known as the bond's yield to maturity, is computed by solving the following equation (the bond valuation model) for r:

$$V = \sum_{t=1}^{n} \frac{1}{(1+r)^t} + \frac{M}{(1+r)^n} = I \times T_4(r,n) + M \times T_3(r,n)$$

Example 40.3

Assume a 12 percent coupon rate $1,000 par value bond selling for $960. The current yield is:

$$\$120/\$960 = 12.5\%$$

The problem with this measure of return is that it does not take into account the maturity date of the bond. A bond with 1 year to run and another with 15 years to run would have the same current yield quote if interest payments were $120 and the price was $960. Clearly, the one-year bond would be preferable under this circumstance because you would not only get $120 in interest but also gain $40 ($1,000 – $960) with a one-year time period, and this amount could be reinvested.

The yield to maturity takes into account the maturity date of the bond. It is the real return you would receive from interest income plus capital gain assuming the bond is held to maturity.

Finding the bond's yield r involves trial and error. It is best explained by an example.

Example 40.4

Suppose you are offered a 10-year, 8 percent coupon, $1,000 par value bond at a price of $877.60. What rate of return could you earn if you bought the bond and held it to maturity? Recall that in Example 40.1, the value of the bond, $877.60, was obtained using the required rate of return of 10 percent. Compute this bond's yield to see if it is 10 percent.

First, set up the bond valuation model:

$$V = \$877.60 = \sum_{t=1}^{10} \frac{80}{(1+r)^t} + \frac{\$1,000}{(1+r)^{10}}$$
$$= 80 \times T_4(r,10) + M \times T_3(r,10)$$

Since the bond is selling at a discount under the par value ($877.60 versus $1,000), the bond's yield is above the going coupon rate of 8 percent. Therefore, try a rate of 9 percent. Substituting factors for 9 percent in the equation, we obtain:

$$V = \$80(6.418) + \$1,000(0.422) = \$513.44 + \$422.00 = \$935.44$$

The calculated bond value, $935.44, is above the actual market price of $877.60, so the yield is not 9 percent. To lower the calculated value, the rate must be raised. Trying 10 percent, we obtain:

$$V = \$80(6.145) + \$1,000(0.386) = \$491.60 + \$386.00 = \$877.60$$

This calculated value is exactly equal to the market price of the bond; thus, 10 percent is the bond's yield to maturity.

The formula that can be used to find the approximate yield to maturity on a bond is:

$$Yield = \frac{I + (M - V)/n}{(M + V)/2}$$

where

I = dollars of interest paid per year
M = par value, typically $1,000 per bond
V = bond's current value (price)
n = number of years to maturity

This formula can also be used to obtain a starting point for the trial-and-error method.

Example 40.5

Using the same data as in Example 40.4 and the shortcut method, the rate of return on the bond is:

$$Yield = \frac{\$80 + (\$1,000 - \$877.60)/10}{(\$1,000 + \$877.60)/2}$$

$$= \frac{\$80 + \$12.24}{\$938.80} = \frac{\$92.24}{\$938.80} = 9.8\%$$

As can be seen, since the bond was bought at a discount, the yield (9.8%) came out greater than the coupon rate of 8 percent.

 HOW TO VALUE PREFERRED STOCK

Preferred stock carries a fixed dividend that is paid quarterly. The dividend is stated in dollar terms per share or as a percentage of par (stated) value of the stock. Preferred stock is considered a hybrid security because it possesses features of both common stock and a corporate bond. It is like common stock in that:

- It represents equity ownership and is issued without stated maturity dates.
- It pays dividends.

Preferred stock is also like a corporate bond in that:

- It provides for prior claims on earnings and assets.
- Its dividend is fixed for the life of the issue.
- It can carry call and convertible features and sinking fund provisions.

Since preferred stocks are traded on the basis of the yield offered to investors, they are in effect viewed as fixed income securities and, as a result, are in competition with bonds in the marketplace. Convertibles, however, trade more like common stock, depending on conversion prices.

The value of preferred stock is the present worth of a series of equal cash flow streams (dividends), continuing indefinitely. Since the dividends in each period are equal for preferred stock, the valuation model can be reduced to this relationship:

$$V = D/r$$

where

V = present value of a preferred stock
D = annual dividend
r = investor's required rate of return

Example 40.6

ABC preferred stock pays an annual dividend of $4.00. You, as an investor, require a 16% return on your investment. Then the value of the ABC preferred stock can be determined as:

$$V = D/r = \$4.06/0.16 = \$25$$

How to Calculate Expected Return from Preferred Stock

In computing the preferred stockholder's expected rate of return, we use the valuation equation for preferred stock just presented. Solving it for r,

$$r = D/V$$

indicates that the expected rate of return of a preferred stock equals the dividend yield (annual dividend/market price).

Example 40.7

A preferred stock paying $5.00 a year in dividends and having a market price of $25 would have a current yield of 20%, computed as:

$$r = D/V = \$5/\$25 = \$20$$

HOW TO VALUE COMMON STOCK

Common stock is an equity investment that represents the ownership of a corporation. It corresponds to the capital account for a sole proprietorship or capital contributed by each partner for a partnership.

The corporation's stockholders have certain rights and privileges, including:

■ *Control of the firm.* The stockholders elect the firm's directors who in turn select officers to manage the business.
■ *Preemptive rights.* These are the right to purchase new stock. A preemptive right entitles a common stockholder to maintain his or her proportional ownership through the opportunity to purchase, on a pro rata basis, any new stock being offered or any securities convertible into common stock.

The value of a common stock is the present value of all future cash inflows expected to be received by the investor. The cash inflows expected to be received are dividends and the future price at the time of the sale of the stock.

Single Holding Period

For an investor holding a common stock for only one year, the value of the stock would be the present value of both the expected cash dividend to be received in one year (D_1) and the expected market price per share of the stock at year-end (P_1). If r represents an investor's required rate of return, the value of common stock (P_0) would be:

$$P_0 = \frac{D_1}{(1+r)^1} + \frac{P_1}{(1+r)^1}$$

Example 40.8

Assume an investor is considering the purchase of stock A at the beginning of the year. The dividend at year-end is expected to be $1.50, and the market price by the end of the year is expected to be $40. If the investor's required rate of return is 15 percent, the value of the stock would be:

$$P_0 = \frac{D_1}{(1+r)^1} + \frac{P_1}{(1+r)^1} = \frac{\$1.50}{(1+0.15)} + \frac{\$40}{(1+0.15)}$$

$$= \$1.50 \times T_3(15\%, 1) + \$40 \times T_3(15\%, 1)$$
$$= \$1.50(0.870) + \$40(0.870)$$
$$= \$1.31 + \$34.80 = \$36.11$$

Multiple Holding Period

Since common stock has no maturity date and is held for many years, a more general multiperiod model is needed. The general common stock valuation model is defined as:

$$P_0 = \sum_{t=1}^{\infty} \frac{D_t}{(1+r)^t}$$

where D_t = dividend in period t

Two cases of growth in dividends, zero growth and constant growth, are explained next.

Zero-Growth Case

In the case of zero growth (i.e., $D_0 = D_1 = \ldots = D$), the valuation model reduces to the formula:

$$P_0 = \frac{D}{r}$$

This is the case with a perpetuity. This model is most applicable to the valuation of preferred stocks, as was discussed earlier, or the common stocks of very mature companies, such as large utilities.

Example 40.9

Assuming dividends (D) equals $2.50 and r equals 10 percent, then the value of the stock is:

$$P_0 = \frac{\$2.50}{0.1} = \$25$$

Constant Growth Case

In the case of constant growth, if we assume that dividends grow at a constant rate of g every year [i.e., $D_t = D_0(1 + g)^t$], then the general model is simplified to:

$$P_0 = \frac{D_1}{r - g}$$

In words,

$$\text{Common stock value} = \frac{\text{Dividend in year}}{\text{Required rate of return} - \text{Growth rate}}$$

This formula is known as *Gordon's valuation model*. This model is most applicable to the valuation of the common stocks of very large or broadly diversified firms.

Example 40.10

Consider a common stock that paid a $3 dividend per share at the end of the last year and is expected to pay a cash dividend every year at a growth rate of 10 percent. Assume the investor's required rate of return is 12 percent. The value of the stock would be:

$$D_1 = D_0(1 + g_T) = \$3(1 + 0.10) = \$3.30$$

$$P_0 = \frac{D_1}{r - g} = \frac{\$3.30}{0.12 - 0.10} = \$165$$

What is the expected return on common stock?

The formula for computing the expected rate of return on common stock can be derived easily from the valuation models.

The single-holding-period return formula is derived from:

$$P_0 = \frac{D_1}{(1+r)^1} + \frac{P_1}{(1+r)^1}$$

Solving for r gives:

$$r = \frac{D_1 + (P_1 - P_0)}{P_0}$$

In words,

$$\text{Rate of return} = \frac{\text{Annual dividend} + \text{Capital gain}}{\text{Beginning price}}$$

$$= \frac{\text{Annual dividend}}{\text{Beginning price}} + \frac{\text{Capital gain}}{\text{Beginning price}}$$

$$= \text{Dividend yield} + \text{Capital gain yield}$$

Example 40.11

Consider a stock that sells for $50. The company is expected to pay a $3 cash dividend at the end of the year, and the stock market price at the end of the year is expected to be $55 a share. Thus the expected return would be:

$$r = \frac{D_1 + (P_1 - P_0)}{P_0} = \frac{\$3.00 + (\$55.00 - \$50.00)}{\$50.00}$$

$$= \frac{\$3.00 + \$5.00}{\$50.00} = 16\%$$

or:

$$\text{Dividend yield} = \frac{\$3.00}{\$50.00} = 6\%$$

$$\text{Capital gain yield} = \frac{\$5.00}{\$50.00} = 10\%$$

$$r = \text{Dividend yield} + \text{Capital gain yield}$$
$$= 6\% + 10\% = 16\%$$

(continued)

Assuming a constant growth in dividends, the formula for the expected rate of return on an investment in stock can be derived as:

$$P_0 = \frac{D_1}{r - g}$$

Solving for r gives:

$$r = \frac{D_1}{P_0} + g$$

Example 40.12

Suppose that your company's dividend per share was $4.50, and it was expected to grow at a constant rate of 6 percent. The current market price of the stock is $30. Then the expected rate of return is:

$$r = \frac{D_1}{P_0} + g$$

$$= \frac{\$4.50}{\$30.00} + 6\% = 15\% + 6\% = 21\%$$

PRICE/EARNINGS RATIO APPROACHES

A more popular pragmatic approach to valuing a common stock is to use the price/earnings (P/E) ratio (or multiple). You can use the simple formula:

Expected stock price = Selected P/E ratio × Projected earnings per share (E_1)

Comparing the current price against the computed expected value price could help indicate if the stock is under- or overvalued.

Example 40.13

The XYZ Corporation had EPS of $5.00. The earnings per share (EPS) is expected to grow at 20 percent. The company's normal P/E ratio is estimated to be 7, which is used as the multiplier. Estimated EPS is $5.00 × (1 + 0.20) = $6.00. The value of the stock is:

$$7 \times \$6.00 = \$42$$

It is important to realize that for the P/E method to be effective in forecasting the future value of a stock, (a) earnings need to be projected correctly and (b) the appropriate P/E multiple must be applied. Forecasting EPS is not an easy task. Furthermore, there is no agreed-on method of picking a meaningful P/E ratio. Some analysts use an average of historical earnings; some normalize earnings; some come up with a P/E ratio relative to the market's P/E ratio; and so on. Following are three methods for forecasting EPS.

1. The first approach is simply to look at historical P/E ratios. A 5- or 10-year average P/E ratio is a useful benchmark because it will smooth out fluctuating earnings and prices during both economic expansions and recessions. Exhibit 40.1 illustrates this approach. It shows the calculated high, low, and average P/E ratios of each of the last five years. You can estimate a range of stock values by using these five-year average high, low, average P/Es with an earnings estimate. This approach, however, does not take into account market factors, and we should adjust for them.

EXHIBIT 40.1   Normalized Price/Earnings Ratio Example

Stock Price ($)						
	2X07	*2X08*	*2X09*	*2X10*	*2X11*	*2X12*
High	24.50	40.90	45.40	45.00	51.30	——
Low	16.30	21.30	35.60	37.50	38.90	——
EPS ($)						
	2X07	*2X08*	*2X09*	*2X10*	*2X11*	*2X12*
	——	1.22	1.43	1.68	2.00[a]	2.30[a]
Normalized P/E Ratio (Stock price/Next year's EPS)						
	2X07	*2X08*	*2X09*	*2X10*	*2X11*	*2X12*
High	20.1	28.6	27.0	22.5	22.3	——
Low	13.4	14.9	21.2	18.8	16.9	——

Average Relative P/E ratios:

24.1 = Five-Year High

17.0 = Five-Year Low

20.6 = Five-Year Average

Stock Valuation

High	$2.30 × 24.1 = $55.4
Low	$2.30 × 17.0 = $39.1
Average	$2.30 × 20.6 = $47.4

[a] Value line estimated earnings.

2. The second approach gets around this problem by looking at market-relative P/E ratios. The relative P/E ratio examines the relative relationship of the P/E ratio of a stock to the P/E ratio of the overall market or the stock's industry. It simply compares them with the overall market's P/E by dividing a company's P/E ratio by the market's (Standard & Poor's [S&P] 500), as shown below. *Note:* A relative P/E ratio of 1.0 would indicate a P/E ratio that is equal to the market's. A relative P/E ratio above 1.0 would indicate that a company's P/E ratio is above the market's. By tracking the P/E ratio over a number of years, you can estimate a P/E ratio that a stock tends to follow.

(continued)

$$\text{Relative P/E ratio} = \frac{\text{Company P/E}}{\text{Market P/E}}$$

$$\text{Company P/E} = \text{relative P/E ratio} \times \text{current market P/E}$$

Exhibit 40.2 illustrates this approach.

EXHIBIT 40.2   Relative Price/Earnings Ratio Example

In this example, the relative ratio is based on the most recent 12 months of earnings divided by the year-end market P/E ratio.

Trailing P/E Ratio

(Stock price/EPS)

	2X07	2X08	2X09	2X10	2X11	2X12
High	24.0	33.5	31.7	26.8	25.7	__
Low	16.0	17.5	24.9	22.3	19.5	__

S&P Trailing P/E Ratio

(Stock price/EPS)

	2X07	2X08	2X09	2X10	2X11	2X12
High	17.3	26.1	21.1	21.5	17.6	__
Low	13.9	19.5	18.0	19.6	16.1	__

Relative P/E Ratio

(Company P/E ÷ S&P 500 P/E)

	2X07	2X08	2X09	2X10	2X11	2X12
High	1.4	1.3	1.5	1.2	1.5	__
Low	1.1	0.9	1.4	1.1	1.2	__

Average Relative P/E Ratios:

1.4 = Five-year high

1.2 = Five-year low

1.3 = Five-year average

Also note:

24.9 = Current P/E ratio of market

$2.30 = Expected next annual EPS

P/E ratio, based on a relative ratio and current market ratio:

High: 1.4 × 24.9 = 34.9

Low: 1.2 × 24.9 = 30.0

Average: 1.3 × 24.9 = 32.4

Stock valuation:

High: 34.9 × $2.30 = $80.3

Low: 30.0 × $2.30 = $69.0

Average: 32.4 × $2.30 = $74.5

3. The third approach, developed by Graham and Dodd, is another market-adjusted P/E approach. The adjustment is based on (a) a statistical relationship between P/Es and growth; that is, P/E= 8.5 + 2g, and (b) an interest adjustment; that is, 4.4%/Y, where Y = corporate AAA bond yield. The adjusted P/E ratio is:

$$P/E \times \frac{4.4\%}{Y}$$

$$(8.5 + 2g) \times \frac{4.4\%}{Y}$$

Example 40.14

Assume:

E = $2.30, expected next annual EPS
g = 15%, annual growth in EPS
Y = 8%, current AAA corporate bond yield

P/E ratio:

$$[8.5 \times (2 \times 15\%)] \times \frac{4.4\%}{8\%} = 21.2$$

Expected stock price = P/E ratio × projected EPS (E_1)
= 21.2 × $2.30 = $48.76

What are the determinants of the price/earnings ratio?

What determines the P/E multiple is very complex. Empirical evidence seems to suggest these factors:

▪ Historical growth rate in earnings
▪ Forecasted earnings
▪ Average dividend payout ratio
▪ Beta (the company's systematic [uncontrollable] risk
▪ Instability of earnings
▪ Financial leverage
▪ Other factors, such as competitive position, management ability
▪ Economic conditions

What does it mean when a firm's stock sells on a high or low P/E ratio?

To answer this question, the Gordon's growth model can be helpful. If a company's dividends are expected to grow at a constant rate, then

$$P_0 = \frac{D_1}{r - g}$$

where

P_0 = current price of stock

D_1 = expected dividend next year

r = return required by investors from similar investments

g = the expected growth in dividends

In order to find the P/E ratio, dividing through by expected EPS yields:

$$\frac{P_0}{EPS} = \frac{D_1}{EPS} \times \frac{1}{r - g}$$

Thus, a high P/E ratio may indicate any of the following:

▪ Investors expect high dividend growth (g).
▪ The stock has low risk, and therefore investors are content with a low prospective return (r).
▪ The company is expected to achieve average growth while paying out a high proportion of earnings (D_1/EPS).
   Exhibit 40.3 shows P/E ratios of certain companies.

EXHIBIT 40.3 P/E Ratios

Company	Industry	March 1, 2011	Industry Average
Boeing (BA)	Aerospace/Defense—Major Diversified	16.21	16.9
Google (GOOG)	Internet Information Providers	23.19	31.5
Toyota (TM)	Auto Manufacturers—Major	63.72	14.7
Nordstrom (JWN)	Apparel Stores	16.54	17.7
Intel (INTC)	Semiconductor—Broad Line	10.88	15.0
Walmart (WMT)	Discount, Variety Stores	13.87	14.4

Source: MSN Money Central Investor (http://moneycentral.msn.com/investor/invsub/results/compare.asp?Page=PriceRatios&symbol=BA).

OTHER PRAGMATIC APPROACHES

In valuing a stock investment, you may employ several pragmatic techniques: price/sales (P/S), price/dividends (P/D), and price/book (P/B) value ratios.

Price/Sales Ratio

The P/S ratio is an increasingly popular tool for determining underlying stock value. It is computed as:

$$\frac{\text{Market price per share}}{\text{Sales per share}}$$

A P/S of, say, 0.83 means you are paying 83 cents for every dollar of sales. The P/S ratio reflects a company's underlying strength. A company with a low P/S ratio is more attractive while one with a high ratio is less attractive. *Note:* As a rule of thumb, you should avoid stocks with a P/S ratio of 1.5 or more. Further, you should sell a stock when the ratio is between 3 and 6.

You can use the simple formula:

$$\text{Expected price} = \text{Projected sales per share} \times \text{Average P/S ratio}$$

Example 40.15

The XYZ Corporation projects sales to be $3.50 per share. The company's five-year average P/S ratio is 14.4, which is used as the multiplier. The value of the stock is $51.00 ($3.50 × 14.4).

Price/Dividends Ratio

The P/D ratio is another popular tool for determining underlying stock value. It is computed as:

$$\frac{\text{Market price per share}}{\text{Dividends per share}}$$

You can use the simple formula:

$$\text{Expected price} = \text{Projected dividends per share} \times \text{Average P/D ratio}$$

Example 40.16

The XYZ Corporation projects dividends to be $0.88 per share. The company's five-year average P/D ratio is 61.3, which is used as the multiplier. The value of the stock is $53.94 ($0.88 × 61.3).

Price/Book Ratio

Book value (net asset, liquidation value) per share is the amount of corporate assets for each share of common stock. It is calculated by dividing total stockholders' equity by total shares outstanding.

You may benefit by uncovering stock that is selling below book value or whose assets are significantly undervalued. A stock may represent a good value when its market price is below or close to book value because the security is undervalued. Companies with lower ratios of market price to book value have historically earned better returns than those with higher ratios.

Example 40.17

You are thinking of investing in a company that has a market price per share of $40. The book value per share is $50. This may be a buying opportunity, since market price ($40) is well below book value ($50) or P/B ratio of .9 ($40/$50), and an upward movement in prices may occur.

You can use the simple formula:

Expected price = Projected book value per share × Average P/B ratio

---

Example 40.18

The XYZ Corporation projects sales to be $5.50 per share. The company's five-year average P/B ratio is 10.4, which is used as the multiplier. The value of the stock is $57.20 ($5.50 × 10.4)

Various financial services track industries and companies. They offer expectations as to future earnings, sales, dividends, book value, and even market prices of stock. For example, reference may be made to Standard & Poor's *Stock Reports* and Value Line's *Investment Survey. Institutional Brokers Estimate System* (I/B/E/S) is a database that provides consensus earnings estimates on over 3,400 publicly traded corporations. *Zack's* performs a similar service and is available through Dow Jones News/Retrieval. These services provide a thorough analysis of companies and clues as to future expectations and a source of earnings estimates.

 THE BOTTOM LINE

Several valuations have been presented so far. The key is to decide which valuation model or models is best suited for a company you are interested in. For example, if your company is a mature, dividend-paying stock, such as a public utility, which is

generally a low-growth stock, the dividend-based models make sense. If your company is a growth-oriented company, you should use an earnings-based model since the stock's price will be driven by earnings potential rather than dividends. Nonetheless, it is a good idea to perform sensitivity analysis and obtain a range of estimates. Any final decision on your valuation estimates should, however, be based on a better understanding of the company, its management, and its competitive environment.

CHAPTER FORTY-ONE

Financial Statement Analysis: Key Financial Ratios and Metrics for Nonprofits

FINANCIAL STATEMENT ANALYSIS reveals how well a nonprofit organization (NPO) has done in meeting its targets. Interrelated ratios reveal the financial standing and areas of financial trouble. Each ratio should be compared over the years for a trend, to an industry norm (e.g., healthcare standard ratio), and to comparable NPOs to obtain a relative standing. Ratios vary depending on the service provided, complexity of operations, funding sources, and donor restrictions. A cost-benefit analysis should be undertaken for new programs. Risk-return analysis is also essential.

When evaluating the service efforts of an NPO, look to see how much of every dollar goes to the primary mission as opposed to the fundraiser's commissions and the executive director's salary. Carefully monitor the relationship of supporting services to program services expenses.

Financial statement analysis is undertaken by those working within the NPO, such as managers, and outsiders evaluating the NPO's financial statements. Financial statement users are provided with red flags as to impending financial problems that need to be identified and corrected. Areas of strength are also identified and taken further advantage of. Financial statement users include resource providers, such as contributors and grantors. They want to know how well their funds are being spent for the purposes solicited. Financial statements reveal this fiduciary trust. Further, donors do not want to pour money into a sinking ship. Suppliers and loan officers analyze the financial statements to determine whether to give credit and, if so, how much and for what time period. Companies and government (federal and local) agencies awarding contracts appraise financial statements as to whether contractual provisions are being adhered to. Government regulators (watchdogs) evaluate the financial statements to ascertain if compliance is being made to prescribed regulations and limitations. An NPO serves the public, so concerned citizens may want to analyze its financial statements to determine if service goals are being met.

This chapter has two primary objectives. First, it focuses on ways NPOs can assess the progress and health of their businesses. It takes readers through step-by-step procedures in performing financial statement analysis. The procedure involves:

- Appraising the balance sheet for financial position and flexibility
- Analyzing the statement of activities for operating performance
- Evaluating the statement of cash flows for cash position
- Referring to footnote information
- Evaluating the auditor's opinion
- Reviewing internal documents related to financial health
- Reviewing budgets to determine if plans are practical and for future directions

Second, the chapter discusses some key financial ratios that are critical for assessing the financial health of NPOs. It also introduces some key financial metrics for NPOs.

As a giver or donor, you need know how to distinguish among NPOs in the same field. You want to address this question: How do you figure out who does the most with the contributions and who spends inordinate sums, however well intentioned, on raising the money and excessive overhead? Several indexes are helpful to answer those questions: charity commitment, fundraising efficiency, and donor dependency.

A case study, presented at the end of the chapter, analyzes a nonprofit organization using including trend analysis, ratio computations, and analytical evaluation.

 TREND ANALYSIS

Trend (horizontal) analysis is a time-series analysis of financial statements of the NPO covering more than one accounting period. It looks at the percentage change in an account or category over time. The percentage change equals the change over the prior year. For example, if salaries expense increased from $140,000 to $165,000 from 2X11 to 2X12, the percentage increase is 18 percent ($25,000/$140,000). The reason (or reasons) for such an increase should be determined. Does the increase indicate more staff was needed because operations improved, or does it indicate a lack of cost control, or is there some other cause? Is the situation an unfavorable one requiring management attention? By evaluating the magnitude of direction of a financial statement item over the years, the analyst can appraise its reasonableness.

Example 41.1

Membership fee revenue declined from $100,000 to $80,000 over the last year. The percentage decline equals:

$$\frac{\text{Amount of change}}{\text{Base year amount}} = \frac{\$20,000}{\$100,000} = 20\%$$

Why has there been such a significant decline in membership fees? Is this a problem peculiar just to this NPO, or does it affect all NPOs in the industry? Is the problem controllable or uncontrollable by management? Is the decline due to dissatisfaction among members of the NPO who object to its policies, or was it caused by overall poor economic conditions? Trend analysis reveals direction, positive or negative, requiring further study of the causes. The decline may indicate a problem requiring corrective action.

 ## ANALYSIS OF THE BALANCE SHEET

Evaluation of the balance sheet considers the NPO's liquidity, asset utilization, solvency, financial flexibility, and capital structure. Assets, liabilities, and net assets (fund balance) must be scrutinized.

 ## LIQUIDITY ANALYSIS

Accounting Standards Codification (ASC) 958-205, *Not-for-Profit Entities: Presentation of Financial Statements* (FAS-117, *Financial Statements of Not-for-Profit Organizations*) requires NPOs to present information about their liquidity. *Liquidity* is the ability of the NPO to pay current debt as it comes due. It indicates how fast the NPO's assets turn into cash. A liquid asset has less risk than an illiquid one. In evaluating liquidity, exclude restricted funds because they are unavailable for use.

Liquidity considers the seasonality of cash flows. Wide fluctuations in cash flows may result in a liquidity problem. Liquidity ratios are explained next.

Working Capital

Working capital = Current assets – Current liabilities.

The higher the working capital amount, the better the liquidity.

Current Ratio

The current ratio is a measure of liquidity equal to:

Current assets/Current liabilities

Current assets are those assets to be converted to cash within one year or the normal operating cycle of the NPO, whichever is greater. Current liabilities are due within one year.

In general, the current ratio should be a minimum of 2:1. A low ratio means poor liquidity. An excessively high ratio may also be a negative sign because it may indicate too much money is being tied up in current assets rather than invested in noncurrent assets for a higher return.

A limitation of the current ratio is that not all current assets have the same degree of liquidity. For example, accounts receivable is more liquid than inventories of suppliers. Prepaid expenses are not redeemable for cash but rather a prepayment for future benefits (e.g., prepaid advertising).

Current unrestricted assets include cash and cash equivalents (marketable securities), accounts receivable, investment income receivable, inventories of supplies, and prepaid expenses. Current unrestricted liabilities include accounts payable, prepaid services, and the current portion of mortgage payable.

Current ratio for unrestricted current assets and current liabilities = Current unrestricted assets/Current unrestricted liabilities

Temporarily Restricted Assets

Temporarily restricted assets should also be considered. An example is pledges receivable arising from gifts to finance operating activities. However, another type of pledges receivable exists, namely unconditional and unrestricted pledges receivable. Another temporarily restricted asset is grants receivable.

With respect to temporarily restricted net assets, determine when the resources will be available. For example, if temporarily restricted net assets include term endowments and annuities, it may be best to consider them permanently restricted. The current ratio for unrestricted and temporarily restricted assets is calculated as:

$$\frac{\text{Current unrestricted assets} + \text{Current temporarily restricted assets for operations}}{\text{Current unrestricted liabilities}}$$

A determination should be made as to the nature of the restrictions on pledges receivable.

Acid-Test (Quick) Ratio

The quick unrestricted assets are the most liquid assets. Excluded are inventories of supplies and prepaid expenses. The quick unrestricted assets include cash and cash equivalents, accounts receivable, and investment income receivable.

Quick ratio = Quick unrestricted assets/current unrestricted liabilities

A higher ratio is better. It should be at least 1:1.

Accounts Receivable Ratios

Turnover and the collection period are useful ratios.

Accounts receivable turnover = Fees for services on credit/Average net accounts receivable

Net account receivable = Accounts receivable – Allowance for uncollectible accounts

The ratio shows the number of times average net accounts receivable turn over relative to fees generated. The more turnover, the better.

$$\text{Days to collect on receivables} = 365/\text{Turnover}$$

The ratio indicates the amounts owed the NPO as well as its accounts receivable management success. A lower ratio is better because it takes fewer days to collect on receivables. Cash received earlier can be reinvested for a return. A high ratio is bad because money is being tied up in receivables that could be invested elsewhere. Further, the longer days receivables are held, the greater is the chance of uncollectability. Perhaps billing is deficient. Receivables must be kept under control.

In looking at the collection period, consider terms of sale, account profile, service mix, collection policies, and the collection period of comparable NPOs.

An aging of receivable balances should be prepared broken down by current, past due (0 to 30 days), past due (31 days to 60 days), past due (61 days to 90 days), and past due (91 days to 120 days). The aging listing should be in both alphabetical order and by magnitude of receivable balances outstanding. The older the receivables are, the less the chance of collection. A determination should be made of both time distribution and size distribution. How many billing periods has a particular account been unpaid?

A determination should be made of what percent receivables are to total assets equal to:

$$\text{Total accounts receivable}/\text{Total assets}$$

A high ratio is a problem, especially if most of the accounts receivable are from a few sources.

Pledges Receivable Turnover

The turnover ratio for pledges receivable is similar to that of accounts receivable.

$$\text{Turnover} = \text{Net contributions from pledges}/\text{Average net pledges receivable}$$

A lower turnover for pledges receivables means a longer collection period.

$$\text{Collection period} = 365/\text{Turnover}$$

Is the collection period for pledges less than expected? If so, is it because of inadequate collection efforts? Compare to industry averages. Determine the reasonableness of the provision for uncollectible pledges. Analyze pledges receivable in terms of time and size diversification.

The turnover and age of grants receivable should be determined in a similar way.

Inventory

Inventory may have a low turnover because items are too costly, poor quality, or lack appeal.

Days in Cash

The days in cash is the number of days the NPO can continue in operation if cash inflow stops. It is the number of days of average cash payments the NPO can manage without cash inflow. The higher the number, the better. The days in cash ratio equals:

$$(\text{Cash} + \text{Cash equivalents}) \times 365/\text{Operating expenses} - \text{Depreciation}$$

Example 41.2

An NPO expends $30,000 daily on average in a one-year period. If it has $900,000 of cash and cash equivalents on hand, it has 30 days' cash.

Cash Flow to Total Debt

The ratio of cash flow to total debt equals:

$$\frac{\text{Net income} + \text{Depreciation}}{\text{Total liabilities}}$$

The ratio indicates how much of internally generated cash is available to pay debt. A higher ratio is better because there is better liquidity, in that cash flow from operations is being generated.

Days Purchases Unpaid

The ratio of days purchases unpaid equals:

$$\text{Accounts payable/Daily purchases}$$

where Daily purchases = Purchases/360

The ratio is used to evaluate trade credit. It shows how long (how many days) trade credit remains unpaid.

If the suppliers' payment terms are 30 days and the NPO pays in 90 days, on average it may mean there are liquidity problems.

Current Liability Coverage

The ratio equals:

$$\frac{\text{Cash} + \text{Marketable securities (unrestricted)}}{\text{Current liabilities}}$$

The ratio reveals how much of current liabilities can be paid from cash and short-term investments if cash inflows cease.

Financial Flexibility

The greater the amount of unrestricted net assets, the greater the amount of financial flexibility. NPOs with huge permanently restricted endowments and minimal unrestricted net assets may not enjoy much flexibility. Can the NPO respond and adapt to financial adversity and unexpected needs and opportunities? Which resources are available when needed?

Asset Utilization

Asset utilization applies to the efficiency with which the assets are used in the operating activities of the NPO. For example, a higher ratio of revenue to assets indicates more efficiency of assets in generating profit. What assets are excessive relative to the optimal level?

The efficiency usage of supplies may be determined as:

$$\text{Turnover of supplies} = \text{Annual total supplies expense/Average total inventory of supplies}$$

A low turnover is a negative sign because it means supplies are excessive and are not being used efficiently.

$$\text{Available days of supplies' use} = 360/\text{Turnover}$$

What is the rate of supplies' usage? How fast would the current usage level deplete supplies inventory?

$$\text{Average daily total supplies expense} = \text{Annual total supplies expense/Average number of days of supplies' use}$$

The ratio shows how often supplies are used such as in a particular program.

Analysis of Fixed Assets

In the long run, buying assets is cheaper than renting. NPOs also have more control by buying because they do not have to concern themselves with lessors unexpectedly raising rental rates or demanding certain prohibitions of using the property.

The average accounting age of equipment (e.g., computers) can be determined as:

$$\text{Accumulated depreciation/Depreciation expense}$$

The ratio reveals how old the equipment is. It shows the rate equipment is being used and replaced. A lower ratio is better.

The ratio is of particular interest to hospitals because they must buy expensive up-to-date technological medical equipment and keep facilities in good working order for the best patient care.

A low depreciation charge may indicate that the NPO is making significant use of rentals. Does a reduction in fixed assets mean there is less capacity and utilization?

Analysis of Liabilities

Short-term borrowing can be used to fill the gap resulting from the temporary shortfall in contributions or other sources of cash inflow.

If long-term debt is used to finance fixed assets, the NPO has greater financial leverage risk. The NPO must be able to pay principal and interest.

Analyze the long-term indebtedness of the NPO including:

▪ Interest rate being charged.
▪ Excessiveness of debt.

- Reason for borrowings. How is the money to be used?
- Maturity dates of debt. Are debt payments staggered? Can the debt be repaid?
- Lines of credit.
- Loan restrictions such as collateral requirements. Are such restrictions tying the hands of the manager?
- Understated liabilities, such as the liability for severance payments or for earned but unused vacation time

 ## APPRAISAL OF SOLVENCY, CAPITAL STRUCTURE, AND NET ASSETS (FUND BALANCE)

A healthy capital structure will help ensure the NPO's ability to engage in its daily activities. High leverage (debt to net assets or fund balance) means risk. The debt ratio will increase if the NPO must finance fixed asset expansion with borrowed funds.

The ratio of long-term debt to total unrestricted net assets (fund balance) reveals the NPO's long-term commitments to its ability to pay the debt. This ratio relates borrowed funds to owned funds. A ratio over 1 may indicate a problem in handling additional debt. Can the NPO pay existing interest and principal payments?

Analysis of the net assets (fund balance) depends on the facts and circumstances. A surplus indicates better financial health than a deficit. An increasing trend in the surplus is a favorable sign. Surpluses provide savings for financing the future and the ability to pay off debt.

 ## EVALUATION OF THE STATEMENT OF ACTIVITIES

An NPO should communicate to the users of the financial statements which specific revenues and expenses are included as the operating revenues and expenses. If the NPO's use of the term "operating" is not clear from the details on the face of the statement, ASC 958-205 requires a footnote describing the nature of the measure of operating performance. The financial analyst should carefully review the NPO's definition of the operating measure and compare it with that used by similar NPOs; the definition should be consistently applied. Generally, the operating income measure is a subtotal in arriving at the net change in unrestricted net assets.

In analyzing the statement of activities, determine:

- Whether the entity is self-sustaining and operating well
- If service efforts are being successful
- Whether management has discharged its stewardship responsibilities

In the long run, if an NPO does not spend all of its revenues, it is not funding as much services as possible to the public. However, if it keeps spending more than its revenues, it will go bankrupt.

In analyzing an NPO, consider *operating capital maintenance*, a concept that refers to whether the NPO is maintaining its capital by having its revenues at least equal to its expenses. Why did a surplus or deficit occur?

An NPO should not report a profit consistently each year. If it always shows a profit, the NPO may not be accomplishing its objective of providing as much service as possible with available resources. It should either provide more service and thereby increase its costs or reduce prices it charges for services. The objective of an NPO's financial policy should be to break even.

An NPO (such as a membership organization) may have a policy of having an operating excess one year but a deficit in another year, which balances out. For example, member dues may be increased only once each three years. In the year of the dues increase, an operating surplus may arise. In the second year, there may be a break-even point, and in the third year a deficit may exist. Dues are then increased again.

In a similar vein, an NPO may want an operating excess one year to eliminate a deficit from the previous year.

An operating surplus may also be desired to have adequate funding for expansion, to subsidize programs, or as a result of a lawsuit. A surplus may be desired as a contingency for unexpected problems and to replace assets.

An NPO may want to operate at a deficit in one year to reduce an accumulated surplus or to meet a special need.

In conclusion, an NPO does not have to break even each year. It may have a surplus in one year(s) and a deficit in another year(s) to meet its unique circumstances as long as it balances out over a number of years.

Revenue

The revenue base should be diversified to reduce risk. For example, overdependence on one revenue source (e.g., grants) may be dangerous.

A decline in revenue may indicate ineffectiveness. For example, a decline in college tuition may mean problems in attracting students at a college. How does actual revenue compare to expected revenue?

Total revenue needed daily on average equals:

$$\text{Total revenue (prior year)}/365$$

Costs

Expenses should be analyzed in terms of program and object of expense. Variances between actual and budgeted expenses should be investigated.

Determine the reason for a sizable increase or decrease in an expense. For example, a significant increase to a specific expense may not be due to a change in organizational plan but may reflect contributed services instead.

Determine the cost per unit of service. A lower rate means better cost containment. When costs need to be reduced, the first thing to cut is lower-priority programs that least accomplish the NPO's goals. However, consider how changes in program activities would affect donor contributions and volunteer support. Identify controllable and uncontrollable costs. Ask these questions:

- Can costs be reduced by replacing obsolete and/or inactive equipment?
- Can costs be reduced by improved technology?
- Will an improved repairs and maintenance program lower costs?
- Can staff improvements be made to lower costs?
- Can energy costs be reduced through improved traffic management?
- Can productivity be improved?

Ratios include:

$$\text{Operating expenses/Total revenue}$$

A lower ratio indicates better cost control.

$$\text{Fundraising costs/Total donations}$$

The ratio evaluates the effectiveness of fundraising efforts. Is fundraising cost excessive for funds obtained?

U.S. GAAP requires a statement of functional expenses from voluntary and health organizations. The statement is helpful to the financial analyst because it provides a detailed breakdown of expenses by program. It is analogous to segment reporting in business enterprises.

Profitability

NPOs trying to expand and enter new areas need to be profitable. Profitability measures include:

$$\text{Profit margin} = (\text{Revenue} - \text{Expenses})/\text{Revenue}$$

A higher ratio shows better operational performance (profit).

$$\text{Operating margin} = (\text{Operating revenue} - \text{Operating expenses})/ \text{Operating revenue}$$

Operating revenue excludes nonoperating sources, such as fundraising revenue, dividends, and extraordinary items. The operating profit is derived solely from operating activities without having to rely on contributors. A higher ratio is better.

$$\text{Return on net assets (fund balance)(Net assets)} = (\text{Total revenue} - \text{Total expenses})/ \text{Average net assets}$$

The ratio shows how efficiently the net assets (fund balance) have created the year's profit.

Ratios of investment performance include:

$$\frac{\text{Interest and/or Dividend income}}{\text{Investments at cost}}$$

$$\frac{\text{Interest and/or Dividend income}}{\text{Investments at market value}}$$

Higher ratios indicate better returns on investments.

Disclosures

In examining footnote disclosures, identify contingencies, including positive and negative developments affecting the NPO. Disclosure of possible future funding problems is a red light. An example is changing political policies directed toward reducing government funding.

A lawsuit against the NPO is a negative sign, particularly if it is reasonably possible that the NPO will lose.

 ## PERFORMANCE METRICS

We have to examine the quality of the services and programs offered by the NPO, not just look at dollars. The NPO's objective is to render an amount and quality of services. For example, measures of performance (or metrics) for a college include number of enrollments, number of courses, and ratio of faculty to students. Some general performance measures to keep in mind include:

- Capital per unit of service
- Number of patients treated daily by a doctor
- Number of welfare cases handled by a social worker
- Input/output relationships, such as the cost and time of performing a service and the quality and quantity of service provided
- Number of complaints

How do you figure out who does the most with the contributions and who spends inordinate sums, however well intentioned, on raising the money and excessive overhead? Several indexes, including charity commitment, fundraising efficiency, and donor dependency, would be helpful to answer those questions.

Charity Commitment

Charity commitment percentage =
$$\frac{\text{Charitable expense (program support or program service expense)}}{\text{Total expenses}}$$

Essentially, the resulting figure excludes such overhead as management and fundraising.

Fundraising Efficiency

Fundraising efficiency measures how much of the money raised from private sources remains after accounting for fundraising. It is computed by taking the total funds raised from the public through direct contributions, indirect contributions (such as from United Way), and proceeds from one-time special events, subtracting fundraising costs, then expressing the result as a percentage of the total amount from the public (private support).

Donor Dependency

Donor dependency tries to assess how badly a charity needs contributions—as opposed to money raised from selling products or tickets or reaping investment gains—to fund its current operations. It is figured by subtracting a charity's annual surplus (excess of revenue over expenses) from public donations (private support), then dividing this figure by the public donations (private support). A percentage at or above 100 percent means that the nonprofit is totally dependent on donations and is not salting away funds for a rainy day. A *negative* index number means that surpluses exceed all donations for the reporting year.

Exhibit 41.1 presents these indexes for a selected charity organization.

EXHIBIT 41.1 Charitable Commitment, Fundraising Efficiency, and Donor Dependency

Alzheimer's Disease and Related Disorders Association

(Alzheimer's disease research)

Chicago, IL (www.alz.org)

All figures in $ millions except where otherwise noted.

Private Support	Govt. Support	Total Support	Other Income	Total Revenue
97	0	97	17	114

Program Service Expenses		Management and General	Fundraising	Total Expenses
84		9	16	109

Surplus (Loss)	Net Assets	Charitable Commitment[a]	Fundraising Efficiency[b]	Donor Dependency[c]
5	95	77.1%	83.5%	94.8%

[a] 77.1% = 84/109
[b] 83.5% = (97 − 16)/97
[c] 94.8% = (97 − 5)/97
Sources: IRS Form 990; annual reports, statements of individual charities; www.guidestar.org.

Note

Donors are becoming increasingly discerning about how charities spend their contributions, thanks to the growing availability of information about nonprofits on the Internet. In particular, donors are looking at two metrics. One is the efficiency ratio, which compares how much a nonprofit spends on fulfilling its mission (known as its programs) with what it spends on overhead and fundraising. The other is the fundraising ratio, which compares fundraising costs as a percentage of contributions. The higher a nonprofit's efficiency ratio and the lower its fundraising percentage, the more comfortable donors will feel about giving money, as they know that most of it will be spent on programs. ■

Fundraising Ability

Creditors evaluate an NPO's fundraising ability as a major source of debt repayment for non–revenue-generating projects. Donated funds are important to consider when appraising the NPO's creditworthiness. Refunding is issuing new debt to replace existing debt and may occur if (1) market interest rates have decreased, (2) excessive restrictions exist in current debt, or (3) there is a desire to lengthen debt maturity.

Analysis of Pledges

In appraising pledges, consider these questions:

- Are pledges decreasing among a particular category of donors or all donors?
- Does poor economic activity result in fewer pledges?
- Have new tax laws made gift giving less advisable?
- Do donors feel the objectives of the NPO no longer match with their views?

Creditors may not assign a value to pledges receivable when analyzing the NPO because donors are not legally bound to honor their dollar pledge or time promised. For example, if the donor goes bankrupt, although unlikely, the promise will not be kept. The donor may change his or her mind in giving because of a change in circumstances. However, the creditor should examine who the donors are, their past history of giving, their current financial status, and their reliability. If the donor's profile indicates a high probability of giving the amount promised, creditors will give loans based on security or the pledges receivable. For example, pledges may be used to secure debt service or construction loans.

The analyst considers pledges due within one year of higher quality than pledges due in five years. Thus, the shorter the time period associated with the pledge, the less risk involved.

Analysis of Contributions

A potential cash problem is indicated when actual contributions fall significantly short of expectations. Restricted contributions are unavailable for operating purposes and to pay short-term debt. How much funds are available and when? What are the restrictions (e.g., scholarship fund, building fund)? Are the restrictions very specific or excessive? It is better to have a higher ratio of unrestricted contributions to total contributions because unrestricted contributions are available to be used by the NPO in its regular activities. Restricted contributions do little to improve the NPO's liquidity unless the donor's terms allow for the transfer of funds for operating purposes.

NPOs with substantial contributed services need special attention. The footnote on contributed services should be closely read because it describes the program or activities that use volunteer services, the nature and extent of contributed services in monetary and nonmonetary terms, and the amount of contributed services recognized as revenue for the year.

Looking at Endowments

An endowment represents long-term investments. Investment income from the endowment may be unrestricted and available to finance operating activities or restricted as to use. Donors want financial feedback as to whether the NPO has expended resources received, if expenditures are in accord with promises made, if services and activities provided are of high quality, and the remaining balance of resources. Constraints and commitments made to donors regarding fund use are disclosed in the financial statements. For example, are legal requirements being met?

A decrease in endowments is a negative sign because it may indicate less interest or dissatisfaction with the NPO. However, poor economic conditions may be the reason.

Answer these questions about the portfolio in which endowment funds are invested:

■ How much fluctuation exists in the securities portfolio?
■ Is diversification of the portfolio adequate?
■ Are the securities negatively or positively correlated?

Total return on endowment investments may be estimated by computing it as a percentage of the average balance of endowment investments.

Example 41.3

The return on an endowment portfolio is $60,000. The beginning and ending balances are $1,000,000 and $1,200,000, respectively.

$$\text{Return rate} = \frac{\text{Return}}{\text{Average balance}} = \frac{\$60,000}{\$1,100,000} = 5.5\%$$

A lower return rate is a negative sign.

The return on the endowment investment should be higher as the risk of the investment increases.

Evaluation of Grants

In analyzing grants, answer these questions:

■ Has there been a sufficient attempt to obtain public and private grants?
■ Was reference made to suitable sources, such as *The Foundation Directory?*
■ Does the foundation's objective match the grant proposal?
■ Are matching funds required to receive the grant?
■ Was the proposal completely done (e.g., detailed information, clear discussion of how funds will be used)?
■ Were due date filings met?

Perform a *risk-return analysis*. Is the return sufficient to justify the risk? The greater the risk, the greater should be the return. *Risk* means the probability of an activity accomplishing its objective. For example, there may be a high degree of risk associated with a new specialized academic program in a university or a new medical procedure at a hospital. There is always risk in allocating human and financial resources to new programs.

To control or reduce risk:

- Use agents and representatives, including volunteers.
- Carry adequate insurance protection. For example, insurance should be sufficient relative to the value of the insured property.
- Carefully hire qualified staff to avoid damages and injuries to others.
- Have written policies and communicate them carefully through the organization.
- Have proper supervision over new hires.
- Have protective provisions in contracts to limit the NPO's liability for contractor malfeasance.
- Have proper security over assets to guard against theft or destruction.
- Diversify operations.
- Avoid dealings with selected groups that may result in legal liability problems, such as young children when dealing with hazardous items.

Audit Reliability

Many state and local governments require audits to be conducted of NPOs. Have the NPO's financial statements been subject to an audit, review, or compilation? A big difference exists between these processes in terms of the reliability of the NPO's financial statements. An audit provides the highest level of reliability and testing. No testing is performed in a review; rather, a determination is made as to whether the financial statements make sense. A compilation, the least reliable type of assessment, involves just collecting and reformatting financial records.

In looking at the audit opinion, an "except for" qualification or a disclaimer may indicate a problem. An unqualified opinion is best.

Software

Software exists to analyze NPOs. For example, the Functional Cost Analysis Program develops credit union income and cost information along functional lines and compares data among credit unions and banks.

 ## SPOTTING POTENTIAL BANKRUPTCY AND AVOIDING FINANCIAL PROBLEMS

Negative net assets (fund balance) indicate a worrisome deficit position that is an indicator of potential bankruptcy. Cash forecasts showing expected cash outflows exceed expected cash inflows may point to financial distress. If cash is a problem, timely steps may be needed to improve cash flow and solve problems. How long will the current cash position last if all cash inflows were to cease?

A balanced budget, using conservative revenue estimates, is its own way to avoid financial ruin. A balanced budget requires difficult choices, such as curtailment or elimination in certain services or programs.

Answer these questions to gauge the NPO's probability of potential failure:

- Is there adequate insurance?
- Does excessive legal exposure exist? What is the nature of pending lawsuits? Is the NPO abreast of all current laws and regulations affecting it?
- What government adjustments are expected regarding rate charges and reimbursements?
- Is there inadequate control over expenditures?
- Is there deferred maintenance that can no longer be postponed?
- Are loan restrictions excessive?
- What effect will contractual violations have?
- Are costs skyrocketing? Why?
- Are bills past due?
- Is debt excessive?
- Are debt repayment schedules staggered?
- Should maturity dates be extended?
- Is the public or government criticizing the NPO?
- Is there a decreasing trend in donor interest?
- To what extent are donor contributions restricted? Restricted donations cannot be used to pay current expenses unless the restriction is satisfied or lifted.
- Is there less community interest in the NPO (e.g., fewer members, patients)?
- Are fewer volunteers available?
- Are more grant applications being rejected?
- Is there a cash shortage?
- Is the NPO anticipating future trends (e.g., social, political, technological)?
- Does the NPO have sufficient expertise in the areas it is involved in?
- Is there a buildup in assets (e.g., receivables)?
- Is a hedging approach used to finance assets by matching the maturity dates of liabilities against them?
- Are long-term fixed-fee contracts hurting the NPO?
- Is there a sharp increase in the number of employees per unit of service?
- Are there open lines of credit?
- Does a lack of communication exist?

Ways to avoid financial problems include:

- Merging with another financially stronger similar NPO. Will a merger aid in financing, lower overall operating costs, synergy and efficiency, and program expansion?
- Restructuring the organization.
- Selling off unproductive assets.

- Deferring the payment of bills.
- Discarding programs and activities no longer financially viable.
- Implementing a cost reduction program, including layoffs and attrition. But will doing so eliminate programs that will be hard to start up again? Are you getting rid of scarce talent? Such cuts are referred to as irreversible reductions, which in the long run may not be wise.
- Increasing service fees.
- Increasing fundraising efforts and contributions.
- Applying for grants.
- Stimulating contracts.

Example 41.4

A nonprofit organization provides the following financial information.

Summary of Income, Expenses, and Cash Balances			
	2X11	2X12	Percentage Change
Income			
Membership and program fees	$125,000	$130,000	4%
Contributions	126,000	130,000	3
Other	13,000	35,000	169
Total income	$254,000	$295,000	12
Expenses			
Salaries	$100,000	160,000	60
Rent	40,000	70,000	43
Insurance	10,000	20,000	100
Supplies	20,000	40,000	100
Total expenses	$170,000	$290,000	71
Excess of income over expenses	94,000	$5,000	95
Cash balance, beginning of year	50,000	144,000	
Cash balance, end of year	$144,000	$149,000	

From 2X11 to 2X12, total expenses have increased 71 percent while total revenue has increased only 12 percent. This is a very negative sign. It may indicate a failure to control costs or declining fees for services, possibly due to membership dissatisfaction. Why have contributions increased only by 3 percent: Are donors upset with the NPO's policies, objectives, or management?

It is particularly alarming that profitability has declined by a stunning 95 percent. The sharp increase in each expense category must be closely scrutinized for causes, and corrective action must be taken immediately. Unless something is done to correct this unfavorable trend, the NPO is in serious trouble.

CASE STUDY IN FINANCIAL STATEMENT ANALYSIS

Family Service Agency of Utopia

This case study is based on a sample NPO provided by the Internal Revenue Service in Form 990. A sample tax return is prepared for illustrative purposes and presented at the end of this chapter.

TREND ANALYSIS
(All line references are to Form 990)

	12/31/2009	12/31/2010	Percent Change
Total cash (Lines 45 and 46)	$248,700	$228,500	−8.1%
Pledges receivable (Line 48c)	$46,000	$58,900	28.0%
Grants receivable (Line 49)	$4,600	$5,800	26.1%
Inventories (Line 52)	$6,100	$7,000	14.8%
Fixed assets (Line 57c)	$168,500	$174,800	3.7%
Total assets (Line 59)	$916,000	$964,800	5.3%
Total liabilities (Line 66)	$111,200	$112,300	1.0%
Current unrestricted fund (Line 67)	$446,300	$485,100	8.7%
Current restricted fund (Lines 68 and 69)	$358,500	$367,400	24.8%
Total net assets (fund balances) (Line 73)	$804,800	$852,500	5.9%
For the Year Ended			
	2009	**2010**	**Percent Change**
Contributions, gifts, and similar amounts (2010 from Line 1)	$742,300	$710,800	−4.2%
Membership dues (2010 from Line 3)	$1,100	$1,600	45.5%

An analysis of the trends from 2009 to 2010 reveals:

- The cash position declined having a negative effect on liquidity.
- Pledges and grants receivable have both significantly increased, reflecting success in obtaining pledges and grants to the NPO, which is a favorable sign. However, it may be that there is a problem in collecting the pledges and grants due to higher receivable balances.
- The buildup in inventories may mean greater realization risk.
- Fixed assets were fairly constant.
- The increase in total assets is a favorable indicator.
- Total liabilities were about the same.
- While the balance in current unrestricted funds increased, a favorable sign, there was a decline in the current restricted fund. However, the dollar amount of the decline is small even though it is a higher percentage.
- More funds are available for fixed asset expansion.
- The NPO has been successful in having more endowment funds.
- The increase in total net assets (fund balances of about 6 percent) is a positive sign.
- Contributions, gifts, grants, and similar items decreased about 5 percent. The reasons for the decrease should be determined. Is there less interest in the NPO among donors? If so, why?

- The membership revenue almost doubled, reflecting greater interest in the NPO's policies as indicated by more enrollments or an increase in per member fees. Perhaps there was a successful membership drive.

Liquidity Analysis

$$\frac{\text{Total current assets (BS)}}{\text{Total assets (BS)}}$$

$$\frac{\$315,600}{\$964,800} = 0.33$$

Each $1 of total assets is comprised of $0.33 of current assets.

$$\text{Current ratio} = \frac{\text{Current assets (BS)}}{\text{Current liabilities (BS)}} = \frac{\$315,600}{\$98,900} = 3.2$$

The high ratio means good liquidity.

$$\text{Unrestricted liabilities} = \frac{\text{Current unrestricted assets (BS)}}{\text{Current unrestricted liabilities (BS)}} = \frac{\$304,400}{\$98,900} = 3.1$$

The high ratio further indicates good liquidity.

$$\text{Quick ratio} = \frac{\text{Quick unrestricted current assets (BS)}}{\text{Current unrestricted liabilities (BS)}} = \frac{\$283,600}{\$98,900} = 2.87$$

where Quick unrestricted current assets = Total current assets – Inventories – Prepaid expenses = $304,400 – $7,000 – $13,800 = $283,600

Because the quick ratio (2.87) exceeds the norm of 1.0, good liquidity is evident.

$$\text{Accounts receivable turnover} = \frac{\text{Program service revenue (Form 990, Line 2)}}{\text{Average net accounts receivable (Form 990, Line 47c)}}$$

$$= \frac{\$2,600}{\$1,700} = 1.5$$

Receivables turn over 1.5 times per year relative to fees generated. The low turnover rate indicates less liquidity. Perhaps there is risk in collecting.

$$\text{Days to collect on receivables} = \frac{365}{\text{Turnover}} = \frac{365}{15} = 243 \text{ days}$$

It takes 243 days to collect on receivables, indicating a possible collection problem.

$$\frac{\text{Total accounts receivable (Form 990, Line 47c)}}{\text{Total assets (Form 990, Line 59)}} = \frac{\$1,600}{\$964,800} = 0.2\%$$

The very low ratio means receivables are insignificant relative to total assets.

Pledges Turnover = Net Contributions from Pledges (From
Statement of Revenue, Expenses, and

$$\frac{\text{Changes in Net Assets/Fund Balance (SRECF)}}{\text{Average Net Pledges Receivable (Form 990, Line 48C)}} = \frac{\$473,700}{\$52,450} = 9 \text{ times}$$

The high turnover rate means faster collection on pledges, which is a favorable liquidity indicator.

$$\text{Collection period on pledges} = \frac{365}{\text{Turnover}} = \frac{365}{9} = 40.6 \text{ days}$$

It takes about 41 days to collect on pledges. This is favorable.

$$\text{Cash flow to total debt} = \frac{\text{Net income} + \text{Depreciation}}{\text{Total liabilities}}$$

$$= \frac{\text{Form 990, Line 18} + \text{Line 42}}{\text{Form 990, Line 66}}$$

$$= \frac{\$47,700 + \$5,200}{\$112,300} = 0.47$$

This computation indicates that $0.47 of internally generated cash is available to pay $1 of debt.

$$\text{Current liability coverage} = \frac{\text{Cash} + \text{Marketable securities (unrestricted) (BS)}}{\text{Total current liabilities (BS)}}$$

$$= \frac{\$221,100}{\$98,900} = 2.2$$

For each $1 in current liabilities, there is $2.20 of cash and short-term investments available to pay it.

$$\frac{\text{Total current liabilities (BS)}}{\text{Total liabilities (BS)}} = \frac{\$98,900}{\$112,300} = 0.88$$

Current debt is a high proportion of total liabilities. This is an unfavorable liquidity indicator.

Analysis of Solvency

$$\frac{\text{Total assets (Form 990, Line 59)}}{\text{Total liabilities (Form 990, Line 66)}} = \frac{\$964,800}{\$112,300} = 8.6$$

There is $8.60 in assets for each $1 in liabilities, indicating a good solvency position.

$$\frac{\text{Total liabilities (Form 990, Line 66)}}{\text{Total net assets/Fund balance (Form 990, Line 73)}} = \frac{\$112,300}{\$852,500} = 0.13$$

The low ratio of debt to net assets/fund balance is a favorable indicator of the ability of the NPO to meet its obligations. It indicates less risk.

$$\frac{\text{Long-term debt (BS)}}{\text{(Total unrestricted net assets)/Fund balance (BS)}} = \frac{\$13,400}{\$485,100} = 2.8\%$$

This ratio is a further indication of a solid solvency position. The NPO is able to fulfill its long-term debt commitments.

Analysis of the Statement of Activities

$$\text{Daily revenue (2010)} = \frac{\text{Total revenue for current year}}{365}$$

$$= \frac{\text{Form 990, Line 12}}{365} = \frac{\$760,300}{365} = \$2,083$$

$$\text{Daily revenue (2009)} = \frac{\text{Total revenue for prior year}}{365}$$

$$= \frac{\text{From 990, Schedule A, Line 23}}{365} = \frac{\$800,600^{a}}{365} = \$2,193$$

[a] Given from year 2009.

The declining revenue per day from 2009 to 2010 is a negative sign for operating performance.

$$\frac{\text{Total expenses (Form 990, Line 17)}}{\text{Total revenue (Form 990, Line 2)}} = \frac{\$712,600}{\$760,300} = 93.7\%$$

Total expenses are a high percentage of total revenue, cuttings into surplus.

$$\frac{\text{Fundraising costs (Form 990, Line 15)}}{\text{Total donations (SRECF)}} = \frac{\$65,400}{\$473,700} = 13.8\%$$

Fundraising costs as a percentage of contributions is reasonable, indicating an effective fundraising campaign.

$$\text{Profit margin} = \frac{\text{Excess of revenue over expenses (Form 990, Line 18)}}{\text{Total revenue (Form 990, Line 12)}}$$

$$= \frac{\$47,700}{\$760,300} = 6.3\%$$

The profit margin should be compared to other similar NPOs. If it is lower, it indicates less operational performance.

$$\text{Return on net assets (Fund balance)}$$
$$= \frac{\text{Excess of revenue over expenses (Form 990, Line 18)}}{\text{Average ne tassets (Form 990, Line 59)}}$$
$$= \frac{\$47,700}{\$940,400^a} = 5.1\%$$

^{a} ($964,800 + $916,000)/2 = $940,400

This ratio reflects reasonable efficiency of the net assets/fund balance in generating yearly surplus for the year.

$$\frac{\text{Dividends and interest from securities (Form 990, Line 5)}}{\text{Investments (Form 990, Line 54)}} = \frac{\$16,400}{\$474,400} = 3.5\%$$

The rate of return earned on the investment portfolio is low.

Exhibit 41.2 summarizes financial statement analysis covered throughout the chapter.

EXHIBIT 41.2 Financial Ratio Analysis

	12/31/2009	12/31/2010
Assets		
Total Cash (Lines 45 and 46)	$248,700	$228,500
Accounts Receivable (Line 47c)	1,800	1,600
Pledges Receivable (Line 48c)	46,000	58,900
Grants Receivable (Line 49)	4,600	5,800
Other Receivables (Line 50)	—	—
Other Notes and Loans Receivable (Line 51c)	—	—
Inventories (Line 52)	6,100	7,000
Prepaid Expenses and Deferred Charges (Line 53)	9,600	13,800
Total Current Assets (Line 45 through Line 53)	316,800	315,600
Investments—Securities (Line 54)	430,700	474,400
Investments—Land, Buildings (Line 55c)	—	—
Fixed Assets (Line 57c)	168,500	174,800
Other Fixed Assets (Line 58)	—	—
Total Assets (Line 59)	$916,000	$964,800
Liabilities		
Accounts Payable and Accrued Expenses (Line 60)	$46,000	$39,300

(continued)

EXHIBIT 41.2 *(continued)*

Grants Payable (Line 61)	—	—
Support and Revenue Designed for Future Periods (Line 62)	61,600	59,600
Loans from Officers (Line 63)	—	—
Total Current Liabilities (Line 60 through Line 63)	107,600	98,900
Tax-Exempt Bond (Line 64a)	—	—
Mortgages (Line 64b)	3,600	3,200
Other Liabilities (Line 65)	—	10,200
Total Liabilities (Line 66)	$111,200	$112,300
Net Assets or Fund Balances		
Current Unrestricted Fund (Line 67a)	$446,300	$485,100
Current Restricted Fund (Line 67b)	10,000	6,400
Land, Buildings, and Equipment (Line 68)	156,800	166,200
Endowment Fund (Line 69)	191,700	194,800
Other Funds (Line 70)	—	—
Capital Stock (Line 71)	—	—
Paid-in Capital (Line 72)	—	—
Retained Earnings (Line 73)	—	—
Total Net Assets (Fund Balances) (Line 74)	804,800	852,500
Total Liabilities and Fund Balances (Line 75 = Line 66 + Line 74)	$916,000	$964,800

	For the Year Ended	
	2009	2010
Program Service Revenue (Line 2)		$2,600
Dividends and Interest from Securities (Line 5)		16,400
Total Revenue (Line 12)	$800,600[a]	760,300
Fund Raising Costs (Line 15)		65,400
Total Expenses (Line 17)		712,600
Excess or (Deficit) (Line 18)		47,700
Depreciation (Line 42)		$5,200
Liquidity Analysis		
(1) Total Current Assets/Total Assets		0.33

(continued)

EXHIBIT 41.2 *(continued)*

(2) Current Ratio = Current Assets/Current Liabilities	3.2
(3) Accounts Receivable Turnover = Program Service Revenue/Accounts Receivable	1.5
(4) Days to Collect on Receivables = 365 days/Accounts Receivable Turnover	239
(5) Total Accounts Receivable/Total Assets	0.2%
(6) Cash Flow to Total Debt = (Net Income + Depreciation)/Total Liabilities	0.47
(7) Total Current Liabilities/Total Liabilities	0.88

Analysis of Solvency

(8) Total Assets/Total Liabilities	8.6
(9) Total Liabilities/Total Fund Balance (Net Assets)	0.13
(10) Long-Term Debt/Total Unrestricted Fund Balance	2.8%

Analysis of the Statement of Activities

(11) Daily Revenue = Total Revenue/365 days	2,193	2,083
(12) Total Expenses/Total Revenue		93.7%
(13) Profit Margin = Excess of Revenue over Expenses/Total Revenue		6.3%
(14) Return on Net Assets (Fund Balances) = Excess of Revenue over Expenses/Net Assets		5.1%
(15) Dividends and Interest from Securities/Investments		3.5%

[a] Given from the previous year.

Conclusion

The NPO's liquidity is favorable, meaning it is able to pay its short-term obligations. Its solvency is also favorable, meaning it can satisfy its long-term debt when due. The NPO is having difficulty in its operating performance, as indicated by declining daily revenue, high expenses to revenue, and low investment return. However, fundraising costs are being controlled, resulting in successful fundraising efforts. Profit margin and return on net assets or fund balance appear reasonable. There is more interest in the NPO, as indicated by the increasing membership base.

EXHIBIT 41.3 Return of Organization Exempt from Income Tax

Form **990**	**Return of Organization Exempt From Income Tax**	OMB No. 1545-0047
	Under section 501(c), 527, or 4947(a)(1) of the Internal Revenue Code (except black lung benefit trust or private foundation)	**2010**
Department of the Treasury Internal Revenue Service	► The organization may have to use a copy of this return to satisfy state reporting requirements.	Open to Public Inspection

A	For the) calendar year, or tax year beginning	and ending	, 20

B Check if applicable:	Please use IRS label or print or type. See Specific Instructions.	**C** Name of organization Family Service Agency of Utopia, Inc.	**D** Employer identification number 12 : 3456789
☐ Address change		Number and street (or P.O. box if mail is not delivered to street address) Room/suite 1414 West Ash Drive	**E** Telephone number ( )
☐ Name change		City or town, state or country, and ZIP + 4 Utopia, PA 11111	**F** Accounting method: ☐ Cash ☑ Accrual ☐ Other (specify) ►
☐ Initial return			
☐ Final return			
☐ Amended return			
☐ Application pending	• Section 501(c)(3) organizations and 4947(a)(1) nonexempt charitable trusts must attach a completed Schedule A (Form 990 or 990-EZ).	**H** and **I** are not applicable to section 527 organizations. H(a) Is this a group return for affiliates? ☐ Yes ☐ No
G Website: ►			H(b) If "Yes," enter number of affiliates ► ....
			H(c) Are all affiliates included? ☐ Yes ☐ No (If "No," attach a list. See instructions.)
J Organization type (check only one) ► ☑ 501(c) ( ) ◄ (insert no.) ☐ 4947(a)(1) or ☐ 527			H(d) Is this a separate return filed by an organization covered by a group ruling? ☐ Yes ☐ No
K Check here ► ☐ if the organization is not a 509(a)(3) supporting organization and its gross receipts are normally not more than $25,000. A return is not required, but if the organization chooses to file a return, be sure to file a complete return.			**I** Group Exemption Number ►
L Gross receipts: Add lines 6b, 8b, 9b, and 10b to line 12 ►			**M** Check ► ☐ if the organization is not required to attach Sch. B (Form 990, 990-EZ, or 990-PF).

Part I Revenue, Expenses, and Changes in Net Assets or Fund Balances *(See the instructions.)*

1	Contributions, gifts, grants, and similar amounts received:			
a	Contributions to donor advised funds	1a	$483,300	
b	Direct public support (not included on line 1a)	1b	227,500	
c	Indirect public support (not included on line 1a)	1c		
d	Government contributions (grants) (not included on line 1a)	1d		
e	Total (add lines 1a through 1d) (cash $_____ noncash $_____)		1e	$710,800
2	Program service revenue including government fees and contracts (from Part VII, line 93)		2	2,600
3	Membership dues and assessments		3	1,600
4	Interest on savings and temporary cash investments		4	14,800
5	Dividends and interest from securities		5	16,400
6a	Gross rents	6a		
b	Less: rental expenses	6b		
c	Net rental income or (loss). Subtract line 6b from line 6a		6c	
7	Other investment income (describe ►)		7	
8a	Gross amount from sales of assets other than inventory	(A) Securities 24,200 8a	(B) Other	
b	Less: cost or other basis and sales expenses	23,700 8b		
c	Gain or (loss) (attach schedule)	500 8c		
d	Net gain or (loss). Combine line 8c, columns (A) and (B)		8d	500
9	Special events and activities (attach schedule). If any amount is from **gaming**, check here ► ☐			
a	Gross revenue (not including $_____ of contributions reported on line 1b)	9a	28,400	
b	Less: direct expenses other than fundraising expenses	9b	18,000	
c	Net income or (loss) from special events. Subtract line 9b from line 9a		9c	10,400
10a	Gross sales of inventory, less returns and allowances	10a	1,400	
b	Less: cost of goods sold	10b	1,000	
c	Gross profit or (loss) from sales of inventory (attach schedule). Subtract line 10b from line 10a		10c	400
11	Other revenue (from Part VII, line 103)		11	2,800
12	**Total revenue.** Add lines 1e, 2, 3, 4, 5, 6c, 7, 8d, 9c, 10c, and 11		12	$760,300
13	Program services (from line 44, column (B))		13	$577,400
14	Management and general (from line 44, column (C))		14	57,400
15	Fundraising (from line 44, column (D))		15	65,400
16	Payments to affiliates (attach schedule)		16	12,400
17	**Total expenses.** Add lines 16 and 44, column (A)		17	$712,600
18	Excess or (deficit) for the year. Subtract line 17 from line 12		18	$47,700
19	Net assets or fund balances at beginning of year (from line 73, column (A))		19	804,800
20	Other changes in net assets or fund balances (attach explanation)		20	0
21	Net assets or fund balances at end of year. Combine lines 18, 19, and 20		21	$852,500

Revenue (label on left side spanning lines 1–12), *Expenses* (lines 13–17), *Net Assets* (lines 18–21)

For Privacy Act and Paperwork Reduction Act Notice, see the separate instructions.   Cat. No. 11282Y   Form **990**

A

EXHIBIT 41.3 *(continued)*

Form 99

Part II | **Statement of Functional Expenses** — All organizations must complete column (A). Columns (B), (C), and (D) are required for section 501(c)(3) and (4) organizations and section 4947(a)(1) nonexempt charitable trusts but optional for others. (See instructions.)

Do not include amounts reported on line 6b, 8b, 9b, 10b, or 16 of Part I.		(A) Total	(B) Program services	(C) Management and general	(D) Fundraising
22	Grants and allocations (attach schedule) (cash $ 35,900 noncash $)	22	$ 35,900	$ 35,900		
23	Specific assistance to individuals (attach schedule)	23	45,800	45,800		
24	Benefits paid to or for members (attach schedule)	24				
25	Compensation of officers, directors, etc.	25	62,800	46,600	$ 8,800	$ 7,400
26	Other salaries and wages	26	184,700	131,000	24,300	29,400
27	Pension plan contributions	27	300	200	100	
28	Other employee benefits	28	13,000	9,400	2,100	1,500
29	Payroll taxes	29	23,800	17,700	3,000	3,100
30	Professional fundraising fees	30				
31	Accounting fees	31				
32	Legal fees	32				
33	Supplies	33	30,000	26,500	1,800	1,700
34	Telephone	34	15,400	11,600	1,500	2,300
35	Postage and shipping	35	23,100	13,100	1,000	9,000
36	Occupancy	36	37,750	34,900	1,500	1,350
37	Equipment rental and maintenance	37	8,750	5,900	1,500	1,350
38	Printing and publications	38	14,100	12,200	300	1,600
39	Travel	39	22,000	16,700	2,300	3,000
40	Conferences, conventions, and meetings	40	17,700	12,800	4,500	400
41	Interest	41	900		100	800
42	Depreciation, depletion, etc. (attach schedule)	42	5,200	4,200	600	400
43	Other expenses (itemize): a Dues	43a	500	500		
b	Professional Fees	43b	127,900	124,500	2,600	800
c	Insurance	43c	26,300	25,650	600	50
d	Miscellaneous	43d	4,300	2,150	100	2,050
e		43e				
44	Total functional expenses (add lines 22 through 43) Organizations completing columns (B)-(D), carry these totals to lines 13-15	44	$700,200	$577,400	$57,400	$65,400

Reporting of Joint Costs.—Did you report in column (B) (Program services) any joint costs from a combined educational campaign and fundraising solicitation? ▶ ☒ Yes ☐ No
If "Yes," enter (i) the aggregate amount of these joint costs $ 9,600 ; (ii) the amount allocated to Program services $ 2,800 ; (iii) the amount allocated to Management and general $ 700 ; and (iv) the amount allocated to Fundraising $ 6,000

Part III | **Statement of Program Service Accomplishments** (See instructions.)

	Program Service Expenses (Required for 501(c)(3) and (4) orgs. and 4947(a)(1) trusts; but optional for others.)
What is the organization's primary exempt purpose? ▶ Family counseling. All organizations must describe their exempt purpose achievements. State the number of clients served, publications issued, etc. Discuss achievements that are not measurable. (Section 501(c)(3) and (4) organizations and 4947(a)(1) nonexempt charitable trusts must also enter the amount of grants and allocations to others.)	
a Counseling - The organization provided 5,954 hours of counseling to individuals and families. A total of 635 cases were assisted involving 2,426 individuals. The agency also made a grant to its national affiliate for a research project. (Grants and allocations $ 3,000)	$257,800
b Adoption Services - The agency placed 50 children in adoptive families. This included counseling for 189 birth parents. Five adoptions involved children from foreign countries. There were 65 home studies completed during this year. (This program was assisted (Grants and allocations $)	
c by $8,000 of donated services in 1994.) Under the Adoption Services program, the agency made grants to three organizations for related services. (Grants and allocations $ 21,000)	187,800
d Foster Care - The agency placed 28 children in 16 foster homes. The agency also made grants to two other organizations providing foster home care for hard-to-place children. (Grants and allocations $ 11,900)	131,800
e Other program services (attach schedule) (Grants and allocations $)	
f Total of Program Service Expenses (should equal line 44, column (B), Program services) ▶	$577,400

B

EXHIBIT 41.3 *(continued)*

Part IV Balance Sheets

Note: *Where required, attached schedules and amounts within the description column should be for end-of-year amounts only.*

			(A) Beginning of year		**(B)** End of year
	Assets				
45	Cash—non-interest-bearing		$ 4,000	45	$ 6,400
46	Savings and temporary cash investments		244,700	46	222,100
47a	Accounts receivable	47a	¢ 1,800		
b	Less: allowance for doubtful accounts . . .	47b	200	1,800	47c	1,600
48a	Pledges receivable	48a	70,100		
b	Less: allowance for doubtful accounts . . .	48b	11,200	46,000	48c	58,900
49	Grants receivable		4,600	49	5,800
50	Receivables due from officers, directors, trustees, and key employees (attach schedule)			50	
51a	Other notes and loans receivable (attach schedule)	51a			
b	Less: allowance for doubtful accounts . . .	51b			51c	
52	Inventories for sale or use		6,100	52	7,000
53	Prepaid expenses and deferred charges		9,600	53	13,800
54	Investments—securities (attach schedule)		430,700	54	474,400
55a	Investments—land, buildings, and equipment: basis	55a			
b	Less: accumulated depreciation (attach schedule)	55b			55c	
56	Investments—other (attach schedule) . . .			56	
57a	Land, buildings, and equipment: basis . . .	57a	188,000		
b	Less: accumulated depreciation (attach schedule)	57b	13,200	168,500	57c	174,800
58	Other assets (describe ▶ _____)			58	
59	**Total assets** (add lines 45 through 58) (must equal line 75)		**$916,000**	59	**$964,800**
	Liabilities				
60	Accounts payable and accrued expenses		$ 46,000	60	$ 39,300
61	Grants payable			61	
62	Support and revenue designated for future periods (attach schedule) . .		61,600	62	59,600
63	Loans from officers, directors, trustees, and key employees (attach schedule)			63	
64a	Tax-exempt bond liabilities (attach schedule)			64a	
b	Mortgages and other notes payable (attach schedule)		3,600	64b	3,200
65	Other liabilities (describe ▶ Payable under capital lease)			65	10,200
66	**Total liabilities** (add lines 60 through 65)		**$111,200**	66	**$112,300**
	Fund Balances or Net Assets				
	Organizations that use fund accounting, check here ▶ ☒ and complete lines 67 through 70 and lines 74 and 75 (see instructions).				
67a	Current unrestricted fund		$446,300	67a	$485,100
b	Current restricted fund		10,000	67b	6,400
68	Land, buildings, and equipment fund		156,800	68	166,200
69	Endowment fund		191,700	69	194,800
70	Other funds (describe ▶ _____)		-0-	70	-0-
	Organizations that do not use fund accounting, check here ▶ ☐ and complete lines 71 through 75 (see instructions).				
71	Capital stock or trust principal			71	
72	Paid-in or capital surplus			72	
73	Retained earnings or accumulated income			73	
74	Total fund balances or net assets (add lines 67a through 70 OR lines 71 through 73; column (A) must equal line 19 and column (B) must equal line 21)		$804,800	74	$852,500
75	Total liabilities and fund balances/net assets (add lines 66 and 74) . .		$916,000	75	$964,800

Form 990 is available for public inspection and, for some people, serves as the primary or sole source of information about a particular organization. How the public perceives an organization in such cases may be determined by the information presented on its return. Therefore, please make sure the return is complete and accurate and fully describes the organization's programs and accomplishments.

C

TABLE A.1 Future Value of $1.00 (Compounded Amount of $1.00)

$$(1 + i)^n = T_1(i, n)$$

Periods	4%	6%	8%	10%	12%	14%	20%
1	1.040	1.060	1.080	1.100	1.120	1.140	1.200
2	1.082	1.124	1.166	1.210	1.254	1.300	1.440
3	1.125	1.191	1.260	1.331	1.405	1.482	1.728
4	1.170	1.263	1.361	1.464	1.574	1.689	2.074
5	1.217	1.338	1.469	1.611	1.762	1.925	2.488
6	1.265	1.419	1.587	1.772	1.974	2.195	2.986
7	1.316	1.504	1.714	1.949	2.211	2.502	3.583
8	1.369	1.594	1.851	2.144	2.476	2.853	4.300
9	1.423	1.690	1.999	2.359	2.773	3.252	5.160
10	1.480	1.791	2.159	2.594	3.106	3.707	6.192
11	1.540	1.898	2.332	2.853	3.479	4.226	7.430
12	1.601	2.012	2.518	3.139	3.896	4.818	8.916
13	1.665	2.133	2.720	3.452	4.364	5.492	10.699
14	1.732	2.261	2.937	3.798	4.887	6.261	12.839
15	1.801	2.397	3.172	4.177	5.474	7.138	15.407
16	1.873	2.540	3.426	4.595	6.130	8.137	18.488
17	1.948	2.693	3.700	5.055	6.866	9.277	22.186
18	2.026	2.854	3.996	5.560	7.690	10.575	26.623
19	2.107	3.026	4.316	6.116	8.613	12.056	31.948
20	2.191	3.207	4.661	6.728	9.646	13.743	38.338
30	3.243	5.744	10.063	17.450	29.960	50.950	237.380
40	4.801	10.286	21.725	45.260	93.051	188.880	1469.800

TABLE A.2 Future Value of $1.00 (Compounded Amount of an Annuity of $1.00)

$$[(1 + i)^n - 1]/i = T_2(i, n)$$

Periods	4%	6%	8%	10%	12%	14%	20%
1	1.000	1.000	1.000	1.000	1.000	1.000	1.000
2	2.040	2.060	2.080	2.100	2.120	2.140	2.200
3	3.122	3.184	3.246	3.310	3.374	3.440	3.640
4	4.247	4.375	4.506	4.641	4.779	4.921	5.368
5	5.416	5.637	5.867	6.105	6.353	6.610	7.442
6	6.633	6.975	7.336	7.716	8.115	8.536	9.930
7	7.898	8.394	8.923	9.487	10.089	10.730	12.916
8	9.214	9.898	10.637	11.436	12.300	13.233	16.499
9	10.583	11.491	12.488	13.580	14.776	16.085	20.799
10	12.006	13.181	14.487	15.938	17.549	19.337	25.959
11	13.486	14.972	16.646	18.531	20.655	23.045	32.150
12	15.026	16.870	18.977	21.385	24.133	27.271	39.580
13	16.627	18.882	21.495	24.523	28.029	32.089	48.497
14	18.292	21.015	24.215	27.976	32.393	37.581	59.196
15	20.024	23.276	27.152	31.773	37.280	43.842	72.035
16	21.825	25.673	30.324	35.950	42.753	50.980	87.442
17	23.698	28.213	33.750	40.546	48.884	59.118	105.930
18	25.645	30.906	37.450	45.600	55.750	68.394	128.120
19	27.671	33.760	41.446	51.160	63.440	78.969	154.740
20	29.778	36.778	45.762	57.276	75.052	91.025	186.690
30	56.085	79.058	113.283	164.496	241.330	356.790	1181.900
40	95.026	154.762	259.057	442.597	767.090	1342.000	7343.900

TABLE A.3 Present Value of $1.00

$$1/(1 + i)^n = T_3(i, n)$$

Periods	4%	6%	8%	10%	12%	14%	16%	18%	20%	22%	24%	26%	28%	30%	40%
1	.962	.943	.926	.909	.893	.877	.862	.847	.833	.820	.806	.794	.781	.769	.714
2	.925	.890	.857	.826	.797	.769	.743	.718	.694	.672	.650	.630	.610	.592	.510
3	.889	.840	.794	.751	.712	.675	.641	.609	.579	.551	.524	.500	.477	.455	.364
4	.855	.792	.735	.683	.636	.592	.552	.516	.482	.451	.423	.397	.373	.350	.260
5	.822	.747	.681	.621	.567	.519	.476	.437	.402	.370	.341	.315	.291	.269	.186
6	.790	.705	.630	.564	.507	.456	.410	.370	.335	.303	.275	.250	.227	.207	.133
7	.760	.665	.583	.513	.452	.400	.354	.314	.279	.249	.222	.198	.178	.159	.095
8	.731	.627	.540	.467	.404	.351	.305	.266	.233	.204	.179	.157	.139	.123	.068
9	.703	.592	.500	.424	.361	.308	.263	.225	.194	.167	.144	.125	.108	.094	.048
10	.676	.558	.463	.386	.322	.270	.227	.191	.162	.137	.116	.099	.085	.073	.035
11	.650	.527	.429	.350	.287	.237	.195	.162	.135	.112	.094	.079	.066	.056	.025
12	.625	.497	.397	.319	.257	.208	.168	.137	.112	.092	.076	.062	.052	.043	.018
13	.601	.469	.368	.290	.229	.182	.145	.116	.093	.075	.061	.050	.040	.033	.013
14	.577	.442	.340	.263	.205	.160	.125	.099	.078	.062	.049	.039	.032	.025	.009
15	.555	.417	.315	.239	.183	.140	.108	.084	.065	.051	.040	.031	.025	.020	.006
16	.534	.394	.292	.218	.163	.123	.093	.071	.054	.042	.032	.025	.019	.015	.005
17	.513	.371	.270	.198	.146	.108	.080	.060	.045	.034	.026	.020	.015	.012	.003
18	.494	.350	.250	.180	.130	.095	.069	.051	.038	.028	.021	.016	.012	.009	.002
19	.475	.331	.232	.164	.116	.083	.060	.043	.031	.023	.017	.012	.009	.007	.002
20	.456	.312	.215	.149	.104	.073	.051	.037	.026	.019	.014	.010	.007	.005	.001
21	.439	.294	.199	.135	.093	.064	.044	.031	.022	.015	.011	.008	.006	.004	.001
22	.422	.278	.184	.123	.083	.056	.038	.026	.018	.013	.009	.006	.004	.003	.001
23	.406	.262	.170	.112	.074	.049	.033	.022	.015	.010	.007	.005	.003	.002	.001
24	.390	.247	.158	.102	.066	.043	.028	.019	.013	.008	.006	.004	.003	.002	
25	.375	.233	.146	.092	.059	.038	.024	.016	.010	.007	.005	.003	.002	.001	
26	.361	.220	.135	.084	.053	.033	.021	.014	.009	.006	.004	.002	.002	.001	
27	.347	.209	.125	.076	.047	.029	.018	.011	.007	.005	.003	.002	.001	.001	
28	.333	.196	.116	.069	.042	.026	.016	.010	.006	.004	.002	.002	.001	.001	
29	.321	.185	.107	.063	.037	.022	.014	.008	.005	.003	.002	.001	.001	.001	
30	.308	.174	.099	.057	.033	.020	.012	.007	.004	.003	.002	.001	.001	.001	
40	.208	.097	.046	.022	.011	.005	.003	.001	.001						

TABLE A.4 Present Value of an Annuity of $1.00

$$(1/i) \times [1 - 1/(1 + i)^n] = T_4(i, n)$$

Periods	4%	6%	8%	10%	12%	14%	16%	18%	20%	22%	24%	25%	26%	28%	30%	40%
1	0.962	0.943	0.926	0.909	0.893	0.877	0.862	0.847	0.833	0.820	0.806	0.800	0.794	0.781	0.769	0.714
2	1.886	1.833	1.783	1.736	1.690	1.647	1.605	1.566	1.528	1.492	1.457	1.440	1.424	1.392	1.361	1.224
3	2.775	2.673	2.577	2.487	2.402	2.322	2.246	2.174	2.106	2.042	1.981	1.952	1.923	1.868	1.816	1.589
4	3.630	3.465	3.312	3.170	3.037	2.914	2.798	2.690	2.589	2.494	2.404	2.362	2.320	2.241	2.166	1.849
5	4.452	4.212	3.993	3.791	3.605	3.433	3.274	3.127	2.991	2.864	2.745	2.689	2.635	2.532	2.436	2.035
6	5.242	4.917	4.623	4.355	4.111	3.889	3.685	3.498	3.326	3.167	3.020	2.951	2.885	2.759	2.643	2.168
7	6.002	5.582	5.206	4.868	4.564	4.288	4.039	3.812	3.605	3.416	3.242	3.161	3.083	2.937	2.802	2.263
8	6.733	6.210	5.747	5.335	4.968	4.639	4.344	4.078	3.837	3.619	3.421	3.329	3.241	3.076	2.925	2.331
9	7.435	6.802	6.247	5.759	5.328	4.946	4.607	4.303	4.031	3.786	3.566	3.463	3.366	3.184	3.019	2.379
10	8.111	7.360	6.710	6.145	5.650	5.216	4.833	4.494	4.192	3.923	3.682	3.571	3.465	3.269	3.092	2.414
11	8.760	7.887	7.139	6.495	5.938	5.453	5.029	4.656	4.327	4.035	3.776	3.656	3.544	3.335	3.147	2.438
12	9.385	8.384	7.536	6.814	6.194	5.660	5.197	4.793	4.439	4.127	3.851	3.725	3.606	3.387	3.190	2.456
13	9.986	8.853	7.904	7.103	6.424	5.842	5.342	4.910	4.533	4.203	3.912	3.780	3.656	3.427	3.223	2.468
14	10.563	9.295	8.244	7.367	6.628	6.002	5.468	5.008	4.611	4.265	3.962	3.824	3.695	3.459	3.249	2.477
15	11.118	9.712	8.559	7.606	6.811	6.142	5.575	5.092	4.675	4.315	4.001	3.859	3.726	3.483	3.268	2.484
16	11.652	10.106	8.851	7.824	6.974	6.265	5.669	5.162	4.730	4.357	4.033	3.887	3.751	3.503	3.283	2.489
17	12.166	10.477	9.122	8.022	7.120	6.373	5.749	5.222	4.775	4.391	4.059	3.910	3.771	3.518	3.295	2.492
18	12.659	10.828	9.372	8.201	7.250	6.467	5.818	5.273	4.812	4.419	4.080	3.928	3.786	3.529	3.304	2.494
19	13.134	11.158	9.604	8.365	7.366	6.550	5.877	5.316	4.844	4.442	4.097	3.942	3.799	3.539	3.311	2.496
20	13.590	11.470	9.818	8.514	7.469	6.623	5.929	5.353	4.870	4.460	4.110	3.954	3.808	3.546	3.316	2.497
21	14.029	11.764	10.017	8.649	7.562	6.687	5.973	5.384	4.891	4.476	4.121	3.963	3.816	3.551	3.320	2.498
22	14.451	12.042	10.201	8.772	7.645	6.743	6.011	5.410	4.909	4.488	4.130	3.970	3.822	3.556	3.323	2.498
23	14.857	12.303	10.371	8.883	7.718	6.792	6.044	5.432	4.925	4.499	4.137	3.976	3.827	3.559	3.325	2.499
24	15.247	12.550	10.529	8.985	7.784	6.835	6.073	5.451	4.937	4.507	4.143	3.981	3.831	3.562	3.327	2.499
25	15.622	12.783	10.675	9.077	7.843	6.873	6.097	5.467	4.948	4.514	4.147	3.985	3.834	3.564	3.329	2.499
26	15.983	13.003	10.810	9.161	7.896	6.906	6.118	5.480	4.956	4.520	4.151	3.988	3.837	3.566	3.330	2.500
27	16.330	13.211	10.935	9.237	7.943	6.935	6.136	5.492	4.964	4.524	4.154	3.990	3.839	3.567	3.331	2.500
28	16.663	13.406	11.051	9.307	7.984	6.961	6.152	5.502	4.970	4.528	4.157	3.992	3.840	3.568	3.331	2.500
29	16.984	13.591	11.158	9.370	8.022	6.983	6.166	5.510	4.975	4.531	4.159	3.994	3.841	3.569	3.332	2.500
30	17.292	13.765	11.258	9.427	8.055	7.003	6.177	5.517	4.979	4.534	4.160	3.995	3.842	3.569	3.332	2.500
40	19.793	15.046	11.925	9.779	8.244	7.105	6.234	5.548	4.997	4.544	4.166	3.999	3.846	3.571	3.333	2.500

About the Authors

Jae K. Shim, PhD, is one of the most prolific accounting and finance experts in the world. He is a professor of accounting and finance at California State University, Long Beach, and CEO of Delta Consulting Company, a financial consulting and training firm. Dr. Shim received his MBA and PhD degrees from the University of California at Berkeley (Haas School of Business). He has been a consultant to commercial and nonprofit organizations for over 30 years.

Dr. Shim has over 50 college and professional books to his credit, including *Barron's Accounting Handbook*, *Barron's Dictionary of Accounting Terms*, *GAAP 2012*, *Dictionary of Personal Finance*, *Investment Sourcebook*, *Dictionary of Real Estate*, *Dictionary of Economics*, *Dictionary of International Investment Terms*, *Encyclopedic Dictionary of Accounting and Finance*, *2011–2012 Corporate Controller's Handbook of Financial Management*, the *Vest Pocket CPA*, and the best-selling *Vest Pocket MBA*. Thirty of his publications have been translated into foreign languages, including Spanish, Chinese, Russian, Italian, Japanese, and Korean. Dr. Shim's books have been published by Prentice-Hall, McGraw-Hill, Barron's, CCH, Thomson Reuters, John Wiley & Sons, American Management Association (Amacom), and the American Institute of CPAs (AICPA).

Dr. Shim has been frequently quoted by such media as the *Los Angeles Times*, *Orange County Register*, *Business Start-ups*, *Personal Finance*, and Money Radio. He has also published numerous articles in professional and academic journals. Dr. Shim was the recipient of the Credit Research Foundation Award for his article on financial management.

Joel G. Siegel, PhD, CPA, is a financial consultant and professor of accounting and finance at Queens College of the City University of New York.

He was previously employed by Coopers & Lybrand, CPAs, and Arthur Andersen, CPAs. Dr. Siegel has acted as a consultant to many organizations, including Citicorp, International Telephone and Telegraph, United Technologies, American Institute of CPAs, and Person-Wolinsky Associates.

Dr. Siegel is the author of 67 books and about 300 articles on accounting and financial topics. His books have been published by Prentice Hall, McGraw-Hill, HarperCollins, John Wiley & Sons, Macmillan, International Publishing, Barron's, Southwestern, Aspen, Richard Irwin, Probus, American Management Association, and the American Institute of CPAs.

Dr. Siegel's articles have been published in many accounting and financial journals, including *Financial Executive*, *Financial Analysts Journal*, *CPA Journal*, *Practical Accountant*, and *National Public Accountant*.

In 1972 he was the recipient of the Outstanding Educator of America Award. Dr. Siegel is listed in *Who's Where Among Writers* and *Who's Who in the World*. His international reputation led to his appointment in 1992 as chair of the National Oversight Board.

Allison I. Shim is CFO of Delta Consulting/Investments Company. She is a finance expert and a PhD candidate at the University of California, Irvine.

Index